REPORT

UPON

THE RECONNAISSANCE

OF

NORTHWESTERN WYOMING,

INCLUDING

YELLOWSTONE NATIONAL PARK,

MADE IN

THE SUMMER OF 1873

BY

WILLIAM A. JONES,

CAPTAIN OF ENGINEERS U. S. A.

WITH APPENDIX.

WASHINGTON:
GOVERNMENT PRINTING OFFICE.
1875.

NOTE.—Chapters IX to XV, inclusive, of Professor Comstock's Geological Report were prepared after the Congressional Document [H. R. Ex. Doc. No. 285, 43d Cong., 1st sess.] had gone through the press, and consequently do not appear in that edition of the report. See Appendix.

TABLE OF CONTENTS.

LETTERS OF TRANSMITTAL.

GENERAL REPORT.

CHAPTER I.

DESCRIPTIVE JOURNAL.

CHAPTER II.

PHYSICAL GEOGRAPHY.

CHAPTER III.

THE YELLOWSTONE ROUTE TO MONTANA.

CHAPTER IV.

METEOROLOGY.

ASTRONOMICAL REPORT.

BY LIEUT. S. E. BLUNT, THIRTEENTH UNITED STATES INFANTRY.

GEOLOGICAL REPORT.

BY PROF. THEO. B. COMSTOCK.

CHAPTER I.

INTRODUCTION.

CHAPTER II.

PHYSICAL GEOGRAPHY.

CHAPTER III.

STRATIGRAPHY, METAMORPHIC AND PALEOZOIC.

CHAPTER IV.

STRATIGRAPHY, CONTINUED—MESOZOIC AND TERTIARY.

CHAPTER V.

STRATIGRAPHY, CONTINUED—POST-TERTIARY AND RECENT.

CHAPTER VI.

STRATIGRAPHY—RECAPITULATION—GENERAL REVIEW, WITH ECONOMIC GEOLOGY.

CHAPTER VII.

DYNAMICAL GEOLOGY—ELEVATION, EROSION, AND DENUDATION.

Page.

CHAPTER VIII.

DYNAMICAL GEOLOGY, CONTINUED—BIOLOGICAL AND CHEMICAL ACTION.

CHAPTER IX.

THERMO-DYNAMICES—IGNEOUS ROCKS AND HOT SPRINGS.

CHAPTER X.

THERMO-DYNAMICES, CONTINUED—DESCRIPTION OF HOT SPRINGS, CONTINUED.

CHAPTER XI.

THERMO-DYNAMICS, CONTINUED—DESCRIPTION OF HOT SPRINGS, CONTINUED.

CHAPTER XII.

THERMO-DYNAMICS, CONTINUED—DESCRIPTION OF HOT SPRINGS, CONCLUDED.

CHAPTER XIII.

THERMO-DYNAMICS, CONCLUDED—DESCRIPTION OF GEYSERS AND SUMMARY.

CHAPTER XIV.

ARCHÆOLOGY, WITH MANNERS AND CUSTOMS OF EASTERN SHOSHONES.

CHAPTER XV.

PHILOLOGICAL NOTES ON THE EASTERN SHOSHONE DIALECT.

REPORT ON MINERAL AND THERMAL WATERS.

BY ASSISTANT SURGEON C. L. HEIZMANN, U. S. A.

BOTANICAL REPORT.

BY DR. C. C. PARRY.

ENTOMOLOGICAL REPORT.

BY J. D. PUTNAM.

APPENDIX.

MAPS.

Map of Western Wyoming, showing region traversed; scale $\frac{1}{600000}$; forty-nine trail-maps, showing detailed topography; geological map, (colored;) scale $\frac{1}{600000}$.

LETTER

FROM

THE CHIEF CLERK OF THE WAR DEPARTMENT,

TRANSMITTING

A report upon the reconnaissance of Northwestern Wyoming, made in the summer of 1873 *by Captain William A. Jones, Corps of Engineers.*

The Chief Clerk of the War Department, in the absence of the Secretary of War, has the honor to transmit to the House of Representatives, in compliance with resolution of the House of the 20th ultimo, report of a reconnaissance made by Captain W. A. Jones, Corps of Engineers, in the year 1873, for a wagon-road from the line of the Union Pacific Railroad, in Wyoming Territory, to the Yellowstone National Park and Fort Ellis, Montana Territory, together with letter of the Chief of Engineers, of the 13th instant, transmitting the same.

H. T. CROSBY,
Chief Clerk.

WAR DEPARTMENT, *June* 16, 1874.

OFFICE OF THE CHIEF OF ENGINEERS,
Washington, D. C., June 13, 1874.

SIR: In compliance with the reference to this Office of a resolution of the House of Representatives of the 20th ultimo, I have the honor to transmit herewith a copy of a report of a reconnaissance of Northwestern Wyoming, made in the summer of 1873, by Captain W. A. Jones, Corps of Engineers, chief engineer of the Department of the Platte, under the orders of Brig. Gen. E. O. C. Ord, commanding that department.

It would appear from the report of Captain Jones that the wagon-road to Montana, by the Yellowstone Park, proposed by him, would open a route that, whatever may be the advantages of the Missouri River route, would tend to keep down rates, and would prove advantageous to the Government in the transportation of military and Indian supplies.

The route passes the military posts of Camp Stambaugh and Camp Brown and the Crow Indian agency, and is stated to be the shortest and most practicable route to the Yellowstone Park and Montana; traversing a fine mineral and agricultural country in the Wind River Valley; an extensive area of well-timbered and well-watered country about the upper valleys of the Snake and Yellowstone Rivers, where the soil is fertile and the rain falls equably through the season; and also a fine agricultural country in the valley of the Yellowstone below the falls.

It would give an outlet to the mineral and agricultural resources of Montana, which is stated by Captain Jones to be one of the most productive mining regions of the West; and, in that connection, it is to be noted that this route would save two hundred and fifty miles of railroad transportation, or the distance from Point of Rocks to Corinne, which is the present point of departure on the Union Pacific Railroad for the posts in Montana.

Very respectfully, your obedient servant,

A. A. HUMPHREYS,
Brigadier-General and Chief of Engineers.

Hon. WM. W. BELKNAP,
Secretary of War.

Unexpected delay has occurred in the copying of the maps by which the report is accompanied, and they will be transmitted within a few days.

HEADQUARTERS DEPARTMENT OF THE PLATTE,
OFFICE OF THE ENGINEER OFFICER,
Omaha, Nebr., May 9, 1874.

SIR: I have the honor to transmit herewith my final report upon the military reconnaissance of Northwestern Wyoming, made during the summer of 1873.

I take great pleasure in thanking my associates in the field-work for their uniform courtesy and devotion to duty; the officers of the department staff for their kindly and efficient assistance while I was preparing my outfit for the field; the officers and men of Company I, Second Cavalry, for their constant and willing assistance; Lieut. R. H. Young, Fourth Infantry, for his extremely arduous and efficient services as acting assistant quartermaster and assistant commissary of subsistence for the expedition; and Mr. Charles Curtis, pack-master, for his untiring energy and enthusiastic devotion to duty.

The report is accompanied by the following reports, viz:

Botany, by Dr. C. C. Parry;

Geology, by Professor T. B. Comstock;

Astronomy, by Lieut. S. E. Blunt, Thirteenth Infantry;

Entomology, by J. D. Putnam; and

One map (in the preparation of which valuable information was obtained from the maps of Professor Hayden and Captains Barlow and Heap, United States Engineers) showing the region traversed, and forty-nine trail-maps, showing, on a large scale, the topography along each day's march.

Considering the extremely successful results in that field, the report upon botany is rather more meager than I had anticipated. Ten new species were collected, none of which are described.

Dr. Heizmann's report upon mineral and thermal waters has not yet reached me; delayed, I suppose, by his sickness. It will be transmitted as soon as I receive it.*

In conclusion, permit me, sir, to thank you for your kindly interest and constant and intelligent assistance, to which much of our success must be ultimately attributed.

I am, sir, very respectfully, your obedient servant,

W. A. JONES,
Captain of Engineers.

Brig. Gen. E. O. C. ORD,
Commanding Department of the Platte.

---

* Report since received, and is appended hereto.

HEADQUARTERS DEPARTMENT OF THE PLATTE,
Omaha, Nebr., May 11, 1874.

SIR: Captain Jones's report and accompanying maps of an exploration of Northwestern Wyoming are herewith inclosed. He received from me, besides the written instructions stated in the report, verbal directions to find, if possible, a good route from the south, via the Wind River Valley and Upper Yellowstone, into Montana, which the report shows he accomplished.

The trail-maps give a correct and detailed picture of the country passed over; the reports of the geologist and botanist, with Captain Jones's description, explain its resources and capacity to support a large population, and show that the country to the south and west, and in the vicinity of Yellowstone Lake, will not, for agricultural purposes, require irrigation, as does the most of Wyoming and Montana.

Valuable minerals were found, especially in the Wind River and Shoshone Mountains.

The fact that this route, north of the Wind River Valley, passes through a timbered country, over which the mild southwest winds prevail in winter, renders it probable that, even at great elevations, it is not liable to drifting snows. Its shortness compared with the present traveled route via Corinne, the mildness of the climate, fertility of the soil, and abundance of water, coal, wood, &c., in the Wind River Valley, are strong reasons for opening the route for the use of the military posts, and the people of Montana, which section is languishing for the want of an outlet for its valuable mineral and agricultural productions.

I therefore recommend that Congress be asked for an appropriation of $60,000 to open a wagon-road from Camp Brown, or some convenient point on the Union Pacific Railroad, to Fort Ellis, or Helena, Montana.

I am, sir, very respectfully, your obedient servant,

E. O. C. ORD,
Brigadier-General Commanding.

The ADJUTANT-GENERAL UNITED STATES ARMY,
Through Headquarters Military Division
of the Missouri, Chicago, Ill.

[First indorsement.]

HEADQUARTERS MILITARY DIVISION OF THE MISSOURI,
Chicago, May 15, 1874.

Respectfully forwarded to the headquarters of the Army.

P. H. SHERIDAN,
Lieutenant-General Commanding.

[Second indorsement.]

HEADQUARTERS OF THE ARMY,
Washington, May 18, 1874.

Respectfully forwarded to the Adjutant-General.

By command of General Sherman:

WILLIAM D. WHIPPLE,
Assistant Adjutant-General.

[Third indorsement.]

WAR DEPARTMENT, ADJUTANT-GENERAL'S OFFICE,
Washington, May 19, 1874.

Respectfully referred to the Chief of Engineers. *To be returned.*

E. D. TOWNSEND,
Adjutant-General.

CHICAGO, *May* 16, 1874.

COLONEL: The inclosed order* was issued in order to give Capt. William A. Jones, Engineer Corps, a chance to have his work of last summer published; but I wish it to be distinctly understood that I in no manner can indorse the contemplated road from the Point of Rocks, on the Union Pacific Railroad, to Fort Ellis, via Yellowstone Lake, as a military necessity.

If the Government desire to make appropriation for the benefit of the mining population at Atlantic City, and the settlers in and about Camp Brown in the Popo Agie Valley, I have no objection; but I am not prepared to give even a shadow of support to anything so absurd as the military necessity for such a road.

The land-transportation now, via Carroll on the Missouri River, to Fort Ellis is only two hundred and twenty miles, over a good road.

I am, colonel, very respectfully, your obedient servant,

P. H. SHERIDAN,
Lieutenant-General Commanding.

Col. W. D. WHIPPLE,
Assistant Adjutant-General,
Headquarters of the Army, Washington, D. C.

[First indorsement.]

HEADQUARTERS OF THE ARMY,
Washington, May 19, 1874.

Official copy respectfully forwarded to the Secretary of War.

W. T. SHERMAN,
General.

[Second indorsement.]

WAR DEPARTMENT, ADJUTANT-GENERAL'S OFFICE,
Washington, May 20, 1874.

Respectfully referred to the Chief of Engineers, to whom was referred the report of Captain Jones of his explorations in Northwestern Wyoming, on the 19th instant. To be returned.

By order:

E. D. TOWNSEND,
Adjutant-General.

---

* Special Order No. 30, Headquarters Military Division of the Missouri, May 15, 1874.

GENERAL REPORT.

CHAPTER I.

DESCRIPTIVE JOURNAL.

Fort Bridger—Pacific Springs—Hostile Indians—South Pass—Sweetwater River—Camp Stambaugh—Camp Brown—Shoshonee agency—Hot Sulphur Spring—Wind River—Owl Creek Mountains—Valley of the Big Horn—Discovery of the Sierra Shoshonee—Ascent of the Washakee Needles—Shoshonee Village—Washakee—Indian Scouts—Stinkingwater River—Crossing the Sierra Shoshonee—Stinkingwater Pass—Yellowstone Lake—Great Falls on Grand Cañon—Explanation of origin—Hot Springs on Orange Creek—Great Hot Springs on Gardiner's River—Description and explanation—Fossil gas-bubbles—Amethyst Mountain—Fossil trees with hollows containing crystals of amethyst—Geyser basins—Yellowstone Lake—"Our Twenty-eighth Hop"—Ascent of Mount Sheridan—A deserted camp—Trouble with Indian scouts—Upper Yellowstone River—Discovery of "Two-Ocean Water"—The Three Tetons—Discovery of Togwotee Pass—Teton Basin—Head of Wind River—Return to Camp Brown.

[Special Orders No. 80.—Extract.]

HEADQUARTERS DEPARTMENT OF THE PLATTE,
Omaha, Neb., May 15, 1873.

4. Capt. William A. Jones, Corps of Engineers, will proceed as soon as practicable to Northwestern Wyoming, and there make a reconnaissance of the country within the territory about the headwaters of the Snake, Green, Big Horn, Grey Bull, Clark's Fork, and Yellowstone Rivers. He will organize and equip his party at Fort Bridger.

Second Lieut. S. E. Blunt, Thirteenth Infantry, will accompany Captain Jones as assistant.

Assistant Surgeon C. L. Heizmann, United States Army, will report to Captain Jones for duty with the expedition, and to the commanding officer of the escort as medical officer for the troops.

The acting assistant quartermaster and *assistant* commissary of subsistence appointed by the commanding officer of the escort for his troops will perform the duties of *assistant* quartermaster and *assistant* commissary of subsistence for the expedition.

5. Company I, Second Cavalry, (*Noyes's*,) is detailed as escort for the reconnaissance of Northwestern Wyoming by Captain Jones, Corps of Engineers. The company will proceed by rail on the 4th proximo to join Captain Jones's party at Fort Bridger.

The Quartermaster's Department will furnish the necessary transportation.

* * * * * * *

8. Second Lieut. R. H. Young, Fourth Infantry, will report in person to Capt. H. E Noyes, Second Cavalry, for temporary duty with his company.

* * * * * * *

By command of Brigadier-General Ord.

GEO. D. RUGGLES,
Assistant Adjutant-General.

In compliance with the above order I organized an expedition in Omaha, Nebr., consisting of the following persons, viz: Professor T. B. Comstock, geologist; Dr. C. C. Parry, clerk, botanist, and meteorologist; Assistant Surgeon C. L. Heizmann, U. S. A., chemist; Second Lieut. S. E. Blunt, Thirteenth Regiment of Infantry, astronomer; Second Lieut. R. H. Young, Fourth Regiment of Infantry, acting assistant quartermaster and *assistant* commissary of subsistence; four topographers, one astronomical assistant, one meteorological assistant, three general assistants, one chief packer, two guides, and two laborers.

The party was concentrated and went into camp at Fort Bridger, Wyoming, June 5, the escort joining the same date. The officers on duty with the latter were Capt. H. E. Noyes, Lieutenants C. T. Hall, F. W. Kingsbury, and R. H. Young.

The sum of $8,000 had previously been allotted to me from the appropriation for "surveys for military defenses," for the purpose of making the reconnaissance, and proved sufficient.

The transportation, as furnished by the Quartermaster's Department, consisted of eight wagons and sixty-six pack and saddle mules, in charge of one pack-master and ten packers; also three six-mule teams and wagons were turned over to me for transfer to Camp Stambaugh.

Until June 12, the time was occupied in equipping the party, making final preparations for the march, and completing the preparatory work of the several field-parties. From Colonel Flint, the commanding officer of the post, I received the most cordial and hearty assistance, which contributed not a little toward our success.

An expedition for an ascent of the Uintah Mountains, at the head of Henry's Fork, was sent out, but on account of the great quantity of snow and the limited time at their disposal, was obliged to return unsuccessful. On the 6th of June the water rose so high in Black's Fork as to force us to abandon our first camp and seek a drier one.

Thursday, June 12.—The expedition broke camp at 8 a. m. and took up its line of march, moving northeasterly to the Big Muddy River, a distance of eighteen miles.

On the march the party was organized as follows: geologist, with one assistant; meteorologist, with two assistants; astronomer, with one assistant; medical officer, with a complete outfit for the analysis, in the field, of mineral and thermal waters and gases; chief topographer, with two parties of two each, one on the general triangulation and the other in charge of the odometer measurements and general description of the line of march. The odometers (three) were carried on a wheel attached to a pair of shafts, arranged for facility in moving over bad trails through timber.

The train, consisting of eleven wagons with the packers as teamsters, was in charge of Lieut. R. H. Young, acting assistant quartermaster for the expedition. These wagons carried a four months' supply of provisions, a complete outfit for a pack-train, and ten days' half-forage, besides the usual stores and camp-equipage. All supplies and train-material were concentrated at Fort Bridger in preference to the Wind River posts, because of the greater certainty with which it could be done in a limited space of time.

The triangulation was carried on with a small transit-theodolite, starting from points established by me in 1871, and using the prominent landmarks along the route as signals. The system worked well, the topographers having no difficulty in keeping up with the column in any march it could make. The odometers did not work well, three of them on the same wheel failing to record a like number of revolutions or even any approach to it.

The unusually high water in Black's Fork had seriously undermined the abutments of the bridge north of the post, but fortunately nine of the wagons crossed it with safety. The tenth broke through, but was quickly rescued, and the hole repaired, valuable and timely assistance being rendered by Captain Noyes and his command.

The line of march lay across the country known as Colorado Desert, flanking the southeastern extremity of the Wind River Mountains, and thence following up the Wind River Valley to Camp Brown. As far as these mountains the region is almost rainless, but the extraordinary spring rains had extended over it and fallen as snow in the surrounding mountains in enormous quantities. As a consequence, the streams were swollen to a remarkable extent, and rendered well-nigh impassable.

At this camp there is no wood, but little grass, and the water was excessively muddy.

Friday, June 13.—Broke camp early and commenced the passage of the Big Muddy. This was attended with great difficulty, as the stream, barely fordable, was running very swiftly, and the bottom was soft. The first wagon mired in the rapid current, and the mules were rescued with much difficulty, great skill and energy being displayed by the men in charge. After this accident a line was led from each wagon to the opposite bank and manned by Captain Noyes's men, and only the best teams hitched to them. The passage, though tedious, was effected successfully, and a march of 13.2 miles made to Ham's Fork by 3.30 p. m. Here the water was so high that the valley was largely overflowed and the ford absolutely impassable. Fortunately an old abandoned bridge, with its middle piers washed away, was found across the main channel, and this was successfully used in making a passage. The teams were unhitched and the wagons lightened to 1,000 pounds, and a detachment from the escort was then stationed on the opposite side, who drew them over the shaky bridge with great caution by means of a line. The unloaded material was then carried over by these men, and the teams led over with extreme care. There remained about one-fourth of a mile of low bottom, of alkaline soil, which was considerably overflowed and cut up with sloughs, over which the greatest difficulty was experienced. Work continued until nightfall, which found six wagons with their cargoes safely across, while the remainder were mired in the bottom, which was strewn with material unloaded from them.

Good grass and wood at this camp.

Saturday, June 14.—Commencing early, the passage was completed by 1 p. m., but the men and animals had worked so hard that it was not deemed advisable to make any march, and we went into camp. I consider this passage quite a feat, the success of which was very largely due to the conception and energy of Captain Noyes and to the untiring efforts of Mr. Curtis, wagon-master.

During the night some horse-thieves, who had been prowling around us, succeeded in getting two horses belonging to the escort. A party was sent out but failed to find them. Before leaving, however, the services of a citizen of Granger were secured to capture them if possible.

Sunday, June 15.—Marched 18.9 miles to Green River, which was at flood-height. Excellent road and good camp.

Monday, June 16.—Moved 3.3 miles down the river to the stage-ferry, by means of which we effected a crossing by 1 p. m., and went into camp. Green River flows through a narrow flat valley which is covered with sage-brush interspersed with good meadow near the water and on the islands in the stream. Groves of the inevitable cotton-wood are numerous. The stream is here of considerable size at any season of the year, but generally is fordable at a few places. Good camp.

Tuesday, June 17.—Moved 12.4 miles to the Big Sandy and commenced crossing it at 11 a. m. This stream was at flood-height, and the ford difficult from moving sands in deep water. The wagons were unloaded and reloaded after their beds had been lined with tarpaulins and tent-canvas. Teams of eight and ten mules were then hitched on, and they were carefully drawn through the swift current, the water coming up above the middle of their beds. The passage was effected by 2 p. m., and we went into camp. One mule was drowned. The two stolen horses were brought in this afternoon, having been recaptured near Black's Fork. The country passed through is a flat plain marked by a few buttes and benches; soil dry and sandy in many places, and the whole covered with a thick growth of sage-brush.

Big Sandy River is a stream having its source in the Wind River Mountains, and runs through a narrow sandy valley with but little grass and no trees.

This camp is at a stage-station on the route from Bryan to South Pass City and the Sweetwater mines. A little grass and no wood.

Wednesday, June 18.—Moved 17.1 miles to the second crossing of the Big Sandy. The ford was much more difficult than that at the first crossing on account of holes and quicksands. The channel was very much wider, though the water was hardly so deep. Twelve mules were hitched to one wagon, and hauled it safely across; but as this exposed too many mules to the danger of getting tangled in the harness and drowned in the rapid current, a line was led across to the opposite side, to which a ten-mule team was hitched, besides being manned by all of the men of Captain Noyes's command. By this means the wagons were pulled across, but not without much difficulty and very hard labor. One wagon was overturned in the stream, but its contents, except a few insignificant articles, were saved by prompt and skillful action. Fortunately they were not of such a nature as to be damaged seriously by being wet for a short time. One mule became entangled in the harness amid-stream and was drowned.

The ford was reached 12 m., and the crossing completed by 4 p. m., when we went into camp.

This is an eating-station on the stage-route. Water and grass; no wood.

Thursday, June 19.—Marched ten miles to the Little Sandy, where the crossing was made by 12 m., and camp was made. There is plenty of grass here, but no wood. The country traversed in the past two days is a hot, sandy plain, supporting a thick growth of sage-brush and grease-wood, and swept by strong winds from the southwest daily after about 10 a. m., during the hot season.

Commenced immediately laying out a secondary base-line. This work was finished by noon of—

Friday, June 20, when we broke camp and marched 13.8 miles to the Dry Sandy. Gnats were extremely troublesome at this camp, where there is but little grass, and no wood. It is a stage-station. The Dry Sandy is an insignificant stream which goes dry except at the stage-station, where there is a spring. The country traversed has the same characteristics as that passed through on the previous days.

Saturday, June 21.—Broke camp at 5.30 a. m., in the midst of a driving storm of cold rain, which soon turned into snow, and marched 10.6 miles to the stage-station at Pacific Springs. Here the storm turned into a severe gale of cold wind. Wood, grass, and water at this camp, which is on the northern border of the hot sage-brush plain over which we have been traveling. This vicinity is the "South Pass" of the early geographers, about which there has been so much fictitious writing and picture-making. As there are no mountains about it, and as the old road hardly crosses a hill of any magnitude, the misnomer is evident. The road, however, crosses at this point the divide between the Atlantic and the Pacific flowing waters, and this gave origin to the name.

Captain Noyes, Lieutenant Hall, and a small escort went ahead to Camp Stambaugh.

At this point I received a communication from the commanding officer of Camp Stambaugh, informing me of the presence of hostile Indians in his neighborhood. Rumors had already reached us of their depredations, and I had already commenced precautionary measures by keeping my guides in the morning and evening on the lookout for signs.

Sunday, June 22.—The night was very cold, the minimum thermometer registering 21° F. Broke camp at 1 p. m. and marched four to six miles to the Sweetwater River, crossing over a bridge that is used in high-water seasons. The stream is generally fordable. Evidences of a recent and considerable fall in the water were abundant. The river here runs through a narrow, flat-bottomed valley, with sharp rugged sides of metamorphic rock. The soil is rich in garnets of small size, with slight indications of gold. The road traversed thus far from Fort Bridger has been excellent.

Monday, June 23.—Broke camp at 6.30 a. m., and marched sixteen miles to Camp Stambaugh.

The route passes through the mining-towns of South Pass City and Atlantic City, and traverses the greater portion of the Sweetwater gold-mining region across the slopes of the southeastern extremity of the Wind River Mountains. These mines are in a belt of metamorphic schistose rocks that occupies the axial line of the mountains. They are very favorably located for working, and good roads are within easy reach, although water is so scarce that placer-mining does not prosper as it certainly otherwise would. On Strawberry Creek, near Camp Stambaugh, it was found remunerative to haul the dirt several miles to water. The gold occurs singularly free in veins of a bluish, impure quartz, generally rather thin. For some reason, or reasons, this industry is in a languishing condition. This was partly caused by a great silver excitement in Utah, which drew away a large portion of the miners to that ever-fascinating new country that they do not happen to be occupying. There is every indication here of gold in paying quantities, but a stage has been reached where capital is needed for further development.

Camp Stambaugh is situated on the southeastern extremity of the Wind River range, where it has run out to an elevation of about 8,000 feet above the level of the sea, and is exactly on the divide. Thus elevated in position, it lies between and commands the two lines of approach and escape over which the marauding parties of Sioux, Arapahoes, and Cheyennes, from about Fort Laramie and Fetterman, make their almost regular annual descents upon the Wind River and Sweetwater settlements and stage-stations, lying respectively to the north and south of it. These two lines are connected by difficult trails over the high foot-hills of the range, above and to the northwest of Camp Stambaugh and the exposed mining settlement, so that either can be chosen as a line of escape after an outrage.

The obvious mode of getting at these Indians, after their presence has been made known in the usual manner by some depredations, is to move the troops with the utmost celerity to some point near the junction or convergence of these lines, which probably would not be more than one hundred miles to the east or north of east from Camp Stambaugh, and there throw out an efficient line of signal-pickets. By this means, if they did not reach their objective point in advance of the escaping Indians, they would not be unlikely to stumble over them on the way.

Indians travel over a country guiding themselves by the prominent or noticeable landmarks, and when these are not sufficient, they build piles of stones on a hill or in a doubtful pass. As a consequence, their trails of general travel must almost of necessity converge or diverge at or near some of these points, and however much a party may scatter, it will come together again in the vicinity of some such place. These are really strategic points in Indian warfare, because the most difficult part of the matter is to get at the Indian, and he can best be reached through a thorough knowledge of his modes of travel.

About Camp Stambaugh and the Sweetwater mines the grazing is generally good, but the country is nearly barren of timber, which, however, is abundant higher up in the mountains. The climate is very severe, and strong winds are almost constantly prevalent.

Until June 28 the time was occupied in shoeing animals, repairs, &c., and as many as possible of the mines were examined by Professor Comstock and myself. Both of the box-chronometers, which had been carried by a mounted man in a basket attached to a sling, had been so erratic in their rates that they were left behind here, and the remainder of our work was done with pocket-chronometers. Three wagons and teams which we had brought from Fort Bridger were turned in.

We were received at this post with the utmost courtesy and attention, and the commanding officer, Lieutenant-Colonel Brackett, cheerfully accorded us every assistance in his power.

Friday, June 27.—Starting at 6 a. m., we marched 8.2 miles to Twin Creek. The road passed through Miner's Delight, the most thriving of the mining-towns in this locality, was very hilly, and in some places quite boggy from the late-melting snows. The long slopes of the foot-hills of the mountains are here covered with a splendid growth of grass, and there is a scattering growth of timber, pine, spruce, and aspen. It is a region admirably adapted for grazing.

Saturday, June 28.—Broke camp and marched 12.2 miles to Murphy's ranche, on the Little Popo-Agie River, which latter had very recently fallen so as to just permit us to ford it. There is here a small but well-sheltered valley of rich soil, where vegetables and hardy cereals are successfully cultivated.

Sunday, June 29.—At 6 a. m. we broke camp and marched 15.5 miles to the North Fork of the Big Popo-Agie River, crossing the valley of the principal stream on the route. This latter is of considerable size, has a rich soil, lies well for irrigation, and is well watered. The climate is quite mild. It is the old site of Camp Brown, and is now occupied by a small settlement of whites, among them several women.*

The valley of the North Fork is quite similar, although the land does not lie so well for irrigation. The grazing-land everywhere around is very fine.

Monday, June 30.—Marched eleven miles to Camp Brown. The road from the crossing to the Little Popo-Agie follows a monoclinal valley parallel to the mountains, and is excellent. The country is rolling, with a good soil, supporting a fine growth of grass, but no trees. Camp Brown is situated on the right bank of Little Wind River, just above the mouth of its north fork. The stream has just emerged through a short cañon from the long rolling outlines of the mountains, and shows a broad, flat, and well-watered valley of rich soil. A large area of land in this valley can be irrigated with but little expense. The climate is very mild and, so far as observation has yet gone, but little snow falls during winter. The mild and dry climate is easily accounted for from

* Shortly afterward hostile Indians made a descent upon this settlement and butchered two of these women. They also attacked Murphy's ranche, but were driven off.

its situation under the lee of a very high range of mountains, which catches the prevailing storms on its southern face and deflects them to the south, whence they are drawn down the Sweetwater Valley as through a funnel, making a fierce eddy and the corresponding severe climate over South Pass City and Camp Stambaugh.

On the river, two miles below the post, there is a large, hot sulphur spring in a small lake, which has remarkable properties for bathing. An analysis of the water, by Dr. Heizmann, discovered chloride of lime as one of the constituents. The temperature is usually 110° F. Near by there is a running oil-spring, and also large beds of gypsum and alabaster. There is also a cold sulphur spring a few miles southwest from the post.

Near by is the agency of the Eastern bands of the Shoshonee Indians. Their chief, Washakee, is thoroughly well known on the plains, and is a man of considerable ability and foresight. He expressed a strong desire to see a railroad come through his country as a result of this expedition, and took great interest in it.

Table of distances.

	Miles.
Fort Bridger to Camp Stambaugh	135
Bryan, on the Union Pacific Railroad, to Camp Stambaugh	99.5
Bryan to South Pass City	93
Bryan to Camp Brown	146

Bryan is the point from which supplies are shipped to the Wind River posts.

Until July 10 we were engaged in turning in the wagons and wagon-train material, rigging up the pack-train, and in measuring out a base-line and carefully locating the principal landmarks with a large transit-theodolite. An expedition for the ascent of the Wind River Mountains went out on the 5th and returned on the 10th. Ten Shoshone Indians were enlisted as scouts, and Narkok, a petty chief, was employed as guide. These Indians stipulated that their families should be permitted to accompany them. To this I had no objection, as it insured their good behavior, and they could easily travel as fast as we would be likely to.

We received the utmost courtesy and attention from the officers at the post, and the most cordial assistance from the commanding officer, Captain Torrey, and Lieutenant Guthrie, post quartermaster. On the 10th of July we broke camp early and attempted to make a march, but many, in fact most, of the train-mules were entirely new to packing, and created such havoc, that we were quite content to move one half of a mile across the river and go into camp again. It took all day to accomplish even this much, and there was great amusement and excitement over the desperate struggles of the frightened and frenzied mules. Mules require a season of training before packs should be put on them for a march, but this we had no time for, and were obliged to break them in while on the march. This involved the breaking of nearly every breakable article in our outfit, and many a sigh was mingled with the laughter over the antics of some wild mule as one after another of the fragile luxuries of camp-life disappeared from usefulness.

Friday, July 11.—The morning was spent in repairing the damages of yesterday's attempt at a march. Made a start at 2.30 p. m. and marched 8.4 miles to Sage Creek. This small stream has a bottom of soft mud and runs between almost vertical banks of alluvium. Our camp was at the nearest point to Camp Brown where it is fordable. There is no ford below it. Poor camp. There is a little grass, no wood, and poor water.

Saturday, July 12.—Marched 10.7 miles to Wind River. Passed over a high plateau covered with sage-brush, from which there is a considerable descent to the valley of the river. This was swollen to a great height and was not considered fordable. We were prepared to make a raft-ferry over it, but I thought it advisable while looking for a suitable spot to also see if a ford could be possibly found.

Sunday, July 13.—This morning the Indians set at work with the utmost spirit in search of a ford. They stripped off all clothing except the soldier's blouse, with which they had been furnished, and, mounting bare-back, drove their ponies into the stream at every possible point, where they soon became involved in many dangerous as well as ludicrous situations. Three or four hours of this sort of work was followed by the announcement that they had found a possible ford. The line wound around and up and down among the islands and shoals in the channel in the most tortuous manner, and displayed an intuitive knowledge of the effects of flowing water that was remarkable. It was really a skillful feat. Great care had to be observed in this crossing, as the line frequently ran along narrow shoals amidstream, where the rapid current was more than sw mming-deep a few steps on either side. Six hours were occupied in effecting it, when we went into camp on the opposite side.

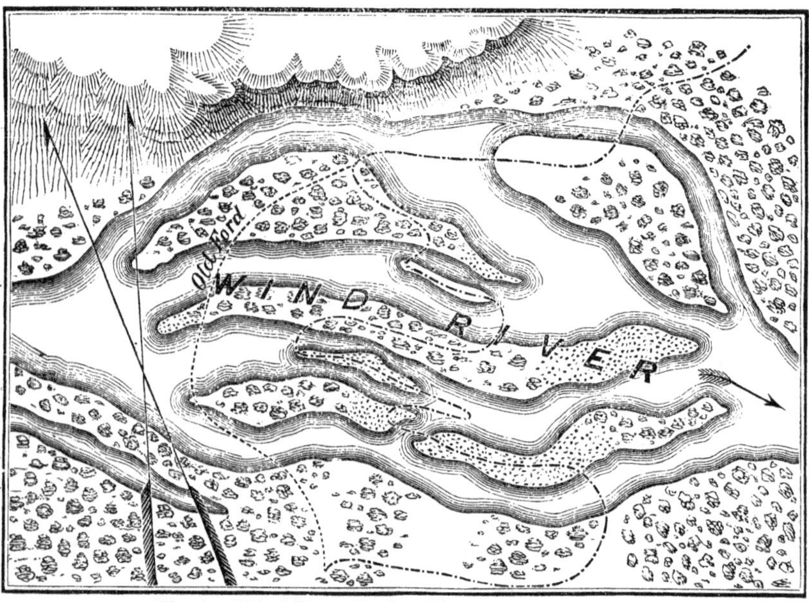

Fig. 1. Wind River Ford. (Shown by broken line.)

A fine specimen of gold quartz (*float*) was found near this camp, washed down probably from near the summit of the Wind River range.

Crossing the river afforded a rare spectacle; for a while, the long, tortuous ford was completely lined with the motley crowd of soldiers, citizens, pack-mules, and gaudily-dressed Indians, with their squaws, children, and numerous loose ponies. Among them was a colt which, on account of the deep water, was strapped legs up, to the pack carried by its mother. The presence of these Indians, who formed a small

ERRATA.

The following paragraph should follow immediately after Figure 1, page 12:

In the vicinity of this crossing, Wind River flows through a broad riband of meadow, of varying width, with numerous groves of cottonwood, which grows to quite a large size. The approach by the right is over very high terraces of soft earth. These plateaux are so high that their cultivation by irrigation is probably out of the question. The soil is rich, and is covered with sage-brush and the characteristic bunch-grass, which latter is of quite superior size. Wild licorice occurs in the valley. On the left bank these terraced deposits are mostly worn away, leaving many buttes and benches, among them Crow Heart Butte, whose height and characteristic features render it a very noted landmark in the valley.

village, gave us a rare opportunity of studying their habits and mode of life. They proved to be extremely vigilant, and their conduct was unexceptionable.

Monday, July 14.—Marched 14.8 miles up Dry Creek, on which we made our camp. The country rapidly grows coarse, dry, barren, and very dusty. No water, except in the creek, where it is poor; wood and grass are scarce.

Tuesday, July 15.—A topographical party which had been sent to a station in the Wind River Mountains overtook camp at 10 a. m., when we took up the march and moved 10.3 miles along the same creek, going into camp at a spot where there was plenty of wood, tolerable grass, and poor water. Dry Creek, from its name, probably does not always carry water through the season.

Wednesday, July 16.—Broke camp 9 a. m., and marched 18.5 miles through the foot-hills of the Owl Creek Mountains. The line of march lay through a country extremely desolate and quite mountainous in its character, the rocks being frequently tilted vertically, with some very large dikes of quartzite. Some quite extensive beds of gypsum and alabaster occur, with deposits of iron-ore, (brown hematite.) These give to one cañon on the route a highly variegated appearance, which led us to call it "Painted-Rock Cañon." Along the route, water, wood, and grass are very scarce, and only one stream (the Little Muddy) was crossed. It was almost dry thus early in the season. At camp the water was from springs that were nearly dry, and was quite alkaline; and the grass was thin and poor. There is no wood. In this region the rocks are tilted and flexed in quite a remarkable manner, apparently by forces from two directions, making a considerable angle with each other. I saw indications of coal, but may be mistaken.

Thursday, July 17.—Broke camp at 9.30 a. m., and marched across the Owl Creek Mountains, camping on the Middle Fork of Owl Creek. Distance 10.5 miles, over an easy trail. Wagons from Camp Brown have been taken across at this point and as far north as the Grey Bull River.

The mountain-slopes are generally rounded, and covered with a fine growth of grass; timber, aspen, pine, spruce, and hemlock, occurs in extensive groves, and there are many springs and small streams on the northern water-shed.

At 5.30 a. m. I took a small topographical party, with an escort and some Indian scouts, and started to make the ascent of the peak which forms the climax of the range, and reached the summit by 9 a. m.

I have named this peak Phlox Mountain, from the extensive fields of white phlox that its slopes display. From this point it was seen that we were entering the Big Horn Valley close under the eastern flank of an enormous range of mountains whose existence, although suspected, was unknown. Subsequent observations showed it to be the same as that bordering Yellowstone Lake on the east, and connected with it by a belt of massive peaks fully sixty miles in width. To the north and east lay the Big Horn Valley, visible through nearly its whole extent, with its streams running transversely from the unknown range to our left into the Big Horn River northward. As far as the eye could reach could be seen a grand and endless series of faces of broken strata of the sedimentary rocks looking up to and dipping away from the Owl Creek range. Strangely enough no strata could be seen dipping from the vastly larger range on our left. Toward the southeast the Owl Creek range evidently ran out in the vicinity of their crossing of the Big Horn River; to the northeast were the Big Horn Mountains, of which little could be seen except Cloud Peak and a few peaks in its vicinity, distant one hundred miles. Subsequent and frequent examinations of this range from a distance of eighty miles, and from many high points, show that, with the exception of the cluster of culminating points just mentioned, the range must be a low one, with the general line of the summit much below the timber-line. North of Cloud Peak this summit appears remarkably even and free from peaks, from which I infer that it is a high, rugged plateau. Very little water drains from their western slopes, and the country appears quite desolate and barren. To the southeast lay the "bad lands" that are inclosed within the angle of the "big bend" of Wind River, coming quite up to the foot of the Owl Creek range. The quantity of water that drains from the south slopes of this range is quite small, and from the north slopes but little is supplied to Owl Creek, which is in reality a drain from the mountains to the westward; to the south, across the valley, the Wind River Mountains stand out in massive grandeur, with snow-clad peaks along their whole length. From the Indians I learned that the snow disappears during the summer from all except in the vicinity of Union Peak. Along their flank, and sweeping up to their summit from the valley below with wonderful symmetry and regularity, lay the huge layers of Silurian, Carboniferous, Triassic, Jurassic, Cretaceous, and Tertiary rocks, forming immense ridges, and forcing one to the simile of the petrified waves of a mighty geological ocean.

I noticed in this vicinity that along the summit, in the neighborhood of Phlox Mountain, the metamorphic rocks are similar and are arranged similarly to those at the summit of the Wind River range. Good camp.

Friday, July 18.—Left camp at 6 a. m., with a topographical party, accompanied by Professor Comstock and Lieutenant Blunt, to make the ascent of what appeared to be the highest peak in the range west of us, distant about fourteen miles. The approach appeared to be one of great difficulty, and when I asked the Indians if they could guide me to a point somewhere near it, they said they knew of no way to get there at all. I had examined the country for an approach the day before from Phlox Mountain, and could see none except by following along the south slopes of the Owl Creek range. This varied considerably from a direct line, but seemed to be free from cañons. The question was a serious one, as the peak was so far away, and evidently of such a difficult character, that a mistake would be attended with a considerable loss of time. At 12 m., after a rapid march of six hours, I ascended one of the peaks in the Owl Creek range to reconnoiter for a further approach, and was fortunate in picking out one by which we could probably reach the foot of the peak by night-fall. In a short time we reached Owl Creek, just above its grand cañon along the anticlinal axis of the mountains, and at 6 p. m., thinking ourselves near enough for the assault to-morrow, we made our bivouac, after a pretty hard day's work.

Saturday, July 19.—Taking an early start, we commenced examining the peak for a feasible point of attack, and marched up Owl Creek until 9 a. m. before finding one. We then secured our animals, and at 9.30 a. m. the ascent was commenced.

This peak, to which I have given the name of the "Washakee Needles," is a terrible crag. Its appearance from the valley of Owl Creek, above our camp, is simply frightful, sheer precipices of whitish lamellar granite rising up from the valley fully 2,500 feet high. From this side it is unassailable, and we spent the best part of the morning in looking for a way across to the other side, expecting to find there a slope of some kind. After five hours of severe and extremely dangerous climbing, three of the party—two of the topographers, very fortunately, and to my astonishment, with the barometer and theodolite—and myself found ourselves at the limit of progress toward the summit. The peak is formed by several huge plates of granite, whose summit-lines are serrated with teeth at which the edges are generally vertical. The summits are so narrow that in places one can actually sit astride, with legs dangling over great precipices on either side. We were upon the serrated summit of the plate adjacent to the highest one, whose summit loomed with precipitous sides fully 200 feet above us. Between was an immense gulf separating the plates. Not only was further progress impossible, but we could see now that the summit was absolutely inaccessible except with the aid of appliances for climbing, and probably not even with them. We took the angle and estimated the distance to the summit; finished our instrumental work upon a ledge a little below our highest point, for there was not room on top to set up an instrument and use it, and were very glad, indeed, to commence the descent. The situation upon our perch—no one dared stand up on it—was anything but pleasant, and we left it only with the burning regret that it had not been the summit. Messrs. Putnam and Bond, who carried the instruments up, certainly deserved success. The approximate altitude of the peak is 12,250 feet. From our dangerous perch the view, spread out to the north and west, was grand and even terrible. As far as could be seen lay a jagged mass of peaks of dark-brown volcanic *ejectamenta*, which showed black in the shadows of the falling sun, giving to the whole that appearance of black shadow and mystery which always produces such strong impressions on the mind.

Later observations lead me to the belief that we were looking upon the headwaters of the Snake and, possibly, the Yellowstone Rivers. We were upon the highest peak in sight in this range.

By 5 p. m. we had completed the descent, and found the rest of the party, one of whom, Lieutenant Blunt, had narrowly escaped with his life.

We marched back over our trail until after dark, and then made our weary bivouac for the night.

Owl Creek, above its cañon, runs through a splendid park, abounding in game—mountain sheep, bear, elk, deer, and buffalo.

Sunday, July 20.—Started back a. m. for camp over a route selected from the mountain yesterday, and reached it 1.30 p. m.

Monday, July 21.—Marched north-northwest eighteen miles to Cottonwood Creek. The line of march lay through the grassy and well-watered foot-hills of the mountains. Scrub-cedar grows upon the hills, and cotton-wood along the streams, both somewhat sparsely. This country is a favorite range for buffalo. The grass is very fine. At camp we found a very cold spring, temperature 41° F. Wood is scarce, and there is an outcrop of coal near by. I have renamed this stream Mee-yer-o Creek, giving it an Indian name. The early trappers, following the Indian practice of referring to streams by means of the natural features about them, have inflicted the country with numberless Cotton-Wood, Willow, Sage, &c., Creeks, which is sure to lead to much confusion hereafter. From what I could gather, I am of the opinion that the Shoshonees do not have distinct names for the streams and mountains, but refer them, where they are not in sight, to prominent landmarks or characteristic natural features in their immediate vicinity; thus, the Stinking Water River would be spoken of as "the stink-water in such a direction and near such a landmark;" the South Fork of the Stinking

Water, as "the water with a peculiar-shaped rock close by it;" Beaver Creek, as "the little water near such a landmark, where there are many beavers;" Wind River, as "the big water by such a landmark, where the wind blows very hard," &c. I do not think that they have names for the mountain-ranges at all. As there is a remarkable sameness among the natural features along the streams in the plateaus of the Rocky Mountains, it results that a large number of streams are named alike. On this account I have changed a few names.

Tuesday, July 22.—Marched 13.6 miles to Beaver Creek, and went into camp 12.30 p. m., where we found good grass, wood, and water. The country is still high-rolling, with fine grass all over it, and few trees. Extensive patches of the wild gooseberry grow along this stream. I have renamed it Gooseberry Creek, feeling little apprehension that the name will be duplicated.

Wednesday, July 23.—I find that by making marches in the forenoon everybody becomes too tired to work to advantage in the afternoon, and have therefore decided to make them in the afternoon, starting about noon. Were we simply marching through the country it would be different, but in cases of this kind the marching should be made subsidiary to the work of examining and describing the country. As our marches are short, it is not too fatiguing to travel in the heat of the day, and we are thus enabled to examine the country about camp during the forenoon, obviously to greater advantage. Another advantage is that the animals have plenty of time to graze before starting on the march, which they do not have when an early start is made, and it is very important that pack-animals should eat their fill before starting on a march.

Some Shoshonee Indians came in from Washakee's camp near the Stinking Water River. They report immense herds of buffalo lower down in the valley, and that the village is having a grand hunt. We have seen a number of straggling buffalo in the past few days, and several have been killed.

Marched 10.7 miles to Grey Bull River. This is a stream of considerable size, running through a narrow valley, which two or three miles above widens out very much and encroaches into the mountains. An expedition of miners, called the "Big Horn Expedition," came into this country from the South in 1870, and brought one wagon as far as this stream. Here they disbanded and the most of them returned to the settlements *via* Camp Brown, while a few made their way into Montana by the way of Clark's Fork and Rosebud.

Thursday, July 24.—Marched seventeen miles to a small tributary of the Stinking Water, which I have named Mee-tee-tsee Creek—a Shoshonee name. Grass and water are a little scarce. About three miles ahead of us, at the foot of a huge spur from the mountains, the Shoshonee village is encamped. The divide between the Grey Bull and the Stinking Water is quite high, and the descent into the valley of the latter rather abrupt.

We have had all day a good view of the Big Horn Mountains, and I am satisfied that, with the exception of Cloud Peak and a few peaks about it, the range is comparatively a low one. The valley of the Big Horn appears very desolate, except along the valleys of the streams, which are fringed, as usual, with cotton-woods and narrow, grassy bottoms.

Friday, July 25.—This morning Washakee, with a large party of his braves, in full dress, made me a state call. He was much interested in the expedition, but did not seem so well pleased at having so many of his best young men go with us as soldiers.

At 2 p. m. we moved camp 4.4 miles, to a point near the Shoshonee village. Five more of them were enlisted by Captain Noyes, and one joined us as a volunteer, raising the number of Indians with our party to seventeen. The captain also swapped off a poor unfortunate fellow who had developed a case of hopeless sore eyes for a healthy one. The tribe is terribly afflicted with syphilitic affections. The village was perched well up on the mountain-side, on a small stream which here opens out into a diminutive valley, just above a long, gloomy cañon. Its existence would never be suspected from below. From the lookouts the view of their sentinels swept all possible approaches thoroughly. Unobserved approach was impossible, and a better place for defense could not well be selected. Constant incursions into this valley of large war-parties of Sioux gave wisdom to their precautions.

To our surprise, the mountain-spur above us is composed almost, if not entirely, of volcanic matter, which, in some places, contains fossil trees of considerable size. Its measured altitude is 8,607 feet, which is 3,400 above the valley of the Stinking Water. Grass is thin and wood scarce.

Saturday, July 26.—Marched 18.8 miles to the North Fork of the Stinking Water River, crossing the South Fork, or Ish-a-woo-a River. I have given this stream the Indian name of a peculiar-shaped rock, by means of which they distinguish it. It is a remarkable, finger-shaped column of volcanic rock, standing alone in the valley, about three miles above our crossing. The valley of the Stinking Water has here an elevation of 5,273 feet above the sea, and is the lowest point touched by the expedition. Just below the junction of the two forks, and about a mile below our crossing, the river, by a deep and rugged but short cañon, cuts off the point of a sharp and high anticlinal ridge of yellow limestone which stands vertical along the summit, leaving a high, bold peak on the right bank, which the Indians use as a landmark. They refer to it as the "mountain with many cedars." I have, therefore, called it Cedar Mountain. High up on its southern face is a remarkable hole, which the Indians called my attention to, and said it was very deep. I could, with my glass, see that it was a hole, and intended to visit it after reaching camp, but was prevented from doing so by more urgent business. About twenty miles northeast from this point is a small, isolated cluster, which is probably the Heart Mountain of the early trappers and guides.

To-day we began meeting with huge spurs running out from the mountains at about right angles; also evidences of tremendous volcanic action. The drift in the valley is composed of the *débris* of volcanic rock. We passed the remains of a large depositing-sulphur spring. The water oozed from a cylindrical mound of soft mud, a little hardened on its rim and held together by the roots of a rank growth of water-grasses. It lies close to the Ish-a-woo-a River, on the south side near where our trail crosses, and probably at one time contributed largely to the odorific title of the main river. A few miles lower down, below the cañon, a mass of sulphur springs occur which still give good cause for the river's name. On the North Fork we found the extinct remains of a mass of depositing springs; the whole hill-side was covered with the large sedimentary mounds of soft black and brown earths, having a good deal of transparent gypsum in crystals and small pieces scattered through them.

On the mountains there is a tolerably heavy growth of coniferous trees, and along the streams the everlasting cottonwood flourishes. The valley of the North Fork for a considerable distance above the cañon has very little grass except a very tall, coarse kind, that grows in patches near the water, and is not sufficiently nutritious to induce the animals to eat it. The soil has a peculiar greasy, yellowish look, and only supports a stinted growth of grease-wood and sage-brush. The Stinking Water is a river of considerable size, and, probably, is rarely fordable below the junction of its two main forks. We had considerable difficulty in finding a ford across the Ish-a-woo-a, even this late in the season, and probably neither of the forks are fordable much earlier.

Above the cañon the waters of both streams are perfectly pure and have no smell. Fine trout are abundant and game has been very plentiful. The tracks indicated that the elk and mountain-sheep have lately moved higher up into the mountains.

Sunday, July 27.—Marched 14.7 miles up the North Fork of the Stinking Water, and camped at the mouth of its grand cañon. We entered the mountains yesterday. Along the trail the soil is rather poor and the grass is thin. Wood is abundant. The latter part of the trail, for about six or eight miles, is quite rough, and crosses a small but remarkable bed of tertiary deposits of colored marls and clays.

The mountains are very rugged. The rocks are mainly limestone, sandstone, and a coarse volcanic conglomerate. The sedimentary rocks soon disappear, and the peaks are composed of, apparently, horizontal layers of volcanic ejectamenta. The prevailing color is a dark-reddish brown, which gives the mountains their marked black haze in shadow and bronze tint in the light. The conglomerate weathers into the most fantastic pinnacles, needles, and grotesque forms. When interstratified with the rich brown sandstones it weathers into characteristic rounded columns, displaying tier upon tier, reaching above the timber-line into the clouds, of sculptured balconies supported by long processions of pilasters and clustered columns, while, clambering up from below, forests of spruce and pine, growing on seemingly impossible slopes, cover the mountain-side to the upper limit of forest-growth. Compared with any mountain scenery that I have seen, the effect is quite peculiar, and even magnificent. The massive grandeur of the huge peaks is suffused with a rare beauty of form and color. At the mouth of the cañon, upon either side, stand two lofty and slender peaks of similar form, which I have named "The Sentinels."

Monday, July 28.—Marched up the stream 9.1 miles. The trail enters the cañon, and is very difficult, leading along steep and seemingly impossible slopes above the river, with frequent precipices below and above. To avoid a huge precipice which reached quite into the river, unfordable through the cañon, it made a detour to the right over the most difficult hill met with on the trip. It did not seem possible for animals to climb it, and the mishaps to the pack-train were quite numerous.

The grotesque forms of the conglomerate previously alluded to afforded great amusement to the party. It is really something remarkable.

After the hill came a short, broad bottom of sage-brush, and then the huge precipice-walls of the cañon closed in upon the river, leaving only a narrow bank, first on one side and then the other, densely covered with cottonwoods, brush-willows, and scattering pines. It was necessary to ford the river repeatedly—no easy matter—and the dense undergrowth of brush made progress anything but pleasant. Earlier in the season this stream is in all probability unfordable, and progress along our trail therefore impossible. At last we came to a patch of grassy bottom, just large enough for the party to camp upon, and a halt was cheerfully called.

The cañon-walls are streaked with dikes and veins. To-day and thenceforward it was found necessary to send a pioneer party from the escort ahead of the main body to clear and make the trail. Captain Noyes generally took charge of this party, and to his untiring efforts the expedition owes much of its successful progress.

During the day the Indians have been following the fresh trail of two white men with two led horses, who have ascended the valley just ahead of us. After reaching camp one was sent ahead to reconnoiter, and about three miles farther on he found them, just as they had predicted; two white men with two spare horses, which were packed. They were prospectors from Clark's Fork, and were greatly relieved when they found we were not Sioux, as they had supposed upon first sight of our Indian scout.

Tuesday, *July* 29.—Laid in camp. The pack-train was so badly used up that it was necessary to give the animals rest, and replace the lost shoes and tighten the loose ones.

Wednesday, *July* 30.—Broke camp and marched 14.5 miles up the stream. The trail was extremely difficult and beset with danger, both upon land and in the water. In one place it was so dangerous that even the Indians dismounted and led their ponies over it. Those who understand how Indians stick to their ponies in the most unheard-of places rather than dismount, will appreciate the difficulties of a situation that induced them to travel on foot. The stream was forded seven times. At one of these crossings, which was quite difficult, a pack-mule lost his footing and floated, pack and all, some distance down stream. Through the extraordinary exertions of Mr. Curtis, our chief packer, this animal was saved, though at the expense of its cargo and aparejo. Mr. Curtis came very near drowning, and broke one of the bones of his right hand—a serious accident.

On this march we emerged from the cañon and came into the park that is usually found near the head of mountain-streams. At camp there was splendid grass and plenty of wood. Along the stream is a thick growth of cottonwood, pines, cedar, and willow. The mountain-slopes are densely timbered.

We are passing through what appears to be one ridge of maximum elevation in the mountains. They seem to be composed entirely of material thrown from or poured out of volcanoes, and yet no distinct craters, or anything that looks like them, can be seen. Estimating from the timber-line, many of these peaks are over 12,000 feet high, and some carry at this season vast fields of snow on their northern slopes. From the precipitous character of the weathering about their summits, many of them will probably be found inaccessible.

Thursday, *July* 31.—The Indians say that I can make one "big march" to the divide, or two easy ones, and get across it. I choose the latter, and we start at 12.30 p. m., marching eleven miles up the river.

The trail leads through a perfectly lovely country of open pine forests, carpeted with long soft grass and the mountain-huckleberry. This berry is quite small and red, and has a very delicate flavor. We camped in a spot that was absolutely perfect, having ice-cold water, a broad meadow of thick grass, with dark forests of spruce and pine close around, carpeted with a long grass that makes our camp-bed feel like down. Elk, deer, and trout are abundant. A mule deer was killed.

I find to-day that we have crossed the highest ridge of the mountains and that the pass at the head of the Stinking Water is probably through a secondary ridge, and not the main divide.

At this point it became necessary to ascend a neighboring peak to do some important topographical work, and it was decided to lay over one day for the purpose. In this connection the question of provisions asserted its importance. It appeared that by making all possible haste to Yellowstone Lake, and sending the pack-train from there to Fort Ellis for supplies, the party left behind would be out of provisions before it could get back. As one day more or less in a case of that kind would not make much difference, it was decided to lie over, do the necessary work, and meet the consequences by shortening the allowance of provisions, should it become necessary. An examination showed that the soldiers had eaten more than their allowance of flour; that my party had consumed considerably more than its allowance of everything, and that the Indians had devoured their rations long ago and were subsisting on the country. They frankly confessed that the supplies thus obtained were rather scanty, and that they were getting hungry. Just here may be explained the secret of the tremendous marches made by war-parties of Indians. Having the power of going several days without food, they have no need of a train to incumber their progress.

Friday, August 1.—Started at 5.30 a. m. with a party consisting of Dr. Parry and Messrs. Bond and Putnam, with the theodolite and barometer, to make the ascent of the peak before mentioned, and reached the summit after three hours of pretty stiff and some dangerous climbing. The point proved a very good one for examining the eastern slope of the divide between the Big Horn and Yellowstone drainage. We were in the midst of a mass of wild and rugged peaks, seemingly thrown together in the direst confusion. To the west, and not far distant, was a line of peaks which evidently formed the "divide," and through a depression in it, to the northwest, we could see mountains, which were evidently upon the farther side of the Yellowstone Valley. The day was spent in work at the summit, and we reached camp at 7 p. m. very tired and hungry. This peak we have named "Sailor Mountain."

Saturday, August 2.—Broke camp at 8.30 a. m. and marched 14.4 miles, across the divide and into the Yellowstone basin, about one mile from the pass. The trail was excellent, except the short spurt of ascen into the pass, which was severe. This slope is on a friable volcanic sandstone, carrying but little soil, and smooth and bare in many places. The horse in the odometer-cart broke down completely at this spot, and the cart had to be left behind.

After the Indian guides, I was the first to reach the summit of the pass, and, before I knew it, had given vent to a screeching yell, which was taken up with a wild echo by the Indians; for there, seemingly at their feet, and several miles nearer than I had expected, was spread out a scene of exceeding beauty—Yellowstone Lake—embosomed in its surrounding plateau, and a mass of green forest extending as far as we could see. Slowly, and in single file, the remainder of the party came toiling and panting up, leading their animals, and, spite of lack of breath, each gave the same involuntary yell as the wonder-land burst upon their view. Perhaps there was something that moved us in the broad and startling contrast between the dreary deserts, the sage-brush plains, the awful and majestic mountains, and that broad expanse of fresh, hazy, and sensuous beauty that looked up so invitingly at us from below; but there was also the proud feeling that we had crossed the "impassable" mountains.

There was no time to be lost, however, and I ascended a neighboring peak in company with the theodolite-and-barometer observers, to do the important work that was now presented to us. From this point it could be seen that Yellowstone Lake lay in a broad and high rolling plateau, densely covered with trees; that from it, to the west and south, there are *no mountains* except Mount Sheridan and the Tetons, and that the country probably slopes off gradually in those directions into the basin of Snake River. We found fresh tracks of mountain sheep exceedingly numerous, but there was so much noise that they took the alarm in time to get out of sight. Two bears came down to witness our passage, but the hostile demonstrations of our Nimrods scared them away.

We reached the camp of the main party at sundown, when it appeared that Dr. Parry and the two white guides were missing.

I have named these mountains "The Sierra Shoshonee," because the right to name them is clearly mine, as I have been the first to cross them and mark out their geographical position and extent. Professor Hayden has called what he has seen of them and their western border sometimes the "Snowy Mountains" and sometimes the "Yellowstone Mountains," but he has also applied the latter name to a range lying south of Yellowstone Lake, that has no existence.*

Sunday, August 3.—Owing to a miserable *contretemps*, this day was lost. The trail to the lake was not found by 2 p. m., so I had the train unpacked, and went into camp without making any move. This camp was in a small opening in the forest, near a very large, gushing spring, whose temperature was 38° F. There are also, close by, some bubbling gas-springs from pools of water at 38° F., that have regular one-minute intervals between times of maximum action. The gas is sulphurous acid.

Grass was very scarce and poor about camp. Measures were taken in the morning to discover our whereabouts to the supposed lost members of the party, and the odometer-cart was brought in. At 2.30 p. m. I took four packers and went back to the old trail, which we rapidly followed down to the prairie on Pelican Creek that was open to the lake. Returned to camp at 6.30 p. m., where I found a note from Captain Noyes, informing me that he had made his way to the lake, and that the three missing persons were there, and not likely to suffer, as they had killed an elk.

Monday, August 4.—Broke camp at 9 a. m., and marched about eighteen miles, to the outlet of the Yellowstone Lake. The last of the three odometers gave out to-day. About six miles from camp we came upon a lake of warm water, with a multitude of diminutive hot sulphur and gas springs on its eastern shore, and some large springs breaking out from beneath the water near this shore. It is the recipient of quite a stream of pure cold water from the mountains, and has an outlet into Yellowstone Lake. On the south side of the lake is a small mud-puff, steaming and fuming away, depositing various forms of sulphur. Two kinds of rock seem to be forming in its immediate vicinity; one a conglomerate from the surface-material. A careful study of the way in which rocks are decomposed and others formed from the resulting material by the hot steam and gases from the springs of this basin ought to throw light upon the dark subject of metamorphism.

On Pelican Creek, in the timber about six miles farther on, there is another system of depositing-springs, supplying a large mass of red earths and recently-formed rocks. An analysis showed the existence in those deposits of chromium, a rare mineral.

The trail down the mountain side was through a dense forest, very

* See Report of United States Geological Survey, 1871, and map of Yellowstone Lake, p. 101, and also same report for 1872.

much obstructed with fallen timber. Along Pelican Creek is a strip of rolling prairie, with marsh close by the stream, while near its junction with the lake the greater portion of its valley is marsh. This prairie is the home of great numbers of field mice and moles, which have burrowed up the ground to such an extent that it is traveled over with difficulty. The same is true of a great deal of the open country in the Yellowstone basin. Along the north shore of the lake the timber is interspersed with many grassy openings.

Tuesday, August 5.—I sent the pack-train to Fort Ellis for supplies. It was accompanied by Captain Noyes and the escort. Lieutenant Hall and a few men remained with us. There is very little, if any, danger from hostile Indians in the park at present. Small parties of Bannacks, Mountain Crows or Snakes, ("Sheep-eaters,") might try to steal something, but they are arrant cowards.

As far as my observation went, good camping-grounds for parties of ordinary size can be found almost anywhere in the basin.

At this camp a complete series of astronomical and hourly meteorological observations was instituted and continued during our stay.

Two p. m. found the beach sprinkled with explorers, spread out at full length, with strained eyes close to the sand, waiting for a crystal to "pop up." The sand is full of clear, sharp but diminutive crystals of different minerals, mostly silica. These crystals are perfectly shaped, and quite beautiful. They come from a porphyritic-trachyte porphyritic with glassy feldspar and silica, that occurs among the igneous rocks of this region. Much of the quartz is amethystine. The north shore of the lake has a long, shallow, sloping beach of soft sand, very convenient for bathing. The temperature of the water varies between 50° F. in the morning and 65° F. in the evening. It is influenced considerably by the heat of the sun, but at any time is cold enough to break down the constitution of the strongest bather if persistently applied. I have ventured to name this place Crystal Beach for the benefit of future poets and sentimentalists.

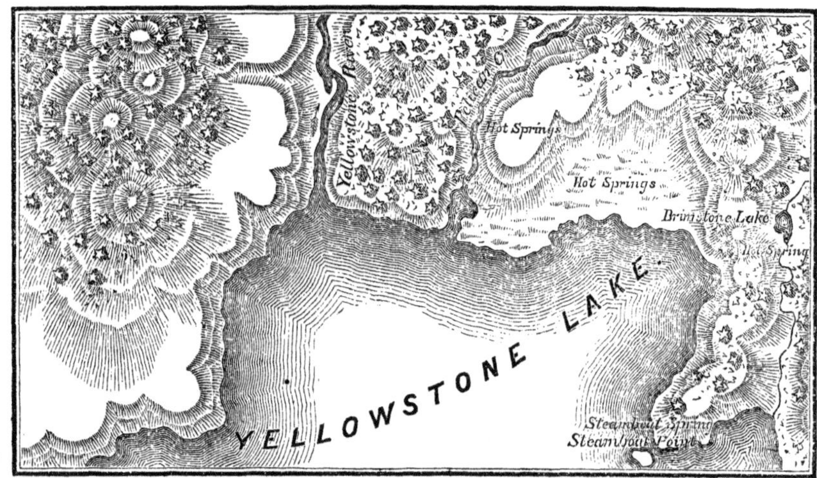

Fig. 2. Crystal Beach.

We find, as others before us, that the trout of the lake are perfectly splendid in size and condition, but are full of parasitic intestinal worms, which leave the intestines and enter the flesh.

The forest here is made up almost exclusively of pine, (*P. contorta.*) Toward the lake their branches are stunted and bent upward toward the trunk, while on the north side (from the lake) they grow out long and free. The contrast is very noticeable, showing that the prevailing storms come from the south (southwest ?). This is to be expected as the basin is all open toward the south and west, and is completely hemmed in by high mountains on all other sides.

Thursday, August 7.—While breaking camp this morning a party of horsemen were discovered upon the other side of the river. They proved to be a party of officers from Fort Ellis.

After placing in a *cache* a lot of provisions and material, for which we did not have transportation, we started at 12 m. and marched fifteen miles to Yellowstone Falls. The river near the lake is not fordable, and generally between the lake and the falls is unfordable. Just below the mud volcano there is a ford that can be used late in the season. Our Indians stopped here, where they crossed the river to await our return upon the other side.

Two of my topographers started down the river upon a rude raft which they had constructed, expecting to get down to the falls before the main party. They were to sketch the stream and make soundings. Unfortunately about six miles below the lake they were swamped in some rapids, whose existence they had not discovered in time, and were obliged to abandon their raft, from which they escaped with much difficulty. They did not reach camp that night.

The trail is very good, about eight miles of it next to the falls being through open country. Some very fine springs occur opposite and a little below the mud volcano. Along the streams there is considerable marsh, and also along the river just above the rapids.

Friday, August 8.—Decided to remain at this camp two days. We are following the trail of Captain Noyes, which here runs into the direst confusion, branching off here and there, but each part always returning upon itself. They have evidently lost the trail and have been hunting for it. We had no guides who were conversant with the country about the lake, and I had trusted to our ability to pilot ourselves by the map of Captains Barlow and Heap, United States Engineers, who were here in 1871. I sent the guides out to find a continuation of the trail, and afterward visited the upper falls and examined the rocks in the cañon and about the falls with much care. With Lieutenant Blunt I went below the fall. This required some pretty nasty climbing along the water's edge about the immediate approach, perhaps not so much from the actual danger as from the moral effect of the terrible torrent just below, which seemed to clamor and roar at the prospect of a misstep by the human intruders upon a smooth, slimy shelf of rock, scarcely wider than the foot, which had to be passed at one place. Ten or fifteen feet from the mass of falling water, just on its flank, and a little to the rear, farther progress became impossible, for here the loose *débris* which occurs at intervals along the torrent's edge gives out, and one stands against the face of the vertical wall of the fall gazing into the cauldron of unknown depth, which the impinging water has worn into the igneous rock, softened and disintegrated by the heated gases and vapors from God's awful laboratory beneath. By the barometer the height of this fall is 150.2 feet. Its beauty is really remarkable. The water contributes beauty of form and color, and the rocks grandeur, as from their vertical jointage they weather and are worn into vertical walls, sheer and straight, of tremendous height. Just before taking the leap there is a sharp bend in the channel, which narrows considerably and wears out below, and to the right a huge semicircular precipice. The rocks are a porphyritic trachyte, and a loose conglomerate containing quite a large variety of igneous rocks. This conglomerate will repay future study.

We then went to the lower fall, but became separated on the way. He descended to the bottom of the cañon below, while my progress became obstructed at the verge of a precipice about 80 feet high, springing up from the seething waters close by the flank of the fall. The rocks, like those about the upper falls, weather vertically, and, from greater decomposition, into pinnacles and isolated slopes of *débris* lying thin on the softened and disintegrated surface.

I did not enjoy the sight of this fall at all, as my attention was constantly diverted to the steep and narrow gulch in the rock, at whose foot I stood, fearing that Lieutenant Blunt, whom I expected down every moment, might, by accident, start a loose stone from the *débris*, a mishap which would have inevitably knocked me into the waters below. Besides, there was just above me a huge drift of snow, and I began to feel certain that the time had come for it to be a small avalanche. I scrambled up the gulch with considerable difficulty, and soon found myself in camp with clothing thoroughly saturated from the spray about the falls.

During the early morning I had visited a mass of hot springs and gas-vents on the sides of a hill near camp. It seemed to me that I saw here evidences of the disintegration of the rocks by the hot waters, gases, and vapors from the springs.

I have noticed that whenever there is a mass of gaseous springs, either in action or extinct, if they come from a hill-side, the whole mass of rocks adjacent is disintegrated and of yellowish and white color.

Some of the party, while walking down the river along the edge of the grand cañon, stumbled across what is probably Captain Noyes's trail. Progress in this direction had been considered impossible. It afterward appeared that he had pushed ahead, making his own trail, after having lost half of one day in looking for the old one, which had become indistinct.

Saturday, August 9.—I sent back to the *cache* for extra supplies, and taking a small party, including Lieutenant Blunt, Mr. Hitt, and Mr. Putnam, returned to the lower fall, where we descended to the bottom of the grand cañon. We could not approach nearer than about 100 feet from the fall. The water in the river is quite high for this season, and probably at a low stage a nearer approach can be made; but not much nearer, for soon the rocks at the water's edge slope smooth and almost vertical into the torrent, and no *débris* can remain along the edge of such a tremendous current; besides, there is such a dense cloud of spray that nothing could be seen even if a nearer approach were made.

I have noticed no hot springs along the river between the falls, although there is abundant evidence of their former action; but immediately below the lower, or great falls, they are quite numerous, oozing and spouting from holes in the solid rock. Here I saw three that threw up slender columns (about half an inch in diameter) of very hot water, two or three feet high, like a fountain. The flow was continuous. A similar one across the river was just below the water's edge, and is only seen as the waves recede. Down the river little columns and clouds of steam gave evidence of the existence of numerous others. I infer that there are many of these hot gas and water springs, active and extinct, along the channel of the river through the grand cañon. Other explorers report their existence wherever they have reached the bottom of it.

Of those that we could examine, the greater number issued from clean holes in the hard, smooth, (water-worn,) rock. Probably the material deposited from the water gets washed off, while the gases stain the neighboring rocks. One spouting spring, however, had built for itself quite a symmetrical bee-hive-shaped mound of silica. An idea of the shape can be gained from the sketch below, (Fig. 3.)

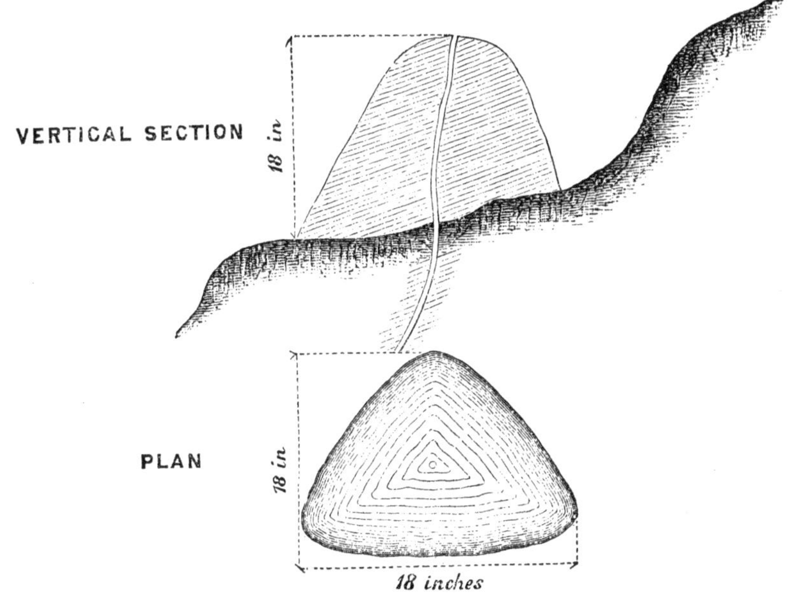

Fig. 3. Spouting Silica Spring, Yellowstone Falls.

By improvising a horizontal sight we set up the barometer at about the level of the bottom of the fall, after which we ascended to its crest. We were on the right bank, where there is a narrow ridge, very steep, with loose dirt on it, which leads down to the crest of the fall. We set up the barometer here, with the feet of the tripod in the water, at the only spot where the water's edge can be approached at all. The sharp ledge of rock here overhangs the precipice, and may fall off at some future day.

From this point one gets the fullest idea of the grandeur of the fall. The depth of the cut seems immense, and the effect is heightened by the tremendous vertical wall on the right, which has a sheer height of fully 500 feet. On the face of this mighty gash in the rocks the column of falling water dwindles and appears small, and this, perhaps, is the reason the effect of the fall is not so impressive from below, or even from the bottom of the cañon; the volume of water appears small in comparison with the great height and mass that encompass it. The fall is so great that the whole volume of water seems to break into drops and spray before it reaches the bottom, and the chasm for one-third of the height from the bottom is filled with a mass of white vapor which very much lessens the apparent height to the eye looking from below. But looking down from the crest, one gets the full effect of the great height. The chasm is so deep that the trees along the bank have but a slight effect in the beauty of the surroundings. The height of the great fall from our measurements (barometrical) is 328.7 feet. This differs from the results obtained by previous parties, but from the satisfactory manner in which our altitude work checked itself, I think it can be relied upon as a reasonable approximation. After examining the rocks from the top of the cañon above the upper fall to the bottom of that below the lower fall, with a view of arriving at an explanation of their origin and the attendant phenomena, I find that at the upper fall the rock is mostly a hard porphyritic trachyte, and Professor Comstock saw two or three dikes of trap. Higher up, and outcropping between the falls, a layer of coarse, soft sandstone, (conglomerate,) apparently horizontal, and distinctly stratified, occurs. It carries a good deal of obsidian in coarse grains, and its *débris* covers a good deal of the country on both sides of the river. Below this, and to the bottom of the upper cañon, occur an amygdaloidal conglomerate; a very coarse conglomerate, (rather breccia,) containing reddish-brown sandstone and obsidian, with well-marked cleavage; a coarse, friable stone, made up of grains of spherulitic obsidian; and the hard porphyritictrachyte observed above the fall. Between the falls I observed no marked change in the character of the rocks. A yellowish color appears over the whole just above the lower fall, but it is onlyon the outside, and is evidently a stain. About and in the Grand Cañon the rocks are nearly all tinged a brilliant yellow, and along the walls are weathered largely into pinnacles with their summits tinged reddish brown. Everywhere that I broke the rocks the fracture showed clearly that the yellow color was only a tinge, and revealed their igneous character, and I tested some of the most marked specimens. I found the same hard porphyritic trachyte and granular obsidian rock that occurs above. Close by the hot springs in the cañon the trachyte carries the strongest tinge of yellow, (sometimes whitish,) and is sometimes converted into a cellular rock, the imbedded crystals having evidently been destroyed.

I therefore suggest, in explanation of this phenomenon, that during a former period, when Yellowstone Lake covered a much more extensive area than now, the line now occupied by the river below the lake, especially from the falls downward through the Grand Cañon, became the line of escape for the hot gases, vapors, and chemical waters from the volcanic depths below; that their action softened and disintegrated the rocks until the waters of the lake could wear them away and form the present river-channel. There is evidently a sudden break in the quantity of this action at the falls, with its maximum effect below; consequently the Grand Cañon commences in a very marked manner. This view is further supported by the fact before alluded to, that generally where these hot springs come out of the side of a hill, that side is excessively eroded and the rocks stained yellow. In the deep tranverse gulches that lead into the Grand Cañon from the east, there is an excessive quantity of thermal and gaseous spring action. In many of these spots I have noticed what appeared to be solid rock, with the greatest similarity of outward contour to the undoubted igneous rocks close by, into which the finger could be thrust with ease, although the interior would be found very hot. A further examination than I had time to make would prove whether or not these are igneous rocks disintegrated by heat and chemical action, as I am much inclined to believe.

As the jointage is vertical, or nearly so, the walls of the cañon weather vertically.

Notwithstanding the remarkably extensive evidences of volcanic action, we have seen nothing yet that could be satisfactorily identified as an extinct crater.

Deer-flies, (a kind of horse-fly,) mosquitoes, and gnats are very numerous below the lake, and future travelers should be well supplied with netting, both for themselves and animals. They are not troublesome at night, owing to the cold. In other mountain localities they disappear with the extremely cold nights of July, but here, in the vicinity of the hot springs, they find plenty of warm rocks to roost upon when the nights are cold, so they can live on for an indefinite lateness of season.

Sunday, August 10.—Started on the march at 10 a. m., with the pack-mules very heavily loaded. The trail, for a considerable distance, follows close to the cañon through a dense wood, and is quite difficult. Marched twelve miles to Orange Creek. Much of the cargo had to be thrown off on the way, to be sent back for on the following day. The chief difficulty was in getting through the thick timber, which had not been sufficiently cleared away.

Monday, August 11.—Remained in camp. Provisions are getting low; sent back to the *cache* for what was left there. One of our cooks was lost in the forest, and remained out over night. I felt much worried, because it is a serious thing for a man to get lost in these forests as there are no landmarks visible from which he can determine his position.

Tuesday, August 12.—Sent parties out to the highest neighboring points to fire signals, and also sent out a guide to make a circuit around camp and find, if possible, the trail of the lost cook. Rain had been falling all night, and was still falling. Our efforts were successful, and the poor fellow came in about 10 a. m. in a pitiable plight, having had neither fire nor food. Rain was falling so hard that it was not considered advisable to move camp. It cleared up, however, by 1 p. m., when, with Lieutenant Hall, I started, with a few pack-mules and such of the cargo as was not required for immediate use, to carry it forward on the trail as far as possible. Our means of transportation were so limited that it took us two days to make one march. We moved fourteen miles to the East Fork divide, and returned to camp by sundown, leaving the cargo under proper guard.

Hot springs are very numerous along this trail, and the whole atmosphere is saturated with their vapors to that extent that we were somewhat nauseated by them. The trail follows for a while an old Indian trail, which, becoming too difficult, Captain Noyes had evidently abandoned it, and tried to get around by the head of the sharp ravines. It led in a very tortuous manner through heavy forests and over very steep hills. Along the bank of the Grand Cañon, by bridging a few of these ravines and deep gulches, a very easy road could be made.

Wednesday, August 13.—Broke camp at 9 a. m., and marched twenty-eight miles, directly over the highest point of the East Fork divide, to the East Fork of the Yellowstone River, one mile from the bridge over the latter stream. Through the ranchman at the bridge we have news of Captain Noyes and the train. Knowing that we would be short of provisions before he could get back to us, he had made a very rapid march into Fort Ellis and would probably get back to us in five or six days.

While on the high summit of the East Fork divide we were greeted with quite a severe mountain-storm. During the march along the trail among the numerous hot springs we were again nauseated as on the day before.

On Orange Creek, near our last camp, occurs a notable mass of springs that have so cut down and discolored the rocks that I named the locality Orange Rock Springs. Orange Creek is a wild mountain-stream, running at this point through a picturesque cañon whose walls are fully

200 feet high. From the bed and banks of the stream, and at the foot of the cañon walls, countless springs are issuing. The air is saturated with gases; the noise deafening, and the smell sickening. The spot has most of the physical characteristics of our best authenticated conceptions of hell; and one of our guides, who discovered it, did not tarry, for he felt certain that "the devil was not far off." The stream dashes over a series of rapids and cascades. The rocks are disintegrated and discolored with the greatest variety of hues—white, yellow, red, various shades of green, brown, and drab. Along the summit of the cañon walls lie huge blocks ready to drop off, while the foot of the slope is strewn with masses of fragments of the trachytic rock. On the northeast side, close by the water, is an exceedingly large jet of steam, escaping under such pressure from a narrow fissure that the noise is deafening. The steam smells of a sulphur gas, and is excessively hot. Close around it are three large hot springs with steam issuing from them, one of which is turbid white and quiet, while the other two are boiling and geyser-like. Very little water escapes from them by the surface into the stream. Directly across the stream, a little to the west, is a large boiling fountain spring, with an outlet whose channel is lined with silica. Besides, there are multitudes of small gas-jets, depositing sulphur in a variety of forms.

Where the trail crosses a small tributary of Broad Creek is another active mass of springs. Among them, one elliptical in shape and about 20 by 30 feet in opposite diameters, is quiet, has a whitish scum, and emits a sulphur gas. It has a slight overflow. Another of dark drab mud is 15 by 31 feet across, and is constantly in violent ebullition, throwing the mud 2 and 3 feet high. Steam and gas escape from it.

I decided to wait in this vicinity until the return of the train from Fort Ellis.

Thursday, August 14.—Sent back for the cargo left on the trail yesterday.

Across the stream, to the north from our camp, is a high ridge of granite, whose direction is not at first sight apparent. It runs across the creek close by camp, where it is quite low, and the surface *débris* can be seen for some distance to the south. A little east from us it shows two well-marked crags close by the south bank of the creek, which latter makes through it a sharp cañon, commencing about two miles from its mouth. About 200 yards farther up it cuts through a layer of sandstone, carrying numerous fossil plants, which rest upon a bed of volcanic conglomerate. This latter crops out extensively along the stream above, and its *débris* is scattered over the rounded hills to the south. It is certainly peculiar. We have seen it in varied conditions and structure. All of the way across, from one side of the mountains to the other, at the Washakee Needles, and, in fact, everywhere that we have come in contact with these mountains, it can be recognized in the distance by its columnar and fantastic weathering, and somber brown, sometimes almost black, hue. It is made up of a smoothly-rounded *débris* of a great variety of volcanic rocks, in sizes varying from a pebble to enormous bowlders. I have seen these latter in position that were from 10 to 15 feet in diameter, and others that clearly came from it very much larger. Along this stream it carries large bowlders of granite and basalt. Being so near to the granite ridge just mentioned, I was doubtful about the source of the granite bowlders until I found a huge one in the bed of the stream with some of the matrix still clinging to it, and shortly afterward numbers of them stuck along a vertical wall of the conglomerate. It is probable that the blocks of granite strewn over

Fig. 4.

Structure of Hot Springs Deposit
Gardiner's River.

the country south from camp are from this source, because they appear to be rounded from wear rather than from concretionary structure, while the granite of the ridge is lamellar, and gneissic in structure. A notable feature of the conglomerate is, that it is frequently stained and its constituents sometimes thoroughly impregnated with a green mineral (silicate of iron,) which might easily be mistaken for carbonate of copper.

As far up East Fork as can be seen from these granite knobs the valley is quite open, fairly timbered with spruce, pine, and aspen, and is clothed with excellent grass on the rolling country between the cañons where the stream cuts through some minor ridges. On these there are many ponds of stagnant water. To the north and northeast the mountains are very high and rugged.

Friday, August 15.—I started at 7 a. m. with a small party, carrying rations and bedding on our saddles, for the Great Hot Springs on Gardiner's River, distant twenty miles down the Yellowstone. We made our nooning near a lovely fall on the east fork of Gardiner's River, after traversing a beautiful country of high, rolling hills, well watered, with excellent grass everywhere, and wood scattered here and there in groves and masses. At the fall the rock is basalt, stained to a dull yellowish hue. The weathering about it and in the cañon below is quite similar to that about the Upper Falls of the Yellowstone.

A beautiful effect is produced about half-way down the face of the fall, where a horizontal dish-like ledge juts out from the wall. Some of the falling water rushes down and into the dish of the ledge, so that its impetus throws it up again at several points in low, heavy, fountain-like jets, while another portion jumps clear over and beyond the ledge, in a thin transparent sheet whose convex surface looks exceedingly like a glass cover preserving the little fountains beneath from defilement.

We reached the springs at 3 p. m., and spent the afternoon in looking over this very interesting and beautiful phenomenon. A settlement has sprung up here for the purpose of accommodating sight-seers and bathers. I have not much confidence in the bathing properties of the water.

Saturday, August 16.—Completed an examination of the springs and the surrounding country, and started back to camp, which we reached at 8.30 p. m. As the Great Hot Springs have been described and thoroughly photographed, I will only offer an explanation of their structure, as my views materially differ from any that I have yet seen advanced. The maximum temperature of the water given (164° F.) was obtained by Dr. Heizmann and myself by penetrating through the clouds of steam and over the hot and dangerous crust to the main fissure, from which the water was escaping with considerable violence. Looking back at this performance it seems foolhardy; for no one can tell, in such a mass of steam, whether the crust under their feet about the edge of the fissure is firm, or thin and overhanging, a common feature. These springs (see sketch, Fig. 4) are the source of a small stream which empties into a sink near Gardiner's River, a short distance above where the latter joins the Yellowstone. The water comes out at temperatures varying from 92° F. to 164° F.; the latter at the fissure, where the maximum quantity of water is escaping now, and is strongly impregnated with certain minerals, principally calcite, which latter it deposits profusely upon exposure in thin layers to the atmosphere. The springs originally came out at the top of the hill above them, which I should judge to be fully 1,000 feet above those in action now.

The effect of the rapid deposition from the water is quite remarkable, there being formed by this agency level-topped hills, sometimes 200 feet high in successive terraces, one below the other down the slope of the hill—probably along a line of rupture in the rocks—their faces showing

Ideal section of spring and its deposits.

beautifully corrugated surfaces which imitate very closely the Meandrina coral, and display, while the water is flowing over in thin sheets, delicate and coarse tints of carmine, pink, rose, yellow, and brown.

The proof that the progress of these formations is from the *top downward*, and not from the bottom upward, as explained by Professor Hayden,* is conclusive; at the top, the springs are all dead, and the deposits are decayed and almost hidden beneath vegetable loam from the dense forrest that has overgrown them, while *all of the active springs* are at or near the bottom. He saw the dead remains at the top, but after observing closely their characteristics as hot-spring deposits, he falls into the strange error of saying: "But in what manner was it formed? I believe that the limestone was precipitated in the bottom of a lake, which was filled with hot springs, much as the calcareous matter is laid down in the bottom of the ocean at the present time. * * * * * The deposit was evidently laid down on a nearly level surface and the strata are horizontal."

After the water ceases flowing the surface bleaches snow-white or bluish-gray.

The process commences with the water running from one hole or fissure, (Fig. 5,) or several, under sufficient pressure to rise as a column to a height varying with the pressure, and from thence flowing off down the hill, with its surface covered with concentric ripples, caused by pulsations in the current; along the scolloped lines of these ripples lie the minimums of velocity in the flow, and the maximums of deposition of sediment; consequently, little wave-lines of ridges commence forming very soon, and once started, another check to the velocity is introduced whose value is continuously increasing. This, in time, makes shallow pools, which are soon filled up with sediment, and in time the upper

* Report United States Geological Survey, 1871, p. 68; ibid., 72.

ones merge into one large one around and below the orifice, on a level with it and bordered by a scolloped rim, over which the water flows in a continuous sheet, (Fig. 5.) The water flowing over this rim and downward, builds up, as the rim rises and advances outward, a steep slope with the maze of corrugations on its surface that result from its rapid throbbing flow. Any serious obstruction on this slope will bring about the formation of a seconday pool on the face of it, a feature of common occurrence. This process builds up a large hill, with the large shallow pools on top of it, but everywhere on its slopes and top-surface the slightest cause tends to produce the general results just described in miniature. Hence, on top we find the large pools whose surfaces are literally meshed with the scolloped rims before described, and the slopes are studded with little shallow basins with scolloped rims and corrugated sides, the hill itself in miniature.

It was along these rims that Dr. Heizmann and I made our way to the very edge of the largest orifice and took the temperature of the water in it. The spring thus builds for itself a characteristic mound of great beauty, both of form and color, which ultimately becomes its tomb.

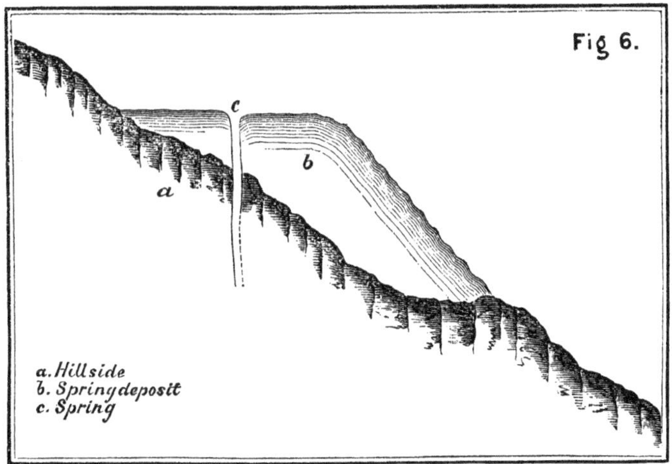

For, in due course of time, the level surface about the orifice becomes raised so high that the water can no longer flow out and over it, whereupon the deposition gradually chokes it up with thin, cellular curved layers of calcite.

Now, if the cause of this action were continuous and of constant power, the spring would break out again in a favorable spot, and build up another mound of about the same height, and the process would be repeated so long as there remained any possible means of escape for the confined waters in that locality. But, although the cause is thus far continuous, the power is actually decreasing, as is evidenced by the extensive distribution of the dead relics of former volcanoes and the multitude of extinct and waning thermal springs; consequently, where the spring breaks out afresh, it must, in this case, be at some point lower down, as the line of rupture in the crust of surface-rock evidently runs downward toward Gardiner's River, and a new mound will be built up of less height than the last one. Sometimes small vents have broken out below the level of maximum action, producing a fountain-spring, throwing a jet of water nearly as high as the level of the principal spring. The deposition from this would produce a cylindrical column, with the top narrower and rounded. (Fig. 7.)

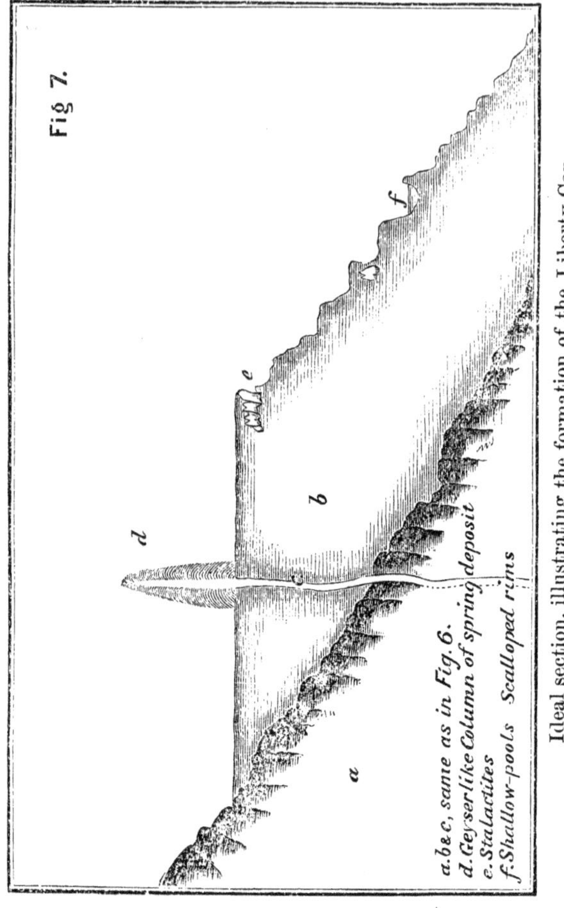

Ideal section, illustrating the formation of the Liberty Cap.

The "Liberty Cap" described by Hayden, and a similar column near it, are illustrations of this, and there are other examples higher up. If, instead of such an orifice, there should be a narrow fissure, a sharp, rounded ridge would result, of which there are numerous examples. Local circumstances may concentrate the force in certain small orifices or fissures, and thus keep up the action in a feeble manner at a level where the principal action is extinct. Thus there is now feeble action on three or four levels above the principal one, which at one place has produced an illustration of all the structural peculiarities on a diminutive scale.

Sometimes the water has found a vent lower down, before the orifices above have closed over, thus leaving the craters bare, displaying numerous small caves.

I infer that the hill of maximum action now has about reached maturity, from the fact that the water from the principal orifice is only thrown a little above the surface. We may, therefore, expect springs to break out lower down the hill, if indeed they have not already done so.

Among the peculiarities of deposition are delicately-beautiful hollow spheres, about one-eighth of an inch in diameter, sometimes open on the top, with a lid. They are so thin and fragile as to break at the slightest touch. I put forward with some hesitation a curious explanation of their origin. From the soft sediment at the bottom of the pools about the main orifice, small bubbles of carbonic-acid gas are constantly but quite sluggishly arising. Now, the deposition is here so rapid that any bubble that lingers a certain length of time on the bottom—as many of them can be seen doing at any time—receives a coat of it over its film of surface sufficient to keep it there, thus forming a fossil bubble. Lying there on the bottom, it is soon surrounded and covered up with the ordinary material of deposition. This is the origin of the small spherical cells which are so marked a feature of the rocks deposited from these springs. Certain forms of coral are imitated, notably the *Madrepores* and *Meandrina*; stalactitic forms are common, and the soft deposit in the pools seems to harden into an irregular interlaced mass of strings and fibers.

Sunday, August 17.—I went out to-day with the miners at the bridge to a place called by them "Specimen Mountain," a noted locality for amethysts, forms of chalcedony, opal, and silicified wood. We were fortunate in finding some notably fine specimens of amethysts and yellow crystals of quartz. The containing-rock is the igneous conglomerate, before mentioned. In it, at this locality, are a good many silicified trees, the hollows of which are frequently lined, in short sections, with varieties of quartz in very beautiful and perfectly-preserved crystal forms; rock-crystal, yellow, blue, amethyst, and opal, and many kinds of chalcedony. The amethysts seem to predominate. In the process of silicification these trees generally become divided into short sections by cleavage planes at right angles to their length. It is these sections that are occasionally hollow and lined with crystals, the adjacent sections being plain, unpretentious petrified wood. Much of the latter is perfectly black, as though it had been carbonized by heat before the fossilizing material came in.

Loaded with specimens and very tired, I reached camp a little after dark. Camp had been this day moved three miles across the river, to meet the train from Fort Ellis. Mr. John Baronett has built here a very substantial bridge across the Yellowstone River for the use of miners visiting the head at East Fork. It is only suitable now for pack-animals.

Monday, August 18.—Pack-train in charge of Lieutenant Young arrived at 3 p. m. from Fort Ellis, with twenty days' supplies for the escort and twenty days' supplies for my working-party.

Tuesday, August 19.—Moved camp seventeen miles, across the Elephant's-back Mountains to Yellowstone Falls. The trail proved very bad; many animals fell down hill, and there was considerable bad bog. The train was pretty badly used up, and two mules were lost; all this, too, after leaving half the cargo at the old camp to be sent back for. The odometer is again in use, having been repaired at Fort Ellis. Camped on Cascade Creek. Along the trail the country is pretty open north of the mountains, with excellent grass, plenty of water, and groves of trees. Across the divide the forest is quite thick, with small openings of meadow, There are three trails across the divide, and we unfortunately took the worst one. I made the ascent of Mount Wash burne with a topographical party.

Wednesday, August 20.—Sent back to the old camp for the cargo left behind yesterday. The lost mules were found. Lieutenant Kingsbury with the escort arrived at 2 p. m. from Fort Ellis; they had staid behind to get their horses shod. Captain Noyes had been taken sick and could not join us. He proposes to meet us at Camp Brown.

Thursday, August 21.—We remained in camp, shoeing the animals and resting them. Rain fell during the whole day. Sent to the *cache* for the remainder of the cargo left there.

Friday, August 22.—In camp; rained all day.

Saturday, August 23.—Moved camp thirteen miles to the Hot Springs, on Warm Spring Creek, where it emerges from the timbered hills. The Indians were in camp on this stream waiting for us. Our party, with the exception of Captain Noyes, was now altogether again. The country along this creek, for about eight miles from Yellowstone River, is an open, rolling prairie, extensively burrowed by moles and field-mice. About the springs the water of the creek and its tributaries is either hot or sour, frequently both. We found good water, after a little search, in a marsh above the springs, on the South Fork.

Sunday, August 24.—Marched 13.3 miles across the divide between the Yellowstone and the Madison, to the Lower Geyser Basin, on Fire-Hole River; met two parties of sight-seers from Montana. The trail passes by a small lake, very near the summit, and down a sharp but short hill, on the west side of the divide, and soon strikes the waters of the Madison. The size of this stream has been exaggerated; it is from two to three feet deep. A depth of 10 feet, as reported, would overflow its banks and the whole valley. Along this stream there is a good deal of marsh, meadow and many groves of timber. Good water can be easily found in the Geyser Basin by hunting for it.

Monday, August 25.—Marched ten miles to the Upper Geyser Basin. The trail from the Lower to the Upper Geyser Basins is very bad from marsh; with a little trouble it could be carried along the hillside through the timber and made very good. Fire-Hole River is the principal East Fork of the Madison. Its waters in the Geyser region are generally quite warm, sometimes hot; just above Old Faithful, in the Upper Basin, it becomes cool and potable again.

The boiling water from the silica springs was used for cooking and found very convenient. The structure of the geysers or silica springs is quite similar to that of the calcite springs on Gardner's River, except that the silica deposits slowly, while the calcite deposits rapidly, making a corresponding difference in the size and shape of the mounds formed. There is a good deal of silica (geyserite) about the springs in a soft, pasty condition from solution in the presence of alkaline salts, which ought to throw light upon the formation of chalcedony. Other explorers have devoted much of their time and attention to the description and explanation of these geysers and springs, to which, in my hasty visit, I have seen nothing to add. Further elucidation must be the result of careful observation and study, over greater periods of time than are at the disposal of exploring parties; besides, the question of getting back to Camp Brown is becoming rather serious; the pack-train is badly used up, from traveling excessively laden, over bad trails, (the cargoes average over 250 pounds,) and there is considerable doubt whether the rations will hold out while we are making way through the "impassable" country at the head of Wind River, described by our forerunners.

The immediate difficulty, however, is, that the Indians have failed to find the trail back to Yellowstone Lake. They seem to be nonplussed and are depending upon me, and this evening informed me that we were lost. The explanation of this is, that they are "plains Indians," and are wholly unaccustomed to travel among forests like these, where all landmarks disappear. It will, therefore, be necessary to make a trail—no pleasant prospect in such a country, where one has so many people and animals dragging along after, to multiply the consequences of getting caught out in the dense forest without any camping-place. An individual or an animal might easily stray a short distance from the trail and get lost, if there was any halting or confusion, and to get lost in this dense forest, where the hills are so rounded that nothing can be seen from their tops, would be a terribly serious matter.

Tuesday, August 26.—Taking a picked party of Indians, the guide Smith, and the escort as pioneers to blaze and clear the trail, I started out early in the morning, with the intention of making a trail to Yellowstone Lake, if the old one could not be found. The train was to wait until 10 o'clock before starting. After a short and fruitless search I took out a compass, and giving the Indians the direction, told them to go that way all the time, and pick out the best way. This they did with great skill, but as our route lay directly across the water-drainage, the hills were frequent, and the trail pretty rough.

An Indian seems to have an instinct which enables him to pick out the best country to travel over, and to avoid natural obstacles.

Four p. m. found the advance party at the lake, at the spot we had set out for, but it was perfectly certain that the train would have to stop on the way. Fortunately there were suitable camping-places along the trail. With empty stomachs, and saddle-blanket lodgings, we made a large fire, and spent a remarkably long night in vain efforts at sleep.

Wednesday, August 27.—The minimum thermometer last night registered 13° F., the greatest cold we have yet experienced. At 8 a. m. an orderly arrived with a message from Lieutenant Hall, commanding the escort, informing me that the mules of the train were so badly used up that it could not move to-day. Much of the cargo had been thrown off along the trail, and one loaded mule was lost. Later in the morning Lieutenant Hall himself arrived and further informed me of the state of affairs. The odometer-cart had worn out completely and was abandoned. The packers had gone back on the trail to gather up the cargo and find the lost mule. Sending all back to camp except the Indians, my orderly, and the guide, I remained to look up the trail ahead.

By noon, having gone without food since morning of the day before, the pangs of hunger overcame a violent prejudice and I ate some fish from the lake worms and all. The Indians have been eating these wormy fish all along and I doubt whether there is anything injurious about them. I might have obtained something to eat from them, but there is a feeling in the average white man's breast which prevents him from asking such a favor from an Indian. It is very unreasonable, but it is there. The Indian, on the other hand, asks favors from the white man, feeling within himself that all that the white man has belongs to him, and he is therefore only getting back his own. He never returns thanks for such favors.

The principal difficulty on the trail yesterday was that it was not sufficiently cleared to allow the pack-mules to get through without getting frequently stuck between trees—a mishap in which a mule will waste strength enough to carry him and his pack several miles.

I have often been struck with the philosophical way that a packer proceeds from the grass that a mule eats to the work that it will do. In his eyes so much grass represents so much mule-work, and no grass represents pretty nearly no work, while it is true that very little work can be expected of a train of pack-mules that have not eaten pretty nearly their fill of grass or something else before starting.

Thursday, August 28.—The train came in during the morning and went into camp at the Hot Springs on the lake three miles ahead. The trail was good, but somewhat obstructed with timber along the shore of the lake. There is a first-rate trail along the west side of the lake, over which I would have sent the greater part of the expedition had I known of its existence, thus avoiding the Fire-Hole Basin, and our trials in getting away from it. It would have been perfectly easy to get a small party from that basin to the lake.

Along the west shore of the lake are numerous small streams with meadows and marsh.

The lost mule, with a cargo of flour, beans, and coffee, was not found yesterday, although the search was carried back to our camp in the Fire-Hole Basin. Word was left with some gentlemen visiting the geysers, who were coming across on our trail, to take this mule back to Fort Ellis in case it should find its way back to the trail before they came along. Our rations were too short to permit any more time to be spent in search and it was therefore abandoned.*

The flour belonged to the escort and is a severe loss, necessitating half rations of bread for them during the remainder of the trip.

At night the Indians in camp up the valley had a scalp-dance over two Sioux scalps that had been given by the Crows to two of the Indians with Captain Noyes's party going to Fort Ellis, who had visited the Crow agency. They invited everybody to join, which invitation was eagerly accepted by the young men of my party, the guides, packers, and soldiers. This dance gives every one a chance to sing and yell with all his might, and they literally made the welkin howl. There was considerable lung-power in action. The waves of sound were echoed back and forth from the woods and hills on either side of the narrow grassy valley, and came billowing to the lake with a tremendous effect, which was heightened by the lurid glare from the numerous camp-fires standing out in the darkness against the mass of black forest behind. The West Pointers in the party called it "Our twenty-eighth hop."

Friday, August 29.—I made arrangements for the main party to move along the south shore of the lake toward the river, and started at 11 a. m. with Professor Comstock and a topographical party to make the ascent of Mount Sheridan, about ten miles south of the lake.

The country is covered with a dense mass of timber on low rounded hills, with the fallen timber so bad as to make much of the country impassable for animals. There was no trail and no one who knew anything about the country. I went ahead, steering by the compass, going around the masses of fallen timber and picking out the highest ground and ridges to travel over. We were lucky enough to make camp at the foot of the mountain after a march of between three and four hours. We could not see it at all at starting, and only caught one glimpse of it on the way before we came directly upon it, and yet it towers to a height of 3,000 feet above the surrounding country.

Saturday, August 30.—Started up the mountain 7 a. m.; a very late start for such work. As there was no chance to reconnoiter, we had the ill luck to take the longest and most laborious line of ascent. The party becoming separated, to my great surprise I reached the summit first at 9.45 a. m., and the rest of the party an hour later. Thinking myself

* This mule was found by them and turned in to the quartermaster at Fort Ellis.

behind I had made great haste so as to reach the summit before the others were ready to come down.

Mount Sheridan is a high mountain mass, rising alone from the rapidly sloping hills of the Snake River drainage, just south of the Yellowstone divide. All the rocks seen were igneous, sometimes stained and decomposed from hot-spring action. Springs and feeble geysers being still in action along the streams from its north and east slopes.

To the east and southeast is a ridge of high timbered hills, which sweeps around to the northward and terminates in Promontory Point at the south end of the lake. To the south, as far as the Wind River range, about sixty miles distant, the country is a mass of high timbered ridges, formed by the erosion of the waters of Snake River, all rapidly sloping down to the eastern base of the Tetons, which lie south 10° west, about forty miles distant.

Westward, and from the Tetons, there are no mountains, only low, rounded, heavily-timbered hills, as far as the eye can reach. To the northwest commence the high ridges of bald mountains which lie between the different tributaries of the Gallatin and Madison Rivers. Between Mount Sheridan and the lake, the divide between the Snake and Yellowstone waters—the Continental Divide—is certainly not more than 300 feet above the lake, and in many places runs within a mile of the latter. It is a broad, comparatively low, gently rounded stretch of country, so flat on top that the opposite-shedding waters are frequently interlocked. It is dotted with lakes, some quite large, and carries a good deal of marsh and strips of meadow along the streams. All of the lakes in sight, except one, drain into the Snake River.

The divide between the waters of the Madison and the Yellowstone, above the falls, is a stretch of smooth hills, rising but little above the Yellowstone Basin, and having steep, rocky slopes only in few places. All of the country in the basin about Yellowstone Lake and extending far to the westward is very densely timbered, with only small openings along the streams and about the marshes.

There is a great deal of fallen timber, such as to sometimes completely obstruct progress, but I have observed that the most and the worst of it lies in the immediate neighborhood of water, either in lake, stream, or marsh, and can be very largely avoided by traveling high up on the hills and ridges. Along the shores of Yellowstone Lake a great deal of water is held in the numerous swamps which afford a constant supply to the multitude of small brooks feeding into the lake. There is, consequently, here an excessive quantity of fallen timber.

The huge mass of the Sierra Shoshonee Mountains closes in and around to the northward of the basin, showing a comparatively low granite ridge running from the East Fork with a northerly trend down the right bank of the Yellowstone River. The highest portion of this mass seems to be that northeast from the basin, about the headwaters of Clark's Fork and the Rosebud. Northward from there it soon runs out and makes way for the valley of the Lower Yellowstone River. Its structure seems to be buried beneath the most extensive outpouring of lava and volcanic matter yet observed on the globe. Along its eastern base we gained only an inkling of its structure from the dip of the upper-lying rocks. Probably the key lies in the country on the Muscle-Shell River, to the northward. It is probable that the southern portion of this volcanic overflow at one time overlaid the northeastern slopes of the Wind River range, and that the erosion of the drift period has cut a channel through on this flank, forming the Wind River Valley and leaving the extensive deposits of volcanic *débris* in the valley as well as tremendous precipices of castellated basalt, trachytes, conglomerates, and sandstones that fringe and seemingly seal its head and northern border. I had the topography of the country in sight from this station sketched with great care and reasonable precision. It is the best geodetic station in the region traversed. My topographical party has now inspected the Yellowstone Lake Basin from mountain-peaks favorably situated on its eastern, northern, and southern borders.

We commenced the descent at 12.30 p. m., and as soon as possible took up the march for the main party. Their trail was struck at 5 p. m., and followed until sundown, when we camped on the spot they had left in the morning.

The smoke was still rising from the smouldering fires and the ground still fresh on their departing trail. As I rode up to the scene so lately rife with the jest; the coarse shouts of laughter; the murmuring of many voices; the bugle's blast; the loud words of command; the round-toned, cadenced shouts of the Indians; the shrill, clarionet-like cry of the squaws; the crying of papooses; the barking of dogs; neighing of horses; braying of mules; the roaring and crackling of great camp-fires; and the occasional rifle or pistol shot at some misguided squirrel—it seemed utterly cheerless and desolate. What can appear more desolate than a freshly-deserted camp?

Sunday, August 31.—We have now only twelve days' rations, and between us and Camp Brown is the "impassable barrier never scaled by white man or Indians." If it were not for the question of provisions I would laugh at it, because we have an outfit that can go almost anywhere; but the question of time now assumes an unhappy importance, and I begin to feel much worried.

We arose at daylight, cooked a hasty breakfast, and started off at sunrise, overtaking the main party at 9 a. m. on Yellowstone Lake, just as they were preparing to start on the march. They had made one march of ten miles over a good trail, and the one of the day before of nine miles, which had been beset with difficulties, owing to the attempt to follow the lake-shore too closely. There was no trail, but a great deal of marsh and fallen timber.

Owing to some misunderstanding, the Indians had become angry with Lieutenant Hall, and considerable jealousy had sprung up among themselves, whereat the greater portion of them had left our camp and gone off.

After a short rest I started off with the guides to make a trail. It was pretty rough for a few miles, but after that we struck a good trail, with many freshly-blazed trees marking it. A queer freak of the disaffected Indians was here displayed. They had deserted the main party and gone on ahead, when, finding this excellent trail, they had freely blazed it with their hunting-knives for quite a distance until the work and slow progress involved became monotonous. I regarded this as an olive-branch, and treated them very kindly, as though nothing had happened, when we passed them. They staid away two or three days and then came back in driblets, but I never, by word or sign, let them know that their absence had been thought of. Their own jealousy continued a few days longer, and then everything went on as happily as before.

We marched ten miles and camped at the extremity of the arm of the lake that we left this morning. There is a well-marked beach along this shore of the lake, but it is frequently deceptive and dangerous from quicksands where the water comes in from marshes above; the timber gradually becomes more open and meadows replace the swamps; the country to the south rises rapidly into hills of considerable magnitude, and the water drains off too rapidly to permit the formation of much marsh.

Monday, September 1.—Broke camp and marched ten miles into the valley of the Upper Yellowstone River. The trail strikes the southeast arm of the lake, thence following up the valley of a small tributary of the lake whose course is parallel to the river to a point high up on the hills bordering the west side of the valley. The latter part is pretty bad from marsh and underbrush. Our camp was about ten miles from the mouth of the river.

The valley about the mouth is very marshy, with numerous small ponds and sloughs. There is also a great deal of timber on the low grounds on the west side, but from its proximity to water there must be in it a great deal of fallen timber to impede progress.

While the advance was quietly following a first-rate trail, it was suddenly observed to lead up a high hill to our right. I sent an Indian to see what became of it up there, who came back with the information that it led to an open rocky place on top, and was after that "kaywut," (played out.) It now appeared that the top of the hill was used as a stamping-ground for elk, and they had made such a broad trail leading up to it as to completely deceive us. Sending back word to the train to go into camp, we started in search of our lost trail, which was soon found considerably lower down in the valley.

We have now reached a country from which one of our Indians says he knows the way back to Camp Brown by the head of Wind River. He belongs to a band of Shoshones called "Sheep-eaters," who have been forced to live for a number of years in the mountains away from the tribe. A heavy rain-storm set in about night-fall.

Tuesday, September 2.—Broke camp a. m. and marched up the Yellowstone River thirteen miles. The trail leaves the timber and goes into the open valley. This latter is probably quite marshy earlier in the season. It is also probable that the river is not fordable in the spring.

The storm of last night burst out about noon with great violence and continued during the day and night. A good deal of snow fell in the mountains about 1,000 feet above us.

We camped in the edge of a grove of pines with a dense fringe of fallen timber on its border. It was a cold, wet camp in the border of the timber, and considerably mixed withal. As it was raining hard when we reached it, everybody dropped into the first place that presented itself; the fallen timber monopolized nearly all of the ground, so that there was little choice; the result was, that Indians, soldiers, citizens, and officers were all camped together in the direst confusion, on a small spot that it seemed possible almost to cover with a blanket.

All through this basin game-tracks have been very abundant, but our party from its size makes a good deal of noise, which will account for the fact that we did not see a great deal. A magnificent elk crossed the valley in advance of us, and in plain sight to-day. He was a royal fellow, indeed, and seemed to resent our intrusion upon his chosen rutting-ground. The party was too much drenched and too cold from the driving rain to make any attempt to get him; the first instance of the escape of anything (except bear) that came in sight of it. The trail was very good except the last mile, which was quite marshy.

Wednesday, September 3.—The storm continued. Broke camp 8 a. m. and marched thirteen miles. The trail soon leaves the main stream and follows up a small tributary that comes in from a little west of south, crossing a low divide to a tributary of the Snake.

At this divide occurs a curious phenomenon, probably the one referred to by the early trappers as the "Two Ocean Pass."

Marching at the head of the column where the trail approached the summit, I noticed that the riband of meadow in which the stream lay we had been following suddenly dropped away in front of us with a contrary slope. I could still see the stream threading it, and for a moment could scarcely believe my eyes. It seemed as if the stream was running up over this divide and down into the Yellowstone behind us. A hasty examination in the face of the driving storm revealed a phenomenon less startling perhaps, but still of remarkable interest. A small stream coming down from the mountains to our left I found separating its waters in the meadow where we stood, sending one portion into the stream ahead of us, and the other into the one behind us—the one following its destiny through the Snake and Columbia Rivers back to its home in the Pacific; the other, through the Yellowstone and Missouri, seeking the foreign water of the Atlantic by one of the longest voyages known to running water. On the Snake River side of the divide the stream becomes comparatively large at once, being fed by many springs, and a great deal of marsh.

While the small advance party were approaching camp two of our Indians discovering three elk close by gave us an illustration of skillful hunting by crawling up and killing the three with four rifle-shots. They were extremely large and fat. As examples of Indian generosity to white men are becoming rare, I wish to put on record this one where one of them made me a present of the whole carcass of one of these elk. Being hungry enough to eat it all myself, after the long march in the cold rain, I had a vivid appreciation of the gift.

The trail was good, passing around a beautiful lake in the Yellowstone Valley, which is probably the Bridger Lake of the old maps.

The valley of the Upper Yellowstone is quite flat, and lies between grand and rugged walls of bare, broad mountains of volcanic *ejectamenta*. It is from one to three miles wide, and interspersed with broad meadows, and groves of pine and spruce. The amount of water that it receives from the slopes on either side is astonishing, and accounts sufficiently for its marshy character.

There is a remarkable discrepancy between the volumne of water in the river above and below the lake. The storm prevented us from making observations for a comparison, and I can only say that above the lake the stream seems ridiculously small compared to what it is below. The volume of water which the lake receives from small streams and the numberless marshes along its border must be very great.

Thursday, September 4.—There is only one Indian in the party who knows the country between here and Wind River, and he seems to be getting proud of the power he has over us and wants to exercise it a little. When all ready for the start it was discovered that he was enjoying all the comforts of a home in the bosom of his family and taking a quiet smoke after having been told to get ready an hour before. Here was a dilemma. It was his second offense, and must be noticed, but to rebuke him and rouse his anger might be followed by his certain departure, followed in all likelihood by all of his dusky brethren. It was no easy matter to make them understand us when we were perfectly quiet. How much misapprehension must occur in case all should become excited and angry. I sent another message to him, and rode along myself trying to look solemn and determined during its delivery. To our great gratification he surlily saddled up his pony and struck off on the trail, assuming from thence forward a winning smile and air of boyish oblivion.

We marched fourteen miles across the high rolling outliers of the Sierra Shoshonee, with the mountains close on our left, and camped on another tributary of Snake River.

The hills between the valleys are quite large but considerably worn, so as to present accessible slopes. The dense timber which has caused us so much trouble and labor is rapidly thinning out so that the trail can be picked out mostly clear of it. Magnificent slopes of grass and luxuriant flowers are becoming numerous.

In getting through the timber and over the terrible trails that we have seen so much of, it has been my custom to start first on the march with a small party, consisting of the guides, a few of the best Indians, and two soldiers with hatchets to blaze our trail. Immediately after comes a pioneer-party from the escort with axes and shovels to clear the trail that has been blazed; cutting away trees and fallen timber; cutting down steep banks, filling bogs with brush, and making a passable way for the crowd of animals and pack-mules that were to start two or three hours later. How necessary it was to keep the clearing party well ahead of the train will appear when it is known that the pack-train could not stop in the dense forest without great danger of losing some of the animals, as it would be impossible to keep them on the trail; and, once off of it, there was little hope of finding them.

Ont he march, a train of pack-mules travels as a unit,—as though each mule were connected with the one in front,—but let a halt be called, and each one becomes a free and independent creature to hunt for grass, or the bell-mare, at will.

Just before reaching camp, two of the Indians and one of the white guides killed three bears after a lively skirmish. There are wood, water, and grass all along the trail, which is excellent.

Friday, September 5.—The Indian difficulty came up early. The fellow after being told to get ready in time to start with us, went off up the stream to trap for beaver. It was evidently time to deal with him. Calling the one who acted as interpreter, and several of the most prominent Indians about me, I endeavored to make them understand that this fellow was not doing as he had agreed to with me; that we had to travel back to Camp Brown as fast as we possibly could or else our rations would give out, and there was not game enough in the country to feed such a big crowd; that I could go back without his assistance, only it would take longer to find the way, and we might get very hungry before we got back to Camp Brown; that I had sooner do that than have any more nonsense from him, and that he either must do as he had promised, or I would have him tied up and carried back to Camp Brown and put in the white man's jail there. I then sent out two Indian runners to follow up his trail, find him as soon as possible, and tell him that he must come in as fast as he could—well knowing that they would tell him all that I had said. To my utter relief, in about half an hour they were discovered away up the valley returning with him, and driving their horses at desperate speed; without a word he took his place in advance of the column, and soon appeared perfectly cheerful and contented. Still I had a fear that he might in resentment lead us out of the way, and watched him with much apprehension. The few days following proved my fears groundless. He as well as the others were overawed, and said that "the captain" was "heap mad." The only misunderstanding that arose from my talk to them was an impression that I was going to put him and a few of his intimate friends in jail upon our return. We did get into a great deal of trouble on this day's march, but no one worked harder than he to help us out of it.

We broke camp at 8 a. m., and after a march of nine miles the trail led across a large densely-timbered hill. About half way up it the fallen timber lay so thickly across the trail that it soon appeared to be a herculean task to get through it. Everybody took hold, officers, men, guides, and, to the astonishment of all, even the Indians who were with the advance, but before we had any hope of getting through, the train came up with us, making it unnecessary to go into camp.

Sending back word to it to camp before attacking the hill, I sent out the Indians and guides to look up a better place for crossing, and in the mean time scrambled ahead on foot over this trail far enough to see that it would take at least a day to clear away the fallen timber so as to make it practicable.

Toward night the Indians returned, having been successful in finding a way across. They pointed it out to me, and I am free to confess it seemed about as feasible as to lead the train over a squirrel-trail up a tree. It boldly attacked the hill by way of numerous openings at its steepest part.

The trail to camp was good, with wood, water, and grass abundant The vegetation is luxuriant.

All of the Snake River drainage above the Tetons concentrates in a low-lying tract along their eastern base, called Jackson's Hole. For this reason I have called this partial water-shed the Teton Basin.

Viewed from the east, the Tetons rise from a low elevation, and, being projected against a low country, their appearance is truly majestic. From their aspect at this distance, I should judge their structure in altitude to be the same as that at the Washakee Needles, *i. e.*, lamellar granite, forming numerous acicular pinnacles.

Saturday, September 6.—Broke camp at 7 a. m., and making a trail over the tremendously-steep hill by continual zigzags, up which it took the train one hour and a half to climb, we marched ten miles over a very good trail, and camped close by the pass to Wind River.

I rode ahead into the pass with the Indian guide, who pointed to me Wind River Valley displayed at our feet in its full length, with evident pride and satisfaction. Dismounting, I climbed the high mountain south of the pass with much difficulty, and had a view that seemed to unravel a good deal of the mystery in which this region has been wrapped. I found myself on the extreme point of the southwestern angle of the Sierra Shoshonee, and at the very head of Wind River.

Along their southern wall to the southeast lay the Wind River Valley, in which I could see Crow Heart Butte, not far from Camp Brown. Across came the grand Wind River Mountains, sweeping up to a climax in Union Peak and running out at a point ten miles south from me. From just south of this extremity, running west as far as Snake River near the southern extremity of the Tetons, and culminating in snow-clad peaks along the western half, lay a range of mountains which have hardly attracted notice before as such, and which I have named the Wyoming Mountains. From the south they appear as a continuation of the Wind River Mountains. To the west, distant forty miles, the Tetons seemed to pierce the sky with their needle-like spires; between and to the northwest and north lay the Teton Basin, a semi-funnel-shaped region of high, rolling, green-clad hills, narrowing to a focus in Jackson's Hole at the foot of the Tetons, and far beyond was just a glimpse of Mount Sheridan —a grand mountain, which will always do honor to the general's name.

The culminating point of the Tetons has for a very long time been called the Grand Teton. It is a good name, and I see no reason for changing it, although some members of Dr. Hayden's party of 1872 have seen fit to rename it after him. I know of no man who is more worthy of having his name left behind him in the Rocky Mountains than he;

but certainly, among the "thousand peaks worthy of a name" which he describes, along the western face of the Sierra Shoshone, some one might have been selected which would have gone down to posterity with a clearer title.

The Teton Basin is notable for the abundance of its streams, the luxuriance of its vegetation, and the happy distribution of immense areas of low-lying timber-land among a liberal display of grassy slopes and valleys.

Togwotee Pass lies between the head of Wind River and a small tributary of Snake River. It has an altitude of 9,621 feet above the sea, but, notwithstanding this altitude, the approaches to it are quite easy. A railroad could be carried over it without extraordinary expense. Just south of it is the last peak of the Sierra Shoshonee in this direction. It is composed of horizontal layers of volcanic *ejectamenta*, (sand, sandstone, and conglomerate,) and rises to an elevation of 10,625 feet above the sea.

Sunday, September 7.—We crossed the divide and camped on Wind River, after a march of fifteen miles. The trail is good, except about two miles of fallen timber on the Wind River side. After this there is no more timber in the Wind River Valley, except the cottonwood along the streams. Grass occurs in meadows along the streams and sparsely over the rolling hills, on either side.

A marked change of climate is noticeable immediately upon entering Wind River Valley. It is considerably warmer, both by day and night, and the relative humidity is very much less. The effect of this is noticeable in the comparative scarcity of springs, streams, and marshes, in the dry and dusty character of the soil, in the sun-cured grasses, and in the gray and sun-dried appearance of the face of the country so peculiar to the rainless region of the Rocky Mountains. In the Teton and Upper Yellowstone Basin the grasses look fresh and green; there are numberless marshes, springs, and small streams, and the black soil does not fly into a cloud of dust at first touch. Indeed, our whole train rarely broke the soil enough to raise the dust. These considerations, taken in connection with the weather observations made on the trip, lead me to infer that we may find in these basins a region of equable precipitation of rain—a phenomenon of rare occurrence in the great Rocky Mountain plateau. I think it quite probable that here the soil can be cultivated without irrigation; and it may be as well to remark just here that the soil of this great plateau is generally quite rich, however unpromising it may appear at first sight; but in these basins, coming, as it does, from the decomposition of volcanic rocks, it is peculiarly fertile.

Monday, September 8.—Broke camp at 10 a. m., and marched seventeen miles down Wind River. The trail is good and well marked, being the one used by the Indians in their trips to Snake River and Fort Bridger. There is good camping-ground almost anywhere in Wind River. The heat and dust are oppressive.

Tuesday, September 9.—Sent a small party of Indians to Camp Brown to announce our return and obtain information regarding the presence of hostile Indians. Broke camp at 9.45 a. m. and marched twenty miles.

Wednesday, September 10.—Lieutenant Hall and a small party started at 5 a. m. for Camp Brown, expecting to get in before night. Broke camp at 10 a. m., and marched twenty miles to a point about three miles above the mouth of Bull Lake Fork; grass rather thin.

Thursday, September 11.—Broke camp at 9.30 a. m., and crossed Wind River, moving on down to Lake Fork. After crossing the latter we struck across a very high plateau to Sage Creek, coming upon our outgoing trail and camping near a former camp. Distance traveled, seventeen miles; grass and poor water; no wood.

Friday, September 12.—Broke camp at 8.30 a. m., and marched eight and one-half miles to Camp Brown.

September 17, 18, *and* 19.—The expedition marched back to Camp Stambaugh, where it was disbanded.

I take the greatest pleasure in according to Captain Noyes the credit that is due him for having, by his skill and energy in assisting us, contributed very largely to whatever of success that has attached to the expedition. Perhaps this will be better understood when I state that a delay of three days at the Big Muddy and Ham's Fork, which might very easily have occurred, would have been followed by a delay of two weeks at Green River on account of the freshet. This delay would have brought us into the Big Horn Valley after the arrival there of a powerful war-party of Sioux, which, it is known, came in shortly after we went out, and who certainly would have driven us back to Camp Brown, and, perhaps, made the expedition a failure.

In conclusion, I may perhaps be pardoned for referring to the opinions that previous explorers have held with regard to the character of the undertaking accomplished by this expedition.

From the report for the year 1872 of N. P. Langford, superintendent of the Yellowstone National Park, I extract the following:

> The park is only accessible from Montana. *It is impossible to enter it from Wyoming.* Attempts to scale the vast ridge of mountains on the eastern and southern borders have been made by several expeditions across the continent, commencing with that of Wilson G. Hunt, the chief of Astor's overland expedition in the year 1811. As late as 1833 the indomitable Captain Bonneville was thwarted in a similar effort, and, after devising various modes of escape from the mountain-labyrinth in which he was lost, determined to make one more effort to ascend the range. Selecting one of the highest peaks, in company with one of his men, Washington Irving says:
>
> "After much toil he reached the summit of a lofty cliff, but it was only to behold gigantic peaks rising all around, and towering far into the snowy regions of the atmosphere. He soon found that he had undertaken a tremendous task; but the pride of man is never more obstinate than when climbing mountains. The ascent was so steep and rugged that he and his companion were frequently obliged to clamber on hands and knees, with their guns slung upon their backs. Frequently exhausted with fatigue and dripping with perspiration, they threw themselves upon the snow, and took handfuls of it to allay their thirst. * * * As they ascended still higher, there were cool breezes that refreshed and braced them; and springing with new ardor to their task, they at length attained the summit.

As late as 1860, Captain Raynolds was foiled in repeated efforts to cross the barrier. While camped on Wind River, at the southeastern base of this formidable mountain, he wrote, (Senate Ex. Doc. No. 77, 40th Congress, 1st session:)

> To our front and upon the right the mountains towered above us to the height of from 3,000 to 5,000 feet in the shape of bold, craggy peaks of basaltic formation, their summits crowned with glistening snow. * * * * * Directly across our route lies a basaltic ridge rising not less than 5,000 feet above us, its walls apparently vertical, and no visible pass, or even cañon. On the opposite side of this are the headwaters of the Yellowstone. Bridger remarked triumphantly and forcibly to me upon this spot: "I told you you could not go through. *A bird cannot fly over that without taking a supply of grub along.*" I had no reply to offer, and mentally conceded the accuracy of the information of the "old man of the mountains."

Dr. F. V. Hayden, in his Report for 1871 of the Geological Survey of the Territories, p. 134, says:

> The range of mountains on the east and south of the Yellowstone Basin * * * * seems to be entirely of volcanic origin; they are also among the ruggedest and most inaccessible ranges on the continent. From the valley of Wind River they present a nearly vertical wall from 1,500 to 2,000 feet high, which has never been scaled by white man or Indian, but are covered with perpetual snows to a greater or less extent. From any high point a chaotic mass of peaks may be seen.

CHAPTER II.

PHYSICAL GEOGRAPHY.

General description—Green River basin—North Platte basin—Wind-Big-Horn basin—Yellowstone-Teton basin—Indian trails.

The region traversed by this expedition lies in the western extremity of the Territory of Wyoming, including the whole extent of the Territory from the southern to the northern boundary. It lies between N. latitude 41°, along the base of the Uintah Mountains,—a little south of the Union Pacific Railroad,—and 45° at the north boundary of the Yellowstone National Park, and W. longitude 108° at the Big Horn River, and 111° near the western boundary of Yellowstone Park, and the eastern base of the Wahsatch Mountains. It forms a trapezoid, with the longest dimension running north and south, with an area of about 41,925 square miles. Distance across, at the southern boundary, one hundred and fifty-seven miles; at the northern boundary, one hundred and forty-seven miles; and length from south to north about two hundred and seventy-six miles.

It is a portion of the plateau from whose surface rise the numerous ridges which, taken together, form the Rocky Mountains. Between north latitude 41° and 46°, the general trend of these ridges changes from a northerly to a northwesterly direction, and in the obtuse angle thus formed the ridges themselves are so broken and scattered that the eastern water-shed breaks quite through and takes a considerable portion of the drainage from the western slopes, while between them, and extending as far west as the Wahsatch Mountains, in west longitude 111° 30′, the plateau itself is exposed, opening out into the great plains of the Missouri on the east, through the valley of the North Platte River; across the gap between the northern extremity of the Black Hills and the Big Horn Mountains; and on the north through the valley of the Big Horn River between the Sierra Shoshone and the Big Horn Mountains. The Black Hills of Dakota form a remarkable outlier nearly opposite the eastern opening and the point of the angle—lying between the two main forks of the Big Cheyenne River, a tributary of the Missouri, in latitude 43° north and longitude 109° 30′ west from Greenwich.

Hypsometrical observations enough have now been taken by the numerous parties that have traversed it, to show a fair approximation to the mean height of this plateau above the sea, but they are not available for my reference, as this writing is done at a place where the necessary means of reference upon scientific subjects are very scant indeed. Enough has come within my observation, however, to lead me to estimate it at about 6,500 feet.

Its breadth from east to west along the parallel of 42° north latitude is three hundred and nine miles, and its length along the meridian of 108° 30′ is three hundred and forty-five miles. The area described is, as a rule, semi-barren and treeless, although the soil is quite rich and supports a scanty growth of extremely nutritious grass in connection with a few very hardy shrubs.

The line of the Rocky Mountain divide, or water-parting, passes through this region. This line, after traversing the country from Mexico in a northerly direction between the meridians of 106° and 108° west longitude, is deflected from its course in north latitude 40° 30′, where bending around the head of North Park it soon leaves the ridge of maximum elevation—in fact leaves the mountains altogether—and, taking a northwest-by-northerly trend, follows a low line at an elevation of about 7,500 feet across the plateau just described to the Wind River range, making a sharp detour about the head of the Sweetwater River, which here breaks through the low ridge and intrudes upon the Pacific water-shed, giving a poor excuse for the name of South Pass; thence following the summit of the range to its northwestern extremity; thence by a tortuous course about the heads of the Wind, Snake, and Yellowstone Rivers in the Sierra Shoshone range, from which it shortly emerges into the Yellowstone Lake Basin; thence northwesterly, skirting the southern border of Yellowstone Lake, at an altitude, in some places, of between two and three hundred feet above it, running—still a very tortuous line,—between Shoshone Lake and the Upper Geyser Basin, on Fire-Hole River, to the low ridge, with a deep flexure to the southeast, which surrounds the sources of the Three Forks of the Missouri; thence returning to the line of direction departed from it takes a north-northwesterly course into the British Possessions. It will be seen that for the greater portion of this distance the continental divide is a comparatively low line, with high mountain-ridges arranged on either side of it, on the opposite slopes of the great plateau.

Including the portion of this divide between the parallels of 44° and 51° north latitude, we have the crown of the water-shed of the continent, from which the water is shed literally in all directions, as from a point; to the north through the Mackenzie River, to the Arctic Ocean; to the east, through the Saskatchewan and Lake Winnipeg, to Hudson's Bay; to the east and south, through the Missouri, Yellowstone, Wind, and Big Horn, to the Atlantic Ocean; to the south, through the Green and Colorado, to the Gulf of California and the Pacific Ocean; and to the west, through the Snake and Columbia, to the Pacific.

The table-land of Wyoming, previously described, forms, in the southern half, the most important pass through the Rocky Mountain chain. It is a belt about one hundred and forty miles broad, from north to south, and is traversed by roads along its northern and southern borders and through the middle, the latter being the line of the Union Pacific Railroad.

The principal water-sheds formed are five, viz: 1st. The Mackenzie-Saskatchewan; 2d. The Missouri-Mississippi; 3d. The Colorado-Snake; 4th. The Columbia; and 5th the remarkable region lying between north latitude 33° and 43° and west longitude 111° and 121°, where the surface-waters are either carried into lakes without outlets or into "sinks," where they disappear from the surface. To give a description of these water-sheds would lead me beyond the scope of this paper into a field for which sufficient material for reference is not available. The description will, therefore, be confined to the subordinate basins lying near their superior limits and within the field of the reconnaissance. These are the Green River, the North Platte, the Wind River, the Big Horn, the Upper Yellowstone, and the Teton Basins.

THE GREEN RIVER BASIN.

This basin is formed by the Wyoming and Wind River Mountains and the continental divide on the north and east, and by the Wahsatch and Uintah Mountains on the west and south. Its dimensions are two hundred and twenty-three and one hundred and seventy-five miles along the forty-first parallel and the one hundred and tenth meridian, respectively.

The Wyoming Mountains form a spur, which leaves the Wind River range near Union Peak, in latitude 43° 25′, longitude 108° 50′, running in a westerly direction to Snake River. The highest elevation is Mount Leidy, near the western extremity. Near their junction with the main range the altitude becomes quite low, forming one of the passes through which the Shoshonee (Snake) Indians reach the head of Green River. The Wind River Mountains rise from the continental divide, in latitude 42° 30′, longitude 108° 48′, at Camp Stambaugh, and run, with a north-northwesterly trend, at an elevation of about 13,000 feet, to latitude 40° 37′, longitude 109° 55′. The culminating points are: (1) Union Peak, near the northwestern extremity, with an estimated altitude of 14,000 feet; and (2) Fremont's Peak, near the southeastern extremity, whose altitude is 13,750 feet. This range is one of the principal elevations in the Rocky Mountains. It is a huge ridge, with the sedimentary rocks sweeping up in long, broken slopes to a broad belt of crystalline schists at the summit. This belt is estimated to be about eight miles broad, and is very much cut up by fissures. Numerous veins of quartz occur in it. The Sweetwater mines are found in these rocks, on the southwestern extremity of the ridge.

Along the northern slope deep monoclinal valleys occur, from which the waters escape to the plains below through short, but very sharp and deep, cañons. Only a few of these openings occur, and between them the long, smooth slopes have suffered comparatively little from erosion, and are probably seen now in something like the original shape. The principal valleys are longitudinal, and not transverse, as is usually the case. Considerable timber occurs, but it is in the valleys above the lower ridges.

There is a pass across to the head of Green River, near Union Peak, and another across to the Gros Ventres Fork of Snake River. Animals have been ridden across from the head of Green River to Camp Brown, but it is probably quite a difficult task.

The continental divide is simply the line of superior elevation of the plateau itself. Its altitude is about 7,500 feet; but little above the surrounding country. South Pass is where the Sweetwater breaks through, and does not deserve the name of pass at all.

The Wahsatch range in Northern Utah has a trend that bears a little west from north; toward the southern extremity the direction of the range seems to bear off considerably to the west, but I surmise from a hasty personal examination that this is caused by a number of the parallel ridges, so characteristic in Utah, lapping over each other thus:

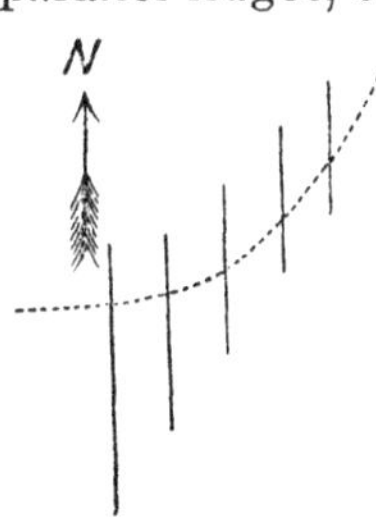

The range comprises a series of three or more parallel ridges, which terminate in about latitude 43°, although it is probable that the Tetons, much farther north, really belong to it. Its southern limit has not been very well defined yet, but it will not be far wrong to place it in latitude 37°. In Northern Utah the peaks are generally from 10,000 to 12,000 feet high, the latter limit being reached in the Twin Peaks, a little southeast from Salt Lake City. The range is not more than fairly timbered.

The Uintahs are considered a spur from the Wahsatch, but it is more probable that they are one of the transverse ridges of the Rocky Mountain chain. Their elevation is considerably greater than the Wahsatch. They leave the latter in the vicinity of latitude 40° 30′, thence trending northwesterly by a curved line, which turns a little to the south before reaching Green River, where it practically terminates. The extreme elevation is attained in the vicinity of Gilbert's Peak, where Mount Hodges and Mount Toh-kwana have an elevation of about 13,500 feet. Gilbert's Peak is 13,250 feet. The range forms an immense ridge, with an almost level but badly-broken-up ridge on top, having a width of from twenty-five to thirty miles, and an altitude of about 6,000 feet above the table-land on the north, and about 7,000 feet above the similar table-land on the south.

The valleys are numerous, deep, and narrow, except at the head, and extend quite up to the summit. Between them, on the north, are the transverse and generally unbroken ridges, by means of which the summit can be reached by a gradual ascent. On the south these ridges are badly broken toward the summit. Ranged on either side of the summit-line are enormous basins of erosion at the head of the valleys. They have a direction considerably oblique to that of the prevailing winds, and in consequence the amount of snow that drifts in during the winter must be enormous. At such an altitude this snow melts comparatively slowly and furnishes an almost continuous supply of water to the very numerous mountain-streams, much of which is first caught in the multitude of small lakes that are sprinkled around the border of the basins. On the north slope there is a good deal of marsh in these basins, but on the south the water, having to make about 1,000 feet more descent in reaching the plains, runs off much more rapidly, and leaves but little marsh. This circumstance, combined with the greater heat of the southern exposure, makes many of the smaller streams run dry early in the season.

The opposite valleys frequently start from about the same point and have between their sources only a thin precipitous wall, which erosion is slowly removing. Gilbert's Pass, at an elevation of 11,000 feet, is such a point. Here the wall has been sufficiently worn away to admit of the construction of a road across it. There are probably few such places at present. The broad belt or strip along the summit is broken and eroded enormously; ridges of high peaks extend across it between the valleys, and many narrow precipitous cañons occur, both along the valleys and transversely to them. The sides of these ridges are generally masses of broken rock. The country along the base of the mountains, both on the north and south, is an elevated, highly-terraced plateau of soft earth, the slopes of the terraces being generally as steep as the earth will stand, and frequently quite barren.

The timber-line, or superior limit of forest-growth, is at an altitude of 11,000 feet. Below this these mountains are covered with a dense forest, very much interspersed with small openings of meadow.

Of the northwestern outline of this basin comparatively little is known. It is probable that the divide here between Green and Snake Rivers is a low ridge of mountains—a continuation of the Wahsatch system.

Of the mountain-ranges described, none rise to the limit of perpetual snow. Only a few large banks or drifts on their northern slopes remain from one winter to another.

The basin itself is a broad highly-terraced plain, the bed of an ancient lake. Away from the immediate vicinity of its scanty streams the excessive erosion of the soft soil has left many isolated buttes and patches of bad lands, and there is everywhere the appearance of barrenness given by the gray hue of the universal sage-brush and grease-wood. The soil, however, as a general rule, is quite rich, and produces splendid crops where sufficient water can be supplied to it by irrigation, and when the unseasonable frosts do not interfere. Bunch-grass, which is extremely nutritious, grows sparsely among the sage-brush.

The water comes entirely from the surrounding mountains, springs being very rare indeed. Some very fine springs occur near South Pass, at Pacific Springs.

The valleys of the streams are narrow, with meadow and pasturage near the mountains, but toward the interior the vegetation is rather sparse. No trees grow except a few cottonwoods along the streams, and away from the mountains even these are rare. The region is infested with great swarms of grasshoppers. In and near the mountains the valleys are fertile, well watered, and, together with the lower slopes, furnish an extensive and abundant pasturage. Some rain falls, but probably not sufficient for cultivation of the soil without irrigation.

All of the hardy cereals and vegetables can be successfully cultivated both in the mountains and on the plains.

In the mountains extensive forests of coniferous trees occur, but as the streams are generally not large enough to float logs, they are, or rather will be, for some time inaccessible.

The rivers are Green River and its tributaries. Green River rises in the southwestern slopes of the Wind River Mountains and southern slopes of the Wyoming Mountains. Its course through the basin is generally southerly until it strikes the base of the Uintah Mountains, where its course is deflected to the left in seeking for a passage through them in longitude 108° 53′. It receives numerous tributaries from the outliers of the Wahsatch on the right, and, with the exception of Bear River, the whole drainage from the north slopes of the Uintahs, and a few on the left from the continental divide.

Of those on the right the principal ones are: (1) Black's Fork, which drains the angle between the Wahsatch and the Uintahs; and (2) Henry's Fork, which drains the middle slopes of the Uintahs. On the left we have: (1) The Big Sandy with its tributaries draining the southern slopes of the Wind River range and a short portion of the continental divide; (2) Bitter Creek, which rises in the continental divide and traverses a country where the soil generally carries a considerable quantity of alkaline salts, giving their character to the few streams that flow through it; and (3) the Little Snake River, which drains that portion of the continental divide which lies south of the Union Pacific Railroad.

THE NORTH PLATTE BASIN.

This region is bounded on the south and west by the continental divide and the southeast extremity of the Wind River range; on the north by the low divide that separates the Sweetwater and North Platte Rivers from the Wind and Powder Rivers; on the east by the Black Hills. Its greatest dimensions are 204 miles along the parallel of 42° 30′, and 173 miles along the meridian of 106° 30′.

The Black Hills form the continuation of the easternmost ridge of the Rocky Mountains beyond the point where the line of general direction of the range is deflected to the northwest. Their northern limit is near Laramie Peak, in latitude 42° 10′ and longitude 105° 25′; from this point their direction is almost due south to latitude 41°, where the Cache-la-Poudre, a tributary of the South Platte, breaks through the ridge. The general altitude is between 8,000 and 9,000 feet. It is a low range with gently rounded slopes, and a ridge of granite crags along the summit, culminating in Laramie Peak, one of the noted landmarks of the West. The western slopes, running down into a tableland whose elevation is about 7,000 feet, are much shorter than the eastern, which leave the plains at an altitude of 6,000 feet—1,000 feet lower. The axis-line lies quite close to their western border. But little water is drained from their western slopes, while the eastern is quite well watered, furnishing many fine valleys susceptible of cultivation. There is good grazing all over the range. Timber occurs, but somewhat sparsely. The ridge is crossed by numerous roads.

The Medicine Bow Mountains are the continuation of another ridge of the Rocky Mountain chain in Colorado, which extends as an isolated ridge into the basin of the North Platte, between the Black Hills and the continental divide. This high range has its northern limit near Elk Mountain, in latitude 41° 40′, longitude 106° 30′. From this point the range has a southeasterly trend to its southern extremity, which is imperfectly known, and indeed but little is known of the range itself.

The basin has very nearly the same surface characteristics as the Green River Basin. Whether the ancient lake that once occupied the latter extended across the divide into this, to cut it up into terraces during its subsidence, is still an unsettled question. This much is certain, that the country is smoother and not characterized by terraces to anything like the extent of the former.

The Laramie plains is a bight of land extending in a southerly direction between the Black Hills and the Medicine Bow Mountains. This is the most favored spot in the whole plateau; the surface of the country is rolling, and thinly covered with grass, while the valleys of the streams through it afford excellent pasturage. Irrigation is necessary in the cultivation of the soil. Quite a noticeable feature of the whole plateau is that grazing is possible during the whole year; and although but little rain falls, yet the grasses become sun-cured, and are always very nutritious. The North Platte River rises in North Park, an elevated valley of the Rocky Mountains, in latitude 40° 30′, longitude 106°, and flows in a northwesterly direction, carrying the drainage of the Medicine Bow range and the continental divide, to latitude 41° 30′, where it bends to the north—passing the Union Pacific Railroad at Fort Steele, as far as latitude 42° 20′, when it enters a deep cañon of inconsiderable length, and, sweeping around in a semicircle to the east and south, marks out, perhaps, the northern limit of the easternmost ridges of the Rocky Mountain chain.

On the right its principal tributaries are: (1) Medicine Bow River, which drains the north slopes of the range of that name and the south slope of the hills in the great bend of the river; and (2) the Laramie River, which drains the eastern slopes of the Medicine Bow Mountains and the slopes in the angle between the latter and the Rocky Mountain range, and flowing northerly through the Laramie plains makes a short bend to the eastward, in latitude 42°, cutting a cañon quite through the Black Hills, and joins the North Platte in latitude 42° 12′, at Fort Laramie. On the left its only tributary of importance is the Sweetwater River, which takes its rise in the southern slopes of the Wind River Mountains and flowing in an easterly direction joins the North Platte in latitude 42° 25′.

The roads that cross the two basins just described in the direction of the parallels of latitude have already been mentioned. They are also traversed by—(1) a road from Medicine Bow Station, on the Union Pacific Railroad, in a northerly direction to Fort Fetterman; (2) one from Point of Rocks, on the railroad, northward to South Pass City and the Wind River Valley; (3) one from Bryan, on the railroad, northeasterly to the Sweetwater mines and Wind River Valley; (4) one from Fort Bridger to South Pass in a northeasterly direction, (the old emigrant-road to Salt Lake City and the Pacific coast;) and (5) one from Evanston, on the railroad, northward along the valley of Bear River to the Mormon settlements at Bear Lake to Soda Springs, and to Fort Hall, in the Snake River Valley.

THE WIND-BIG HORN BASIN.

This basin opens into the basin of the Lower Yellowstone on the north; has the Big Horn Mountain on the east, the low divide between the Sweetwater and the Wind-Big Horn on the south, and the Sierra Shoshone and Wind River ranges on the west. Its longest dimensions are one hundred and seventy-five miles along the meridian of 108° 30′, and one hundred and twenty-six miles along the parallel of 43° 30′.

Of the Big Horn range but little that is reliable is known. The probability is that the axis is a curved line. Commencing very low, about in latitude 43°, longitude 107° 30′, the line of direction runs northeasterly as far as Cloud Peak, the summit of the range in latitude 44° 23′, longitude 107°, and thence northwesterly to the Big Horn River in latitude 45° 10′, longitude 108° 7′. The culmination seems to be a cluster of peaks. To the north of these the range sinks to a low elevation, where the summit has something of the character of a plateau, and to the south also the elevation seems to be quite low. The streams that flow from their eastern slopes are very numerous and water a fine country along their base, while from the western slopes scarcely a stream flows that is worthy of the name, and the bordering country is a barren waste.

The Sierra Shoshonee range sends off a light spur, half-way across the basin, in the Owl Creek Mountains, whose line of direction is about south 27° east from latitude 43° 40′, longitude 109° 10′, from whence they run with an average elevation of about 8,250 feet as far as the Big Horn River, attaining a maximum elevation of 9,136 feet in Phlox Mountain. The foot-hills on the south are much more rugged than the mountains themselves, showing many sharp ridges where the rocks are tilted vertically, apparently in two directions, one parallel to the range and the other making an approach to a right angle with it. Above these, and on the north, the slopes are smoothly rounded and support a fine growth of grass and sparse groves of aspen, hemlock, spruce, and pine. The summit is formed by ledges of the sedimentary rocks, arranged, in a measure, alternately along the opposite sides of the axis-line.

The amount of water that is shed from the south slopes is extremely small, while the north slopes are comparatively well watered. A strange freak occurs at the western extremity of the range, where Owl Creek, after taking its rise at the Washakee Needles, cuts through to the anticlinal axis of the Owl Creek range, which it follows for quite a distance through a wild precipitous cañon, from whence it emerges into the plains seemingly from a source in this range, whereas its source is really in the Sierra Shoshonee Range. The Sierra Shoshonee range is probably the most remarkable one in the great Rocky Mountain chain. The original range, if there ever was one, and of this there are many indications, lies buried beneath an outpouring of material from the fluid interior of the earth, which it is safe to estimate as being now from 4,000 to 5,000 feet thick. This statement is warranted by the fact that the section cut through by the Stinking Water River shows only this volcanic material down to an elevation of 5,500 feet, while the peaks are all over 10,000 feet, and many reach an elevation of over 12,000 feet, and are composed entirely, so far as our observation went, of this material, (except the Washakee Needles, which is granite.) It will be more appropriate to speak of it as a mountain mass, which extends from latitude 43° 10′ in a northerly direction, to 45° 10′, with a general width of over sixty miles in peaks that will certainly average over 10,000 feet in elevation. The culminating points are at the Washakee Needles, near the southeastern extremity, where the elevation is 12,253 feet, and in a cluster of peaks, in latitude 45°, whose elevation is not known. Between these, however, there are probably quite a number of summits that equal and, perhaps, exceed them in elevation.

It is doubtful whether any of the craters, from which this enormous mass of once-fluid material escaped, have yet been discovered. There are many appearances of volcanic cones, but a close examination will probably show them to be simply peaks of erosion. This mountain mass has been eroded to a remarkable extent, and the streams have cut their channel into it accordingly in the most irregular manner. The Snake cuts clear through from the west to the east side, and the Grey Bull and Stinking Water on the east have their sources in the very westernmost rim. Their valleys are simply huge cañons, except the usual park-like opening near their sources.

The mountain-slopes are covered with forests of coniferous trees, wherever it is possible for trees to grow, and streams are very numerous. Perhaps more water is shed from this mass of mountains than from any of equal size in the Rocky Mountain chain.

There are no roads across the Sierra Shoshone range, and this expedition is the first that ever crossed it, a feat that had been previously considered very difficult, if not impossible. Three passes were found across: one along the Ishawooa River to the head of Yellowstone Lake; one by the North Fork of the Stinking Water to the foot of Yellowstone Lake; and one from the head of Clark's Fork to the East Fork of the Yellowstone.

The basin is divisible into, 1, the Wind River Basin; and 2, the Big Horn Basin.

1. The former is triangular in shape and traversed by the Wind River and its tributaries. It is characterized by high benches, dropping off by steep slopes to the river. Along the right bank of the river, as far down as Bull Lake Fork, a great deal of bowlder drift occurs, and the soil, away from the narrow bottoms along the streams, is quite rocky. On the left bank there is not so much of this drift-soil, and it disappears below Crow Heart Butte, a noted landmark in the valley, which seems to have been left to point toward the amount of erosion that has taken place. The favored portion of the valley is along the foot of the Wind River Mountains, in the region watered by Wind River, below Crow Heart Butte, Little Wind River, and the Popo-agies. The mountain-slopes are clothed with grass, and the valleys of these streams are quite fertile and lie well for irrigation. North of Wind River the country is generally rather barren.

2. The Big Horn Basin is generally barren, except the narrow belts along the streams, the foot-hills of the Sierra Shoshonee and Owl Creek Mountains, and the strip of country along the base of these mountains, which is tolerably well watered, fertile, and clothed with grass. Except along the streams, but little timber occurs. The general aspect of the country is rugged, parched, and barren.

The Wind-Big Horn River rises in the angle between the Sierra Shoshone and the Wind River Mountains, in latitude 43° 40′, longitude 110°, and, with the name of Wind River, runs in a southwesterly direction for nearly the length of the Wind River Mountains, whence, rounding to the northward, making the "big bend," it proceeds northerly to its cañon through the Owl Creek Mountains; here it loses its first name and is called, thenceforth, the Big Horn River, which flows northerly to its cañon through the extremity of the Big Horn Mountains, and thence to its junction with the Lower Yellowstone. The name "Big

Horn" comes from the Indian name for the mountain-sheep, which are quite numerous in the mountains about this basin. The Indians call them "big horns." It was the custom of early trappers to name localities from such circumstances as the abundance of certain kinds of game, trees, &c., in their vicinity. The principal tributaries, on the right, are Campbell's Fork, Bull Lake Fork, Little Wind River and its tributaries, the two Popo-agies and Beaver Creek from the Wind River Mountains, and Bad Water Creek and No Wood Creek from the Big Horn Mountains. On the left, De Noir Fork, North Fork, and Dry Fork, from the south slope of the Sierra Shoshonees; Muddy Creek from the south slopes of the Owl Creek Mountains, and Owl Creek, Meeyer-o Creek, Gooseberry Creek, Grey Bull River, and Stinking Water River, from the Sierra Shoshonee.

A wagon-road, opened by James Bridger, leaves the old North Platte road from Fort Laramie near Red Buttes, follows up Poison Spring Creek, and thence across to the Big Horn River, which it follows up a short distance and then strikes across the basin to Heart Mountain, from whence it proceeds in a northwesterly direction to the settlements in Montana. It traverses a very barren country, in which good water is very scarce for a considerable portion of the distance.

THE YELLOWSTONE-TETON BASIN.

As the region here to be described is quite small, it is thought advisable to treat it as a whole, although it is traversed by the main divide of the Rocky Mountains—here very low—and part of the divide between the Upper Yellowstone and Missouri Rivers. It includes the Yellowstone National Park. It has the Sierra Shoshonee range on the north and east, the Wyoming Mountains on the south, and the Tetons on the southwest. All but the latter have been described. This range is quite short, and extends in a northerly direction between the parallels of 43° 30′ and 44° 15′, in longitude 110° 35′. A few peaks are quite acicular in character, and attain in the Grand Teton and Mount Moran the altitude of 13,835 and 12,800 feet respectively, as given by Professor Hayden. The figures are largely in excess of what the previous estimates of these altitudes had been. This region is an elevated plateau, lying about the sources of some of the principal rivers of the continent. It has a surface of high, rolling hills, covered with dense forests, with many lakes, some quite large, about the sources of the streams which lower down have cut very deep valleys.

The northwestern portion about the sources of the Gallatin and Madison is mountainous, culminating in Mount Washburn, overlooking the Grand Cañon of the Yellowstone at an elevation of 10,105 feet. About 10 miles south of Yellowstone Lake is Mount Sheridan, a small knob, with an elevation of 10,156 feet. The soil is quite rich, and vegetation flourishes, although there are indications of a severe climate. At the foot of the Tetons, on the east, is a large, fertile valley called Jackson's Hole. In the midst of it is Jackson's Lake, a considerable body of water. The whole region is thoroughly well watered and is notable for the quantity of timber which it carries on low-lying land. Its greatest dimension is one hundred and four miles from north to south, and there is an area of over five thousand square miles. Southwest from Yellowstone Lake is a cluster of small lakes—of which the largest is Shoshonee Lake—all at the sources of Snake River.

Yellowstone River rises in the Sierra Shoshonee range about fifty miles above the lake, to which it flows in a northwesterly direction.

Shortly after leaving the latter it makes a fall of about 500 feet into its Grand Cañon, through which it flows in a curved line, emerging with a northwesterly direction, and afterward makes a grand detour around the northern extremity of the Sierra Shoshonee, from whence it joins the Missouri by an easterly and northeasterly course.

Within the limits of the region described, the only tributaries of consequence are Pelican Creek and East Fork, on the right, flowing from the Sierra Shoshonee.

Snake River rises along the Continental divide, between latitude 43° 50′ and 44° 30′, in a large number of streams that spread out like a fan from a base at the foot of the Teton Mountains. The principal ones are: 1st, Lewis Fork, rising in a series of lakes lying southwest from Yellowstone Lake; 2d, Barlow's Fork, a tributary of the latter from the east; 3d, Pacific Creek, rising near Two-Ocean Pass; 4th, Buffalo Fork, rising far to the eastward, in the vicinity of the Washakee Needles; and 5th, Gros Ventres Creek, rising near the head of Wind River.

There are no roads traversing this basin. One from Fort Ellis leads to the Great Hot Springs, just inside of its northern limit.

INDIAN TRAILS.

The following are some of the important Indian trails traversing the region visited by the expedition:

1. From Camp Brown, up Wind River Valley nearly to its head, and across the divide to the Gros Ventres Fork of Snake River. Here it forks, sending one branch down the stream as far as Jackson's Hole, where it forks in turn, one portion leading down the Snake River to Fort Hall, and the other, bending sharp around to the northeast, follows up Pacific and down Atlantic Creeks to the Yellowstone River, down which it follows, passing, to the east of Yellowstone Lake, to the Crow country in Montana—a branch of it following Lewis Fork and the west side of the lake and river; the other branch leaves the Gros Ventres near its head, and, bending to the south, crosses a low pass in the Wyoming Mountains to the headwaters of Green River, which it follows down to the open country and thence to Fort Bridger.

2. From Camp Brown to the North Fork of Wind River, which is followed up, and two divides—one to the headwaters of Snake River—crossed to reach the headwaters of Yellowstone River, which is followed down to Yellowstone Lake, where it joins the trail previously described. The divides crossed are extremely difficult.

3. From the "big bend" of Wind River along the left bank to Dry Fork, which is followed up to its head, and a low divide crossed to the headwaters of Owl Creek near the Washakee Needles, whence it passes up this stream to its source, passing through a remarkably fine hunting-ground for mountain-sheep. There is here one of those luxurious mountain-parks which Nature seems occasionally to throw off in the very midst of her most forbidding works. Its existence would never be suspected from without, as there is about it nothing but the most desolate and forbidding scenery, while Owl Creek, the natural approach, after leaving it, flows for a long distance through a tremendous cañon along the very axis of the Owl Creek Mountains, from whence it emerges into the plains, seemingly from a source near their summit; a higher source would scarcely be suspected. This park bears many evidences of having been used as a hiding-place. Our Indians knew nothing of it, and yet there are all through it numerous trails, old lodge-poles, bleached

bones of game, and old camps of Cheyennes and Arapahoes. We may expect to hear from it some day as a hiding-place for horse-thieves and other marauders.

4. From Camp Brown northward over the Owl Creek Mountains, and still further north to the buffalo-grounds of the Big Horn Valley and the Stinking Water River, near Heart Mountain, thence up the North Fork of that river and over the divide to the trail along Yellowstone Lake.

5. From the "big bend" of Wind River eastward along the northern face of the Sweetwater Valley, by the head of Powder River to the Sioux country east of the Big Horn Mountains.

6. From the "big bend" of Wind River northerly into the Big Horn Valley.

7. From Camp Brown to the head of Wind River, thence through Togwotee Pass, and northerly across the drainage of Snake River, striking at Pacific Creek, a previously-described trail from the Tetons to the east side of Yellowstone Lake.

8. From the Wind River Valley across the Wind River Mountains, above Union Peak, to the headwaters of Green River.

CHAPTER III.

THE YELLOWSTONE ROUTE TO MONTANA.

A short route to the Yellowstone National Park.

The discovery of Togwotee Pass, at the head of Wind River, is pregnant with results to the future commerce of the West and Northwest, as it discloses in all probability one of the principal highways that will in the future bind their interests with those of the Mississippi Valley and the Atlantic States.

One important object of the expedition was to discover, if possible, a practicable approach to Yellowstone Lake from the south or southeast, an approach which would not only furnish the shortest route to the Yellowstone National Park, now practically inaccessible, but would open a new route to Montana by a wagon-road but little, if any, longer than the present one from Corinne, Utah, that would save a considerable distance by rail. In this it has met with a gratifying success.

In the first place, it was ascertained that there are three passes through the Sierra Shoshonee affording approaches to the Yellowstone Basin from the east. These are: 1st, from the head of Clark's Fork to the East Fork of the Yellowstone; 2d, from the head of the North Fork of the "Stinking Water, entering the basin opposite the foot of Yellowstone Lake, (the route of the expedition;) 3d, from the head of the Ishawooa River, entering the basin opposite the head of Yellowstone Lake. These passes aer all difficult.

Also one at the head of Wind River, a little southeast from Yellowstone Lake, which affords a perfectly *practicable passage to the Yellowstone Valley, via Wind River Valley and the head of Wind River.* I have named it Togwotee Pass, preferring to attach easy Indian names, wherever possible, to the prominent features of the country. It lies in latitude 43° 46′ 29″, longitude 110° 1′, and has an altitude of 9,621 feet above the sea. Notwithstanding this altitude the slopes approaching the summit so long and regular that a railroad could be built over it at a reasonable cost.

At present there are two routes to Montana, over which the interchange of products between that Territory and the East is carried on, and government supplies shipped to the military posts and the Indians in that country. These are: 1st, the Missouri River route, by which supplies are carried by steamboat as far as Fort Benton, Montana, and from thence distributed through the Territory by wagons; and, 2d, the Union Pacific Railroad route, over which supplies are carried by rail as far as Corinne, Utah, and from thence northward, by wagons, to Idaho and Montana. In the Government's freighting contracts of 1873, the rates from Fort Benton to points in the Territory, and from Corinne to the same points, are exactly the same. Of course, so far as *rates* are concerned, the land-route cannot compete with the water-route; but the river-route is only open during a few months of the year, and during the remainder of the time the land-route is not brought into competition with it. Furthermore, during the season that the river is open, its navigability is far from being certain and reliable at all times; so that shipments over it are detained a very long and wholly uncertain length of time *in transitu*. As the business of the country is now conducted, men can ill afford to have their money lying idle for months, or weeks, or even days, locked up in goods *in transitu*. Every day saved on goods, of *whatever character*, is the equivalent of money gained. It is this element of *time and its money equivalent* that underlies the astounding success of railroads as competitors with water-lines of traffic—success through which the steamboat is disappearing from our rivers; success that is proving to us that there is no such thing as slow freight; that men want some kinds of freight shipped *faster* than others, but that there is none they want shipped in a slow and unreliable manner.

These considerations are so potent that, were a railroad constructed to Montana from some point on the Union Pacific Railroad, it would, in all probability, be followed by virtual disappearance of steamboat-traffic from the Missouri River; and it is by no means improbable that the great saving in distance effected by the new Yellowstone route will, even without any more railroad, enable the land-route to compete successfully with that *via* the Missouri. In all events, the proposed route is fraught with benefit to the people of Montana, through the bringing of the rival lines into a closer competition.

The present land-route leaves the Central Pacific Railroad at Corinne, Utah, and runs in a northerly direction through Idaho to Montana, crossing the Bannack Mountains on the divide between the Snake and Missouri Rivers. The distance from Corinne to Fort Ellis, Montana, is four hundred and three miles. The proposed road should leave the Union Pacific Railroad in the vicinity of Point of Rocks, Wyoming, and run about north into the Wind River Valley; thence following up that valley to its head, and through Togwotee Pass, northerly, to Yellowstone Lake, and through the Yellowstone National Park to Fort Ellis. This route would pass directly by all of the principal phenomena of the park—except the geysers, which could easily be reached by a short side-road. By it, the distance from Point of Rocks to Yellowstone Lake is two hundred and eighty-nine miles, and to Fort Ellis four hundred and thirty-seven miles.

COMPARATIVE TABLE OF DISTANCES.

Omaha, Neb., to Corinne, Utah	1,055	miles.
Omaha, Neb., to Point of Rocks, Wyo	805	"
Distance saved by rail	250	"

Omaha, Neb., to Yellowstone Lake.

Omaha to Corinne	1,055 miles.	
Corinne to Fort Ellis, Mont	403 "	
Fort Ellis to Yellowstone Lake	118 "	
Omaha to Yellowstone Lake, (present route)		1,576 miles.
Omaha to Point of Rocks	805 "	
Point of Rocks to Yellowstone Lake	289 "	
Omaha to Yellowstone Lake, (proposed route)		1,094 "
Proposed route shortens distance to Yellowstone Lake		482 "

Omaha, Neb., to Fort Ellis and Bozeman, Mont.

Omaha to Corinne	1,055 miles.	
Corinne to Fort Ellis	403 "	
Omaha to Fort Ellis, (present route)		1,458 miles.
Omaha to Point of Rocks	805 "	
Point of Rocks to Fort Ellis	437 "	
Omaha to Fort Ellis, (proposed route)		1,242 "
Proposed route shortens distance to Fort Ellis		216 "

It is fair to presume that the freight and passenger rates will be about the same over the proposed as they are over the present route, as the distances are nearly the same. A reasonable comparison between these rates can therefore be made from the following table, showing those paid by the Government to the Union Pacific Railroad.

TABLE OF RATES.

Transportation of persons—(amount for each person.)

Omaha to Corinne	$79 25
Omaha to Point of Rocks	57 25
Amount per man saved by the proposed route	22 00

TRANSPORTATION OF FREIGHT.—THIRD CLASS.*

(4 cents per ton per mile.)

Omaha to Corinne, (1,055 miles,) per ton	$42 20
Omaha to Point of Rocks, (805 miles,) per ton	32 20
Amount per ton saved by the proposed route	10 00

SHIPMENTS OF FREIGHT TO MONTANA.

Shipments to Montana via Union Pacific Railroad.

Years.	Amount.
1869	1,125,960 pounds.
1870	6,896,723 pounds
1871	7,501,280 pounds.
1872	6,129,644 pounds.
1873	(about) 6,000,000 pounds.

Shipments from Saint Louis to Montana, via all routes

Years.	Amount.
1871	13,000,000 pounds.
1872	10,000,000 pounds.
1873	6,000,000 pounds.

*Based upon present rates of Union Pacific Railroad from Omaha to Ogden.

The proposed route will not be blocked by snow so much as the present one, as the snow-belt lies in a heavily-timbered country, in which the snow will not drift much. This will include a distance of fully one hundred and fifty miles north from Wind River Valley. It will open up a body of 2,000,000 acres of timber-land, well watered, and with a rich soil. Observations thus far indicate that this is a region of equable precipitation of rain, and that irrigation will not be necessary in cultivating the soil. There is considerable frost even during the summer, but in spite of it the vegetation is always quite luxuriant.

There is good reason for believing that the Yellowstone National Park will, in time, become the most popular summer-resort in the country, perhaps the world. This, of itself, is a sufficient reason for opening the way to it at once.

To sum up, the proposed route will save two hundred and fifty miles of distance by railroad; four hundred and eighty-two miles in reaching Yellowstone Lake, and two hundred and sixteen miles in reaching the principal cities of Montana; is a direct route to the Yellowstone National Park, which at present is practically inaccessible, and will eventually be the shortest railroad line to Montana; it opens up a very large tract of low-lying timber-land, a feature of rare occurrence in the great Rocky Mountain plateau; it will open up to settlement the Wind River Valley, the Teton Basin, and the valley of the Upper Yellowstone; and, finally, will throw open the Yellowstone National Park to the wonder-seekers of the world.

CHAPTER IV.

METEOROLOGY.

Instruments—Climate of Green River, Big Horn, and Yellowstone—Teton basins—Probable region of equable precipitation of rain—Table of altitudes—Table of weather-observations.

Observations were taken with barometers, (two cistern and three small aneroids,) thermometers, hygrometer, maximum and minimum thermometers, and solar and terrestrial radiation-thermometers. In all possible cases, the temperature of springs, including thermal springs, was taken. The temperature of the latter will be treated in the report of Dr. C. L. Heizmann, assistant-surgeon U. S. A. Observations were generally taken by Mr. J. D. Putnam, under the direction of Dr. C. C. Parry, and are, in my opinion, thoroughly reliable. Mr. Putnam deserves special mention for having carried cistern-barometer No. 1972 (Green) the round trip, frequently in very difficult mountain climbing and marching, without getting it injured in any manner that could affect the reliability of its readings. The terrestrial radiation thermometer was unfortunately broken on the march to Camp Brown. The minimum-thermometer was also broken, but afterward observations were taken to get the minimum just before sunrise, which I think can safely be relied on. Observations for maximum are not so numerous as I wished to have them, because the column was generally on the march at that period of the day when it usually occurs. All altitudes are deduced from readings of the cistern barometer.

A careful comparison of the aneroids with a cistern, (1972,) in the office and on the march from Fort Bridger to Camp Brown, in all the circumstances of rapid and wide variations of temperature incident to hypsometrical observations, led me to look with suspicion upon their reliability. In bringing them down from great elevations, they require a long and erratic period of time for returning to their normal indications, while in going up they indicate the decrease of pressure too rapidly, thus leading to the excessive altitudes usually resulting from their use. It would seem as though the corrugated metallic box offers less resistance to expansion than compression, and that at high altitudes it is likely to take a set, thus preventing a complete return to the shape which it held at the lower level. Furthermore, where the diurnal variations of temperature are very wide, these aneroids, although compensated, were visibly affected by heat, and there is nothing to show to what extent. The result of office-comparisons is given below in Tables I, II, and III.

COMPARISON OF BAROMETERS.

TABLE I.

Omaha, Neb., altitude	1,000 feet.
Error of cistern-barometer No. 1972	+0.005
Error of cistern-barometer No. 1854	—0.042
Capillarity	+0.004
Mean of 44 comparisons with 1972	—0.038
Fort Bridger, Wyo., altitude	6,639 feet.
Error of cistern-barometer, (1854.)	
Mean of 14 comparisons	—0.039
Probable constant error of No. 1854	—0.038

TABLE II.

*Aneroids.**

Omaha, Neb., elevation	1,000 feet.
Error of aneroid No. 1, (mean from 34 readings)	—0.118
Error of aneroid No. 2, (mean from 34 readings)	—0.043
Error of aneroid No. 3, (mean from 34 readings)	+0.034

TABLE III.

*Aneroids.**

Fort Bridger, Wyo., altitude		6,639 feet.
Mean from 23 comparisons	Error of aneroid No. 1	+0.524
	Error of aneroid No. 2	+0.667
	Error of aneroid No. 3	+0.646
Mean from 115 comparisons	Error of aneroid No. 1	+0.632
	Error of aneroid No. 2	+0.818
	Error of aneroid No. 3	+0.728

N. B.—These aneroids were compensated.

On the 16th of May I sent Mr. Putnam to Fort Bridger with all the barometers and other necessary instruments for making (before the expedition took the field) a thorough comparison of their readings. This he did very faithfully, and the result showed that my aneroids were not reliable, although I still hoped to use them for special trips, by comparing them immediately before leaving and at once after returning to camp. It soon appeared, however, that they were not fit even for this. The aneroid is a good weather-glass, but is hardly fit for hypsometrical work; this is a great pity, for there is great merit in its portability where mountains are to be climbed, and in its non-liability to breakage.

* Compared with No. 1972, (cistern,) at 32° Fahrenheit.

On the march from Fort Bridger the mercury in cistern-barometer 1854 leaked a little through the bag. The oxidation of this mercury between the threads of the elevating-screw soon clogged it, so that it could not be turned without great difficulty. Mr. C. T. Creary, who was carrying it, very ingeniously remedied the difficulty by making a wooden screw to work in its place. This answered the purpose admirably until we arrived at Camp Stambaugh, when he made a new screw of iron, that answered its purpose during the rest of the trip.

The leakage was caused by attempting to screw up the mercury until it filled the tube, in putting it up for transportation. This brings too much pressure on the bag of the cistern, and the mercury is crowded through it. It should only be screwed up until the cistern is full. The small motion in the mecurial column that is thus permitted does not endanger the instrument so much as the leakage when it is screwed up too tight. Works on meteorology do not call sufficient attention to this point, but rather convey the idea, if they do not positively direct, that the tube should be filled. The Smithsonian directions for meteorological observations, under the head of Barometer, say, page 17: "If circumstances compel this (moving) to be done, we should begin, before taking it from its place, by raising the mercury in the cistern by means of the screw so as to fill the cistern *and the* tube." Now, for transportation in the field, when at high altitudes, a comparatively large portion of the mercury gets into the cistern. This will not do at all, and, indeed, I should not think it advisable ever to screw up the mercury more than enough to fill the cistern.

In comparing these barometers, my attention has been particularly called to the unsatisfactory manner in which the attached thermometer registers the temperature of the mercury in the tube. Its bulb is placed in a small metallic case fastened to the outside of the brass frame of the barometer, which has a small hole sometimes cut in it opposite the bulb. It makes but little difference whether the hole is cut or not; the thermometer registers the temperature of a small inclosed space that receives the impress of increments or decrements of heat, somewhat less rapidly than the air outside, and the whole would make no sensible change in the readings. But the column of mercury is very slow to receive impressions of heat, and yet it is the temperature of this mercury that we *must* have in order to proceed with certainty to a common point of comparison for all observations. Here is undoubtedly the reason why no satisfactory results can be obtained in the comparison between two barometers. The true difference can only appear from the mean of a good many observations. In hypsometrical work this must be the cause of serious error, and when it is remedied the barometer will indeed be a remarkable leveling instrument.

Through the courtesy of the Chief Signal-Officer of the Army I have obtained the barometer-readings at Cheyenne, Corinne, and Fort Benton for the period covered by our trip. They have been plotted, and the results are shown in the accompanying chart. From these I was enabled to refer Camp Brown, our field-base, to Salt Lake City, at a time when the whole region was equally affected by barometric disturbance, thus insuring excellent altitude results, as an examination of the table of altitudes will show. To instance this I will call attention to the altitudes of Yellowstone Lake. We camped upon its shore five times, making almost the circuit around it. By leaving out one observation, that was not made at a proper time in the day for nice work, as the others were, it will be seen that the results compare quite closely. The mean of these gives 7,564 feet for the altitude of the lake, which, there is good reason for

APPROXIMATE HORARY BAROMETRIC CURVES.

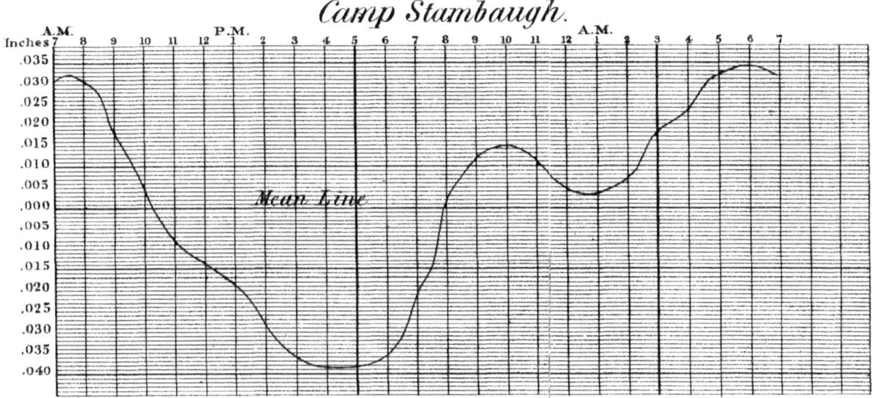

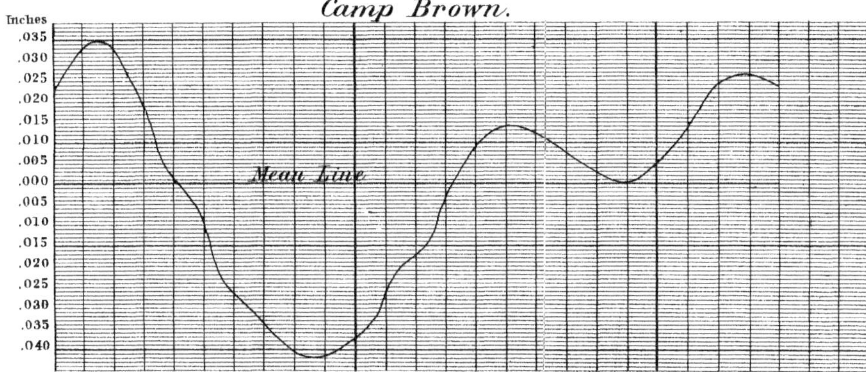

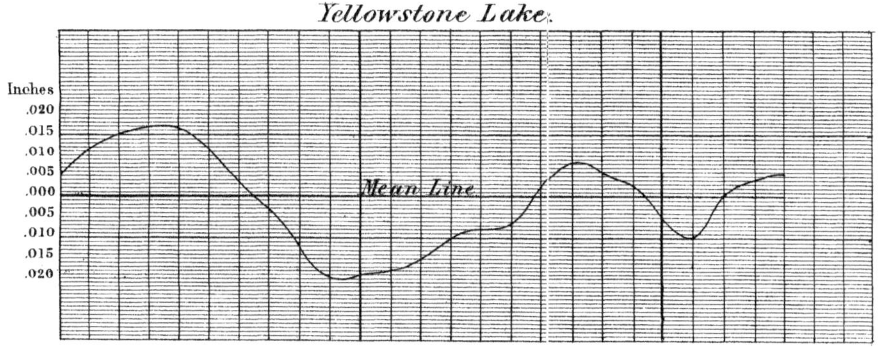

Camp Stambaugh elevation	*7767 feet,*	*Lat. 42° 30′,*	*Long.*	*108° 48′.*
" Brown	*" 5498 "*	*" 42° 59′,*	*"*	*108° 54′.*
Yellowstone Lake	*" 7564 "*	*" 44° 35′,*	*"*	*110° 22′.*

believing, is a fair approximation. I am somewhat specific on this point, because these figures differ so widely from those obtained by Professor Hayden, who, in 1871, finds this altitude to be 7,427 feet, and in 1872 finds it 7,788.

At Fort Bridger, Camp Brown, and the outlet of the Yellowstone Lake, I had hourly observations taken, for the purpose of getting an approximate horary curve for each. The results are given in the annexed chart, and will be of much interest.

The barometric readings at Corinne, Fort Benton, and Cheyenne, show that over the field embraced by the reconnaissance, the abnormal barometric oscillation was very nearly uniform. The computations for altitude were made by Lieut. S. E. Blunt, Thirteenth United States Infantry.

GREEN RIVER BASIN.

In the Green River Basin the diurnal temperature varies between pretty wide limits. This is largely owing to the extreme dryness of the atmosphere, which leaves almost nothing interposed to interfere with the radiation from the sun and earth. The relative humidity is very low, and dew and frost are quite rare. Rain seldom falls. The amount of solar radiation, as will be seen from the observations, is large, and the same causes that produce it will also probably produce a correspondingly large terrestrial radiation; all this indicates a severe climate.

The winds, with remarkable unanimity, are from the southwest and west, and the quantity of motion is great; a gale of wind can be confidently expected every day, commencing a little before noon. The natural tendency of the winds to come from the southwest over this region, is augmented by the local configuration of the ground. The west end of this basin is a *cul-de-sac*, with high mountains nearly surrounding it—the Uintahs on the south, the Wahsatch on the west, and the Wind River range on the north. The annexed sketch will illustrate it, (Fig. 8.)

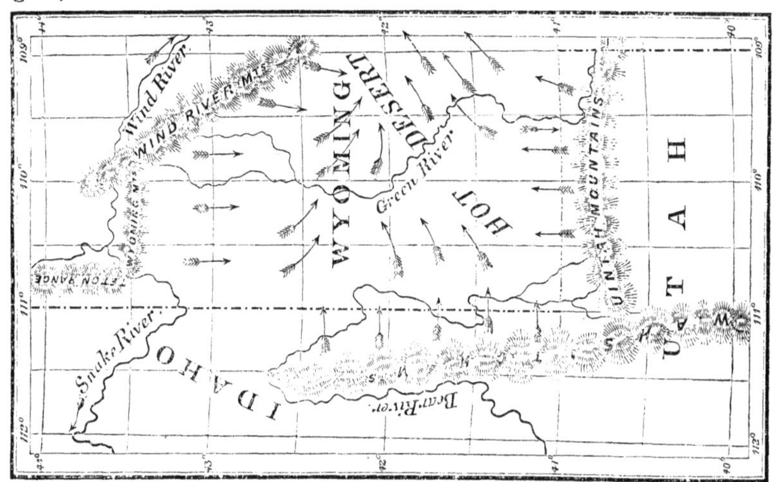

FIG. 8.—Explanation of winds in Green River Basin.

The air over the plateau becomes inordinately heated from radiation, while the cold air from the mountains rushes in to take its place, as it rises, and restore the equilibrium. The resultant motion thus produced is in a northwesterly direction, and as this is about the mean direction of the general currents of the air in this latitude, it will be seen that the different causes that tend to set the air in motion mutually re-enforce each other, producing the high winds that are such a well-known feature of the climate.

There are times when this local disturbance must be excessive, and perhaps we may look here for the origin, or at least a clew to it, of the storms that sweep across the continent to the eastward, and spend their fury on the Atlantic Ocean.

Local storms and squalls from the mountains sometimes descend a short distance into this basin, but generally clouds are rare, except the low fringe of cumuli on the horizon, that is so characteristic of fine weather.

WIND RIVER BASIN.

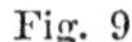

Fig. 9.

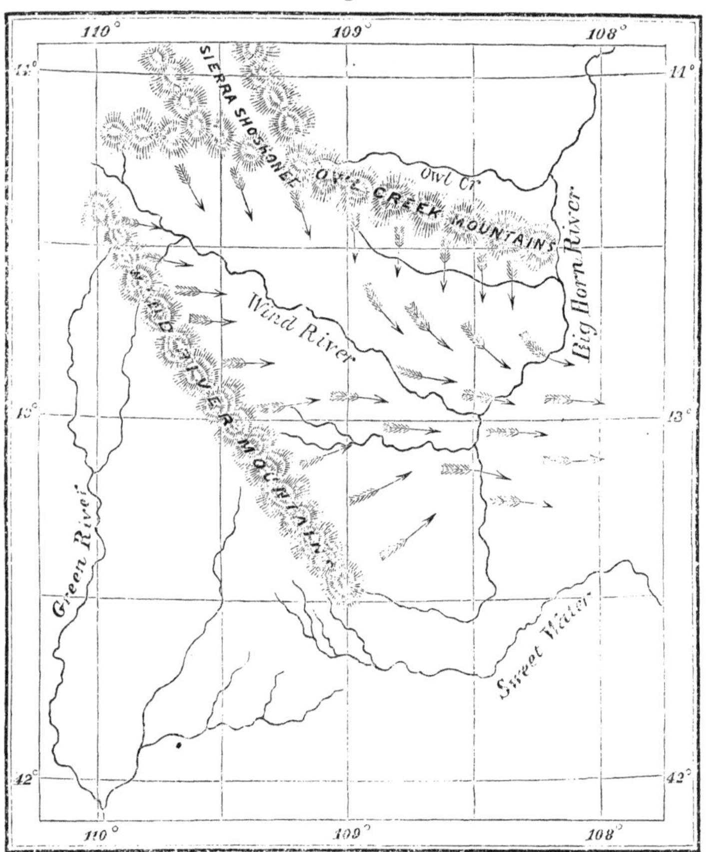

Explanation of winds in Wind River Basin.

The climate here is comparatively mild. The diurnal temperature has not such a great range as on the other side of the Wind River range, although in summer the air gets exceedingly warm about mid-day. The solar radiation is still very great, but terrestrial radiation is smaller, as the nights are warm. The relative humidity is also extremely low, causing a rarity of dew and frost. The mountains lying so close around, a slight rain-fall is caused by the summer showers from them, but the quantity of water that falls is very small. The general prevailing winds are entirely intercepted by the mountains, but the local disturbance caused by the air getting highly heated over the valley, and the rush of the cold air from the mountains to establish an equilibrium, is very great, causing daily currents of such strength and persistence as to give origin to the name of the river and mountains. This action is illustrated in the annexed sketch, (Fig. 9.)

THE BIG HORN BASIN.

The climate here is probably quite similar to that of the Wind River Valley; as far as our observations go such are the indications. There is the same and perhaps a somewhat greater cause for violent winds. The Indians repeatedly called my attention to the fact that it was very windy here, even more so than in the Wind River Valley. This is sufficiently accounted for by the fact that the mountains are very extensive, and the country at their feet and across to the Big Horn Range is mostly bare soil and rock, capable of becoming very strongly heated under the effects of the great solar radiation.

Away from the western face of the basin where the summer-squalls hang down from the edge of the mountains, the region is probably largely exempt from rain. This is further indicated by the fact that an extremely small quantity of water is drained from the western slopes of the Big Horn Mountains. The streams are of rare occurrence, and are frequently dry. On account of the scarcity of water, travel in the lower part of this basin, and more especially along its eastern face, is attended with much inconvenience.

UPPER YELLOWSTONE-TETON BASIN.

These two basins, although on opposite sides of the main divide of the Rocky Mountains, are yet subject to the same climatic influences; for this divide is so low between them as to lose its mountainous character almost entirely. This is supplied by the Sierra Shoshonee range which borders them on the east, the Wyoming Mountains to the south, and the Tetons which lie to the west.

This region is also characterized by wide extremes of diurnal temperature, although the day temperature is generally rather low, making an agreeable summer climate. The freezing-point seems to obtain quite commonly just before sunrise; and late in August, different parties, in three consecutive years, have noted at this time of the day such very notable temperatures as 14° F., 13° F., and 12° F. The nights are extremely cold as a rule. An approximation to the mean annual temperature obtained from the temperatures of some springs east of Yellowstone Lake, and one between the lake and the falls, is 37°.5 F.

The relative humidity is remarkably high for the Rocky Mountain region, which is so generally characterized by the small proportion of aquous vapor in its atmosphere; as a natural attendant upon this exceptional feature, the whole region is densely timbered.

There is ample evidence of a moderately copious rain-fall in and around this basin, especially about the headwaters of Snake River, the vegetation is always fresh and tolerably luxuriant; the country is amply supplied with water in marsh, spring, stream, pond, and lake, and the meteorological records of parties who have visited it for three years in succession point clearly to it. We had several rainy days while traversing it, days in which the rain fell almost continuously during the night and day. This is a notable fact.

It is probably a region of severe storms; for an inspection of a general map, together with the annexed sketch, shows that the principal

Fig. 10.

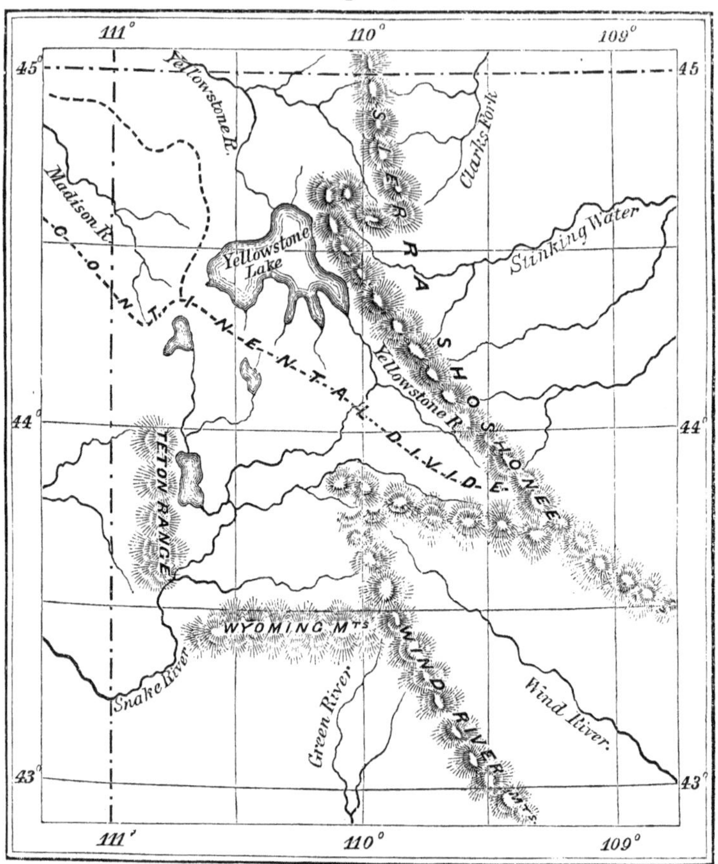

Yellowstone—Teton Basin.

southwest air-current, moving over a low portion of the mountain mass of the Pacific coast, reaches the Teton's and Sierra Shoshonee range without being deprived of much of its vapor. It is not only checked in its course by this high, cool wall, but the tremendous acicular ridge of the Tetons stands in such a position as to produce a strong eddy about the headwaters of the Snake and over the lake basin.

The equable precipitation favors the growth of forest and rank vegetation, while the latter stores up the water, to be constantly vaporized and held ready for reprecipitation, the cause and effect each favorably acting upon the other. The indications are that this region along the western base of the Sierra Shoshone Mountains,* and lying between

* I use the word "mountains" in connection with *sierra* in deference to the custom of considering them words of different shades of meaning. To the majority of English-speaking people mountain is the only word that completely covers the idea involved.

the parallels of 43° 30′ and 45° 30′ north latitude, is one of equable precipitation. The severity of the summer frosts, however, will prevent any extensive tillage of the soil, which, by the way, is a rich black loam. The prevailing winds are westerly, and mild in their character.

Table of altitudes.

All observations with mercurial barometer.

Place.	Altitude.
	Feet.
Fort Bridger	6639.0
Camp No. 3	6308.3
Camp No. 5	6314.9
Camp No. 6	6210.2
Camp No. 8	6257.0
Camp No. 9	6569.2
Divide between Big Sandy and Little Sandy	6685.6
Camp No. 10	6657.6
Camp No. 11	6742.6
Camp No. 12	7134.0
Summit of South Pass	7480.0
Camp No. 13	7400.2
Camp Stambaugh	7767.1
Triangulation Station No 43	8267.1
Camp No. 15	6937.3
Bench at head of Red Cañon	6848.0
Camp No. 16	5407.1
Ranch on Big Popo Agie, (old Camp Brown)	5311.0
Camp No. 17	5447.3
Camp Brown	5498.4
From Camp Brown to Wind River Mountains:	
Foot of first hill	6600.0
Top of first hill	8034.0
Top of second hill	8857.0
Summit of Bald Mountain	9897.4
Timber-line	10760.0
Summit of Chimney Rock	11853.0
Camp No. 20	5792.7
Divide Sage Creek and Wind River	6096.5
Camp No. 21	5553.1
Camp No. 22, (across the river from Camp 21)	5556.5
Camp No. 23	6140.2
Camp No. 24	6320.0
Camp No. 25	6208.0
Pass over Owl Creek Mountains	7836.0
Summit east of pass	8233.0
Summit of Phlox Mountain	9136.0
Camp No. 26	6168.1
Camp on headwaters of Owl Creek	8610.0
Timber-line on the Washakee Needles	10683.0
Summit of the Washakee Needles	12253.0
Last divide before Camp No. 27	7074.7
Camp No. 27	6471.0
Hill south of Camp No. 27	6783.0
Camp No. 28	6120.8
Camp No. 29	5780.0
Camp No. 30	6166.4
Spur from the mountains	8607.1
Camp No. 31	7423.0
Camp No. 32	5273.2
Camp No. 33	5845.0
Camp No. 34	6041.6
Ridge S. S. W. from Camp 34, 1st point	7203.0
Ridge S. S. W. from Camp 34, 2d point	7284.0

Table of altitudes—Continued.

Place.	Altitude.
Ridge S. S. W. from Camp 34, 3d point	8062. 0
Camp No. 35	6318. 7
Camp No. 36	6683. 0
Summit of Sailor Mountain	10046. 0
Timber-line on Sailor Mountain	9746. 0
Stinking-water Pass	9444. 3
First triangulation-point north of pass	9938. 1
Second triangulation-point north of pass	10027. 9
Camp No. 37	8940. 0
Yellowstone Lake, (at outlet)	7564. 0
Camp No. 39	7491. 8
Height of Upper Falls of the Yellowstone	150. 2
Height of Great Falls of the Yellowstone	328. 7
Camp No. 40	7908. 0
Camp No. 41	5762. 1
Jack Baronett's cabin	5741. 5
Yellowstone River at bridge	5695. 0
Camp No. 42	5813. 7
Summit of Mount Washburne	10105. 3
Camp No. 43	7724. 0
Camp No. 44	8985. 8
Camp No. 45	7132. 4
Camp No. 46	7373. 3
Camp No. 47	8301. 7
Camp No. 48, (Yellowstone Lake)	7565. 9
Camp No. 49, (Yellowstone Lake)	7564. 0
Camp No. 50, (Yellowstone Lake)	7552. 3
Camp No. 51, (Yellowstone Lake)	7563. 1
Yellowstone Lake, (mean adopted)	7564. 0
Summit of Mount Sheridan	10150. 0
Camp No. 52	7787. 7
Camp No. 53	7847. 7
Camp No. 54	8080. 9
Camp No. 55	7574. 6
Camp No. 56	6892. 4
Hill above Camp 56, (crossed by trail)	6892. 4
Camp No. 57	8917. 4
Togwotee Pass	9621. 3
Mountain S. W. of pass	10625. 4
Camp No. 58	7498. 2
Camp No. 59	6942. 0
Camp No. 60	6172.
Camp No. 61	5750. 1
Camp No. 62, (Camp No. 20)	5799. 6

TABLE I.—*Meteorological record of Northwest Wyoming Expedition from May 19 to September 13, 1873.*

Station.	Date.	Time.	Barometer.	Attached thermometer.	Detached thermometer.	Dry bulb.	Wet bulb.	CLOUDS. Kind.	CLOUDS. Amount.	WIND. Direction.	WIND. Force.	Remarks.
Fort Bridger, (elevation 6,639′)	May 19	9 0 a. m.	23. 400	43		44. 5	39. 5					Rain.
		10 0 a. m.	23. 400	44		44	39. 5	Cumulus	2			Rain.
		12 0 m	23. 390	45		45	39	Cumulus	5			
		1 0 p. m.	23. 390	48		47. 5	41	Cumulo-stratus	9			
		2 0 p. m.	23. 410	48		47	39	Cumulo-stratus	8			
		4 0 p. m.	23. 426	47		46	38	Stratus	6			
		6 0 p. m.	23. 460	44		46	37	Cumulus	1			
	May 20	8 0 a. m.	23. 480	40		41. 5	35. 5	Cumulus	1			
		9 0 a. m.	23. 476	44. 5		44	38	Cumulus	1			
		10 0 a. m.	23. 475	47		47	39	Cumulus	5			
		11 0 a. m.	23. 470	48		47	39	Cumulus	7			
		1 0 p. m.	23. 443	51		51	42	Cumulus	6			
		2 0 p. m.	23. 415	56		53	43	Cumulus	6			
		3 0 p. m.	23. 404	56		55	45	Cumulus	5			
		4 0 p. m.	23. 371	57		56	45	Cumulus	4			
		5 0 p. m.	23. 332	55		54	43	Nimbus	10			
		6 0 p. m.	23. 332	52		52	43. 5	Nimbus	10			Light rain.
	May 21	8 0 a. m.	23. 340	37		38. 5	34	Cumulus	2			Snow.
		9 0 a. m.	23. 320	38		38. 5	34	Cumulus	4			
		10 0 a. m.	23. 320	39		39	35	Cumulus	1			
		12 0 m	23. 313	40		40	35	Cumulus	1			
		2 0 p. m.	23. 356	45		43	36. 5	Cumulus	8			
		4 0 p. m.	23. 358	41		42	37					
	May 22	10 0 a. m.	23. 480	48		49. 5	43	Cumulus	1			
		11 0 a. m.	23. 472	47		49	43	Cumulus	1			
		12 0 m	23. 461	49		49	43	Cumulus	2			
		3 0 p. m.	23. 440	53. 5		54	47	Cumulo-stratus	6	North	2	
		4 0 p. m.	23. 438	53		54	46	Cumulus	9			
		5 0 p. m.	23. 423	53		53. 5	43. 5	Cumulus	9			
		6 0 p. m.	23. 426	51		52	44	Cumulus	9			
		7 0 p. m.	23. 432	50		52	45	Cumulus	9			
	May 23	6 0 a. m.	23. 397	44		46	40. 5	Stratus	8	East	2	
		7 0 a. m.	23. 386	45		47	42	Cumulus	6	East	2	
		8 0 a. m.	23. 372	46. 5		49	44	Cumulus	5	East	2	
		9 0 a. m.	23. 348	49		50	45	Cumulus	4	East	2	
		10 0 a. m.	23. 321	50		53	47	Cumulus	3	East	2	
		11 0 a. m.	23. 387	51		52. 5	46. 5	Cirro-cumulus	5	East	2	Storm to west.
		12 0 m	23. 254	52		55	48	Cumulus	8	East	1	Storm to west.

TABLE I.—*Meteorological record of Northwest Wyoming Expedition from May 19 to September 13, 1873*—Continued.

Station.	Date.	Time.	Barometer.	Attached thermometer.	Detached thermometer.	Dry bulb.	Wet bulb.	CLOUDS. Kind.	CLOUDS. Amount.	WIND. Direction.	WIND. Force.	Remarks.
Fort Bridger	May 23	2 0 p.m.	23.282	52	......	51	46	Cumulo-nimbus	9	Southwest	3	Storm to southwest.
		3 0 p.m.	23.302	50	......	50	45	Cumulo-stratus	10	West	3	
		4 0 p.m.	23.335	48	......	49	44	Nimbus	10			Rain.
		6 0 p.m.	23.352	48	......	50	44	Nimbus	10			Rain.
		7 0 p.m.	23.364	48	......	50.5	44.5	Nimbus	9	West	2	Clearing.
	May 24	6 0 a.m.	23.380	42	......	44	40	Nimbus	9	South	0	
		7 0 a.m.	23.386	43	......	45	40	Nimbus	9	South	0	Snow.
		8 0 a.m.	23.397	44	......	46	41	Nimbus	10		0	Snow.
		9 0 a.m.	23.401	46.5	......	47	42	Nimbus	9	West	1	
		10 0 a.m.	23.413	47	......	47	42	Nimbus	10	West	1	Snow.
		11 0 a.m.	23.416	45.5	......	47	42	Nimbus	10	West	2	Snow and rain.
		12 0 m	23.408	45.5	......	45	42	Cumulus	6	West	2	Sleet.
		1 0 p.m.	23.415	46	......	46	42	Nimbus	10	West	3	Rain.
		2 0 p.m.	23.418	45.5	......	46.5	42.5	Cumulus	5	West	3	
		3 0 p.m.	23.418	47	......	47	43	Cumulus	4	West	3	
		4 0 p.m.	23.437	48	......	46.5	44	Cumulus	7	West	3	
		5 0 p.m.	23.448	48	......	50	45	Cumulus	8	West	3	Light rain.
		6 0 p.m.	23.452	47.5	......	48	44	Cumulo-stratus, nimbo-cirrus	4	West	2	Light rain.
		7 0 p.m.	23.464	47.5	......	48	43.5	Cumulo-stratus, nimbus	6	West	1	
	May 25	6 0 a.m.	23.504	42	......	45.5	41	Cumulo-stratus	6	West	1	
		7 0 a.m.	23.509	44	......	45	40.5	Cumulus	4	West	2	
		8 0 a.m.	23.523	44	......	45.5	41	Cumulus	9	West	2	
		9 0 a.m.	23.523	45	......	45.5	41.5	Cumulus	8	West	2	
		10 0 a.m.	23.521	47	......	48.5	43.5	Cumulus	3	West	1	
		11 0 a.m.	23.523	50.5	......	51	45.5	Cumulus	6	West	1	
		12 0 m	23.520	50	......	50	44.5	Cumulus	8	West	1	
		1 0 p.m.	23.520	51	......	50	45	Cumulus	8	West	1	
		3 0 p.m.	23.508	50	......	51	45	Cumulus	3	North	2	
		4 0 p.m.	23.504	50	......	50.5	44	Cumulus	3	North	2	
		7 0 p.m.	23.520	53	......	53	46	Cumulo-stratus	3	West	1	
	May 26	7 0 a.m.	23.492	44	......	45.5	40		0	North	1	
		8 0 a.m.	23.491	46	......	46.5	41		0	North	1	
		9 0 a.m.	23.476	48	......	48	43	Cumulus	1	West	0	
		10 0 a.m.	23.472	49	......	48	43	Cirrus	2	West	2	
		11 0 a.m.	23.447	52	......	52	45	Cirro-stratus	5	West	2	
		12 0 m	23.440	53	......	52	45	Cumulus, cirro-stratus	5	West	2	
		1 0 p.m.	23.440	55	......	54.5	45	Cirro-cumulus	7	West	2	
		6 0 p.m.	23.418	52	......	55	48	Cumulo-stratus	8	West	2	
	May 27	6 0 a.m.	23.436	48	......	47	42		0		0	

Fort Bridger		7	0 a. m.	23. 444	48. 5	......	50	44. 5		0			
		11	0 a. m.	23. 418	51	......	53	46. 5	Cumulus	1	Northwest	1	
		1	0 p. m.	23. 392	54	......	56. 5	49	Cumulus	6	West	2	Light rain.
		6	0 p. m.	23. 323	50	......	51	46. 5					
	May 28	6	0 a. m.	23. 176	39	......	46	44. 5	Fog		Southeast	1	Heavy dew.
		8	0 a. m.	23. 137	51	......	56	51	Cumulus	2	Southeast	1	
		10	0 a. m.	23. 158	67	......	70	54	Cumulus	2	West	2	
		12	0 m.	23. 140	58	......	65	50. 5	Cumulo-nimbus	9	South	3	Storm to south.
		1	0 p. m.	23. 124	62. 5	......	62. 5	50	Cumulus	9	West	3	Light rain.
	May 28	2	0 p. m.	23. 120	68	......	70	52. 5	Cumulus	5	West	3	
		3	0 p. m.	23. 187	49	......	51	43	Cirro-cumulus, cirro-stratus.	3	Northwest	3	
		6	0 p. m.	23. 198	45	......	48	41	Cumulo-stratus	9	Northwest	2	
	May 29	6	0 a. m.	23. 337	36	......	39	37	Cirro-cumulus, cumulo-strat.	8	West	3	Ice one-eighth inch.
		7	0 a. m.	23. 369	44. 5	......	46	41. 5	Cirro-cumulus	7	West	1	
		11	0 a. m.	23. 377	52	......	53	44	Cirro-cumulus	3	East	2	
		12	0 m.	23. 361	55	......	56	45					
		2	0 p. m.	23. 326	55	......	69	55	Cirro-cumulus, cumulo-strat.	8	North	1	
		4	0 p. m.	23. 267	63	......	63	49	Cumulus	8	South	1	
		6	0 p. m.	23. 244	56	......	......	......	Nimbus	9	West	2	
		8	0 p. m.	23. 248	45. 5	......	47	42	Nimbus	9	West	2	
	May 30	5	0 a. m.	23. 347	32. 5	......	34	32. 5	Cumulo-stratus	6	Southwest	1	Ice one-eighth inch.
		6	0 a. m.	23. 349	33. 5	......	35	33	Cumulo-stratus	6	Southwest	1	
		7	0 a. m.	23. 363	36	......	37	35	Cirro-stratus	4	North	1	
		10	0 a. m.	23. 434	50. 5	......	52	45	Cumulus	8	West	3	
		1	0 p. m.	23. 488	54	......	54	46	Cumulus, nimbus	9	West	4	
		2	0 p. m.	23. 540	59	......	63. 5	51. 5	Cumulus	7	West	3	
		6	0 p. m.	23. 583	47. 5	......	45	38	Cirro-cumulus	2	West	2	
		7	0 p. m.	23. 597	50	......	50. 5	44	Cirro-stratus	1	West	2	
		8	0 p. m.	23. 597	39	......	38	35. 5	Stratus	1	West	2	
	May 31	7	0 a. m.	23. 664	41	......	46	37		0	North	1	
		8	0 a. m.	23. 670	44	......	44. 5	35		0	East	1	
		11	0 a. m.	23. 676	62	......	67	......		0	East	1	
		12	0 m.	23. 669	62	......	74	55	Cirrus	1			
		2	0 p. m.	23. 665	79	......	82	61	Cirrus	3	Northwest	1	
		5	0 p. m.	23. 600	60	......	60	48					
		6	0 p. m.	23. 606	61	......	63	51	Cumulo-stratus	6	West	2	
		7	0 p. m.	23. 602	50	......	50	44	Stratus	9	West	3	
		8	0 p. m.	23. 608	48	......	49	......	Cumulo-stratus	9	West	3	
	June 1	7	0 a. m.	23. 670	48	......	53	46		0	West	1	
		8	0 a. m.	23. 682	58. 5	1	64	......		0	West	1	
		1	0 p. m.	23. 684	71. 5	......	75. 5	57		0	West	2	
		4	0 p. m.	23. 656	72. 5	......	72. 5	......	Cirrus	1	West	2	
		6	0 p. m.	23. 649	70	......	69	......		0	West	2	
		9	0 p. m.	23. 622	37	......	37	......		0	West	1	
	June 2	6	0 a. m.	23. 660	48. 5	......	52. 5	46. 5		0	Northwest	1	
		7	0 a. m.	23. 678	57	......	59	48. 5		0	Northwest	1	
		8	0 a. m.	23. 683	69	......	61	49		0	East	1	
		9	0 a. m.	23. 683	64	......	67	52		0	East	2	
		2	0 p. m.	23. 665	75	......	75	56	Cumulus	1	West	2	
		7	0 p. m.	23. 622	62. 5	......	60. 5	47	Cirro-stratus	1	Northwest	2	
		8	0 p. m.	23. 614	51. 5	......	50	41		0	West	1	
		9	0 p. m.	23. 604	40	......	40	35		0	West	0	Slight aurora.

TABLE I.—*Meteorological record of Northwest Wyoming Expedition from May 19 to September 13, 1873*—Continued.

Station.	Date.	Time.	Barometer.	Attached thermometer.	Detached thermometer.	Dry bulb.	Wet bulb.	CLOUDS. Kind.	CLOUDS. Amount.	WIND. Direction.	WIND. Force.	Remarks.
Fort Bridger	June 3	7 0 a. m.	23. 689	58		62	51	Cirrus	1	West	0	
		8 0 a. m.	23. 689	58		59	47	Cirrus	1	Northeast	1	
		9 0 a. m.	23. 689	61. 5		62. 5	47		0	Northeast	1	
		10 0 a. m.	23. 689	64. 5		65. 5	50	Cumulus	1	Northeast	1	
		11 0 a. m.	23. 683	69		73	55	Cumulus	1	North	1	
		1 0 p. m.	23. 683	80		87. 5	63	Cumulus	1	North	1	Showers in mountains.
		2 0 p. m.	23. 664	79. 5		82. 5	61	Cumulus	1	West	1	Do.
		4 0 p. m.	23. 635	79		76	53	Cumulus	2	West	1	
		7 0 p. m.	23. 603	65		63	52	Cirro-cumulus	1	Northwest	1	
		8 0 p. m.	23. 584	52		50	44	Cirrus	5	North	1	
	June 4	6 0 a. m.	23. 681	50. 5		52. 5	46. 5		0	West	1	
		7 0 a. m.	23. 691	58		59. 5	51		0	West	1	
		2 0 p. m.	23. 532	76. 5				Cumulo-stratus	2	West	1	
		7 0 p. m.	23. 509	61. 5				Nimbus	1	Northwest	1	Showery to east.
		9 0 p. m.	23. 505	44					0	South	1	
	June 5	7 0 a. m.	23. 574	63				Cirrus	1	North	1	
		10 0 a. m.	23. 594	78				Cirro-cumulus	1	Southwest	1	
		12 0 m.	23. 588	78				Cumulus	2	West	2	
		3 0 p. m.	23. 567	79				Cumulus	1	West	1	
		6 0 p. m.	23. 538	72. 5						West	2	
		9 0 p. m.	23. 539	47		47	42		0	South	1	
	June 6	5 0 a. m.	23. 532	47. 5		50			0	West	1	
	June 7	12 0 m.	23. 564	74	74			Cumulus	3		0	
		6 0 p. m.	23. 574	69	65			Nimbus	3	West	0	
	June 8	7 0 a. m.	23. 652	49	50							
		9 0 a. m.	23. 664	61. 5	69							
		11 0 a. m.	23. 686	71	70							
		12 30 p. m.	23. 674	73	70							
		3 30 p. m.	23. 634	64	62							
		6 0 p. m.	23. 610	54	57							
		9 0 p. m.	23. 634	48. 5	48							
	June 9	7 0 a. m.	23. 668	47. 5	47				0		0	
		2 0 p. m.	23. 666	76	72			Cumulus	1	West	1	Instrum'ts exposed to sun.
		6 0 p. m.	23. 629	65. 5	63. 5			Cumulus	1	Southwest	1	Do.
		9 0 p. m.	23. 614	44	45				0		0	
	June 10	6 0 a. m.	23. 624	46. 2	50							
		7 0 a. m.	23. 668	63. 5	56				0	West	1	Do.
		12 30 p. m.	23. 653	78. 5	78. 5				0	West	1	Do.
		2 0 p. m.	23. 644	86	86. 5			Cumulus	1	West	2	Do.

	June 11	9 0 p. m.	23. 596	51. 5	54	......	......	....	0	West	1	
		6 0 a. m.	23. 592	53	54	......	......	Cirro-cumulus	2	South	1	
		12 15 p. m.	23. 644	79	74	......	......	Cumulus	4	West	2	Do.
		2 0 p. m.	23. 632	73	71. 5	......	......	Cumulus	8	Southwest	2	Instrum'ts exposed to sun; a few drops of rain.
		9 0 p. m.	23. 634	50	45	......	......	Stratus	1	South	1	
	June 12	7 0 a. m.	23. 728	71. 5	65. 5	......	......	Cirrus	2	West	1	
Camp 3, (6,308′)	June 12	7 30 p. m.	24. 004	63	62. 7	......	......	Cirro-stratus	1	West	1	
	June 13	8 15 a. m.	24. 013	72	67	......	......	....	0	West	1	
Camp 5, (6,315′)	June 14	9 0 a. m.	24. 016	78	......	68	57	Cumulus	1	....	0	
		12 m	23. 982	80. 5	......	80. 5	59. 5	Cumulus	6	South	1	
		3 0 p. m.	23. 948	85. 5	......	78	......	Cirrus	2	West	2	
		7 0 p. m.	23. 922	65	......	64	53. 5	Cirrus, cumulo-stratus	7	West	1	
Camp 6, (6,210′)	June 15	4 30 p. m.	24. 038	77	73	......	......	Cumulus, cirrus, nimbus	8	East	2	
		6 0 p. m.	24. 036	71	70. 5	......	......	Nimbus, cumulus, cirrus	8	Southeast	2	Thundering.
	June 16	7 0 a. m.	24. 049	57	55. 5	......	......	Cumulus, nimbus	6	East	1	Instrum'ts exposed to sun
Camp 7	June 16	11 0 a. m.	24. 057	85	78	93	70	Cumulus, cirrus	2	South	2	Do.
		12 m	24. 046	86	83	96. 5	......	Cumulus, nimbus	7	Southeast	3	Do.
		2 0 p. m.	24. 032	86. 5	82	93	68	Cumulus, nimbus	6	West	3	Do.
		6 0 p. m.	23. 995	71	67	65	55	Cumulo-stratus	8	West	1	Do.
Station-house south side of Big Sandy	June 17	12 m	23. 962	80. 5	81. 5	......	......	Cirro-stratus	7	West	2	
		1 0 p. m.	23. 949	77	78	......	......	Cirro-stratus	7	West	2	
Camp 8, (6,257′)	June 17	8 0 p. m.	23. 898	57	55	......	......	Cirro-stratus	1	West	0	
	June 18	4 30 a. m.	23. 810	41	41	......	......	Cirrus	1	East	0	
Station-house crossing of Big Sandy	June 18	2 30 p. m.	23. 642	77. 8	78. 2	......	......	Cirrus	4	West	2	
		4 30 p. m.	23. 640	77	76. 5	......	......	Cirro-cumulus	4	West	2	
Camp 9, (6,569′)	June 19	5 30 a. m.	23. 705	57	48	......	......	Cirrus	1	Southeast	0	
Camp 10, (6,658′)	....	2 0 p. m.	23. 634	88	88	88	60	Cumulus	1	East	2	Do.
		6 0 p. m.	23. 573	84. 8	82. 6	82	56. 7	Cumulus	1	Southwest	2	
		9 0 p. m.	23. 534	57. 5	52. 5	54	47	Stratus	1	....	0	
	June 20	6 0 a. m.	23. 558	59. 3	55	59	49. 5	Cirro-stratus	1	North	0	
		12 m	23. 570	85	......	90	60. 5	Cumulus	1	South	3	
		2 0 p. m.	23. 510	88	92	89	59. 5	....	0	South	4	
		8 0 p. m.	23. 472	68	66	67	48	Cumulo-stratus	1	West	2	
	June 21	12 m	23. 442	81. 5	83	79. 5	55	Cumulus	4	South	4	
Camp 11, (6,743′)	June 21	7 30 p. m.	23. 102	61. 2	58. 5	......	......	Stratus	3	....	0	
	June 22	5 0 a. m.	23. 110	48	45. 5	......	......	Nimbus, cumulo-stratus	8	West	2	A few drops of rain.
Dry Sandy station-house	June 22	7 0 a. m.	23. 138	40	41	......	......	Nimbus	10	Southwest	3	Hard rain and snow.
Camp 12, (7,134′)	June 22	4 0 p. m.	22. 986	52	50. 5	......	......	Cumulus	7	West	4	
		5 0 p. m.	22. 992	49	48	......	......	Cumulus	6	West	3	
	June 23	6 0 a. m.	23. 126	52	55	49	41	....	0	West	2	
		12 m	23. 148	56	57	57	......	Cumulus	1	South	2	
Summit of South Pass, (7,480′)	June 23	3 30 p. m.	22. 788	59	52	......	......	....	0	West	2	
Camp 13, (7,400′)	June 23	6 30 p. m.	22. 858	55	51	......	......	....	0	West	1	
	June 24	5 0 a. m.	22. 830	36	29	......	......	Stratus	1	East	2	
Camp Stambaugh, (7,767′)	June 24	7 20 p. m.	22. 516	65. 5	60. 5	......	......	Cumulo-stratus	1	West	1	
	June 25	7 0 a. m.	22. 567	62	62	......	......	....	0	West	2	
		9 0 a. m.	22. 568	77. 5	78	......	......	....	0	Southwest	2	
		10 0 a. m.	22. 575	70	69. 5	......	......	....	0	Southwest	2	
		11 0 a. m.	22. 572	70	71	......	......	....	0	Southwest	3	

TABLE I.—*Meteorological record of Northwest Wyoming Expedition from May 19 to September 13, 1873*—Continued.

Station.	Date.	Time.	Barometer.	Attached thermometer.	Detached thermometer.	Dry bulb.	Wet bulb.	CLOUDS. Kind.	CLOUDS. Amount.	WIND. Direction.	WIND. Force.	Remarks.
Camp Stambaugh, (7,767′)	June 25	12 m	22.576	73.8	76.5				0	South	3	
		1 0 p. m.	22.568	74	79				0	South	3	
		2 0 p. m.	22.576	73	74.5	75	46		0	Southwest	4	
		3 0 p. m.	22.562	75					0	Southwest	4	
		4 0 p. m.	22.594	74.5	74				0	Southwest	4	
		6 0 p. m.	22.598	73	70	70.5	44.5		0	Southwest	3	
		8 0 p. m.	22.640	68	60			Cumulo-stratus	1	Southwest	2	
		9 0 p. m.	22.610	69	57.5				0	Southwest	2	
		10 0 p. m.	22.690	68	63				0	Southwest	1	
		11 0 p. m.	22.676	68.5	54							
		12 m	22.680	67.5	51.5							
	June 26	1 0 a. m.	22.708	67.5	46.5							
		2 0 a. m.	22.710	66.5	44.5							
		3 0 a. m.	22.735	65.5	42.5							
		4 0 a. m.	22.740	65	41.5							
		5 0 a. m.	22.764	62	42.5							
		6 0 a. m.	22.758	61	51	64.8	45.5		0	West	1	
		7 0 a. m.	22.774	64	61				0	Southwest	2	
		8 0 a. m.	22.790	68	65.5				0	Southwest	2	
		9 0 a. m.	22.806	69.5	68				0	Southwest	2	
		10 0 a. m.	22.808	72.5	71				0	Southwest	2	
		11 0 a. m.	22.815	74	70.5				0	Southwest	2	
		12 m	22.810	75	77.5	75	47.5		0	Southwest	2	
		1 0 p. m.	22.811	75.5	81.5				0	Southwest	3	
		2 0 p. m.	22.811	74	75	76.5	47.5		0	Southwest	3	
		3 0 p. m.	22.813	75	74.5				0	Southwest	2	
		4 0 p. m.	22.808	76	76				0	Southwest	1	
		5 0 p. m.	22.816	73.5	73.5				0	Southwest	1	
		6 0 p. m.	22.820	71.5	70	71	45.5		0	West	1	
		8 0 p. m.	22.838	69	57				0	Southwest	0	
		9 0 p. m.	22.848	67	54				0	West	0	
	June 27	7 0 a. m.	22.875	65	64.5				0	Southwest	1	
		8 0 a. m.	22.884	69	68.5				0	Southwest	1	
		9 0 a. m.	22.880	72	72				0	West	1	
		12 m	22.882	75	80	76.5	48		0	Southwest	2	
		2 0 p. m.	22.873	74.5	74	75	46		0	West	3	
		6 0 p. m.	22.850	74	69	69.5	43.5		0	West	2	
		8 0 p. m.	22.848	70	57				0	West	2	
		9 0 p. m.	22.851	68	56			Stratus	1	West	2	

	June 28	6 0 a. m.	22. 838	61. 2	58	......	......	Cirro-cumulus	1	Southwest		
Camp 15, (6,937′)	June 28	7 15 p. m.	23. 332	53	44	......	......	Cirrus	1	Southwest		
Camp 16, (5,407′)	June 29	12 m	24. 713	88	76	......	......	Cumulus	1	Southeast		
		2 0 p. m.	24. 663	87	76	......	......	Cumulus	1	North	1	
		6 0 p. m.	24. 573	75	74	74	57	Cumulus	1	......	0	
	June 30	4 15 a. m.	24. 533	46	45	......	......	Cumulo-stratus	3	......	0	
Ranch on Baldwin Creek, (5,311′)	June 30	12 30 p. m.	24. 620	67. 5	66	......	......	Cumulus	8	South	1	
		1 15 p. m.	24. 630	71. 5	70. 5	......	......	Cumulo-stratus	7	South	1	Light rain.
Camp 17, (5,447′)	June 30	3 45 p. m.	24. 551	66	64	......	......	Cumulus	3	West	1	Rain.
		8 0 p. m.	24. 531	51	51	......	......	Cumulo-stratus	6	South	1	
	July	5 0 a. m.	24. 468	41. 5	42	......	......	......	...	......	...	
		6 0 a. m.	24. 472	48. 2	54	......	......	Cirro-cumulus, cirro-stratus	1	......	0	
Camp Brown, (5,498′)	July 2	12 m	24. 420	76. 5	79	78. 8	56	Cumulus	8	West	2	
		2 0 p. m.	24. 406	78. 5	80	80. 5	54. 5	Cumulus	3	West	2	
		8 15 p. m.	24. 440	73	66	......	......	Cirrus, cumulo-stratus	2	West	1	
	July 3	7 0 a. m.	24. 472	63	58	67	52. 5	......	0	......	0	
		8 0 a. m.	24. 507	68	64	......	......	......	0	East	1	
		9 0 a. m.	24. 510	72	68	......	......	......	0	East	1	
		10 0 a. m.	24. 509	73	71	......	......	Cirro-stratus	1	East	1	
		11 0 a. m.	24. 508	75. 5	74	......	......	Cirro-stratus	1	......	0	
		12 m	24. 510	77	78	78. 9	51	Cirrus	1	West	2	
		1 0 p. m.	24. 508	77. 8	80	......	......	Cirrus	1	West	2	
		2 0 p. m.	24. 510	79. 5	81	82	52. 5	Cirrus	1	West	2	
		3 0 p. m.	24. 512	81	83	......	......	Cirrus	1	West	2	
		4 0 p. m.	24. 512	83. 5	84	......	......	Cirrus	1	West	2	
		5 0 p. m.	24. 532	81. 5	82	......	......	Cirrus	1	West	2	
		6 0 p. m.	24. 544	82	79	......	......	Cirrus	1	West	1	
		7 0 p. m.	24. 557	78. 3	74	72	51	Cirrus	3	West	1	
		8 0 p. m.	24. 586	75	67	......	......	Cirro-stratus	2	West	1	
		9 0 p. m.	24. 592	72. 5	64	......	......	......	...	......	...	
		10 0 p. m.	24. 600	70. 5	62	......	......	......	...	......	...	
		11 0 p. m.	24. 608	72	62	......	......	......	...	......	...	
		12 m	24. 610	70	60	......	......	......	...	......	...	
	July 4	1 0 a. m.	24. 616	69. 5	59	......	......	......	...	......	...	
		2 0 a. m.	24. 620	68. 5	62	......	......	......	...	......	...	
		3 0 a. m.	24. 626	67. 6	59	......	......	......	...	......	...	
		4 0 a. m.	24. 622	66. 7	52. 4	......	......	......	...	......	...	
		5 0 a. m.	24. 664	66	52	......	......	......	0	......	0	
		6 0 a. m.	24. 673	64. 5	56	......	......	......	0	West	1	
		7 0 a. m.	24. 672	66	61	69. 5	52. 5	......	0	West	0	
		8 0 a. m.	24. 676	69. 5	66	......	......	......	0	East	1	
		10 0 a. m.	24. 670	75. 5	72	......	......	......	...	......	...	
		11 0 a. m.	24. 664	78. 5	76	......	......	......	...	......	...	
		12 m	24. 652	81	79	......	......	......	...	......	...	
		2 0 p. m.	24. 640	83	84	86	55. 2	......	0	West	2	
		7 0 p. m.	24. 628	83. 5	77	73	55	......	0	West	2	
	July 5	9 20 a. m.	24. 680	78	75	......	......	......	...	......	...	
		12 m	24. 652	84. 5	87	86	60. 5	......	...	......	...	
		2 0 p. m.	24. 646	86. 5	89	87. 5	59. 5	......	...	......	...	
		4 0 p. m.	24. 628	86	87	87. 5	61	......	...	......	...	
		6 0 p. m.	24. 634	86	85	85. 5	60. 5	......	...	......	...	
		9 0 p. m.	24. 612	72. 5	66	63	53	......	...	......	...	

TABLE I.—*Meteorological record of Northwest Wyoming Expedition from May 19 to September 13, 1873*—Continued.

Station.	Date.	Time.	Barometer.	Attached thermometer.	Detached thermometer.	Dry bulb.	Wet bulb.	CLOUDS. Kind.	CLOUDS. Amount.	WIND. Direction.	WIND. Force.	Remarks.
Camp Brown, (5,498′)	July 6	7 0 a. m.	24. 682	71. 5	68	71. 5	58					
		9 0 a. m.	24. 680	76. 5	75. 5	76. 5	58	Cumulus	6			
		12 m	24. 666	86. 5	87	88. 5	62	Cumulo-stratus	8			Few drops of rain.
		2 0 p. m.	24. 688	80. 5	78	78	56. 5	Cumulo-stratus	9			Light rain.
		7 0 p. m.	24. 678	76	77. 5	76. 5	57. 5	Stratus, nimbus	2			
		10 0 p. m.	24. 670	70. 5								
	July 7	7 0 a. m.	24. 698	66. 5	54	54. 5	33					
		8 0 a. m.	24. 696	70	73	73	56					
		9 0 a. m.	24. 708	75. 5	74							
		10 0 a. m.	24. 710	77	76							
		11 0 a. m.	24. 710	80	78. 5							
		12 m	24. 692	82	80. 5	81. 5	60					
		1 0 p. m.	24. 674	84. 5	83	84. 5	61					
		2 0 p. m.	24. 658	88	87. 5							
		3 0 p. m.	24. 652	87	82			Nimbus, cumulo-stratus	9	Southwest	0	Showering.
		4 0 p. m.	24. 636	85	81	81	61. 5	Nimbus, cumulo-stratus	9			
		5 0 p. m.	24. 620	82	79	89. 5	59	Nimbus, cumulo-stratus	9			
		6 0 p. m.	24. 634	81. 5	77. 5	77. 5	57. 5	Nimbus, cumulo-stratus	7	East	1	
Camp Brown, (5,498′)	July 8	7 0 a. m.	24. 674	68. 5	67	67. 5	57. 5					
		9 0 a. m.	24. 676	75. 5	76							
		12 m.	24. 674	85. 5	82. 5	83. 5	60					
		2 0 p. m.	24. 654	85. 5	82							
		5 0 p. m.	24. 622	90. 7	84. 3			Cumulus	2	West	2	Wind-storm between 3 and 4 p. m.
		6 0 p. m.	24. 636	80. 5	77	77. 5	58	Cumulus, nimbus	2	Northwest	2	
		9 30 p. m.	24. 723	73	68			Cumulus, nimbus	9	North	3	
	July 9	7 0 a. m.	24. 749	67.	66	66. 5	56		0	North	0	
		12 m.	24. 766	80. 5	77. 5			Cumulus	1		0	
		6 0 p. m.	24. 730	89. 9	81. 5	83	61	Cirro-cumulus	1	North	1	
	July 10	7 0 a. m.	24. 700	69. 5	67	68	58. 5	Cirro-cumulus	5	North	1	
Camp 19	July 11	7 0 a. m.	24. 640	66. 5	69			Cumulo-stratus	8		0	
		12 15 p. m.	24. 603	87	90			Nimbus, cumulus	4	Southeast	1	
Camp 20, (5,793′)	July 12	7 0 a. m.	24. 348	63	62			Cumulus	1	West	1	
Camp 21, (5,553′)	July 12	8 0 p. m.	24. 412	67. 5	68			Stratus	4	South	1	
	July 13	6 0 a. m.	24. 515	53	56			Cirro-cumulus, cumulo-strat.	8	South	0	
		7 0 a. m.	24. 532	66. 5	61. 5	59. 5	50. 5	Cirro-cumulus, stratus	3	East	1	
		12 15 p. m.	24. 515	72	72	71. 5	51. 5	Cumulus, cumulo-stratus	6	West	3	Shower in Wind River Mountains.
		3 0 p. m.	24. 546	74. 6	75			Cumulus	2	West	1–3	Wind westerly.

Camp 22, (5,556′)	July 13	8 0 p. m.	24. 563	62	56			Cumulus	1	South	1	
	July 14	6 0 a. m.	24. 605	59	53				0	Southwest	1	
		7 0 a. m.	24. 610	63. 6	61				0	South	0	
Camp 23, (6,140′)	July 14	7 0 p. m.	24. 007	73. 7	72. 5				0	West	2	
		8 0 p. m.	23. 996	65. 5	65				0	West	1	Brilliant meteor at 8.35 p.m.
	July 15	7 0 a. m.	24. 030	66. 3	65. 5			Cumulus	1	West	0	
		12 m.	24. 030	86	84			Cirro-stratus	5	West	1	
Camp 24, (6,320′)	July 15	7 0 p. m.	23. 511	74	72			Cumulo-stratus	7	South	2	
	July 16	7 0 a. m.	23. 590	69	76. 5				0	West	2–4	
Camp 25, (6,208′)	July 16	8 0 p. m.	23. 798	62	61				0	Northwest	2–3	
	July 17	7 0 a. m.	23. 949	62. 5	57				0	Southwest	1	
Highest point on trail over Owl Creek Mountains, (7,836′)	July 17	10 0 a. m.	22. 636	67	60			Hazy		North	2	
Summit, east of pass, (8,233′)	July 17	11 15 a. m.	22. 303	60. 1	58			Hazy		North	2	
Camp 26, (6,168)	July 17	6 0 p. m.	24. 080	71	68				0	East	1	
	July 18	4 30 a. m.	24. 084	46	47				0	Southeast	1	
Camp on Dry Creek	July 18	2 0 p. m.	22. 859	69. 8	69. 5				0	Southwest	1	
Headwaters of Owl Creek, (8,610′)	July 18	8 0 p. m.	22. 142	43. 5	44				0	West	1	
	July 19	4 30 a. m.	22. 092	36	34				0	West	1	
		6 0 a. m.	22. 108	51. 5	51. 5				0	West	1	
Highest point reached on Washakie Needles, (12,053′)	July 19	2 0 p. m.	19. 406	57. 5								
Timber-line on Washakie Needles, (10,683′)	July 19	3 0 p. m.	20. 608	62								Light rain.
Camp 26, (6,168′)	July 20	2 0 p. m.	23. 864	89	91			Cumulus, stratus	8	West	2	
		7 30 p. m.	23. 802	77. 5	77				4	West		
	July 21	6 45 a. m.	23. 730	72	71			Cirro-cumulus, cumulo-strat.	8	West	2	
Last divide before reaching Camp 27, (7,075′)	July 21	3 0 p. m.	23. 196	84	77. 5			Cirrus, cumulo-stratus	8	West	2	
Camp 27, (6,471′)	July 21	6 30 p. m.	23. 884	69. 5	68			Nimbus	9	North	1	
		8 0 p. m.	23. 886	62. 5	65			Cumulo-stratus	7		0	
	July 22	4 45 a. m.	23. 968	47. 5	45. 5			Cirro	½	Northwest	0	
		6 0 a. m.	23. 991	65	65			Cirro	¼	Northwest	0	
Camp 28, (6,121′)	July 22	2 0 p. m.	24. 232	82. 3	81			Cirro	4	West	1	
		8 0 p. m.	24. 245	59	58			Cumulo-stratus	8	West	1	
	July 23	5 0 a. m.	24. 260	52	54			Cirro-stratus	1	West	2	
Camp 29, (5,780′)	July 23	5 0 p. m.	24. 434	84	83	83	58. 5	Nimbus, cumulus	9		0	Rain in mountains.
	July 24	8 0 p. m.	24. 486	65				Cumulus, stratus	7	East	1	
		5 30 a. m.	24. 556	49	50				0	West	0	
		7 0 a. m.	24. 609	62	62. 5	62. 5	54		0	West	1	
		10 0 a. m.	24. 620	71. 5	72. 8	72. 8	57. 5	Cirro-cumulus	1		0	
Camp 30, (6,166′)	July 24	6 30 p. m.	24. 235	70. 3	66. 5	66. 5	51		0	North	1	
	July 25	6 0 a. m.	24. 222	63	64			Cumulus	1	Southwest	2	
		7 15 a. m.	24. 230	67. 3	66. 4			Cumulus	1	N. N. E	1	
Summit of mount south of Camp 30, (8,607′)	July 25	11 0 a. m.	22. 320	72. 5	75			Cumulus	4	North	1	
Camp 31, (7,423′)	July 25	7 0 p. m.	24. 099	64	59. 5			Cumulus	1		0	
	July 26	6 15 a. m.	24. 047	59	59. 2			Nimbus	9		0	Light rain,
Camp 32, (5,273′)	July 26	2 15 p. m.	24. 956	68. 5	65			Nimbus, cumulus	9		0	Showery.
		6 45 p. m.	24. 962	60. 9	59. 5			Cumulus, cumulo-stratus	1	West	0	
	July 27	5 0 a. m.	25. 048	47. 5	47			Stratus, cumulus	4	Northwest	1	
		7 0 a. m.	25. 066	56. 5	57			Cumulus	1	West	1	

TABLE I.—*Meteorological record of Northwest Wyoming expedition from May 19 to September 13, 1873*—Continued.

Station.	Date.	Time.	Barometer.	Attached thermometer.	Detached thermometer.	Dry bulb.	Wet bulb.	CLOUDS. Kind.	CLOUDS. Amount.	WIND. Direction.	WIND. Force.	Remarks.
Camp 32	July 27	11 0 a. m.	25. 078	70. 8	67. 5	......	......	Cumulus	3	Southwest	1	
Camp 33, (5,845′)	July 27	6 0 p. m.	24. 536	69. 1	67	......	......	Cumulus, nimbus	6	......	0	
		7 0 p. m.	24. 544	66. 5	65. 7	......	......	Nimbus, cumulus	9	South	1	Heavy shower to south.
	July 28	7 15 a. m.	24. 537	60. 3	59. 6	......	......	Cumulus	1	South	2	
		11 0 a. m.	24. 529	76	68. 5	......	......	Cumulus	7	Northeast	1	
Camp 34, (6,042′)	July 28	6 0 p. m.	24. 357	71	67	......	......	Cumulus, cirrus, nimbus	7	Northeast	1	
		7 0 p. m.	24. 344	58. 6	59	......	......	Cumulo-stratus	4	......	0	
	July 29	6 15 a. m.	24. 322	52. 6	52. 5	......	......	Cumulus	1	West	2	
		1 0 p. m.	24. 263	79	74. 5	......	......	Cumulus	5	West	1	
		2 0 p. m.	24. 240	74. 4	72	......	......	Cumulus	7	North	2	
		6 0 p. m.	24. 203	65. 7	64. 5	......	......	Cumulus, nimbus	9	North	1	Thunder to north.
	July 30	6 20 a. m.	24. 213	53. 9	65. 5	......	......	Cumulo-stratus	4	West	1	
Camp 35, (6,319′)	July 30	2 0 p. m.	23. 800	75	72. 3	......	......	Cumulus	5	......	0	
		6 0 p. m.	23. 784	66	65. 6	......	......	Cumulus, nimbus	8	West	2	Light showers.
	July 31	5 0 a. m.	23. 790	35. 5	36. 5	......	......	......	0	......	0	
		7 0 a. m.	23. 818	71. 5	56. 5	......	......	......	0	West	1	
		10 45 a. m.	23. 822	74. 6	72. 5	......	......	Cumulus	2	West	2	
Camp 36, (6,683′)	July 31	4 35 p. m.	23. 500	67. 5	66. 5	......	......	Cumulus	3	North	1	
		7 0 p. m.	23. 492	58	57. 4	......	......	Cumulus	1	Northwest	1	
	Aug. 1	4 30 a. m.	23. 509	34. 2	34	......	......	......	0	......	0	Light dew.
		5 15 a. m.	23. 530	33. 5	33	......	......	Cirro-cumulus	1	Northwest	1	
Summit of Sailor Mount, (10,046′)	Aug. 1	9 30 a. m.	20. 880	61	56	......	......	Cumulus	1	South	1	
		10 0 a. m.	20. 893	64. 5	58	......	......	Cumulus	2	South	1	
		12 m	20. 893	62. 7	60	......	......	Cumulus	7	South	1	
Camp 36, (6,683′)	Aug. 2	5 0 a. m.	23. 599	34	34	......	......	......	0	North	0	Light frost.
		6 30 a. m.	23. 616	35	35. 5	......	......	......	0	North	0	Smoky.
Summit of Pass, (9,444′)	Aug. 2	2 0 p. m.	21. 340	67	......	......	......	Cumulus	1	West	2	
Camp 37, (8,940′)	Aug. 2	7 45 p. m.	21. 786	56. 2		......	......	......	0	East	0	
	Aug. 3	6 30 a. m.	21. 706	44	44. 5	......	......	......	0	East	0	
Summit of Pass, (9,444′)	Aug. 3	9 0 a. m.	21. 288	60	59. 5	......	......	......	0	West	1	
Camp 37, (8,940′)	Aug. 3	12 40 p. m.	21. 766	75	67. 5	......	......	Cumulus	2	......	0	
		6 0 p. m.	21. 709	61	60. 6	......	......	Cirrus	1	North	1	Thunder; a few drops rain.
	Aug. 4	5 0 a. m.	21. 640	47. 5	48. 5	......	......	Cirro-cumulus	8	Southeast	1	
		6 30 a. m.	21. 648	50. 5	52	......	......	Cirro-cumulus	9	......	0	
Camp 38, (7,564′)	Aug. 4	4 0 p. m.	22. 692	56. 8	56. 5	57. 5	51. 8	Cumulo-stratus	10	Northwest	1	
		7 0 p. m.	22. 702	51. 2	51. 2	53. 1	50	Nimbus	10	......	0	Drizzling rain.
	Aug. 5	7 0 a. m.	22. 798	48	48. 3	51	49	Cumulo-stratus	10	North	0	
		12 m	22. 839	63. 8	64. 1	62. 5	55	Cumulus	5	East-southeast	0	Thundering in the north.
		2 0 p. m.	22. 848	62. 5	62	......	......	Cumulus, nimbus	8	East-southeast	1	

		6 0 p. m.	22.825	61.8	61.8	62.7	54.3	Cumulo-stratus	5		...	
		9 0 p. m.	22.828	54.5	53.5			Cumulo-stratus	7	West	...	
	Aug. 6	7 0 a. m.	22.846	51.5	50.5			Cumulus	2	South	0	
		2 0 p. m.	22.838	67.5	66			Cumulus	4	South	0	
		6 0 p. m.	22.794	62.2	62.7	63	50.1	Cumulus	1	Southeast	0	
		9 0 p. m.	22.760	46.5	46.5	48.3	43	Cumulus	2	North	0	
	Aug. 7	7 0 a. m.	22.734	49	47	51.4	46.5		0	South	0	
Camp 39, (7,492′)	Aug. 7	7 0 p. m.	22.701	61.4	53				0		0	
	Aug. 8	6 0 a. m.	22.734	35	37				0		0	
		12 m	22.813	66.5	65				0	South	1	
	Aug. 9	7 0 a. m.	22.851	47.5	40	40	37	Cirro-stratus	1	South	1	
		2 0 p. m.	22.886	67.5	72			Cirro-stratus	9	South	1	
		3 0 p. m.	22.892	72	70.8	70.8	49.5	Cirro-stratus	9	South	1	
		6 15 p. m.	22.870	66	66.5	66.5	50.5	Cirro-stratus	8		0	
	Aug. 10	5 30 a. m.	22.844	33	31.5	31.5	30.5	Cirro-stratus	1		0	Thin layer of ice.
Camp 40, (7,908′)	Aug. 10	6 0 p. m.	22.491	67	62.6	62.6	51.5	Cirro-cumulus	3	West	0	
	Aug. 11	7 0 a. m.	22.484	51.5	52	52	47	Cirro-stratus	3		0	
		2 0 p. m.	22.478	71	68.5	68.5	49	Cirro-stratus	10	Northwest	0	
		6 0 p. m.	22.455	60.2	60.4	60.4	52.5	Cumulo-stratus	10	Northwest	0	
	Aug. 12	5 15 a. m.	22.389	47.6	48.5			Nimbus	10		0	Drizzling.
		2 0 p. m.	22.407	61.5	59.5	59.5	54.5	Cumulus, nimbus	9	West	1	Clearing up.
		7 0 p. m.	22.409	54.7	52.6	52.6	49.5		0		0	
	Aug. 13	6 0 a. m.	22.450	43.1	44			Cumulus	10	East	1	
Camp 41, (5,741′)	Aug. 13	7 20 p. m.	24.283	63	57.1			Cumulo-stratus,	1	South	1	
	Aug. 14	9 30 a. m.	24.374	60.5	63.1	63.1	55	Cumulus	9	North	1	
		1 0 p. m.	24.355	67.6	66.5			Cumulus, nimbus	8	North	2	
		2 0 p. m.	24.373	60	59.5	59.5	52.5	Cumulus, nimbus	10	West	3	Threatening.
		6 40 p. m.	24.421	56.8	55	55	51	Cumulo-stratus	1	Northwest	1	Steady rain from 2 to 4 p. m.
	Aug. 15	12 m	24.404	66.2	65			Cirrus, cumulus	2		0	
		6 30 p. m.	24.330	64.5	64.5			Cirrus, cumulo-stratus	9	West	1	
	Aug. 16	6 0 a. m.	24.335	43.5	43.5				0		0	
		2 10 p. m.	24.302	79.5	77	77	61.5	Cumulus	2	West	1	Thunder-shower with hail, 2.30 to 3 p. m.
	Aug. 17	5 30 a. m.	24.342	39.5	39.5				0	Southeast	1	
		10 50 a. m.	24.334	70	67			Cumulus	4		0	
Camp 42, (5,813′)	Aug. 18	7 0 a. m.	24.198	48.8	49.1				0	Southeast	0	
		2 15 p. m.	24.166	81.5	80				0	Northwest	1	
		7 30 p. m.	24.110	56	53.6			Cumulus	1	East	0	
Mount Washburn, (10,105′)	Aug. 19	1 0 p. m.	20.835	64.5				Cumulo-stratus	2	South	3	
Camp 43, (7,724′)	Aug. 19	6 0 p. m.	22.599	62.7	59			Cumulus	2		0	
		7 15 p. m.	22.574	50.5	50.5			Cumulo-stratus	2		0	
	Aug. 20	7 0 a. m.	22.592	48.5	48.5	48.5	44	Cirro-cumulus	1		0	
		2 0 p. m.	22.594	65.5	64	64	46	Cumulo-stratus	6	Southwest	2	
		6 0 p. m.	22.578	63	64	64	51	Cumulo-stratus	2	North	0	
	Aug. 21	7 0 a. m.	22.548	50	39.5	39.5	36		0	Southeast	0	
		7 0 p. m.	22.511	56.1	56.5	56.5	45.8	Stratus	0		0	
Camp 43, (7,724′)	Aug. 22	5 30 a. m.	22.484	40.6	40.2	40.2	38.9	Stratus	10	Northwest	0	
		7 0 a. m.	22.490	46.2	46.0	46.0	42.7	Stratus	10	Northwest	0	
		2 15 p. m.	22.490	56	56.0	56	51	Nimbus	10		0	Drizzling rain.
		6 10 p. m.	22.475	48.8	48	48	48	Cirro-stratus	6		0	
	Aug. 23	7 0 a. m.	22.590	38.5	38.8	38.8	37.8	Cumulo-stratus	9	North	0	
Camp 44, (8,986′)	Aug. 23	6 30 p. m.	22.615	54	53.9				0		0	

TABLE I.—*Meteorological record of Northwest Wyoming expedition from May 19 to September 13, 1873*—Continued.

Station.	Date.	Time.	Barometer.	Attached thermometer.	Detached thermometer.	Dry bulb.	Wet bulb.	CLOUDS. Kind.	CLOUDS. Amount.	WINDS. Direction.	WINDS. Force.	Remarks.
Camp 44	Aug. 24	5 15 a. m.	22. 616	36	38	......	......	Stratus	8	....	0	
Camp 45, (7,132′)	Aug. 25	7 0 a. m.	23. 214	38. 5	37	......	......	Fog	10	West	0	
Camp 46, (7,373′)	Aug. 25	2 0 p. m.	23. 049	71. 1	69. 2	......	......	Cumulus	7	North	1	
	Aug 26	5 40 a. m.	22. 999	42	41. 5	......	......	Cumulus	3	....	0	
		9 30 a. m.	23. 016	66	65. 8	......	......	Cumulus	2	West	2	
Camp 47, (8,302′)	Aug. 27	5 15 p. m.	22. 253	53. 9	54. 5	......	......	....	0	South	3–4	
Camp 48, (7,[illegible]65′)	Aug. 28	7 0 p. m.	22. 852	50	46. 5	......	......	Cirro-stratus	1	West	1	
	Aug. 29	7 0 a. m.	22. 825	39	34	......	......	....	0	Southwest	1	
		9 45 a. m.	22. 835	58	50	......	......	....	0	Northeast	1	
Camp near base of Mount Sheridan	Aug. 29	6 35 p. m.	22. 560	54	52. 3	52. 3	42	....	0	West	0	
	Aug. 30	5 15 a. m.	22. 556	43	44	......	......	Stratus	1	West	1	
Summit of Mount Sheridan, (10,156′)	Aug. 30	11 0 a. m.	20. 840	64	57	......	......	Cirro-stratus	1	West	1	
		12 m	20. 842	65	60. 4	......	......	Cirro-stratus	1	....	...	
Camp 49, (7,564′)	Aug. 30	7 0 p. m.	22. 840	57	52	......	......	Stratus	4	South	0	
Camp 50, (7,552′)	Aug. 31	9 30 a. m.	22. 859	57. 5	56. 2	......	......	Cirro-stratus	3	East	1	
Camp 51, (7,563′)	Aug. 31	4 0 p. m.	22. 836	69. 5	68. 5	68. 5	53	Cumulus	2	South	1	
		6 0 p. m.	22. 829	63. 5	62	62	52	Cumulo-stratus	8	....	0	
	Sept. 1	6 0 a. m.	22. 773	51	46	......	......	Cumulo-stratus	9	South	3	
Camp 52, (7,788′)	Sept. 1	6 0 p. m.	22. 604	58	50. 5	......	......	Cumulus, nimbus	8	....	0	Threatening rain.
Camp 53, (7,848′)	Sept. 2	7 30 a. m.	22. 558	60. 5	52. 8	......	......	Cirro-cumulus	1	....	0	
	Sept. 3	8 30 a. m.	22. 590	50	45. 6	......	......	Cumulus, nimbus	9	....	0	Drizzling.
Camp 54, (8,081′)	Sept. 3	6 30 p. m.	22. 396	40. 5	36. 6	......	......	Cumulus, nimbus	9	....	0	
	Sept. 4	7 30 a. m.	22. 462	43	44	......	......	Cumulus	7	Northwest	1	Fog on mountains.
		9 0 a. m.	22. 480	46	46	......	......	Cumulus	9	Northwest	0	Do.
Camp 55, (7,575′)	Sept. 4	6 0 p. m.	22. 846	48. 5	45	45	43	Cumulus	7	West	0	
		7 0 p. m.	22. 820	42	41	41	39. 5	Stratus	1	West	1	
	Sept. 5	7 0 a. m.	22. 890	37. 7	34. 5	34. 5	33	Cirro-cumulus	1	North	0	Slight frost.
Camp 56, (6,892′)	Sept. 5	3 0 p. m.	23. 496	64	64	......	......	Cumulus	5	Southwest	1	
		6 30 p. m.	23. 496	50	50	50	46	Cumulus	5	....	0	
	Sept. 6	6 0 a. m.	23. 567	30. 0	32	33	33	Fog	10	....	0	
		8 0 a. m.	23. 580	38. 5	38	38	37. 5	....	0	South	0	
Camp 57, (8,917′)	Sept. 6	6 30 p. m.	21. 884	47. 5	44	......	......	....	...	....	...	
	Sept. 7	7 0 a. m.	21. 809	33	33. 5	33. 5	32	Cirrus, cumulus	4	South	0	
Mountain southwest of pass (10,625′)	Sept. 7	10 35 a. m	20. 568	61	49. 5	......	......	Cumulus	2	....	0	
Togwotee Pass, (9,621′)	Sept. 7	11 30 a. m.	21. 376	62. 1	51. 5	......	......	Cumulus	1	Northwest	1	
Camp 58, (7,498′)	Sept. 7	6 0 p. m.	22. 997	59. 5	53. 8	......	......	Cumulus	0	South	0	
	Sept. 8	6 0 a. m.	22. 980	31	32	......	......	....	0	....	0	
		9 0 a. m.	23. 017	69. 5	62. 5	......	......	Cirro-stratus	1	East	0	
Camp 59, (6,942′)	Sept. 8	6 0 p. m.	23. 536	59	58. 5	58. 5	44. 5	Cirrus, cumulo-stratus	1	....	0	

	Sept. 9	6 0 a. m.	23. 500	42. 5	42. 5	42. 5	36. 5	Cirrus	1	West	1
		7 30 a. m.	23. 518	63. 5	53	53	43. 5	Cirrus	1	West	0
		9 0 a. m.	23. 524	67. 5	66	66	51	Cirrus	1		0
Camp 60, (6,172′)	Sept. 9	6 0 p. m.	24. 120	70. 5	70			Cirro-cumulus	1	West	2
	Sept. 10	6 0 a. m.	24. 105	50. 5	48. 5	48. 5	40. 5		0	West	2
		8 0 a. m.	24. 115	59. 5	59	59	46. 5		0	West	0
		9 0 a. m.	24. 113	66. 7	67	67	51	Cirrus	1	West	1
Camp 61, (5,750′)	Sept. 10	6 10 p. m.	24. 392	73	67. 5			Cumulus, stratus	1	West	0
	Sept. 11	7 0 a. m.	24. 438	57	53. 5			Cirro-cumulus	3		0
Camp 62, (5,799′)	Sept. 11	6 15 p. m.	24. 518	64	65. 5			Stratus, cumulus	8	Northwest	1
	Sept. 12	7 0 a. m.	24. 636	57	55. 1				0	West	0
Camp Brown, (5,498′)	Sept. 12	6 0 p. m.	24. 750	67. 5	61						
	Sept. 13	8 0 a. m.	24. 744	58	51. 2	59	49. 6		0		0
		2 0 p. m.	24. 658	78	76	83. 2	56. 1	Cirrus	2	Southwest	1
		6 30 p. m.	24. 634	72	68	67	49	Stratus	2	West	1

TABLE II.—*Record of radiation, maximum and minimum thermometers.*

Station.	Date.	Heat.		Radiation.	
		Max.	Min.	Solar.	Terrestrial.
	1874.				
Fort Bridger	June 9	79.5	61	126.75	58
	June 10	82	29	133	28.5
	June 11	82.5	45.5	142.5	45
	June 12	....	39.5	....	....
Camp 5	June 14	96	....	140.5	....
Camp 6	June 15	115	....	170 (?)	....
Camp 7	June 16	88.5	....	150.7	....
Camp 8	June 18	....	38.5	....	....
Camp 9	June 19	97	45.5	152.5	....
Camp 10	June 20	....	41	148	....
	June 21	90	37	149.25	....
Camp 12	June 23	62	23	....	....
Camp 13	June 24	....	21	....	....
Camp Stambaugh	June 25	78.5	68	....	....
	June 26	83	36	140.75	....
	June 27	83	38	143.8	....
Camp Brown	July 2	82	....	138.6	....
	July 3	83	66	147.2	....
	July 4	86	49	148	....
	July 9	82	50.5	....	....
Camp 26	July 19	....	....	161.25	....
	July 20	....	....	129.5	....
Camp 34	July 29	....	46.5	....	....
Camp 35	July 30	....	44.5	....	....
	July 31	....	36.5	....	....
Camp 36	Aug. 1	....	33	....	....
	Aug. 2	....	34	....	....
Camp 38	Aug. 4	58.5	....	....	....
	Aug. 5	67.8	39.7	....	....
	Aug. 6	69	46	....	....
	Aug. 7	....	37	....	....
Camp 39	Aug. 9	....	22.5	....	....
	Aug. 10	....	30.2	....	....
Camp 40	Aug. 11	....	38.5	....	....
	Aug. 12	....	46.6	....	....
	Aug. 13	....	37	....	....
Camp 41	Aug. 15	....	....	146.5	....
	Aug. 16	....	38.5	....	....
	Aug. 17	....	38	....	....
Camp 42	Aug. 18	....	31	....	....
	Aug. 19	....	35	....	....
Camp 43	Aug. 20	....	32.5	....	....
	Aug. 21	....	26	....	....
	Aug. 22	....	40.2	....	....
	Aug. 23	....	33	....	....
Camp 44	Aug. 24	....	38	....	....
Camp 45	Aug. 25	....	35	....	....
Camp 46	Aug. 26	....	41.5	....	....
Camp 47	Aug. 27	....	48	....	....
	Aug. 28	....	13.5	....	....
Camp 48	Aug. 29	....	24.5	....	....
Camp 49	Aug. 30	....	27	....	....
Camp 50	Aug. 31	....	27.5	....	....
Camp 51	Sept. 1	....	38	....	....
Camp 52	Sept. 2	....	36	....	....
Camp 53	Sept. 3	....	37	....	....
Camp 54	Sept. 4	....	35	....	....
Camp 55	Sept. 5	....	29	....	....
Camp 56	Sept. 6	....	27	....	....
Camp 57	Sept. 7	....	28.5	....	....
Camp 58	Sept. 8	....	26	....	....
Camp 59	Sept. 9	....	42	....	....
Camp 60	Sept. 10	....	46	....	....
Camp 61	Sept. 11	....	46.5	....	....
Camp 62	Sept. 12	....	34.5	....	....
Camp Brown	Sept. 13	78.5	39	....	....

TABLE III.—*Temperature of springs, waters, &c.*

Date.	Time.		Temperature.
1873.			°
June 13	12 0 m.	Sand, on ridge between Big Muddy and Ham's Fork	126
June 19	9 30 a. m.	Sand, on divide between Big and Little Sandy	112
June 19	6 0 a. m.	Water in well at station-house, near Camp 9	36
June 19	6 0 a. m.	Water in Big Sandy	53
June 26	2 0 p. m.	Water in well at Camp Stambaugh	40
June 29	5 0 a. m.	Spring near Camp 15	42
July 21	7 0 p. m.	Spring at Camp 27	44
July 25	2 0 p. m.	Spring near Camp 30	37. 5
Aug. 3	6 30 a. m.	Spring at Camp 37	37
Aug. 4	4 0 p. m.	Yellowstone Lake	60. 5
Aug. 5	7 0 a. m.	......do	56
Aug. 6	6 0 p. m.	......do	65. 5
Aug. 7	6 0 a. m.	......do	58

ASTRONOMICAL REPORT.

By Lieut. S. E. Blunt, *Thirteenth United States Infantry.*

Instruments—Failure of chronometers—Examples of computations.

Engineer Office,
Omaha, Neb., January 1, 1874.

Sir: I have the honor to make the following report concerning the astronomical work of the expedition to Northwestern Wyoming during the summer of 1873. The observations were taken by myself, assisted by Mr. George C. Hitt.

The only instruments used were one sextant, one reflecting circle, and one artificial horizon; two box-chronometers, one regulated on mean solar time, and the other on sidereal time, were used in connection with the sextant at Fort Bridger, and part of the way to Camp Stambaugh. The boxes containing the sextant and reflecting circle were carried on the backs of men in the saddle; thus transported, the instruments remained in good order, and, though they were always examined before taking an observation, adjustment was but seldom found necessary. The box-chronometers were also packed in the usual manner for field transportation and carefully carried on the back of a man in the saddle; but it was our experience that the slight motion that they were thus unavoidably exposed to, so impaired their rate as to render them worthless as a means of determining longitude. They were left at Camp Stambaugh, and a pocket-chronometer (Frodsham, 9898) was used during the remainder of the trip, and gave satisfaction; its rate had been determined at Omaha, and also at Camp Brown, before leaving and after returning; all three results closely agreeing.

Longitude at the following places was obtained by means of lunar observations; the distance of the moon from the sun, and also from a planet or star, or from both, being taken.

At Fort Bridger, mean of two lunars; Camp Brown, mean of fourteen lunars; outlet of Yellowstone Lake, mean of four lunars; Camp 49, on Yellowstone Lake, mean of four lunars; Camp 56, on Buffalo Fork of Snake River, mean of three lunars.

Some of the lunars at Camp Brown were taken before departure for the Yellowstone, the remainder after our return—the fourteen observations being taken on four different days.

To show the manner of taking the observations for longitude by lunar distances, and for field-work the closeness of the results obtained, I give the observations at the outlet of Yellowstone Lake, (Camp 38.)

Observations for longitude by lunar distances, moon, Mars. Outlet of Yellowstone Lake, Camp 38, August 6, 1873.

Observed double altitude of moon, lower limb.	Observed double altitude of Mars.	Distance of Mars from moon, near limb.	Time of observation noted by watch.	Watch fast of mean solar time.	Mean solar time of observation.	Deduced longitude west of Greenwich in time.
° ′ ″	° ′ ″	° ′ ″	h. m. s.	h. m. s.	h. m. s.	h. m. s.
23 14 00	34 43 30	67 47 50	9 41 42.5	1 0 9.5	8 41 33	7 21 25
29 25 30	29 12 40	....	....	....	....	....
29 25 30	29 12 40	67 57 40	10 5 3	1 0 9.5	9 4 53.5	7 21 15.5
30 40 00	23 10 10	....	....	....	....	....
30 40 00	23 10 10	68 4 00	10 18 7	1 0 9.5	9 17 57.5	7 21 35.5
31 58 10	21 57 50	....	....	....	....	....
31 58 10	21 57 50	68 7 10	10 25 32.5	1 0 9.5	9 25 23	7 21 35
32 30 00	20 00 00	....	....	....	....	....

Index error of sextant, 00″. Barometer, 22.824 inches. Error of eccentricity of sextant, 00″. Attached thermometer, 55°.5. Detached thermometer, 54°.5.

The altitudes of the moon were taken at equal intervals before and after the time of observing for distance—the same in regard to Mars; the means of the altitudes thus obtained were used as the altitudes at the time the distance was measured, this being more accurate than any other method that could be adopted by a single observer.

The computations were made according to Chauvenet's method of correcting lunar distances.

Longitudes for other points were determined from the error of the pocket-chronometer on local mean solar time, its error on the mean solar time at Camp Brown being found by computation; lunars serving as checks upon these where the longitude was obtained by both methods, and the two determinations agreeing closely; the longitudes by time can be regarded as close approximations.

The mean solar-time at place of observation was found either from equal altitudes of the sun or of a star; Arcturus, *a Serpentis*, *a Ophiuchi*, or *a Aquilæ* being generally used.

Latitude was obtained by circum-meridian altitudes of the sun, or of the same stars as used in the observations for time. Whenever the party remained more than one day at the same camp, latitude was determined each noon, as well as by the stars at night. Here, too, very satisfactory results were obtained, remembering that no other instrument but a sextant was used in the observations.

I give one of the observations, and the mean of the deductions from four others, to show how closely the results agree with each other.

Determination of the latitude, from observed double circum-meridian altitudes of the sun. Camp 38, (outlet of Yellowstone Lake,) August 5, 1873.

Time of observation by watch.	Observed double altitude of sun.	Latitude deduced from each observation.	Remarks.
h. m. s.	° ′ ″	° ′ ″	
0 55 4	123 46 40	44 34 51.26	Barometer 22.803 inches.
58 30.5	52 30	34 57.94	Attached thermometer 65°.
1 1 4	55 30	34 58.30	Detached thermomer 65°.
4 31.5	57 40	34 55.64	Index error of sextant +40″.
6 23.5	57 50	34 55.47	Error of eccentricity of sextant 00″
8 24	57 20	34 53.19	Watch fast of mean solar time, 1h 0m 13s.57.
10 40	55 30	35 00.76	Approximate longitude, 33° 15′ west from Washington.
13 22.5	52 20	35 00.01	Approximate latitude, 44° 34′.
15 42	48 30	34 56.77	

The latitude deduced from the mean of these nine observations on the sun is 44° 34′ 56″.59, and from the other four sets 44° 34′ 47″.2; 44° 34′ 52″.23; 44° 34′ 53″.56, and 44° 34′ 49″.97, respectively, giving a mean for the final result of 44° 34′ 51″.91.

The following is the list of latitudes and longitudes determined:

List of astronomical stations.

Stations.	Latitude.			Longitude.		
	°	′	″	°	′	″
Fort Bridger	41	15	37	110	22	39
Camp No. 8	41	54	36			
Camp No. 10	42	7	43			
Camp Stambaugh	42	29	56	108	48	28
Camp Brown	42	59	11	108	53	51
Camp No. 21	43	12	25	108	57	28
Camp No. 26	43	41	00	108	50	22
Camp No. 28	44	2	30	108	51	22.5
Camp No. 30	44	19	15	109	7	54
Camp No. 32	44	30	16	109	14	4
Camp No. 33	44	28	48	109	30	34
Camp No. 34	44	28	6	109	39	14
Camp No. 35	44	28	11	109	52	13
Camp No. 36	44	33	46	109	59	15
Camp No. 37	44	32	45	110	10	46
Outlet of Yellowstone Lake	44	34	52	110	21	56
Camp No. 42	44	56	13	110	23	30
Old Faithful, (Upper Geyser Basin)	44	28	30	110	53	51
Camp No. 49	44	22	26	110	18	50
Camp No. 55	43	56	47	110	5	20
Camp No. 56	43	51	13	110	9	10
Togwotee Pass	43	46	29	110	00	57
Camp No. 59	43	33	13	109	38	10
Camp No. 60	43	26	45	109	14	36
Camp No. 61	43	17	15	109	2	51

The magnetic variation could not easily be obtained very accurately with the instruments at my command; three or more observations, however, were taken whenever the declination was obtained, in order to eliminate errors as much as possible, and a mean of the results adopted as the final result. They can probably be depended upon to within 5′.

Table of magnetic variations.

Date.	Stations.	Declinations.	
		°	′
June 9	Fort Bridger	17	30
June 17	Camp No. 8	17	30
June 19	Camp No. 10	17	32
June 26	Camp Stambaugh	17	25
July 4	Camp Brown	17	33
August 6	Outlet of Yellowstone Lake	19	1
August 9	Yellowstone Falls	19	0
August 22	......do	19	1
August 26	Upper Geyser Basin	19	33
September 6	Camp 56, (Teton Fork, Snake River)	19	6
September 9	Camp 59, Wind River	18	43
September 10	Camp 60, Wind River	18	36
September 11	Camp 61, Wind River	18	27
September 13	Camp Brown	17	35

I am, sir, very respectfully, your obedient servant,

STANHOPE E. BLUNT,

Second Lieutenant Thirteenth Infantry.

Capt. W. A. JONES,

Corps of Engineers.

GEOLOGICAL REPORT.

BY PROF. THEO. B. COMSTOCK.

CHAPTER I.

INTRODUCTION.

Explanation—General plan of geological report—Narrative of special trips.

Before proceeding to the more special and detailed account of the geology of the district traversed by Captain Jones during the summer of 1873, it will be proper to devote a little space to a hasty review of some points connected with the trip itself, which come justly within the scope of this report, and which, if not here introduced, might leave unexplained some matters of greater significance. It is also desirable that some explanation should be given of the causes which have led to the appearance of the report in its present shape.

Upon my return from the field with an abundance of material, in the form of notes and specimens, for the preparation of a report upon the geological structure of the greater portion of the western third of Wyoming Territory, it very soon became evident that the labor of arranging and elaborating completely the whole of the work done in the field would require much more time than could well be allowed me. This difficulty would have been grave enough had the region explored been of no more than ordinary interest; but when the wonderful extent and variety of this section is fully realized and considered, it will be seen that my task has thereby been greatly increased. In addition to this difficulty, circumstances beyond my control have compelled me to work with very few advantages of reference or comparison. As a natural result, regretted by no one more than by the writer, the following pages will be found lacking in several important particulars, among which two interesting subjects require some notice in this place. I refer to paleontology and chemical geology, in both of which departments much material was collected, but which, for the reasons mentioned, have been necessarily treated quite summarily. So far as I have been able, I have identified the fossils collected, and, in most cases, I have thus been enabled to determine with certainty the formations from which they were obtained.

PLAN OF GEOLOGICAL REPORT.

In the preparation of this report I have sought to arrange its component parts in such a manner as to combine utility with conciseness of expression and ease of reference. In a work which is intended merely as a *résumé* of the more important results of field-labors, it is excusable, not to say necessary, that events and discoveries should be narrated in the order of their occurrence, but, however easier it may be to thus send forth the final results, such a report can only be accepted as the forerunner of a more complete and elaborate treatise in the future. Though indulging the hope that the ample material now in my possession may yet yield richer fruit under more favorable circumstances, I have yet felt, in the absence of such assurance, that the present work should have as much of the air of a finished production as can well be given to it within necessary limits. For this reason the plan of arrangement adopted in the following pages is the grouping of facts and conclusions under appropriate heads, with little or no regard to sequence of observation, except when essential to the complete elucidation of any subject. Each broad division of geology and related subjects is discussed in succession, each occupying as many chapters as may be deemed expedient. In each chapter the several prominent topics are plainly indicated by head-lines in the text, and these, with minor topics, will readily be found by referring to the copious index at the close of the report. This method, which, I believe, will prove most satisfactory to the majority of those who will use this report, will necessitate a somewhat more careful attention than would be required by an arrangement which would allow of more frequent repetition; but I am persuaded that if this treatise be incapable of resting upon its own merit, nothing in the way of mere composition can make it any more deserving of generous approval. It has been thought desirable, however, in one or two instances, to give a brief *résumé* or recapitulation of several chapters, as in chapter VI, which is devoted to a general review of local geology, systematic and economical.

The order of arrangement of the several chapters is in a measure natural and progressive. Beginning with a notice of the physical geography, or the resultant of all the various forces which have combined to produce the present surface features, then proceeding to the discussion of geological structure or the resistance encountered, the determination of the forces themselves comes next in order, after which such special subjects as are not directly connected with the geology of the region are considered. To the latter class belong the chapter of archæological notes and the notes upon the Shoshone tribe, with a vocabulary.

NARRATIVE OR ITINERARY OF SPECIAL TRIPS.

It would be entirely superfluous to write anything like a narrative of the occurrences from day to day along the line of march; nor have I thought it necessary to transcribe the greater portion of my field-notes in the form of a journal. I found it necessary, however, upon several occasions, to make independent side-trips for the purpose of obtaining more extended information than was possible at all times in the immediate vicinity of our trail. As the incidents and observations of these sorties will not be elsewhere related, it will be well to describe them without amplification in this place. Each is numbered in the order of its occurrence.

I.—TRIP TO THE UINTAH MOUNTAINS.

June 6.—A delay of several days at Fort Bridger, incident to preparation and organization, afforded an opportunity for a somewhat extended trip, of which I availed myself by a run to the Uintah Mountains for the purpose of observing the structure of that range, and with the intention of learning as much as possible of the intervening country and its geology. I was accompanied by Mr. J. D. Putnam, who carried a mercurial barometer and an aneroid, with which frequent observations were taken. We were piloted by William Somers, a guide of much experience in this section of country. Our route, which was as direct as possible so early in the season, lay across the southwestern corner of the great Green River Basin, in a general south-southeastern direction. When we left the post the water of Black's Fork at that point was unusually high, causing serious damage to bridges, and knowing ones predicted the failure of our little expedition. A ride of eight miles brought us to the crossing of Smith's Fork, which was found to be too high for fording, and we went some distance above, where the creek divides into several smaller streams. Even these proved difficult to cross. One must see these swollen torrents and ford them to fully appreciate their force and the consequent amount of sediment held in suspension. In seasons of heavy floods many of the mountain-streams are veritable rivers in size, and such they are usually named, to the great wonder of those who have seen them only in midsummer, when many are almost dry. All the streams that we were obliged to cross in our progress toward the mountains were very much swollen, and we were not infrequently obliged to cast about for suitable places to ford. After crossing Smith's Fork we bore southward for several miles, passing through a portion of the Grizzly Buttes,* a "bad lands" district now made famous as the scene of the labors of Professors Marsh, Leidy, and Cope, resulting in the discovery of numerous remains of extinct vertebrates. This formation is more or less restricted, flanking the edges of quite extensive benches as a kind of fringe at this point about one mile in width. The buttes are usually capped by grotesque masses of weathered rock in the form of columns or pyramids of various shapes, which often bear a fair resemblance to familiar objects, such as huts, anvils, chimneys, steeples, monuments, nestling birds, &c.

Continuing our course over benches becoming broader and more extended nearer the mountains, we finally reached and crossed Cottonwood Creek, one of a dozen so named within a limited area in the West. From this point we continued our course across sage-brush plains, with little of variety, except an occasional alkali bog, in which our mules sank to their bellies, or an alkali hole, filled with a sloughy mass of the consistency of soft-soap, with irregular streaks of blue and yellow.

Pushing onward rapidly we crossed the divide to the slope toward the west branch of Henry's Fork, camping just at dusk near a fine cold spring, in a sheltered depression upon the hill-side. This camp was at an elevation of about 2,000 feet above the valley of Black's Fork at Fort Bridger, and it was distant by an air-line nearly nineteen miles, and by our course about twenty-two miles from the same point.

June 7.—Left camp quite early, bearing east of south toward the mountains. On our way we encountered quantities of fallen timber, which very seriously impeded our progress. Between two wide belts of this we were obliged to climb a steep bluff strewn with bowlders, largely of red sandstone, but with a beautiful grassy summit almost level. Passing through a narrow opening in the timber which skirts this ridge there is brought to view an inclosed pasture of several acres, evidently a favorite resort of the elk, judging from the number of shed antlers which lie strewn over its surface. The view from this point is very fine, and quite extensive. The ridge slopes rather abruptly upon both sides to the streams below, one of which ripples through a grassy bottom, apparently walled in upon all sides, with a narrow gap where the water

* In a paper entitled "On the Geology of Western Wyoming," published in the American Journal of Science and Arts, vol. VI, December, 1873, I have offered an explanation of the origin of this name, which proves to be erroneous. Judge W. A. Carter states that the name originated from a report that an old hunter had there discovered a petrified grizzly.

flows out. This was pointed out by our guide as one of his favorite places for wintering stock. Beyond this we passed through an extensive tract of fallen timber, part of it scattered over the surface of a hill which we descended to reach the valley of a small creek to which I have given the name of Bog Creek, merely for convenience of reference. The left bank of this stream for several miles has a very gentle slope toward the creek, and it is, therefore, very boggy and dotted with standing pools, at least early in the season. The slope upon the right bank is very much greater and the bulk of the stream flows along that side of the valley. Passing up the stream by a gradual ascent we suddenly reached a small belt of timber stretching across the valley. This was but a few rods in width, and very quickly the water was found running off rapidly in the opposite direction by a series of small cascades, extending nearly to the junction of the west branch of Henry's Fork, not a great distance below.

The west branch, or Burns' Fork, runs through a broad alluvial valley, very irregularly, frequently, as at this point, splitting into four or five parts, which again unite and separate indefinitely, causing constant changes in the channels by the formation and destruction of islands, peninsulas, ponds, &c. This valley is in many respects the counterpart of the Lower Amazon, but on a very small scale. Even the fluctuations of level caused by the tides in the mighty Brazilian stream, which I have observed at a distance of five hundred miles from the Atlantic coast, are simulated in this average mountain-stream in the rise and fall produced by the alternate melting and freezing of the snows.

Directly opposite our point of approach a side valley opens, but its stream, hugging the right bank, enters Burns' Fork some rods below. Crossing the latter, we ascended this tributary. The upper portion of the valley was very miry, and we were soon in the midst of immense drifts of the slowly-melting snows. For at least two miles our mules fairly floundered, sinking above their knees at almost every step, until we finally reached a high hill covered with loose bowlders, which we ascended by a very steep course to a height of about 4,000 feet above Fort Bridger. Descending upon the other side, a still greater slope, not less than 1,000 feet in height, we reached the main stream of Henry's Fork, which here runs through a comparatively narrow gorge. It was my original intention, after crossing, to push on as far as good forage existed, and there leaving the mules in charge of the guide, to proceed with Mr. Putnam to make the ascent of Gilbert's Peak, one of the most accessible elevations, with an altitude of 13,250 feet. To accomplish this I soon saw was impossible; for the swollen creek, with its fierce current, was rapidly rising, and we dared not attempt its passage. Indeed, we had barely time to kindle a fire and partake of a hasty meal ere we were forced to climb the hill by the flooding of the narrow valley. Baffled in our purpose, we could only make up for our disappointment by returning by a different route. We retraced our steps, however, with little divergence until we reached the valley of West Branch, which we crossed, camping near the entrance of the Cascade Creek before mentioned.

Game in great variety is plentiful in this section; deer, elk, bear, and grouse of several kinds being quite common, particularly in the neighborhood of Burns' Fork, while antelope, and some varieties of grouse, frequent the grassy benches nearer the plains. While at this camp a large drove of elk came very near to feed upon the rich grassy bottom, and all of the game in this vicinity seemed remarkably tame.

June 8.—We crossed the low divide to Bog Creek, following it down near its junction with one of the forks of Sage Creek, to which I will refer under the name of Meadow Brook. Bog Creek Valley continued swampy upon its left bank, widening gradually until we left it, when it descended more rapidly from 50 to 100 feet into the terraced valley of Sage Creek. Crossing the latter, we bore northwest for several miles, gradually veering to the north and northeast, crossing benches, descending as by an irregular succession of steps, until we reached our camp at Fort Bridger. A short distance beyond Sage Creek we came upon a small camp of friendly Ute Indians returning to their reservation from a visit to Fort Bridger for trading purposes. We found our party in Camp 2, having been driven from Camp 1, on lower ground, by the overflow of the stream during our absence. The whole distance traveled upon this trip was not far from one hundred miles.

II.—RED CAÑON ROAD ALONG DEEP CREEK.

June 29.—Just beyond Camp 15, on Twin Creek, the road forks; one branch, called the Red Cañon road, passing by a very steep hill down into the narrow valley of Deep Creek, while the other follows a monoclinal valley farther from the mountains, which leads by a more direct course to the crossing of the Little Popo-Agie near Murphy's Ranch. The train took the latter route, and I followed the former with a small escort. Deep Creek flows through a narrow valley or cañon, originally a monoclinal valley, bounded upon one side by a carboniferous ridge with precipitous bluffs of Triassic red sandstone upon the right, probably extending upward into conformable beds of Jurassic sandstone of a lighter color. The whole valley, for a considerable height, has been filled in with red drift material, through which the stream has cut nearly to the base, leaving a series of terraces high up on the ridges. The name appropriately refers to the manner in which the present stream has cut through its bed; for in some places the narrow creek runs through a gorge with almost vertical sides, at least 20 feet in height, making a veritable cañon in the soft material of the drift, a form of erosion which is somewhat peculiar under such circumstances.

This valley lies very favorably for irrigation, as it receives several fine streams from the mountain-side of the cañon, where the descent is rather gradual. Several fine gardens are here tilled, affording a choice and varied supply of "truck" for consumption at Camp Stambaugh, Miner's Delight, and the settlements in the vicinity of South Pass. Six or seven miles below its source, Deep Creek joins the Little Popo-Agie, almost at a right-angle, just beyond the point at which the latter emerges, with considerable force, from a grand old cañon cut through the limestone ridge. From this point we followed down the left bank of the Little Popo-Agie River to Murphy's, where the main party joined us, and made Camp 16. The valley of the river, as it may be styled, pursues a nearly straight course away from the mountains until it reaches a point below Murphy's Ranch, when it is deflected greatly to the left for some distance, cutting diagonally through the next ridge. This, and other interesting features of these streams, have a peculiar interest to the student of dynamical geology, and they will be further considered in connection with that subject in another chapter.

III.—TRIP TO NUCLEUS OF WIND RIVER MOUNTAINS FROM CAMP BROWN.

July 5–8.—Left Camp 18, at Camp Brown, with Doctor Parry, Messrs. Le Hardy, Putnam, and Jewett, and Somers, my own object being the study of the structure of the range at this point from nucleus to exterior. As in all other cases, I give here only the incidents and general observations of the trip, reserving for future chapters the discussion of geological structure and topics of a special nature. At the kind suggestion of Doctor Irwin, the much-esteemed and highly-successful Indian agent of the eastern Shoshone reservation, we directed our course toward a prominent land-mark in the nucleus known in the neighborhood as Chimney Rock. Passing for five miles over a comparatively level tract, with abundant evidence of ancient glacial action, we followed a well-worn wood-choppers' road, which led us upward for three-quarters of a mile over the regular surface of a ridge of carboniferous limestone with a slope of 20°, (1,900 feet to a mile.) From the top of this we descended several hundred feet only to climb another ridge of older rocks, and so on, ridge after ridge, until the last (*i. e.*, the earliest formed) exposures of the unchanged sedimentary rocks had been passed, when we struck through the metamorphic series, and thence into the granitic nucleus. We were fortunate enough to find our way into a magnificent park, which afforded fine pasturage for our mules, which we rode as far as practicable, leaving them at our second camp to make the ascent of the ridge on foot. This feat proved much more tedious and difficult than we had anticipated, though it was accomplished in a shorter time than we had supposed possible. Mr. Le Hardy and myself left the camp toward evening, hoping to reach a point half way up the first ridge before dark; but we were much surprised to find that the distance to the summit was less than estimated from below, so that we were able to build our signal-fire just at dark, near the edge of the timber-line, at an altitude of 10,500 feet. The first part of our way lay for a short distance through a treacherous bog, partly covered with icy-cold water, which, safely crossed, gave place to a long stretch of huge granite bowlders irregularly tumbled together, making it necessary to make steps of unequal lengths, occasionally leaping, now up, now down, in places where a misstep was of serious consequence. Oftentimes it became necessary to force our way through dense thickets of small but springy undergrowth, reminding one strongly of the impenetrable laurel-brakes of the Alleghanies. After this experience, the long steep climb, through a forest strewn with the dead pine-needles, rendering a sure footing all but impossible, was welcomed as a pleasant variety. This was succeeded by a long, perilous stretch of melting snow, in huge drifts, covering quantities of bowlders, ready at any moment to start from their places and go hurling down the almost vertical declivity thousands of feet into one of those clear, cold lakes that are to be found only in these far-off mountain-fastnesses. It was impossible to climb directly up this slope, and we were obliged to pursue a long diagonal course to the summit. Finally, we passed beyond the snow, continuing our course over less dangerous but not less tiresome bowlders, until we had reached a point several hundred feet above the timber-line, where there grew some small patches of straggling cedars. Here we kindled a roaring fire, and spent the night. Next morning very early we pushed on and succeeded in reaching the "chimney" before the mist had completely obscured the surrounding country. The summit of this isolated mass of rock can only be reached by climbing in the rear to a narrow cavernous opening well toward the top, through which it is necessary to crawl, or, more properly, to drag one's self. The front of this is a very narrow ledge, more than 500 feet from the *débris* below, which leads to a series of rough, irregular steps by which the top can be gained with caution. From this point, 11,853 feet above the level of the sea, we obtained a view of the whole country north and east of the mountains for a distance of one hundred and fifty miles. In front lay the Owl Creek Mountains, with the Wind River like a thread between, and far in the background the Big Horn range with its prominent peaks towering high in air. To the north the Sierra Shoshone and the extension of the Rocky Mountain divide appeared to meet, and no doubt we saw many high peaks far beyond, which seemed to form portions of one of these chains.

The return-trip was but a repetition of the experiences already narrated, with the addition of much discomfort arising from the short supply of provisions, which gave out before we started backward. The total distance traveled was about thirty-five miles.

IV.—TO WASHAKIE NEEDLES, SIERRA SHOSHONEE.

Long before reaching the Owl Creek Mountains we had in view what appeared like a double peak lying beyond, and rising much higher than the main crest of that range, and this assumed so much importance in the topography and geology of the country that a party was organized under the direction of Captain Jones for the purpose of visiting it. Though one of the most interesting excursions made during the trip, there is no call for description here, as it will be given in the general report of the expedition. We left Camp 26 on the 18th of July, traveling in all more than sixty miles, and returning July 20. The peak was ascended to a greater or less height by each member of the party, the highest point reached being over 12,000 feet above sea-level. The geological results of this excursion will be found in the recapitulatory chapter on the general geology of the whole trip.

V.—TO STEAMBOAT SPRINGS, ON YELLOWSTONE LAKE, ETC.

August 6.—From Camp 38, at the outlet of Yellowstone Lake, I went alone to Steamboat Springs, an interesting locality upon the lake-shore, about three miles above the mouth of Pelican Creek. In order to make much headway in this vicinity it is necessary to follow, as closely as possible, in most cases, the lake shore or the valleys of the larger streams. By crossing the marshy valley of Pelican Creek rather near its mouth and crossing a wide belt of fallen timber, I saved two or three miles in the distance by the usual trail, but the time occupied in reaching my destination was largely increased. The groups of hot and cold springs at Steam Point and in the neighborhood are rather numerous, but many of them are very insignificant when compared with those in other localities. Like nearly all of the groups within the Yellowstone Park, however, they present peculiar and distinctive features of their own. Among these none is more interesting than the Steamboat, the noise of which so closely resembles the puffing of a small lake-steamer that one involuntarily casts a longing eye over the surface of the water in the hope that such is really there. This sound is produced by the escape of vapor, under pressure, from a small orifice in a cavernous opening in the rocks. A short distance beyond the vapor issues from a kind of cavern near the water's edge, with a seething sound as it comes in contact with the waves, and this adds greatly to the effect, simulating very closely the escape of waste-steam from a boiler on a windy day.

My work at the springs was completed by 4 o'clock, when I endeavored to pass in a straight course to a point on Pelican Creek, several miles above its mouth, but I was so delayed by the fallen timber that I was barely able to reach a favorable camping-spot on Sulphur Pond, not more than two miles in a direct line from Steam Point, before night set in. I selected a delightful place at the edge of a small grove of trees near the mouth of the eastern inlet of the pond. My camp was upon a well-worn game-trail, which led up a bluff within a few feet of the fire. Being much fatigued, I turned in early, but, when fairly in a doze, I was aroused by the frightened movements of my mule picketed near by, and I presently heard the doleful howl of a large wolf, which was slowly approaching along the trail. In anticipation of a trifling adventure, I lay down again with my carbine close at hand. It was late in the morning when I woke, and all was quiet; but a little investigation showed that the animal had been lying in the grass at the edge of the bluff, just above my head. This locality seems to be a favorite resort of many animals. Our train approached it by following a prominent game-trail, at least a dozen of which, extending for miles into the forest, meet at this point. Upon my first visit to this place, the day before the passage of the train, fresh tracks and other unmistakable signs of their presence were visible. To-day I started numbers of elk while passing through the fallen timber, not far from some active boiling springs. This is probably explained by the fact that there are here a number of cold springs containing sodium chloride, or common salt.

During the night a very heavy mist enveloped the pond like a cloud. It was quickly dispelled by the heat of the sun in the morning.

August 7.—Followed up the small creek near camp for two miles and attempted to cross the divide to Pelican Creek, but I was obliged to return nearly to last night's camp, on account of a comparatively narrow belt of fallen timber, which baffled my utmost endeavors to pass. Nearly the whole of the summit of the ridge was blocked by long windrows of blasted pines, not infrequently forming impenetrable walls four or five feet in height. Reaching the valley of Pelican Creek, I ascended the stream for two or three miles, then crossing, returned, taking Hayden's so-called Sulphur Hills and the hot springs of Lower Pelican Creek on the way. Arriving at Camp 38, and finding it deserted, I followed the trail to Camp 39, which I reached soon after dark.

VI.—FROM CAMP 40 BACK TO CAMP 38, THENCE UP PELICAN CREEK AND DOWN EAST FORK TO CAMP 41.

August 12.—Discovering, while at Camp 40, that a necessary portion of my outfit had been placed in a *cache* at Camp 38 during my absence, I determined to return for it, extending my trip so as to reach the next camp of the main party by a circuitous route. With Mr. Creary as an assistant, I followed back upon our trail as rapidly as possible to Camp 38, at the outlet of Yellowstone Lake, securing my goods, and camping in a grassy spot upon the bank of the river. As we emerged from the timber into the open space about Camp 39, a badger, (*Taxidea Americana* Waterh.,) unwittingly approached quite near to us, but I did not succeed in killing it, although I fired twice at it. About 1 p. m. we stopped for lunch nearly opposite a group of hot springs, about seven miles below Yellowstone Lake, upon the west bank of Yellowstone River. Here Mr. Creary shot with a Colt's revolver a fine male of *Erithizon epixanthus* Brandt, commonly known as the yellow-haired porcupine, of which I obtained the skull and some of the quills. From the size of the testicles, and the presence of a peculiar white, soft, waxy secretion on the exterior of the urinary orifice, as well as the strong skunky odor of the animal, I judge that it was at the beginning of the rutting season. It was also remarkably fat. When shot it was lying in the crotch of a tree, about 10 feet above the ground. Some of our Indians, who were then encamped upon the opposite side of the river, were rejoiced at the gift of the offensive carcass; Luisant remarking that it was "*Heap good eat.*"

August 13.—Left camp early, making a short cut through the timber to Pelican Creek, which we followed up along the right bank for several miles, until, when near some hot springs, at the junction of two of its forks, we struck a prominent trail, evidently that of Doctor Hayden's party of 1871. This we followed for a number of miles, but left it before crossing the divide, choosing another route which led us over the ridge in another place. After struggling through much fallen timber we again struck the trail upon the other slope of the divide, near the point at which it makes an abrupt descent to a tributary of the East Fork of the Yellowstone. From the forks of Pelican Creek the trail leads rapidly upward, passing a series of cascades with one interesting waterfall, the valley for the most part being rather broad and grassy. Plentiful tracks of game were noticed, but we saw very little until near the summit, when we met a large drove of elk and some deer. After reaching the south branch of the East Fork, our course lay through a belt of fallen timber, all but impassable for some distance, when we succeeded in keeping clear of the greatest difficulties by following the most open of the very numerous game-trails high above the stream. By this means, however, we passed unawares the junction of the north and south branches, at which point I had proposed to camp for the night. It had been raining hard all day, and we camped at dark in the mud near a mountain torrent in the midst of a dense forest, our exhausted animals refusing to proceed farther.

August 14.—Continuing our course, four miles of excessively difficult travel through marshes with tangled undergrowth and fallen timber, brought us opposite the mouth of Soda Butte Creek, where we met the well-traveled miners' trail leading to the mining district of Clarke's Fork of the Yellowstone. Beyond this point our ride of nine miles to Camp 41 was comparatively easy. This we reached at 3 p. m., having traveled, since leaving Camp 40, about seventy-five miles.

VII.—FROM CAMP 41, ON EAST FORK OF YELLOWSTONE, TO GARDINER'S RIVER HOT-SPRINGS, AND RETURN.

This excursion, though made independently of Captain Jones's party, was practically over the same ground, and, therefore, requires but little attention here.

August 15.—Left Camp 41, with Mr. Creary, and crossed the bridge over the Yellowstone River. At the foot of a steep hill, which we ascended, about a mile beyond the bridge, three fair-sized California raccoons (*Procyon hermandez*, Wagler,) crossed our path. This neighborhood seems to be well supplied with these animals, as I noticed others at points not far distant. We reached the falls upon the East Branch of Gardiner's River soon after 1 o'clock. I spent the greater part of the afternoon in the examination of the structure between this point and the springs, reaching Captain Jones's camp, near the latter, toward evening.

August 16.—Spent the whole day in the study of the springs, leaving our camp upon the return about 5 p. m. Being very anxious to gain time, we rode the whole distance back to Camp 41 the same night, reaching it soon after 11 p. m., being obliged to move upon a walk on account of the darkness and the fragile nature of the specimens which I had collected.

VIII.—FROM CAMP 42, ON YELLOWSTONE RIVER, TO HELL-ROARING CREEK, THENCE BACKWARD TO AMETHYST MOUNTAIN, RETURNING TO CAMP 43.

August 19.—With Mr. Creary as assistant, I went back from Camp 42, crossing East Fork just above Camp 41. Here we found a trail which led us, by a very direct course, to Hell-Roaring Creek, one mile above its junction with the Yellowstone. On the way we met with several large droves of antelopes feeding upon the fine pasturage here afforded with much security, owing to the irregular topography, which enables them to seek immediate shelter upon the approach of danger. At the time of our visit the great antelope country along the left bank of East Fork was remarkably free from their presence, which may doubtless be explained by the recent passage of several parties of miners. Near the mouth of Hell-Roaring Creek we met another raccoon, which quite savagely resisted an attack until it was forced to beat a hasty retreat. After spending the greater portion of the day in the study of the geology of this section, we returned to East Fork to camp, reaching a favorable spot opposite Camp 41 long after dark.

August 20.—Crossed East Fork, and followed the miners' trail up along the left bank of the river to Amethyst Mountain, which we ascended nearly to the summit, collecting a number of fine mineral specimens, and returning to Camp 42, where we found a small guard in charge of supplies left behind by the train. We proceeded to Tower Creek and spent the remainder of the day in its examination, camping in its cañon for the night.

August 21.—Left camp quite late in the morning, and followed the trail over Mount Washburn to Camp 43, on Cascade Creek, where I packed my collections and prepared for an advance movement on the following day.

IX.—FROM CAMP 43 VIA GEYSER BASINS TO CAMP 47.

August 22.—In order to gain as much time as possible for investigation among the geysers of the headwaters of Madison River, I pushed ahead of the train with Mr. Creary, in a drizzling rain, which continued with occasional heavy showers throughout the day. The route followed was mainly that taken by the train during the following days. Our first camp was in the vicinity of a few prominent silica springs or jets, near the point chosen by the main party next day as Camp 44. Owing to the storm, we did not reach our destination until nearly dark.

August 23.—Took notes and collected specimens from the springs, starting forward at 8 a. m. Passed an area of sulphur jets, and soon struck the old trail of Captain Barlow, (1871,) leading over the divide to a branch of East Fork of Madison River. We then left the trail, crossing the stream much above Barlow's Ford, and striking across the country in a nearly direct line to East Fork, crossing the latter twice via Barlow's trail. After a hasty review of the springs and geysers of the East Fork we visited the lower geyser basin of Fire-Hole River, camping toward its upper end, near the White Dome Geyser.

August 24.—Visited the springs and geysers not previously examined.

About noon we hastened by a short cut through the timber to the Upper Geyser Basin, examining the intervening springs by the way. Camped near the lower end of Upper Basin.

August 25.—Pushed on very early to the upper end of the basin, leaving heavy articles near the spot designated as Camp 46. With my assistant the whole day was spent in a careful study of the principal geysers, until too dark to work.

August 26.—Remained in the Upper Basin until 5.30 p. m., the train having moved on to Camp 47. Rode until after dark, when we picked our way for two or three miles on foot, leading our mules until we could no longer *feel* the trail, and were finally compelled to camp about 9 miles from Camp 46.

August 27.—Moved on at daybreak nine miles to Camp 47, reaching it just in time for a late breakfast.

X.—FROM CAMP 48 TO MOUNT SHERIDAN, THENCE TO CAMP 50.

On this trip I made one of a small party led by Captain Jones from Camp 48, at the southwestern extremity of Yellowstone Lake, to Mount Sheridan, a prominent elevation near the sources of Snake River. We left camp August 29, reaching a camping-spot in the vicinity of some hot springs at the base of the mountain, about 3 p. m. The ascent of the peak was made by all but myself on the following day. With considerable difficulty I succeeded in reaching a prominent point, several hundred feet below the summit, when I was forced to relinquish an attempt which had been made against the advice of my friends, on account of previous over-exertion.

The total distance traveled by myself in these ten excursions, exclusive of that portion over the trail of the main party, was very nearly four hundred miles.

CHAPTER II.

PHYSICAL GEOGRAPHY.

General surface features—mountains—plateaus or table-lands—river systems.

While it is true that the examination of the minute topography of a country, the contour and forms of relief of its surface, falls somewhat out of the domain of the geologist engaged in the study of the past history of the earth, it is evident that a thorough appreciation of the causes which have produced the present external configuration of our globe is only possible after study of the results. In other words, we have no means of judging of the past except by comparison with the present. It becomes necessary, therefore, at the outset, to devote a little space to a consideration of some of the results of the action of natural forces over the area embraced by our reconnaissance. Moreover, the physical geography of any portion of the earth's surface is closely related to its geology, and it is consequently necessary to examine, with some degree of care, the external features before proceeding to the investigation of internal structure. A full discussion of this subject in all its bearings would, however, lead to encroachment upon the field of others engaged upon the survey, and it is only intended in this chapter to refer to those features which bear more or less directly upon the solution of questions concerning the geology of the district.

Few Americans at the present day are so ignorant of the general topography of their country as not to know that the approach to the central portion of the Rocky Mountain chain from the east is very gradual in most places, but it is very doubtful whether this fact is fully realized by those who have never visited this region, and yet the traveler in the West, unless he be provided with a list of elevations of the principal points, would scarcely be prepared to acknowledge that in passing westward from Omaha to a distance of five hundred miles he had reached an altitude of 5,000 feet above his starting-point, while apparently traversing a level prairie. Southward, along the line of the Kansas Pacific Railroad, the slope is even less, averaging little more than eight feet per mile, while northward, near the latitude of Saint Paul, Minn., it is not more than two feet to the mile.

The ridges of the Rocky Mountain system, considered separately, appear to trend quite irregularly, as if all attempts to arrange them into a general system would prove futile, but when viewed as parts only of a vast whole they are all seen to be subordinate ranges of a great system or chain, with an average northwest-southeast trend.

The district comprising the field of our labors during the summer of 1873 is included between the forty-first and forty-fifth parallels, and the meridians of 108° 14′ west and 111° west. The whole of this tract is within the limits of the two counties of Uintah and Sweetwater, in the western third of the present Territory of Wyoming. For our purpose, though not strictly correct, on account of the convergence of the meridians northward, it may be considered in outline a parallelogram with a length of two hundred and seventy-eight miles, and a width of one hundred and thirty-nine miles. By reference to the topographical map it will, then, be seen that the parallel of 43° north divides this district into two equal squares, each containing 19,300 square miles, the northern division containing the bulk of the mountain-masses, while the southern square is proportionately free from extreme elevation, being mainly occupied by a continuous plateau. Again, if the diagonal from the northwest to the southeast corner of the parallelogram be drawn, it will be noticed that the greater portion of the mountainous country lies within the limits of the northeastern half. The central meridian of this tract (109° 37′ west) cuts the northern square into two such halves that the western portion contains the bulk of the westward, or Pacific-bound waters, and the eastern half contains the greater portion of the Atlantic-bound streams within the district, but each half also contains a certain amount (about equal in each) of the headwaters of rivers belonging to the opposite slope. This latter feature is somewhat remarkable from the fact that it is caused not so much by the distribution of the mountain-masses, as by the operation of apparently insignificant forces, which have produced extraordinary results. In the southern square but a small proportion of the precipitated moisture is carried off by way of the eastern slope, although less is carried westward than might be imagined from the examination of an orographical chart of this region.

ROCKY MOUNTAIN SYSTEM.

The whole of this district may be said to constitute a portion of the great Rocky Mountain chain, as generally understood, although, geologically, this term cannot properly be applied so loosely, because it would imply that over this area all the secondary ranges belong to a single system of upheaval; that is to say, from such a term one might justly infer that the whole tract was occupied by those mountains only which were simultaneously elevated, which is not the case. It will, however, be convenient to use the name in this sense, and chiefly because the only portions of other determined systems which lie within this area are upon its borders, and have not received as much attention as the remaining ranges from the members of our survey. The main crest of the Rocky Mountain system, strictly speaking, passes tortuously across our field, in some places so nearly upon a level with the surrounding country that its true course has only been determined after extended and laborious study upon the part of many explorers; at other points rising abruptly from the plains to a lofty height, with prominent peaks towering high above the mass of the chain. The eastern slope is so gradual that the irregularities of the crest are rendered much more noticeable than similar variations in chains, such as the Appalachian, which rise quite abruptly from base to summit, and at the same time these variations are in reality more extensive. This is one reason that names of purely local application are so common among the western mountains, being almost necessary in order to avoid difficulties which would arise from the confusion of the main divide with ranges which, though more conspicuous, may afterward prove to be subordinate to it, or even of another system. A glance at any ordinary map of Western North America will show the force of these remarks, and their application is perhaps nowhere more manifest than in the section of country now under consideration.

The Rocky Mountain crest has been traced and mapped with considerable accuracy throughout the greater part of its winding course through the territory of the United States, from the thirty-fifth to the forty-ninth parallel. The general direction of the axis of the chain, northward from the thirty-fifth to the forty-first parallel, is nearly north, but at this point it bends gradually to the west until South Pass is reached, in latitude 42° 25′ north, longitude 109° 43′ west, when it is continued northwest in the Wind River Mountains, beyond which it follows a flexuous course, crossing the forty-ninth parallel ten degrees of longitude west of its intersection with the thirty-fifth parallel.

The elevations of passes through the crest vary greatly throughout its length; Vermillion Pass, in British America, having an altitude of less than 5,000 feet, while in Colorado the pass between Gray's and Parry's Peaks is reported by Whitney to be 13,623 feet above sea-level, which is higher than any recorded *peak* of the divide in Wyoming or Montana. The point of greatest elevation in the Rocky Mountain crest within the limits of this survey is Fremont's Peak, of the Wind River Mountains, with an altitude of 13,570 feet.

OTHER RANGES AND SECONDARY RIDGES.

The Wahsatch range and the Uintah Mountains belong, geologically speaking, to a different period of upheaval to that in which the eastern ranges were elevated, a conclusion first adopted by Prof. J. D. Whitney, of the California survey, with respect to the Sierra Nevada range, which was synchronously thrown up, and afterward extended to the Wahsatch and its parallel ranges with their connected ridges, by Prof. Clarence King, in charge of the survey along the line of the fortieth parallel. Very little more than the foot-hills or outlying ridges of either the Wahsatch or the Uintah ranges lies within the district comprising our field, but the relations of both to the geology of this region are so close and important that a general review of their features will be useful.

The Wahsatch Mountains form the boundary between the so-called Great Basin and the basin of the Green River, including the upper portion of the valley of the Colorado. The basin of the Green and Colorado Rivers is divided into two parts by the prolongation eastward, near the forty-first parallel, of the Uintah Mountains. The upper portion of this basin (*i. e.* the portion north of the Uintah Mountains) is commonly called the Green River Basin, and the southern portion has received the name of Uintah Basin. Rising abrubtly from the plains, the Wahsatch Mountains stand out prominently in the topography of the country, although their elevation above the Green River Basin is comparatively small in amount. The culmination of the crest is, however, south of the forty-first parallel in Central Utah. A peculiar ruggedness is produced by the deep-cut cañons which abound, not infrequently extending nearly or quite down to the base of the mountains, which is but little above 4,000 feet in many places at the foot of the western slope. The Union Pacific Railroad in its course through this range, along the cañons of Bear and Weber Rivers, nowhere reaches an elevation as much as 1,750 feet above its crossing of Green River.

The Uintahs present much the same general features as the Wahsatch Mountains, but with less of ruggedness in outline, owing partly to the existence of fewer and less eroded cañons, but principally to the trend of the range and its consequent structure. It should be explained that the Wahsatch chain runs north and south with a series of parallel ridges separated by synclinal valleys, while the Uintah range trending at a right angle forms one immense anticlinal extending across a basin which sheds its water southward. This fact, to a student of dynamical geology, is alone sufficient to account for a very large portion of the existing topography. In the Uintah range there are several peaks with elevations above 13,000 feet, and the greater portion of the crest rises certainly above 11,000 feet. The altitude given by Clarence King for Mounts Hodges and Tohkwano is 13,500 feet, and Gilbert's Peak, according to the same authority, has an altitude of 13,250 feet.

Among the secondary ridges lying directly in our line of march, the Sierra Shoshone and Owl Creek ranges are the most important.

The Sierra Shoshone in its present aspect can scarcely be termed a range of mountains, being more properly an irregular mass of elevated territory, longer than broad, with a succession of isolated points appearing above the general surface in irregular curves. The causes which have produced this configuration have operated since the original formation of a range which is now greatly obscured. Remnants of this partly obliterated range are to be seen in some localities, but in most places it is entirely concealed by a thick formation of volcanic material subsequently deposited. Several imperfect prolongations of the underlying range seem to stretch southward across the upper portion of the valley of Wind River, even in one or two instances extending quite to the foot-hills of the Wind River Mountains. This subject constitutes, however, one of the most important structural problems of the trip, and as such it will be more fully treated under the head of dynamical geology in the section upon the elevation of mountain-ranges.

In physical features, there are some points of resemblance between this Sierra and the Wahsatch chain, but the comparison must not be extended too far, for the similarity is less real than might be imagined from the perusal of finely-wrought descriptions of the scenery, which is, indeed, impressive and remarkable. A comparison of any well-executed map of the region traversed by the Wahsatch chain with the topographical map of Captain Jones will render this more evident. Unlike the chain of the Wahsatch, the Sierra Shoshone, though not a simple anticlinal, has no prominent series of folds which would cause the cañons to be cut through the mass, more or less, longitudinally, but the streams follow the general slope nearly transverse to the length of the Sierra, but with a very irregular northward tendency. The whole area is, to the last degree, rugged, and scored by numerous deeply-cut gorges and cañons.

From the southeastern portion of the area occupied by the Sierra Shoshone the Owl Creek range extends eastward as far as the Big Horn River. This ridge is much less elevated and generally more regular in outline than any of the preceding, although it is not unlike the Uintahs in some respects. The highest point is but little more than 9,000 feet above sea-level, while in the Sierra Shoshone many peaks exceed 10,000 feet, and Washakie Needles, a high point north of the junction with the Owl Creek range, attains an altitude greater than 12,000 feet.

Besides the foregoing there are several other ridges of more or less importance which require at least a passing notice. These are:

1. The Téton range, a most jagged and apparently inaccessible ridge, with a nearly meridional trend, lying in longitude 110° 48′ west. This culminates in a peak known as the Grand Téton, which is the highest point within the limits of our parallelogram. Messrs. Langford and Stevenson, of the Snake River division of Doctor Hayden's party of 1872, report that they ascended to the summit, 13,858 feet above the sea.

2. The Wyoming Mountains, a transverse range, trending latitudinally almost along the line of the parallel of 43° 30′ north, west of the main divide of the Rocky Mountains. This ridge is sometimes called the Green River Mountains.

3. The Sweetwater Mountains, lying east of South Pass and trending eastward from that point.

4. Far to the northeast lies the Big Horn range, concerning the relations of which much too little is known.

PLAINS, PLATEAUS, OR ELEVATED TABLE-LANDS.

The lowest point reached during the trip was not far from 5,000 feet above sea-level. All that portion of country lying between the various mountain-ranges, and partaking of the nature of plains, must, therefore, be classed under the head of elevated plateaus or table-lands. Of the 19,300 square miles composing the southern half of the district under consideration, more than three-fourths belong to this class. The area of plateau-surface within the limits of the northern square will scarcely exceed one-third of the entire area of the square. Thus it will be seen that the total area of table-land is not more than six-tenths of that of the whole district; the remainder being occupied by mountains.

It will be unnecessary to describe in detail the several divisions of the plateau-surface, for they will require attention in various places in the following chapters, where their special features can be more fully discussed. Some general remarks in this place will, however, be useful to those who may be more particularly interested in the subject of this chapter, and it will also be found that some subjects will be explained by this means which would otherwise require much useless repetition.

The table-lands comprised within the limits of this district, excluding such as are of small extent or of minor importance, are four, viz: The Green River plateau, the Wind River plateau, the section to which I shall refer as the Shoshone plateau, and the Park plateau, occupying a portion of the Yellowstone Lake Basin.

The Green River plateau, as here understood, embraces the ellipsoid tract north of the Uintah Mountains, which, under the name of Green

River Basin, will be frequently referred to in this report, extending from the main divide of the Rocky Mountains westward to the Wahsatch range and bounded on the north, in its northwest corner, by the Wyoming Mountains. For the purposes of this review, it is convenient to take as its eastern boundary that portion of the continental divide between South Pass and the latitude of the Uintah Mountains. In reality, however, this is a semi-arbitrary line of division, and the separation of the Green River Basin from the Laramie plains east of the divide is rather geological than otherwise. Accepting this water-shed, then, as its limit, the Green River plateau occupies an area of not less than 16,500 square miles, its greater diameter extending from northwest to southeast. Its surface is now very much broken into low buttes and benches with intervening vales, so that the elevation varies greatly; but as this configuration has been accomplished mainly by the action of running water, we need now consider only the elevations of the various divides between the principal streams. A comparison of these shows that the plateau, as a whole, has an average elevation of about 7,000 feet above the level of the sea, and that there are several points upon the plain exceeding in altitude some portions of what is generally considered the Rocky Mountain divide.

The Wind River plateau, as the name indicates, lies upon both sides of the Wind River, between the Owl Creek and Wind River Mountain ranges, extending as a triangle from below Tó-gwo-te Pass as far as the Big Horn River, beyond which it passes out of the limits of this sketch. Its topography is even more irregular than that of the Green River plateau, and though not more than one-sixth of the latter in extent, it varies much more in extremes of elevation. It is safe to say, however, that the average altitude is considerably less than that of the Green River Basin. The whole tract lies upon the eastern slope of the Rocky Mountain chain.

The Shoshone plateau, extending east of the Sierra Shoshone and north of the Owl Creek Mountains, is irregular in outline as well as in its topographical features. In general shape it approaches the form of a narrow quadrangle, with its length in a north and south direction. Its extent beyond the limits of our survey cannot be great, at least toward the east. There are several prominent mountain-peaks over this district, but aside from these it is probable that the average elevation is less than in either of the two cases before mentioned.

Much of the area within the district reserved for the national park comes properly under the head of table-lands, and it will be convenient to describe the whole of such area as the park plateau. This will then include all the non-mountainous country comprising the Yellowstone Lake Basin, with the broad valleys of many of the large streams connected with or adjacent to it. A careful description would necessitate the division of this region into a number of districts, none of which would be of wide extent, but which differ so greatly in position and in altitude that they cannot well be correlated in any but the most general manner. The physical features of the Yellowstone Lake Basin may be mentioned here, leaving the minor areas to be treated elsewhere as occasion may require. To the south and southeast of the Yellowstone Lake the great continental divide, or watershed, is quite low, compared with the surrounding country, in many places, where it must be regarded as forming a part of the plateau which we are now discussing. Including this, the lake-basin has an average elevation exceeding by several hundred feet that of the Green River Basin. Its area is not great, and it differs from the three foregoing tracts in the amount of timber and other vegetation, which is doubtless a result of the more abundant supply of water. Its topography is more rounded and regular than is the case upon the "plains" before alluded to.

RIVER-SYSTEMS.

In this rapid review of those physical features of the water-courses of Western Wyoming, upon the cognizance of which a full understanding of many points in its geology depends, it will be advantageous to narrate the facts, as nearly as possible, in their geographical order, that they may be the more readily compared with the general topography as previously indicated. The whole of the district being highly elevated, we shall meet only with the headwaters portion of the great river-systems, but the number of the streams will be large.

In the extreme southwestern corner of the Green River plateau, the junction of the Wahsatch and Uintah ranges forms a double water-shed, which, according to the laws of the composition of forces, causes the resultant stream to flow off in a direction west of north. At this point rises Bear River, which pursues its tortuous course northward between the parallel ridges of the Wahsatch Mountains, occasionally cutting through them, until it reaches latitude 42° 42′ north, at a point about thirty-five miles west of its source, when it turns abruptly southward and works its way out of the range upon the western side to pour its contents into the northeastern prolongation of the Great Salt Lake, known as Bear River Bay. East of the main sources of Bear River the water-shed from the Wahsatch Mountains is unfelt, and the streams run northward, escaping to the plains nearly at right angles to the Uintahs. This is notably the case with Black's Fork, which rises well up in the Uintah Mountains, and, in a lesser degree with Muddy, Smith's, and Cottonwood Forks, which have their sources nearer the plains. East of these is Burns' Fork, and other tributaries of Henry's Fork start northward, but joining Henry's Fork, and finding no immediate escape from the mountains, they follow its cañon eastward, which receives all the mountain-streams along its course to the junction with Green River. All the streams originating east of the sources of Bear River, upon the northern slope of the Uintahs, flow directly or indirectly into Green River. The main sources of Green River, however, originate upon the southwestern slope of the Wind River Mountains, but it receives important tributaries from the east, and several, which come in from the west, rise in the outlying ridges of the Wahsatch Mountains, north of the Union Pacific Railroad. The main river flows across its basin in a general southeastern course. Green River and its tributaries may be said to drain the whole of the plateau, for the streams of other systems merely catch a portion of the surplus water from the corners, and, although in each case a source of an important river, they do not to a great extent determine the main course of their systems. They are, however, peculiar and important for some reasons, but it will be unnecessary to dwell upon them now, as they will be more fully treated in another chapter.

Passing to the Wind River plateau, we find that it is almost completely drained by the Wind River system, which receives nearly all the precipitation between the crests of the Wind River Range and the Owl Creek Mountains. All the tributaries of Wind River, with their affluents, which rise near the nucleus of the Wind River range, emerge from the mountains through narrow cañons in the outlying ridges, cut at right angles to the axis, or nearly so; hence it may happen that the separate sources of one of these rivers originate many miles distant from each other, and flow together from nearly opposite directions, until they meet to pass to the plains as one stream, by a narrow gateway, as it weie. Near latitude 43° north, longitude 108° 30′ west, the Wind River turns abruptly northward, pursuing a very direct course to its junction with the Yellowstone River. Beyond this bend it is known as the Big Horn River. The tributaries of the Big Horn which rise in the Sierra Shoshone, viz, Owl Creek, Meeyera and Gooseberry Creeks, Grey Bull and Stinking Water Rivers, pursue a general easterly course, with a northward tendency, the latter increasing and continuing so that Clarke's Fork, the main Yellowstone below the lake, the three forks of the Missouri, &c., are found to flow almost due north for a considerable distance. The sources of the Stinking Water are so far to the west of the more southern tributaries of the Big Horn that it drains a very large proportion of the whole Sierra Shoshone, its branches extending far to the southward of the main head. Still farther to the south, however, this range is drained by some of the headwaters of the Snake and Upper Yellowstone Rivers, and it is in the vicinity of the point where these several streams originate that we have that peculiar water-shed which has been not inaptly termed the "Crown of the Continent."

The preceding review gives but the bare outlines of the physical geography of a most interesting region, and many subjects have been passed by without notice, while others have received but little attention; but enough has been written to make a detailed review of the geological structure of the region more comprehensible and valuable than it could be without a general knowledge of the facts related in this chapter.

There are many of the finer features or lineaments of the surface, particularly in mountainous countries, which are apt to be overlooked or lightly treated because of their apparent insignificance; and yet it not unfrequently happens that careful scrutiny will prove that they have been instrumental in shaping the outlines of a vast expanse of territory. It would be interesting to review these in a chapter by themselves, but it has been thought best to defer special mention until they can be more carefully noted in connection with the subject of dynamical geology.

CHAPTER III.

STRATIGRAPHY—METAMORPHIC AND PALEOZOIC.

Introduction—Pre-silurian era—Silurian system—Potsdam sandstone—Quebec group—Niagara limestone—Devonian system—Carboniferous system.

In collating and arranging the results obtained in this department of our subject, it has been deemed advisable to adhere strictly to the plan adopted in other portions of the report, and to present topics in chronological order rather than in the order of observation. This method will cause us to wander from point to point; but it will prevent much useless repetition, and give something like system to the work, which will render it more easy of reference; and it will also render more permanent whatever of value the report may possess.

As we proceed, it will become more and more evident that the chief value of the determinations in this department will depend almost wholly upon the relations which are found to exist between the rock-formations of this section and those of other parts of the country and of other countries; and particularly will it depend upon their relations to the formations of neighboring districts.

Fortunately for the writer, the explorations which have been made of late years in this region, under the direction of Hayden, King, and others, have rendered the tracing of the latter class of relationships much less difficult and more certain than could have been the case under less favorable circumstances. Although much yet remains to be done in various directions, it is but due to these men that grateful acknowledgment should be made of the value of the information which has been derived from the perusal of such of their reports as have been consulted in the preparation of this treatise.

To show at a glance the proper relations of the geological formations of Western Wyoming, the accompanying synoptical table of the deposits of the various epochs has been prepared, giving the formations representing them in different parts of the world as they are commonly named, in which one column is devoted to the deposits now to be described. This table is so arranged that each formation is placed in its proper relative position to all the others; at least, so far as it can be done with our present knowledge of the strata, and beyond this no explanation of its use is necessary.

METAMORPHIC ROCKS.

The question naturally arises, what is the earliest act of which any record has been discovered within the territory embraced by the reconnaissance? Such records must evidently be sought in the lowest rocks which are exposed over this area. It is now scarcely doubted that our globe has passed from a gaseous condition by successive stages to its present form.

Accepting this view, we are prepared to find that many of the rocks which were formed during earlier stages of the earth's history have been greatly altered since their deposition by the various kinds of action to which they have been subjected. Wherever, then, as in some parts of the district under consideration, sufficient force has been employed to rend apart or wear away the superincumbent strata, but without disturbing their relative positions, we may expect to meet with exposures of the underlying metamorphics. These exist in quantity throughout the region of the Rocky Mountains, but they are not well exposed in all of the ranges. In that portion of the Uintahs visited by the writer, they are mostly concealed by the overlying purely sedimentary rocks, as they are also in the Owl Creek range, though in the latter one or two fair exposures were noticed by Captain Jones from the summit of Phlox Mountain. In the Sierra Shoshone, it is almost impossible to determine whether the metamorphic series ever came to light; for, with few exceptions, the whole section is now covered by a formation which has been deposited since the elevation of its primary ridges. The Wind River Mountains furnish abundant opportunities for the study of these rocks, however, and they are extensively exposed in the Wahsatch range, according to the reports of Clarence King, Hayden, and other geologists. The central portions of the Rocky Mountain system, or, more properly, the crests of the Rocky Mountain chain, furnish the best exposures of these rocks.

In the Wind River Mountains, as in most other portions of the Rocky Mountains, the nucleal rocks occupy an irregularly-exposed belt along the axial line of the range. It is at least doubtful whether any true *igneous* rocks are here exposed; for the gradations between the compact and the gneissoid granites, and between the latter and the gneisses and schists, are so close as to point toward the aqueous or sedimentary origin of the whole series, At any rate, there can be little question that the exposures of purely igneous rocks, if any exist, are of very limited extent. It will, therefore, be convenient to consider the whole series as composed of metamorphic rocks, although the massive granites are so far changed from their original condition as to be *structurally* inseparable from igneous granites by any method of analysis known at present.

The rock most nearly approaching the igneous is a compact, fine-textured granite, containing an abundance of mica, apparently *muscovite*, with more or less of black *biotite* distributed through the mass; the latter, in places, becoming so abundant as to give character in color and mode of weathering to separate portions of the rock. These granites seem to be associated with gneisses and gneissoid granites, varying considerably in texture and composition; and these again pass somewhat gradually into the metamorphic schists, upon both sides of the anticlinal. Beds of quartz and reddish and flesh-colored feldspathic seams are met with, and quartz veins traverse the slaty metamorphics, charged with the gold which is mined in the neighborhood of South Pass. Some portion of these metamorphic rocks contains, besides the magnetic iron, (Fe_3O_4,) which is abundant, garnets, mostly quite small, but occasionally of fair size. These were accidentally discovered in large quantities in the bed and alluvial bottom of the Sweetwater River, at Camp 13. The feldspar seams in this section are mostly filled with nuggets, as it were, of muscovite. The quartz, in many instances, is quite pure and white; in other cases it is darker colored and frequently contaminated by the decomposition of pyrites.

Beginning below, or at the center of the mountain-nucleus, we have then the following succession of the metamorphic rocks:

1. Gray and reddish granites, with masses of black interspersed.
2. Gneissoid granites, passing through granitoid gneiss to—
3. Gneisses of varying composition and feldspathic seams.
4. Metamorphic slates and schists, with quartz veins containing gold and silver.
5. Pre-Potsdam metamorphics.

This will serve to show the general character of the series, though by no means intended as a complete section, which would require much more investigation than is possible in a mere reconnaissance. It is not improbable that a closer study would reveal many interesting facts in connection with the origin of many of these rocks. For instance, there is some ground for the belief that some apparently local actinolite schists and other allied forms may have originally been the trap-dikes of the early sedimentary strata now metamorphosed. Some rocks here classed among the metamorphics may be proved more recently trappean, but it is probable that such cases are very exceptional.

Other exposures of the metamorphic rocks occur along the route of the expedition. The granites appear at the surface over a considerable area in the valley of the East Fork of the Yellowstone, and in the valley of the Yellowstone River, between the mouths of East Fork and Hell-Roaring Creek. The structure of this section is deserving of close attention, for it cannot fail to add greatly to our knowledge of the dynamical history of a large portion of the Rocky Mountain system. North of latitude 43° 45′, and west of longitude 109°, every exposure of the deep-seated rocks is to be welcomed as an aid in the solution of difficult problems connected with the mountain-geology, because such exposures over a vast territory are rare indeed. There is here, perhaps, some evidence that a portion of the granites are igneous intrusions, or, rather, it should be said that there is less evidence to the contrary; and yet, upon the whole, I am strongly inclined to the opinion that they are no less metamorphic than those of the nucleus of the Wind River Mountains. Here we find the same general characteristics, with a similar succession of gneissic and schistose rocks, wherever full exposures can be reached. There is this difference, however, that not only the overlying metamorphic and sedimentary beds, but the granites themselves, bear traces of further change, owing, probably, to the subsequent ejections of molten volcanic products, which have flowed over them. This view is partially supported by the fact that in this region there occur granites composed of the same varieties and proportions of mineral ingredients as some from the Wind River Mountains, but differing in their arrangement, and consequently in texture. This feature is also noticeable in many of the micaceous sandstones, and in the schists, which have become more friable, and, like some of the granites, have the appearance of having been burned or baked. Quartz veins of various sizes occur in these rocks, and gold has been obtained from some of them in what appears to be a continuation northward of this system of ridges.

Between the Two-Ocean Pass and Tógwote Pass there are exposures of a metamorphic group, which undoubtedly represent the ridge of some mountain-range or its spurs, though it is a difficult matter at present to define its relations to the main chains; and the same remark will apply also to the section just discussed. Here, again, the same conclusions may be drawn from facts quite similar; and such trifling differences as are found to exist between these formations in the two localities may, I think, be readily reconciled by referring them wholly to differences in the amount of the pre-volcanic erosion. This will be rendered more apparent as we proceed, as it will be necessary to refer more than once to the evident changes in texture which have been produced in the rocks by the outflow of the later igneous material from volcanoes.

Age of the metamorphics.—Sufficient data for determining the exact age of this series have not been collected; nor is it by any means certain that this can ever be done. On account of the complete change which most of these beds have undergone since their deposition as sediments, it is possible that future research can do little more than to extend downward the series of rocks of known age by the transfer to it of one or two restricted groups from the upper beds of the metamorphic series. The structure of the Wind River Mountains is, however, so regular that it affords convincing proof of the *relative* age of such of these beds as are exposed in the nucleus of that range, at least in one direction. In other words, although it would be unwise to assert that they are identical with either the Saint John's, the Huronian, or the Laurentian system, as elsewhere known, without a wider knowledge of their relations, we may confidently affirm that no portion of the whole series was deposited later than the formation of the Potsdam sandstone in the Rocky Mountain region. There is a possibility that the comparison of facts from a large number of localities in the West may hereafter lead to some very interesting developments concerning these undetermined rocks. Certain it is that the succession of the strata throughout the Rocky Mountains is remarkably uniform, and a careful examination of the metamorphic rocks over an extended area would do much toward unraveling their history. Uniformity of lithological characters over broad districts is rare, even when the metamorphosed rocks were originally identical in composition, because slight differences in the amount or quality of action or resistance may cause great differences in the results.

There are some slight reasons for placing a portion of the oldest of these rocks in a group nearly equivalent to the Laurentian system of the East, but it must be confessed that none of them are based upon much better foundation than a certain similarity to that formation in lithological characteristics. Their position upon the stratigraphic chart is, therefore, entirely provisional.

SILURIAN SYSTEM.

As before remarked, no proof has been obtained of the existence in recognizable form of a set of beds which can be referred to the horizon of the Saint John's group of the Canadian geologists; although it is not impossible that some of the upper beds of the metamorphic series may be of that age. So far as can be determined from the hasty review which is rendered necessary in a simple reconnaissance, there are few, if any, indications of unconformability between any of these lower beds; but this is a question which can only be settled after careful examination over a wide space. In the valley of a small branch of Beaver Creek, at a point where the overlying sandstones have been cut through, the metamorphic slates appear in such a manner as to suggest unconformability between themselves and the Lower Silurian sandstone, but the exposure was so narrow and weather-worn that it was impossible to determine the physical relations of the two groups to each other. In most localities, the sub-sedimentary beds dip at a much greater angle than the overlying rocks, some of the former being very nearly vertical, while the adjacent strata are much less inclined. This, of itself, is not sufficient to prove the unconformability of deposition, however. Until we know more of the rocks comprising the metamorphic series, this subject of their "lie" is of minor importance, though it will be of consequence in determining their geological relations. One great difficulty in working out such problems in connection with a reconnaissance is that the route of the expedition must necessarily lie through the least rugged portions of the country, in which the geological structure is frequently obscured by drift and other later formations of mere local extent.

The Silurian system is represented by several important formations in the region of our survey, most of which probably underlie a vast extent of country west of the Mississippi, but which are concealed by the more recent deposits except in places where they have been brought to light by the upheaval of the mountains; and even here they have been again largely buried by the accumulations of later formations of non-sedimentary character. The lowest formation yet recognized is that of the widespread—

POTSDAM SANDSTONE.

Beds of a reddish sandstone, of varying thickness, with the structural and mineralogical characteristics of the Potsdam sandstone east of the Missouri River, were noticed some years since by Dr. Hayden at various places in the Rocky Mountains, from which a few characteristic fossils were obtained in some instances. The first discovery of these remains, announced by Meek and Hayden in March, 1858, in a paper read before the Philadelphia Academy of Sciences, was made in the region of the Black Hills, Wyoming, (then Nebraska.) Subsequently, Dr. Hayden reported other fossils, collected in the Big Horn range, near the head of Powder River, and in his report for 1870 he mentions the discovery of others in this formation near South Pass. On the geological map accompanying his report in connection with the expedition of Col. Wm. F. Raynolds, published in 1869, this formation is represented as an irregular band bounding the nuclei of all the prominent mountain-ranges. In the colored map which I have prepared to accompany this report, some modifications have been made in the distribution of these rocks, in certain sections, but they are not of sufficient importance to call for special notice. Unfortunately, though satisfied of the age of such rocks as I have referred to this formation by reason of their order of sequence, and their lithological features, I was unable to obtain any fossils from any of the exposures along our route.

In the Wind River Mountain district, there is a succession of beds of a loosely granular, almost friable sandstone, varying in color from red or brown below to white above; in texture, from a mere loose aggregation of the siliceous particles to fairly compact sandstones; in structure, from thinly-laminated or obliquely-laminated to thickly-bedded massive rock. The parallelism of these beds with much of the Potsdam sandstone of the East, even to minor peculiarities, is quite remarkable. The following statement concerning this formation is taken from the Wisconsin Report, (Hall and Whitney, vol. 1, 1862, page 141,) being a portion of Prof. J. D. Whitney's contribution to that work:

> The lower sandstone occupies the same position as the Potsdam sandstone of the New York geological survey, and is the exact equivalent of it. As developed in the Northwest, and especially in the State of Wisconsin, where it occupies a large extent of surface, it is made up of an almost chemically pure siliceous sand, in minute grains, hardly larger than a pin's head, which are held together by the minutest possible quantity of a calcareous or ferruginous cement. Frequently even this small quantity of cementing-material is wanting, so that the rock can be readily crumbled between the fingers, like a crystalline granular sugar. Where the ferruginous material, which is the peroxide of iron, becomes more abundant, so as to form 2 or 3 per cent. of the mass, the sandstone acquires a dark-brown color, and frequently affords a solid and durable building-stone.

This description will apply to the rocks of this group along the eastern slope of the Wind River Mountains. In the same relative position to the metamorphic rocks, there occurs, in the valley of Lava Creek, along the western base of the Sierra Shoshone, a thick formation, composed mainly of a compact red sandstone, almost a quartzite, portions of it being entirely made up of coarse grains of bright quartz, with quite small quartz pebbles distributed irregularly through the mass. Hayden also mentions a similar outcrop east of South Pass; and other exposures of apparently the same group as that on Lava Creek are referred to by Hayden and Bradley in the report of the Department of the Interior survey of 1872. The rock seen upon the right bank of Lava Creek is very hard, but it has the appearance before noticed of a partially-metamorphosed sediment, as if it had been modified by the outflow of the eruptive material, which has largely covered this section, and its imperfect jointing and consequent mode of weathering have probably been induced by the same cause.

Other geologists have described beds of this formation in other sections, and their remarks will often be found to apply almost equally as well to the exposures along our route. Emmons and the Canadian geologists, as well as Hall, Owen, and others, allude to peculiarities of this sandstone and its associated rocks, which are strikingly repeated in the Rocky Mountain region. Among these may be mentioned the peculiar lamination of some of the harder brown beds, which contain a considerable quantity of the ferric oxide cement. A short distance beyond Miners' Delight, the present wagon-road from Camp Stambaugh to Camp Brown passes through a hollow, upon the edge of which the reddish-brown beds are exposed and weathered in such a manner as to present something of the appearance of crowded shelves in tiers. This is roughly represented in Fig. 1, which is a diagrammatic section in the direction of the *strike* of the rocks.

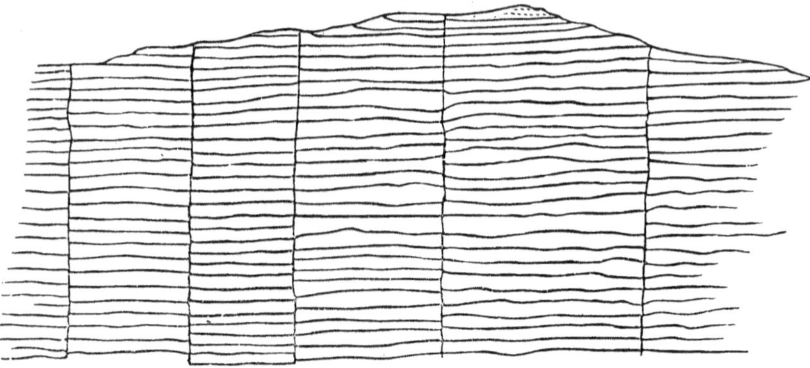

Fig. 1—Style of weathering of cliffs of Postdam sandstone, Wind River Mountains, near Miners' Delight. The lines all represent the uneroded portions; the spaces between representing the eroded portions. A portion of one stratum only is shown, hence there are no lines of bedding.

This form of weathering is doubtless owing partly to variations in the texture of the rock, which have produced the lamination or alternation of the fine and coarse materials, but, also, to other peculiarities induced by the erosive agencies.

The greatest thickness of the Potsdam sandstone over the area described is about 200 feet, in the region of the Wind River Mountains. All the beds bear evidence of deposition in shallow seas, or upon beaches or sand-flats.

QUEBEC GROUP.

Above the Potsdam sandstone in some sections, and probably in most places directly superimposed, occurs a set of beds which, for reasons that will presently be given, are referred to the horizon of the Canadian Upper Calciferous strata, known as the Quebec Group. As exposed along the eastern flank of the Wind River Mountains, these beds differ widely from the underlying sandstone-formation, and they furnish abundant proof of the deepening of the sea over the area in which they were deposited. Their distribution is not yet fully determined; but some interesting hints in this connection may, if they have been correctly interpreted, go to show that, though a wide-spread formation, it extends less regularly over the country than most of the beds below and above it. This conclusion cannot be considered final until the numerous missing links in the chain of the western geological history have been supplied by the more careful surveys of the future. The facts upon which it is based are briefly these: The geology of the eastern portions of the Rocky Mountain region has been *traced* over an extended space from north to south without the discovery of important exposures of this group of strata, which fact, to one acquainted with the differences of weathering between most sandstones and limestones, seems remarkable if such strata exist. Again, Hayden, after several good opportunities of observation, has expressed the opinion that no strata between those of Potsdam and Carboniferous age occur along the eastern slope of the Wind River range. This, as we shall see, is certainly an error, but it was based upon an examination of well-exposed sections at each end of the range, and there are some indications of the thinning-out of the Calciferous beds in the neighborhood of South Pass, which would partly justify his opinion. West of the Rocky Mountain divide, beds of the age of the Quebec group have been observed by both Hayden and Bradley; but, as is the case in several places on our trail, the supposed Potsdam is also to be seen immediately overlaid by rocks of more recent date.

The best exposure of these rocks which was reached during our trip, and, in fact, the only one from which the main facts were gathered, is situated near the central portion of the Wind River Mountains, a little

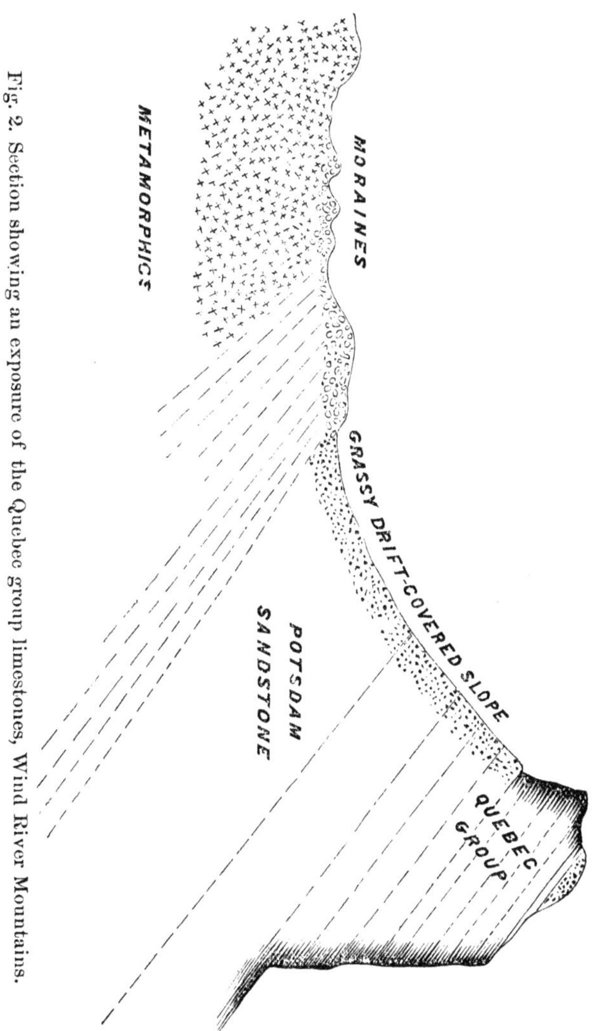

Fig. 2. Section showing an exposure of the Quebec group limestones, Wind River Mountains.

south of west from Camp Brown. The connection with the rocks below is entirely obscured by heavy drift-deposits, as will be seen from the accompanying section taken at a point where the overlying beds have been worn away, (see Fig. 2.) The thickness of the exposed Quebec limestones is about 200 feet, which will constitute two-thirds of its whole amount, if it be true, as supposed, that there is only a thickness of 200 feet of Potsdam sandstone between this formation and the metamorphic series, but which is not exposed in this section.

This supposition is not of much value, for there is no means of determining from this section the nature of the 300 feet which is covered by drift. One thing, however, is certain: there is nowhere in the Wind River range such a development of this formation as is reported by Bradley from several localities farther west, unless it be in a very restricted section.

The rock varies somewhat in composition and texture, but in general it may be described as a ferrous-magnesian, or dolomitic, limestone with an öolitic structure, although large portions of it are not öolitic. In some of the layers there is a considerable amount of siliceous material intermixed with the calcareous, and occasionally there is a bed which might better be called a calcareous sand-rock. Local bands or streaks of ferruginous shale are common, in some instances almost constituting separate layers, but generally irregularly dispersed through the limestones.

The greater part of the silica, which is contained in the dolomitic limestones, is exceedingly fine, but there is scattered through the rock a small amount of what appears to be the minute fragments of some silicates of black and orange-red colors. Occasional globular masses of *pyrites* ($Fe\ S_2$) are found distributed through the öolite, and "drusy" cavities lined with rhombohedral crystals of *calcite* are very common. Many of the fossils seem to be connected with the mineralization of the rock by the introduction of special ingredients in the place of their component minerals. The change of the calcic carbonate of the shells to *dolomite*, and the alteration of other shells into ferric oxide, or the filling of their cavities with the same mineral, are of common occurrence, and in some layers a species of *Theca* (?) is now almost invariably largely composed of a green mineral resembling *glauconite*, (silicate of iron.)

Organic contents.—The beds of the Quebec group in this region contain an abundance of fossil remains of a Lower Silurian cast, such as would require for their existence the conditions under which these beds were formed, viz, a comparatively clear sea, not necessarily of extreme depth, nor free from occasional slight turbidity, but highly charged with calcareous matter. As a rule, these fossils are quite badly broken, although the fragments are remarkably well preserved with few exceptions. In the öolite they are apt to be less broken than in the other limestones. From the few specimens collected I have been able to identify a trilobite of the genus *Dicellocephalus*, several specimens of *Orthis-tritonia* (?) and a quantity of a species of *Theca* (?). Fragments of other fossils are present, some of which could, doubtless, be identified, with more careful study and comparison with better-preserved remains, but this has been impossible under existing circumstances.

NIAGARA LIMESTONE.

Until the time of the present reconnaissance, all of the rocks of Silurian age north of South Pass, and east of the main crest of the Rocky Mountains, were referred to the epoch of the Potsdam sandstone. Hayden discovered evidences of the existence of strata of Upper Silurian age near South Pass as early as 1860, but he did not meet with any indications of their presence elsewhere in the Wind River Mountains. The trip to Chimney Rock, made by the writer from Camp Brown, which is mentioned in Chapter I, proved very fortunate, as it resulted in the discovery of several important groups of strata not heretofore suspected in that region. The junction of the Quebec group with the underlying formation is still unsettled; but very near the section shown in Fig. 2 its connection with the formation above is rendered plain by an exposure, which shows the two groups in contact. Fig. 3 is a section illustrating the prominent facts as there exhibited.

Several other outcrops of a similar limestone along our trail have been referred provisionally to this formation on account of their relative position to other beds. Near the summit of the Owl Creek range, where

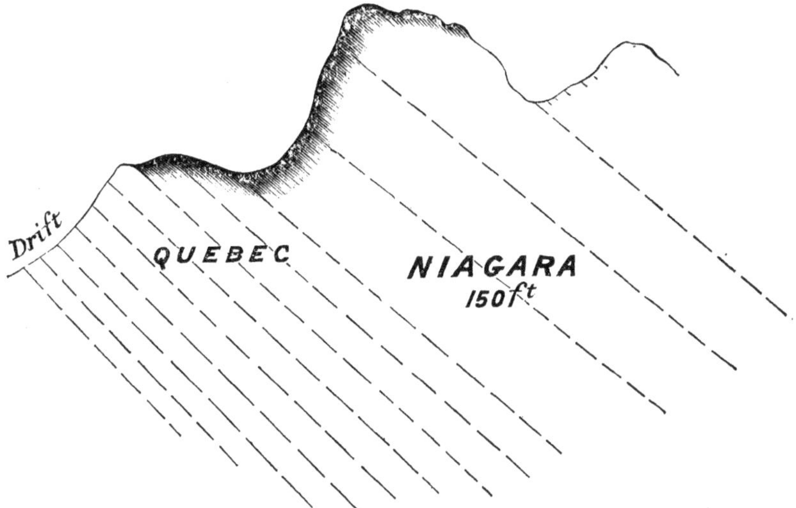

Fig. 3.—Section showing the connection of the Niagara and Quebec formations, Wind River Mountains.

we crossed it, there is an exposure of compact crystalline limestone, overlying a thinly-bedded shaly rock, which does not greatly resemble the limestones of the Quebec group lithologically, but which may be of the same age, though there are, perhaps, better grounds for considering it of later date. There are several exposures of thick limestone formations in the valley of the East Fork of the Yellowstone which have yielded no paleontological evidence of their true horizon; but, as they appear to lie not far above the metamorphic series, it seems more likely that they were deposited during the Niagara period than that they are of Carboniferous age, the rocks of which in this region they do not so closely resemble.

On Lava Creek, a locality before mentioned, the red sandstone which I have referred to the Potsdam epoch is directly overlaid by limestones, the upper portions of which are probably of Upper Silurian age, being very similar in many respects to the fossiliferous Niagara beds of the Wind River range. This opinion is strengthened by the discovery of a co-incident arrangement of strata in the neighborhood of the Téton range, forty miles west of this point, by Prof. Frank H. Bradley, geologist of the Snake River division of Doctor Hayden's expedition of 1872.

The lithological characters of this formation are very similar to those of some of the more eastern rocks of the same age. It is possible that a few beds of an arenaceous nature will eventually be included in the group, but, so far as its limits have been determined over the area which we are discussing, it is entirely made up of a compact cherty dolomite of a color varying from white to gray or light-drab. Some portions of it are inclined to weather brownish-yellow, but much of it only assumes a darker gray color upon exposure to atmospheric agencies. Large masses of the dolomite frequently weather into turreted or castellated forms, and sometimes huge blocks are left standing by themselves or tumbled down steep declivities into the ravines. Caverns of various sizes are also not scarce, affording fine shelter even for quite large animals.

Beautiful siliceous crystals are abundant in the rock in "drusy" cavities, many of them being highly ferruginous, while others are opalescent, and some are concretionary, with an agate structure. Portions of the rock are also traversed by thin veins of chalcedony, interlacing and studded with minute and brilliant crystals of quartz. An occasional fossil is almost completely transformed by this process. Nodules or flakes of *hornstone* are also found sometimes approaching in color the *carnelian.*

Organic contents.—Unfortunately, some of the most characteristic fossils belonging to the rocks of the Niagara period are not sufficiently characteristic of a single formation to enable one to refer the beds containing them to their exact horizon. A cursory glance at the specimens collected in 1873 might cause considerable doubt whether these beds would not be as appropriately regarded as synchronous with the Clinton limestones of the East, but a more careful review of all the evidence shows that the affinities are largely in the direction of the more recent limestone of the Niagara epoch. In the interior basin, in the valley of the Mississippi, where the limestone-beds are more extensive than at points farther east, the lithological features, the mode of weathering, and other characteristics of the Niagara limestone strikingly resemble the peculiarities which have just been described. But the comparison does not end here, for the character of the fossils also points to the more recent date of this formation in the Rocky Mountain region.

Perhaps the most common organic remains are those of the well-known *Halysites catenulatus*, Linn., or "chain-coral," which can be obtained in quite large masses. Other corals, of the genera *Cyathophyllum* and *Zaphrentis*, are not rare in the lower beds, and a brachiopod, poorly preserved, resembling a cast of the interior of *Pentamerus* (*galeatus?*) was collected, besides one specimen of an *Orthoceras.*

The fossils, with the exception of the brachiopods, are usually silicified and very well preserved; but they are difficult to collect on account of the extreme hardness of the rock.

ABSENCE OF THE DEVONIAN SYSTEM.

Overlying the Niagara dolomite there is a series of beds which are mostly arenaceous, but which promise to prove of much geologic interest when they shall have received their due share of attention at the hands of those who will not be obliged to merely "skim" the country. In a paper published in the *American Journal of Science*, (vol. vi, December, 1873,) I have too hastily referred certain of these arenaceous strata in the Wind River Mountains to the Oriskany Period of the Devonian age. Prof. James Hall, of Albany, N. Y., who has since kindly examined two specimens obtained from this locality, writes that one proves to be identical with *Spiriferina pulchra*, Meek, a form originally described from Nevada; while, concerning the other, he remarks,

"Strange as it may appear, I am unable to refer it to any other than *Spirifer cameratus*, from the ordinary forms of which it differs considerably. The characters of the specimen are certainly obscure, and the determination may admit of doubt; but * * * I should give it the relations I have indicated, and, if not *Sp. cameratus*, it is to me unknown at the present time." It is probable, therefore, that the Devonian system is not represented by any considerable formation in this section of the West, although there is a wide field for research here; and, if this view be correct, the development of the Upper Carboniferous is quite remarkable.

CARBONIFEROUS SYSTEM.

Above the Niagara limestone, there is a well-developed and widely-distributed formation, which was early referred to the Carboniferous system. Beds of this age are quite generally exposed all along the flanks of the principal ranges of the Rocky Mountain chain, and occasional exposures of beds, which are usually considered synchronous with them, occur in many places west of the main crest, where it is often difficult to determine their relations to the adjacent rocks. Recent discoveries have made it doubtful whether such reference has not too often been based upon the previous supposition that there were no beds in this region between the Potsdam sandstone and the Carboniferous rocks, so that it is possible that some outcrops of an earlier date have been inadvertently reported as of Carboniferous age.

SUBCARBONIFEROUS ??? LIMESTONE.

The limestones of the Carboniferous age, flanking the ranges of the Rocky Mountain system, with one or two exceptions, have been generally regarded as of the horizon of some portion of the Carboniferous period, (the terms *age* and *period* being technically employed here.) In another place,* the writer has expressed the opinion that this formation, as exposed in a portion of the Wind River Mountains, north of South Pass, is of Subcarboniferous age. That statement was made from a review of the notes taken in the field, without the opportunity of further examination of the specimens collected, and it is now so far modified as to be less confidently expressed, for reasons which will presently appear.

The rock in question (the arenaceous beds before mentioned being excluded from the present review) is a bluish-gray dolomitic limestone, quite compact and thickly bedded, with numerous crystalline facets and geodes of *calc-spar*, besides occasional minute crystals of some foreign minerals. Some beds which seem to belong to this age are exposed in the cañon of the North Fork of the Stinkingwater River, showing, in an interesting manner, the effects produced by the molten volcanic outflows, portions of which have passed in between the upturned layers, transforming the sedimentary rocks into forms with peculiar characters.

Organic contents.—Much of this limestone is quite fossiliferous, but there is so little difference in the mineral composition of the rock and its contained remains that it is often difficult to procure specimens which can be readily identified, and this difficulty is not lessened by the irregular manner in which the fossils are crowded together. Several recorded specimens, containing remains from a favorable locality, have been

---

* In a paper "On the Geology of Western Wyoming," by Theo. B. Comstock, published in the American Journal of Science and Arts, vol. vi, December, 1873.

lost, so that the material on hand for final determination is far from complete. Among the missing were a crinoid of the genus *Poteriocrinus?* and two or three specimens of *Lithostrotion*, as recorded in the field-notes. If my determinations of the remaining forms are correct, this limestone also contains *Spirifer biplicatus*, and a *chonetes* closely allied to *C. variolata.*

By some this might be deemed sufficient ground for the omission of the interrogation-marks after the word Subcarboniferous at the head of this section, but in view of the novelty of such a designation, as well as the doubt, which must be confessed, as to the validity of all the determinations, it is best that it should stand as it is.

There is also another reason for doubt. It is known that limestones of the age of the Coal-Measures occupy the position of this formation over a very large area in the mountainous region of the West, and it is difficult to imagine such a state of things as would have been necessary for the deposition of a restricted Subcarboniferous group immediately followed by a period in which the absence of any deposition was geographically identical, without some marked evidence being visible in the arrangement of the strata. So far as known at present, there is no ground for the belief that there is any break of this kind structurally, unless it be that an observed change in the character of some of the Carboniferous beds in the Big Horn range, reported by Hayden, may indicate a difference in horizon. As the subject now stands, it would be unwise to press too strongly an opinion of the Subcarboniferous age of this group; and it will be best to regard the whole series as Upper Carboniferous, according to previous authorities, until the matter can receive more thorough investigation.

CARBONIFEROUS LIMESTONE.

Near the head of Wind River, overlying conformably the Subcarboniferous? limestone, there is a thick formation of arenaceous and calcareous beds underneath the brick-red sandstones usually regarded as Triassic. Toward the base of the group, from a non-homogeneous dark-gray limestone, I obtained a portion of a tooth of *Psammodus*, and shells undetermined, which have led me to place it in the Carboniferous group or Coal-Measures. The rock resembles limestones of this horizon in Illinois and Indiana. This was met upon the return trip, and no opportunity afterward occurred for reaching another exposure. Its reference must, therefore, be regarded as provisional. If the limestone referred doubtfully to the Subcarboniferous be really the equivalent of Hayden's Carboniferous east of our district, this formation would seem to occupy the position of his Permian. The determination of the *Carboniferous* eastward rests on such good authority as Prof. F. B. Meek, and cannot be questioned without better evidence than I can offer. These difficulties can readily be settled by those who may hereafter have occasion to work in this region, by the collection of more material from each formation.

The sandstones and arenaceous limestones before mentioned, from which the supposed *Spirifer cameratus* was obtained, *underlie* beds which are apparently continuous with those which have been referred very doubtfully to the Subcarboniferous period, which fact adds another element of uncertainty to the determination. Accepting, therefore, the opinion of previous explorers, the thickness of the Carboniferous limestones, the equivalent of the Upper Coal-Measures of the Eastern United States, is not less than 2,000 feet (probably much more) in the

Wind River Mountains. The entire absence of coal and the prevalence of calcareous strata, as well as the widespread distribution of the formation, all point to the existence of an extensive sea of considerable depth during the period of their formation; and no evidence has thus far been collected of a shore-line in any part of this region during the era in question. The upper limestones are massive and very compact, forming prominent ridges, with even, well-worn slopes, while the underlying strata are more thinly bedded, being usually less calcareous.

Organic contents.—Besides those already mentioned, no fossils have been identified. But few opportunities occurred of obtaining a good supply, and the general toughness of the rocks renders it difficult to procure them in excellent condition. As a rule, they are much crowded, and poorly preserved also.

OBSERVATIONS ON THE PALEOZOIC STRATA.

There is yet too much to be learned concerning the geology of our district to make any but the most broad generalizations useful, but the results of this expedition, in a geological way at least, will prove barren indeed if they do not furnish future explorers with a few hints of some of the unsolved problems yet remaining, that they may know where to seek for new facts for their elucidation.

It has been already remarked that the Potsdam sandstone and the Carboniferous limestone are widespread formations in the region of the Rocky Mountains, and that over the greater portion of the area east of the main divide these two formations have heretofore been reported in contact. Knowing now that several other formations intervene in certain sections, it is natural to seek a reason for their apparently local distribution. Two or three explanations are suggested by the facts as far as they have been gathered. First, it will be noticed that few competent geologists have traversed this region, even in such a manner as to collect all the data necessary for the mere tracing of the prominent outcrops of the successive formations, and none have been able to obtain more than a bare outline of the geological structure of any portion. It seldom happens in a reconnaissance—and territorial surveys are usually nothing more—that one can obtain information to any extent at a distance from the trail of the expedition; and the route pursued must of necessity be mostly away from the rugged country, making it impossible to reach the most instructive sections in all cases. Thus it may have happened that many exposures of the Quebec and Niagara strata have been entirely overlooked. This supposition, however, to one who has engaged in western field-work, will have little weight, and the wiser conclusion will be that such strata do not exist where they have not been reported, except it may be in small patches. But there is another question which is not so easily decided. Did these formations once spread over this whole area, or were they deposited in patches as we suppose them to exist at present? An examination of the limestones and their fossils shows that they were deposited in saline-waters of considerable depth and extent, as a sea or ocean. Moreover, during the Quebec epoch the shore need not have been very far distant from the present position of the Wind River Mountains. A comparison of the statements concerning that group in this chapter with the reports of Hayden and Bradley shows that this formation rapidly *thickens* westward, while there is no doubt that it *thins out* southward and eastward, so that it is very thin, if not entirely absent, in the vicinity of Miner's Delight. The same features are noticeable with the

Niagara dolomite, which, as before stated, probably extends farther eastward than the Quebec group.

If this idea be correct—and it seems well supported—there was an ancient shore-line during the deposition of the Quebec and Niagara groups, of uncertain trend, but a portion of which lay near the longitude of South Pass. This opens a new field for research in this region, one which will doubtless add much to the great mass of facts which are now helping on the settlement of the theories of mountain elevation, and it also suggests the possibility that the history of the far-past in the West is not as simple as many have believed.

CHAPTER IV.

STRATIGRAPHY, CONTINUED—MESOZOIC AND TERTIARY.

Triassic system—Jurassic—Cretaceous and Tertiary systems—Age of the lignite formation.

We have seen that over much of the region north and west of South Pass the earlier Paleozoic rocks were deposited in a sea at first shallow, but somewhat gradually deepening until toward the close of the epoch of the Niagara dolomite, when comparatively shallow seas were the rule. During a considerable portion of the Devonian and Carboniferous ages, it is probable that dry land existed over at least a portion of this region; and east of the Big Horn River, it would seem that, during much of the era between the deposition of the Potsdam sandstone and the Carboniferous beds, the land was not covered by the sea. However this may have been, there is abundant proof that the barrier was overflowed at least as early as the close of the Carboniferous age, since which time the geological history of the whole area has been essentially the same, generally speaking.

TRIASSIC SYSTEM.

Directly overlying the limestones of Carboniferous age a thick series of brick-red sandstones forms one of the most peculiar and conspicuous features of Rocky Mountain geology. In most places where these beds are well exposed they stand out prominently by themselves, their separation from the underlying hard limestones being extremely distinct, on account of the great difference in the texture of the formations and the consequent greater erosion of the so-called Triassic strata. The brick-red sandstones are generally considered Triassic, though full proof of their age cannot be said to have been obtained. Notwithstanding the fact that these beds are among the best exposed of any of the western formations, less is probably known of their true relations than of those of all the others, except the metamorphic series.

Frequent exposures of the red sandstones occur over our district, but often the forces which have operated to bring them to light have also aided in again obscuring their structure. The most simple outcrop, not complicated by folds or subsequent deposits, is to be seen in the cañon of Deep Creek, at the base of the Wind River Mountains. Figure 4 is intended to represent a section across this cañon at a right angle to the axis of the range, but it also includes a portion of the exposures upon each side as they are seen along the banks of the Little Popo-Agie River.

Some outcrops in deeply-eroded vales in the Owl Creek range are quite similar, but many of the finest exposures are in eroded folds, several of which occur in the Wind River Valley, between the two mountain-ranges. In these, the dip of the red beds is often very great. Ripple-marks, and other evidences of deposition in shallow water, abound in most of the strata.

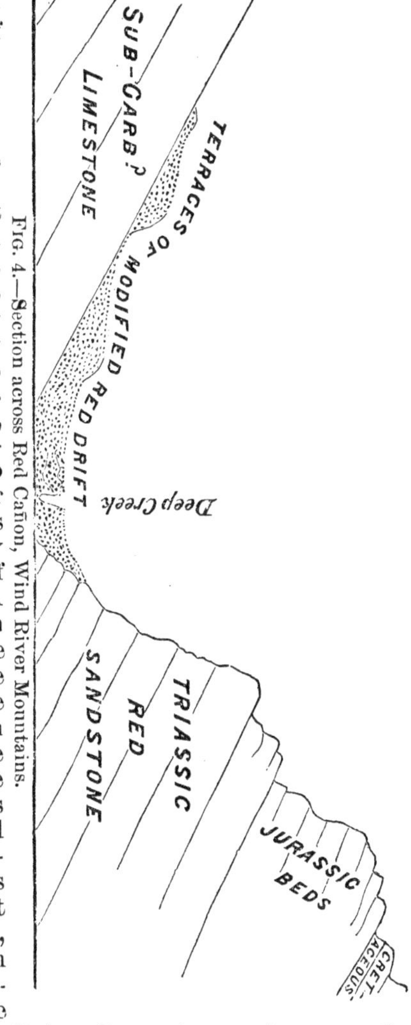

FIG. 4.—Section across Red Cañon, Wind River Mountains.

The rock appears to vary but little over broad areas, though occasional beds of a different nature from that of the red sandstones have been observed. Besides the ferric oxide, to which the color is mainly due, much of the rock contains a considerable quantity of iron in spots scattered through the interior like fossils, but showing no structural markings. Many of the layers are fairly compact, and being traversed by a double system of regular joints, they break into blocks of a form and size suitable for building-purposes. Large quantities of bedded gypsum occur, apparently interstratified between the layers of the sandstone in many places. A short distance below Camp Brown on the Little Wind River, this is quite abundant, and it bids fair to become of much economic importance in the future. At the head of Lake Fork, in the cañon, there are also extensive outcrops of this mineral, which are very accessible. The greater part is probably in the form of saccharoidal or compact alabaster, but some portions closely resemble in properties the finer varieties of anhydrite, and it is not impossible that other portions, in places where the rocks have been folded, may prove valuable as a partial substitute for marble, as is the case with the vulpanite of Northern Italy. In most cases, however, the anhydrite has been broken into quite small blocks by the heat accompanying the uplift. Some extensive beds of selenite were also observed. Beds of limonite, some of which appeared to be of the argillaceous variety known as yellow ocher, were noticed in the outlying ridges south of the Owl-Creek range, a portion of which may be of Triassic age.

Above the brick-red beds two or three hundred feet of lighter-colored sandstones, containing less ferric oxide, lie beneath arenaceous limestone-beds, affording a transitional series between the so-called Triassic beds and the succeeding strata of undoubted Jurassic age.

Organic contents.—The rocks of this age in Northwestern Wyoming are as barren in the evidences of life as the Potsdam sandstone, and it is seldom that one is so fortunate as to collect any fossils from them, except when making a specialty of their study. None were obtained by the writer in 1873, hence no new facts were elicited concerning the age of this formation. There can be no doubt that it is older than the Fossiliferous-jurassic of this section, for it is invariably found beneath it wherever both are exposed, but its limits cannot at present be clearly defined, although it is undoubtedly Post-Carboniferous, for it has been reported in some sections as lying unconformably upon beds which have been referred, with good reason, to the Permian period.

JURASSIC SYSTEM.

Wherever good sections can be reached, the brick-red and buff-colored sandstones, which constitute the provisional Triassic system, are almost always found covered by the Jurassic limestones, a group which attains a thickness of nearly 1,000 feet in some localities. Many fine outcrops of these strata are to be seen in the Wind-River country, particularly in the neighborhood of the mountains, upon both sides of the plateau. The first exposures upon the northeastern slope of the Wind River Mountains are in the main as simple as on the Little Popo-Agie near Red Cañon, (see Fig. 4), where there are no complications in the way of folds, and the structure is not obscured by accumulations of drift or other material. Passing across the plateau several prominent folds have so tilted the strata that the Jurassic beds outcrop at different angles to the horizon, but frequently dipping almost vertically, in which case the harder layers jut above the softer intermediate beds, often to a height of many feet, stretching like so many irregular walls across the country. The formation is very widespread, its distribution in the Rocky Mountain region being nearly identical with the supposed Triassic, at least so far as our district is concerned. West of the main divide, on our route, no exposures were observed of rocks, which can with certainty be referred either to the Jurassic or the Triassic, but the existence of the former in that section has been proved by the explorations of Hayden and Bradley, who have obtained characteristic fossils of this group from localities comparatively near.

The formation as a whole might be characterized as one of impure limestones, the nature of the fossils, as well as the composition of most of the strata, indicating that the beds were deposited during an epoch of marine subsidence in comparatively shallow water. The beds composing the walls, before mentioned as occurring in certain sections, are generally quite hard and compact, but they are not remarkably homogeneous. The proportion of *silica* is always large, seldom extremely fine, but often quite coarse. In the more calcareous strata, containing fossils, *alumina* seems to be present only in small quantity when compared with the amount which is contained in less arenaceous rocks of earlier date. The fossiliferous limestones are dolomitic and often somewhat ferruginous. Crystals of *calcite* and *dolomite* are very commonly distributed through all the rocks, and much of the magnesian limestone is traversed by numerous very thin joints, filled with veins of *calcite*.

The prevailing color of the rocks is a dull leaden or ashy gray, weathering from darker gray to brown and dark brown. Occasional beds of quite pure yellowish-white limestone are seen, also yellow and brown arenaceous limestones. It is probable, also, that this formation in the neighborhood of the Owl-Creek range, upon its southern flank, includes some valuable iron-ore beds; but, as before remarked, they cannot be properly placed until the boundary between the Triassic and the Jurassic shall be more definitely fixed, and this cannot well be accomplished until more complete paleontological evidence has been collected from the lower series of arenaceous beds.

Organic contents.—Characteristic Jurassic fossils have been more than once collected from the region of the Rocky Mountains, and the announcement of those collected from the Wind River Valley by Dr. Hayden, while acting as the geologist of Captain Raynolds' expedition, was made as early as 1861. These remains present strong resemblances to many of the species which characterize the lower strata of the Jurassic system in Europe. A good supply was collected from the various exposures seen upon the trip of 1873, but inopportune circumstances have made it absolutely impossible to work them up with any degree of care, so that it must be acknowledged that there are a number of forms which have not been made out which it is believed will add some new members to the list of the characteristic organic remains of the American Jurassic. Enough has, however, been learned to determine the age of the containing beds, without a doubt, for their separation from the overlying group is very distinct, stratigraphically and paleontologically, as has been well remarked by Meek and Hayden.

Among the forms which are most readily recognizable, there is a species of *Gryphaea*, bearing some resemblance to the European Liassic *G. Arcuata*, Lam., but perhaps nearer *G. Calceola*, Quenstedt, (which I have not seen represented.) Fairly preserved specimens of *Monotis curta* (?) were obtained, besides a few of a species of *Rhynchonella*, specimens of the genera *Lingula* (*brevirostra* ?) *Modiola*, etc., and two specimens of *Belemnites*, near *B. densus*.

CRETACEOUS AND TERTIARY SYSTEMS.

Perhaps there is no question of greater interest connected with western geology, nor one which has attracted more attention of late years, than the determination of the upper limit of the Cretaceous deposits. The beds of this age are usually found to be so distinct from the Jurassic strata that it is seldom very difficult to define the boundary between these two formations, but there is an important group lying between the known Cretaceous and the undoubted Tertiary rocks, the age of which has not yet been conclusively settled. Some geologists, with much apparent reason, are disposed to regard the majority of these intermediate beds as Tertiary, while perhaps a larger number are of the opinion that the weight of evidence thus far obtained places them more properly within the limits of the Cretaceous system, and not a few, taking a middle view, favor the idea that they are largely transitional in character. The opportunities afforded for the collection of facts bearing directly upon this question were not many during our trip, as the route followed was not such as to offer good outcrops of the beds under discussion. No opportunity has since occurred for the elaboration of any of the material which might throw light upon the subject, and it will therefore be necessary in this place to pass it by with much less notice than it deserves. Leaving the matter for some further consideration at the close of the chapter we will now proceed to a review of the Cretaceous beds, as far as full evidence exists of their true age.

CRETACEOUS STRATA.

As a rule, the Jurassic beds are conformably overlaid by the members of the Cretaceous series, and the distribution of both formations is, in the main, identical east of the Wahsatch chain, although the Cretaceous system is made up of several more local groups. In the Wind River Valley the beds overlying the Jurassic strata are exposed in much the same manner, but there are fewer good outcrops, owing to the more extensive covering of the Cretaceous by the Tertiary rocks, in the neighborhood of the Wind River Mountains, and to the greater erosion of the Cretaceous beds when they occur in the uncovered folds. North of the Owl Creek range it is probable that these strata are favorably exposed for study over a wide district, but in many places they have been so much folded and eroded that their stratigraphical relations to the adjacent formations cannot be satisfactorily worked out in a single trip across the country. Sufficient evidence was obtained, however, to show that there is no want of conformity between the Jurassic and the Cretaceous within a considerable distance of our trail. About half-way between Pacific Creek and Lava Creek the trail crosses the deep gorge of a small stream, where some of the Cretaceous beds are to be seen dipping southwest 57°, and in the cañon of Buffalo Fork, just below Camp 56, similar beds, with additional members, are found dipping in the opposite direction 89°. Between these points no Cretaceous exposures were noticed, but, judging from the dips of the lower sedimentary strata, which were observed on Lava Creek between Camps 55 and 56, there must be one or more folds intervening.

The lithological characters of the included members are almost as variable as possible, with intimate mixtures of arenaceous, argillaceous, and calcareous ingredients, in different proportions. There are very few beds of limestone, and such are always very thin, but there are some shaly layers, and even occasional beds of clay, though the formation, as a whole, would best be designated as an argillo-arenaceous group. Some of the shales, as well as many of the sandstones, are highly ferruginous, while other layers are quite free from the presence of iron. Much of the ferric oxide can be traced directly to the plant-remains which abound in parts of the group, but a large portion is undoubtedly due to the decomposition of pyrites. Passing up through a thick series of strata, with the arenaceous material somewhat gradually increasing in proportion, several beds of lignite, or impure bituminous coal, are reached, which are well exposed for working in many places. More will be said of their economic value in another chapter, but it may be mentioned here that the beds are of considerable thickness, and that they contain much sulphur and ferric oxide, besides a notable quantity of gypsum, all resulting very largely from the decomposition of iron pyrites, which is abundant in the coal. Beautiful grains or drops of amber, usually not larger than a pea, are also rather common, and, rarely, a short piece of the stem of a plant, several inches in circumference, will be found so completely carbonized as to approach somewhat closely to anthracite. These lignite beds are usually separated by several feet of soft sandstone, frequently of a yellow color, and they are directly underlaid by a peculiar hardened clay, or soft, clayey shale, to which it is, as it were, cemented, the lignite becoming browner below, and running into the shale almost gradually.

Three of these coaly layers are exposed upon the northeastern flank of the Wind River Mountains, and what appear to be the same beds can be traced by numerous exposures across the country to the southern flank of the Owl Creek range, while, perhaps, similar outcrops over the area beyond, as far as the Stinking Water Cañon, North Fork, may not be improperly referred to the same horizon. There is more or less of variation in character and quality over this district.

These lower lignitiferous seams are generally included in the Cretaceous groups by those who have studied them, whatever may be their views concerning the age of the doubtful beds which occur higher in the series; and this conclusion seems supported by the paleontological evidence. In the Wind River region, as well as over the district traversed in 1873, north of the Owl Creek range and east of the Sierra Shoshone, the great bulk of the Cretaceous formation appears to lie below the lignite beds, and it is supposable that the whole group, as there exposed, was deposited before the changes took place which resulted in the deposition of the strata of doubtful age.

Organic contents.—It will be impossible now to give even the genera of the distinctively Cretaceous fossils, but this lack will be less felt from the fact that Hayden long ago gathered evidence that the Wind River Valley deposits underlying the horizontal Tertiary strata are mainly of Cretaceous age. The remains of marine life are of Cretaceous types, and there is, as yet, little or no evidence of a great thickness of uncertain beds of brackish or fresh water origin. Still it must be confessed that this formation has been, at the best, but hastily examined, and changes in the character of the beds above appear to begin toward the head of Wind River, and to increase in importance westward. Near Gray Bull River some interesting plant-remains, mostly leaves of angiosperms, were obtained, and some very fine leaves in shale were obtained near the top of the section exposed upon the left bank of the cañon of North Fork of Owl Creek. The latter resemble so closely in character and position, and in the nature of the rock, some very good specimens collected in a bluff upon the left bank of Wind River, a short distance below Camp 58, that there can be little doubt that they are from the same horizon. In both cases I am disposed to regard them as Cretaceous, though the dip of the beds is much less than that of many of the underlying rocks. At any rate, the overlying Tertiary beds in the Wind River Valley are horizontal, or nearly so, and unconformable to these beds, while it is impossible to draw a similar line of unconformability between any two of the lower formations, although some of the beds dip much more than the plant-layers. The same relative arrangement of the principal formations was also observed north of the Owl Creek Mountains, where there are variations in degree but not in the order of superposition.

The outcrop before mentioned, which is exposed in the cañon of Buffalo Fork, affords a fine section of arenaceous and carbonaceous strata, with abundant remains of plant and animal life, which seem to bear affinities to Cretaceous types. These will be more fully discussed in connection with the remarks upon the age of the doubtful lignite group.

TERTIARY DEPOSITS.

Passing over the debatable ground for the present, we find that sufficient land had appeared above the sea at the close of the era of the lignite deposition for the existence of extensive fresh-water lakes over much of the Rocky Mountain region. Some of the lake-basins far exceeded in area the largest of modern depressions containing fresh water, and in them were deposited immense quantities of the detritus brought in by the streams from the surrounding country. This process in some places continued until the sedimentary material had accumulated in the bottom of the lakes to a thickness of hundreds, and even thousands, of feet. The important chapters of the earth's history, in which the records of these events are minutely recorded and profusely illustrated, might have remained a sealed volume had not the later history of our globe required for its records the waste of what had been built up during the long Tertiary period. As it is, the draining of most of the old Tertiary lake-basins has been accompanied with erosion upon a scale so vast that it is often possible to obtain a nearly complete section of these enormous accumulations by merely passing across the basin in which they were deposited. A very few years since it was scarcely believed that the Tertiary deposits of our country were capable of yielding as rich a harvest as had been reaped from beds of this age in Europe, but it is now ascertained that they are not surpassed in interest or prospective importance by any known group of strata in the world. To one at all familiar with the general geology of the United States it is only necessary to mention the names of Newberry, Lesquereux, Marsh, Leidy, Cope, and Meek to call to mind the rich results already obtained by the careful study of specimens collected from this horizon in the West. One of the most remarkable sections, the favorite field of several of the most experienced collectors, is situated in a portion of the territory embraced by our reconnaissance, and it therefore claims a share of our attention.

The greater portion of the Green River Basin, (as defined in Chapter II,) is now occupied by fresh-water deposits of the Tertiary period. A section of these beds from top to bottom will, however, include a considerable thickness of the lignite formation. Excluding this from the review, we shall have to consider here only that part of the series which is exposed in the vicinity of the road traveled between the Uintah Mountains and South Pass.

EOCENE STRATA.

In view of the discrepancies found to exist between supposed synchronous strata in different parts of the world, the plan of employing local names to designate the various epochs and periods represented in the United States, has wisely been adopted by field geologists. Strangely enough, however, the evident advantages arising from this method when applied to the Paleozoic rocks have been overlooked in the classification of the later formations, so that our Tertiary nomenclature is now encumbered with terms which are even less appropriate than would be the names, "Lingula Flags," "Llandeilo Flags," and "Wenlock Beds," applied to American Silurian strata of the same adjudged horizons. The terms *Eocene*, *Miocene*, and *Pliocene*, are particularly objectionable in American geology, and it must be distinctly understood that they have no more literal significance at present in the West than does the term *Triassic* when applied to the formation succeeding the Permian.

There has been some doubt concerning the proper disposition of the beds overlying the lignite or coal group, which were referred to the Middle Tertiary (Miocene) by Hayden in his report for the year 1870. This reference was largely based upon the supposd Eocene age of the coal-formation of the Green River Basin. Dr. Newberry, after examining a very few of the fossil plants from near Green River station, remarked that they hinted of an earlier period than the Lower Miocene. Professor Cope pronounced the age of the Green River fishes to be more likely Eocene, and during the same year (1870) that Hayden crossed the basin, Prof. O. C. Marsh determined to his own satisfaction that some still higher beds are Eocene, since which time he has two or three times visited the locality (Grizzly Buttes) and obtained more evidence. Professors Leidy and Cope, who have also collected and described numerous vertebrate remains from this section, regard them as Eocene. The weight of authority thus seems to favor their reference to the Lower Tertiary. My own conclusions, somewhat tardily adopted, were partially formed in the field, but have not heretofore been advocated for want of decisive proof. I can now express more confidently the opinion that these beds are of Eocene or Lower Tertiary age, although the paleontological evidence which I have collected is less satisfactory on account of the fresh-water type of the invertebrate remains, than would be the case were there more vertebrate forms. The collections have not yet been carefully examined, and it is therefore impossible to speak of them in detail.

Hayden has provisionally divided the beds comprising this remarkable formation into two groups, which may be conveniently recognized in the present state of our knowledge concerning them, though no definite line of separation can be drawn between them.

GREEN RIVER GROUP.—(Lower? Eocene.)

This name is at present used to designate that portion of the fresh-water Tertiary strata which lies directly above the coal group, and which is the present surface formation over a large portion of the Green River Basin north of Fort Bridger. If it be true that the coal-beds are of Eocene age, this group holds a position which will entitle it to be ranked as Middle Eocene, but if, as many believe, the former group be really Cretaceous, these beds may be considered Lower Eocene, there being in this case no Middle Eocene, unless it shall be found that the whole series is made up of three well-marked groups, which does not now seem probable, to say the least.

The upper limit of the Green River group is not readily definable at present, the transition between the beds of this and the overlying group being rather gradual, but the general character of the two formations, both lithologically and paleontologically, differs greatly. The Green River beds are mainly composed of a series of shales, marls, and harder calcareous strata, the latter, especially, containing quantities of the remains of fresh-water forms of life, with laminated layers literally filled with the remains of land-plants of the Phænogamous series. The famous "petrified-fish beds," so well exposed near Green River station, Union Pacific Railroad, belong to this group.

The outline of the ancient lake-basin in which these strata were deposited is not fully determined, but there are indications that its eastern boundary was outside of the present limits of the Green River Basin, and there is no room for doubt that the Uintah Mountains and the Wahsatch chain then, as now, towered above its surface. Northward it is equally clear that the Wind River range formed the shore of the great lake, with probably more or less of gently sloping border during a portion of the era of Lower Eocene deposition. This formation is now exposed over our route from Fort Bridger to near South Pass, the excessive erosion over this area causing the rocks to be laid bare in most places, so as to afford favorable opportunities for study, but they do not yield as plentifully the interesting remains which are characteristic of these beds in the neighborhood of Green River City, though it is highly probable that rich harvests will hereafter be reaped by collectors who may be able to examine the outcrops with some degree of thoroughness.

Generally speaking, the rock contains a considerable portion of calcic carbonate, with an abundance of ferric oxide produced by decomposition and oxidation. *Gypsum* and *calcite* of different varieties are abundant, frequently occurring as thin, papery seams between the rock-layers, at other times forming masses of considerable extent. These features are scarcely as characteristic of this formation, however, as of the Bridger group. Some of the layers are little more than a pure clay shale, while there are a few quite arenaceous beds and some compact limestones. The mineral peculiarities are so generally the result of chemical and other changes in the rocks of a secondary nature, that they will be more properly considered in that part of the report which treats of the action of atmospheric agencies, under the general head of dynamical geology. The texture of the different beds is quite variable, but, in general, the streams which have cut their channels through them are walled by nearly vertical cliffs, and the buttes and benches for the most part have quite precipitous sides. Numerous joints occur in many of the strata, particularly in the more compact kinds, and fine examples of concretionary structure or weathering are not rare. The tendency of the thick beds of marly sandstone on the banks of Green River, at the crossing, to weather spheroidally is very noticeable, and this is repeated in various degrees in the argillaceous and calcareous rocks as well.

Organic contents.—In the absence of adequate knowledge of the affinities of the fossil-plants collected, it is impossible to state with certainty their bearing upon the age of the beds now under consideration. Indeed, after the abundant material of this nature which has passed through the hands of Dr. Newberry and Professor Lesquereux, it is scarcely probable that the meager collections made by myself in 1873 will furnish cause for the changing of opinions so strongly held by these vegetable-paleontologists. Some remarks regarding the manner of occurrence of these remains will, nevertheless, not be out of place. The finest specimens were obtained from an exposure in a bluff just below the stage-station at First Crossing, Big Sandy, on the left bank of the river, near the top of the bluff. A few good specimens were obtained from a cliff upon the left bank of Green River, about one mile and a half below the crossing at Robinson's Ferry. Outcrops of plant-beds at other localities were not rare, but the remains were seldom as well preserved as in these places. The rock containing these is usually a very fine-grained white or yellowish shale, often more or less ferruginous. The leaves, the most common form in which the relics exist, are mostly spread out smoothly, giving most perfect impressions of the ribs and veins, making their identification a matter of comparatively little difficulty. In some places the plant-layers are composed of comminuted fragments of leaves and other vegetable matter crowded together in an indefinable mass, and again mere bits of water-worn pieces were scattered thinly over the shale, seldom sufficiently distinct for determination, while even more frequently the shales are traversed by irony streaks of ferric oxide, without a trace of the original vegetable tissue.

The animal remains gathered during the summer of 1873 are mostly well preserved, consisting mainly of Lamellibranchs and Gasteropods, of the genera *Unio*, *Corbicula?* *Melania*, *Viviparus*, and *Turritella?* with possibly others, including, perhaps, some undescribed specific forms. In a bluff on the right bank of Ham's Fork, less than half a mile below the old toll-bridge at the main crossing, a bed remarkably rich in *Unio*, associated with immense quantities of *Viviparus*, occurs, half way to the top, directly above the stream. Directly opposite Camp 3, on Muddy Fork, a few feet above the water, there is a bed almost completely made up of Gasteropods—*Melania*, *Vivipara*, and *Turritella?* This is but a few rods north of the Union Pacific Railroad. A somewhat similar

Gasteropod bed underlies a thinner layer, apparently almost wholly made up of *Cypris* remains, which is exposed on the left bank of Black's Fork, a few rods below the lower bridge across that stream at Fort Bridger. This exposure is near the point at which the telegraph-line to Carter crosses the creek. Back in the cliffs, on the right bank of Green River, nearly south from Camp 6, (three miles above Robinson's Ferry,) in a thin calcareous shale partially saturated with *petroleum*, I obtained a single specimen of the vertebra of a fish. This bed is probably of the same horizon as the petroleum beds not far from Green River station.

In the present state of geological science, there are few who will not acknowledge that vertebrate remains are a better criterion of the age of a formation than fresh-water molluscs, or the leaves of plants. No one doubts that the beds of the Green River group are Tertiary; and more recent beds, with abundant remains of the higher vertebrates, being referred to the Eocene by the best authorities, it will be seen that the reference of the Green River strata to the Lower or Middle Eocene is tolerably well founded. This classification receives additional support from the statement of Prof. E. D. Cope, before given, concerning the affinities of the fossil fishes collected from this formation near Green River City.

BRIDGER GROUP.—(Upper Eocene.)

The beds overlying those of the Green River group are closely related to them in age, for the transition from one to the other is not abrupt, whether we regard their structure or their contents. All who have had occasion to study the features of both groups, in the field or the closet, have agreed in this, that they have regarded them as representatives of a single Tertiary epoch, the point of controversy being only the question whether they together represent the Eocene or the Miocene era. After all, it will be found that the whole difficulty originated mainly in the doubt concerning the true age of the coal group beneath, the settlement of which seems just now to be the chief desideratum of American geology. Hayden provisionally referred the Bridger group to the period of the Upper Miocene, which must have been proper had the Green River group proven to be of Lower Miocene age, as he at first supposed. Those who hold to the Eocene age of the lower strata will, therefore, also be unanimous in the avowal of the Upper Eocene age of the members of the Bridger group.

This formation is exposed at the surface over a considerable extent of country, northward and eastward from Fort Bridger as far as Little Sandy River and beyond, forming the top layers of numerous isolated buttes. Along our route they are nearly horizontal or dip very slightly. Perhaps the most instructive section observed on the trip, south of South Pass, is in the vicinity of the Uintah Mountains, where the beds of the Bridger group may be seen in their connection with the tilted strata of earlier date. Figure 5 gives a general view of the structure of the country lying between Fort Bridger and the Uintah Mountains although it does not strictly represent a section in a direct line between the post and Gilbert's Peak, but, more properly, it is a representation of the principal facts with the surface features exaggerated, but mainly correct, as far as the cañon of Henry's Fork. Gilbert's Peak is then included to show its geological relations, although it is really out of the line of the section.

During the epoch of the Bridger group, it is probable that the land was covered with fresh water in a lake as large as in the previous era, if not more extensive. It may have been that the northern shore was farther south than during the time when the Green River beds were deposited, but the mere fact that few of the Bridger strata now cover the

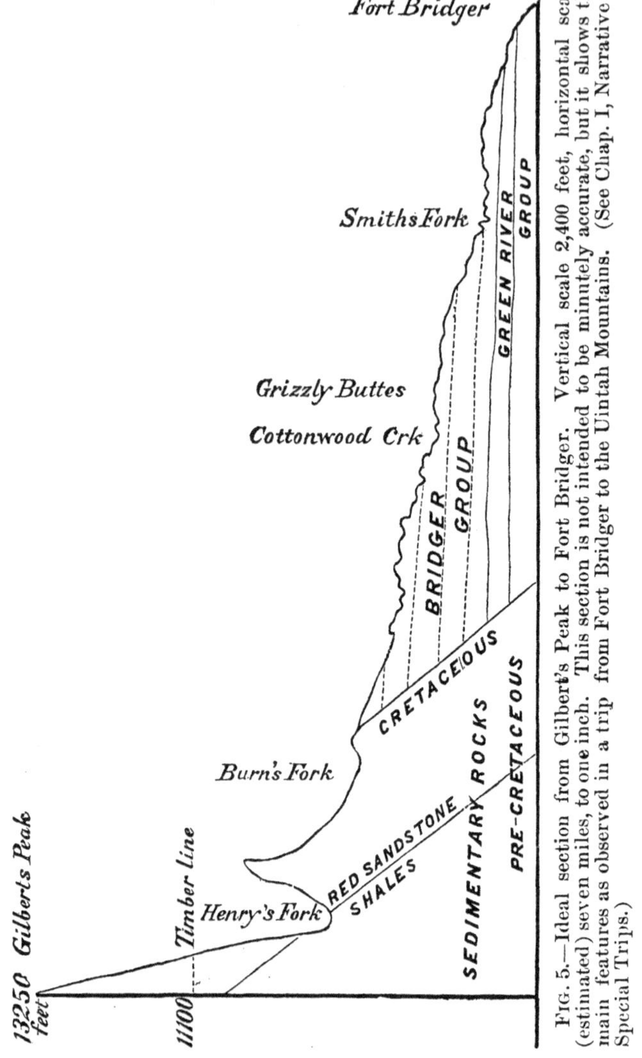

FIG. 5.—Ideal section from Gilbert's Peak to Fort Bridger. Vertical scale 2,400 feet, horizontal scale (estimated) seven miles, to one inch. This section is not intended to be minutely accurate, but it shows the main features as observed in a trip from Fort Bridger to the Uintah Mountains. (See Chap. I, Narrative of Special Trips.)

underlying group north of the Little Sandy, on our road, does not afford sufficient proof of this. There is, doubtless, much yet to be learned from the field study of that section of the Green River Basin, as yet unexplored geologically, which lies north of the forty-second parallel and west of longitude 109° 30′. It may, however, be safely stated that the lake of this epoch did not extend across the divide of the Wind River Mountains. There is also no doubt that the Uintah Mountains formed a portion of the southern boundary, though Professor Marsh discovered evidence of a synchronous basin south of this range, which, having been much lower, may have received the outflow from the ancient Bridger Lake, though he remarks that the outlet was not through the present channel of Green River. If the Washakie group of Hayden, east of the present continental divide, be synchronous, and *continuous* with the Bridger group, the eastern boundary of the basin in which both were accumulated was far outside of the present Green River Basin, but this supposition is little more than a surmise thus far. The western limit could not have been beyond the Wahsatch higher ridges, for reasons which will be obvious to those who read the remarks upon the age of that chain, in the section treating of the subject of the elevation of mountains.

The beds of the Bridger group, as a whole, are readily distinguishable from those of the Green River group, being mainly composed of dull-colored indurated clays, and arenaceous layers of considerable thickness, the latter usually brownish, or dull yellow or gray, often with more or less of a concretionary structure. The clays are generally compacted, but they become disintegrated upon exposure to the atmosphere, and readily yield to the eroding forces. Some thinner layers of more calcareous material, with siliceous seams often affording interesting concretions, are interspersed, but they are rather exceptional than otherwise. These two groups of strata may also be readily distinguished wherever seen by the great difference in the effects produced by erosion in each case. As before remarked it is the tendency of the beds of the lower series to present nearly vertical cliffs, so that the general impression received in passing across the section in which they compose the surface formation is that of traveling over an ordinary plain with occasional descents by a succession of terraces to the narrow valleys of the streams; on the contrary, the topography of the country wherever the Green River beds are concealed or only occasionally capped by the members of the Bridger group, is very irregular, often simulating that peculiar aspect which has received the appropriate name of "bad lands" in other regions. In some places at a distance from the mountains, as in the neighborhood of Church Buttes, and between that point and Bryan along the Union Pacific Railroad, the beds of this formation have been so eroded without complete denudation, that they now stand out in buttes by themselves, often with some slight resemblance to rude architectural forms. The now famous "Grizzly Buttes" southeast of Fort Bridger belong to the Bridger group, and in that section the same essential features are observable, but the buttes are much more crowded, and seldom so completely isolated as are those farther northward. This intensely interesting subject will receive more attention in another chapter. (See Erosion.)

The mineral characteristics of these Upper Eocene beds are generally similar to those of the Lower group, but they are exhibited upon a much larger scale, which may no doubt be mostly accounted for in the more extensive erosion to which the Bridger group has been subjected, especially as there are numerous indications of changes of a secondary nature. The subject can be more appropriately discussed beyond, (see Chemical Geology,) but a brief review of the more common mineral forms will be now given. Gypsum, in the forms of *selenite*, *satin-spar*, and, more rarely, as *alabaster*, is very common. One of the most striking features of many of the buttes is the silvery, glistening appearance which they present in the clear light of the sun, giving them at a little distance a very pleasing aspect. Closer investigation shows that this is produced by the reflection from enormous quantities of bits of *selenite* which lie strewn over the surface of the slopes. When found *in situ* it usually occurs in thin layers between more extensive beds of other material, or in masses, the fibrous forms not unfrequently being rather geodiferous in their formation. Joints and planes of loose lamination are commonly filled with *selenite*, or even with gypsum in the form of small crystals, which are often ferruginous, or coated with ferric oxide. *Calcite* is abundant in several crystalline varieties, or *calc-spar*, also in other interesting forms, occurring in similar manners to the gypsum, of which it occasionally appears to be a pseudomorph. The presence of iron in considerable quantity is shown by the reddish color imparted to many of the rocks upon weathering, also by the accumulations of ferric oxide in the crevices, and in connection with imperfect organic impressions. *Pyrites* is probably commonly distributed, though scarcely ever obtained in distinct crystals. Silica, in its remarkable development in these rocks, constitutes one of the most interesting subjects which claim the attention of the chemical geologist in this section. Saline efflorescence, and the connection of the so-called "alkali" deposits with much of the history of the region, are topics which naturally fall within the imits of another portion of this report, where they will be further treated.

Organic contents.—The scientific public, at least, are already familiar with the great results which have accrued from the studies made by our vertebrate-paleontologists of the remains which have been obtained in such great abundance from the beds of the Bridger group, more especially from the vicinity of the Grizzly Buttes. The organic remains which I have myself obtained from these strata are not numerous, but they were obtained from new localities, as a rule, and may embrace one or two new specific forms, though this is quite doubtful. From a ruggedly weathered exposure of loosely compacted sandstones and conglomerates, with some harder beds of white and slightly red sandstones, half a mile northeast of Camp 10, on Little Sandy River, some poorly preserved specimens of gasteropods (*Melania?*) were collected, with numerous small fragments of turtles, which were found partially imbedded in the soil upon a small raised flat. At the foot of a prominent butte standing entirely alone near Soublette's road, three miles or more back from Camp 10, across the Big Sandy, a fragment of a costal plate of the carapace of a *Trionyx* was obtained from about the same horizon. B. D. Smith, one of our guides, who had collected for Professor Marsh, brought from a locality above Camp 10, on the Little Sandy, at nearly the same level, a caudal vertebra of a crocodile, a portion of the ilium of a turtle, and the proximal extremity of the left humerus of a turtle. Much higher in the series specimens of *Planorbis* were collected from a bluff exposure at the foot of the Uintah Mountains west of the Grizzly Buttes. It was possible only to collect from these beds, in the most superficial manner, but enough was observed to convince the writer that a richer harvest than has yet been reaped awaits the future collectors in this field.

CONCERNING THE AGE OF THE WIND RIVER TERTIARY DEPOSITS AND SOME OTHERS.

During one or more of the long Tertiary epochs, there was deposited over the space included between the Wind River and Owl Creek ranges, a lacustrine formation of great thickness, composed of beds of arenaceous and argillaceous material. The general character of the strata is, on the whole, more like that of the Bridger group than that of the Green River beds, and yet the formation cannot be said to closely resemble the former, nor would such a similarity between the two series in lithological features furnish, in itself, the least proof of identity of age. The sandy marls of the Wind River deposits are frequently variegated, *i. e.*, bands of a bright red or a pinkish color are associated with the blue, greenish, and light-colored beds of this material. But few fossils have ever been obtained from this formation, and it will be wise to make no definite statement regarding its age until it has been more carefully studied. The whole group lies in a nearly horizontal position, and the erosion has been so extensive that the beds are well exposed for observation, provided one can regulate his course so as to seek the most favorable localities; hence it may be hoped that the future development of this region may greatly add to our knowledge concerning them.

The arenaceous nature of most of the strata, and the oblique lamination of the sandstones and conglomerates, prove that they were deposited in quite shallow water; and these facts will account for much of the lack of organic remains. The thick deposits, on the other hand, of more alluvial material, would suggest the probability of the preservation of some vertebrate remains. Hayden has reported the discovery of fragments of the skeletons of *Trionyx* and *Testudo*, but diligent search along our route was unrewarded by the sight of a single bone of any kind. It is proper to mention here that a more definite statement concerning these beds, published elsewhere,* was based upon the supposition that some underlying beds, now believed to be Cretaceous, were of Tertiary age.

In the same unsettled state must be left the Tertiary beds which are exposed north of the Owl Creek Mountains, of small extent at present, but in many respects resembling the Wind River deposits. There is here, however, stronger proof that these are of later than Eocene date, and it may be suggested that the Wind River deposits may prove to have been laid down nearly simultaneously, but certainly in a separate basin.

In all of these beds there is an absence of the great deposits of *gypsum* and *calcite*, as would be readily supposed from their arenaceous character. The topography, also, is different, from a similar cause, although the erosion has been great, and interesting forms have been produced.

PLIOCENE DEPOSITS.

In the neighborhood of South Pass, extending across the water-shed, is a deposit which apparently represents the closing scenes of the lake period in the Green River Basin. It would seem that during the Miocene epoch, or near its close, while, perhaps, extensive but shallow lakes existed in the Wind River Valley, a portion of the Sweetwater Valley, and north of the Owl Creek range, the waters upon the western slope of the Rocky Mountains had so far been drained off as to allow of partial denudation of the old lake-bottom. During the next epoch (Pliocene) a shallow lake spread over the northeastern portion of the Green River Basin across the outlying metamorphic ridges, and connecting with a body of fresh water which more or less covered the area occupied by the Miocene (?) lake of the Sweetwater Valley. Figures 6, 7, and 8 are intended to explain this idea, without giving the slopes, elevations, or distances with any degree of accuracy.

It should be understood that the Pliocene deposits are represented as if local, merely because their boundaries are not known positively. In these deposits in the Sweetwater Basin, Dr. Hayden has obtained fos-

* In a paper "On the Geology of Western Wyoming," in Amer. Jour. Sci., vol. vi, December, 1873.

sils which show close relation to those of the Niobrara River beds of Pliocene age. On the left bank of Little Popo-Agie River, some distance below the entrance of Deep Creek from the right bank, there is a similar deposit of marls and laminated sandstones and conglomerates to that near South Pass, which may be of Pliocene age. The South Pass beds, as shown in Fig. 8, cross the outer portion of the metamorphic rocks, and some of the beds contain pebbles from those beds of the mountain nucleus.

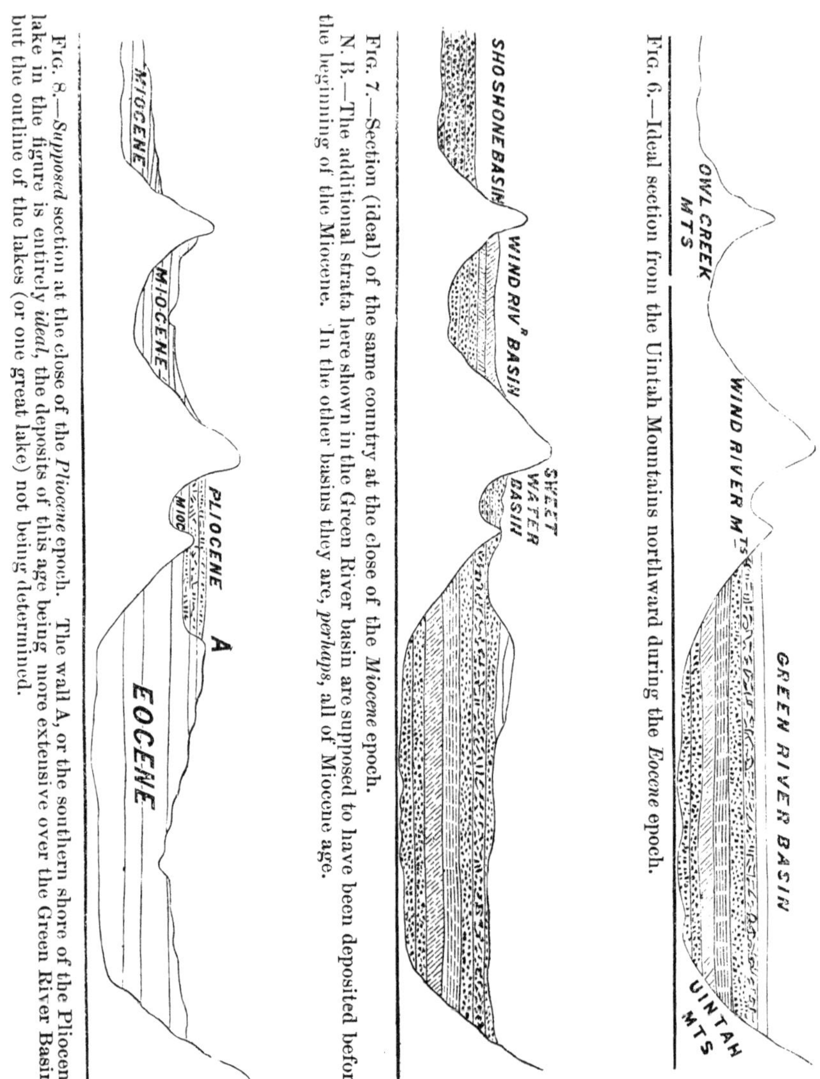

Fig. 6.—Ideal section from the Uintah Mountains northward during the *Eocene* epoch.

Fig. 7.—Section (ideal) of the same country at the close of the *Miocene* epoch.
N. B.—The additional strata here shown in the Green River basin are supposed to have been deposited before the beginning of the Miocene. In the other basins they are, *perhaps*, all of Miocene age.

Fig. 8.—*Supposed* section at the close of the *Pliocene* epoch. The wall A, or the southern shore of the Pliocene lake in the figure is entirely *ideal*, the deposits of this age being more extensive over the Green River Basin, but the outline of the lakes (or one great lake) not being determined.

The deposits in the Yellowstone Lake Basin and in the valley of the main river and its tributaries, which may be regarded as Pliocene, are mainly the sediments of an ancient lake, of which the present body of water is the representative on a much reduced scale. Beautiful and highly instructive sections of the old beach formations are exposed in the valleys of the streams, particularly in the lower valley of Pelican Creek, and far down the Yellowstone River, where they become more complicated, but on that account all the more interesting. An examination of these shows that the lake formerly extended over a much larger area, and that it has held its place amid changes of great importance. It is impossible for the most enthusiastic and imaginative person to go beyond the truth in the description of the remarkable events which are here recorded in this one page, as it were, of the world's history; but this is but the beginning of the end, for the mind, even of the careful observer, fails to grasp in its entirety the vastness of the variety which is here displayed.

It was during the later portion of the Tertiary age that much of the volcanic activity took place which was so general over this portion of the country, though probably only the closing stages of the lava flows are represented by the eruptive deposits of the Pliocene epoch. As it will be necessary to speak somewhat in detail of the history of those accumulations in a section specially devoted to the subject of volcanic action, a mere *résumé* of the deposits of Pliocene age will here be presented. A section of the lake sediments, taken on the present lake-shore, between Bluff Point and Steam Point, is as follows in descending order:

1. Grass-covered soil passing gradually to loose sand, 2 feet.
2. Various sand, gravel, and spring deposits, with scattered irony concretions, 6 feet.
3. White and dark lake sand, very thinly laminated, with beach structure, and occasional irony layers, 5 feet.
4. About 15 feet of thinly laminated, blue-black clay, locally contorted and beautifully cut by a small rill emanating as a spring from one of the irony layers in No. 3. The water is slightly chalybeate.

Other sections in this vicinity show the same general features with more or less of variation. They represent the upper portion of the Pliocene series, deposited toward the close of the era of volcanic activity, hence the occasional beds of volcanic ejectamenta which were poured out into the lake are mainly composed of volcanic sand and the finer textured conglomerates, as may well be seen near Steamboat Springs. As we descend the valley of the Yellowstone River we find the lower members of the group well exposed and the beds of unmodified* non-molten material becoming more common, with increasing proportions of the molten or lava series, until the latter are almost universal, and doubtless represent an earlier period, though frequently largely concealed by the subsequent spring deposits. Near the close of the Pliocene epoch the internal fires had so far died out that the igneous ejections were of fitful occurrence, and geysers, solfataras, fumaroles, &c., abounded to an almost incredible extent, giving rise to enormous deposits of siliceous and calcareous material, which has continued to be deposited with decreasing vigor until the present day. From the nature of the circumstances under which these rocks were deposited but few fossils will be expected, and yet there are some interesting facts which lead to the belief that not a few organic remains now entombed in these strata are really the relics of the Pliocene epoch and not of an earlier date. For a more complete elaboration of this and other subjects of great interest connected with this group the reader is referred to the dynamical portion of this report.

---

* The term *modified* will be a convenient one to apply (as in the case of drift deposits) to those lake or stream deposits which have been re-arranged by aqueous action, after having been deposited in beds by eruption from volcanoes. *Unmodified* in this sense applies to beds of volcanic sand and ashes thrown out into a lake without subsequent re-arrangement.

CONCERNING THE AGE OF THE COAL OR LIGNITE GROUP.

It is not pretended that the true horizon of the contested coal series is to be settled by the scraps of evidence which are now brought together, nor is it probable that the little that the author can present in the shape of newly obtained facts, will materially aid in promoting a decision of the mooted question. The least that can be done, however, is to place on record the field-notes of the writer, as far as they may bear upon the subject, and to show the grounds upon which they have been referred to the Cretaceous epoch in this report. It would be presumptuous to attempt, from so few opportunities of observation, to solve a problem

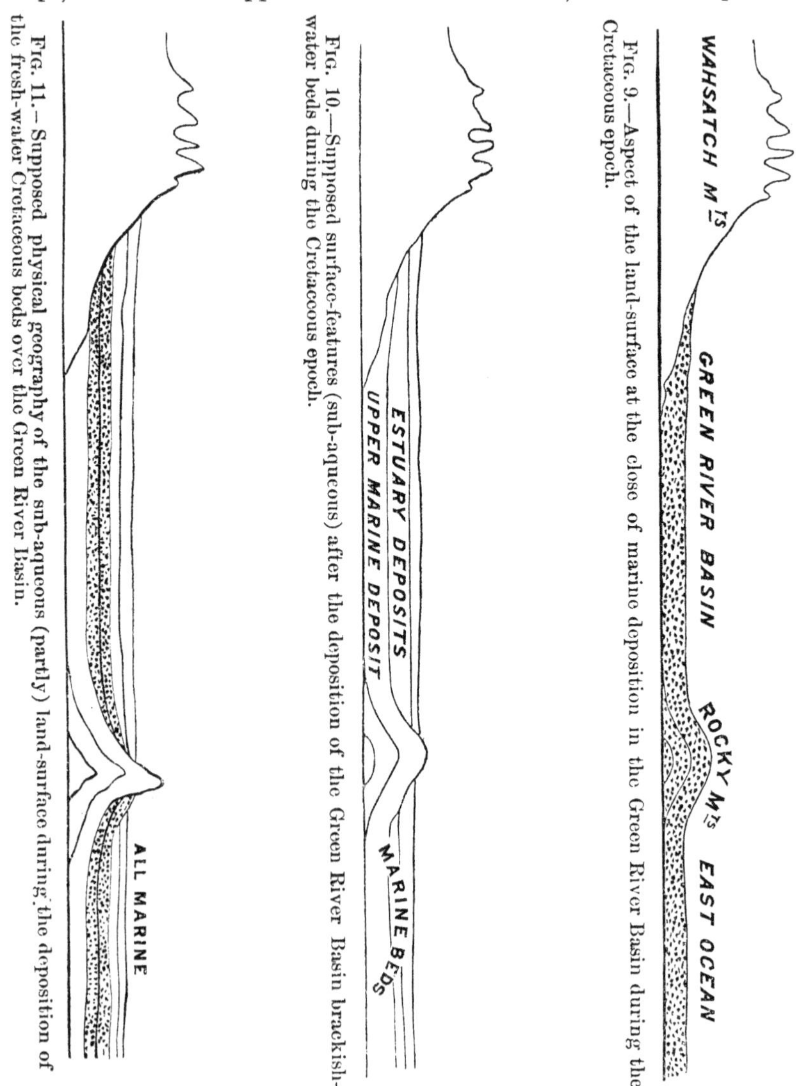

Fig. 9.—Aspect of the land-surface at the close of marine deposition in the Green River Basin during the Cretaceous epoch.

Fig. 10.—Supposed surface-features (sub-aqueous) after the deposition of the Green River Basin brackish-water beds during the Cretaceous epoch.

Fig. 11.—Supposed physical geography of the sub-aqueous (partly) land-surface during the deposition of the fresh-water Cretaceous beds over the Green River Basin.

which has received the thoughtful consideration of the ablest minds without satisfactory settlement. It will, therefore, not be expected that the question will be treated here, except with extreme brevity.

The investigations of Clarence King, in particular, have shown that the westward continuation of the known Tertiary strata of the Green River Basin is in a series of broad folds, and that the beds do not lie horizontally, as is the case farther east. It has also been determined that the Eocene series is there unconformable to the underlying coal group, while the latter rests conformably upon the rocks of undoubted Cretaceous age. Again, the formation of the coal was begun during the Cretaceous epoch, probably while the Rocky Mountains were slowly rising, and several lignite beds were deposited during the marine era. It is not difficult to believe that the elevation of a prominent chain in the eastern ocean, which then beat upon the flank of the Wahsatch, would gradually cut off the Green River Basin from free communication with the sea, causing it to be occupied by a brackish-water estuary, while marine deposits were still accumulating in the east; for it must be borne in mind that the Unitah Mountains then existed as a prominent range, as remarked by Clarence King. Continued gradual elevation would finally completely shut off the estuary basin from the ocean by raising it higher, when the liquid contents would gradually become fresh, provided that the outlet was not closed, as would probably be the case, the elevation being gradual. The three accompanying sections will show the idea more clearly, although some of the beds are necessarily represented as unconformable because it is impossible to show in a drawing the gradual nature of the upheaval. Subsequent to the deposition of the fresh-water beds here referred to the Cretaceous, the whole series was disturbed westward, and the Tertiaries were afterward unconformably deposited upon them. The question must at length be decided upon the evidence furnished by the organic remains, no doubt; but in the absence of conclusive evidence of this nature, it is not unreasonable to suppose that such marked physical changes as took place after the deposition of the fresh-water beds which underlie the Green River group, would have been unnaturally local if they had transpired between two of the fresh-water sub-epochs of the Tertiary period. It would certainly be difficult to account for the deposition of the estuary beds in the Green River Basin without the existence of a sea to the eastward at nearly the same level, and in view of all the facts thus far collected, to the writer at least, the belief that the coal-group is of Cretaceous date seems much less difficult to support than the opinion that the strata were formed during the Eocene epoch.

It is unnecessary to make more special mention of the coal-beds which, it has been previously observed, are exposed in the cañon ot Buffalo Fork of Snake River, for the foregoing remarks are largely based upon a study of that section, and no special features have been elicited from them.

CHAPTER V.

STRATIGAPHY, CONTINUED.

Post-Tertiary and recent Glacial and Champlain epochs—Terrace epoch.

From the numerous organic remains entombed in the strata of the Eocene epoch, we learn that the climate over a large portion of the Rocky Mountain region was tropical or subtropical; but the gradual elevation of the mountains to a considerable distance above the sea-level, with, perhaps, other causes now too little understood, produced also more or less gradual changes in the climatic conditions. Hence we find that the plants and other relics collected from the Miocene beds indicate a climate cooler than that of the Eocene epoch, though milder than that of the present day. This condition of things continued with little apparent change during the Pliocene epoch, or until near its close. In Eocene times there roamed over the western continental hills and plains vast numbers of peculiar mammals, and in the dense forests innumerable birds filled the air with sonorous notes, while reptiles of the most varied forms sought the darker recesses of the murky swamps, and fishes and molluscs in wonderful variety inhabited the great fresh-water lakes. Then was presented a scene in many respects similar to what may now be viewed in some of the more elevated portions of the tropics where lakes abound, but on a scale more vast than has ever been witnessed by human eyes. The "struggle for existence," ever more severe in tropical regions than in milder climes, resulted in the destruction of millions upon millions of individuals, the remains of which, as Dana remarks, are now coming to a new "existence" through the researches of our eminent paleontologists. Slowly but steadily the growing severity of the climate doubtless compelled the dominant forms to maintain their positions by successively more vigorous contests until they were finally compelled to seek the lower latitudes nearer the sea-level, and finally to succumb to their inevitable fate when the climate had reached the climax of severity, thus forcing them into a small area southward. Dr. Newberry (Hayden's Report on Wyoming, 1870, p. 337) has well suggested that exposure to such vicissitudes would have less effect upon some of the more hardy plants than with animals, on account of the smaller space required by the former for support; hence, as he concludes, the cause of the greater similarity of our flora than of our fauna to that of the Miocene epoch. The rise of the land continued during the Pliocene epoch, and the more elevated lakes were gradually drained, thus adding to the increasing rigor of the climate. There are probably few who will insist, after a careful study of the facts, that the period of extremely low temperature which undoubtedly succeeded the Pliocene epoch, was wholly the outcome of the mountain elevation. However this may be, this is not the place for discussing the influence of cosmical causes in bringing about the results which followed. We will, therefore, turn our attention directly to the main features of the deposits of the more modern periods, without here entering deeply into the subject of the forces employed in their accumulation.

POST-TERTIARY, OR QUATERNARY SYSTEM.

We have now reached a point in geological history beyond which it will be impossible to divide the separate formations into so many distinct and related groups, and we shall find, as we proceed, that we have entered upon the discussion of a series of events of a more modern character than those which have preceded, many of which still continue with diminished energy and effect. The close of the Pliocene epoch left the country in the neighborhood of the mountains in a partially exposed condition. During all the previous periods erosion had taken place upon a grand scale, but the material transported had been only removed to short distances from the mountain eminences, and it was then accumulated at their bases in such a manner as to add largely to the elevations of the surrounding plateaus. The streams were so small and so swollen at intervals by large lakes, not remarkably high above the level of the sea, that their erosive power was comparatively slight, except for short distances. It is probable that the lakes were fed by numerous small tributaries from all sides, rather than by one large inlet receiving the contributions of many branches.

The draining of the lake basins, and the elevation of the land, with the accompanying decrease of temperature, would increase the amount of erosion by giving greater slope to the surface, and by combining more extensively into river-systems the hitherto independent streams. This would also be facilitated by the precipitation of the moisture as snow in the place of rain, as before. Such, in brief, were the conditions at the close of the Pliocene epoch.

GLACIAL AND CHAMPLAIN EPOCHS.

Evidences are not rare in the west, north of the 41st parallel at least, of the former existence of a period during which there occurred the principal phenomena which have had such an important influence in shaping the surface-features eastward. However difficult it may be to fully account for the important climatic changes which succeeded the Tertiary period, there is now no reason to doubt that the Pleistocene, or Post-tertiary period, was opened by an epoch of frigidity with a climate similar to that of the subarctic regions at present. In seeking for the causes of such an apparent difference in temperature between these contiguous eras, it is necessary to bear in mind the fact that the cold of the glacial epoch was universal over the northern portion of our globe; hence it is unnecessary to suppose that that portion of the Rocky Mountain region lying south of the forty-fifth parallel was elevated much, if any, higher above the level of the sea than in the Pliocene epoch, for the extreme severity of the climate farther north would have had a chilling influence upon the temperature in the lower latitudes. Judging from the observations of others southward, it is concluded that the lower limit of the ancient glaciers of this age in the west was not far from its latitude in the east, *i. e.*, about 39° N., or in Colorado, near the latitude of Pike's Peak.

Inasmuch as the drift-deposits in many portions of the Rocky Mountain chain are often of comparatively small extent, and usually bear evidence of transport for short distances only, it would seem that the glaciers from which they came were more local in character than were those which then existed farther to the east. Dr. Hayden, whose opportunities of observation have been very extended, has repeatedly remarked in his reports that he has "never been able to find any evidence in the Rocky Mountain region of what is usually termed a northern drift."

There is, however, little doubt that the glacial deposits in this section are synchronous with those which exist in the east, and it is the opinion of the present author that the causes of the actual differences can mostly be explained. This will be rendered more plain as we proceed; but, first, it will be well to take a cursory glance at the deposits as they occur in Western Wyoming.

In passing southward from Fort Bridger toward the Uintah Mountains, the buttes are frequently found covered with small fragments of various rocks, which are quite firmly imbedded so as to resemble a variegated pavement. Many of them represent the more recent formations, being largely siliceous, and these may owe their present position to the action of water, or other causes, not entirely during the glacial period, which is probably the case when found upon the terraces of the streams.

Associated with these in many places, however, are undoubted drift-pebbles, composed of materials from the earlier strata, and deposits of the finer and coarser mixed gravels of considerable thickness are not infrequently exposed along the banks of the streams. The remarkable extent of the erosion over the Green River Basin, and its relations to the surrounding mountains, make it unsafe to generalize upon all the phenomena of the Drift period in this section, without extended observation of the facts; but it may be said that the features already mentioned rapidly increase in importance as the Uintah Mountains are approached, showing clearly that much of the material was transported from that direction. Much of the structure of the Uintah range, particularly near the line of junction between the tilted strata and the nearly horizontal Tertiary beds, is obscured by very thick deposits of drift-material, and the harder formations of the outlying ridges have been eroded into rounded hills by glacial agency, as is shown by the quantities of bowlders which are strewn over their summits and down their sides.

Northward from Fort Bridger the drift-deposits seem to thin out, and finally almost to disappear until pebbles of the metamorphic series begin to be seen beyond Green River, and they gradually increase in size and amount northward to South Pass, in the vicinity of which some of the rounded hills of Pliocene strata are covered with numerous heavy bowlders. One mile south of Dry Sandy Creek a bowlder thirty inches in diameter was observed lying over beds of probably Eocene age, though now well imbedded in the soil. The water-divide at South Pass is composed of Pliocene rocks, which were deposited in a lake which covered the upturned edges of the metamorphic group, and it is evident that the erosion of the valley of the Sweetwater, in at least a portion of its extent at this point, was accomplished during the glacial epoch, for the stream has since, in some places, cut its way through the drift-deposits. Over the district from South Pass to Camp Stambaugh, the erosion has been great, and numerous local valleys have been formed, many of which are now filled in with moraine-deposits, or occasionally with modified drift. Bowlders are scattered over the surface in many places, but they are, perhaps, less numerous than might be expected. Between South Pass City and Camp Stambaugh, particularly near Atlantic City, a very fine road has been laid out through the accumulations of the fine material, and over several quite large moraines.

Much drift, composed of quartz, quartzites, and a great variety of fragments of the metamorphic rocks, largely covers the slopes of the hills above Beaver Creek. The two forks of Twin Creek are separated by part of a moraine, jutting out from the hills in a direction nearly northeast, (N. 40° E.) Deep Creek Valley (Red Cañon, see Fig. 4,) was probably cut during this epoch, and it was then partially filled with the detritus of the Triassic brick-red sandstones, which was modified by the action of the water. Between the Little Popo-Agie and the North Fork of the Popo-Agie River erosion has been extensive, and heavy drift deposits occur. The same may be said of the country lying between North Fork and Camp Brown, where these features are noticeable on a larger scale. On the trip from Camp Brown to Chimney Rocks, described in Chapter I, the evidence of ancient glacial action was abundant. At intervals along the northeastern slope of the Wind River Mountains, the various streams emerge from the mountains through narrow cañons with nearly vertical walls hundreds of feet in height, but an examination of the country inside of the great ridge of limestone of the Carboniferous age shows that each of these cañons receives the accumulated waters of several prominent tributaries which rise in the mountain nucleus far to the northward or southward. Moreover, the higher points of the nucleus stand as islets hundreds and often thousands of feet above the sources of the streams at their base. Clearly, then, we have here complete proof of an amount of erosion since the elevation of the range which, without this evidence, would seem almost incredible. But this is but a small part of it, for there are in this section magnificent and extensive parks; long and high moraines, composed of huge granitic bowlders, stretch like vast walls across the way, with intervening lakes or ponds; scattered bowlders of other material, and immense blocks of the tougher sedimentary strata of Silurian age, are to be seen in the greatest profusion; yawning chasms many hundreds of feet in depth have been scooped out of the very summits of the highest ridges, and the numerous water-courses now follow channels which they could never have cut for themselves.

The deposits of the drift are in general abundant across the Wind River plateau, decreasing in amount toward the main stream until an increase is again apparent upon approaching the Owl Creek Mountains. Northward from Camp Brown the coarser bowlder ingredients are more common, and the streams which flow out from the Wind River range, including Bull Lake Fork, are often seen passing directly to the main river by continuous cañons, at right angles to the trend of the mountains. Such streams are usually bounded by heavy deposits of drift-bowlders, composed of granitic and metamorphic rocks from the nucleus of the Wind River range. Frequently these accumulations are found filling large hollows which had been previously eroded in the Tertiary and lower stratified rocks, and in one case the valley of Wind River has been cut for some distance through an extensive deposit of this nature. This is shown in Fig. 12, which represents a section across the main stream, between the mouths of North Fork and a smaller stream from the right bank a short distance above.

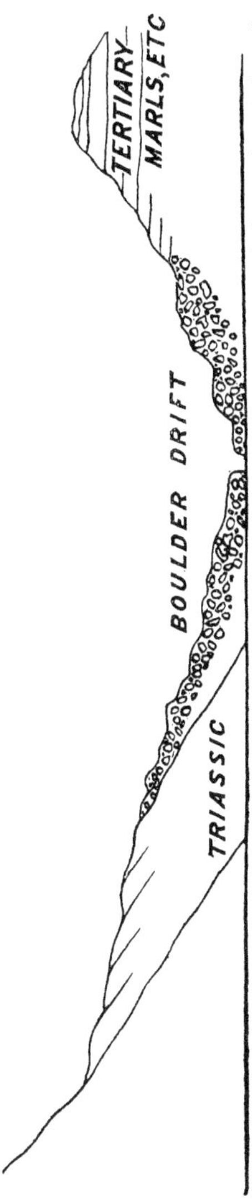

Fig. 12. Section across Wind River above the junction of North Fork. The outline of the surface below the bowlder drift is ideal. The formations lying between the Triassic and Tertiary systems are not exposed.

Passing up the Wind River Valley from this point the materials are found to become gradually finer, with occasional exposures along the river-banks of some modified drift. The materials also appear to change character somewhat, and to partake more of the nature of the volcanic rocks of the Sierra Shoshone.

To return to the Owl Creek range: The evidences of glacial action are not rare, and the erosion and deposits of this epoch have greatly added to the complications in the structure of the outlying ridges. It would appear that the greater effect has been produced upon the northern slope, although it is often much less rugged than upon the southern side. As good a place as could be desired for the study of the dynamics of the early Quaternary period is the region inclosed by the trail of our party during the two months' absence from Camp Brown. The remarkable cañon of the main stream of Owl Creek, far more deserving of the name of river than three-fourths of the larger streams of the district, now undoubtedly marks the course of a former glacier of great power, for the remains of the ancient drift-deposits are abundantly exposed in many places along its borders, where they have been cut through by the stream. The same may be said of many other channels originating in the Sierra Shoshone, and in lesser degree of nearly all the minor or secondary water-courses, but it is only when we pass across to the main upper tributaries of Snake River that we can form an adequate idea of the enormous amount of the material which must have been worn away during the glacial era. In numerous places between the Two-Ocean Pass and the Tógwote Pass, the finer materials of the drift are well exposed in sections along the streams, showing that a formation at least 500 feet in thickness was deposited during this epoch.

The study of the Rocky Mountain drift, when it can be entered upon without special regard to other subjects, will fully reward those who may undertake it. It would greatly exceed the limits of this work to attempt anything like a complete discussion of its history, and the most that can now be done is to give very briefly an outline of the author's conclusions so far as they seem warranted by the facts. We must believe, from the enormous thickness of the Tertiary strata which were deposited at the base of the higher elevations, that the denudation which had been produced at the beginning of the Quaternary period was very great, and this view is well corroborated by the records which have come down to us. Before the close of the Miocene epoch the anticlinal of the Wind River Mountains had so far been eroded that the Sweetwater Basin then, as now, formed a portion of the Atlantic drainage system; and the same is true of the Wind River Basin. The Green River Basin during at least the latter part of the Eocene epoch was occupied by a lake which probably shed its water into the Uintah Basin, though by a different channel from that of the present Green River. The existing cañons through the hard limestone ridge upon the northeastern slope of the Wind River range were doubtless begun during the Cretaceous period, toward its close. We may, then, with good reason suppose that a section across the main chain at the beginning of the glacial epoch would be essentially as indicated in Fig. 13 by the broken line. The dotted lines may be taken to represent, in a general way, the relative positions of the bed of the main branch of Little Wind River along its course through the mountains, though it is obvious that this cannot be done with great accuracy. It would require a dozen sections to show the variations in the transverse outlines of this range at different points, but it is believed that the most prominent features are fairly exhibited in the accompanying figure. Leaving the reader to supply the details of the argument from the facts which have already been given, it may be remarked that the conclusion seems natural enough that the main glacier of this region followed a course very nearly coincident with the axis of the range, probably gradually increasing in size, from a mere cap at the summit until it had spread so as to fill a large portion of the space between the flanking Carboniferous ridges, thus wearing for itself an irregular channel in a southeasterly direction. At various points along its sides the material inclosed in the ice was separated from the main glacier and carried down into the plains and distributed. There is also some reason for believing that the northeastern slope of the mountains was in many places denuded by glacial action so as to leave small lakes outside of the limestone-ridge, or, perhaps, one or more larger lakes, with very irregular outline, and quite uneven bottom, in which the bowlders and finer material were deposited. Be this as it may, there is abundant evidence that the glacier escaped over this edge of the range at several points.

For my own part, after the careful review of a large number of facts, collected at every point along our route, I am disposed to regard the period of drift-deposition, over a considerable portion of the Rocky Mountain region, as made up of two epochs, and it is highly probable that they were nearly synchronous with the Glacial and Champlain epochs in the east. This view has been adopted in the arrangement of these deposits in the Stratigraphic Chart accompanying Chapter III. To express this idea more clearly, but much too briefly, it is probable that the Pliocene epoch was followed in this section by a gradual diminution of heat, which caused the lower limit of perpetual congelation to descend by degrees from near the summit of the mountains.

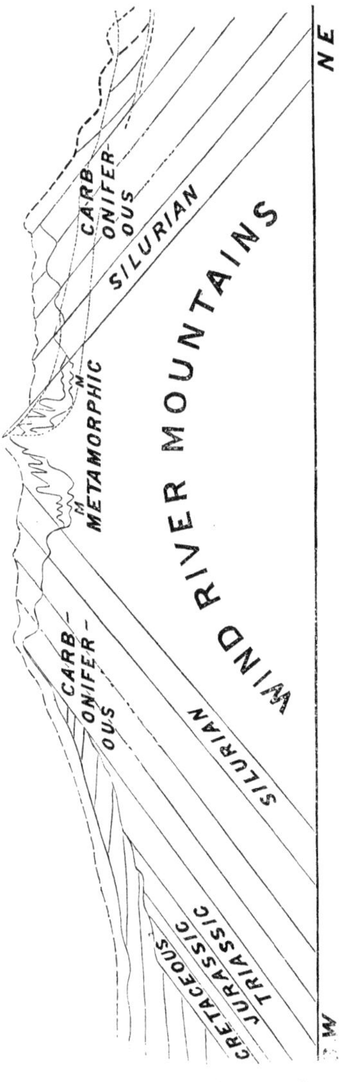

Fig. 13. Ideal section across the Wind River Mountains. The broken line represents the outline at the beginning of the glacial epoch. The lower unbroken line gives the present outline. The surface-features of the northeastern slope were obtained on the trip to Chimney Rocks, and those of the southwestern slope are partly made to correspond, though probably different *in detail*. The drift deposits are not shown, except the moraines, which cover the metamorphic series at M M. The darker crumpled line represents, roughly, the outline of the central portion northward.

The first erosive effects were therefore produced near the axes of the ranges, and the courses of the channels produced in each case would very largely depend upon the surface features, but with a prevailing southern direction. At first one of the great causes of glacier motion—the difference between summer and winter temperature—would probably be almost wanting, but this would also continue to increase, though perhaps never becoming so great as in many other parts of the country. For a long time the erosion of the tilted strata remote from the axes would be accomplished by water from the melting snows, and thus channels would be cut and the river-courses upon the plains would be marked out. As the snow-line came nearer the plains the glacial action would become apparent also; and still later smaller side-glaciers would, doubtless, partly follow the larger valleys or cañons, widening them and often slightly altering their courses. Through some of these valleys and in places over the ridges through which the water-cañons had been cut, some portions of the main glacier would finally escape. It might happen that one of the side-glaciers would dam up the main valley below the mountains, forming a lake above itself, which would distribute the bowlders and finer material according to size. In places along the Wind River Valley, above Lake Fork, this feature is displayed, and elsewhere in the narrower portions of other valleys. Later still, the melting of these ice-streams gave rise to accumulations of fine and coarse materials which were afterward re-arranged by the streams, according to the force of their currents, in the upper valleys usually being stratified irregularly as *modified* drift, while the very fine particles were often carried below and deposited in the undrained lakes.

To sum up, then, it is the author's opinion that these deposits may be conveniently divided into two groups, sufficiently distinct in character and origin to warrant the belief that they represent the two eastern epochs, generally known as the Glacial and the Champlain—the *freezing* and the *thawing* eras, as they may not inaptly be termed.

During the freezing or Glacial epoch, glaciers spread widely over the more elevated portions of the Rocky Mountain region, and the effects produced by them were enormous, but mainly local.

The general direction of the motion was from the northwest, but greatly modified by the slopes of the country. Erosion by water and ice was very great, and in some places immense deposits of bowlders and detritus were formed.

The deposits which I have referred to the Champlain epoch may belong in part to the Glacial epoch, for it can hardly be said that it is proper, in all cases, to separate these eras. All over the Green River Basin, in the Wind River Valley, and elsewhere upon the plains, away from the mountains, the materials of the drift are widely but thinly scattered, the particles gradually increasing in size as the mountains are approached. Thus, fine pebbles of red sandstone from the Wahsatch or the Uintah range, twenty to fifty miles distant, may be obtained from the summits of some of the higher benches north of Fort Bridger, and the metamorphic series of the Wind River range begins to be represented before these disappear. Clearly these are not the direct products of a glacier, but the facts would seem to indicate deposition by re-arrangement in the waters of a shallow lake, as Hayden has remarked. The agency of small icebergs might be suspected, but the arrangement of the materials according to size is too regular for the support of that supposition. The large isolated bowlder noticed south of Dry Sandy Creek, with some others nearer the mountains, may have been thus transported for a short distance, but these are quite exceptional. The principal reason which can at present be offered for referring these accumulations in the Green River Basin to the Champlain epoch is, perhaps, not very conclusive, but it affords some little ground for such a provisional classification. It is this: If the lake over the bottom of which they were spread, had existed during the glacial epoch, it is but reasonable to suppose that in this long period of time a considerable thickness of material of various sizes would have been deposited from the wear of the mountains, but this has not been observed; hence it is probable that this lake was a later body of water caused by the melting of the glaciers upon its borders, and the accumulation of morainal *débris*, which were assorted, as it were, according to weight, by its waters. But there are other deposits of greater thickness in various localities, which, by their position overlying the drift, show that they are of more recent date. It is impossible to do more than to enumerate them here. They are—

1. Deposits of *modified* drift of varying thickness, mostly exposed along the banks of existing or ancient streams.
2. Deposits of "till," sometimes of great thickness, evidently deposited during the melting period in the deeper portions of the lakes, or in *other* more local lakes.
3. The connection of the *graduated* drift, as it may be called, with the other Quaternary deposits in the Wind River Valley renders the reference to this age of similar accumulations in other localities more probably correct.

TERRACE EPOCH.

The transition from the Drift era, including the Glacial and Champlain epochs, to the succeeding epoch in the earth's history, was certainly not abrupt, and inasmuch as we are now dealing, as in the whole of this chapter, with surface-formations which are still being subjected to great changes by reason of their exposure to destructive agencies, it is often difficult to determine correctly the synchronism of results. Moreover, the forces which were at work during the epoch immediately succeeding the Drift era are still active, and many of them had produced such great effects previous to the Quaternary period that the glacial denudation was insufficient to eradicate them. There is no lack of proof that the present drainage-system over the southern portion of our district was at least outlined as early as the close of the Cretaceous epoch, while over the northern portion changes have probably been produced by the igneous outflows, but still the present courses of the streams are mainly through channels of ancient erosion. But even in these regions there is enough to indicate that the epoch of the Champlain deposits was followed by a period during which the valleys were cut deeper, apparently by a succession of impulses imparted to the streams, and the records of this time are now to be seen in the form of terraces which more or less regularly follow the general courses of the present river-channels. The erosion of the valleys by the stream still goes on, but there was evidently a long era in the past when this action was upon a grander scale, and to this indefinite and transitional period it is convenient to give the name of Terrace epoch.

Concerning the causes of the fluctuations of level in the stream-beds, little can be said in a work of the local nature of this report, for it is necessary to accumulate evidence from a wide extent of country, in order to fairly discuss the subject; but the author may, perhaps, be pardoned for the expression of an opinion in this place, not hastily formed, but greatly confirmed by observations in the upper valley regions of a large number of streams during our trip. There are yet a large number of geologists who, though ever ready to acknowledge the inconceivable length of geologic time when found necessary to explain many phenomena, are still prejudiced to the old theories, which refer *all* great changes in the surface-features of the earth to the action of internal forces. There is, however, a growing conviction in numerous minds that this is a serious error, and it is the candid opinion of the writer that the production of these terraces, except in rare instances, is very largely the result of external causes.

Many interesting varieties in the forms of the terraces may be observed, some of which will be again referred to when considering the subject of erosion. A few only of the more common examples will be mentioned here. In many portions of the Green River Basin, particularly in sections in which the lower or Green River group is the surface-formation, the approach to the larger streams upon each side is made over a succession of extensive and quite regular terrace-benches; and in some places the same regularity is noticeable in the minor valleys. Elsewhere in this basin, and perhaps much more commonly, the surface of the terraces bordering ancient streams has been much changed, so that it is not always an easy matter to determine their courses. Fine examples of regular benches are also to be seen in the Wind River Valley and in other places away from the mountains.

Even in the gorges of the streams issuing from the rugged Sierra Shoshone, this structure is often observable, though now much obscured by the growth of trees. In the valley of the Yellowstone River, at many points, the terraces can be readily made out, but their surface is largely scored by gulleys, which cause them to appear less regular than they really are. One of the best places for the study of the effects of running water upon the beds of streams is the section of country between the Two-Ocean Pass and Tógwote Pass, where there is probably as much variety in the results as could well be found over an equal area elsewhere.

HUMAN PERIOD.

The close of the Terrace epoch brings down the history of the earth to a time when the present conditions were in force, and the changes which have since taken place are of comparatively slight extent, although much has been done in the way of denudation, transportation, and deposition, from which important local formations have not unfrequently resulted. Some very prominent recent deposits, which have been in process of formation during several of the preceding epochs, have been lightly passed over, that their history may be more clearly elucidated by comparison with similar action now in progress. Such are the hot-spring and geyser deposits, many of which doubtless originated long before the present epoch, but, being now active and of special interest from their comparative rarity, it has been thought desirable to devote one or more chapters to their exclusive consideration. It is also proposed in succeeding chapters to treat as completely as opportunity will allow of the forces or causes which have produced the effects previously discussed. It is consequently unnecessary to speak very fully of the remaining general deposits of the human period which exist in the district under consideration, for they are almost entirely the direct results of local action, which can usually be traced with little difficulty. The so-called *alkali* deposits, and the rather common dunes, mounds, and furrows of wind-blown sand, will each receive due attention in the part of the work devoted to dynamical geology, and this passing allusion must here suffice. The same remark may be made concerning the prehistoric and other relics, which will receive special mention beyond. There are not a few other topics also about which much of interest and importance might be written, such as come more properly within the scope of the science of zoology. These also must be left for review in another portion of the report, and this chapter may appropriately conclude with some—

GENERAL REMARKS ON THE POST-TERTIARY AND HUMAN PERIODS.

Whatever may have been the cause of the cold of the glacial epoch, there can be but little doubt that by some means the northern portion of the continent was raised to a considerable height above the level of the sea during the period of its continuance. The resulting glaciers extended far to the southward, causing great erosion of the surface over a very wide area, but the effects produced near the summit of the Rocky Mountains, though frequently of much importance, were usually of a local character. The general course of the motion of the ice-sheet between the forty-first and the forty-fifth parallels was about southeast, varying according to circumstances to a greater or less degree. It may be suggested—the writer is not sufficiently familiar with the facts farther south to offer it as a confirmed opinion—that the cause of the local nature of the deposits, resulting from comparatively slight glacier motion, was the gradual change of climate after the Pliocene epoch. In other words, if the decrease of temperature was almost wholly owing to the slow approach of glaciers from the north, we will suppose that the Wind River Mountain glacier, for instance, did not fairly begin its erosive action until one-third of the glacial epoch had elapsed; that is to say, one-third of the whole time during which the bulk of the glacier existed in the north. Now, we know that there was a more or less gradual reversal of these conditions during the Champlain epoch, and it may have happened that the climate at the supposed point farther north would cause the glacier there to continue as much longer as it had before preceded the Wind River Mountain ice-mass. Thus the latter would have just one-third as much time, with much less force for the performance of its work of erosion and transportation. Upon this supposition, it is not necessary that the effects produced should be found to decrease quite gradually as we go southward, for the amount of erosion or transportation effected at any one point depends quite as much upon the resistance as upon the power employed. The author must not be understood to imply by these remarks that the formation of the more southern portions of the great ice-sheet was separated from the Pliocene epoch by a greater interval of time than was the case farther north, though this may have been true. In such a case, it is more than likely that all the southern Pliocene beds are not synchronous with what might be called the *parachronous* beds farther north, using the latter term in the sense of beds of the same *relative* age.

The Champlain epoch, as a whole, was one of relative approach of the land elevations to the sea-level, and during this era the climate gradually became more mild from the diminished amount of surface above the sea. There was then a partial return toward Lower Tertiary conditions, and the valleys were partially filled with material washed from the deposits of the melted glaciers, which was afterward partly removed by the action of the streams during the Tertiary epoch. The fauna of the west became enlarged, and finally man entered upon the scene, leaving behind him relics of his rude skill, with monuments of his superstitions. Passing down thus through the prehistoric period, we next find proofs of the existence of later tribes, who have left us far too little of themselves, and by degrees we come to the present Indian families spread apart by fortune and misfortune until their tribal relations are even less understood by each other than by the white man who makes them his study.

Accompanying man, or rather accompanied by man, in his nomadic condition, large herds of ruminating animals next crowd the plains, deriving therefrom their sustenance. With remorseless hand, the wily savage drives them from their haunts, and in a few short years spreads their bones far and wide across the country. Literally exterminating as he goes, for a brief while he rules supreme, when, pushing eastward to seek the food-supply of which his reckless waste has deprived him, he is met by other tribes more savage than himself, pressed westward by a power greater than hunger—the onward march of civilization. Then begins another conflict, and the records which have hitherto been the property of the geologist and the archæologist are silently placed in the keeping of the historian, where we must leave them.

CHAPTER VI.

STRATIGRAPHY—RECAPITULATION.

General review, with economic geology—Fort Bridger and Uintah Mountains—Northward to South Pass and Camp Stambaugh—Sweetwater gold-mines—To Camp Brown and across Wind River Valley—Owl Creek Mountains—Sierra Shoshone, &c.—Yellowstone Park and return.

It is only intended in this chapter to give a very general description of the geology of the district traversed by Captain Jones in 1873, for the benefit of those who may require a concise statement of the facts in local order. In connection with this review, some few topics bearing upon the economic geology of the region will also be very briefly considered. Should fuller information upon any special subject be desired, it will usually be found more completely discussed in another portion of the report, which may readily be ascertained by reference to the alphabetical index at the close of the work.

From Creston, on the continental divide, at an elevation of 7,030 feet above the sea, the traveler on the Union Pacific Railway passes down to the valley of Green River, and beyond across the plains to the Wahsatch Mountains, over and among the fresh-water Tertiary deposits of the great Green River Basin, striking in the western portion the tilted brackish and fresh-water strata, containing large deposits of coal, which are referred in this report to the Cretaceous period. Leaving the railroad at Carter station, nearly sixty miles west of Green River City, a wagon-road is found running eleven miles southward, to Fort Bridger, which pursues an undulating course over successive benches of the lowest Tertiary formation, known as the Green River group. This represents the Lower Eocene epoch in the earth's history, and is well exposed over a wide extent of country.

FORT BRIDGER AND THE UINTAH MOUNTAINS.

Fort Bridger is pleasantly located in the well-watered valley of Black's Fork, having been a prominent station on the old overland stage-route to California. This was the initial point of our reconnaissance; but the writer was able to pass in review the country southward to the Uintah range, which forms a prominent natural boundary in this section, and it will be well to notice its peculiarities. South of west from the Post, the principal feature in the landscape is a flat-topped hill or bench, called Bridger Butte, rising to a height of more than seven hundred feet above the valley-level at the Fort. This is also interesting from the fact that its upper portion is composed of mostly arenaceous beds of the Upper Eocene formation, or Bridger group, while its base contains more calcareous beds of the Green River group. The Green River beds are exposed in part in the vicinity of Fort Bridger, and to some extent southward; but as we pass toward the mountains, the sandstones and the indurated clays of the Bridger group appear at the surface, and finally entirely conceal the underlying formation. Still farther south, the denudation has been less effective, and a great thickness of the Bridger beds is revealed in the sides of the buttes and benches. In some places, as at the locality known as Grizzly Buttes, the erosion has produced remarkable forms, and the argillaceous strata are cut through so extensively as to afford numerous exposures of their fossil contents, which are very largely made up of the remains of extinct vertebrate animals.

The Tertiary beds in the vicinity of the mountains dip very slightly, and they jut against the northern slope of the Uintahs in a manner which plainly indicates that they were deposited after the upheaval of that range. Thick accumulations of the fine and coarse materials of the drift are so common that the structure of the point of junction is much obscured; but examinations of sections at several points show that the sedimentary rocks to the close of the Jurassic period were represented in the main upheaval. The Mesozoic rocks seem to cover the underlying formations to a greater extent in the Uintah range than is common in the Rocky Mountain system.

Drift is abundant and coarse toward the central portion of the Uintahs, somewhat gradually decreasing in size and quantity northward. It is very difficult, however, without extended examination, to determine the amount of this material which may have been the result of glacial action in the Wahsatch Mountains. Accumulations of some extent exist in the vicinity of Fort Bridger, to the origin of which a hasty review of the country southward furnishes little or no clew. There are very interesting questions connected with the history of similar deposits over the whole district, which deserve careful attention in the future.

The return from the mountains is much more satisfactory to one desirous of gathering only general facts, for it enables the observer at many points to obtain views of the country extending over a wide area. The traveler across the Green River Basin can obtain but an inadequate idea of the vast amount of erosion which has taken place since the deposition of the horizontal strata, without passing down through the valleys of the northward-bound streams from the present summit of the Bridger group of beds.

FROM FORT BRIDGER, VIA SOUTH PASS, TO CAMP STAMBAUGH.

Along our route, the Bridger group is exposed at the surface over a considerable extent of country northward and eastward from Fort Bridger, and numerous isolated buttes, largely composed of the strata of this formation, are met before reaching Little Sandy River, while a number exist beyond this point, which are merely capped with these beds. Between Bryan and Church Buttes, on the railroad, there is an interesting collection of buttes which are weathered into forms slightly resembling the Grizzly Buttes, but much less crowded and irregular. The Green River beds are exposed beneath the Bridger group over the whole country north of Fort Bridger, and beyond the Little Sandy they are at the surface almost to Pacific Creek. This formation is now noted for the abundant and finely-preserved remains of fishes and land-plants which it has yielded, particularly in the railroad-cuttings not far from Green River City. A shale highly charged with petroleum is also found, containing the remains of fishes. This was met upon our trip above Robinson's Ferry on the right bank of Green River. Its fuel-properties are fair, but no economical methods of utilizing it have yet been proposed on account of the great amount of waste which clogs the furnace and smothers the fire. It is not probable that it will soon be brought into use, as the supply of better material near at hand will be sufficient for all demands for a long time.

The coal of this country occurs in a group which underlies the fresh-water Tertiaries. It is not exposed along the road between Fort Bridger and South Pass; but it is worked at several points along the railroad east and west. In the neighborhood of the Wahsatch Mountains, the strata are much tilted and the coal is easily reached. East of Green River City, the coal-bearing group is nearly or quite conformable to the overlying Tertiary series, and is occasionally found by boring at some distance beneath the surface. East of the continental divide, similar beds underlie a large area of the country, and a thriving mining-town has sprung up at Carbon station, half-way between Creston and Laramie.

Shallow-water lacustrine beds of the Pliocene epoch are seen in quantity near Pacific Springs, though not extending far southward over the plains. These have spread across the outlying portions of the metamorphic series of the Wind River Mountains near South Pass, and they have been greatly denuded since their deposition. Remnants are now left standing in the shape of immense buttes, forming prominent landmarks to the traveler in this region.

Passing northward from Fort Bridger, the drift-material thins out gradually, then increases by degrees until it is rather abundant near South Pass, its size increasing in about the same proportion. Alkali deposits, chalcedonic masses and concretions, deposits of gypsum and calcite, and interesting changes in the minor surface-features by wind and water action, are among the more important peculiarities which claim a share of the attention of those who shall make the Green River Basin the field of geological labors.

The low divide at South Pass might readily be crossed without being observed, except by the most watchful traveler; for there is no high ridge to mark the passage from the Pacific to the Atlantic waters, and the change in direction of the streams upon each side would scarcely be noticed, unless special attention were given. The water-divide is not the geological divide, or axis of the anticlinal, which is situated some little distance beyond, and is often lower than portions outside the nucleus of the mountains. It will thus be seen that the Sweetwater River rises upon the southwestern slope of the Wind River range, but cuts its way across to join the Atlantic water-system without escaping to the plains of the Green River Basin. Near the point at which the road crosses, it runs in a narrow cañon through the metamorphic slates and schists, occasionally meeting with a swell or basin filled with Pliocene strata, or the more recent accumulations of the Post-Tertiary period. Below this it meets with the fresh-water sediments of a lake which existed probably in the Miocene epoch, occupying what is now termed the Sweetwater Basin.

The metamorphic slates pass rather gradually through the common forms to the granites, which compose the axis of the Wind River range, which here constitutes the main crest of the Rocky Mountain chain. The geological divide is crossed before reaching South Pass City, and it is here comparatively low. The same gradations in the metamorphics are noticed beyond in reversed order until the overlying sedimentary rocks make their appearance upon the northeastern slope. Quartz and feldspathic seams are abundant upon both sides of the anticlinal. Heavy drift-deposits fill many of the variously-eroded valleys, and excellent roads are built without difficulty on this account. South Pass City and Atlantic City are located in deep valleys occupied by tributaries of the Sweetwater, which were in part at least cut out during the Glacial epoch, and afterward more or less completely filled with the finer drift-deposits, probably to some extent during the Champlain epoch. The Pliocene deposits extend to a remarkable distance over the metamorphic series, being discovered where wells have been dug in places where they are covered by the drift, as at Camp Stambaugh, which is almost directly upon the divide between the Sweetwater River and Wind River.

SWEETWATER GOLD-MINES.

Some opportunities of observation having occurred, the gold-mines of this section, known as the Sweetwater mining country, were examined in company with Captain Jones, with as much care as time would allow. It should be here stated that the writer is greatly indebted to the proprietors of the mines now in operation, and particularly to Mr. James Smith, of Atlantic City, for facilities given, in every case very courteously rendered and without hesitation.

The gold of this region occurs in thick veins of impure quartz among the schists and gneissic slates of the northeastern side of the anticlinal. The greater portion is disseminated through the matrix, but it not unfrequently is found in cavities in the quartz in fair-sized flakes or scales. Silver is frequently associated with it, and iron-pyrites in varying proportions is rarely absent. There are at least two prominent lodes, which may be called the Cariso and the Miners' Delight. The mining-section is locally divided into two portions, known as the Shoshone and the Miners' Delight districts. The Shoshone district, in particular, has been the scene of great excitement, and signs of comparatively recent prosperity are evident in the numerous fine dwellings, hotels, factories, and other concomitants of mining-settlements, which mark the sites of the now deserted Atlantic and South Pass cities. The mines have not been exhausted, and some are yet in operation; but so far as could be learned, the entire lack of capital and the cost of transportation of the ore to points where it can be worked, have caused their gradual abandonment or suspension. The small number of remaining inhabitants of the two cities—not more than thirty in all—are very sanguine of ultimate success, and it is quite probable that a railroad through this country would add the necessary incentive to the profitable development of these mineral resources.

The notes upon these mines, active and abandoned, will be given in order, beginning at South Pass City, in the Shoshone district. The natural facilities for placer-mining are very good, and the channels of former ditches are by no means uncommon. Some of these exist in the neighborhood of South Pass City. Numerous "prospect-holes" are to be seen in all directions.

Cariso mine.—Not now in operation. This mine has yielded well, and much labor has been spent in its working. Very good buildings, with good but not extensive machinery, are still standing above the main shaft. The shaft has been sunk two hundred and ten feet, in a tough, dark quartzite with numerous thin, quartz veins. Marshall's shaft is ninety feet in depth, and has a tunnel along the vein, toward the main shaft, one hundred and sixty-five feet in length. The vein is here four or five feet in thickness, dipping 70° to the northeast, being conformable to the adjacent rocks. Some free gold is found in the cap and wall rock, and the shafts and tunnels have been excavated partly in these. A rich specimen from the hanging-wall represents a reddish or speckled, rather friable, quartzose layer, with the gold finely disseminated. This rock very readily splits into thin laminæ upon exposure to the air, owing, doubtless, to the quantity of ferric oxide which it contains. The average of the gangue is more refractory quartz or quartzite. Iron pyrites is more or less abundant, occasionally being found in the form of cubes in the *attle*, or refuse. Very little water was met before reaching a depth of two hundred feet, but the reason given for suspension of the work is inability to supply pumping-machinery, which is now rendered necessary.

Young America mine.—Suspended or abandoned. Across a ravine, easterly from the Cariso mine, the Young America shaft, ninety feet in depth, has struck the same lode. Considerable silver is found in the attle, but it has never been worked, though said to exist in sufficient quantity if the more valuable gold were not present. This mine has not yielded as well as the Cariso; the average being not more than $25 per ton.

Irishman and Sheridan mine.—Not in operation at present. Two mines, consolidated under this name, have a shaft ninety feet in depth. The rock which was worked yielded fairly, but it is not extremely rich in gold. In general, it is an impure, hard quartz, but much decomposed, in parts containing pyrites.

There is apparently a "horse" in this mine, containing a considerable quantity of magnetite.

Below this mine a few rods, the Grecian Bend mine was opened, with the hope of reaching the same lode, but was finally abandoned. Tennessee, Golden Gate, and Flora are the names of other mines, which were opened and prosecuted with comparatively little success, though with fair prospects. The Barnaby prospect-pit, farther eastward, was sunk with a view of striking the lode on which the Duncan mine is located.

Duncan mine.—Worked on a small scale in summer; James Smith, of Atlantic City, proprietor. The approach to this mine, sixty-five feet in length, is roughly timbered, and its continuation in a tunnel seventy-five feet in length along the vein enters the hill about eighty feet below the summit. The mean width of the tunnel is four and one-half feet, with a large expansion or pocket, ten feet in width, near the inner end. The height is about six and one-half feet, and it slopes inward about three feet. Above this tunnel, on the hill, a shaft twenty feet in depth has been opened, with a tunnel at the bottom fifteen feet in length, striking along the same vein, and a "slope" to the surface eastward. A windlass worked by hand constituted the motive-power. A layer occurring near the middle of the vein contains an abundance of iron-pyrites and ferric oxide, mostly in small pockets. In large swellings or pockets in the vein, there occurs a soft irony layer, much decomposed, very rich in gold, most productive near the northern or hanging wall. Another hard quartzy layer is rich, and is also abundant in pockets on the side of the hanging-wall. Along the northern side of the vein, more prevalent eastward, runs a streak of quartz containing notable quantities of a blue salt of (apparently) copper, probably some silver, and much ferric oxide. An "arrastra" has been in use at this mine, and it is very favorably situated for obtaining a supply of water. The yield of gold is less than at the Cariso, but it will probably average $20 or more to the ton if properly worked.

Mary Allen mine.—Suspended. This mine is located one mile and a half eastward from the Duncan, apparently striking the same lode, which seems to turn very slightly to the north in that direction. It was not visited during our trips.

Buckeye mine.—Now being worked by McBurk, Lawn, and Dawkins. The metamorphic rocks are here nearly vertical, but the vein appears to have filled joint-fissures near the surface, making the dip of the lode at this point from 34° to 39° southwest. They have apparently, by sinking a shaft, also struck and worked another smaller vein or branch below, with much the same direction, which does not come so near to the surface. Along the upper vein, and penetrating in the same way the lower, a thin foreign seam occurs, with a fine example of "slickensides," where it comes in contact with the quartz vein. The upper vein near the surface is about nine feet in thickness. At the lower end of an incline, seventy-six feet from the entrance, it is about four feet in width, but the gangue is richer. The gold-bearing rock from the bottom of the shaft and on the side of the incline is a tough but broken quartz, with some visible particles of gold.

Between this mine and Camp Stambaugh, the Caribou mine, not far distant, and a few placer and other mines in Promise Gulch, were hastily passed for lack of time to examine them.

Young America mine, (East End, Miners' Delight.)—Now in operation. The dip of the lower wall averages 72°, S. 65° E. The shaft, which follows the vein, is one hundred and eight feet in depth; first level, sixty feet below the surface, the portion of the shaft above being on an incline. The width of the vein varies from nothing to four feet. The lower wall of the workable portion is quite quartzy, and there is much adhering quartz in many places on the hanging-wall. The average yield is about $15 per ton, and the working is easy. The proprietors run a twenty-stamp mill, and the hoisting-machinery and the timber-work are in good order and substantial. At a depth of less than one hundred feet, the shaft runs vertical for twelve feet, and then bears northward. In the center or to one side of the vein, often in pockets, occurs a blackish rock-material, which decomposes readily. At a depth of one hundred and five feet, water issues from the wall in a good-sized stream. The gold is here often found in large scales in the quartz.

The Miners' Delight district is now more thickly settled than the Shoshone district, and more or less of an impulse has been given to this section by the success of those who have opened mines. Several other prominent mines are worked, which could not be examined for want of time. These few notes give but a bare outline of the facts; but the report of Captain Jones will, doubtless, contain other items of information connected with their economy. Mr. R. W. Raymond, United States Mining Commissioner, has given these mines due attention, and he has already published more complete accounts of them.

FROM CAMP STAMBAUGH TO CAMP BROWN, THENCE ACROSS THE WIND RIVER VALLEY.

On the western slope of the Wind River Mountains, near South Pass, no signs of strata older than the Tertiary were discovered; but upon the northeastern slope many fine sections were afforded, exposing representatives of the great groups of the western sedimentary rocks, from the Silurian to the Cretaceous, inclusive. By comparing and elaborating the materials collected from various points, it is ascertained that the following formations are represented in ascending order, above the metamorphics:

1. Potsdam sandstone.
2. Quebec group limestone, &c.
3. Niagara limestone, (cherty and dolomitic.)
4. Carboniferous group.
5. Triassic red sandstones.
6. Jurassic limestones, &c.
7. Cretaceous beds.
8. Tertiary (miocene ?) beds.
9. Pliocene? clays and soft or loose arenaceous beds.
10. Drift-deposits of glacial epoch.
11. Champlain deposits.
12. Terrace-formations.
13. Recent accumulations of blown sand, &c.

The streams flow down from the mountains by a very direct course to the plains through the sedimentary strata, including the Cretaceous and occasionally the Tertiary. A fold in these rocks is then met, which turns the more southern of the streams more or less to one side, sometimes for a short distance in a direction opposite to the general course of the Wind River. Several of these folds stretch along the Wind River plateau, being variously eroded at different points.

There are several places between the Little Popo-Agie and Camp Brown where the Triassic gypsum-beds are thus exposed in a manner which makes them quite accessible, as well as the valuable building-stone, which would otherwise have been kept concealed. Several extensive seams of coal outcrop in the Cretaceous series, and a portion of it may hereafter prove of economic value, though it is mostly of an inferior quality so far as observed. Just beyond the Little Popo-Agie, and on the Little Wind River below Camp Brown, oil-springs exist, which bid fair to become of importance in the future. That near Camp Brown has already furnished a quantity of asphaltum by its evaporation as it flows over the ground, and this has been extensively employed at the post for pavement and roofing purposes. The Hot Spring, two miles below Camp Brown, is a very interesting feature of this section, and cold sulphur-springs are found in other localities. Camp Brown itself is located in the midst of a rolling country, which has been much planed down since the upheaval of the mountains, so that the geological structure is much obscured by drift-accumulations.

The fresh-water Tertiary beds jut against the older deposits, almost exactly as those of the Green River Basin overlie the red sandstones of the Uintah Mountains, and like them they are nearly horizontal. They form the surface rocks across the Wind River Valley to near the junction of Spring and Dry Creeks, when they are replaced by the underlying strata, which are much folded and eroded, making their study rather difficult. Fine exposures of the Jurassic and Cretaceous beds are seen in the outlying ridges of the Owl Creek Mountains, with numerous fossils in the former. A species of the *Lamellibranch* genus *Gryphæa* is remarkably abundant in some of the nearly vertical Jurassic limestones. The Triassic brick-red sandstones are also exposed in places. The mineral contents of all these formations are intensified, as it were, in quality and in number of exposures by the excessive folding to which they have been subjected.

OWL CREEK MOUNTAINS, SIERRA SHOSHONE, ETC.

The metamorphic nucleus of the Owl Creek range is not well exposed, being covered, except in a few isolated localities, by the early sedimentary rocks. Glacial action and the consequent deposits of bowlders and finer material are abundantly manifested, but especially upon the northern side and in the cañons or narrower valleys of the streams.

The country between Owl Creek and the Gray Bull River is very rugged. Beds similar to those south of the Owl Creek Mountains continue. Lignite or coal, some probably valuable, iron-ore, and gypsum are not scarce. The Tertiary beds are very scanty, and it is difficult to determine their original distribution. Drift continues abundant, and interesting studies in dynamical geology, including water-erosion, wind-action, and other subjects, could hardly be more favorably presented than in this section. Cretaceous strata are most common along our route, but lower beds are occasionally seen.

From Gray Bull River to the Stinkingwater Valley, the surface is less rugged, but it still shows great erosion. No new developments of structure can be made out until the divide above Short Fork is reached, when we are obliged to descend by a very steep trail to the tributaries of the Stinkingwater. Here the volcanic conglomerate, which makes up such a large portion of the mass of the Sierra Shoshone, is seen as detached fragments scattered upon the hills, and to some distance upon the plains. An examination of the main portion as it is exposed back upon the higher ridges near Washakie's temporary camp, reveals large quantities of silicified wood, sometimes in small pieces, but often as large logs and trunks of trees. Passing beyond across Ish-a-woó-a River to the North Fork of the Stinkingwater River, more outcrops of coal are met, and a dying sulphur-spring. Near this point, a fair section is afforded, including the Triassic beds.

As we pass up the North Fork, the volcanic rocks increase in quantity, at first covering the sedimentary rocks, without obscuring them, but shortly becoming so thick that the streams have not cut to their base, thus continuing for many miles, completely concealing the structure of the original range. In fact, little or nothing was learned of the underlying rocks, while passing through this cañon, except what was gleaned from a very few exposures toward the lower end, with an occasional outcrop of some of the later strata in most unexpected places. The eruptive rocks extend westward over a vast extent of country far beyond the limits of our reconnaissance, and they constitute one of the most interesting features of the geology of the West beyond the Rocky Mountains. The cañon of North Fork has been cut to a depth of many hundreds of feet in this material.

The Stinkingwater Pass is a narrow opening between two high points on the divide between the North Fork and the Yellowstone Lake.

THE YELLOWSTONE PARK AND RETURN TO CAMP BROWN.

The geologist who reaches the park from the east, by way of the Stinkingwater Pass, will soon find his attention drawn from the study of the more ancient deposits to the consideration of the rare and too little understood phenomena attendant upon the closing stages of volcanic activity. Almost the whole tract is covered with hot springs and geysers in the greatest variety, and in many places the older stratified deposits are not visible. The Pliocene lake-deposits are very prominent, high above the present sheet of water, and they extend to a considerable distance northward, where their connection with the volcanic outflow opens a field for careful investigation. At other points, particularly northward, the earlier sedimentary strata outcrop in some cases as far back as the Silurian and even to the metamorphic rocks. Following down near the lake-shore to the river, and descending the latter for fifty miles to the bridge, one has the advantage of meeting with the facts in such order as to obtain an understanding of their significance in the best manner possible in a limited time. Then making the trip to Gardiner's River, where the hot springs are at work upon the grandest scale, he is better able to comprehend what he sees, and to apply the knowledge thus gained to the future study of the geysers in another section. It is unnecessary to dwell here upon any of these phenomena, which are to be discussed by themselves, and which are of such special interest that no general statement concerning them would be at all satisfactory. We will, therefore, hastily review the country southward and eastward to Camp Brown, the closing point of our labors.

South of Yellowstone Lake, although the volcanic rocks still continue, there are numerous places in which the sedimentary strata are revealed beneath them, or are uncovered by them. These occur mostly on the banks of streams which are tributary to the Snake River. On Lava Creek the granites are exposed, overlaid by a quartzose sandstone, which is probably Potsdam, and this by limestones, which may be of the ages of the Quebec group and the Niagara limestone. Cretaceous strata are exposed before reaching Lava Creek on our route; also the coal-bearing series on Buffalo Fork. The strata containing the coal are nearly vertical and in folds, so that the beds are several times exposed along the cañon within a stort distance. Much of this coal is very good, and will, doubtless, some day be of value. Drift is very abundant in some places between Two-Ocean Pass and Tógwote Pass. Near the latter point, the eruptive rocks are largely denuded, if they ever covered the lower strata, and the sedimentary rocks are finely cut through diagonally by the Wind River, exposing numerous good sections. Before reaching North Fork, this river has passed through the later formations, and is then almost entirely walled by the Tertiary beds for the remainder of its course. The drift-accumulations are very abundant, both as bowlders and gravels and as modified drift. The details of its distribution are in many respects very similar to the synchronous deposits of the Green River Basin. It would seem that the Pliocene beds, if any were formed in the Wind River Basin, were quite local in extent, but the evidence of action during the Champlain epoch is much more conclusive. Well-formed terraces mark the courses of the streams here as elsewhere, and recent surface-deposits are, perhaps, as well shown as anywhere over our district.

ECONOMIC GEOLOGY.

It has not been the main purpose of the writer to collect statistical information, nor to examine the country with special reference to its capabilities for improvement, but such data have not been entirely neglected, and the following summary of facts in this connection will not be without some interest to a large class of people.

The Sweetwater gold-mines have certainly not been worked to their full capacity, and the introduction of capital and machinery consequent upon the increase of railroad facilities, which must no doubt take place at an early day, will probably add to their productiveness. In such an event, markets will be produced for the garden-truck which can be very readily raised in many parts of the Wind River Valley, where the facilities for irrigation are of the best. The deposits of coal and oil can doubtless then be utilized; the inexhaustible store of building-material, of stone, and the abundant supply of timber will furnish ample accommodations for the settlers, as it has already done at Atlantic City, South Pass City, Miners' Delight, Camp Stambaugh, and Camp Brown. The gypsum-deposits will be found valuable and easily obtainable, while at no very great distance iron-ore may be cheaply worked. The main railroad through this country will probably be on the regular route to the National Park from the East, and distant markets could be supplied with the products of this section. The Potsdam sandstone, it is very possible, is in some parts well calculated to be used in the manufacture of glass, and a good quality of lime can be produced from much of the limestone.

Everything considered, the Wind River Valley is the most favorable locality for this development, but it can be extended across the Owl Creek Mountains to the Shoshone plateau and beyond without difficulty.

The rich fuel-deposits along the line of the Union Pacific Railroad will some day demand the introduction of an agricultural population to furnish the food-supply. Very many localities are now very favorable for grazing purposes, and the soil is, as a rule, very rich in the necessary ingredients of plant-food. In most places irrigation is all that is needed to turn the desert wastes into productive fields, as has been done in the Salt Lake Basin, and on the Rio Virgin, by Mormons. The possibility of irrigation is a deeper question, but it is certain that much can be done in this direction even now, while the capabilities of the future will very largely depend upon the measures which are adopted to husband and distribute the water-supply. There are those, and the author is one, who believe that the results to be obtained in this way will be almost exactly commensurate with the time and money which may be spent in diligently working out the problem of the influences of vegetation upon atmospheric precipitation. This is not the place for argument upon this subject, and this reference to it is all that can here be made. Enough has been said, however, to show that the possibilities of advancement are far greater than many have imagined, and it will be found that these views are shared in common with the great majority of observers in this region, who are competent to form an opinion from the facts.

CHAPTER VII.

DYNAMICAL GEOLOGY—ELEVATION, EROSION, AND DENUDATION.

Mountain Elevation—Erosion and Denudation—Glacial Action—Aqueous Action—Peculiar Effects of Erosion—Wind Action.

In all the preceding chapters we have dealt mainly with results, studying the history of each epoch from its completed works, and paying but little attention to the forces which have aided in their production. In Chapter II, when reviewing the general surface-features of the country, it was stated that there are many physical peculiarities which are at first sight remarkable, and which must be, in a measure, explained, before one can fully appreciate the great changes which have taken place in this portion of the Rocky Mountain region since the formation of the earliest strata. This portion of the report is, therefore, devoted to a consideration of the causes of these changes, with a more complete account than has previously been given of the direct effects; that is to say, the indirect, or ultimate effects, will require little notice, as they have already been discussed in the chapters on stratigraphy. In other words, we are now to deal, in a general way, with forces which have been at work more or less permanently, and we shall endeavor to trace their action in the production of results, many of which have been already considered. The subject will be topically discussed, somewhat systematically, but with scarcely any regard to local or chronological sequence, except in the treatment of minor or special topics.

ELEVATION OF MOUNTAINS.

It has been elsewhere remarked that the elevation of the Wahsatch and Uintah ranges was accomplished before the chain of the Rocky Mountains eastward had risen to any extent above the ocean. This conclusion was reached by Clarence King, from the fact that the Cretaceous beds extend up to the eastern base of the Wahsatch chain, but they are not found upon the western slope. The relation of the Cretaceous strata to the underlying rocks in the neighborhood of the Wahsatch and Uintah ranges also favors this belief. Previous to the deposition of the Paleozoic strata, an uplift of limited extent occurred in Arizona, according to the published reports, and some statements have been made in Chapter III of this report, which point toward the conclusion that there may have been a slight elevation somewhere in the neighborhood of South Pass during early Paleozoic times. This latter supposition requires further evidence, however, for its support. The Wahsatch and Uintah ranges, then, were uplifted toward the close of the Jurassic period, with a broad area westward, the whole of which was thrown into a series of parallel folds, with a general north-south trend.

The upheaval of the ranges composing the Rocky Mountain chain, east of the Wahsatch range, took place at a later date. The disturbance appears to have commenced during some portion of the Cretaceous period, and to have continued gradually until its close. King also reports a later uplift affecting Green River Tertiary beds in the neighborhood of the Wahsatch Mountains. It is very difficult to determine the complete orographic history of the northwestern portion of our district, but the uplift of the whole region seems to have been completed before the opening of the Miocene epoch, although large additions have since been made to its height by the accumulation of material poured out over its surface.

The Jurassic upheaval, as well as that of the Cretaceous period, was accompanied by sufficient heat to transform or metamorphose a great thickness of strata below the Potsdam sandstone, and almost to melt some of the lower beds, if the granites be rightly considered a part of the metamorphic series. North and west of the Wind River Mountains, the heat accompanying the later upheaval was so intense as to lead to outflows of igneous material from fissures, upon a scale of such magnitude that whole ranges were concealed and a new aspect was given to a vast extent of territory. These ejections of molten matter continued with greater or less force during the Miocene epoch, and probably through the Pliocene, or even later, gradually diminishing in quantity until the fissures were covered by lines of volcanoes, from the craters of which the lava poured down upon all sides at irregular intervals. The remnants of many of the cones now stand as clustered peaks, to mark their former positions. These volcanoes finally became extinct, and geysers, fumaroles, and solfataras, in almost inconceivable numbers, were left through succeeding ages to attest by the accumulation of enormous mineral deposits the persistency of the subterranean heat. Many of these still remain, but they are slowly dying out, and it is evident that they represent the last stages of the volcanic action.

The development of the eruptive rocks is very great westward, and the author would here express his obligations to those investigators whose writings have enabled him to obtain additional evidence of the truth of several opinions which were formed in the field, and largely confirmed by the study of notes and specimens. In the succeeding pages these views will be freely expressed, together with the facts upon which they are based.

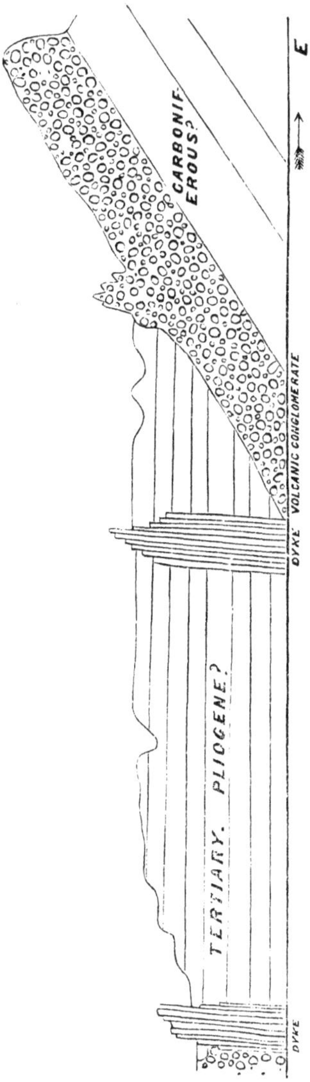

In the lower portion of the cañon of the North Fork of Stinking Water River there occurs a peculiar patch of Tertiary rocks, lying nearly horizontal upon each side of an almost vertical dike of compact andesite, in such a manner as to leave no room for doubt that some of the volcanic rocks were deposited prior to the existence of the fresh-water Tertiary lake in which the horizontal beds were formed. These strata are composed of about 300 feet of clays and light-buff sandstones, very similar to the Pliocene beds in the neighborhood of South Pass. It was impossible to determine whether this basin was continuous with an outside lake during the deposition of these strata, but it appears to have been quite isolated, and not more than a dozen square miles in area. Figure 14 illustrates the section referred to. Similar Tertiary beds, with nearly the same relation to the lower volcanic conglomerate, also occur near the junction of the Owl Creek Mountains and the Sierra Shoshone, at a much higher level than these.

Fig. 14.—Section partly ideal, showing relative position of lower volcanic conglomerate on North Fork of Stinkingwater River, between Camps 32 and 33.

Beyond this point the dikes are very numerous, but usually rather narrow, at first cut through by the stream with a general north-south trend parallelwise to the axes of the folds in the underlying sedimentary rocks, then becoming more abundant and irregular and crossing each other in almost every direction. Figure 15 gives an outlineview of several dikes, as seen in a cliff on the right bank of the sream, a short distance below Camp 34.

The conglomerate frequently contains large masses of the sedimentary rocks, particularly those of Tertiary age, which are often baked so hard as to give a peculiar metallic ring when struck with the hammer. In these not unfrequently finely-preserved specimens of leaves of angiosperms are found, almost indelibly impressed upon the rock, much after the manner of the porcelain print. Logs, stumps, and even trees silicified are found in many places in large quantities.

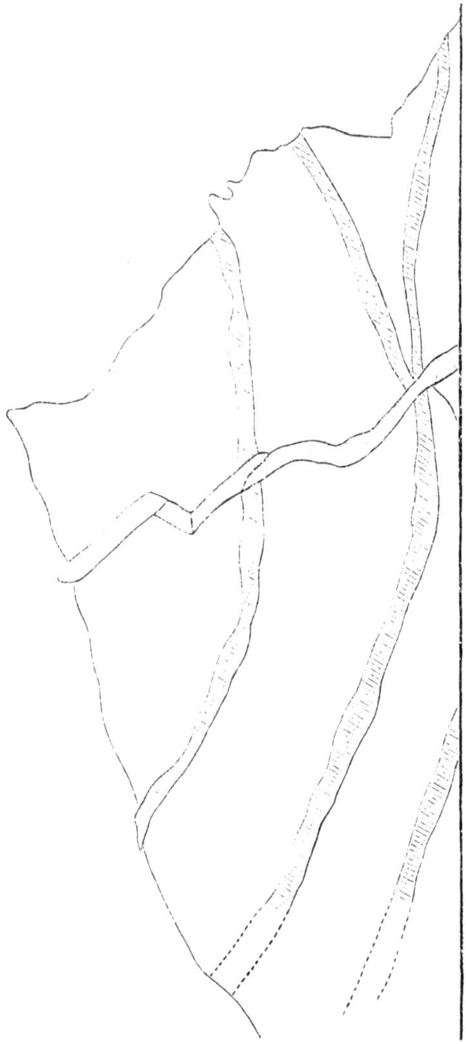

FIG. 15. Andesite ? dikes in breccia-conglomerate, in cañon of North Fork of Stinkingwater River.

The effects produced upon the sedimentary beds by the outpouring of the heated volcanic material upon them are very instructive. Hard limestones have become friable, sandstones have been changed to the texture of quartzite, and beds of gypsum have been very much hardened where they have not been converted completely into anhydrite. Some beds of cherty limestone have also been rendered even more compact and finely-jointed, and apparently some beds of sandy marl have been locally transformed into quite compact but much-jointed rock.

As we pass up the cañon of North Fork the conglomerates are interstratified with and overlaid by thick beds of trachytic material varying in texture and inclosing many minerals. The whole series to the Stinkingwater Pass is of great interest, but few lithological details can herebe given.

Judging from all the facts which have thus far been gathered, we may read the history of these deposits in this region, including as well their continuation beyond the limits of our reconnaissance, briefly as follows: During the Cretaceous period there began a disturbance in the strata east of the mountains which had been elevated at the close of the Jurassic period, resulting in the upheaval of the Rocky Mountain chain. This was gradual in its effects, and, whatever may have been its cause, the trend of the new system was parallelwise to the axis of the previously-formed chains; in some portions of its length the later system is almost exactly parallel in trend with its predecessors. Over a large part of the area now occupied by the Sierra Shoshone a considerable range was probably elevated during the period of the Cretaceous upheaval. This is now so nearly obscured by the igneous deposits that the evidence of its age is difficult to obtain, and it is at best very fragmentary. In some respects it resembles more closely the Jurassic than the Cretaceous mountain-chains, but wherever the Cretaceous beds are exposed in the vicinity of its ridges they are invariably involved in the folds; it must, therefore, be considered a portion of the Rocky Mountain system. From a review of all the facts which bear upon this subject it is inferred that the nucleus of this concealed range is to be found in a belt of granites and other metamorphic rocks extending northward from Tógwote Pass, bearing about 19° to the west, and crossing the East Fork of Yellowstone River just above its mouth. If this be the case, the range formed a part of the northward continuation of the main geological divide of the Rocky Mountains, or the prolongation of the axis of the Wind River Mountains.

The early outflows of igneous material were accompanied by masses of the stratified rocks, broken from the walls of the fissures no doubt in many cases, but also, it is probable, entangled in the liquid stream from the upturned edges of tilted beds, caught from cliffs, and in other ways accumulated until thick beds of conglomerate had been deposited. As a rule, the successive outflows are arranged in a stratified manner, and the lower layers follow closely the inequalities of the pre-existing surface, wherever the latter is exposed. The overlying layers, and especially the lavas, have gradually filled the depressions until the later outflows have passed away from the fissures over a comparatively even course. In some places large patches of stratified rock have apparently been engulfed in the lava-flows without removal from their position; and there may be seen in the left wall of the cañon of the Yellowstone, not far above the mouth of Hell-Roaring River, and at other points, the upright trunks of large trees, which may have grown where they stand. None but the earlier outflows extended eastward to the mouth of the North Fork of the Stinking Water River, or, if so, they were removed from a broad area prior to the deposition of the provisional Pliocene beds. No sudden breaks are noticed, however, westward to the Stinkingwater Pass, but the change from fissure to crater eruption seems to have been rather gradual.

It is possible that the eruptive rocks of the Jurassic upheaval extend eastward beneath a portion of the district under consideration, but this is rather doubtful. A limited outflow took place after the Cretaceous period, and perhaps prior to the Miocene epoch, but the great lava-flows probably occurred during the Miocene. Much more investigation is required before the details of this history can be made out with certainty, but it is believed that the foregoing statements, though of necessity less complete than the material collected warrants, are yet generally correct. Prof. Joseph Leconte, of the University of California, has published, in the numbers for March and April, 1874, of the American Journal of Science and Arts, two admirable articles upon the subject of the lava-floods, with whose conclusions in the main the present author heartily concurs—the chief differences in the facts being due almost entirely to local causes, independently of age. It would be a pleasant task to follow this subject to the end, but the peculiar difficulties under which this report is prepared forbid further discussion, and it is very reluctantly dropped at this point.

The Owl Creek range is a kind of spur or shoot from the angle formed by the bending eastward of the main axis of the Cretaceous upheaval, and, with the many folds of similar date, doubtless served as the mechanical expression of much of the elevating force which would otherwise have been converted into heat for the melting of the rocks.

ANCIENT EROSION AND DENUDATION.

Perhaps the greatest difficulty in the way of generalizing correctly upon the results of field-work is that of determining accurately even the main surface features of the country at any given period in the past. It is rare, indeed, that one will find each successive step in the history so clearly and unmistakably revealed that it may be read with ease in a hasty passage through a complicated district. There can be no doubt that erosion has been as active in past times as at present under like conditions. We must, therefore, believe that each succeeding formation has been built up from the waste of those which have preceded it, wherever the latter have been exposed to disintegrating influences. The evidences of excessive denudation of some portion of the earth's surface during the Paleozoic era are abundant, but there is no proof of the existence of extensive tracts of land high above the sea-level, in Western Wyoming, until the period of the Jurassic upheaval. The elevation of the Wahsatch and Uintah ranges, with the accompanying Sierra Nevada chain, then furnished ample material for the accumulation of the arenaceous and other deposits of the Cretaceous seas, and the succeeding estuaries and fresh-water lakes. Subsequently the uplifting of the Rocky Mountain chain added largely to the superaqueous surface, and, notwithstanding the conservative effects of the luxuriant vegetation during much of the Tertiary period, the country was denuded to an extent sufficient to produce at least three thousand feet of lake-sediment over a very wide area. It is safe to conclude that the average height of the mountains in this section was reduced by denudation fully one thousand feet during the Tertiary period alone, and if we add to this the accumulation at their base of more than three thousand feet in thickness, we shall have a reduction in altitude, from base to summit, of four thousand feet since the Cretaceous upheaval, without taking into account the denudation during the Glacial epoch. There are good reasons for believing that this estimate is much too small, for the Eocene beds of the Green River Basin present a thickness of certainly four thousand feet. Two thousand feet of beds which are probably Miocene occur in the Wind River Valley, and the Pliocene beds near South Pass are fully one thousand feet in thickness. It is almost impossible to decide how much of the material deposited in the Green River Basin was worn from either mountain system, but some clew to the proportionate amount furnished by the Wind River Mountains may be obtained by an examination of the physical features of that range. During the Eocene epoch there seems to have been a comparatively free passage for the waters upon the northeastern slope; and, although the erosion may have been as great as at a later period, very little of the material was deposited until it had passed some distance from the mountains. Upon the western slope a great lake existed during this epoch, and whatever fine material was carried down by the streams was deposited in the Green River Basin. In the Miocene epoch these conditions were almost reversed as far as the opposite sides of the range were concerned, and during the Pliocene epoch both shared in the deposition to some extent. Judging from the present aspect, and taking into consideration the effects of the glacial action, it seems very probable that the Wind River Mountains have always been characterized by greater erosion upon the northeastern slope, though it must be acknowledged that less is known of the southwestern flank.

In the Owl Creek range and the Sierra Shoshone almost nothing can be learned of the early denudation, but in both of these the drainage appears to have been mainly northward and eastward, as at present, though not in all cases through the same channels.

GLACIAL ACTION.

To one accustomed to the heavy drift-deposits of the East, often bearing evidence of transport for many miles, the local nature of the western accumulations, in view of the excessive erosion which has been produced in certain sections, is somewhat bewildering. It is unnecessary to repeat here the facts and explanations which have been offered in Chapter V, but an attempt will be made to give a more satisfactory review of some topics which were there too briefly considered.

It has been remarked that the general course of the glacier movement was southeastward, varying more or less according to the resistance encountered, and spreading out, in some cases, nearly at right angles from the sides. In the Wind River range the main glacier followed a course apparently not strictly parallel with the axis, but trending slightly more toward the east, so that the erosion was usually much greater upon the northeastern slope. From the top of the Chimney Rocks, in the axis of the range, the whole country northward and eastward can be taken in at a glance, but the view in the opposite direction is extremely limited, being almost entirely confined to the exposures of the metamorphic series.

There are many remarkable features in the erosion of channels which, from their form and the partial filling in of undoubted drift-deposits, no one would hesitate to refer to the Glacial epoch, but which it taxes the mind to trace to their special causes. The absence of grooves or striæ from sections in which the volcanic products are almost universal may be accounted for by the rapid weathering; but it is more difficult to understand why they should not be found in the harder and more durable metamorphic rocks. The only instance during our trip in which I was able to detect anything approaching to the nature of a glacial mark, was in the case of a very limited outcrop of a dolomitic limestone above the Niagara, which had upon its surface two or three faint scratches, which may have been quite recent.

In the valley of the East Fork of the Yellowstone, and on Lava Creek, a quantity of very large granitic bowlders are strewn over the surfaces of the higher terraces, and similar masses of granite occur isolated and in moraines, in the central portion of the Wind River range. In the latter, outside of the nucleus, large masses of the stratified rocks are occasionally seen standing by themselves, but usually in such positions as to indicate transportation very gradually, and for short distances only. The bowlders becoming smaller extend out into the plains, and some of them are composed of the material of the sedimentary rocks, sometimes containing fossils.

The general course of the glaciers over the igneous district was not very different, and all the observed peculiarities of the drift in this region are traceable rather to the outlines of the surface and the texture of the rocks than to any important difference in the glaciers from those farther south. In the upper valley of the main fork of Owl Creek there are extensive accumulations of bowlders running down from the east in low ridges, similar to those noticed in the Wind River Valley. The erosion was rather uneven, and the southern-bound glacier seems to have met an insurmountable obstacle in the Owl Creek range, and to have been deflected from its course; or, perhaps, the erosion was effected by separate glaciers existing at different times, and possibly pursuing different courses. At any rate, there is abundant evidence, also, of the final deposition of volcanic-drift material at the base of the mountains, between the upper and lower cañons of Owl Creek, far to the eastward. Mere glimpses were obtained of the wonderful history which is yet to be unraveled in this region, but enough was learned to show that these deposits and their channels are but the subordinate parts of one system, in unison with similar accumulations in other portions of the district.

Between Pacific Creek and Lava Creek, and in the valleys of Lava Creek, Buffalo Fork, and Rock Creek a large portion of the drift is very finely comminuted, and this is often the case elsewhere in the volcanic district, especially where the lavas prevail. Many of the metamorphic bowlders may have come from the volcanic conglomerates. Much modified drift, probably of the Champlain epoch, occurs in the valleys of Buffalo Fork, Rock Creek, and in other places, of which the later terraces have been formed. In these cases, and perhaps in many others, there is evidence that a part, at least, of the valley was cut out by a glacier, and the same may be said of portions of the valleys of the majority of the streams in the Uintah and the Wind River ranges, as well. As before remarked, however, it is almost certain that the narrower cañons of many of the streams have been for the most part, or entirely, cut by running water, partly or wholly since the Glacial epoch. In some places the streams have plainly turned from their original courses to cut deep cañons through solid rock; at other points these cañons, though narrow, bear unmistakable evidence in the shape of drift-deposits that they were partly cut as early as the close of the Glacial epoch, while some even appear to have been in progress during the Tertiary period.

From the facts that have been given in this and a previous chapter, it cannot be doubted that, whether the movement were rapid and evanescent, or very slow and longer continued, the element of power was present, though it seems to have become concentrated in its effects, causing extensive erosion with little transportation, comparatively.

RECENT EROSION.

In discussing the causes of the erosion and denudation which have taken place since the close of the Post-Tertiary period, it is often impossible to separate that part of the effects which properly belongs to the Champlain or Terrace epoch, nor is this necessary for our present purpose. The term *recent* at the head of this division will, consequently, be used to designate all that time which has elapsed since the period of the drift.

AQUEOUS ACTION.

Since the laying down of the fresh-water Tertiary strata they have been denuded to a degree almost incredible to one who has never visited the region in which they occur. The Green River Basin in particular has been subjected to this process, lying as it does almost completely hemmed in by the mountains. The Bridger beds originally covered the Green River formation over the greater part of the basin with at least one thousand feet of clays and sandstones, but now the lower group is laid bare to a remarkable extent by the complete wearing away of the superincumbent strata. The position of the drift-deposits, at least in the southern portion of this tract, indicates that much of the denudation had been accomplished prior to the close of the Post-Tertiary period, and it is probable that local glacial action had much to do with the early erosion, though I have had no opportunities of observation of such effects, except in the vicinity of the Uintah Mountains and near South Pass, in both of which cases there is no doubt that extensive denudation was accomplished during the Glacial epoch. Of the great effects which have since been produced, the largest part must undoubtedly be attributed to the action of running water during the Terrace epoch, in comparison with which the amount is very small which has taken place in modern times. Nevertheless it must not be thought that the erosion now in progress is by any means of trifling importance. On the contrary, it would be a simple matter to bring forward abundant evidence to prove that the amount of the material which is annually removed by the streams is excessive when compared with ordinary standards. There are many causes of this, a few of the more important of which may here be mentioned.

1. *The great altitude of the region.*—Two prominent results accrue from this cause, viz, the accumulation of snow in the mountainous districts, and an increased force to the currents of the streams arising from the greater slope of the surface.

The accumulation of the greater portion of the atmospheric precipitation during a long winter causes powerful freshets in the late spring, which produce greater effects upon the surface than would be accomplished by the same amount of water passing off gradually. The mountain-slopes give free scope to the action of gravity, and the streams strike the plains with a force sufficient to carve out deep channels in the soft strata, and to remove large quantities of the finer material, as sediment, to great distances.

2. *The alternate melting and freezing of the snow by day and night.*—In this section of the country during the months of late spring and summer there is usually much difference in the temperature of the days and nights. The snow in the mountains thus melts by day and freezes by night, causing alternations in the level of the streams of considerable magnitude. In some instances these changes are so regular for days at a time as to closely simulate the ebb and flow of the tide in rivers communicating with the sea, except in the length of the intervals. The frequent importance of very slight differences of this nature, dynamically considered, will be readily acknowledged.

3. *The character of the rocks.*—This influences not only the amount but also the character of the erosion. Accordingly we find that the Bridger beds, where they have not been entirely removed by the long-continued action of the streams, are left standing for the most part as isolated hillocks, though these vary greatly in size and frequency. The harder Green River beds are usually more regularly and perpendicularly worn. Between the extremes nearly every possible form may be met, according to position, and other circumstances which are generally not difficult to understand. To this cause must be mainly attributed the irregularity in the results which have been produced, for the aqueous eroding agencies, though not constant in their intensity, have practically always held about the same relations to each other as at present.

These and other agents acting in concert are steadily degrading the surface by undermining the cliffs, washing out the alluvial deposits from the old stream-beds, and transporting the finer material to points below. One who has only seen these stream-beds in the late summer or early fall, when they are traversed by mere wiry rivulets, can form no adequate idea of the powerful river-torrents which fill and often overflow their banks for several weeks early in the season, so thoroughly charged with sediment as to appear more like mud than water.

The foregoing remarks will apply almost equally as well to the Wind River Valley and to other portions of the Rocky Mountain region where the conditions are similar, but there are usually minor differences, dependent upon a variety of circumstances which are more or less special in occurrence. The sandstones are at the surface over a large portion of the Wind River plateau, which has caused the erosion to result in valleys and gorges similar to those which have been cut through the beds of the Green River group. In some cases peculiar buttes of small size remain, and Crow Heart Butte and another similar to it, in the main valley of Wind River, are in some respects like the more regular ones of the Bridger group. There are also "bad lands," exposures of the indurated green and red marls of the Wind River Tertiary, near the mountains and in the upper valley where the upper sandstones have been worn away, having a peculiarly rugged aspect. These may very appropriately be named the Gothic Buttes. The peculiar mixed structure of some of the sandstone-conglomerates of this formation has given rise to many curious and remarkable forms resembling familiar objects, as urns, pillars, altars, &c., and many of the Grizzly Buttes near the Uintah Mountains are capped by masses even more strikingly similar in outline to other less regular objects. In the volcanic rocks the chasms are lined with caverns, pillars, towers, and steeples, often hundreds of feet in height. In some cases narrow fissures have been produced by water-action through lavas and conglomerates thousands of feet in depth, so that, in numerous places, the whole formation now has an extremely rugged, turreted, and castellated appearance. It seems remarkable that many of these thin chimney-columns can remain in position. In the cañon of North Fork of the Stinking Water, in one locality, there is a vertical block of volcanic material less than fifty feet in length, *two feet* in breadth, and five hundred feet in height, standing alone at a distance of three or four feet from the north wall of the cañon, and this is but one of many similar instances which might be given. Hundreds upon hundreds of lofty pinnacles, deep-worn caverns, and fathomless crevices attest the resistless power of apparently insignificant forces with unlimited time in which to work; they stand as mute witnesses of the almost inconceivable length of the era which has elapsed since the comparatively modern igneous ejections; and they add one more to the long list of proofs of the immensity of geologic time.

Sections taken at intervals across the valleys of the streams would show that the erosion, ancient and modern, has been very unequal at different points, and it may seem rather peculiar that this statement is nowhere more applicable than in the volcanic district. This is no doubt largely owing to the local nature of the glacial action, but it must be partly attributed to the character of the rocks and partly to other existing causes. In the lower part of the cañon of North Fork, hard dikes of trachyte are abundant, many of which are almost vertical. These rarely cross the path of the stream at a right angle to it; but, in most cases, being tougher than the adjacent rocks, they now jut above them, and in a line making a more or less acute angle with the stream. This causes much of the detritus from above to accumulate behind the high walls thus formed, affording lodgment for trees and other vegetation, and allowing of the growth of thickets of symmetrical pines on slopes so steep that there would otherwise be frequent land-slides. This is well shown by the comparative absence of growing timber from lesser slopes which are not thus protected.

Some of the most remarkable and interesting effects of water-erosion are to be seen in the Yellowstone Valley, where the gradual draining of the very large ancient lake has caused the formation of a river-channel of very great depth. The Great Falls, at a distance of fifteen miles below the lake, are a complete study of themselves. (See Fig. 16.) For a number of miles above the rapids the river runs through a broad, level, grassy bottom, made up of sandy lake-deposits and of gravelly deposits of the stream before the period of its present level. Here it pursues a very tortuous course, but the current is visibly rapid, although the water is too deep for fording, except in a few places. Below the mouth of Sour Creek the sandstones and fine beach-conglomerates, largely composed of volcanic material, are cut through by the stream, which is thus narrowed at first, and then turned slightly eastward. It next strikes against ridges or masses of purplish trachyte-porphyry, containing crystals of sanidine. This is made up of alternations of fairly compact and slaggy portions, the latter containing reddish-brown botryoidal geodes and spherulites. Much of the material is very nearly pearl-stone, between which and the trachyte-porphyry there is an almost insensible gradation. The resistance offered to the current by the hard face of the trachytic-porphyry creates a counter-current, which causes a bay-like expansion of the river, in which the water appears almost stagnant. No notice is given of the coming turmoil save the muffled roar from the rapids below. But the rock also feels the shock and it is finally cut through, this action being facilitated by the jointage of the rock. The stream now pursues a general course along one of the lines of jointing, trending north 4° west. It then meets the perlitic trachyte-porphyry, which, being thinly bedded and more loosely arranged, yields more readily to the eroding forces, making swells at the sides and transverse troughs or gullies in the bed of the stream, the action upon the sides being increased by the formation of eddies produced by the striking of the main current against another portion of the tougher or non-perlitic rocks. Here the rapids begin, but they are not yet very boisterous. At each ridge of the more massive material more or less of an eddy is formed by the resistance of the rock, which causes currents to rush in from the sides to join the main current in the center, thus throwing the eroding force by degrees toward one point, concentrating it, and enabling the stream to force its way through the remainder of the section in a straight and narrow gorge. The rapids or cascades are largely due to the irregular erosion along the bottom, as will be seen by examining its general outline represented in Figure 17.

The terraces bordering the river at this point show the same features, but they are much more regular at a distance from the stream, as they have there been cut through the soft sandstones which overlie the porphyry. Upon the right bank, at the gorge, there are low spots or basin-shaped holes which, before viewing the rapids, were almost inexplicable, but were made clear when considered as the positions of eddies in the former stream. A mass of the harder rock also marks the place of a small islet in the stream at a higher level, which then stood in the midst of the rapids.

Figure 18 gives the existing contour of the surface at this point. A similar sketch would, doubtless, properly represent the transverse outline of the present bed of the stream at the lower rapids in the midst of which now stand the islets shown at II, Figure 16.

Below the gorge the river widens, owing mainly to the absence of hard beds in one spot on the left bank, which may have once been at the mouth of a tributary stream. It continues its course, alternately cutting into the right and left bank, according to the nature of the rock. The stream below the rapids, at the last rock islet, is thrown mostly into a deep hole near the right bank; then meeting hard rock, it is thrown across to the left bank against hard rock, which forces it to pass through another gorge by the formation of a powerful eddy. Through this the water rushes with remarkable force in a short series of rapids or cascades, then suddenly plunges by a sheer fall of 150 feet down into a large amphitheater in which the water spreads out shallowly, flowing over a comparatively smooth bottom with little current. The cause of the falls is the rather sudden change in the character of the rock to a fine-jointed argillo-trachyte-porphyry, which gives way more readily to the action of the water than the more massive rock above.

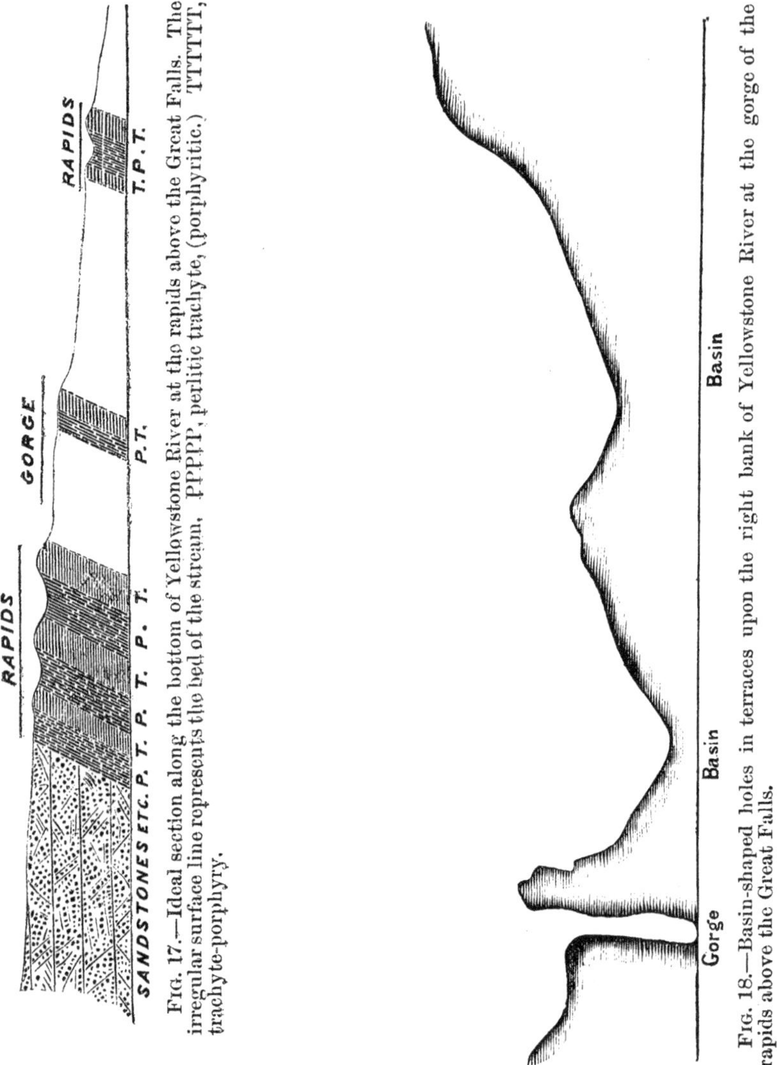

FIG. 17.—Ideal section along the bottom of Yellowstone River at the rapids above the Great Falls. The irregular surface line represents the bed of the stream. PPPPP, perlitic trachyte, (porphyritic.) TTTTTT, trachyte-porphyry.

FIG. 18.—Basin-shaped holes in terraces upon the right bank of Yellowstone River at the gorge of the rapids above the Great Falls.

Less than a quarter of a mile below the upper falls, nearly opposite the entrance of Cascade Creek, the stream again meets with greater re-

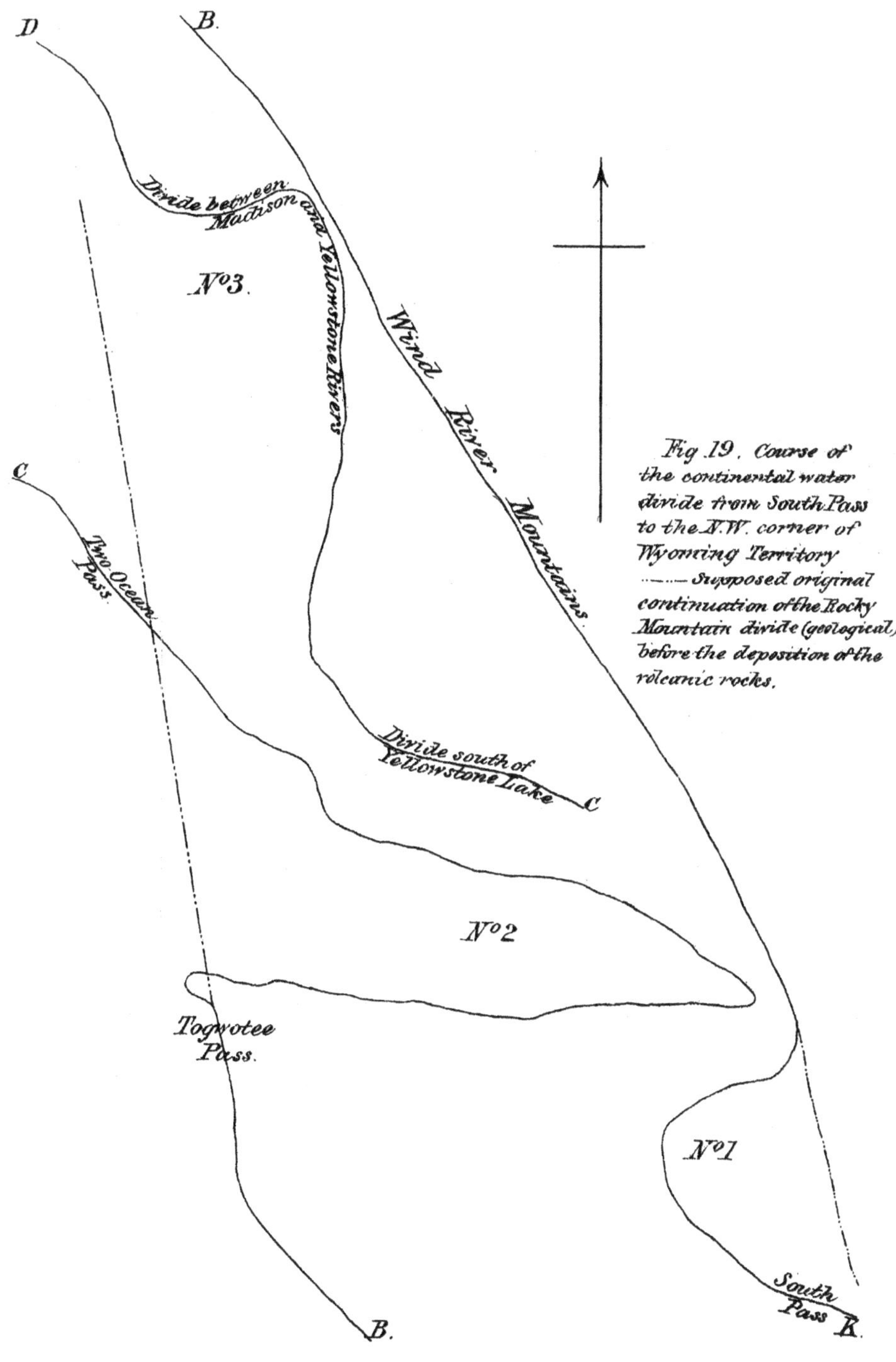

Fig 19. Course of the continental water divide from South Pass to the N.W. corner of Wyoming Territory ·—·—·— Supposed original continuation of the Rocky Mountain divide (geological) before the deposition of the volcanic rocks.

sistance, so that it is deflected very greatly from its course and narrowed at the same time. Just at the verge of the lower falls it is quite suddenly constricted by the protrusion of a hard ledge from the left wall of the gorge, which causes it to leap with redoubled energy over the steep but irregular precipice, (nearly 330 feet) which was undoubtedly caused by the passage to the softer conglomerates which here underlie the porphyries.

Numerous other intensely interesting studies of this character are available to the investigator in this wonderful region, but this one example must serve as the type of the class, and it will convey some idea of the enormous results of the long-continued action of running water, while it will also serve as another reminder of the great length of time which has elapsed since the geologically modern igneous products were deposited in this section. It must not be supposed that the transitions from one kind of rock-material to another are as abrupt in all cases as might, perhaps, be inferred from the foregoing description. On the contrary there are many varieties in the volcanic rocks alone. Between the rapids and a point in the Grand Cañon a few rods below the foot of the lower falls, I collected not less than twenty forms, exclusive of the sandstones and conglomerates, sufficiently distinct to merit special description. These include, besides those already mentioned, obsidian, obsidian-porphyry, various spring deposits, and other varieties which cannot be noticed here. These affect more or less the results of the erosion, but usually only in minor degree.

PECULIAR EFFECTS OF AQUEOUS EROSION.

From what has already been said of the present surface features of much of the country, it will not be matter of surprise to learn that there are many peculiarities in the manner of distribution of the atmospheric precipitation, and in other directions, which seem quite remarkable when portrayed upon any but the most minutely accurate maps constructed upon a very large scale, and even then they can be only imperfectly understood without at least a general knowledge of the geological structure. An examination of Captain Jones's admirable map will show the force of these remarks. One of the most striking features in the topography of the district is the interlocking or overlapping of the headwaters of many of the rivers, particularly in the portion occupied by the volcanic rocks. The continental watershed (see Figure 19) is now very irregular in trend north of South Pass, there being several instances in which the Atlantic waters rise far to the westward of the geological divide, and the Pacific streams *vice versa*. This result may be traced to two main causes, each of which has taken effect since the upheaval of Cretaceous date, *i. e.*, erosion or denudation and deposition. In some cases one of these causes has apparently operated to a much greater extent than the other. In the neighborhood of South Pass, it would seem that the deposition of the Pliocene beds has influenced the course of the headwaters of the Sweetwater River more than the previous extensive erosion, but it is an open question how much of the transfer of the precipitation from the western to the eastern slope through these channels is due to the subsequent glacial erosion. It is quite certain, however, that the latter has exerted a powerful influence, from the fact that the watershed at this place in most points is directly upon the Pliocene beds, which have been glacially eroded between the water-divide and the geological divide, or axis of the range, forming a trough in which the Sweetwater now lies, in part at least.

In the ancient volcanic district it is highly probable that deposition has had the greater share in the marking out of the present stream-channels, though, as we have seen, these have been much enlarged and otherwise modified by the glacial action. The Yellowstone Lake Basin has undoubtedly been partly formed by erosion; but, as remarked by Doctor Hayden, the deposition of the igneous rocks around it has had much to do with its formation.*

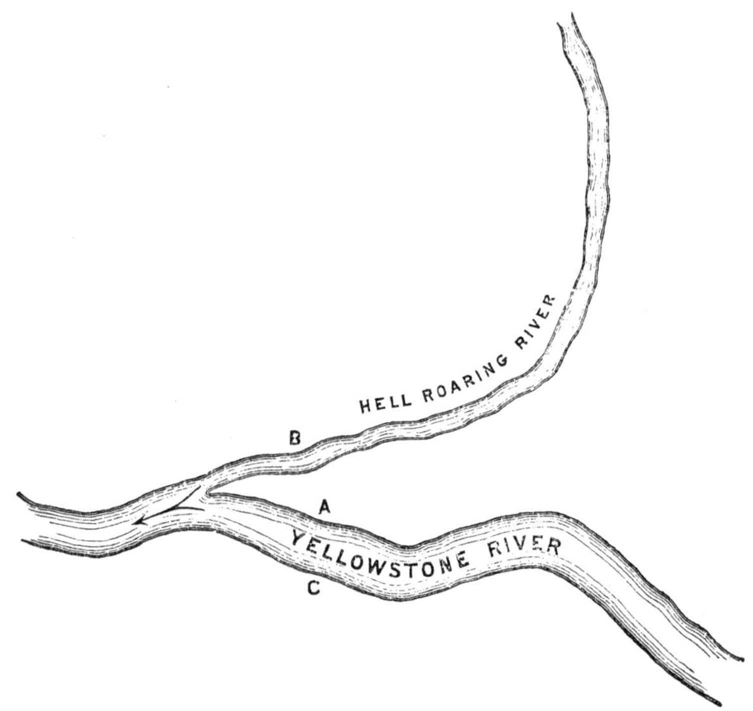

FIG. 20.—Example of acute junction of streams.

The occurrence of low divides in this portion of the Rocky Mountain region is somewhat characteristic. The slight elevation of portions of the water-shed at South Pass may be inferred from the fact that several of our party passed some rods beyond the divide before observing it, although they were at the time specially engaged in its determination. The divide at the Two-Ocean Pass, as the name indicates, is so nearly level that the single mountain-torrent which feeds the divergent streams is passed northward and southward with little disturbance, and an ordinary observer might pass from the Pacific to the Atlantic waters, or *vice versa*, without noticing for a time the difference in the direction of the currents. South of Yellowstone Lake the divide is often quite low, being, in places, scarcely three hundred feet above the lake-level, though some miles distant. Other examples have also been given in the course

* Doctor Hayden, in several places in his reports, has spoken of this basin as largely one of *elevation*. This term is liable to cause misapprehension, for certainly he cannot intend to express the opinion that the basin has been formed partly by its own elevation, but rather by the elevation of its boundaries by deposition. I shall therefore use the less objectionable phrase, *basin of circum-deposition*, which may be conveniently employed to designate such basins or valleys as have been more or less caused by the deposition of beds about them as an inclosing wall or walls.

of this report. In nearly all such cases these effects may readily be traced to the deposition of nearly horizontal beds in such a manner as to cover pre-existing ridges without materially affecting the general course of the drainage. This, at least, will explain the general results; but modifications of greater or less extent have arisen from subsequent erosion in special cases.

Among the many interesting features of this region one or two other peculiarities of the aqueous erosion must suffice for the present. The courses of conjoining streams near their junction are not unfrequently gradually convergent, so that they unite acutely, although often widely divergent in their general courses. As a type may be taken the case of Hell-Roaring River, entering the Yellowstone six miles below the bridge. Figure 20 represents this feature fairly. Slough Creek, the last tributary of the East Fork of the Yellowstone, is another good example, as are also some of the Stinking Water tributaries and other streams, found, as a rule, in the volcanic district, this result being doubtless due to the nature of the crok in a large measure.

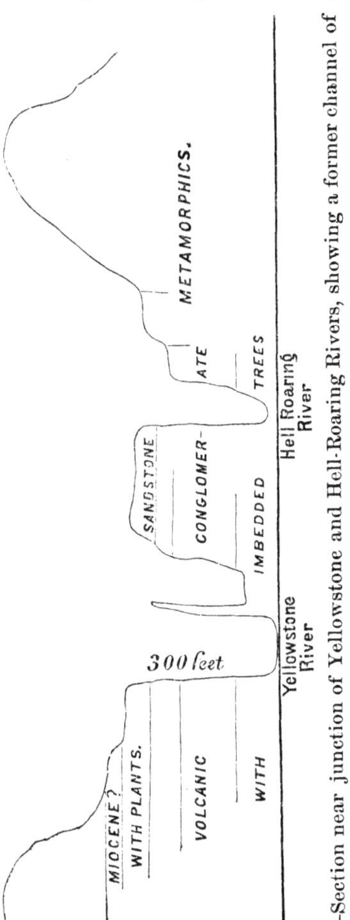

FIG. 21.—Section near junction of Yellowstone and Hell-Roaring Rivers, showing a former channel of the Yellowstone.

At A, Figure 20, there is a curious cutting, the place of a former channel of the Yellowstone, which is separated by a very thin ledge from the present cañon. This ledge is so frail that it is difficult to understand how it could have remained, even had it been but an islet in the middle of the earlier stream. A section across both the Yellowstone and Hell-Roaring Rivers is shown in Figure 21, including this thin wall.

WIND ACTION.

Like the circulation of the water upon the land, the atmospheric movements are also controlled by the topography of the country to a very great extent, and it will not be surprising to find that the results of such action, in a district composed of comparatively level plains, bounded by high walls upon one or more sides, have a certain uniformity about them which could not be expected in more open tracts.

The Green River Basin is, practically, a plain, hemmed in upon all sides but the east by snow-clad mountain-ridges, while the open side communicates with a wide expanse of prairie-surface. During the summer the heated air rises from the plains, causing a current which is kept up by the continued supply of colder air from the mountains. The direction of the wind, or of the surface-currents, will thus depend partly upon the position of the outlet, but even more upon the location of the surrounding mountain-walls. The prominent features, as exhibited in

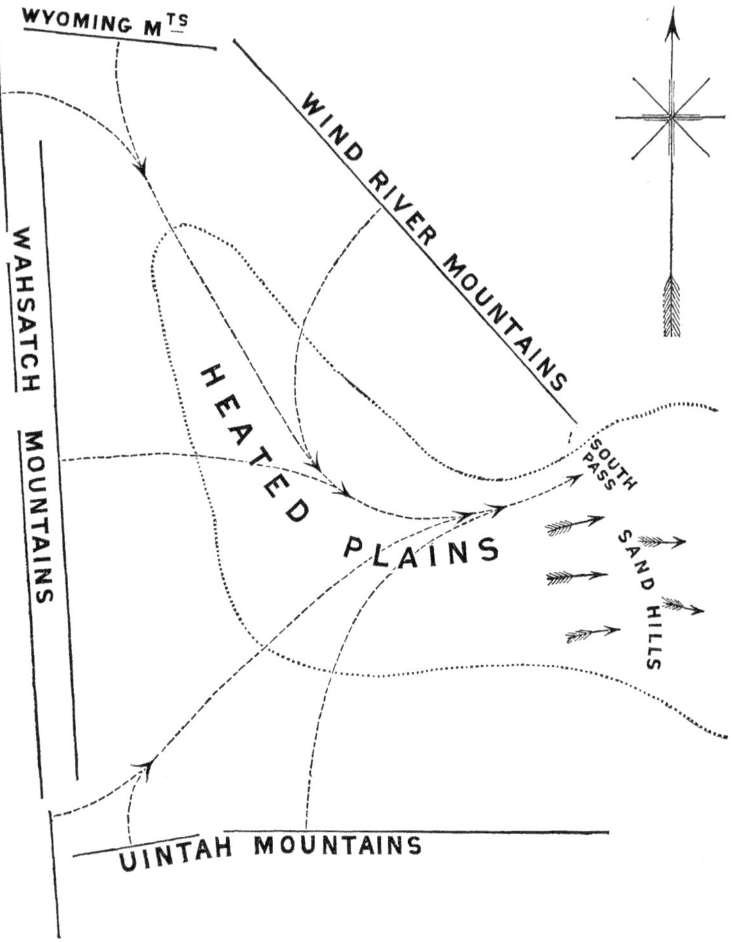

Fig. 22.—Showing cause and effect of wind action in the Green River Basin, Wyoming Territory.

the Green River Basin, are illustrated in Figure 22 and Figure 23 gives an outline view of the main facts as they occur in a portion of the Wind River Valley. The arrow points in both indicate the courses of the prevailing atmospheric currents. The power of the wind is plainly shown in the Green River Basin by the peculiar position of those composite plants which are collectively known as "sage-brush" and "grease-wood" in this section, and by the scooping out of the road-bed in some places to a depth of 3 or 4 feet. These plants, in spots which are well exposed to the wind, now stand upon isolated mounds or small hills, not unlike the potato plants in a well-tilled field, except that the hills are often three or four times the height of a potato hill. In the section marked "Sand Hills," in Figure 22, there is now a very large barren tract extending for miles to the eastward, said to be the abode of innumerable rattlesnakes, but it is entirely destitute of vegetation. When viewed in the reflected light from the sun it closely resembles an immense tract of drifted snow; and if a strong wind be blowing at the same time, as is almost always the case, one could readily mistake the clouds of sand for a driving snow-storm.

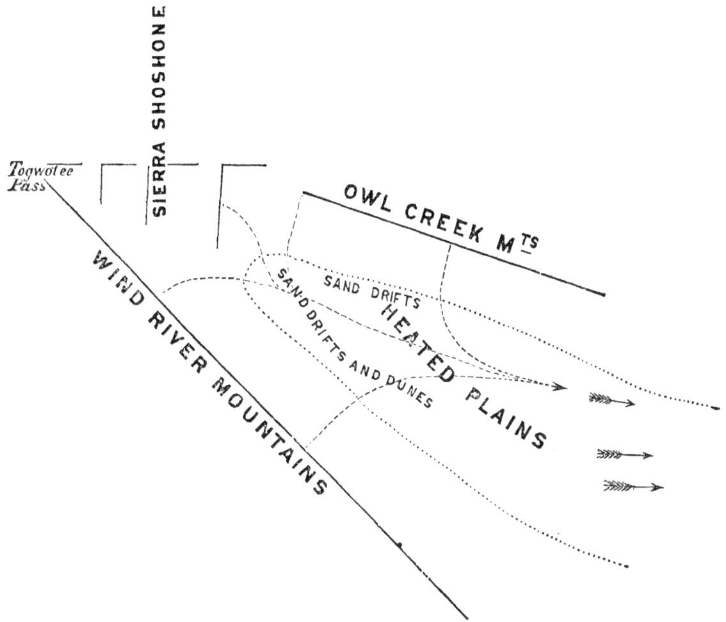

FIG. 23.—Showing cause and effect of wind action in a portion of the Wind River Plateau.

In the Wind River Valley, in the region indicated by the lettering in Figure 23, similar formations exist; but one or two special features deserve notice here. *Dunes*, or sand-hillocks, of considerable size may be seen in places, usually in hollows or along the edges of low cliffs which serve to break the force of the wind and cause the sand to be there deposited. Figure 24 represents the structure of the sand-drifts when only herbaceous vegetation is present. Here the prevailing winds are from the west, or nearly so, and the slope of the hillocks is much less upon that side. As a rule they are less regular than here represented, owing to the growth of clumps of grass upon many of the summits, which finally changes the hillocks into tufty hummocks.

Some peculiar forms of soft sandstone, already referred to as results of aqueous erosion, have no doubt received their finishing touches by the direct influence of the wind or by the abrading action of wind-blown sand. Many of the pinnacles and other irregular masses of rock which cap the conical and pyramidal buttes of the Bridger group in the Green River Basin, as well as the grotesque forms found elsewhere, were probably shaped in part by this force.

Lastly, the action of the winds in the felling of timber in large quantities has produced results the importance of which can scarcely be estimated. To say nothing of the ultimate effects which may be supposed to follow from the decay of the vegetable tissue and the possible or probable accumulation of peat, coal, or other material, there can be no question that the present features of a vast expanse of country in the West are due, in a measure, to the influence of these wind-falls upon the circulation of the water in the streams. The snow which becomes lodged in the intricate masses of logs resists the thawing power of the sun's rays for a longer time, and it is also often prevented from sliding down declivities with force. Streams are not seldom dammed or otherwise obstructed, retarding their progress for a time, only to renew their courses with increased power when the resulting lake overflows the barrier. Swamps are formed in other places, allowing of the growth of denser and more luxuriant vegetation, and the consequent increase of humus by decay. In these and in numerous other ways these all but impenetrable stretches of fallen timber are playing their part in the dynamics of the country, but chiefly by retarding the passage of the atmospheric precipitation from the mountainous districts, and providing for its more equable distribution throughout the year.

W E

FIG. 24.—Section across a sand-drift patch, Wind River Valley, north of Camp 24.

CHAPTER VIII.

DYNAMICAL GEOLOGY—CONTINUED.

Biological and chemical action—Effects of plant and animal life—Weathering of rocks—Chemical changes and products—"Alkali" deposits—Conclusion.

The geological action of plant and animal life, directly and indirectly, is, perhaps, too frequently overlooked in estimating the effects of the various forces engaged in the formation, destruction, and conservation of deposits, although it must be acknowledged that results of importance are often produced by these agents in their growth and decay. There are many questions of the greatest economic interest as yet unsettled which can only be finally solved by the accumulation of facts bearing upon this and kindred subjects. As a single example may be mentioned the opinion now quite commonly, but probably erroneously, held that forests exert an attractive influenec upon the moisture contained in the clouds, but there are other subjects concerning which even less is known, which are more or less connected with the dynamical action of life.

In view of all this, a portion of the present chapter is devoted to a consideration of some of the important effects visible in Western Wyoming, which have been accomplished through the agency of living forms.

EFFECTS OF PLANT LIFE.

The geological results of the growth and decomposition of the members of the vegetable kingdom may be conveniently divided into three classes, viz: 1. Protective or conservative; 2. Formative, or reproductive; 3. Destructive.

I.—CONSERVATIVE ACTION.

In cases in which two or more forces are simultaneously at work in nature, it is often not easy to determine accurately the results which should properly be accredited to each, and even when certain of these agencies are antagonistic, the difficulty is not always decreased. Thus, the sand-hills southeast of South Pass, mentioned in the preceding chapter, (see Figure 22,) were there formed because of the absence of vegetation from that tract, but the lack of vegetation is, doubtless, caused by the power of the wind which has drifted the sand. The protective or conservative effects of plant-life, in the shape of the hardy "sage," and "grease-wood," are well shown in the *hillocky* region to the westward. So, also, in the sand-drift region of the Wind River Valley, before mentioned, (Chap. VII, Figures 23 and 24,) the growth of grasses upon some of the small hillocks has produced similar but less regular features upon a reduced scale. Figure 25 represents a section across the old emigrant-road and overland stage-route, at a point where its course lies in the direction of the prevailing winds. It will be seen that the sand has been blown out of the track, (which has been much worn by use,) to a depth of several feet, while the plants have protected the greater portion of the district, partly by their roots and partly by the resistance offered by their trunks to the wind.

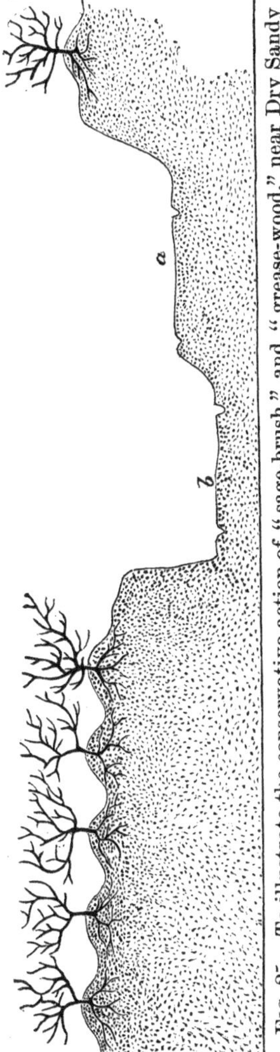

FIG. 25.—To illustrate the conservative action of "sage-brush" and "grease-wood," near Dry Sandy Creek, Green River Basin. *a*.—Newer road-bed. *b*.—Old road-bed. Both in use.

The influence of turf in preserving the surface of the land is well shown in portions of the Yellowstone Basin. A small stream which flows into Pelican Creek a mile and a half above the crossing of our trail illustrates this in a peculiar and remarkable manner. The amount of water which passes through the channel is not very small, but the matted turf layer of considerable thickness has held the stream within narrow bounds, thus preventing great lateral spread at the surface. Were the supply of water uniform at all times the undermining of the banks which is continually taking place might prove more destructive, but the difference in the amounts furnished during the spring and the summer is so great that the channel is overflowed in the flood-seasons, resulting in the production of shallow ponds. Occasionally masses of the overhanging turf (see Figure 26) fall down, damming the stream, and thus in a measure retarding the eroding action behind. In the upper portion the valley is very boggy, and here again the growth of the grasses prevents the soil from being removed, though a treacherous quagmire is the result.

The growth of underwood in numerous places has served to retard the transportation of material to the great advantage of many parts of the country. Accumulation of leaves, detritus, and other loose deposits are swept down in times of freshets in large quantities and retained, thus gradually increasing the depth of the river-channels by thickening the deposits upon the banks. The dense growth of gooseberry-bushes

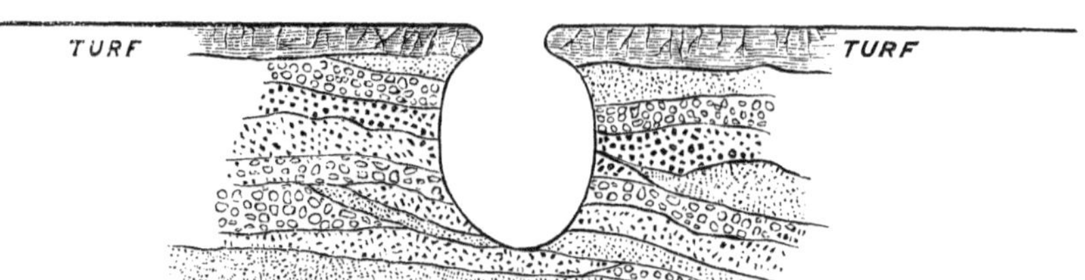

FIG. 26.—Average section across Fool Creek, Yellowstone Basin.

upon the banks, and almost in the bed of the stream of Gooseberry Creek, (tributary of Big Horn River south of Gray Bull River,) as well as the large patches of tall grass, resembling grain-fields, in the same section, are of the greatest value in this way, as is evinced by the less effective action of the stream in wearing away its banks, and by the more extensive accumulation of alluvium in these localities than at other points along the same stream. These and other plants of like nature are frequently met in similar situations, but they are especially characteristic of the volcanic district and of the region about the eastern base of the Sierra Shoshone. The excessive erosion of the Tertiary plains is attributable in a large degree to the general absence of protective vegetation, particularly to its absence from the vicinity of the streams. Numerous examples are in mind, which could be given, of the existence of deep gullies, small "earth-pillars" and other results of water-erosion which would have been almost wholly prevented had there been but a mere covering of turf or other matted vegetation.

Cotton-wood and other forms of *Populus* serve in the same manner as the willow, the gooseberry, &c., to bind the soil by their roots and prevent rapid waste of the land by running water. Fair-sized trees of this genus border the streams in favorable localities, not unfrequently accompanied by a dense undergrowth of the same plant, as upon the Middle Fork of Owl Creek, half a mile above Camp 26, where their value as a restraint upon the action of the water is well indicated by the depth and narrowness of the channel as compared with its limits beyond the extent of their influence.

The importance of accumulations of fallen timber in preventing the sliding and the rapid melting of the snow was mentioned in the last chapter. Growing trees to a certain extent answer the same purposes, and they also protect the surface in other ways. Binding the soil by their roots, even with added weight, they have been the means of retaining much of the detritus upon the steep slopes of the cañon-walls of the North Fork of the Stinking Water, and elsewhere, perhaps nowhere more noticeably than in the Grand Cañon of the Yellowstone. In the nucleus of the Wind River Mountains, huge bowlders have been imprisoned by the gnarled and tangled roots of the pines on slopes so nearly vertical that the snow could not rest upon them were it not for their roughness. The decay of leaves and trunks has covered the rocks in very many places so deeply with vegetable mold that the ordinary processes of weathering have been retarded or almost wholly checked. The ancient spring deposits on Gardiner's River and at other localities are extremely liable to degradation by erosion and decomposition, and yet they have often been remarkably well preserved, owing mainly to the protective action of plant-life and its results.

Lastly may be mentioned the protection afforded the less hardy plants by belts or patches of timber lying upon the side from which come the prevailing winds. It is always difficult to estimate the true value of this element in special cases without more extended observation than it is possible to obtain in a single season spent on the march, but some slight idea of the real importance of this influence may be gained from a single well-marked example. In the valley of Yellowstone River, just southeast of Sour Creek, there is a sand-flat of several acres so exposed as to be frequently acted upon by local wind-currents, while the adjacent timber is well arranged for the protection of much of the contiguous unwooded area from the same currents. The sand-flat is more or less covered with drifts and shifting dunes, but the protected portions are clothed with excellent grass. Similar features are noticeable, with variations according to circumstances, above the forks of Warm Spring Creek and in one or two other sections.

II.—FORMATIVE ACTION.

Allusion has already been made to certain accumulations of vegetable mold or humus, resulting from the decay of leaves and the trunks of fallen trees. There is nothing very peculiar in these formations, except that they are often rather remarkable for their extent and protective power. The thick layer of this material which now covers deeply the ancient hot-spring deposits of Gardiner's River is particularly noticeable on this account. This and other extensive accumulations in the present thickly-wooded districts bear abundant evidence of the coniferous nature of the vegetation, which, as now, has occupied these regions almost exclusively for centuries past. The dry pine "needles" falling upon the ground not only directly tend to increase the deposits, but they also largely prevent water-erosion of their own accumulations by the formation of a kind of thatch which protects the surface and serves to bind the decayed material more firmly together. These facts will probably explain the more abundant humic deposits in pine-clad countries, a feature not confined to the Rocky Mountain region.

Upon the treeless plains, when clothed with turf, the amount of the vegetable mold varies greatly, in some places being but two or three inches in thickness, while in others, more accessible to moisture and less exposed to the winds, accumulations of as many feet in depth have been formed. On the arid Tertiary areas remote from the mountains and away from the streams, especially in districts open to high prevalent winds, there is, practically, no formation of humus, although the soil is usually very fertile.

Many interesting observations concerning other deposits of this character are necessarily omitted here, though often extensive and of great importance. Alluvial deposits in portions of the district have been caused by the damming up of the streams by fallen timber or by driftwood, but much more frequently by the retaining action of growing vegetation in the flood seasons. These latter accumulations are most abundant, perhaps, in the valley of the Upper Yellowstone River, though they are represented in parts of the Wind River Valley, and, markedly, on the tributaries of the Big Horn River north of the Owl Creek range, as well as in the valley of Burns' Fork, (Uintah Mountains,) and more especially on some of its affluents. Small lakes and ponds abound in many sections, and it would require a lengthy chapter for the description of the characteristic deposits of each, to say nothing of other striking peculiarities. To allude to some of these in a very general manner, it will answer the present purpose to divide these minor bodies of water into three not well-defined classes. In the first division may be included those lakes and ponds, with outlets, which are constant or perpetual, *i. e.*, those which retain water throughout the year, however they may fluctuate in level at different seasons. Such basins rarely receive important deposits of purely vegetable matter, except as drift-wood, which occasionally accumulates to a certain extent upon the shores. Leaves and herbaceous stems will, however, become mixed with the alluvium, and thus aid in some slight degree in the formative process, though the comparative absence of deciduous trees from this region prevents such effects to any considerable extent. Another class of lakes, those, with or without outlets, which become dry during a part of the year by drainage or evaporation, may be the cause of not unimportant vegetable-deposits. A single case in point must suffice for illustration, although many might be given from notes taken in the field. About four miles south of Camp Brown, upon our outward march, on the first day of July, we encountered, directly in the road, a still pond of shallow water less than half an acre in extent. Around it, upon all sides, the land surface was exposed to the wind, and consequently mostly barren. Upon our return, in the middle of September, we rode through a slight hollow where the pond had been, now completely dry and clothed with the choicest grass, which was being made into excellent hay for use at the post. The soil in which it grew was quite rich in humus, the result of the decay of many previous crops not reaped by the hand of man. The third division embraces the stagnant pools and ponds of various sizes which are so very abundant in the Yellowstone Basin, though by no means strictly confined to that region. These are usually productive of important cumulative results on account of the continual progress of decomposition, which furnishes abundant food for the growth of many plants. Accordingly we find these places crowded with aquatic forms of vegetation, which by subsequent decay gives rise to noticeable deposits of humus.

Nor is this all. The very large tracts of country covered by fallen timber have so influenced the drainage as to form vast swamps in which the greater portion of the local vegetable products are retained and decomposed. In such places the vegetation is, of course, very luxuriant and of rapid growth, and it is also of such a character that the annual contribution of waste material, such as leaves, stems, and fruits, is much larger than in the drier and more exposed localities. The consequent accumulations of muck are very great, while to all this must be added the enhanced decay of the fallen timber itself, resulting from exposure to conditions brought about by its own prostration, though in many cases this is retarded by the antiseptic properties of the swamp extract, which only serves to increase the bulk of the deposit, however.*

In this connection, the enormous quantity of silicified wood, which is so commonly distributed in portions of the volcanic series, and which is now being formed to some extent by geyser action, may be mentioned in passing as one very prominent example of a vegetable accumulation. In this case, however, the result is due mainly to the exertion of forces elsewhere considered, and to the deposition of preservative material not derived from the vegetable kingdom. The process by which this

* It should be noted that the dryness of the climate and the nature of the vegation together exert a retarding influence upon the decay of the blasted timber, thus adding greatly to the continuance of the above effects.

deposit has been produced will receive attention in a succeeding chapter, to which the reader is referred for further information upon this subject. To avoid repetition one or two other formations of minor importance, resulting more or less directly from the growth and decay of plants, but also dependent upon the action of geysers or hot springs, will be left for discussion beyond.

III.—DESTRUCTIVE ACTION.

So far as Western Wyoming is concerned it does not appear that the destructive effects of plant-life have been at all commensurate with the protective and reproductive influence of vegetation. Land-slides in the mountainous districts are very rare, if we may judge from the absence of frequent proof of such occurrences. There are many places along the walls of the cañon of North Fork of Stinkingwater River, where the loose earth and gravel is almost constantly falling down the steeper slopes, but this bears no resemblance in extent or effect to a real land-slide. Even upon the nearly vertical walls of the Grand Cañon of the Yellowstone, where pines often grow, there is no evidence of frequent or extensive changes of this nature. There is, on the contrary, conclusive proof that the roots of the trees often prevent land-slides by binding the soil and the rocks more firmly together.

The destructive element in connection with vegetation is, therefore, reduced to a small amount. The extensive growth of lichens upon the rocks, giving them at a little distance an unnatural color, shows that the disintegration due to their presence is notable, at least, although it would be difficult to determine the extent of their influence. Large trees, undermined by the wear of the water upon the banks of streams, cause considerable destruction when they fall by tearing up the soil about their roots, and the effect is produced more generally by the prostration of timber by the wind.

EFFECTS OF ANIMAL LIFE.

The geological or dynamical action resulting from the life and death of animals will be treated under three heads, similar in scope to the preceding, viz: 1. Protective effects; 2. Cumulative effects; 3. Destructive effects.

I.—PROTECTIVE EFFECTS.

Animals exert but little conservative influence in any way, and that indirectly, but it is, nevertheless, true that some slight preservation of the surface can be traced to them in this region. To say nothing of the hard-beaten paths or trails made by the domesticated animals of the white man and the Indians, game-trails almost without number are to be seen all over the district wherever the country is not so open as to allow of the scattering of the animals to feed, and one soon learns to detect the character of the animals which have made them, from certain peculiarities in each case. The bison prefers the plains, and the great weight of his body and its clumsiness compels him to climb the heights and knolls by a gradual or zigzag course. The elk often passes high up in the mountains, and the trails made by droves of this animal are quite direct, but never as steep as the courses often taken by the big-horn, or mountain-sheep. At first the passage of large droves of animals over the same course wears the surface, loosening it and causing the dust to be swept out of the trail by the wind, but the final result is to leave the soil so compact that vegetation will not grow upon the path for many years afterward. This protects the surface somewhat, especially if the trails have been made along the edge of a bluff, one above another, as is so commonly the case with the bison-paths. But this conservation is slight compared with the effects produced by another habit of this animal. All over the wide tract which has been traversed by the bison within the past fifty years there may be seen circular patches of grass in greater or less number, often now raised slightly above the surrounding surface in windy sections. Catlin, in his valuable work entitled "North American Indians," refers to these patches in the lower valley of the Missouri, and his explanation of their origin is no doubt correct. Without entering upon a lengthy discussion, it may be remarked that the bison is fond of wallowing in the mud, and no one can travel far in the West without meeting with what are there called "buffalo-wallows." These are shallow depressions, bearing some resemblance to the familiar "hog-wallow" by the roadside in the rural districts, though more nearly circular or semi-oval in outline. On account of the erratic habits of the animal large numbers of these depressions will be left, wherever the herds have rested in a suitable spot, to be filled with water by the rains, which, by evaporation, allows of the growth of grass to fix the soil by its roots, while the surrounding surface, if parched, as is often the case, may be degraded by the winds, leaving the grass-plats at a higher level.

II.—CUMULATIVE EFFECTS.

There are very few recent animal formations of much geological importance to be presented under this head, but there are several interesting and somewhat peculiar deposits of limited extent which deserve a share of our attention in this place. Next to the barren aspect of the great plains produced by the aridity of the climate, there is nothing which has so much to do with their appearance of utter desolation as the widespread accumulations of the bones of the bison and other animals which have been so recklessly slaughtered for the sake of the sport of hunting(?) them, or, at best, for the mere value of their hides. Millions upon millions of the skeletons of these animals now lie bleaching upon the surface, and it is almost certain that very many of them will become entombed much after the manner of their Eocene ancestors buried in the deposits of the Bridger group of strata. The present conditions for their fossilization are less favorable than during the Tertiary period, but many of the bones are already partly or wholly covered by the drifted sands, or by the growth of vegetation around them, and many have, no doubt, been transported by the streams and buried in the alluvial deposits.

"Buffalo-chips," as the dried dung of the bison is called, is common as a thickly-scattered surface-deposit in sections where it has not been covered by wind-action, though it is scarce along the line of the well-traveled roads, on account of its frequent use as fuel for camp-fires. In a few localities small deposits of guano exist in crevices in the rocks not exposed to the action of the rains. Opposite Camp 24, on a short tributary of Dry Creek, (Wind River Plateau,) I noticed in such a crevice a rich deposit of at least half a bushel. In many places in the Sierra Shoshone the weathering of the rocks has produced admirable crevices or fissures for the nests of owls, and frequently the walls of these are lined with a richly-colored glossy deposit of their excrement, mixed with the pellets of indigestible material ejected through their throats, according to their habit. Much of this is very resinous and not in the least offensive to nose or eye of one who does not know its real character. In fact, one of the party expressed a desire to taste a portion of it until informed of its true nature. This very strong resinous odor and quality is rather difficult to explain, except upon the supposition that the crevices are commonly shared by the owls with other birds which feed upon the seeds of the pines, though it is just possible that it is the result of secondary action, caused by the decomposition of the pine "needles" which fall into the crevices and become mixed with the guano.

The beaver may, perhaps, be properly credited with the indirect and unintentional formation of local. deposits of alluvium by the damming of streams, but this effect is more than counterbalanced by its destructive tendencies. A few rather important but not extensive cases of fossilization by immersion in the basins of hot springs were noticed, but they do not require fuller notice in the present chapter, as further mention will be made of them in the section devoted to the geysers and hot springs.

III.—DESTRUCTIVE EFFECTS.

The beaver is probably entitled to take the lead in the work of destruction. These animals are still common in portions of the Yellowstone Park, and elsewhere, but the hand of man is already turned against them, and their works are, in most places, more numerous than themselves. It is unnecessary to describe these structures or their effects, for they are already widely known. Prairie-dogs and other burrowing animals are very commonly distributed throughout the region, and their actions have resulted in more or less destruction to the soil by bringing to the surface deposits of sand, which is scattered by the winds, and by injuring the solidity of the ground above their burrows. The destruction of vegetation by beavers occasionally has been quite general over small areas, but usually it has only accomplished a more or less beneficial thinning out of superfluous growth. Grasshoppers, in some sections, particularly on the Shoshone Plateau, have been instrumental in the destruction of vegetation to a remarkable degree, at seasons of the year when such devastation is often detrimental to the life of the plants.

CHEMICAL GEOLOGY.

A large number of interesting details remain to be considered, concerning which a quantity of illustrative material has been gathered, but which must be very generally treated within the prescribed limits of the present chapter. Much of this material requires careful chemical analysis for its complete elucidation, and this it has been impossible to procure, though the author indulges the hope that opportunity for its elaboration at some time in the future may yield valuable results in a department of geological science which assuredly deserves thoughtful consideration on the part of investigators. In the foregoing pages of the section relating to dynamical geology, very little has been said of the chemical changes which have taken place in the rocks since their deposition or of the important products which have resulted from chemical action.

The remainder of this chapter is, therefore, allotted to these subjects, including also some of the more important effects produced by the action of the atmosphere. No classification can well be adopted, and the various effects will be taken up in convenient order without regard to perfect system. In order to partially supply this lack, minor headings, in italics, are introduced for greater convenience of reference.

WEATHERING OF ROCKS.

It will not be necessary to speak in a detailed manner of the characteristic modes of weathering of the rocks of the various formations, but there are certain peculiarities in the effects of climatic and other influences upon special layers in some sections, which are of sufficient importance to merit attention.

Ozone in the atmosphere.—Many of the sandstones of the Green River group of Eocene beds, though white inside, weather reddish upon the exposed surface. The mere presence of iron in this rock seemed insufficient to account for the very marked change in color, but for several days no clue was obtained toward any more satisfactory solution. While engaged with Dr. Heizman in some preliminary analyses at our camp on Little Sandy River, I noticed that blue litmus-paper rapidly reddened upon exposure to the air, even when moistened with ammonia. Dr. Heizman, then and subsequently, kindly made several tests for ozone with iodized starch-paper, and found it abundant. This, then, may account for the excessive oxidation of many of the rocks of the Green River basin. This action is also noticeable in other sections where similar beds are exposed, but it seems to be mainly confined to the more compact beds, which, is, perhaps, owing to the fact that the more friable beds become more rapidly disintegrated and crumble before they can become colored. This will also explain the otherwise remarkable fact that the reddening effect is seen only upon those rocks not very highly ferruginous, though oxidation has taken place much more extensively in rocks highly charged with iron. If we seek to account for the presence of so great an amount of ozone in the atmosphere, it seems probable that it is due to the strong wind-currents or to some peculiar electrical condition of the atmosphere not accompanied by sufficient heat to prevent its accumulation.

Concretionary structure.

It is in the Tertiary rocks especially that the most interesting examples of nodular and concretionary forms may be found.

It would be no easy matter to enumerate the various peculiarities in the modes of weathering which have been induced by this structure, much less is it possible to describe more than a very few of the leading varieties, within the narrow limits of this section. In the Bridger group of beds large quantities of siliceous material are found, sometimes in compact cherty layers, but often in nodular masses, and frequently in concretionary forms with concentric or *concentring* layers. Sometimes these are lined with minute crystals of quartz, being in effect roughly-shaped geodes; others are little more than the fillings of cavities of irregular form, without separation into bands. Again there will be seen a huge concretion, composed of alternating layers of sandstone and intrusive chalcedony, the latter partly in "tears," partly massive or even crystalline. Very often in arenaceous and marly beds the concretionary structure appears almost to be entirely induced by the weathering of the rock, the oxidation of calcareous or ferruginous material giving rise to more or less concentric bands of color.

In the sub-Tertiary rocks concretions are often common. The Niagara limestone contains *jaspery* flakes and "drusy" cavities filled with beautiful agate concretions; *clay ironstones*, sometimes with plant-fossils, occur in the Cretaceous beds near Gray Bull River and at other points; and geodes of *calc-spar* are abundant in nearly all of the sedimentary rocks.

The volcanic rocks are very well supplied with these secondary formations, as instance the botryoidal geodes of the Yellowstone River, mentioned in the last chapter, and the great variety of interesting forms associated with the masses of silicified wood at Amethyst Mountain, on the south of the East Fork of the Yellowstone. Even the geyser deposits sometimes take on the concretionary, or, more properly, the concentric structure.

The principal forms of concretions will be found more fully described in the chapters relating to stratigraphy, under the heads of the different formations.

Influence of climatic conditions.—In winter the temperature of this region is severe but steady, and the surface is mostly covered with snow, which protects it to some extent from the effects of the various weathering influences. In the early spring and late fall the action of frost, in rending apart the rocks and enlarging the fissures, becomes an important element among the numerous dynamical agents, and it is probable that the alternate freezing and thawing which takes place at these seasons is productive of a large part of the weathering effects which are exhibited upon a scale of great magnitude in many parts of the district. Positive proof of the workings of this force from actual *observations* are wanting, but no one at all familiar with the ordinary results of such action will be disposed to doubt the propriety of the above statement when told that the necessary conditions of thawing and freezing are present during a large portion of the year in a high degree of intensity. Evidences of the slight movement of large masses of rock from the original positions by some force of this nature are very common. Some excellent examples of this action may be seen in the Wind River Mountains, particularly in the neighborhood of the nucleus, though it would be difficult to name a single rock-exposure in the whole district where such effects are not visible. Any person at all familiar with this process and its results in places in which freezing can take place only during a small portion of the year, will be prepared to recognize the dynamical importance of this agent in a country where there are but few nights, even in summer, during which the temperature does not fall below 32° Fahrenheit. In the central portion of the Wind River range the profound chasms have often been choked with immense accumulations of angular granitic bowlders which could never have been thrown down from positions in the cliffs without the intervention of the force produced by the expansion of water in assuming the solid condition. Steep cliffs of the Quebec group and the Niagara dolomite are almost invariably accompanied by large blocks at their base, which have thus been forced from their original places. The same features are observable in jointed exposures of the rocks of all the formations, but not always to the same extent. In many of the Tertiary rocks, as well as with some of the members of the metamorphic series and in certain argillaceous beds of the intervening formations, the strata are traversed by very numerous joints, which in a measure prevents the accumulation of water in the crevices for the formation of ice, and also leaves in the talus much less convincing proof of its mode of origin.

In the volcanic conglomerate in a large number of places there are good-sized cavernous holes, sometimes high above the ground. It is possible that some of these at the bases of cliffs may have been formed by wave action upon the shores of Miocene lakes; but many, and by far the greater number, have, undoubtedly, been caused by other agencies. Not a few show pretty clearly that they are the result of the action of freezing water in fissures, which has caused large masses to be dislodged at the weaker points from time to time without affecting the bulk of the rock adjoining the crevices. The alternate expansion and contraction of the rocks by differences of temperature in the days and the nights is, doubtless, of great consequence as a dynamical agent, although the actual effects produced are usually very difficult to ascertain. No special facts have been collected which can be offered with entire confidence, but the following remarks will enable the reader to form some general idea of the influence which these thermic changes must exert upon the rocks of this section: The difference between the day and night temperature (*i. e.*, maximum for day, minimum for night) upon the plains during the summer months is frequently as much as 30° or 40°, and it often becomes as great as 50° during the month of August. Dr. Livingstone* reports that the rapid contraction by cooling of rocks in Africa heated to a temperature of 137° Fahrenheit during the day, was sufficient to cause the breaking off of masses weighing even two hundred pounds in some instances. It may at least be suggested that this cause has been instrumental in the weathering of the rocks in the Rocky Mountain region to a greater degree than has generally been supposed.

Summary.—In general, it may be remarked that the Tertiary rocks show the effects of erosion and weathering much more clearly and extensively than the earlier rocks. This is due to two things: the greater activity of the eroding agencies, and the more fragile and soluble nature of the later horizontal strata. Another prominent cause is the rather abundant presence of formative and protective agencies in the moister mountainous districts, which are almost entirely absent upon the plains. Again, in the mountains there is greater resistance to the exercise of mechanical force, while below the chemical action is also increased, so that, upon the whole, the later series is exposed to far greater destructive influence, at the same time that its power of resistance is very small in proportion to that of the more ancient deposits.

CHEMICAL CHANGES AND PRODUCTS.

As before stated, a clear and comprehensive elucidation of the important subject of chemical geology cannot be given in these pages, but the present chapter would be incomplete without some reference to the more prominent changes resulting from chemical action, both in the direction of degradation of ancient deposits, and the accumulation of new formations from their waste. Hitherto, the chemical or physical processes of solution, condensation, evaporation, and precipitation, have been scarcely mentioned, in order that their effects might be more systematically considered in this portion of the report. For the sake of convenience, rather than from any natural method of arrangement, these subjects may be taken up in the order which has just been given.

Solvent action of water.—As water, in its passage over the rocks, takes from them the more soluble ingredients, its power to effect similar changes upon the rocks afterward met is more or less modified, according to a variety of circumstances. On this account it will be best for us to begin at the sources of the streams in the mountains and follow them down across the plains, that the ascertained results may be more clearly understood. Chemically speaking, there are two classes of mountain streams, which may be productive of somewhat different effects in the way of solution of the mineral ingredients of the soil and

* "Zambesi," pp. 492, 516. Quoted in "Manual of Geology," Jukes & Geikie, (third edition,) p. 376.

the rocks. To the first group belong those which are the direct products of the melting snows, and which pass off quickly to the plains over the surface of the ground. The second division comprises those which proceed from springs, in which the water has percolated through the soil, and has become partially saturated with the more soluble substances. In the region of the Rocky Mountains, where snow lies in the higher ridges almost perpetually, it is seldom possible to separate these two classes of streams, for very soon they will be found united in the same channels. There are, it is true, in the Yellowstone Basin, some important streams which proceed from springs alone; but in nearly every instance of this kind, the water passes for many miles over rock which is practically identical, mineralogically, with the formation in which the springs occur, so that the observed effects are much the same as in the snow-fed streams, which traverse the same district. A notable and not unimportant exception must be made in the case of the prominent aqueous products of the geysers and hot springs, which will receive special attention.

The extensive accumulations of decomposing vegetable matter in most of the mountainous districts furnish favorable conditions for the absorption of carbonic acid by the water, and this has no doubt had much to do with the excessive erosion which has taken place in the limestone exposures, and it may partly account for the general emergence of the streams from the mountains through cañons cut in the limestone. The absence of thick accumulations of soil is a very noticeable feature of a large part of the country, and this is due to the solution of the limestone, which is then carried off by the streams. Upon reaching the plains the waters become saturated with the more soluble mineral ingredients, though in seasons of freshets this may not take place until the stream has traversed the open country for a long distance. The water at this stage will contain alkaline carbonates which will have increased its solvent power, and even silica will be attacked and dissolved. In the Tertiary rocks there are many cherty beds and layers of the more soluble forms of silica which thus add their quota to the amount. In flood-seasons the banks of the streams are overflowed, and pools and small ponds are left in low spots when the current subsides. Rains and melted snow-water pass down through the crevices of the rocks, and the same ingredients are extracted, but with less of variety in each case than will be found in running water which has passed over many different rocks containing a great assortment of minerals.

Subterranean waters.—The presence of limestone-beds in such great quantity as to form the bulk of the Paleozoic and Mesozoic rocks as well as the regular but extended tilting of the strata, has produced fissures and underground passages, since enlarged by the waters, through which the drainage of the country is now partly effected. When the streams from these subterranean channels reach the surface in limestone districts, or in places where carbonic acid is forming from the decomposition of carbonates or of organic matter, bubbles of this gas (CO_2) are sent off in quantity. Springs of this kind exist in many parts of the Yellowstone Basin and in other portions of the volcanic district. Yellow Water Creek, a southern tributary of Gray Bull River, originates in a chalybeate spring which is very highly charged with carbonic acid. The hot springs below Camp Brown also evolve considerable quantities of this gas. Several cold sulphur-springs issue from the Triassic and other rocks containing gypsum as a deposit or in process of formation by the decomposition of pyrites. Near the left bank of the Little Popoagie, and also at Camp Brown, thick oil issues from the earth, probably connected in some way with the Cretaceous coal or lignite beds not far distant in either case. Both of these springs are located within or near a prominent fold involving the Subtertiary strata. At our camp on Spring Creek, at the southern base of the Owl Creek range, several springs of bitter "alkali" water afforded the only means of quenching thirst. Sour Creek entering the Yellowstone above the falls, from the right bank, Warm Spring Creek, nearly opposite, and all the prominent streams of the geyser basins, are highly charged with mineral ingredients held in solution, largely the result of the action of subterranean waters.

As might be inferred from the horizontal disposition of the Tertiary strata, and from their extensive erosion into buttes and benches, springs are seldom or never present over the area occupied by them, except in cases in which they may originate in other formations and reach the surface through the Tertiary beds.

The most important and extended results of the action of underground water are exhibited in those sections where heat has accompanied its movements, as in the geysers and hot springs of the National Park which fall to be described in a subsequent portion of this work.

Results of condensation and evaporation.—In the Tertiary districts the surcharged streams, and particularly the stagnant pools produced by the overflow, soon become condensed by the heat of the sun and the drying action of the wind. In soils which are not argillaceous, or in those which are covered with turf, this results in the production of a sirupy saline liquid, and finally, if the evaporation be sufficiently extended, the so-called "alkali" deposit is formed. In clays the evaporation is retarded and chemical changes doubtless take place continually. If the saline accumulation be excessive, or if the evaporation be insufficient to dry the clay, a bog or slough is the result, and these are commonly known as "alkali bogs" and "alkali holes." Along the edges of the streams and upon the overflowed grass after the receding of the waters, a deposit is formed which is usually reddish or brown at first, from the presence of iron, becoming white or grayish upon exposure to the air and drying. This is usually called "alkali," although it frequently contains scarcely a trace of potassa or soda. A specimen of this deposit gathered by myself on June 20, 1873, from a fresh accumulation on Little Sandy River, was qualitatively analyzed the same day by Dr. Heizman and myself with the following result:

Alumina, very abundant.
Magnesia, in considerable quantity.
Lime, in small quantity.
Iron, small amount.
Carbonic acid, considerable.
Sulphuric acid, very abundant.

In a peculiarly weathered concretion exposed in a bluff or butte near the same locality a quantity of siliceous marl was inclosed by a deposition of *chalcedony* in "tears." An analysis of the marl yielded:

Alumina, in considerable quantity.
Magnesia, in considerable quantity.
Lime, abundant.
Iron, small amount.
Silica, basis of the marly deposit.
Carbonic acid, in considerable quantity.
Sulphuric acid, in considerable quantity.

The very large quantities of "alkali" which exist so widely over the plains as an efflorescent deposit have probably been formed by the evaporation of former extensive lakes and ponds left over the Tertiary basins by the draining of the ancient lakes which once covered the whole area. Some of these deposits are of great thickness, but none worthy of more special notice were met upon our line of march. The same process is in operation at present, as described above, but the results are small when compared with what was accomplished in ancient times, because the streams now carry off the greater portion of the soluble material. In these old ponds also are found the readily soluble ingredients as well as those which are sparingly soluble, while the streams leave behind only the substances which are not so easily held in solution.

The various deposits of the hot springs and geysers to be hereinafter described might properly be discussed under this head were it not more convenient to consider them in a chapter by themselves.

Precipitation.—The only prominent example of undoubted precipitation occurring in a natural aqueous solution along our line of march was noticed in a portion of Yellow Water Creek.* The water is slightly alkaline, and contains or receives a large amount of iron from an ore-bed near its source. Much of the iron is precipitated as ferric hydrate, (Fe_2O_3, H_2O.) This settles to the bottom, but it entangles carbonic acid which struggles, as it were, to free itself, thus lifting the precipitated mass toward the surface a little way. A few rods below, the water becomes clear and more palatable, from which it would seem that the iron had by this time exhausted the alkaline principle so that the precipitation can no longer take place. This phenomenon is very interesting and quite remarkable.

Nothing but the absolute necessity of completing this report within the allotted time has compelled the omission of not a little in the way of facts bearing upon the important subjects of this chapter. An endeavor has been made, however, to introduce those facts and observations of the writer which are of the greatest interest, and such as will most aid in connecting together the several parts of the report in a harmonious whole.

CHAPTER IX.

THERMO-DYNAMICS—IGNEOUS ROCKS AND HOT SPRINGS.

Volcanic action—Fissure and crater eruptions—Thermal springs: I. Turbid Lake group; II. Steamboat group; III. Green Spring, Sulphur (!) Hills, &c.; IV. Mud-volcanoes and Crater-Hills; V. Forest group; VI. Wayside group, &c.; VII. Bath Spring, near Camp Brown.

In this and the three succeeding chapters, we shall have to deal with subjects which might appropriately have been discussed in part in each of the four or five preceding chapters, but which, from a certain special interest that attaches to them and for other obvious reasons, may be more satisfactorily considered separately. It is fitting that this review should occupy the position here given it on account of its historical and dynamical relations, both of which have been of the greatest moment in

* Precipitation occurs commonly in regions of hot springs and geysers also, but this subject will receive more attention beyond.

shaping the physical features of a vast expanse of western territory, and often in the production of deposits of economic value.

In several places in the course of the discussion of subjects connected with stratigraphy and dynamical geology, in the previous pages of this report, it has been necessary to refer to topics which are now to be considered; but in no case has any subject of this nature been treated with any degree of completeness. It is hoped that the material presented in these two chapters will prove at least as interesting and valuable as that of any chapter which has preceded them, although evidences of haste in their preparation cannot be avoided.

The subject of thermo-dynamics, or the final effects and the passing phenomena of heat-action, naturally divides itself into four heads in the region embraced by our reconnaissance. These are: 1. Fissure-eruption; 2. Crater-eruption; 3. Geyser action; 4. Hot-spring action, including also *solfataras* and *fumeroles*. This arrangement is based upon the general chronological sequence of the phenomena, and it will be seen to represent successive stages in the diminution of thermal intensity. For reasons that may be apparent to those who have followed the author through the preceding pages of this report, the above order will not be strictly observed in speaking upon these topics, but an effort will be made to treat the subject in such a manner as to accomplish the best results possible in a limited space.

VOLCANIC ACTION.

The proper treatment of the highly interesting subject of the history and dynamical effects of the ancient volcanic action would require more time and space than can be devoted to its discussion in these pages. A review of the history will be found in portions of chapters IV, V, and VII, reference to which may be made with little difficulty, and it will, therefore, be unnecessary to repeat it here, though some additional details may be given for the sake of clearness.

Prof. Joseph Le Conte, of the University of California, spent a portion of the summer of 1873 in the field-study of the volcanic rocks west of the Rocky Mountain chain, and his views, which have been published in the *American Journal of Science*, March and April, 1874, are in many respects identical with those held by myself concerning the history of their accumulation. There are many unsolved problems connected with this subject; but the backbone, as it were, of the history seems now to have been largely determined, and with this key to the structure the labors of future investigators will be in a measure simplified.

FISSURE-ERUPTIONS.

The earliest outflows did not pass over smooth surfaces, apparently in all cases, but they appear to have met with large bowlders strewn over the surface and with growing timber and other obstructions, which were cemented together by the igneous material into thick beds. It is probable that masses of the sedimentary beds were occasionally ejected also from the fissures, but I am obliged to differ with Dr. Hayden as to the extent of such effects. In his report for 1871, page 138, he remarks: "My impression is that when the old volcanoes disgorged their contents into the great lake of waters around, they threw out also portions from the sedimentary formations, and thus the silicified wood comes from the Tertiary or Cretaceous beds, which may have formed the upper part of the walls of the crater. To my own mind, there are several prominent objections to this belief; but first, it will be well to explain, more fully than has yet been done in these pages, some of the leading characteristics of the conglomerates in which the immense deposits of silicified wood are contained. In some respects the lower deposits of conglomerate differ from those of later origin; but the dissimilarities are not of sufficient importance to justify the belief that they have been formed under very different circumstances, except, perhaps, in the case of the earliest beds, which often contain many more fragments of the metamorphic and sedimentary rocks than are usually found in the higher beds.

The later conglomerates also lie, for the most part, in a nearly horizontal position, while the lower beds follow quite closely the irregular contour of the surface at the time of their deposition. It is very difficult to conceive of the condition of the surface at the period of the later outflows; nor would it be wise to attempt wholly to explain all the observed phenomena without a much wider knowledge than is at present possessed of the distribution of the various volcanic formations. No other explanation of the horizontality of the upper conglomerates seems at present admissible than that they were deposited, or, at least, arranged, under water, as Hayden has observed. This is partly proved by the occurrence of intervening layers of sands and clays at various points; but it must be acknowledged that many of the facts are not easily accounted for upon this hypothesis.

Often quite large masses of the Tertiary and other strata are inclosed in the cement of the breccias; and these are frequently composed of thin layers, which have not been separated from each other, as must have been the case had they been forcibly ejected. These sedimentary beds, often containing plant-remains, (Miocene probably,) are also usually disposed horizontally, and, even when much broken and widely separated, a certain continuity can be traced, which proves, beyond the shadow of doubt, that they have been covered where they lay before the volcanic outflows took place. It is, then, highly probable that the semi-aqueous breccias and conglomerates, being thrown out into large bodies of water covering the sedimentary strata, have disrupted the latter in places, leaving other portions to be inclosed by the igneous material *in situ*.

The silicified wood exists in enormous quantities in many of the volcanic breccias and conglomerates; and thousands of excellent specimens may readily be obtained beside which the ordinary fragments so often preserved in museums will sink into insignificance. In many instances, large logs and stumps of trees are found entire; and examples have previously been given of the existence of the upright trunks of trees in some of the beds. From Amethyst Mountain I obtained pieces which had been *worm-eaten*, before becoming fossilized, and several logs were observed which had been worn very smooth by water-action previous to the change. In both of these cases there was every reason for believing that the wood had been rather suddenly acted upon, and that it had not been formerly deposited as a sediment; for the worm-holes had apparently never been filled by mud, and the water-worn logs had the appearance of recent drift-wood. As for the large majority of the silicified logs and stumps, I am quite confident that they were contemporaneous with the igneous deposits in which they are now inclosed; and this opinion is based upon a much greater amount of evidence than can be presented here without detriment to other portions of the report. There are other more fragmentary accumulations of this material in the later strata, which have probably been formed to some extent by hot-spring action, and in these *menilite* is not uncommon. The process of silicification, in my opinion, so far as the bulkier masses are concerned, has been that of the infiltration of silica by means of water percolating through the igneous material; for cavities in the wood and in adjacent portions of the conglomerate are now very often lined with perfect quartz-crystals in great variety of color and arrangement, particularly in the vicinity of Amethyst Mountain, on the left bank of East Fork of the Yellowstone River. Quite commonly, the wood shows signs of charring or of lesser heat-action upon the outside, which cannot be explained unless we adopt the conclusion that it was not mineralized at the time of the igneous ejections. Often, large cylindrical masses of very beautifully-banded *opal*, of richly-variegated colors, will be found in cavities with an exterior and interior resemblance to wood; and these very frequently present an irregular surface across one end, as if the tree or log had been broken in two by the force of the flow, leaving a fractured end upon which the concretion was formed and continued beyond the wood. In other cases, it appears that the wood was nearly or quite consumed, but so slowly that an impression was left of the exterior in the volcanic cement, to be afterward filled up with silica with more or less of a concretionary structure. In this way, as well as in cavities formed by other means, geodes and other concretionary forms have been produced in quantity with almost every conceivable variety of structure and coloring.

The position of the ancient fissures cannot be accurately determined except by extended observation. Dr. Le Conte, as the result of special observations in Oregon and westward, is convinced that the principal fissures in that section were located in the Cascade and Blue ranges; but it is probable that others, perhaps of less importance, existed eastward from that region. There is yet the greater part to be learned concerning the deposition of the beds surrounding the Yellowstone basin; and it is with some slight hesitancy that the following views are advanced, although they appear to be well supported by the facts so far as they have been observed. The author hopes yet to do more thorough work in this intensely interesting field; but, in the mean time, it will not be out of place to record here some opinions, which may serve, in some measure, as a basis for future investigations. So far as I am aware, these views do not very widely differ from those held by others who have traversed a portion of this field. In brief, then, it seems evident that the topographical separation of the Sierra Shoshone mass from the volcanic district to the westward is no less a disjunction, geologically considered. It is barely possible that the Yellowstone Lake basin as such was of pre-volcanic origin; but this is, to say the very least, extremely improbable. I think there can be little doubt that Miocene fresh-water lakes extended over a large portion of the area now covered by the volcanic rocks east of the Rocky Mountain divide, though the deposits of that age have been so covered and disarranged by the subsequent igneous outflows that it is now next to impossible to trace the boundaries of the separate basins.

Richthofen, who has proposed a minute classification of the fissure-ejections, claims that the succession of these rocks is fixed and in the following order, beginning with the earliest formed: 1, *Propylite;* 2, *Andesite;* 3, *Trachyte;* 4, *Rhyolite;* 5, *Basalt.* The fine exposures in the deep-cut cañons afford excellent opportunities for the settlement of this subject; for it is possible to obtain a nearly complete vertical section of the whole series, although this will require careful and extended investigation. With the amount of study that I have been thus far able to give the large number of specimens which I have collected from these beds, it is impossible to offer much of value bearing upon this question; but it may be said, in a general way, that the order of succession of such of the layers as appear without doubt to represent the fissure-eruptions is not unlike the above in the district under consideration. The classification proposed by Baron Richthofen separates varieties of igneous rocks which may, in one or two instances, be too closely allied to admit of such distinction; though too little is known of the mineralogical relations of all these rocks to enable a more natural system to be adopted.

The lowest conglomerate bed is propylitic, *i. e.*, it is cemented with *propylite;* and the overlying lavas, as exposed in the lower portion of the cañon of North Fork of the Stinkingwater, are *propylite* until the region of dikes is reached, when *andesite* comes in, apparently having broken through the propylite by new fissures in places. Above the latter, as a rule, occur thick beds of *sanidin-trachyte*, or *trachyte-porphyry*, containing crystals of sanidin. The *rhyolite* beds, probably, in most cases, overlie these, and these are succeeded by layers of *basalt*, often columnar, and sometimes *brick-jointed*. There are many intermediate varieties of these rocks, including compact and cellular, porphyritic and amygdaloidal, quartzose and felspathic, and the lavas are interspersed with tufaceous and other breccias frequently partly formed from the material of the preceding layers.

Judging from sections exposed in the Yellowstone basin and in the valley and the cañon of the Yellowstone River, it would appear that, after the deposition of the Miocene beds, the first outflows of *propylite* had passed across this region, and probably a large part of the succeeding fissure-ejections, including the basalt-flows. I am strongly inclined to believe that at least one prominent fissure existed during the propylitic, andesitic, and trachytic periods (and possibly during the period of basaltic eruption, though this is somewhat doubtful) at a point some miles east of the present watershed on the east of Yellowstone Lake. The location of this fissure need not have been permanent, however; but it may have shifted its position at each period of action. The formation of the Yellowstone Lake basin, according to this view, is, then, readily accounted for by supposing the area now occupied by it to have been situated between the limits of an eastward and a westward lava-stream, which approached each other without meeting, except, perhaps, during the earlier eruptions.

It must be remembered that the fissure-action continued during a very long era, extending from near the close of the Miocene epoch until probably late Pliocene times, or perhaps even into the Post-Tertiary period; and that, between each period of outflow as well as between each separate eruption, erosion of the surface was often very extensive. Add to this the subsequent erosion and obscuring of the structure by various agencies, and some faint idea may be had of the difficulty of obtaining a sufficient number of facts for safe generalization in a single rapid trip through the region. The ideas which have been here presented have, however, been rendered possible by the peculiar and very fortunate course chosen by Captain Jones, which permitted a more extensive view of the district than is often obtained in a single season by exploring-parties.

Several lengthy chapters might easily be filled with results derived from the proper study of notes and collections; but justice to other parts of the report, treating of subjects of equal interest and importance, forbids the expenditure of more time and space upon this review. A few brief remarks upon the results of crater-eruption will be all that can be given at present.

CRATER-ERUPTIONS.

A tracing of the lines of trend of the remnants of the extinct volcanic cones would scarcely represent the true positions of the ancient fissures which have just been hastily considered. Taken together, and in connection with the general history of the volcanic action, it may be said that the phenomena of crater-eruption were of more recent date than the fissure-ejections; but it may be doubted whether all of the products of the cones have been deposited subsequently to those of the extended fissures. In other words, the crater-period, as we may call it, is chronologically later than the fissure-period; but active volcanic cones may have existed to a certain extent during the earlier period also. It has become a custom with some to refer every high peak in the volcanic district to the category of extinct craters, often with little or no regard to propriety; and I cannot believe that there have been as many such centers of emission in the region visited by our party as have been currently reported from that section. In fact, the excessive erosion to which these rocks have been subjected since their ejection from the volcanic vents has so obliterated the original craters that it would be very unwise, in many instances, to attempt their ideal reconstruction or restoration without the closest study. "Sailor" Peak, and many other similar high points in the Sierra Shoshone, numbers of which are in view from the elevations upon either side of the Stinkingwater Pass, have very probably formed parts of the rim of one or more craters; but it would be the height of imprudence to affirm that there had existed in this section a definite number of craters, or to attempt to define their limits, or even to determine their relative ages, without devoting a very great amount of time and labor to the investigation of these special subjects.

There can be no possible gain in reporting, as fact, mere opinions based upon a cursory review of a district teeming with an overwhelming amount of material for study, which it will require years of patient research to develop into anything like perfect system. The present writer has had some slight opportunities of observation of recent but practically extinct craters, while twice passing quite near to several of the principal islands of the Windward group, including Guadaloupe, Dominica, Martinique, and the Barbadoes; also, by two passing visits to the island of Saint Thomas. It is true that there are important points of difference between the phenomena of these widely-separated and non-synchronous accumulations; but it does not seem to me that these are sufficient to account for all the differences in structure, if the ancient craters in Northwestern Wyoming were as numerous as some travelers have imagined. One prominent objection, to my mind, is the fact that in many of these so-called crater-peaks, not only the lavas, but the conglomerate and tufaceous layers, are resting in a horizontal position; and that their continuity in this manner can be often traced to some distance in the surrounding elevations. Besides this, the evidence which should exist in the form of broader valleys, or, at least, of uneroded expansions within the supposed rims, is too often lacking.

Still, there is scarcely room for doubt that important craters have existed in this region; and it is highly probable that the Sailor Peak and its neighboring elevations have once formed portions of one of these, subsequently to the last fissure-flow in that particular section. Near the head of the Yellowstone Lake, upon the eastern and southeastern boundaries, there are also indications of cones; but it is impossible to determine their true limits from a passing view.

The material of the crater-outflows of lava appears to include members of both the felspathic and augitic series; but it cannot be positively affirmed that some well-exposed sections (particularly in the lower end of the Grand Cañon of the Yellowstone and in the magnificent gorge of Gardiner's River, East Branch, below the high falls) do not exhibit intermingled crater and fissure flows. *Obsidian* of several varieties is quite common; in some cases directly overlying the granites, and forming thick layers, which have been denuded so as to leave prominent dark-colored buttes. This is not uncommonly spherulitic, sometimes a compact volcanic glass, splitting into flaky pieces, quite generally porphyritic, and often possessing a more or less perfect columnar structure, varying in color from reddish-brown to dark-brown and black.

Very regretfully, this subject is thus summarily disposed of, although its further elucidation is but a question of time devoted to the elaboration of material in the possession of the writer. Should future leisure allow of the completion of this work, it will be given to the public through the medium of periodical publications. It is *necessary* now to pass to the consideration of topics of more general interest by reason of their present significance.

THERMAL SPRINGS.

In order of time, the hot springs were preceded by geyser-action; the former being the representatives of a later stage in the gradual dying-out of the subterranean heat. It will be more convenient to reverse this order in the examination of their effects; leaving the rather special phenomena of the geysers to be described in chapter XIII, which will be largely devoted to them. In the remaining pages of the present chapter, and in chapters X, XI, and XII, descriptions of the principal thermal springs will be given, including also such cold springs as are the undoubted relics of formerly heated basins or channels. This classification of the results is founded upon extremes of activity, between which it is possible to discover a complete gradation, so that no well-marked line of distinction can be drawn to separate the two main divisions.

The hot springs represent merely the quiescent state of the active geysers; and many of the latter, when dormant, present no features which will enable one to determine their real character. It is, therefore, not certain that a few of the *bowls*,* which have been described heretofore and in this place as hot springs, are not in reality geysers, which have never been observed in action. In most cases, however, as will appear in the sequel, the important dormant geysers can be distinguished from the non-eruptive bowls by the marks left upon the surface of the rim by the falling water. Where convincing proof of this nature exists, the bowls have been referred to the second division; and they will be considered in another chapter.

For purposes of description, it will be advisable to deviate somewhat from the general plan of this report, and take up the groups of thermal springs in local order without special reference to their phenomena or the composition of their products. This method possesses more of system than would at first appear, because each locality is marked by the existence of effects which are in a measure peculiar to itself. We may begin,

* The term *bowl* will be used in this work to designate generally the basins or craters of the hot springs and geysers, regardless of form or size; the term *basin* being restricted to its more general use, as applied to a topographical division; thus, *river-basin*, *geyser-basin*, &c.

then, with the first group which was met after our entrance into the National Park, viz, the salses and solfataras in the vicinity of Turbid Lake, reserving the Bath Springs below Camp Brown for some consideration at the close of this chapter.

I.—TURBID LAKE GROUP.

Three visits were made by myself to this locality, including one night-camp near the shore of the lake, (see chapter I, special trip No. V.) The greater part of the data here recorded were gathered on the occasion of the second visit, made the day of the passage of the main party through this section, on the way to Camp 38, at the outlet of Yellowstone Lake.

The first near view of this group of springs was had on the previous day, when I reached the spot at 11 a. m., but was able to gain but little information, as I was obliged to return immediately to Camp 37. At this time, little or no vapor was rising from the surface; but there was every indication that ebullition had taken place within a few hours; for the ground was wet in many places around the bowls upon the lee side, and the inner surfaces of the bowls themselves above the then water-level were also quite wet.

On the following day, (August 4,) I reached the locality at 8.45 a. m. When two miles distant from the spot, the odor of sulphureted hydrogen from the steaming sulphur was plainly perceptible. When I arrived, there was much vapor arising from various points southeast of the small lake, and the odor was very strong. Near the beach, there was a rather large, deep, saucer-shaped hole, containing muddy water in a violent state of ebullition, (*a*, Fig. 27.) In Fig 27, *b* represents another spring not far distant, with a deep bowl somewhat longer than wide; the sides being nearly vertical. This also contained boiling, muddy water, which produced a rumbling sound beneath the surface at one side, as if a subterranean chamber existed at that point. Occasionally mud was spurted to a height of several inches; but in neither *a* nor *b* did any overflowing take place, though recent marks of such a flow were evident upon the side nearest to the lake. Little sulphur was apparent; but a vapor-vent at one side of *b*, not then in action, was lined with an incrustation of this substance. *c* is a cold spring, the largest and most powerful in the group, boiling up fiercely in the midst of the clear cold water of Game Trail Creek. This is evidently a sulphur-spring, as the water of the stream becomes suddenly somewhat milky at this point, and the gravelly bottom is distinctly colored by it. The creek then flows along the edge of *d*, an area of small, raised vents, resembling diminutive volcanic craters. These have been formed by the breaking-through of the incrusted surface at points subjected to tension by the escaping vapors; and the area covered by them is an excellent model of a region of volcanic activity. Volumes of dense white vapor arose from these numerous orifices, and became condensed in part against the face of a ledge a short distance back from the stream. The whole area was underlaid by boiling and sputtering sulphurous water; and along the line of the creek, upon the edges and within it, there were both cold and hot bubbling springs, some of which were quite clear, others milky from suspended sulphur. In spots, where the springs were somewhat inactive and covered by nearly stagnant water, there has been precipitated a black deposit of ferrous sulphide, (Fe S,) which was doubtless formed by the slow action of the sulphur upon the iron set free by the decomposition of the vegetable matter which has there accumulated. A delicate green *Cryptogam* was found growing upon sticks in the hot

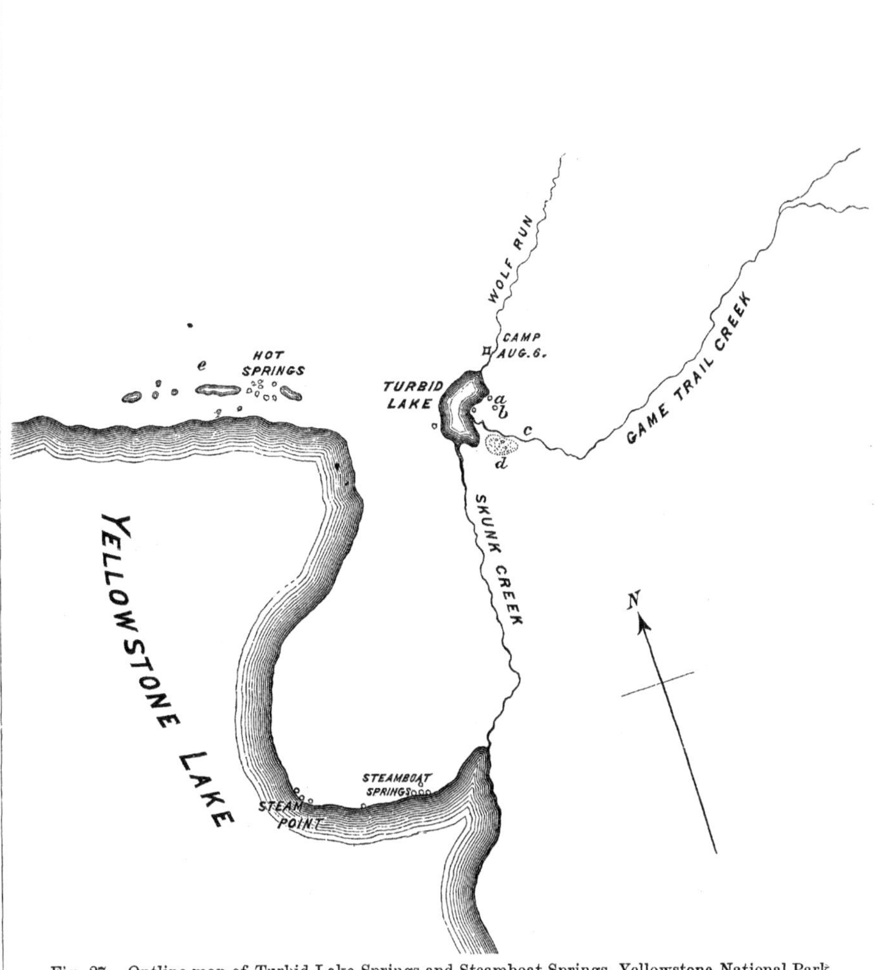

Fig. 27.—Outline-map of Turbid Lake Springs and Steamboat Springs, Yellowstone National Park. *a, b, c, d, e*, springs described in the text.

sulphur region *d*. According to Dr. Heizman's observations, the temperature of the hot springs of the Turbid Lake group varied from 180° F. to 192° F.

Much drift-wood has been brought down by the stream at times, and lodged near the area of activity. Wherever this has been soaked by the sulphurous water, it has changed color, at first assuming a yellow tint, then gradually becoming brown, dark-brown, and finally black. The spring-deposits about this wood also become blackened to a great extent. Indescribable clusters of crystals, needle-shaped, of pure sulphur, are formed by condensation upon the roofs of the miniature caverns beneath the crust, where the heat is retained for a great length of time. Fragments of scoriaceous material, composed of sulphur and other ingredients, with admixtures of various impurities, are scattered over the surface, appearing as if burst from the crust by the sudden increase of tension attendant upon the periodical eruptions.

There are good reasons for placing many of this group in the list of active geysers; but inasmuch as their projectile effects are not great, it has been thought best to include them among the hot springs. Few, if any of them, are entitled to be classed as perfectly clear springs; there being in this locality two principal kinds of turbidity, the muddy and the milky. The mud bowls, or the salses, are situated at some distance from the exposures of igneous rocks, with thick argillaceous deposits at the surface, through which the waters must pass in their exit to the outer air. The sulphur-vents, or *solfataras*, on the other hand, are, in the vicinity of the ancient spring-deposits, derived from volcanic rocks of the trachytic group, from which they may obtain the sulphur, alum, and other substances which they have deposited by sublimation, condensation, and evaporation in such large quantities.

Concerning the periodicity of the action of this group of springs, a few facts only have been collected; but I was fortunate enough to obtain some data upon which to found an opinion. About 3 p. m. of the 2d day of August, I first caught sight of Turbid Lake from a high point north of the Stinkingwater Pass, two thousand feet above the level of the springs. At that time, no vapor was rising from this spot, although the locality of the concealed Steamboat Springs, which emit much less vapor at any time than the Turbid Lake group when in action, could be plainly discerned by the vapor. On the following day, as previously stated, I reached this locality at 11 a. m., and discovered that an eruption had occurred before my arrival. Upon the way, at least two hours before reaching the place, I clearly distinguished volumes of white vapor issuing from the direction of the group, and then the view was obstructed by timber for the remainder of the distance. On the 4th of August, I found the springs in action at 8.45 a. m., and the emission of vapor had almost ceased at 10 a. m.

Returning to spend the night in this vicinity on the 6th of the same month, no notable quantity of vapor was visible, but during the night a heavy mist shut out the springs from view. When this had been dissipated by the sun, I again saw the springs in vigorous action before 6 a. m. From these observations, it seems reasonable to conclude that the increase of activity, or the eruptive throe, takes place in all the springs of this group quite regularly, beginning before 6 a. m. each day and continuing for at least four hours without interruption. It is possible that another period of activity may occur at night; but this I regard as exceedingly doubtful for good reasons, which it will be impossible to give here.

II.—STEAMBOAT SPRINGS AND OTHERS.

The Steamboat or Puffing Spring and its associates are situated on the bank of the Yellowstone Lake, west of south from Turbid Lake, as shown in Fig. 27. At *e*, same figure, are represented several stagnant lakes, with a number of hot and cold springs near Yellowstone Lake, which are apparently dying out, there being few signs of recent activity. These may be included in this second section, on account of their close similarity, except in intensity, to the Steam Point and Steamboat groups. At Steam Point, close to the lake-shore, there is a prominent spring, which emits much vapor, but it does not differ in any marked manner from the Steamboat group, either in its phenomena or in the character of its deposits. Eastward from the point a short distance, another small collection of evanescent solfataras occurs, which, in reality, belongs to the Steamboat group, from which these springs are separated by a minor ridge running down to the lake shore, composed mainly of ancient spring-deposits.

Passing over this ridge, the trail runs above several more springs, one of which is the Steamboat, appropriately named from the peculiar sound emitted, which closely resembles the puffing produced by the escape of steam from the cylinders of a high-pressure steamer. This is caused by the passage of the vapor from a subterranean chamber, under pressure, through a narrow orifice in the hard rock. A few rods farther up the lake, sulphurous vapor issues from a cavern, in conglomerate, with a seething noise, as it comes in contact with the waves, not unlike the sound produced by the escape of steam from the cylinders of a locomotive moving slowly. For purposes of distinction, this will here be called the Locomotive Spring. There are two or three other prominent springs at this point, one in nearly the same vertical position as the Steamboat, but with a larger orifice.

A general section of the rocks in this vicinity, given in Fig. 28, will render more clear the explanation of the facts here observed, and the probable relations of these springs to those of the Turbid Lake group.

An examination of this section will show that the origin of the salses and the solfataras is probably not distinct, but that the nature of the surface-rocks has very much to do with the character of the spring-deposits. In the Turbid Lake solfataras, silica is not a very common ingredient, but it is found in large quantities in connection with the orifices of those springs which pass wholly or partly through the thick mass of ancient hot-spring formations here overlying the lower conglomerate. The salses *a* and *b* encounter this substance also in the beach-deposits, K, which there form the surface-beds; but the various deposits of these springs are very much mixed on account of the constant stirring of the mud by ebullition.

The recent deposits of the Steamboat group contain soda, sulphur, iron, silica, and alumina. Carbonic acid is given off from the dried mud of H, when treated with chlorhydric acid, but not in large quantity. Sulphur is less common than in the solfataric area (*d*) of Turbid Lake, but it is still a characteristic ingredient of the clearer springs. Salses, properly so called, are not present, except near Steam Point, as the water in the simmerers bubbles up through the siliceous mud so gently as not to render it turbid in most cases.

It will be noticed that the present open cavern from which the Locomotive sends out its vapor was probably at one time subterraneous, like the underground swell of the Steamboat channel in the conglomerate.

The action of the waves upon the shore is gradually converting the Steamboat and other springs into Locomotives, and the Locomotive into a boiling spring in the midst of the lake, several of which already exist at different points.

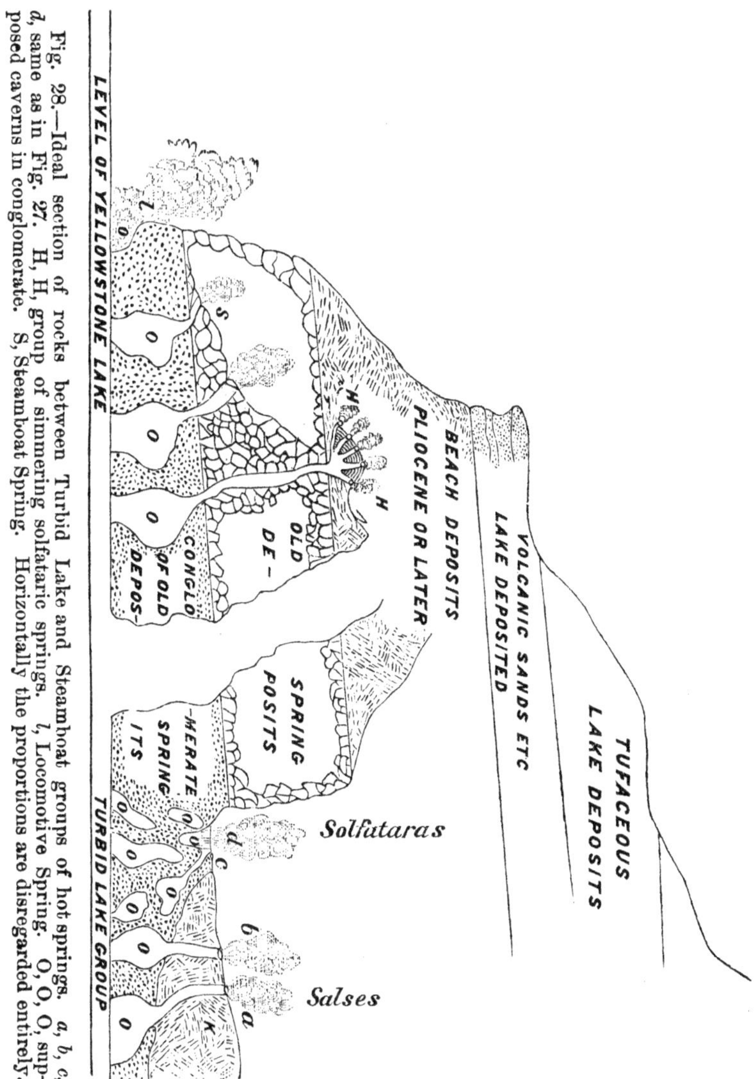

Fig. 28.—Ideal section of rocks between Turbid Lake and Steamboat groups of hot springs. *a*, *b*, *c*, *d*, same as in Fig. 27. H, H, group of simmering solfataric springs. *l*, Locomotive Spring. O, O, O, supposed caverns in conglomerate. S, Steamboat Spring. Horizontally the proportions are disregarded entirely.

Sufficient data for arriving at a satisfactory conclusion in regard to the periodicity of the action of these springs are wanting at present. Some observations have led me to surmise that the emission of vapor is more constant or of more frequent recurrence than in the case of the Turbid Lake group. At any rate, there is no good reason for believing that any underground connection exists between the two groups. It seems probable, also, that while the Steamboat and Steam Point Springs may be subject to nearly the same influences, the group represented at *e*, Fig. 27, is not connected with either. This view is little better than a mere opinion, however; though it may be stated that the members of the latter group were not observed in vigorous action at the time of my visit.

III.—GREEN SPRING AND SULPHUR (!) HILLS.

Less than two miles beyond Turbid Lake our trail crossed Pelican Creek at a point where there occurs upon the right bank an extensive bed of hematite, ($Fe_2 O_3$,) of the variety *eisenrahm*, or *red ochre*, which is evidently the result of deposits from hot chalybeate springs. An iron-spring of cold water empties its contents into Pelican Creek at the crossing, but little or no precipitation takes place. The Indians use the material as a paint, and much of it has been taken from the spot, although our discovery of it was new to the whites.

At the farther edge of this deposit is a magnificent hot sulphur-spring, the stream from which sinks after running a few rods, then passes over the surface again along the edge of the ore-bed, finally discharging into Pelican Creek. The temperature of the water, according to Dr. Heizman, is 104° F. Large quantities of a slimy, green *Cryptogam* grow in the bed of the stream, which suggests the name Green Spring proposed at the head of this section. The study of this locality bids fair to prove of great interest; for there are developments here which cannot be elsewhere observed over the whole region. The hot springs in the valley of Pelican Creek, near the junction of the Three Forks and above, upon the main branch, possess a certain degree of interest, but they are removed from the region of great activity, and may be included in the present division on account of their minor importance.

The mineral products of Green Spring are mainly iron, sulphur, and silica; the iron being apparently of small moment, so far as the accumulation of a ferruginous deposit is concerned. There is, however, much ground for the belief that this substance is of great importance in connection with the growth of the above-mentioned *Cryptogam.* Nowhere near any of the hot springs of this region was there found such an extensive ferruginous deposit as at this place; and the deep-green color of this vegetation was here especially noticeable, as well as the luxuriance of its growth. In many other cases, the amount and exuberance of similar cryptogamic forms was remarkably proportioned to the quantity of iron present in the waters. No opportunity is here afforded for the production of crystals of sulphur by the process of sublimation; there being scarcely any vapor produced. The actual amount of sulphur accumulated is not large, though a small quantity is carried off in the water of the stream. A measurable portion is precipitated as *milk of sulphur*, and retained in hollows in the rough bed of the more quiet portions of the stream. Silica is a common ingredient, forming a beautiful stalagmitic arrangement by gradual accretion along the bottom and the sides of the outlet, affording an excellent attachment for the slimy vegetation.

Sulphur Hills is the quite inappropriate title which has been given to a very prominent ancient group of hot springs not characterized particularly by the presence of that mineral. At this point, there are three deep basins or hollows between ridges of the old spring-deposits, in each of which there is a small group of springs.

From the west side, a powerful stream has issued at one time, draining off the surplus water by a series of interesting cascades. Throughout the whole section between this spot and Green Spring, there has been, during a recent geological period, and probably within the historical epoch, a degree of activity greater than is at present manifested anywhere in this vicinity; and yet it does not appear that the existing phenomena are materially less than they have been for very many years. Small springs at the very bottom of these pits have formed about their orifices deposits which are clearly the result of long-continued action, while there is unmistakable proof that the present level of some is from twenty to fifty feet, at least, below the outlet of comparatively modern ponds, which once occupied the basins. The present outlets are largely of later origin. The history of the accumulation of the extensive deposits, here forming a mass several square miles in area and fully two hundred feet in thickness, is not to be read in an hour; but it will require the patient labor of years to unravel the intricate problems which arise even while viewing hastily a single section like this, which is but one of the lesser of a hundred of this nature. This deposit represents, without a doubt, a period subsequent to the culmination of the crater-eruption, when the Yellowstone Lake extended to a much higher level than now, and the formation may have begun within its waters, afterward becoming a portion of the shore-line. From this and other observations, it cannot be disputed that the early hot-spring action was upon a scale of almost unimaginable magnitude. The mind utterly fails to grasp the reality; and the existing demonstrations, wonderful as they are in many places, we must believe are the mere shadows of the past.

The ridges which now form the rims of the basins are made up of quartzites, conglomerates, and other layers, most of which are mainly composed of materials originally deposited from hot springs. The snow-white aspect of the hills, which enables them to be distinguished from a great distance, is due to the silica which forms the great bulk of the deposit. Sulphur exists in broken masses, mostly amorphous, with some sublimated crystals about the active springs. Occasional brick-red spots are visible, caused by the presence of iron. The mass of the siliceous deposit is a fairly compacted white rock, fine grained, and much jointed; but there is much of a very beautiful tough quartzite, with a conchoidal fracture, and having a pearly luster, or it is sometimes iridescent in a favorable light.

Between 12 m. and 1 p. m. of the 4th of August, a heavy cloud of vapor was observed ascending from this spot while passing along our main trail one mile distant. I visited the locality about two o'clock in the afternoon of August 7th, and also had several other good opportunities of observing such emission if it had occurred, but not near midday. Had I not seen it, I could not have believed it possible for such a quantity to be emitted by such a small number of apparently unimportant springs as were afterward found to occupy this section. Judging from this accidental circumstance, it may not be unfair to suppose that these fumeroles are periodically agitated, though nothing can be predicated concerning the regularity of the action, nor the duration of the quiescent intervals. It may also, with some degree of propriety, be inferred that this group is distinct from those previously discussed.

The springs before mentioned, which are situated in the upper portion of the *flood-plain* of Pelican Creek, near the junction of its forks, and above, are of comparatively little importance, although there are several small fumeroles among them. Like many others of their class, they are noticeable on account of the sulphur which they are the means of depositing about their orifices and distributing through the agency of their overflow. Not infrequently these springs are directly in the bed of the stream, or in the midst of sluggish pools near its edges. Two visits to this locality, about noon on the 7th of August, and at 8 a. m., August 13th, showed that differences in intensity are not lacking; for several fair-sized orifices, which were not seen on the occasion of the first trip, were observed in action on the 13th, some time before reaching the spot. In connection with this statement, it must, however, be remembered that the difference in the temperature of the atmosphere at 8 a. m. and 12 m. is sufficient to account in part for the difference in the quantity of the vapor, and, perhaps, for the whole.

IV.—HOT SPRINGS OF YELLOWSTONE RIVER, BETWEEN THE LAKE AND THE GREAT FALLS.

In passing down the Yellowstone River Valley from the lake, two prominent groups of hot springs are met before reaching the rapids above the falls. Most of these are upon the left bank of the river, however, and they were, therefore, not specially examined. Somewhat detailed descriptions of the principal members upon that side of the stream are given by Dr. Hayden and Dr. Peale in their reports for 1871, under the heads of *mud-volcanoes* and *crater-hills.** Both of these groups are highly interesting and important. They doubtless represent a former more vigorous condition of the Sulphur Hills group. In each case immense deposits have been accumulated, and many springs have ceased their action; but, in the Yellowstone River groups, many powerful, clear and turbid springs and salses are still active. From the right bank, all this may be learned, as well as the fact that sulphur, iron, and silica form portions of the accumulated masses, giving the characteristic yellow, red, and white colors to various portions of the hills. Dense clouds of vapor may be seen issuing from these localities at certain hours, and the thumping noise produced by the throbbings of the agitated mud of the salses may be distinguished without difficulty at a considerable distance. Sulphydric acid gas (H_2 S) is evolved in notable quantity.

There are several mud-bowls and seething springs upon the right bank of the river, directly opposite the upper group, or the mud-volcanoes, six miles below the outlet of the lake. One of these, near the water's edge, strongly reminds one of a large kettle of boiling soap; the resemblance to this uninviting substance being increased by the peculiar streaky appearance, arising from the imperfect mixture of the yellow sulphurous, the red or pink ferruginous, and the blue and greenish argillaceous ingredients of the mud. The mud-paste is in a constant state of sputtering ebullition, and it is occasionally spurted with force to a height of two or three feet. There were some signs about the rim of the bowl of recent more vigorous action, but nothing to indicate a degree of activity nearly approaching the energy displayed by some of the mud-volcanoes across the river.

Both the mud-volcanoes and the crater-hills occupy positions apparently nearly identical in horizon stratigraphically with the Turbid Lake and Steamboat groups, and the variation in actual level is very slight. The exposed formations in the vicinity of the river-groups are clays and sands of lacustrine origin in all respects similar to the deposits along the present lake-shore near Steam Point, in the valley of Pelican Creek, and elsewhere. Overlying these are layers of tufaceous and other volcanic material, many of which bear traces of more or less complete and regular re-arrangement of their component particles by the

* Geological Survey of Montana and Adjacent Territory, 1871. Washington, Government Printing-Office, 1872.

waters of the ancient lake. In some places, above the looser and more finely-comminuted sands and clays, or intermingled with them, occur occasional beds of the more compact trachytic lavas. In the immediate vicinity of these springs, the clays and the trachytes predominate, which fact is sufficient to account for the emergence of the springs, for the most part, as salses and solfataras.

V.—FOREST GROUP.

The foregoing general remarks will apply almost equally as well to an extensive group of thermal springs near the verge of the right wall of the Grand Cañon of the Yellowstone, and the few following details concerning this collection will be found to correspond in most essential points with the descriptions of the two preceding groups which have been given by Dr. Peale and other authorities. This cluster may be appropriately styled the Forest Group, being so nearly surrounded by growing timber that it might easily be overlooked by the passing traveler, or regarded as a section devoid of special interest.

This group comprises representatives of all the great classes of thermal springs, including also a variety of cold springs of varying composition and temperature; while, as a whole, the locality in which they occur may be said to belong to one of the latest stages of thermal intensity. There are some spots in which the activity is much greater than in others, and a considerable stream of water passes off at certain intervals, as the result of the accumulated discharge from a number of the clear and more vigorous bowls. The majority of the active springs, including the salses and solfataras, emerge through the enormous accumulations of ancient hot-spring deposits, which here almost completely obscure the underlying beds of volcanic origin. Not infrequently, two or more salses are seen in close proximity to each other, apparently receiving their supply of heat from the same source, and yet scarcely any two of these agree exactly in all their manifestations. One feature of several of these mud-bowls is especially noticeable, *i. e.*, the thickness or toughness of the mud, which causes it to be arranged in the form of low cones about the centers of ebullition. This represents the stage of transition from the salse proper to the mud-puff, but none of the latter were observed in the basin occupied by the Forest Group. This collection of springs is distributed over an area of considerable extent, and also includes properly several important bowls which are located upon the walls of the Grand Cañon itself, mostly near the bottom of the chasm, not far from the edges of the stream. The majority of the springs, however, are located upon a broad, barren flat of dried mud, sand, and fine gravel, which nearly encircles a short ridge of ancient hot-spring deposits, rising to a height of about two hundred feet above the general surface. It was extremely difficult to make out a satisfactory section of these deposits on account of their great variety and the obliteration of structure caused by washing and weathering. Besides many of the more common varieties of the hot-spring formations, the following-described specimens of rocks were collected from this locality:

1. Rock at the top of the ridge, a fine-grained, yellowish-white sand rock; or, rather, a fine gravel-rock, or conglomerate, apparently formed from material deposited originally by hot springs.

2. White siliceous rock, which gives character to the hill; also, a hot-spring deposit.

3. Lying, apparently, between layers of No. 2, occur bands of reddish

and light-yellow sandstones, probably re-arranged by the waters of the ancient lake subsequent to formation by hot springs.

4. Lower (?) than the preceding, hard, slabby, fine-grained sandstone, which also appears to be composed of hot-spring material.

5. A peculiar hard rock, showing a thin layery structure, occurs in both thick and thin layers.

6. In position probably above No. 5, a conglomerate made up of a rock like No. 5, inclosing fragments of a kind of spring quartzite.

7. Crystalline deposit from a spring toward the eastern base of the ridge. This hot spring is in every respect (except the presence of very little iron) like the Green Spring, on Pelican Creek, before referred to. (Group III, this chapter.)

8. A hard, white, slabby rock, found below in the wash, but occurring *in situ* (?) below the others.

About two-thirds of the distance up the hill fragments of a tufaceous layer were seen, but its position with respect to the above could not be determined.

On the flat below the hill, in the mud washed from the springs, there were imbedded logs of softened wood, and the standing trees for a little distance showed signs of a former flood in the whitening of their trunks at the base. The flat was covered (August 8) with magnificent examples of mud-cracks on a large scale.

As might be anticipated, these ingredients of the accumulations now in progress in this locality are by no means characteristic, but there is scarcely an element which is found in other springs that is not here represented in one or more springs. Sulphur is not formed at present in great quantity, although there are several quite active solfataras; but that this substance has at one time been abundantly produced here is proven by the prevalence of the yellow colors in the walls of the cañon and in the adjacent hills. Silica is abundant in the cliffs, and it is still the principal product of several of the most interesting bowls. One of these in particular is worthy of note. It emerges from the rocks within a very few feet of the river's edge, below the lower fall, hundreds of feet below the level of the majority of the members of the Forest group. Its action is more or less regular, but intermittent, and the water is occasionally ejected to the height of a foot or more above the chimneyed orifices. These chimneys, as I have called them, are small tubular eminences through which the fluid is spouted, and they have been steadily built up by slow accretions from the evaporation of the water as it has fallen down about the original orifice in the rocks. In this case the chimneys are less than a foot in height, tapering from a breadth of six inches at the base to a diameter of only two or three inches at the apex.

It is noticeable that iron is less conspicuous in the recent as well as the ancient spring deposits in this section, although there would seem to be no reason for its scarcity. This may, perhaps, be explained in a measure by the preponderance of other ingredients which give color to the formations, or possibly by the production of salts of iron not common in other localities.

VI.—WAYSIDE GROUP AND ISOLATED SPRINGS.

This name is here proposed for a number of springs of considerable interest situated on the banks of Orange Creek, near where it is crossed by the trail of Captain Jones's party. The path at this point, after crossing the stream, follows it upward for a short distance along the base of a steep hill, and the springs lie upon both sides of the creek quite near the edge of the water, two or three emerging almost directly in the trail. Unfortunately, a mere cursory glance was all that could be obtained, on account of other duties, but enough was learned to prove that this group is well worthy of careful investigation. Sulphur and iron appear to be the prominent products, though it is probable that silica also plays an important part. As a rule these springs are clear, and they mainly emerge from the rocks, leading to the formation of small cavernous openings, which render more audible and resonant the puffing of the vapor as it escapes under pressure. One bowl thus simulates the noise produced at the Steamboat Spring, on Yellowstone Lake, but in a lesser degree. The orange-colored precipitate covering the rocky bed of the stream, from which its name has arisen, is a spring deposit of ferric oxide. This does not seem to originate wholly at this point, but it is probably formed also by other springs, hot or cold, farther up the stream.

Isolated springs.—A few scattered bowls occur over the region south and east of the great Gardiner's River Group, to be described in the following chapter, but a mere statement of their positions is all that is necessary, for nothing is known concerning them which serves to separate them in their features from the groups already mentioned. A few of these may be found at greater or less intervals along the banks of the Yellowstone River below the falls, and, less frequently, in the valley of the East Fork and upon its tributaries. In most cases, these isolated springs are the remnants of more active scenes in the past, and occasionally they serve to mark the location of a once very vigorous group, even including one or more geysers, as in the valley of the East Fork.

VII.—BATH-SPRING NEAR CAMP BROWN.

This description is introduced here simply for the sake of convenience in arrangement, and not because of any direct relation which it is supposed to bear to any of the foregoing groups or springs. Indeed, the question of its relations to other similar bowls in any part of the West is by no means an easy matter to solve. In other words, it would almost seem that the causes of its existence are more apparent, if we consider it as unconnected in any direct manner with the Park groups. Reserving the discussion of this subject for a more appropriate place, we will conclude the present chapter with a description of the principal features of this spring; which is situated near Little Wind River, on the right bank, about two miles northeast from the military headquarters at Camp Brown.

This bowl is, properly speaking, an aqueous basin or pond; which receives the contributions from several prominent orifices opening within its borders. This pond covers an area of considerably more than five thousand square feet, and a continuous supply of hot water is passed off through the channel of a large stream, which connects the springs with the Little Wind River not very far distant. The water is usually clear enough to enable the bottom of the pond to be seen at a depth of five feet or more, but there seem always to be held in suspension, minute particles of a very light-yellow precipitate, which also covers the bottom, and which renders the water turbid when disturbed by the feet of the bathers. The depth of the pond near the center is very great, and one very soon passes beyond one's depth in moving from the edge of the basin.

Carbonic acid is given off abundantly, and Dr. Heizmann finds that calcic hypochlorite (chloride of lime) is present in considerable quantity. The roots of grasses, and such other vegetation as is found in the immediate vicinity of the water, are completely bleached by the agency of the latter. It is a little remarkable, in consideration of the fact that gypsum is so abundant in the neighborhood of this spring, that sulphur and its acids are present only in very small proportions. The temperature, which varies slightly at times, is but a few degrees above "blood heat,' (98° F.,) but it differs from the ordinary day-temperature in the summer sufficiently to cause a feeling of discomfort when first entering the water to bathe. The effects produced are thought to be very beneficial, and the inhabitants of this section consider it especially valuable in the treatment of affections of the skin. The members of Washakie's band of Shoshones, regard it as useful in alleviating the distressing features of syphilis, a disease which is quite generally prevalent among Indian tribes.

This spring emerges at a point where the great gypsum-fold, as it may be termed, has been denuded for the passage of the Little Wind River across it. Without more extended study it is extremely difficult to account for its occurrence without supposing it to be in some way connected with the formation of the fold itself. There are no rocks of volcanic origin within a radius of more than forty miles, so far as is known, and no hot spring, within the volcanic district, is known to exist nearer than one hundred miles from this point.

The next chapter will be devoted to the description of the mammoth springs of Gardiner's River, the most important collection of this nature now known in any part of the world.

CHAPTER X.

THERMO-DYNAMICS, CONTINUED—DESCRIPTION OF HOT SPRINGS, CONTINUED.

VIII.—White Mountain Hot Springs of Gardiner's River—First seven terraces—Eighth terrace—Ninth terrace and beyond.

While the main division of Captain Jones's party was encamped above the mouth of the East Fork of the Yellowstone River, (Camp 41,) a small corps was detached for the purpose of examining the locality referred to at the close of the last chapter, which lies some twenty miles distant to the west of north. At this point there exists the most remarkable development of thermal springs within the limits of the National Park, and certainly there is not its equal in grandeur or in importance elsewhere on our globe, if we may judge from all the accounts of similar manifestations in other parts of the world which have heretofore been published.

VIII.—MAMMOTH (WHITE MOUNTAIN) HOT SPRINGS, GARDINER'S RIVER.

This group lies near the northwest corner of the Yellowstone Park reservation, forming a part of the bluffs above the stream, on the left bank of Gardiner's River, a short distance below the entrance of the West Branch. The springs are situated upon a series of benches of unequal dimensions, arranged rather irregularly after the manner of steps. These benches, of which there are no less than fourteen, with active springs, besides a number more ancient and more elevated, are not ordinary terraces such as those of the Terrace Epoch, but, as we shall presently see, they are almost entirely made up of deposits from extinct and active hot springs.

The first seven steps contain the majority of the largest and most vigorous springs now in action. The upper tiers of benches shed their drainage, for the most part, down upon and across the tops of the lower series, but the greater part spreads out, when it reaches the seventh terrace, so as to pass over the edge in a thin sheet. This is caused by the very slight slope of the surface, and it has resulted in the very peculiar conformation of the bluffs, which is one of the most striking features of this group. The section shown in Fig. 29 will serve to

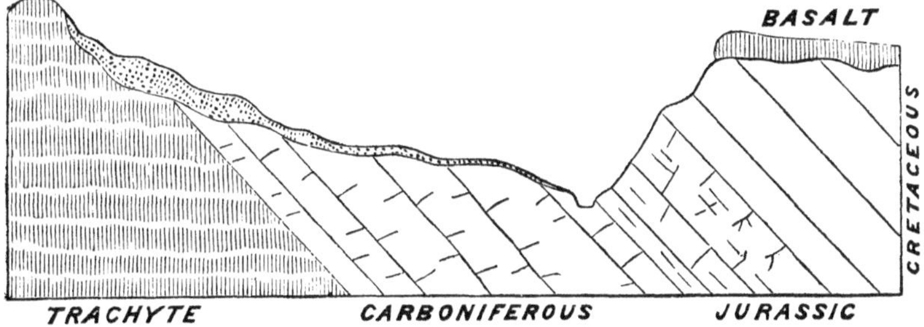

FIG. 29.—Ideal section, across Gardiner's River at White Mountain Hot Springs.

elucidate the structure which has influenced the production of the general features, while the special peculiarities alluded to are diagrammatically represented by Fig. 30. We need not here enlarge upon the causes of the arrangement of the rock-masses which underlie this area, but we will proceed at once to the description of the springs and the phenomena attendant upon their action.

DESCRIPTION OF THE FIRST SEVEN TERRACES.

On the flat below the main tier of terraces there are a number of scattered springs, which do not essentially differ from those at a higher level, and several prominent chimneys mark the positions of former geysers. One of the latter, more than forty feet in height, with a base at least twenty feet in diameter, is the most striking feature to be observed on this plain. From its peculiar shape it received the not inappropriate name of Liberty Cap from members of Dr. Hayden's party of 1871. Besides the geyser chimneys there are also a few dry bowls and fissures, and between this point and the river below there are several active springs of some importance.

Bathing-pools.—Rising to a height of nearly two hundred feet above this flat is the main tier of steps before mentioned, which is fringed with a most remarkable arrangement of shallow pools or bathing-tubs, as they have been styled. This peculiarity cannot be described with any degree of satisfaction to the writer, for it is so unlike any other work of nature or art that it is impossible to convey an adequate idea of its wondrous grandeur or of the almost endless variety of the strange products formed by the action of well-known forces. The study of the physical and chemical changes here in progress is intensely interesting, and rich rewards are certainly awaiting those who may hereafter be enabled to labor in this new field for investigation. Some idea of the structure of this unique formation may be gained from an examination of the dia-

FIG. 30.—Diagrammatic view of "bath-tub" formation on the bluff at White Mountain Hot Springs, Gardiner's River.

gram, (Fig. 30.) A careful study of these pools has led me to believe that they are all formed originally in the same manner, whatever may be their size or shape and without regard to their present depth. If correct in my views, the water, which flows slowly over the surface at the top of the terrace, or elsewhere if the conditions are favorable, spreading out thinly, passes off so slowly as to afford time for evaporation at the edges, and this is hastened by the saturation of the hot solution of calcic carbonate. Very slowly a narrow rim is thus formed about the pool so as to hold it in as by a dam. Once started, this process continues until the basin acquires a considerable depth, provided that a steady but small supply of water is kept up. When this supply ceases, the whole is evaporated to dryness, leaving a deposit of calcic carbonate and other ingredients, the nature of which is dependent upon the conditions under which the evaporation takes place. In the majority of cases this residue is a fine white powder, and it not unfrequently accumulates in large quantities, but occasionally various crystalline and other forms of entirely new structure are found, leading to the belief that a careful investigation will reveal much concerning some unknown laws of crystallization and chemical combinations.

The process of pool-formation in all its stages may be seen in progress wherever the conditions mentioned above are present. The outer surface of the rim of each is ornamented with relief-work similar to the scales of a fish, but more closely resembling the *wave-marks* commonly found on many rocks of beach origin.

These markings are also common over the bottoms of very shallow pools in progress, and in such cases their source is readily traced to the action of the wind blowing over the surface of the water.

The cause of their production upon the nearly vertical surfaces of the walls of the tubs is not so easily deducible, perhaps, but it does not require very close attention to convince the observer that they are the result of the action of the water which trickles or pours over the sides of the cups.

The pools vary greatly in depth and in circumference, those of the greatest dimensions being usually accompanied by the most coarse ornamentation, owing to the fact that they are subjected to the most rapid and powerful action of the descending stream, thus being more abundantly supplied with the ingredients held in solution by the water.

Chemical composition.—As would naturally be expected, when it is known that the principal constituents of the solution at this point are iron, calcium, and magnesium in the form of carbonates, the iron is usually separated locally under specially favorable conditions, while the upper pools, and especially the larger and coarser among them, are built up by the deposition of magnesic carbonate mixed with calcic carbonate; the lower and the more shallow pools being more frequently composed of nearly-pure calcic carbonate. This latter substance, as is common in hot spring districts elsewhere, usually separates as *aragonite*, the greater portion, at least, of the *calcite* in this section being in the form of stalactites, and, consequently, of secondary origin. A careful determination of the mineral composition of these deposits at various elevations would, perhaps, reveal the existence of all the varieties which result from the combination of these three carbonates in different proportions, including true *dolomite* and *ankerite*, with their intermediate forms. This view receives support from the great variety of coloring produced by the weathering of the ancient deposits, nearly approaching black in some cases. Silica is also a prominent ingredient of the spring deposits, and is sometimes obtained almost free from admixture with the others. Sulphuric acid is also perceptibly present.

The tubs, arranged as they are upon the slope of the hill, receive their supply of water mainly from the overflow of the boiling springs above. As the water passes from one pool to another, it gradually loses heat, each tub answering the purpose of a cooling-vat, so that bathers find no difficulty in obtaining almost any desired temperature. This locality has already become a favorite resort of many invalids from the surrounding country, particularly those suffering from cutaneous diseases, for the treatment of which the waters are thought to be very valuable.

Products.—There is a remarkable diversity in the special products of these numerous cooling-pans, owing to the varying conditions of temperature, dimensions, and agitation of the contents. In some, especially near the top, and in the direct course of the outflow from the springs, the water is constantly passing through and does not remain long enough to become perceptibly cooled, and these are usually quite free from precipitations or other deposits, while the external ornamentation is often very coarse. Others more remote from the flow transmit the water more slowly, thus allowing time for a considerable reduction of temperature in transit, and, in such cases, a very fine white deposit of calcic carbonate is formed over the bottom, which often attains a thickness of several inches. Many pools through which the water passes with sufficient rapidity to maintain a temperature as high as can well be borne by ordinary bathers, are thus encumbered by accumulations of this substance, in which the feet sink very perceptibly. Again, there are others in which a high temperature is maintained by a constant but diminished flow, which furnishes the conditions essential to the production of crystalline aggregations of the most peculiar and interesting forms. Twigs, small stones, and other objects placed in such situations eventually become covered with thick deposits of this nature, and the preparation artificially of ornaments of various kinds has already been successfully accomplished with little difficulty. The most delicate and interesting products are, however, so frail as to render their transport impossible, and very many of them cannot be lifted from the pools without demolition. Owing to the presence of notable quantities of iron, magnesia, and other ingredients, the majority of the crystalline and colloidal products are of a dark-brown or reddish color while wet, changing often through pink to a most delicate white upon the gradual evaporation of the water in the pools in which they are formed. It occasionally happens that a flowing tub will become converted into an evaporating pan by the cutting off of its supply of water by some means. In this event, if the condensation be fairly uniform and uninterrupted, stalagmitic pillars, often with a beautiful honey-comb texture, are not uncommonly built up over the bottom of the pool. Two such small and shallow pans occur near the edge of a small stream flowing from the large boiling spring presently to be described, which is situated upon a low terrace above the spring from which the main group of pools is supplied. One of the pans was entirely dry at the time of our visit, the bottom being covered with white pillars of the size of one's finger, three inches in length, arranged at intervals of about two inches. By the exercise of the greatest possible care both in collecting and in packing, I was enabled to transport several of these pillars with no further detriment than a reduction in length by fracture and crumbling at the ends. In a neighboring pool, somewhat deeper and partly filled with water, another set of these columns was observed in progress. They were soft and rather swollen in appearance, of a dark-brown color, and all attempts to raise them out of the "mother-liquor" proved futile. When taken from the water at this stage, the effect is very similar to the collapsing of a "jelly-fish" upon its removal from its natural element, with this difference, that there is left in the hand a more abundant slimy residue in the former instance.

Much of the outflow from the large spring at the top of the bluff passes down over a series of quite regular cascades, which present a rather gradual transition between the tiers of pools on one side and the general absence of such formations upon the other side. Passing southward beyond this stream, we come upon the dry bed of a rill which has at some time coursed down the ridge with a gentler fall than the main stream. Here, again, the running water has left its mark, but in a shape not elsewhere seen. The same feature of overlapping is noticed that was referred to in speaking of the ornamentation of the bathing-pools, but the form of the separate parts, with the minute ramifying channels here observed, is peculiar to this spot. When broken out by a hammer, small fragments are procured which remind one, in a measure, of a bird's wing, the delicate tracery appearing not wholly unlike the feathers with their appendages.

Fucoidal markings.—Still farther toward the edge of the outcrop of the spring-deposits in this direction, over a surface which has clearly been overflowed at times, there occur numbers of raised prominences which bear a striking resemblance to *fucoids*, for which they are sometimes mistaken. A close examination shows that each one of these has a small cylindrical channel through its entire length, and this tube is always occupied by the culm of a species of "rye-grass," which grows abundantly at this point. The deep longitudinal striæ of this grass are distinctly preserved in relief on the walls of the tubes. The size of the prominences varies greatly, from that of a large pipe-stem to those which project two inches or more above the general surface. A rude illustration of the manner in which these incrustations are built up is given in

Fig. 31. In autumn the dead and dried culms fall flat on the ground without detachment from the main stem, and thus the water flows over them without transporting them from the spot in which they have grown. Gradually an incrustation is thus formed by deposition from the sat-

FIG. 31.—Diagrammatic section intended to show the process of formation of incrustations upon "rye-grass" at White Mountain Hot Springs.

urated liquid, and the increase of the resulting prominences is limited only by the amount of water or the time employed in their formation. The texture of these cylindroid masses is compact, and rather uniform, with some tendency to greater looseness of arrangement of the particles toward the surface. A transverse fracture shows lines of imperfect radiation, as though the crystalline structure had been induced by the deep ribs which mark the surface of the grass to follow certain lines in preference to others.

Springs on seventh terrace.—Passing now to the summit of the ridge or bench which we have been discussing, a large active bowl is brought into view, which proves to be the source of a large portion of the water which flows over the cliff into and through the bathing-pools before described. Just below the main outlet of this spring, there was a beautiful pinkish deposit at one side, where it was still wet, but beyond the force of the current. This characteristic color is undoubtedly produced here, as in numerous other instances, by the presence of sufficient iron in the water, as *ferrous carbonate*, to leave deposits of *ferric hydrate* in quiet spots by the evaporation of the carbonic acid on exposure to the air. The spring itself, or, more properly, two very large springs connected by a narrow and shallow strait, are among the most powerful and extensive of the whole collection. Each bowl is nearly 150 feet in one dimension, while the breadth of one is 50 feet and that of the other nearly half its length. The boundaries of both are very tortuous, and the edges are handsomely ornamented by a tasty rim which projects inward some inches. This rim is the lowest of three similar ledges, the water in the bowl having twice receded about four inches in depth, leaving each time a rim to mark its former position. These have been formed by the pulsation of the water in the following manner: Each convulsive throe of the liquid sends across to the edges of the bowl a wave which rises slightly above the general surface of the water and spreads gently over the sides to the distance of several inches. By evaporation a residue is left which forms a thin shelf which projects inward over the surface of the water. The edge of this shelf is kept almost constantly moist, but the rear portion is subjected to more rapid evaporation; consequently, while the latter presents a delicately-glistening surface, resembling clear white porcelain, the edge, being exposed to oxidation with less evaporation, forms an attractive fringe of red, caused by the precipitation of ferric hydrate. Pieces broken from the rims show essentially the same structure, being composed of layers of pink and white irregularly alternating. The temperature of these springs is much below the boiling point of water at this altitude, but the force of ejection is so great as to cause rapid and vigorous ebullition, which is no doubt facilitated, if not in some degree induced, by the presence of much carbonic acid. The water is very clear and of an azure tint, which renders startling and impressive the view obtained upon looking far down into its depths.

In a somewhat quiet portion of the southernmost bowl, removed from the immediate vicinity of the excessive agitation, there was found a white and reddish gelatinous substance, probably colloid in part. Interlaced or included within this are little globules of calcic carbonate formed by the bubbling up of carbonic acid through minute orifices beneath the colloid body. At the edges of the bowl, where the carbonic acid rises with less obstruction, little hollow filmy spheres of calcic carbonate are formed, after the manner of soap-bubbles, which increase in size by the union of several by attraction, until they become too heavy or non-cohesive to remain suspended, when they fall to the bottom entire, or burst and scatter their component particles. Not unfrequently in this vicinity, these are found as hard, shelly globes, intermingled with the general texture of the ancient spring deposits.

In another portion of this bowl, also in a comparatively quiet spot, are a few small clusters of a tough, green, fungoid form of growth, vigorous and prominent. The real nature of this apparent anomaly and other undescribed inmates of these springs is as yet unknown. In common with many of the latter, it possesses characters which would seem, at first sight, to define its position as a member of the vegetable kingdom among the lower cryptogamic orders, but there are other features which seem to place it more properly in the large and ill-defined group of colloids. In either case, however, there is here presented a wide field for study in a little-understood subject. In this connection may be mentioned two other forms which are not only found at this point, but which are also more or less abundant in a large number of the springs throughout the Gardiner's River group. The first of these consists of a collection of white, silky fibers, sometimes coated with a fine, granular substance resembling sulphur, usually forming the bed of a shallow rill, through which quite warm water is flowing. The other is a yellowish-green substance found on the gravelly and rocky bottoms of channels of no great depth, with siliceous or calcareous particles inclosed in its meshes. This form is often seen underlying the first, which is then usually attached to it. Both simulate closely the confervoid forms of vegetation.

On the west side of the larger bowl, and in fewer numbers at the western edge of all the wide bowls, a quantity of grasshoppers were floating, which had probably been blown into the water, for none were observed on the barren land adjoining. They were coating rapidly with an incrustation of calcic carbonate; and doubtless many are thus covered and preserved as fossils by falling to the bottom of the spring, although none were obtained from the old deposits about the extinct springs.

From evidence abundantly present, it is plain that there have been recent extinctions of springs on this terrace, unless it be true that many not in action during our stay were then but dormant representatives of bowls which are vigorously active during certain seasons of the year when more moisture is supplied. In fact, Dr. A. C. Peale, to whom we are indebted for many interesting and trustworthy observations concerning these springs, reports quite important differences in their degree of activity which had taken place within the space of one year, and there was certainly not a little change during the year that elapsed between his last visit and our own in 1873. In one spot I observed water bubbling at the bottom of a hole which had once been filled with the water, as was proven by the ornamentation of its walls. At present there is no visible outlet to this spring, though it may be in some way connected with the large bowls before described, and the same may be said of the frequent long and deep fissures, which are not uncommon, in which the sputtering is continually heard, and from which a quantity of vapor is frequently seen to escape. Several other old spring holes are present, lined with numerous white crystals of exceeding beauty.

The foregoing descriptions have been mainly confined to a review of the first seven terraces.

Eighth terrace.—The eighth bench is raised but five feet above the seventh, and contains but a single spring, about ten by fifteen feet in diameter, and having not more than one-third the depth of the preceding bowls. The water in this spring throbbed fitfully near the center to the height of a foot or more. About the edges there were a number of rather shallow evaporating pans, containing water at different temperatures, in which were being deposited the most beautiful crystals, in wonderful variety, aggregated into masses of the most varied forms, and of several tints—brown, red, pink, white, and yellow. This collection of slowly-forming products of imperceptible forces is not the least impressive of the remarkable features of this little known region. Far abler pens than mine would fail to do justice to a scene beyond the power of language to describe, but one which can never be forgotten by the most careless observer of the workings of nature. In some of these pans there was a quantity of a peculiar reddish-brown fungoid growth, which apparently possessed the texture as well as the consistence of a colloid body. It is especially interesting on account of its rather definite form, which is fairly represented in Fig. 32. The upright shoots are mere tubes, closed at the top, which seem to be distended, if not wholly caused,

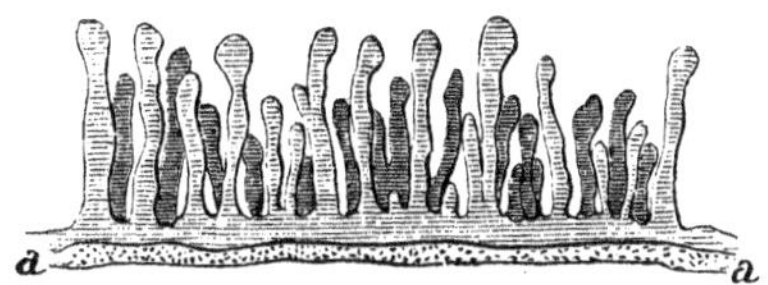

FIG. 32.—A clump of a colloid (?) growth in evaporating-pans on eighth terrace, White Mountain Hot Springs.

by the evolution of carbonic acid from beneath, and when taken out of the water they completely collapse. They are, however, sufficiently cohesive to enable small clumps to be dried, when they are very brittle, and crumble to powder unless handled with care. A comparatively large quantity of solid matter is attached to the under-surface, consisting of the various substances which would naturally be freed from the solution upon the liberation of the carbonic acid. Furthermore, a microscopic examination of the dried gelatinous matter, softened and swollen by soaking in hot water, reveals no trace of vegetable organization, although green is not uncommonly a prevalent color. Add to all this the fact that no amount of steeping in ordinary hot water will suffice to raise the film with its weight of solid matter, as in the evaporating pan, (though the colloidal mass when freed from this encumbrance rises rapidly to the surface,) and there can be no doubt that the conformation illustrated in Fig. 32 is produced by the struggling of carbonic acid to free itself from beneath an obstruction of colloid matter, which probably originates from the organic matter contained in the water. This organic matter may in part arise from the rocks through which the springs reach the surface, but we have already seen that much is introduced into the bowls from without by the action of the wind and in other ways. Amidst so much of novelty, and while closely studying the wonderful variations produced by very slight changes of condition, one is almost overwhelmed with the hundreds of interesting problems which are continually presented for solution on all sides. It is, therefore, impossible, within the limits of a single chapter, to record one-half of the interesting observations made in the field, much less to follow out the discussions to their legitimate conclusions in all cases. On this account, many important features of this region must be omitted altogether, while others can receive but a small share of attention in this report. Some subjects, which cannot be even alluded to in this chapter, will receive some consideration in another place, however.

Before leaving the description of the eighth terrace, it will be well to speak briefly of some very striking results which have been produced by the action of water upon many of the deposits since the extinction of the springs. In some manner not necessary for our present purpose to investigate, there have been produced deep fissures in the material of the benches, and occasionally also quite large caverns have been left. The latter are, doubtless, in some cases the relics of underground chambers belonging to some of the ancient springs. Whenever these are brought to light, the trickling of the water which percolates through the superincumbent mass has formed huge masses of clear white stalactites of the most fragile nature. Whole masses of the adjoining formation also present an appearance very difficult to describe, but not wholly unlike an immense aggregation of long acicular crystals joined together by cementation into a loosely-fibrous rock. This peculiarity will hereafter be referred to as the *acicular structure*. Sometimes this is not clearly defined, when the mass presents more of an amygdaloidal structure, or an appearance resembling some kinds of cream candy which contain numerous air-cavities within their texture.

FROM NINTH TERRACE TO UPPER LIMIT OF ACTIVE SPRINGS.

Above this point there are many active springs, but they are as a rule much smaller and less vigorous than those existing on the lower terraces. A thickness of more than thirty feet of the ancient deposits occurs in a ledge overlooking the eighth terrace, in which the peculiar "wave-line" ornamentations at frequent intervals serve to mark the successive stages as well as the varying positions of the old springs. Large masses of this formation are frequently forced off by the action of frost and other agents, forming by their disintegration a considerable talus of fine material. Not quite half way to the top of this ancient cliff, on a narrow jutting ledge, there are several small orifices from which the hot water issues, one of which deposits internally a little sulphur. Above this a ridge runs out southerly which is deeply split by what appear to have been earthquake fissures. Toward the northern end the bubbling of hot water is plainly heard beneath, and this finds its exit at the other end, where it nearly fills the fissure; still bubbling, it finally passes out, spreading over the sides and ends of the ridge, and finally runs off below in a little stream. In this spring there is also deposited a thin lining of sulphur. In the outflow below, where the water runs over the surface in a shallow stream, there is left a deposit of the most delicate cream-color tinged with pink, and in one spot there may be seen almost every conceivable shade which can be produced by mixture of delicate white, pink and yellow.

Back of this ridge, in a kind of hollow, occur three boiling springs of different composition; one clear with a dark-brown bottom, another with bluish water, and the third slightly yellow.

Here the acicular structure before mentioned is seen in progress, being caused by the gentle overflow from the small orifices slowly running off, as it were, in lines. At one point a curved arrangement of the needles is induced by the meeting of the overflow from two adjacent orifices. The outlets of these three springs join a small rivulet coming from a point above, and the whole falls into a hole below and disappears.

The white silky fibers previously noted, which closely resemble vegetation, if they are not actually of such nature, are abundant in the outflow from the long fissure. At the end of the ridge, half way down, these are covered by a thin streak of sulphur, which is deposited from a rill which here issues from an orifice in the side of the bank.

Below the ridge, there are two extinct geyser chimneys above six feet in height. One of them is a mere mound, with a smaller chimney surmounting it, while the other is more regular and open from top to bottom upon one side. No evidences of recent action are present, and both are gradually, though slowly, becoming wasted through the means of various weathering agencies. This action is, however, retarded in a measure by the irregular arrangement of the overlapping-plates of which the chimneys are composed. On the next bench above, a hot spring runs out of the bluff near the top, which contains much of the silky fibrous material,* and deposits of ferric hydrate are common in shallow places and at the edges of the bowl. This terrace is mainly a region of extinct springs, and many old orifices not now in action may be discovered by careful examination over the area. More or less of earthquake action at different times is apparently indicated by the numerous stopped fissures which are especially prevalent in the small extinct geyser ridges and other similar elevations. The structure adjacent to the fissures is frequently more or less acicular, and sulphur becomes a prominent ingredient above the ninth terrace. Light incrustations of silica are sometimes formed about the smaller orifices, but it is seldom deposited in a pure state, being usually mixed with sufficient foreign matter to give it a dark color not pleasing to the eye. When quite pure, its component grains are usually much finer and more closely arranged than in the majority of instances. The deposition of silica in all the springs seems to mark the declining stages of action, and small extinct orifices are quite commonly filled with a rather fine-grained calcareous sand.

On one old ridge at this height, (eleventh terrace,) there is an extinct shallow bowl four by eight feet, with two very small bubbling springs. Carbonic acid can here be readily detected by the taste, and the silky fibrous material is abundant. The orifices are evidently dying out, and the bubbling is very irregular, the action for a time (sometimes five minutes or more) being very vigorous, then almost or entirely ceasing for about the same interval. There were also two other openings within the rim of the extinct bowl, which appeared to have recently died out, as the sand was still moist about them. No stream issued from the acting orifices. The bowl occupies the summit of the ridge, and dry bathing-pools and evaporating-pans, in all respects similar to those previously described, are ranged below on all sides as on the seventh

*It is to be regretted that the determination of the nature of this substance was not more thoroughly made. The very limited time devoted to this section, and that without assistance except in packing, rendered it absolutely necessary to pass hastily some of the most interesting features. It is worth recording, however, that this substance is always more abundant in the presence of carbonic acid.

terrace. In the walls of some of these, holes were observed, some having served as mere exits for the contents of the pools, while others, which extend downward from the outside below the bottoms of the tubs, doubtless gave rise to small springs at some time in the past.

Below the ridge, on the tenth terrace, there are several hot springs possessing a due share of interest, but none were noticed which differ sufficiently from those already mentioned to require special description. These springs are mostly less active than those on the lower terraces, and they do not overflow to a great extent, though a few are of more than average dimensions. Grass is growing over the terrace quite generally.

The twelfth terrace is a region of greater activity, and in some respects it resembles the seventh terrace in its developments, though the overflow was by no means as great at the time of our visit as at the latter locality.

Dr. Peale particularly speaks of a great reduction in power and overflow on this bench which was observed between the summers of 1871 and 1872. I have no means of comparing accurately the status of any terrace in 1873 with that of the preceding years, but the overflow in 1871, as reported by Dr. Peale, was certainly greater than when visited by us in 1873. Such comparisons will not be considered of much value, however, when it is remembered that our knowledge of the causes upon which the supplies of heat and water are dependent, is extremely limited. The "cooling-vat" structure is here well displayed, but it differs in no important particular from those previously described. Several prominent but not unique bowls occur at different points on the terrace, the various deposits and other products being no less interesting than those which have preceded. No mention has heretofore been made of the occurrence of unmistakable vegetation in not a few of the cooler springs throughout the district, in the form of green filaments of *Confervoidæ*. These are naturally more abundant in the little rills which flow from the springs, but they are also occasionally present within the bowls themselves, and sometimes in water of a high temperature. That this vegetation is less common here than in other hot-spring groups, described in the preceding chapter, is, perhaps, due to the smaller proportion of iron in the water of the White Mountain springs.

The thirteenth and fourteenth terraces are occupied by three classes of springs, viz: 1. The ordinary deep bowls, usually with no raised walls above the surrounding surface. 2. The fissure springs. 3. Those which emanate from ridges or mounds, some of which may have been active geysers at one time.

The common bowls occur almost without exception on the fourteenth terrace, and, like the majority of such springs in the whole group, they evolve sulphureted hydrogen. Few of them are especially interesting on account of their peculiar phenomena, though there is more or less of variety in their products. As a whole they may be regarded as representatives of the closing stages of heat action in this region, and their variations from the generality of the bowls in the group may readily be explained by reference to the somewhat different conditions of soil and geological structure which here prevail. Lying as they do nearer the outcrop of the volcanic rock, the thickness of the ancient spring deposits is increased and the composition of the water more closely approaches that of the springs which directly cover trachytic material. Being comparatively feeble in action, and located at the edge of a thriving forest, in the midst of a recent surface-formation, they also partake to some extent of the nature of salses, or, more properly, several of these springs are more or less turbid. Sulphur is a prominent ingredient and silica is present in fair quantity.

The thirteenth terrace is pre-eminently an area of fissures, there being several of large size, with many smaller. Occasionally these are now occupied by small springs, but the greater number are dry and show signs of great age, as we shall presently see. Most of the fissure springs are of low temperature; and, indeed, this is a characteristic of the whole series upon the thirteenth and fourteenth terraces. The springs themselves possess very few features of special interest, but a careful study of the fissures in which they occur cannot but prove highly advantageous in working out many of the present problems connected with the post-volcanic history of this section. It would be unwise to generalize extensively upon the few facts already obtained, although a number of interesting observations were made which might seem to warrant more definite conclusions than are here expressed.

The mounds are so directly the reverse of the fissures that a cursory view would not lead one to suppose that they could be in any way connected in their origin. A careful examination, nevertheless, reveals a degree of similarity in this respect which is quite surprising when first observed. The fissures very often extend through the axes of ridges similar to the mounds in general shape, and almost every mound, whether closed or not, shows traces of a *fissure-line* (if I may use the term) along its axis, between the spring orifices, if any exist. These and other facts point to the conclusion that the mounds, however formed originally, are produced by the closing of fissures through the agency of hot springs. The whole subject deserves more careful attention than any one has been able to devote to it as yet. Some of the mound springs, though often quite small, are brilliantly colored and very interesting; carbonic acid, as indicated by the sweetish taste, is often present in quantity, and iron and sulphur are common ingredients; occasionally pools are formed on the sides of the mounds, and in one case an ancient pool now gives rise to a spring of some size, containing, besides a quantity of the silky fibers, an amount of the fungoid substance referred to in connection with the large springs of the seventh terrace.

Evidences of age.—The upper benches just discussed may be easily reached from the tenth terrace by following a well-worn trail running up the dry bed of a stream which formerly carried off the waste water from the springs above. Above the tenth bench there begins a fair growth of pines, many of which are so situated with respect to ancient spring bowls as to make it certain that they have grown since the extinction of the springs. Some of these trees, of the species *Pinus flexalis*, are fully thirty inches in diameter below, which, according to Dr. Parry, is equivalent to a growth of five hundred years. In the direction of the cliff to the left, and also partly upon the cliff itself, (twelfth terrace,) there are much younger trees, now dead, appearing as if killed by the springs, some of which probably existed there at a more recent date. The evidence of the very great age of the larger portion of the spring-deposits becomes more marked and abundant as we go upward. The excessive weathering of the rocks, the thick accumulations of soil and detritus, and the heavy growth of very old timber, amply illustrate the truth of this statement. In one broad and extended fissure on the thirteenth terrace the vegetable mold has accumulated to a sufficient depth to allow of the growth of pines fifteen inches in diameter. Above the fourteenth terrace some remains of ancient springs were noticed, more or less obscured by the surface-formations and by the growth of trees, whose roots have often largely filled the old bowls. Still higher the deposits become more worn, and, finally, the vegetable mold becomes so thick that only an occasional exposure of the spring-formation is seen, while the timber becomes so densely crowded as to render progress through it rather difficult.

Bearing in mind the great length of time which must have elapsed after the extinction of the springs before vegetation could have covered the terraces, as well as the extreme slowness with which deposits of vegetable mold are accumulated, we are justified in believing that at least one thousand years have passed since the complete cessation of activity over the upper or oldest terrace. It is, however, more than probable, all things being considered, that this era has extended over many times that period. If now we allow that all the spring-deposits of the first twelve terraces, counting from below, have been formed during this latter epoch, (which is scarcely possible,) we shall certainly not be overestimating the antiquity of the volcanic outflows in this section if we regard their age as fully eight thousand years. To one who has had the opportunity of examining this remarkable formation these figures will appear small indeed, and I am myself convinced that a period of more than twenty thousand years has elapsed since the origin of the earliest springs in this section, at the very lowest calculation consistent with all the facts thus far collected.

The composition of the products of the springs of this group is not difficult to explain if it be true, as there is every reason to believe, that a thickness of hundreds of feet of the limestones of Carboniferous age underlies a portion at least of these deposits. The general structure exhibited in Fig. 29 is ideal only as regards a portion of the section, and sections observed farther to the north are reported by Drs. Hayden and Peale to reveal fifteen hundred feet of the Carboniferous beds in the same relative position as here indicated. Although not positively ascertained, few indeed will be disposed to doubt that the springs originate in the eruptive rocks, and this would cause the water to reach the surface by passing through the limestone, dissolving it in its course and depositing calcic carbonate as its principal ingredient.

Subterranean passage.—Not far from the upper limit of the spring-formed rocks, quite near the trail, which passes high up through the timber, there is a large cavern with a narrow entrance from above at one side. The opening is not prominent, and might readily be passed unobserved by one in search of it. Mr. Creary and myself came upon it quite accidentally, and it was not visited by other members of the party. Two small pine trees had been conveniently placed as a kind of ladder leading downward from one end of this passage. It is highly improbable that these could have fallen into this position, from which it must be inferred that the cave had been entered by some one before our visit; but no reference is made to it in any writings upon the subject of the springs that I have yet seen. As a cavern merely, this is not especially interesting, but its features plainly indicate that it once formed a part of the underground channel of a hot spring, and this renders it important as a means of adding to our limited knowledge of the structure of such as are now in action. A section through the main portion of this cave is given in Fig. 33. The entrance lies at one side of the bottom of a depression which was evidently at one time the surface portion of a fair-sized spring. It is rudely hopper-shaped; that is, it is narrower below than above, and it has a length of about six feet, an average width of three feet, and a depth of about three feet. Crawling through the passage (o) and descending by the rude ladder, we found ourselves in a chamber (c) about nine feet in height, with a steep sloping floor, covered with a thick deposit of vegetable mold, which was carpeted with undecayed pine leaves and the smaller branches.

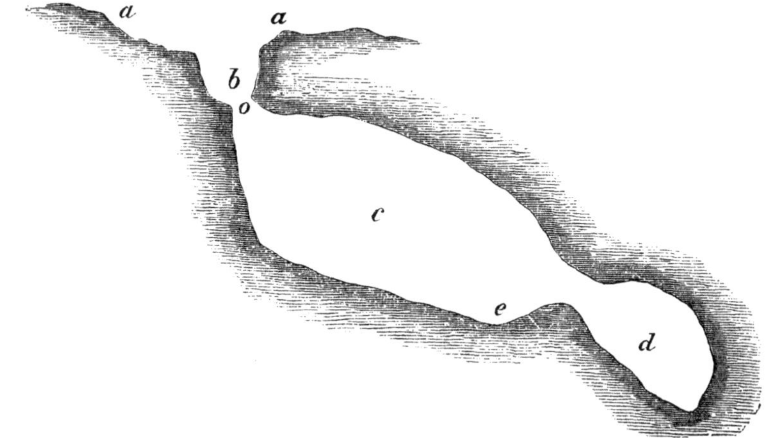

FIG. 33.—General section through cave left by extinction of a hot spring at White Mountain, Gardiner's River.

a, *a*, surface contour, showing ancient pool; *b*, entrance; *c*, chamber; *d*, descending channel, transverse section; *e*, remains of a bison; *o*, passage into cavern, (not quite as large as represented in the cut.)

A section taken along any given line fails to convey an adequate idea of the extent and irregularity of this subterranean channel.

The passage or constriction between *c* and *d*, Fig. 33, leads also to a larger chamber not represented in the cut, which communicates more directly with the descending channel, *d*. It is probable that a careful exploration will reveal one or more external openings, through which springs have once issued, in addition to the one already described. In support of this opinion, not verified for want of sufficient time, it may be mentioned that much more light enters the larger chamber than would seem possible if the one entrance (*o*) discovered were its only source of supply. Some interesting deductions may be made from the structure of this cavern, the more important of which are reserved for use in chapter XIV. In this place it need only be remarked that the observed features point very clearly to the existence of one or more hot springs in this section in very ancient times which received their supply of water through these underground passages, and which obtained the substances deposited from this water by direct solution of the material of the surrounding walls.

At the farther side of the chamber *c*, near the foot of the sloping floor, *e*, (Fig. 33,) I discovered the skull and other bones of a bison (*Bos Americanus* Gmelin,) of such size as to render the question of the manner of its entrance not an easy one to solve. The relative position of the bones, (which did not appear to have been disturbed since the death of the animal,) as well as the general position and posture of the whole, seemed to indicate a certain amount of choice on the part of the individual, from which I conclude that the animal did not die before reaching the bottom of the cavern. This also confirms me in the opinion that there are other external openings to this series of chambers, for I am persuaded that no animal of this size could fall into the opening (*b*) without one of two results: either he would be able easily to extricate himself, or, if too severely maimed, he would remain wedged into the narrow passage (*o*) until death ensued. In the latter case, the carcass would not fall until so far decomposed as to prevent it from reaching the foot of the slope entire, and it is highly probable that the head or some other portions would remain outside. The conclusion seems natural, therefore, that this animal in some way fell through a larger opening, perhaps into the adjoining chamber, from which he passed to the chamber *c*, as the one nearest the surface, trying to force his way through the passage (*o*,) until death finally came to his relief. All the bones found were well preserved, but, in common with the surrounding objects, they were covered with mildew. From the fact that they were well imbedded in the soil, it is not probable that the animal had perished within a number of years, though certainly very much later than the extinction of the springs.

The dampness of the air within the cave will be inferred from the growth of mildew and its allies, but very little water gains an entrance, and this by percolation only. As a consequence, a stalactitic growth takes place very slowly in a few spots over the roof.

This cavern is situated on the highest and most ancient hot-spring terrace, which is adjacent to the outcrop of trachyte forming the high timber-clad ridge above. This terrace is the fourth or fifth, at least, above the fourteenth or highest bench now containing active springs. It is very difficult to determine the exact number of the extinct benches on account of the thick growth of timber and the partial obliteration of the ancient contour of the surface by the various eroding and other agencies.

In leaving a subject of such great interest as that which occupies so large a part of this chapter, it may not, perhaps, be considered wholly out of place to reiterate a portion of the author's views on the benefits to be derived by science from these and other works of nature, within the limits of the tract reserved by the Forty-first Congress under the name of the Yellowstone National Park. These remarks, as given below, are quoted from an article which appeared in the number of the American Naturalist for February, 1874.*

"It is a remarkable fact that the springs in different localities are widely dissimilar in many respects, and even those in the same locality often differ as greatly from each other in some of their characteristics. The White Mountain Hot Springs of Gardiner's River are a noteworthy example of this, and did there exist no other reason for the formation of a park in this region, the fact that here the successive steps in the history of the ancient volcanic action are so clearly portrayed is alone sufficient ground for their protection. I venture to say that nowhere in our country, not even in the truly wonderful cañon of the Colorado, is so much of geological history crowded into such narrow limits as in this portion of the Yellowstone Basin. Nowhere in the world, I had almost said, is there to be found such an infinite variety with so small an expenditure of material. The area within which all this is comprised is much less than ten square miles. Some of the most interesting products are so delicate, and many of them are formed in situations so peculiar, that frequently the work of years might easily be demolished in a very few seconds. It is true that in many cases spoliation may be rectified, but there are numerous formations which have been and are now progressing so slowly that the work of accumulation can barely keep pace with the destructive effects of natural erosion.

* The Yellowstone National Park. I. Its Scientific Value. II. Its Improvement. By Theo. B. Comstock, B. S., American Naturalist, vol. viii, February and March, 1874. A few copies were reprinted in pamphlet form, entitled "The Scientific Value of the Yellowstone Park."

"And yet this remarkable section furnishes but a small portion of the attractions of the Park to the scientific observer. Hot and cold springs, mud-volcanoes, fumaroles, solfataras, and geysers; rapids, water-falls, and torrents; deep-cut cañons and craggy peaks, abound in every direction; lakes, gorges, and cataracts surprise one almost at every turn, and the whole is situated at a point where 'the grand Rocky Mountain system culminates in a knot of peaks and ranges inclosing the most remarkable lake-basin in the world. From this point radiate the chief mountain-ranges, and three of the longest rivers of the continent—the Missouri, the Columbia, and the Colorado.'*

"These being preserved by act of Congress, the earnest student of nature will always find an abundance of fresh matter for research in nearly every department of science. Here he will find ready to his hands a laboratory of physics in which he may observe on a large scale the action of the various forces of attraction and repulsion, and new illustrations of the correlation and conservation of energy cannot fail to attract his attention. He will find the laws of crystallization exemplified in forms novel and instructive, and will, doubtless, witness many new and varied phenomena of heat, light, and electricity.†

"The chemist will interest himself in problems of analysis and synthesis, in the processes of solution, condensation, and evaporation, and the chemical changes incident thereto. To the botanist and the vegetable physiologist the field is open for observation and wide experimentation, but there exists even at this great altitude a store-house of facts bearing upon the distribution and fertilization of plants and the almost indefinite related subjects. The zoologist and the student of comparative anatomy may also hope for rich rewards in but partially explored fields, and the meteorologist, astronomer, artist, and physician may each find here full employment for his peculiar talent. Speaking from a geological standpoint, I can, from my own experience, promise the enthusiastic student of our earth's history a view at once so complete and so overwhelming as to enchain his whole attention."

CHAPTER XI.

THERMO-DYNAMICS, CONTINUED—DESCRIPTION OF HOT SPRINGS, CONTINUED.

IX. Prairie Group, Warm Spring Creek—X. Silica Jets on branch of Warm Spring Creek—XI. Brimstone Group—XII. Hot Springs on East Fork Madison River—XIII. Prominent bowls of Lower Fire Hole Valley—XIV. Half-Way Group.

Returning to Camp 41, on the East Fork of the Yellowstone, the train then proceeded southward along the left bank of the main river, after crossing by the Miner's Bridge, a substantial structure which spans the torrent not far above the entrance of East Fork. No prominent groups of springs are met along our trail until the valley of Warm Spring Creek is reached, more than twenty miles farther up the river. The existence within these limits of three groups, including fifteen bowls, is, however, reported by Dr. A. C. Peale in his report for 1872. These are

---

* "Wonders of the Yellowstone," edited by James Richardson; "Illustrated Library of Travel, Exploration, and Adventure," edited by Bayard Taylor. New York: Scribner, Armstrong & Co., 1873.

† Some interesting observations of others are quoted in the article from which these remarks are copied.

located near the western edge of the Grand Cañon, at the southeastern base of Mount Washburne, and, consequently, at some distance from our trail, which passed to the westward of this point, to avoid recent obstructions in the old path.* In the same volume, Doctor Peale also describes one or two interesting collections which he visited upon a stream to which the name of Violet Creek was given. These springs were not passed by Captain Jones's party, but a glimpse of them was obtained by myself while making the trip from Cascade Creek to the Geyser Basins of Fire-Hole River one day in advance of the train. The route then pursued varied in some respects from that followed afterward by the main party, being less direct and bearing well to the southward, when these springs were seen in the distance. Even the imperfect view thus obtained was sufficient to enable one to judge that the group, as a whole, possesses features not less interesting than those of any other collection within the limits of our reconnaissance, and this opinion is substantiated by the report of Dr. Peale, who describes them as "an important group," and mentions some very striking peculiarities in connection with them. †

IX.—WARM SPRING CREEK, OR PRAIRIE GROUP.

A short distance above the rapids, which occur above the upper falls, two streams enter the Yellowstone River nearly opposite each other. The one flowing from the right bank is named Sour Creek upon the map of Captain Jones, which also forms the basis of the colored geological map accompanying this report.

Warm Spring Creek, rising near the divide between the waters of the Madison and Yellowstone Rivers, enters from the left bank just below the collection of hot springs known as the Crater Hills Group. (Group IV, *ante*, chapter IX; see also Fig. 16.) The valley of this stream is rather narrow, but marshy, the descent being comparatively slight for some distance above the junction of the creek with the river.

The bluffs upon both sides for the distance of a mile or more are clothed with a thick growth of timber; but above this a wide expanse of high-rolling prairie wedges in, as it were, between the forest patches. The springs being almost wholly located outside of the timber, the name Prairie Group suggests itself as not inappropriate for use in designating them.

The first collection of hot springs occurs about two miles above the mouth of the creek. They are situated mostly upon the left bank, not far from the main stream, with which they are connected by a small branch entirely supplied by their overflow. The temperature of the water is sufficiently high to heat the contents of the creek to a very perceptible amount above the previous temperature and to make this influence felt for some distance below. The springs themselves do not differ essentially from others which have already been described not far distant; but such differences as were noticed furnish a clue to the causes of observed dissimilarities in the members of a single group. In other words, we are here given a striking illustration of the principle elsewhere enunciated, that variations in the character of different springs are de-

* A single spring emerges with force in the deep cañon of Tower Creek near its junction with the Yellowstone River, and others are scattered thinly along the banks of the latter. See "Isolated Springs," under section VI, chapter IX.

† See report of Dr. A. C. Peale in United States Geological Survey of Montana, Idaho, Wyoming, and Utah, 1872, pp. 134, 135. Washington: Government Printing Office, 1873.

pendent, not only upon dissimilar geological structure, but also very largely upon variations in the intensity of the subterranean forces. The structure at this point is almost identical with that along the banks of the Yellowstone, in the neighborhood of the salses; but the deposition of sulphur is here more abundant in proportion to the size of the springs. In general, the bowls may be described as sputtering fumaroles, though there are a few fair-sized pools from which little or no vapor ordinarily escapes. The clearness of the water, compared with that usually present in springs emerging from the old lake-deposits, and the marked absence of mud-bowls, is a matter of some surprise to one who has previously visited the groups which lie in similar relations to the lacustrine formation. This seeming discrepancy may readily be understood, however, by referring it to the comparative feebleness with which the water is ejected in most of the members of the Prairie Group.

No new products, structurally or chemically considered, were here observed, nor were there forming any deposits of sufficient extent to merit special consideration.

The presence of iron is less apparent in the coloring of the products than is often the case, but the constancy and rapidity of the outflow of the water, though in comparatively small quantities, is sufficient to account for the absence of such indications. At the same time the small amount of special deposits formed by precipitation from the water after it has become condensed by cooling, points to the conclusion that the solution of the subterranean rocks is less complete than in many localities.

Another important collection of thermal springs occurs two or three miles farther up the valley of Warm Spring Creek. These were just in view from the point at which we (Mr. Creary and myself) turned southward, away from the creek, but the trail of the main party passes the group at no great distance, if I am not mistaken.

The water which flows from them remains quite hot until it has reached a point below our crossing.

The valley has been cut down to the underlying igneous rock at our ford, and the clear water passes over it in a broad shallow stream. So far as we were able to ascertain, the prominent springs of this upper group emerge from the volcanic rock. Quantities of vapor were ascending from the locality at the time of our passing, which was not far from 3 p. m., (August 22.)

X.—BOILING SPRINGS NEAR SOURCE OF WARM SPRING CREEK.

After crossing Warm Spring Creek, we pushed on in a southwesterly course for several miles, until a severe storm of wind and rain (we had been all day exposed to a cold, drizzling rain) forced us to take shelter upon the lee side of a forest. After a time we were able to proceed, when we soon struck a trail (Barlow's, 1871) for which we had been searching, which led us near to the source of the creek. By leaving the trail at a point where it turns to make a considerable détour, we made an advantageous cut-off, not impracticable for riding animals, and quickly reached an interesting group of springs, in the neighborhood of which we spent the night.

The train camped here on the following day, making Camp 44. The stream on which these hot springs are situated probably comes from cold springs some distance above, a number of which also add to its volume from along its sides in a meadow above our camp. Here it also meets with a number of hot springs, which, with the contributions from the numerous boiling springs below, soon render the water excessively hot. This upper meadow is partially separated from another in which we were camped, by a ridge of trachyte, which has been cut through by the stream.

The springs are scattered along both sides of the creek above and below, but the most powerful and interesting bowls occur near the edge of the current, on the left bank, just within the lower end of the short pass or gorge. This set of jets, as they have been called, is the nearest approach to geysers that we have yet noticed, and, in the ordinary acceptation of the term, it would not be improper to designate them thus, but it will be more convenient and, for our purpose, more correct to describe them under the present head. We will therefore consider them merely as *spurters*, a kind of highly active boiling springs in which the water is thrown to a considerable height, but in a manner differing essentially from the eruption of a true geyser, even when the latter is in a state of constant activity. This distinction is one of not a little importance, but, as it will be found more clearly defined in the chapter partly devoted to the discussion of the general subject of the hot springs and geysers, (chapter XIII,) no further attention need be given to it in this place.

These springs vary in size and intensity from furious boiling pools, in which the water spurts but an inch or two, to those in which it is thrown to a height of more than twice that number of feet. One bowl in particular, the largest in the group, is partly surrounded by a chimney nearly five feet in height, and the water is occasionally thrown to a height of more than six feet, so as to pass completely over this rim. The contents of this bowl are continually agitated, and the constant but irregular thud of the successive impulses reminds one vividly of the sound produced by the dashing of the water on a rock-bound coast. The chimney is open on the side next the stream, thus allowing the overflow to pass off freely in this direction. It is difficult to imagine the building up of such a compact and regular wall by the mere accumulation of solid particles derived from the evaporation of the ejected solution, and yet the evidence is abundant and quite conclusive upon this point. Some idea of the antiquity of the spring may, perhaps, be gained from a knowledge of the fact that a small portion only of the water which is projected from the bowl falls in a position to be available for the purpose of increasing the height or thickness of the wall of the chimney. There are several smaller orifices with correspondingly diminished chimneys, but the majority of the minor springs of this group are mere bubbling jets, in which the water is occasionally spurted to the height of a few inches, and these are not usually provided with raised walls. In all of these, however, there is something of an approach to the same structure, and a few differ only in degree from the largest bowl.

The water as it falls and evaporates about the smaller orifices spreads out so as to form a slightly arched covering over the bubbling pool, with an opening near the center, through which the jet is forced; in the large bowls, on the contrary, the volume of agitated water keeps open the space above the pool, and thus only the liquid which falls outside its limits can become evaporated, while the greater rapidity with which the accumulation takes place causes the resulting wall to rise much more nearly in a vertical direction.

Sulphureted hydrogen gas is evolved from some of these springs and small deposits of sulphur are formed in favorable situations, but the chief and most characteristic ingredient throughout is silica, of which the chimneys are mainly composed.

Were we to classify these jets according to the character of the deposits alone, their place would undoubtedly be among the geysers, for we find here not only a composition nearly identical with that of the products in the Fire-Hole basins, but even the peculiar structure of the geyser products is very closely imitated in the formations about the bowls. About some of the smaller jets clear white deposits of the most beautiful geyserite are formed, resembling porcelain beneath, with an upper surface of delicate tracery or of coarser excrescency, according to the force of the falling water. Sometimes a glistening pink surface is disclosed by the fracture of the rougher incrustations, which are usually of a light-brown color. Manganese in the form of pyrolusite (manganic dioxide) is extremely abundant as a coating to parts washed by the outflow and by the falling spray, as well as on portions of the interior walls of many of the bowls. Iron is not scarce, being more particularly present exteriorly, where it gives rise to the brown and pink colors which are visible in the siliceous crust, and it is noticeable that the growth of green cryptogamic vegetation in the water is especially abundant in those spots where iron is most common as a deposit. The proportion of this ingredient is, however, not as great as in many sections, the trachyte being lighter in color in consequence.

The following description of specimens obtained from this locality will serve to explain the special features observed:

a. Igneous rock from the wall of the gorge, a part of the ridge through which the stream has been cut. This is a trachyte of a purplish tint on a surface of fracture and weathers light-colored.

b. An incrustation of *siliceous sinter* or *geyserite*, formed about the orifice of a small jet. The water, falling as a coarse spray, has produced upon the upper service a peculiar kind of ornamentation almost impossible to describe, but which may be compared to a quantity of brown beans, partly imbedded in a rock.

c. Piece broken from the channel of the same jet, where the water flows out. This is coated with a dark yellow incrustation caused by the admixture of sulphur (?) and ferric hydrate, and is very largely composed of manganic dioxide, which give it a soft earthy texture.

d. Small island-masses standing in the bed of the outflow from the largest jet. The top is covered with relief work not unlike a cauliflower-head in general appearance, but more deeply indented, formed by the action of the returning water as it falls from the jet. The upper portion of the side is coated with black, (possibly a sulphide,) and the lower portion is covered with a considerable deposit of aluminic hydrate and ferric hydrate mixed (*bauxite*) of a light coffee-color. A section shows that the whole is composed of a rather irregular alternation of the three minerals *geyserite*, *pyrolusite*, and *bauxite*, there being no mixture of these at any point, on account of their different specific gravities. The deposition of the bauxite and pyrolusite at the same distance from the jet, therefore, indicates some variation in power at different times.* The *siliceous sinter*, or geyserite, which comprises the greater portion of the mass, is compact and glistening and rather dark in color.

e. Portion of the outside of the rim of the lower or open side of the largest jet. Here the surface is exposed to the combined action of the overflow and the falling water; hence the mammillary excrescence is coarser and less regular, while the flowing off of the water has produced

* In some cases the deposition of the manganic dioxide is undoubtedly induced by the presence of foreign organic matter, (as wood, &c.)

much the same features as in specimen *c*, though on a much larger scale. *Pyrolusite* is prominently present as an incrustation, but it does not accumulate on surfaces exposed to the washing action of the water.

f. Fragment of soaked wood taken from the water at the outlet of the largest jet. This does not show signs of silicification after months of exposure to the air, (from August 23, 1873, to September 17, 1874,*) though it had previously become softened and thoroughly permeated by the hot liquid. Its color, as at first, is now a light brown, and it has become toughened by drying, without, however, increasing in brittleness.

g. Earthy moss obtained from beneath the water in the stream below the largest jet, originally formed as an incrustation upon a small branch. The impression of a portion of the wood is left as a groove in the lower side. A deposit of *pyrolusite* was first formed, but this is now covered by an accumulation of *bauxite*, one-quarter of an inch in thickness. The upper or outer surface is ornamented slightly by annular grooves. Here again we have evidence of a change in the force of ejection of the same nature as recorded under *d.* The deposition of *alumina* (as *bauxite*) in a spot previously characterized by the precipitation of *pyrolusite*, indicates a diminution of intensity since the epoch of the formation of the black coating at this point.

There can be but few subjects more interesting or more promising of rich results in the investigation, than the tracing of the numerous hot springs through their various products back to their origin in the igneous rocks. In the present case, we need go no further than the immediate vicinity of the group for eruptive material which contains all the mineral ingredients of the spring deposits, so that we may be justified in believing that the source of these bowls, so far, at least, as their products are concerned, is not far distant. The source of the heat and other possible forces concerned in the movement of the water, is, however, quite another question, and one which can only be answered after a careful review of all the facts, and a comparison of the features and phenomena of a large number of widely-separated springs.

XI.—BRIMSTONE GROUP. (SOLFATARAS.)

Less than a mile distant from the silica jets just described, in a southwesterly direction, an important collection of solfataric fumaroles exists as the main source of another branch of Warm Spring Creek. There are many points of similarity between this group and that on Turbid Lake, described in chapter IX, (group I,) but the salses of that section are here scarcely represented, while the activity of the solfataras is much increased.

The geological structure is much the same in the two localities, although the Turbid Lake Group is more than 1,500 feet below the level of the Brimstone Group. From this fact it may be inferred that a smaller lake has existed in the past, or perhaps a series of lakes at a much higher altitude than the great Yellowstone basin. It is also highly probable that these were drained in the direction of the great lake, though the exact course of the outlet cannot be determined without more thorough and extended investigation. Several ponds and pond-like depressions still remain, and although their relations to the present drainage system cannot, in all cases, be clearly made out in a cursory view, there is still

* Though I can see no reason to suppose that it would cause any difference in the result, it may be well to state that the specimen has been tightly wrapped in paper during the year that has elapsed since it was obtained.

much reason for the belief that all are more closely connected with the Yellowstone slope than with that of the Madison River. A large but not rapid stream passes off from the neighborhood of the springs, which is probably the main source of Warm Spring Creek, the outflow from the silica jets being more properly considered a branch of this. A sulphurous pond not more than one-quarter of the size of Turbid Lake is situated near one side of the group, lying some feet above the flat on which most of the springs are located. Some vapor was arising from a few of the orifices at 8.30 a. m. on the twenty-third of August, but signs of previously greater activity were apparent. It is therefore probable that these springs are subject to periodical agitation, though no facts were elicited which could aid in determining the intervals between eruptions.

The time spent in this locality was not sufficient to allow of much careful work, and the nature of all the products was consequently not ascertained; sulphur, however, is the principal ingredient, being probably produced here in greater quantity than in any other portion of the National Park thus far described by the several authorities. There are some bowls of considerable size, but the most striking feature of the whole area is the occurrence of a large number of small orifices, in which the water bubbles constantly, giving rise to deposits of crystallized sulphur, which are formed upon the walls of numerous cavernous incrustations. The various interesting effects produced by the action of sulphurous water and vapor in other sections are here displayed on a scale of some magnitude, whenever the necessary conditions are present.

The pond and some of the larger bowls occur in a spot which contains a few feet of limestone deposits as a surface formation, while the solfataras emerge more directly from the underlying trachyte. The whole group is, perhaps, one hundred feet above the level of the jets described in section X.

Local deposits of ferric hydrate were observed, but nothing was seen to indicate the deposition of manganic dioxide as a prominent deposit.

In the midst of the dense forest, about half a mile beyond this group, the trail passes partly around a small lake of clear fresh water, not in the least unpleasant to the taste. Its size, late in August, was not less than forty rods in diameter, and the signs of water action extended for some distance up the steep slope of the gravelly beach, showing that it is much larger at times. I could perceive no outlet, and it is not impossible that it has underground connection with some of the neighboring hot springs, although it is lower in position than the Brimstone Group, I think.

XII.—HOT SPRINGS ON EAST FORK OF MADISON RIVER.

Heavy deposits and other evidences of the former existence of springs over a portion of the area drained by the East Fork of the Madison and its tributaries,* occur abundantly along our course, which also here differed somewhat from that afterward taken by the train. No active springs were observed of special importance until a prominent group, on the left bank of the East Fork, was reached shortly before entering the Lower Geyser Basin of Fire-Hole River. There are, however, a large

* On the maps, two streams flowing into the Madison River are named alike (East Fork.) That referred to throughout this report is the more southerly, which has received the name Hayden's Fork from members of the expedition of 1872, though this appellation has not become general.

number of thermal springs, more or less isolated, in the valley of East Fork, which we could not stop to examine, while the existence of others is indicated by the amount of highly-heated water contained in the stream.

Judging from the accounts of other members of the expedition, as well as from the published reports of Dr. Hayden and others, we probably missed many of these by passing in a nearly direct line through the timber for some distance before striking the river.

In the group just mentioned there are more than a dozen large and mportant bowls, some of which are vigorously active, approaching even to the smallest geysers in the force with which their contents are occasionally ejected. At the time of my visit to this locality, (2 p. m., August 23,) the activity was not as great as is sometimes the case, for there were signs of recent overflows much more extensive. Very little vapor was then ascending from the spot, but dense clouds were afterward given off. The springs vary in size from mere orifices less than an inch in diameter, to deep bowls having circumferences of from thirty to forty feet.

There is considerable variety in the phenomena here exhibited, some of the larger bowls being comparatively quiet, others almost incessantly boiling, though quite regularly, while others sputter, and even eject the water in jets. Besides these there are not a few seething solfataras, and the contents of one bowl alternately rise and fall in connection with excessive ebullition. Some of the springs have no rims other than the adjacent soil, but the majority are ornamented in various ways, several being provided with raised chimneys of no great height.

Here again we find the geological structure not widely different from that observed in the neighborhood of the Yellowstone Lake at the Turbid Lake Group, (I, chapter IX,) with, perhaps, a much smaller proportion of alumina in the uncompacted surface-formation. As a consequence of the latter feature, silica predominates in the products of this section. Iron and sulphur are also present in sufficient quantity to give character to some of the highly-colored deposits, and the latter is found lining the interior of many of the smaller orifices in the form of delicate yellow crystals. A green cryptogamic (?) growth is present in some of the larger bowls, which offer favorable conditions of agitation and temperature.

Another small collection of springs, manifesting quite similar phenomena, occurs directly on the trail, just at the entrance by a kind of pass to the Fire-Hole Valley. One or two geysers with low chimneys also exist here, but they were not in action when we passed them. As in the group near the stream, mentioned above, there are some bowls which are quite extinct, while others appear to have been more recently formed than most of those in action. None are sufficiently unique to require special mention, and the two collections may be considered as one so far as essential features and products are concerned.

In passing down to this point from the summit of the divide between the drainage systems of the Yellowstone and Madison Rivers, we obtain a vertical section of two thousand feet of the eruptive rocks, though the structure is greatly obscured in many places by immense deposits of ancient spring products or by thick accumulations of vegetable mold.

Some peculiarly-mixed varieties of rocks of igneous origin occur under circumstances which suggest mere local distribution as veins or dikes; but the general order of arrangement can be made out with some degree of satisfaction. Without attempting an accurate classification, the following may be taken as a representative section; beginning above *a.* Hard and compact trachyte, with a crypto-crystalline texture; underlaid by,

b. Quartzose trachyte, (*? granitic rhyolite*, or *nevadite*, of Richthofen;) which covers,

c. Obsidian; above

d. Volcanic breccias, &c.

XIII.—SPRINGS IN LOWER GEYSER BASIN, FIRE-HOLE RIVER.

Just beyond the locality of the last-described group, a sudden turn to southward brings us quickly in sight of many more hot springs and geysers belonging to several more or less connected clusters which occupy a large area in the lower valley of the so-called Fire-Hole River, covering the district now commonly known as the Lower Geyser Basin. The highly-interesting phenomena of the geysers in this section claim such a great share of the observer's attention that the many non-eruptive springs may readily be overlooked unless some special attention is devoted to them. In attempting to describe the more important of these, we are met at the outset with the difficulty of drawing a close line of separation between the hot springs and the geysers. This subject will be discussed, however, in its proper place, and we may proceed without present delay to take up here such of the bowls as do not properly come under the head of geysers, as defined at the close of chapter XIII.

The remains of ancient, extinct springs are quite as abundant as the deposits of recent formation, covering as they do portions of the igneous rocks of different ages in the neighborhood of the basin. Not a few of the active springs now occupy the summits of mounds which have been built up by former geysers; and the present bowls of such represent the last stages of the warring subterranean forces.

Upon entering the Lower Geyser Basin, we first crossed a broad, flat tract, clothed with a rank growth of grass, except in spots subjected to inundation by the overflow from the hot springs and geysers during the flood-seasons.* Some hot springs have previously existed in certain portions of this tract, and the evaporation of their contents when spread over the surface has left impressions of some interest, though upon a scale of no great magnitude. In a series of quite shallow pools thus formed on the plan of the evaporating-pans of Gardiner's River, the ornamentation and other peculiarities of that region are very closely imitated, while fine examples of mud-cracks are shown in those which have been so recently produced as not to allow of the accumulation of a deposit of sufficient thickness to conceal the soil beneath. Silica is the principal ingredient of all the bowls of this basin.

Extinct geysers.—At the edge of the timber, near the flat, there is a sluggish spring, which issues from the center of a conical geyser-mound four feet in height. By the unequal degrees of evaporation in various parts of the outflow, the top and sides are streaked with shades of red and yellow, which give the whole an appearance very striking, but not suggestive of an agreeable object; for it forcibly reminds one of an ulcerous discharge from a putrid sore. The mound is the accumulation of a geyser long since extinct, and the deposits from the subsequent spring have nearly closed the orifice, so that the present discharge

* There is no lack of evidence here, as elsewhere, both in this valley and in other parts of the National Park, that the amount of the outflow has been recently much more abundant. The term "*flood-seasons*" is used here to designate the period of such increase, without regard to the actual times of such occurrences, or the causes by which they have been produced.

is much reduced in quantity. The vivid colors are produced by the precipitation of ferric hydrate and a small amount of sulphur upon a white ground produced by accumulations of silica and calcic carbonate with more or less of the common impurities.

From this point southward, after crossing a small stream coming in from the east, the surface is covered with a fine calcareous sand, through which progress is made with some difficulty, and this is succeeded by a similar loose deposit, with a thin crust not firm enough to support the weight of a riding-animal. Continuing this course, a low, broad, mound-shaped hill is ascended, upon which there are several geysers not to be distinguished by casual observers from hot-spring bowls, except when seen in action. Upon one side of the eminence over which the greater portion of the drainage passes, the bathing-pools and evaporating-pans of the Gardiner's River Group are represented on a reduced scale, and several small springs of no special importance emerge in their vicinity.

Mud-caldron.—Back of this group of geysers, in a hollow of the ridge to which they also belong, there is a large mud-caldron in a state of violent agitation.

The contents consist of a thick, pasty mud, of a great variety of colors, from clear white to the most brilliant red. The surface of the sputtering mass is several feet below the edge of the bowl, and the interior of the pit thus formed is lined with red, blue, and yellow deposits, caused by the clinging of the mud which is spurted fitfully upon the disruption of many viscous cones temporarily formed by the resistance offered to the ejecting force. The shape of the pit is irregular, approaching the elliptical, with a depth of three or four feet and diameters of about thirty-five and sixty feet. The mud is composed of a rather streaky mixture of siliceous, calcareous, and argillaceous material, with the not uncommon concomitants from which the deep red and yellow colors are derived. Owing to the constant and excessive agitation of this material the union of the ingredients is more complete than in many of the mud-bowls, and the colors are consequently more nearly blended into one. The boiling takes place over a large surface, perhaps more vigorously near one side, and small cones or puffs are raised temporarily at each center of ebullition, which finally burst from the continued pressure, often spurting to a height of four or five feet. Smaller mud-springs occur in the neighborhood, and there is one bowl of clear water, nearly or quite as large as the mud-caldron itself. From my own observations I was led to surmise that the clear spring, and the mud-caldron, or *salse*, are subject to more or less of periodical variation in the intensity of their action, but this supposition is based upon too little knowledge to be of any special value by itself. It is mainly based upon variations noticed in the amount of vapor ascending from the pit.

We next passed across a marshy and slushy valley, down which an important series of geyser clusters shed their surplus water. Camping as near as convenient to the White Dome, (described in chapter XIII,) the remaining springs of the basin here mentioned were visited on the following morning. It should be understood that the writer has placed these bowls in the category of hot springs, according to the best of his judgment, after a review of the geysers in this and other localities; but it should also be borne in mind that some, at least, of those described as mere springs, may be true geysers which we were not fortunate enough to observe in action. Such errors, however, are of trifling importance, when the close connection existing between the two classes of bowls is duly considered.

North Branch.—North of east from our camp, less than half a mile distant, there is a group of powerful geysers among which occur several bowls less evidently eruptive in character. As a rule, the latter do not, apparently, contribute a notable amount of waste liquid to the general outlet of the group; but in one or two cases the overflow is very considerable, if not even equal to the ejections from some of the larger intermittent geysers, owing to the constancy of the flow. One of these thermal springs is much more feeble than it has been at some earlier period of its existence, as is evident from the dryness of a large bowl at the surface, below the bottom of which the present spring is boiling with a marked resonance. Not far from this is a pool in which the water bubbles constantly over the greater part of the surface, but boils fiercely near the edges, as if struggling to free itself from beneath a projecting rim. Another, near the last, has been a powerful geyser at some time in the past, for it is surrounded by the peculiar stalagmitoid prominences, so commonly produced by the water as it falls to the ground after its ejection. The pools about the bowl were quite dry at the time of our visit, but it is quite possible that we have here a geyser in which the eruptions occur only at long intervals, as in the Giantess, elsewhere described, (chapter XIII.*)

Above all of these springs there is a large and deep bowl filled with hot, but not boiling, water, and there seems good reason for the belief that this is not a geyser, in the fact that it contains a quantity of a brown colloid substance, which could not thus accumulate in pools subject to periodical agitation, unless the dormant intervals were extremely long. But again, the water in this bowl is constantly pouring over the edges in a steady stream, though not in excessive quantity. It is possible, it is true, that there may be some underground connection which furnishes direct communication between this spring and one of the neighboring geysers, but such a passage is not clearly apparent in any way. The so-called colloid matter is occasionally found incrusting bits of wood and other similar bodies floating in the water. In such cases it is often almost or quite crystalline in texture, a result which may, *perhaps*, be induced by contact with organic matter. A Coleopterous and a Neuropterous insect were taken from the water of this bowl, and others were found in similar situations in other localities.

South Branch.—A short distance west of the White Dome Geyser the main creek is formed by the junction of two forks; the cluster above mentioned being located on what may be termed the North Branch. For convenience of reference, the main stream will here be designated as White Creek, a name suggested by the prevailing color of the deposits along its sides. The South Branch, besides the geysers which largely supply it, receives the contributions of a number of thermal springs in addition to such bowls as are of doubtful nature. A few are deserving of a fuller notice than can be given in this place, although their peculiar characteristics are mainly the results of combinations of features already described. One who has never remarked the marvelous variety which is not seldom produced by very slight changes in the relations of parts or in the occurrence of physical conditions, can form no adequate idea of the great diversity of delineation which is here displayed. There are springs with ornamented borders and springs which are mere holes in the ground filled with water; some are deep, with azure-tinted contents, while others are almost forbidding in their aspect, reminding one of nothing less disgusting than a tub of sloppy liquid. In some, delicate rims of their own deposits project inward over

* See Unknown Geyser, chapter XIII, 9.

the surface of the water; others are provided with margins no less fragile which project upward as fringing reefs, and not a few are hemmed in by stout walls of coarser composition. There are those with deep pits, in which the water bubbles, or gurgles, or roars, or simmers, or sputters, or spurts, and there are quiet bowls, steadily-flowing springs, and fitful pools. The character and composition of the deposits, the wonderful variety and combinations of their colors, and the numerous conditions under which they have been accumulated and distributed, have resulted in the production of effects impossible to describe, never to be justly interpreted by the most skillful artist. Such, in fact, may be said of each prominent collection throughout the whole district of hot-spring action, no less truly than of the South Branch cluster, which is in some respects exceeded by many of the groups already described. Our passage through this portion of the basin was too rapid to allow of much detailed observation, and a very important cluster of geysers and thermal springs on the main trail, at the junction of White Creek with the Fire-Hole River and below, was necessarily left unexamined.

Desiring to reach the upper basin as early as possible, we pursued as direct a course as practicable through the timber to a point on Fire-Hole River half-way to the next group of springs, (XIV,) thus saving very much in the distance by the usual trail. In the forest an occasional spring was passed, and the remains of extinct bowls were not uncommon. In some places fallen timber is quite abundant, but the greater part of it lies in one general direction, so that progress along that course is not seriously impeded. Upon the higher lands, however, it is almost impossible to make headway against the obstructions of this nature, which are thickly strewn over the surface in inextricable confusion, and one is forced to follow closely the scarcely less objectionable course marked out by the low marshy border of the Fire-Hole River. Less than two miles above, the stream runs through a narrow cañon in the volcanic rock, which renders travel less difficult for a considerable distance along its borders, and just here occurs the prominent collection of springs to which has been given the name of Half-Way Group, on account of its position on the trail, about equidistant between the two geyser-basins of the Fire-Hole Valley.

XIV.—HALF-WAY GROUP—FIRE-HOLE RIVER.

At this point the river is deflected by the wall of igneous rock upon the right bank so as to turn nearly at a right angle to its previous course. The trail, extending along the right bank near the stream, passes close to a number of interesting springs within a distance of less than a mile, scarcely one of which is not deserving of a critical examination. Altogether there are not less than fifteen bowls of considerable size, with several smaller orifices and one or two pools in which the water is thrown up as in a miniature geyser. Upon the left bank of the river, at the lower end of the group, the most important springs are located, and their features are so different in many respects from all others elsewhere observed that even the most casual observer cannot but be impressed with a sense of the wondrous variety of manifestation within such narrow limits. The river in turning westward passes partly around and beneath the edge of a broad siliceous terrace rising forty feet or more above the bed of the stream. On this bench the springs are situated, and the outflowing water is carried over the cliff into the river by the most direct course.

One of the bowls is a mere pond of hot water, one hundred and fifty feet in diameter, but so deep and clear that the view obtained upon looking down into its water is very fascinating, and this effect is very much heightened by the play of the sunlight upon the rippling surface. The water rises by a series of regular and gentle impulses acting in the center, thus causing a kind of pulsating overflow all around the margin of the pool. In this manner the bowl has become slightly raised above the surrounding surface by the evaporation of a portion of the extraverted liquid, and a series of steps, each but a few inches in height, has been formed outside. These present an appearance very much as if a number of immense rings, transversely flattened, with their external dimensions decreasing gradually from the bottom upward, had been placed one above another about the rim of a large pit. Clouds of vapor ascend from the surface at times, but this does not serve to lessen the beauty and brilliancy of the whole, for even these fumes are quite distinctly tinted when viewed in certain favorable lights. Another bowl less than twenty-five feet in diameter is shaped like the interior of a hollow frustum of a cone inverted, and another is the feeble remnant of a once powerful spring, which now exists only as an orifice at the bottom of the ancient pool.

Cliff Spring.—Near the northern edge of the terrace the most conspicuous spring exists, one which is as unique as it is impressive and difficult to describe. At a little distance one sees nothing but a dense mass of vapor rising from one of the largest and deepest pits* to be found in the Fire-Hole Valley. Approaching with some caution, it is possible to pass down into the pit near the outlet, and thence along the southern and western edges of the bowl. The present surface of the water is, in some places, at least 20 feet below the general surface of the terrace on which it is situated. The outline of the pit is very irregular, but we shall be quite safe in estimating the average diameter (if such an expression may be used) at not less than 200 feet. The water is constantly most violently agitated, the greatest commotion being observed atthe western edge, where it is forced out from beneath the overhanging rock, which is composed of laminated ancient spring deposits. It would require some careful study to determine the exact relations which the laminated rock bears to the origin of the existing springs, but the later history of the present bowl is quite clearly revealed by a comparison with its recent manifestations. We thus learn that the subterranean forces have in the past, as now, found an outlet in an easterly direction, while the surplus contents of the bowl have been discharged toward the west, according to the natural slope of the surrounding surface. As the water is thus forced up from below it wears the rock upon the western side in such a manner as to undermine it, the thin lamination of the mass causing this process to take place more rapidly. After a time a kind of cavern is thus formed, as may now be seen at one point, and finally the impending portion falls by its own weight, by so much carrying westward the margin of the pit, the bowl having accomplished its own enlargement while undermining the ledge. Occasionally, also, large blocks of the ancient deposits have become detached from the sides by the action of frost and through other means, and it is highly probable that such masses have not unfrequently been instrumental in changing the location or direction of the subaqueous operations to some slight extent. A constant stream of hot water passes out through a walled channel from the main portion of the bowl, but this soon spreads out thinly and runs off down the slope in many

*The term *pit*, as employed in this report, distinguishes that portion of a spring which is above the surface of the liquid contents from the *bowl* proper, which contains the water or mud.

small rills. According to the shallowness and sluggishness of the flow at different points, upon which the amount of condensation mainly depends, deposits of various colors are formed, affording examples of almost every conceivable shade from delicate white to the darker tints of brown and red. In addition to the mineral deposits, green and brown and red accumulations of growing vegetable matter and of colloidal substances are common here as well as elsewhere upon the bench to which this spring belongs.

The specimens collected from the Cliff Spring, as this may be styled, are described in the following list:

1. A portion of the jutting ledge of the pool, bathed by the water as it washes the edges in successive waves from the centers of ebullition. This is exceedingly delicate and highly colored by the deposition at different points of the silica, containing various proportions of ferric hydrate and other foreign matter. The colors are very largely retained, so that the older portions of the ledge, not now exposed to the action of the water in its ebb and flow, present irregular alternations of the several shades over a surface of fracture. The process of formation of the ledge, and its chief characteristics, remind one strongly of the corresponding portion of the rim of the large bowl on the seventh terrace, at Gardiner's River Mammoth Hot Springs. The richness and softness of coloring, and the delicacy of texture in that section, is, however, much inferior to that of the Cliff Spring, on account of the preponderance of silica at the latter point. Much of the *sinter* here has the glossy appearance of real porcelain, being very compactly and evenly deposited.

2. A soft, dark gray deposit in shallow water, with a finely wave-marked surface, caused by the ripples produced by the agitation in the center of the bowl. The temperature of the water in which this is forming is so high, that specimens can be procured only with great difficulty, although the substance offers no great resistance to blows from a hammer. The mass thus obtained is rather tenacious, and it hardens upon long exposure to the air.

3. Loose pieces of sinter in shallow water, near the edges of the bowl, originally introduced from without, and now more or less coated with an incrustation of No. 2, according to the duration of its exposure to the action of the hot water.

4. Portion of the wall of a shallow pool through which the water passes in escaping from the bowl. This may be regarded as a general combination of the three preceding, being subject to conditions partaking of the nature of all of those under which they have been produced. The result is, therefore, a deposit of a mixed color, with a consistency between that of a hardened sinter and the soft No. 2.

5. Brownish red colloid substance, not uncommon about the edges of the bowl; a pulpy jelly with very slight tenacity, becoming extremely brittle when dried. It presents no peculiarities other than pertain to the numerous masses of a similar character which abound throughout the Hot Spring district.

6. Green confervoid? vegetation in quiet places near the cooler edge of the bowl; also observed in channels of the outlet. Owing, probably, to the presence of iron in the water, this growth is abundant in the springs of the Half-Way Group, when favorable conditions of depth and temperature are offered.

7. More ancient deposit near the base of the wall of the pit, washed by the water as it boils up in the southwestern corner of the bowl. A considerable quantity of ferric hydrate, and other matter, is deposited in the crevices of the wall at this point. The ancient laminated rock is

mainly siliceous, but it resembles the more recent formations in the irregularity of its texture and composition.

8. Pieces from the wall with less trace of recent action than in No. 7. These do not show much change from weathering, except in crumbling more readily than the modern deposits. They were not taken from spots exposed to much aqueous action.

9. Specimen from the old wall, in which the red and green deposits are quite conspicuous. The green is of uncertain origin, but it may be collodial, or even some lowly-organized form of vegetation, and it is possibly not an ancient formation.

10. Portion of the surface layers of the wall, showing a very interesting structure induced by the action of running water and other "weathering" influences. A description can scarcely convey any idea of this, but it may be compared, in general terms, to a series of thin horizontal plates supported and separated by minute pillars closely crowded, the distance between the floors being not more than an inch or two.

The reddish substance, No. 5, is formed in the other springs where the water is not too much disturbed, and in one spot upon the summit of the bench there is a very large deposit of it, some two inches in thickness, possessing all the properties of like aggregations to be seen in every group of importance throughout the whole region of springs. The yellowish-white silky deposit so common at Gardiner's River is also present here in channels of the outlet through which the hot water passes.

Near another bend in the river, a few rods above this spot, there are several bowls upon each bank, one of those upon the right being quite large. The deposits from these are not widely different from those just described, although they are situated in a rather alluvial section.

Above this point the trail passes through a continuous succession of quaggy marshes and fallen timber for three or four miles, with no signs of hot springs until the lower end of the Upper Geyser Basin is reached, when travel becomes much less difficult.

General geological structure between the Geyser Basins.

As before remarked, in passing from the Lower Geyser Basin up the Fire-Hole Valley to the Half-Way Group, a broad alluvial tract is crossed, which is raised so slightly above the bed of the stream as to be kept continually in a marshy condition by the overflow of its banks. The existence of ancient thermal springs over a portion of this area is suggested by the occurrence of several ponds with basins not unlike the bowls of large hot springs, but there is nothing in the aspect of this section which seems to indicate the formation of extensive deposits by such agency within a very great length of time. On the other hand, there is every reason to believe that much of the space included between the Half-Way Group and the Upper Geyser Basin has more recently been the scene of very great activity, for the greater part of the valley from side to side is flooded with ancient siliceous sinter, not very deeply covered by recent humic accumulations. The bed of the river, for nearly the whole distance, is also composed of the same material. The Geyser Basins and the intermediate springs are underlaid by these deposits, and it is apparent that the origin of the post-volcanic thermic action was in the far remote past. We may also learn that, whatever of change has taken place since that period, has resulted rather in diminution of intensity than in movements of base. In several places the opposite walls of the valley approach each other more nearly than usual, so as to form short cañons or passages between somewhat restricted basins.

In the lower valley there has been much erosion, and two prominent hillocks, known as the "Twin Buttes," have been left as relics of the igneous beds which once filled a portion of the present hollow.

In the walls of the upper part of the valley, particularly upon the right bank, the structure can be made out with less of difficulty, but it will require long and careful investigation to determine the relations existing between this and distant sections. High up in the bluffs, on the north, the trachytes appear dipping away from the river at an angle of nearly 15°. The strata upon the opposite side of the valley, so far as could be ascertained by cursory observations, are apparently continuous with these. (See Fig. 34.)

The foregoing facts, incomplete as they are, are offered as important links in the chain of evidence which must some time be gathered from a region which certainly holds as much material of interest to the student in thermo-dynamics as can be found anywhere within the same limits.

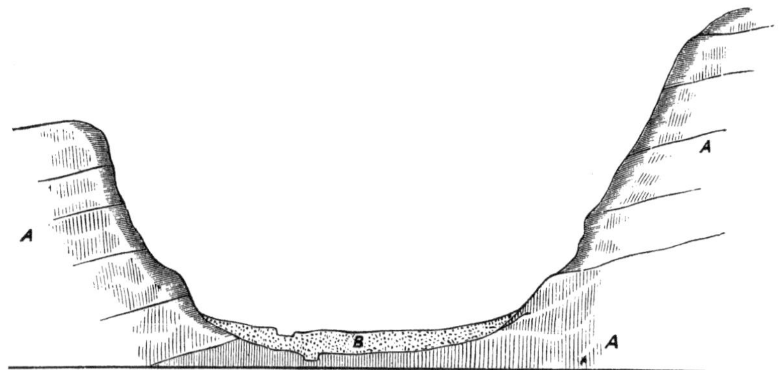

FIG. 34.—Ideal section across upper portion of valley of Fire-Hole River, Yellowstone National Park. *A A A*, trachytes, &c., dipping 15°; *B*, ancient spring deposits, siliceous.

The Hot Springs of the Upper Geyser Basin, and the several remaining groups, will be described in the following chapter.

CHAPTER XII.

THERMO-DYNAMICS, CONTINUED—DESCRIPTION OF HOT SPRINGS, CONCLUDED.

XV. Principal Bowls of Upper Geyser Basin—XVI. Hot Springs on southwest arm of Yellowstone Lake, Group No. 1—XVII. Southwest arm of Yellowstone Lake, Group No. 2—XVIII. Thermal Springs, above Heart Lake, at base of Red Mountains.—Conclusion.

Near the lower end of the Upper Geyser Basin a prominent branch enters the Fire-Hole River from a direction east of south. On the map of the basin, published by Dr. Hayden in his report for 1871, this stream is recorded as Iron Spring Creek, a name which is sufficiently appropriate on account of the reddish deposits of iron which occur in its track. A group of hot springs and geysers is situated just below a fork in the creek, one mile and a half above its junction with the Fire Hole, but we were unable to visit the locality so as to describe them properly. The minor collections of springs remaining to be described in this section are all located in the Fire-Hole Valley, and the geysers and non-eruptive bowls are so generally mingled together that it is even more difficult to separate the members of the two classes than in the Lower Geyser Basin.

XV.—HOT SPRINGS OF UPPER GEYSER BASIN—FIRE-HOLE RIVER.

In a visit of such short duration to a basin containing a large number of the most remarkable geysers in the world, it was impossible to fix the attention strongly enough upon the quiescent thermal springs to obtain all the information concerning them which is essential to accurate description. Enough material was, however, gathered from the study of these bowls to demonstrate, beyond the shadow of doubt, that they are no less important and interesting in their phenomena than those of any other section within the limits of our reconnaissance. Some were examined with sufficient thoroughness to enable them to be described with some degree of fullness, accounts of which will now be given in the order of their occurrence, beginning at the lower part of the basin.

Clusters a, b. On each bank of the Fire-Hole River, just below the mouth of Iron Spring Creek, there is a group of springs of varying temperature, among which are a number of large bowls.

Those upon the left bank lie but a little above the bed of the river, while those of the opposite collection are disposed upon a sloping surface, the upper members being not less than thirty feet higher than the main stream. The former collection comprises several minor geysers, with three or four mere springs; the group upon the right bank including only one bowl with sufficient eruptive power to be properly considered a geyser, but having seven thermal springs of some importance. As a rule the bowls are quite regular in outline, approaching the circular form, and the depth of the upper portion is very considerable. One of the largest, however, at the summit of the hill has formed a bordering rim at some distance outside of the edge of the original bowl, so as to wall in a larger portion of the water, making, as it were, a shallow pond about the inner cup. This fringing pool is mainly upon the drainage-side of the spring, leaving the main bowl nearer the opposite edge. The temperature of the different springs is not uniform, but the average is high, the boiling-point being almost reached in one or two instances. As might be inferred from their similarity in structure, the features and products of the springs in these clusters are not markedly different from those described under section XIV. Iron is prominently present and silica is the principal ingredient. The growth of confervoid vegetation is abundant in favorable spots.

Much vapor is evolved at times from this locality, particularly from the large bowl at the summit of the terrace upon the right bank, but, although a very great difference was observed in the amount of such fumes given off at dusk (August 24) and on the following morning, it was impossible to ascertain how much of this change was due to atmospheric conditions. It may, however, be predicated that this bowl at least is subject to more or less of periodical variation, for there was sufficient evidence to that effect in the marks of recent overflow about the edges of the outlets.

Cluster c.—The next collection of springs is little more than a continuation of cluster *b*, though it is distinct enough to claim separate consideration. As here somewhat arbitrarily defined, this group includes all the bowls upon both sides of the Fire-Hole River between the mouth of Iron Spring Creek and a point half a mile above. Within this area there are seventeen hot springs of noteworthy importance, besides a number of inferior geysers, which might not inappropriately be classed in the same category. Of this number, but five are situated upon the left bank of the stream. Among them all there is, perhaps, as much of variety in ornamentation and mode of action as is to be found in other sections, but their general features and phenomena, as well as their products, are strikingly similar to the members of cluster *a*, which are apparently influenced by nearly the same circumstances of structure, position, and temperature. Indeed, it may be said that the whole description given in the preceding paragraph will apply equally as well to the present group, taken as a whole, for if there be any important difference, it is rather to be found in the degree of activity than in the nature of the springs or the character of their deposits. One point of interest common to all the groups, but more especially noticeable in this cluster, is the frequent occurrence in close proximity of two or more bowls in which the temperature of the contents differs greatly. As we pass up the valley the eruptive effects are more apparent, and the main geyser basin is reached by a kind of transition from the latent bowl to the roaring spouter. In accordance with this, the overflow from the upper members of the cluster under review is more excessive than in the collections below, giving rise at last to well-defined streams, which also receive the surplus from the accompanying geysers. The deposits of silica, contaminated with iron (as hydrated sesquioxide) and alumina, and a slight amount of magnesic carbonate, are consequently rather more abundant than in the lower groups. Owing probably to the easy drainage, which causes the surplus water to be rapidly removed, the finely-ornamented rims and the richly variegated deposits which abound in some sections are here less common, but their place is supplied by heavy accumulations of equal geological importance, and of no less weighty interest when viewed in the light of local history.

Above cluster c.—The remaining springs cannot be grouped satisfactorily; but they will be described as nearly as possible in local order, omitting such as are unimportant or not specially characteristic of some new or interesting feature. At least twenty-five large, and doubtless very significant, bowls must be passed without notice for want of careful observation, while the number of minor orifices and springs thus excluded from this account is many times as great. Not a few of these, it is certain, are but representatives of one or other of the prominent types already described; but many were seen which promised much additional information if they could have been properly examined. Above the upper limit of cluster *c* no noticeable springs occur upon either bank of the river for a space of nearly one-quarter of a mile, when an area of great activity is met, thickly dotted with them, besides a number of remarkable geysers, including the *Fan*, *Riverside*, *Giant*, and *Grotto*.

Pyramid.—From the flat upon the left bank, at a distance of several hundred feet from the river, a large, white mound of silic arises to the height of twenty-five feet. More or less of vapor was almost continually ascending from a vent-hole at the summit, with a periodic increase of intensity, the intervals of which were not determined. This was at one time undoubtedly a very powerful geyser, which has gradually erected an enormous pyramidal chimney, the bowl being closed by degrees as the internal forces have slowly decreased in power. Even now there are unmistakable signs of comparatively modern ejections in the peculiar ornamentation about the bowl, which one soon learns to recognize as the result of the action of the falling water. Some of these markings are quite coarse, clearly indicating to those who have had a little experience in the study of geyser phenomena that the eruptive power was sufficient to project the column of water to a considerable height. There is no evidence of recent great activity, and the mound may safely be regarded as a mere thermal spring of small size surmounting the chimney of an extinct geyser, which it is steadily closing by the accumulation of its own deposits. Near its base are several fumaroles and one fair-sized boiling or spouting spring, which possesses, on a small scale, all the essential characteristics of some of the simpler geysers. The ornamentation of the fumeroles is here of the plainest kind, and there is nothing especially novel or attractive in any of their features, so far as I was able to observe. Back of the pyramid, at twice its distance from the river, much vapor was seen ascending from the vicinity of a series of highly-ornamented springs, with brilliant deposits and unique walls. Several of these were figured by Dr. Hayden in his report for 1871, and they are merely mentioned now to show that they were quite active at the date of our visit to this region. No careful examination could be made on account of the sudden eruption of neighboring geysers, which diverted the attention from them. On this account it will be impossible to describe in detail the numerous other springs in the basin, of which only the positions were noted.

To sum up briefly, then, the results of observations upon the hot springs of this section, it may be remarked that while the diversity in special features, such as size, form, and position of the bowls, the style and degree of ornamentation, and the temperature of the contents, is scarcely less than may be observed elsewhere, the general nature of the deposits and the phenomena of eruption are much the same in all cases. With but a few exceptions, the springs are grouped about active or extinct geysers, and it is not uncertain that a large proportion of those here mentioned have themselves been geysers in the past, while others may yet be proven to be geysers which have never been seen in action heretofore. It should be remarked that sulphur occurs as an ingredient in some bowls, though rarely and in small quantity. Concerning the geological structure of the basin, little need be said in addition to what has already been given in chapter XI, except that there is reason to believe that the basaltic layers of the igneous material are more nearly in the line of the subterranean channels than the purely trachytic rocks.

Before proceeding to the next main division of this chapter, a small group of thermal springs above the Upper Geyser Basin, in the same valley, requires a passing notice. There are only five bowls, and none of these are remarkably large, but they are interesting from the brilliancy of their deposits, and the shape of some of the mounds from which the water emerges. Although the water was spurted in one of the bowls to a height of two or three feet, the degree of activity in the cluster was apparently less than in the majority of the springs of the Upper Geyser Basin. The "Third Geyser Basin of Fire-Hole River," a small area mentioned by Dr. Peale and Professor Bradley, was not seen by our party.

XVI.—FIRST GROUP ON SOUTHWEST ARM OF YELLOWSTONE LAKE.

Three miles beyond Camp 47, Captain Jones's trail strikes the lake-shore near a group of active springs covering a large area along the bank. Like most of the collections within the limits of the ancient lake basin, this cluster contains a number of bowls which emerge directly from the silty deposits, the contents of which are, therefore, more or less contaminated by the admixture of insoluble ingredients. Near the lower end of the group a small muddy flat runs back from the shore which appears to have been the bed of an ancient stream, if not the channel of a recent creek during seasons of flood. On this are situated several mud-bowls and a number of orifices of smaller dimensions, in which the agitation is not powerful enough to render the contents turbid. Nearer the shore there are several large, clear, or nearly clear springs which constantly overflow, sending their surplus into the lake. The little stream which carries off the waste is so highly heated that one cannot bathe with comfort in its track except by wading for some little distance into the lake before venturing opposite its entrance. Several mud-pots occur at a higher level just north of the flat on which the above are located. South of this point, at a still higher level, there are what may be called three clusters of springs, although they are not widely separated. The first collection comprises a set of half a dozen bowls of varying dimensions which emerge from the summit of a kind of terrace of old hot-spring deposits fifteen feet above the level of the lake at low water. In several of these the vapor issues with considerable force, but with a seething rather than a puffing sound.

One spring has a large bowl about four feet in diameter. Back of these the members of the second cluster issue from a silty area, for which reason the contents are mostly turbid or muddy. The third group is farther from the lake and more elevated than the others, and may be said to combine, in a measure, the features of them all. The products are as various as the varying character of the springs would suggest. The mud-pots deposit about the usual proportion of ferric hydrate in addition to the other ingredients, and the amount of iron dissolved in the water of the clearer springs is apparently large, judging from the amount of colloid and confervoid growth which exists wherever favorable conditions are present for such accumulations. The ornamentation of the margins of the clearer bowls is comparatively simple, and raised rims are almost entirely absent. Hydrated alumina is a prominent ingredient, and in some of the ancient deposits it is blended and intermingled with the siliceous accumulations in a very interesting manner. In the past, as now, there has evidently been a close connection between this group of springs and the Yellowstone Lake, for all the bowls are situated in a section which has been worked over by the beating of the waves upon a beach, and the ancient deposits have been greatly modified since their formation by the same action.

There are certain peculiarities of geological structure in this region which should be understood in order to fully appreciate the prominent points of difference between this group and those upon the west of the divide between the Yellowstone Lake and the Fire Hole River.

In passing eastward from the geyser basins high ridges of basaltic rocks are crossed, until, when nearing the lake, important outcrops of dark-brown and black obsidian are reached. This latter material is highly porphyritic, and not unfrequently spherulitic, or even approaching to what is known as *blistered obsidian.*

The heavy accumulations of detritus and vegetable mold obscure the structure within a mile of the lake shore, but the character of the ancient spring-deposits is such as to indicate that the obsidian porphyry predominates over a wide area. The section represented in Fig. 35 was taken on the lake shore south of the muddy flat before mentioned. The lower portion, marked *a* in the cut, is made up of irregular alternations of conglomerates and other beachy formations, largely composed of ancient hot-spring deposits. The following list of the formations exposed in the section includes the more important and peculiar of these re-arranged layers:

1. Heavy conglomerate, composed of siliceous pebbles of hot-spring material, firmly cemented, with smaller particles of obsidian distributed through the mass, occurring near the bottom of the section. This seems to have been formed by the cementation of the particles of a beach-deposit by the action of hot springs containing silica in solution in their water. Some of the sintery pebbles are coated with a glistening layer of silica, and the obsidian particles, though small, are often brilliant. The general color of the mass is gray, with a reddish tinge, and it weathers dark.

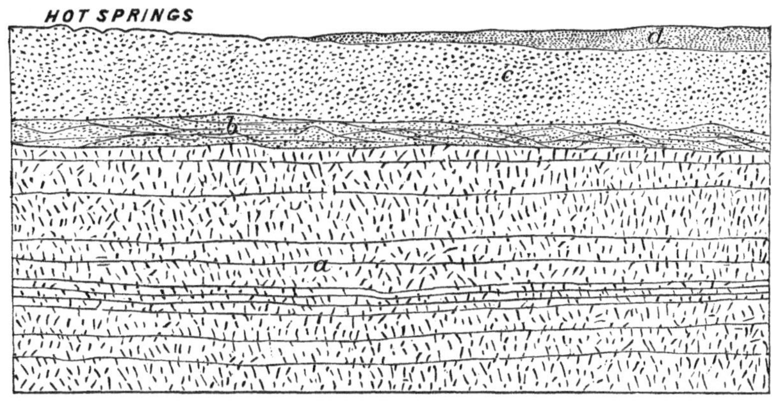

FIG. 35.—Section exposed in a cliff along the shore of Yellowstone Lake, southwest arm, Hot Spring Group No. 1. *a*, several kinds of modified spring deposits, mixed with obsidian fragments; 10 feet. *b*, gravelly beach-deposit of hot-spring material and obsidian; 1 foot. *c*, alumina spring deposits; 3 feet. *d*, vegetable mold covered with timber. The horizontal scale of this section is approximately one-tenth of the vertical scale.

2. Sandy conglomerate near the base, composed of compacted grains of white and gray sand, interspersed with black obsidian sand, and larger particles, and occasional nodular pieces of water-worn spring deposits, appearing as white blotches through the mass. Weathers darker gray than the original color.

3. A bed of light-colored trachyte containing a quantity of irregularly disseminated granules of an undetermined black mineral, the general texture being compact, and the specific gravity high; approaches the augitic series of volcanic rocks, and might be called a *trachydolerite*. At base of the section.

4. Ancient hot-spring deposits, inclosing small stems and roots of grasses and other light vegetation.

5. Conglomerated hot-spring deposits, and pebbles of various kinds. This is rather an *agglomerate*, the arrangement of the component parts being quite irregular throughout the mass.

6. Ancient hot-spring deposits shown at *c*, Fig. 35, modified by percolating water. The bulk of the material is a white mineral tinged with gray, very largely composed of alumina, and possessing properties which ally it closely to the species known as *gibbsite*. Much of it is arranged in layers of several inches in thickness, bound together by alternating layers of siliceous sinter. The main portion is very friable, except in unexposed spots, or where the proportion of combined silica is rather

large. The action of the water and weathering influences has induced an irregular cellular structure, which gives a delicate and attractive appearance to much of it.

The setting-in of a small bay at this point exposes portions of two sides of the terrace to the action of the waves. Large blocks of the ancient deposits have been broken off from the cliff and now lie at the water's edge, to be comminuted for the formation of new lacustrine deposits. This is but the continuation of a process which has long been in operation, and the present bowls are undoubtedly the relics of once powerful thermal springs in this vicinity. Several caverns were observed in the cliffs beyond the present reach of the water, although it is not certain that the waves may not affect them in seasons of high water. It seems probable, however, that they represent chambers in the subterranean passages of long extinct springs, which, like similar expansions at Steamboat Point, and elsewhere, have become exposed by the wearing away of the cliffs.

XVII.—SECOND GROUP ON SOUTHWEST ARM OF YELLOWSTONE LAKE, AT HOT SPRING CAMP.

Camp 48 was made August 28, near the southwestern extremity of Yellowstone Lake, in a grassy park, which has become a favorite resting place for travelers in this section on account of its admirable location at one of the best points for viewing the lake from its shore. The large number of thermal springs in the vicinity, and on the trail between this and the foregoing group, may lack interest to the tourist fresh from the more exciting geysers, but to the student of nature many new and striking facts are here presented of great importance in the solution of intricate problems, while much material may also be gathered which will serve to confirm the results obtained in other localities. Properly speaking, there is no very distinct line of demarkation, structural or geographical, between the collection now to be described and the cluster immediately preceding, for there are many scattered bowls within the intervening space, each of which may, however, be taken as a representative of one or other of the two types.

The springs in the immediate vicinity of Hot Spring Camp, nearly fifty in number, are of two kinds, mud-caldrons, and clear fumeroles.

Those which lie directly upon the shore of the lake are of large size, with deep bowls of limpid water, besides which several emerge from the bottom of the lake itself, their positions being indicated by the rising of bubbles at different points. One of these has built up an inclosing wall, which separates it from the water of the lake which surrounds it, and it has become a rather common practice on the part of visitors to catch the trout from the cool waters and cook them in this spring, without detaching them from the hook, or moving from the spot at which they are caught. This bowl, with two or three others adjacent, which may all be the separate outlets of one large subterranean chamber not far below, are provided with walls of a hard siliceous deposit resembling the sinter of the geyser basins of Fire Hole River, but darker and less homogeneous as well as coarser in general texture. There is also a lack of the delicate ornamentation so common in other sections of the Park. There is, however, the same azure hue to the water when viewed perpendicularly to its surface. Two of the bowls appear to be separated only by a kind of bridge, scarcely three feet in width, but of sufficient thickness to support the weight of as many men as can conveniently stand upon it. The water is not excessively agitated, neither is it very quiet, but it throbs rather regularly, with no great display of force.

The remaining springs to be noticed are situated on the main terrace or flat on which Camp 48 was located, more than twenty feet above the level of the lake. This bench is formed of ancient lacustrine deposits, with relation to which the springs occupy much the same position that the bowls of the preceding paragraph hold with respect to the lake formations now in progress. In other words, it would seem that the upper collection was at one time so near an ancient level of the lake that several of the bowls emerged from beneath its waters as some of the lower bowls do at the present time.

This idea is illustrated in the accompanying section, (Fig. 36,) in which

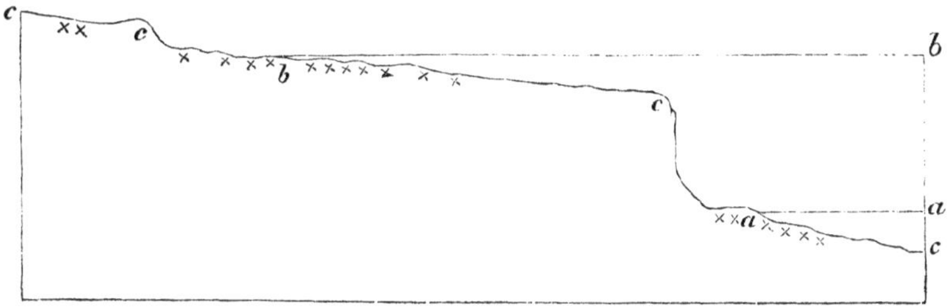

FIG. 36.—Positions of hot springs with respect to ancient and present lake-levels. *a a*, present level of Yellowstone Lake. *b b*, ancient level at a given period. *c c c c*, surface-contour of ancient and recent lacustrine and hot-spring deposits. *x x x x*, positions of existing springs. Note.—For the sake of illustration, the clusters of springs at *a* and *b* are represented on a line perpendicular to the shore of the lake. In reality, cluster *b* is thirty rods or more farther north, *i. e.*, down the lake.

the upper line, *b b*, may be taken to represent a former level of the lake at a period when the low terrace back of the upper cluster of springs formed a portion of the bank. This collection lies in a kind of hollow, showing that its area was included within the limits of a small shallow bay which here set in at that time. In fact, there is a striking resemblance between the ancient condition of this cluster and the present aspect of the small collection upon the lower mud-flat in group XVI, the only important difference being in the height of the adjacent bench, which in the latter case is nearly fifteen feet, while here it is less than five feet. The comparison may also be extended to the character of the bowls in the two districts, but beyond this the parallelism fails, for the springs near Hot Spring Camp are in every respect more vigorous and important than those described in the preceding section.

It will be unnecessary to describe in detail all the clear bowls of this vicinity, of which there are several possessing characteristics which are common elsewhere, but there is one large spring which, if not unique, is sufficiently interesting to deserve special mention in this place. This has a diameter of nearly fifty feet at the surface, tapering gradually downward to a depth scarcely less, forming a funnel-shaped bowl, a form which is not unusual in this region. At the date of our visit (August 28) the cavity was not entirely filled by the water, but the surface of the water was bounded by a narrow sloping shore, a few feet in width. Passing down this to the water's edge, I was about to break a piece of sinter from the wall, when I was forced to retrace my steps rapidly in order to escape from the heated liquid which was suddenly raised in a mass by a steady impulse from below, passing over the shore like a single wave upon a lake-beach. The impelling force exhausted, the water then returned in the same steady manner to about the same level as at first, and the process of ebb and flow was again and again repeated at slight intervals with much regularity. This alternate rising and falling of the contents with an even, throbbing motion, has suggested a comparison with the beating of the pulse in animals, and the bowls in which this action occurs have been not inaptly termed "pulsating springs" on this account. It seems to be partly owing to this continual oscillation of level, that richly-colored deposits accumulate in many spots between what we may call "high and low water marks." As in the bowls upon the shore of the lake, the solution is highly siliceous, but a certain amount of alumina is present, and ferric hydrate is precipitated to some extent. *Confervoidea* and colloid matter do not meet with all the necessary conditions for rapid accumulations in such a place, but they are not wanting in the more quiet bowls.

Mud-puffs.—As before remarked, the great bulk of the formations at this locality is made up of lacustrine deposits, and these are very largely composed of the finer or silty layers, although a fair proportion of gravel is also intermingled in some parts. Fine sections are exposed along the bank of the lake above and below our camp for several miles. The addition and more or less complete admixture of the hot-spring deposits has given a decided siliceous cast to much of the area, which would otherwise show a preponderance of the lighter alumina. Upon the outer edges of the upper collection of springs, and particularly upon the western side, the subterranean waters have burst through the less compact material, issuing from the flat as mud-pots or mud-caldrons, containing pasty masses of somewhat varying consistency. In some of these the contents are thin and but slightly coherent, so that the boiling is continuous and not very irregular, while in others the mud is glutinous or even sufficiently dense to form chimneys about the ebullient centers. Although there is, then, great variation in the tenacity of the plasma within a very limited area, it is owing almost wholly to the varying supply of water, and not, as might be supposed, to any marked difference in the composition of the mud itself in the different bowls. The agitated material is minutely divided and most thoroughly mixed by the constant stirring which it undergoes in the struggling of the subterranean heat to escape through its mass. Some of the most interesting effects are produced in the more viscous bowls, in which the contents retain permanently the cones which are always at least temporarily formed by the pressure from below whenever the tension is overcome. Thus there are exhibited several grades between the simmering spring and the mud-puff of plastic clay. Several of the latter have one or more conical chimneys of different dimensions, the largest being not less than two feet in height, with a circumference at the base of fully four or five feet. From the apex of these, or occasionally at one side of the center, the mud is irregularly spurted, often to a height of several feet above the summit of the cone, and it then falls back upon the outside, serving to increase the size of the cone. The eruptions are accompanied by a peculiar hollow sound, which can be heard for some distance. When moist, the drying mud is usually of a bright pink color from the presence of ferric hydrate, but excessive evaporation soon precipitates the lighter-hued ingredients, in which silica and alumina predominate. It is interesting to note that here, as elsewhere in the Park region, the boiling surface of the mud-bowls is almost invariably from one to five or more feet below the general surface surrounding, although the larger mud-puffs are often raised above the level of the edges of the pits. This fact, it strikes me, is very important as an aid in determining the source of the water-supply of any given group of springs, and, indirectly, the possible position of the heating agencies.

No data were obtained for determining the periods of eruption of any of the springs of this or the preceding group, but some slight indications of more or less uniform variations of intensity were apparent in the adjacent markings, though it would be unwise to draw definite conclusions on this point without more convincing evidence, to be obtained only by continued observation.

The next group of hot springs, the only one now remaining to be described, was visited by a small detached party, which left Camp 48 in advance of the train, for the purpose of making the ascent of Mount Sheridan. A brief account of the trip is given in the narrative in chapter I of this report, (*Special trip No. X.*)

XVIII.—THERMAL SPRINGS AT NORTHEAST BASE OF RED MOUNTAINS, ON SOURCE OF HEART LAKE.

One of the finest points for obtaining a comprehensive view of the country south of Yellowstone Lake is to be found at the summit of the highest peak of the Red Mountains, a limited range of undulating hills which trend nearly north-south between two of the main sources of the Snake River. The highest peak of this wavy ridge has been known as Mount Sheridan since the date of Captain Barlow's expedition, that gentleman having been the first to ascend it and propose a name. Heart Lake lies in a deep depression at the eastern base of the range, three thousand feet below the summit, receiving its water-supply very largely from the snow-fed streams, which pour their contents down through deep-cut cañons among the lower hills. Our little party was camped in a sheltered spot near the brink of a high fall on one of these creeks, at the northern end of the range, several hundred feet above the lake, which was not in sight from that point. We passed a number of interesting springs along the banks of the stream, but the largest and most powerful members of the group were only seen at a distance. This collection has never been carefully examined, and it is probable that many new facts of value will yet be gathered here, if one may judge from the peculiarities of the two following bowls, which received some special attention.

Puffing Spring.—The first to be described is situated on a kind of platform, upon the right bank of the stream, below the main fall, but near the side of a rambling cascade. The orifice is not large, and the vapor, which is constantly emitted, issues from the solid rock, in a manner closely resembling the puffing effusions at the Steamboat Spring, described in chapter IX, section II. The expanded chamber, which probably exists at no great distance beneath, is not visible from the surface. The resonance of the escaping vapor is increased, with the production of a slight echoing sound, by the wall of the gorge, which partially incloses the spot, somewhat after the manner of an amphitheater. The result is a noise not unlike that of a hydraulic-ram in action. The products are largely siliceous, with a fair proportion of iron and some sulphur. Alumina is abundant in several larger bowls lying on an alluvial flat at a lower level.

Sand Spring.—Just above the falls, nearly opposite our camp, there is a depression in the bank of the creek, but a little above the present level of the stream, near its edge, though it rises gradually beyond. This seems to have been, at a time long since past, an area covered by hot springs. The greater portion is now covered with a thick matting of turf, which supports a rank growth of tufted grass. Unsuspicious of the treacherous nature of the subsoil, of which no indications are visible, I incautiously sprang across the creek upon the flat, when I immediately sank nearly to the middle in a hot quagmire, from which it was difficult to extricate myself. The only result of this involuntary bath was a thorough soaking of apparel, including heavy under-garments, no mud adhering to the clothing. This miry patch lies in the track of a small outlet from an interesting boiling spring above, the contents of which seem to be very largely retained beneath the toughened sod, which is thereby provided with an abundance of heat as well as moisture for the support of its vegetation. A very small portion of the water *is seen* to escape into the creek. The spring referred to lies at the upper end of the depression, which is here so narrowed that its walls almost inclose the spring on three sides. There are several centers of ebullition near the edges, the very hot water boiling up with force, greatly contaminated with white sand, with minute black grains interspersed.

But a comparatively small quantity of water overflows the bowl, and this passes off in a sluggish stream, which is soon lost in the quaggy area, after serving for a time as a support for a brownish, scummy, colloid substance, very similar to masses of the same material elsewhere described. Silica is the principal deposit, alumina being present only in small quantity. Some vapor escapes from the surface, but it is not a marked feature of the locality. The ornamentation of the edges of the bowl in places washed by the water is not elaborate, nor is it, either, commonplace; but the decoration is frequently retarded by the mixture of the suspended sand with the precipitates arising from the condensation of the solution.

Hissing Spring.—Just after reaching the basin in which these springs are located, a large spring at some distance down the creek suddenly ejected a dense mass of white vapor to a height of perhaps twenty-five feet, with a rushing noise which startled us all. This may have been a veritable geyser, but we were unable to detect any signs of a column of water from our point of view below the Puffing Spring, one hundred rods distant. The eruption lasted for about five minutes, the action ceasing rather gradually. Time, near 3 p. m., August 29.

The mass of the Red Mountain range at this point, including Mount Sheridan, is made up of trachyte and trachyte-porphyry, the latter predominating. The greater portion is finely brecciated, and very much of the exposed part is red from the oxidation of iron, which is a prominent ingredient. This color prevails when the mountains are viewed from a distance, but a closer inspection reveals the fact that many portions weather white, while not a little of the material presents a dark steel-blue metallic luster. The red and dark varieties are especially characteristic of the higher peaks; the white portion, which is lighter and softer, and thus more easily eroded, being almost wholly confined to the lower eminences. The small fragments of an irregularly-prismatic form, into which the rock readily separates on exposure, lie strewn in immense quantities as a talus over the steep slopes, often completely covering the formations beneath, obscuring their structure while it serves to maintain the mountain physiognomy by preventing excessive erosion. This latter effect is, however, often carried to an extreme, resulting in the production of new and softening features by the enormous accumulation of this material upon the declivities.

So far as observed, the majority of the springs of the present group emerge from alluvial or silty areas, although there is little doubt that all pass through the underlying rock-formations in their course. Many other bowls were observed than those described, some of which were of good size and quite clear, others turbid but not pasty, and a few veritable simmering solfataras, besides a large number which were only seen in the distance while climbing the peak which directly overlooks them.

CONCLUDING REMARKS.

It is believed that the four chapters which have been occupied with the description of the hot springs visited by the writer will be found as full and complete as is necessary or possible in a work of this nature, and that while a very large number of the springs hitherto described from this section have not been here included, a sufficient number of new facts have been adduced to render the generalizations to be propounded in another chapter lucid and intelligible. If it be thought that the five hundred bowls or more, which have furnished the material for the foregoing descriptions, are not enough to afford ground for the conclusions there offered, it must be remembered that the groups examined are widely scattered and of remarkable variety, while but few collections now known have been omitted, and these, with one or two exceptions only, such as possess but a minor degree of interest and few important features of unique character. It should also be borne in mind that almost an equal number of localities were visited by our party, which have not heretofore been described with any degree of accuracy.

In order to *discuss* with freedom the nature and action of what may be termed *minor volcanic phenomena, i. e.*, the phenomena of post-volcanic activity, it will be necessary to include in the same category all the hot springs and geysers, for it will be impossible to divide them into well-marked classes based upon any ground of distinction known at present. The following chapter is therefore devoted to the description of such bowls as may be roughly but conveniently separated for that purpose under the head of Geysers. Before proceeding to that subject, it may be well to call attention to the existence of large tracts of ancient hot spring deposits in many places where there are no signs of present or very recent activity. It is not possible to find words which shall adequately depict the impression left upon the mind of the attentive traveler in this region concerning the enormous amount of vigor which has been displayed in the past by innumerable bowls in almost every part of the district. One is amazed at the remarkable persistency of the heat to the present late epoch, but the imagination is taxed to its utmost capacity to conceive of the magnitude of the manifestations which must have taken place at a remote period, though within recent geological eras. No special description of the ancient accumulations is necessary, for, although there is a variety almost marvelous in their texture and composition, there are few facts connected with them which are not exemplified in one or more of the groups of existing springs.

CHAPTER XIII.

THERMO-DYNAMICS, CONCLUDED—DESCRIPTION OF GEYSERS AND SUMMARY.

Distribution and general remarks—A. Group on East Fork of Madison River—B. Geysers of Lower Basin, Fire-Hole River—C. Geysers of Upper Basin, Fire-Hole River—Generalizations.

The term *geyser*, as employed in this chapter, relates to such bowls as are more or less eruptive in character, in which the water is periodically ejected with force. This classification is in many respects arbitrary and unsatisfactory, for the reason that it often compels a separation of springs which cannot positively be said to differ except in power. The majority of the bowls included under this head will, however, be found to possess certain peculiarities which point to some important modifications in the relations of the supplies of heat and water, rendering them in a measure distinct from the most active of the hot springs previously described.*

A few of the springs mentioned in chapters IX–XII might, perhaps, as well have been considered in this place, but their position in the report has generally been determined as a matter of convenience in discussing them.

DISTRIBUTION OF GEYSERS.

Of the eighteen groups of hot springs reviewed in the four preceding chapters, the first three do not possess a single bowl which approaches the typical geyser. Some of the mud-volcanoes of the fourth group are eruptive in character, but the ejection of the mud is rather the result of the restraining and concentrating influence brought to bear upon the projecting force by the tenacity of the material. No geysers are included in the fifth group, nor in the seventh, ninth, eleventh, sixteenth, or seventeenth groups. The sixth or Wayside Group, on Orange Creek, in the Yellowstone Valley, contains two or three jets which might not inaptly be termed *pseudo geysers*, but their phenomena are essentially different from those of a true *spouting* geyser. The same may also be said of the jets at Gardiner's River, already described, (chapter X,) as well as those already mentioned in connection with groups XIII, XIV, and XV. The silica jets of group X are really minor geysers, which would have been as appropriately described in this chapter as in chapter XI. Thus it will be seen that the bowls which have been reserved for the present chapter belong to three of the hot-spring localities before marked out, all of which are connected and not widely separated. It should, however, be noted that several small geysers are supposed to exist in the imperfectly-known basin of group XVIII, and another important collection was discovered by a portion of Dr. Hayden's command in 1872, on the shores of the lake at the source of the Snake River, now known as Shoshone Lake. It is not unreasonable to suppose that other similar groups will be brought to light by future explorations about the headwaters of the larger rivers.

The most prominent geysers have received settled names, which have become as familiar as the bowls themselves to travelers in this region. These titles are employed to designate them here whenever it has been possible to determine their application. In some instances new names have been proposed, but not with a view to their perpetuation unless they are hereafter found to be original.

A.—EAST FORK (MADISON RIVER) GROUP.

Besides the small jets alluded to in section XII, chapter XI, a few bowls were noticed in which the stalagmitic appearance caused by the falling of the water upon the surrounding surface gave evidence of the existence of real geyser action, although no eruptions were witnessed.

* The points of difference between the hot spring and the *typical* geyser can only be appreciated after a careful review of the prominent characteristics of each. A definition of the term *geyser* is given near the close of this chapter, where this difference is also clearly stated.

This growth, as it may justly be called, is the one distinguishing feature of the active geyser, by which its character may be determined even in its quiescent state. As the formation of this peculiar surface is dependent upon the complete evaporation of the water, it is not absolutely necessary that it should be produced in order to entitle a spouting bowl to the name of geyser, for a large column of water may be shot high into the air from the center of a large pool in such a manner as to return wholly within the rim. In such cases no fungoid tracery will be formed without the bowl, and no evidence of eruption will be found after the ejection has ceased, except in the marks left by the overflow, which, of themselves, are not sufficient to determine the character of the bowl. Judging from the comparative fineness of the excrescences about the spouting springs of this group, it may be inferred that the height of the projected column is never very great, but this criterion cannot be fully relied on in all cases, because the coarseness of the ornamentation is as much dependent upon the amount of the falling water as upon the height from which it falls. In other words, the falling of a large column of water in a mass may produce the same effect as a smaller body dropping from a considerable elevation.

Another result of geyser action is the building up of a chimney about the bowl, usually becoming somewhat narrowed as it ascends, so as to approach more or less closely to a conical shape. In this locality the raised rims are not high, and the bevel is rather slight. The composition of the products is the same as that of the surrounding less turbulent springs, silica predominating, but there is less chance for the precipitation of the iron as ferric oxide, and the red deposits are, therefore, less abundant. The main features of the craters are of essentially the same nature as those described beyond and need not be enumerated here, but we will proceed directly to the next group.

B.—GEYSERS OF THE LOWER FIRE-HOLE BASIN.

Upon the ridge containing the mud-caldron and other springs, between the entrance to the Lower Geyser Basin and our special camp near the White Dome, there are several interesting geysers, some of which were fortunately observed in action. For convenience of reference these, with all the others to be described in this report, are numbered consecutively. Names marked thus * are taken from the reports of Dr. Hayden and corps; those preceded by a † from other authorities, as Doane, Barlow, &c.; the § being used to designate such as are supposed to be named by the writer for the first time. The descriptions are all given from personal observat on, any additional information used being invariably properly accredited.

1. § *Spasm Geyser.*—After reaching the summit of the terrace of sinter, which forms a part of the lower edge of the ridge mentioned above, several quiet bowls were passed before reaching one near the western edge of the bench, which was fitfully spurting a small column of hot water two or three feet into the air. This was at 3.20 p. m., (August 23,) and the same action continued with no apparent diminution until 5.30 p. m., when it ceased altogether rather suddenly. It is impossible to state the length of time it had been playing, before we first observed it, but it will be interesting to note its sympathetical relations to some adjacent bowls, as remarked beyond. The fungoid markings, so common about many of the larger geysers, are here represented by similar excrescences of a rich and delicate structure. The mass of the sintery deposit is composed of an exceedingly fine-grained white

silica, the outer and fresher portions being of a shiny yellowish color when collected, with a surface covered with roughened prominences like an aggregation of minute coral branches. These are sometimes formed as little islands, in small shallow pools surrounding the geyser-bowl, and they appear to have been caused by the interference of opposing waves produced by the falling water, though this is not definitely

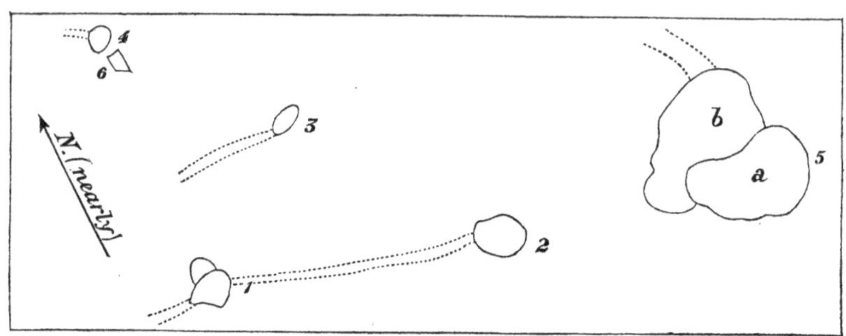

FIG. 37.—Relative positions of geysers on Fountain Terrace, Lower Fire-Hole Basin. The figures refer to bowls thus numbered in the text. The dotted lines represent the general course of the outflow from each bowl.

ascertained. Pieces of rope and cloth left here by previous visitors were picked out of the water in a half-rotten condition, which became tough and spangled with crystalline grains of silica upon exposure to the air until dried. Some pieces of the rope, which were of a brownish-yellow color at the end lying out of the water, were bleached to a most delicate white. Pine cones and chips of wood were also well silicified by immersion. The size of this bowl is not great, consequently the larger portion of the ejected water is thrown beyond the edges and falls without the bowl, mostly upon the lower side. In favorable spots, the characteristic red deposits are precipitated in the track of the outlet.

2. § *Impulsive Geyser.*—While watching the pulsations of the Spasm, a second geyser (2, Fig. 37) suddenly began to spurt, at 3.30 p. m. At first it sputtered sullenly, and the water was thrown upward but a little distance, but gradually the action became more rapid and violent, a small jet occasionally rising with considerable force to a height of fifteen feet. The contents of the bowl were thoroughly agitated, but the greatest activity occurred in the center, the jet being thrown, as it were, through the middle of the main mass ejected, which may be likened to a fountain. The falling spray produces remarkable forms of relief, with a glistening surface, rendered only more attractive by slight discoloration, which gives it the appearance of the richest ivory. It would be impossible, by the most artistic description, to convey an adequate idea of the marvelous richness and beauty of this formation as viewed in the light of the unclouded sun, and we are forced to resort to comparisons, which, at best, are very unsatisfactory. If one can imagine the effect of a million of glittering pearls, large and small, arranged without order over an uneven surface, crowded and jumbled together in irregular masses, the very confusion of which lends an added charm, he may be able to form some faint idea of the surpassing grandeur of nature's workmanship in this lonely spot.

As represented in Fig. 37, a large part of the overflow from the Impulsive Geyser passes into the bowl of the Spasm, which lies at a little lower level. The differences observed in the mechanical deposits, as we may call the peculiar protuberances resulting from the falling of the water, are mainly structural, but the texture, upon which their structure partly depends, is also more or less distinct. Instead of the compacted powder which is eminently characteristic of much of the product from the Spasm, we have here prevailing an impure porcelain texture. The resulting forms of relief may be considered respectively, as illustrations of the *coralline* and the mammillary types of structure.

The eruption of the Impulsive Geyser continued until 5.30 p. m., having been in operation for two hours. The cessation of the boiling was very nearly simultaneous with the close of the eruption in the Spasm.

3. § *Clepsydra Geyser.*—The third member of the group is one of the most regular in the basin, and on this account the name Clepsydra is proposed for it. Like the ancient water-clock of that name, it marks the passage of time by the discharge of water. It would be unwise to number this among the constant geysers without knowing more concerning its movements than has yet been gathered, but it was in action during the whole of the two hours and a half that we were in its vicinity. A large mass of water is forced up in a rolling wave, ending in a vigorous but not greatly elevated spurt, at intervals of three minutes. The mechanical deposit surrounding this geyser is even more delicate than either of the forms above mentioned. It is of the coralline type and may be described in terms of coral-masses, so far as mere general resemblance is concerned, as a close aggregation of madreporic *coralla*,* of small but varying sizes, arranged on a horizontal plane. This parallel can be carried no further, however, for the numerous *corallets** and the connecting *cœnenchyma*,* if we may use these terms, are of course solid, the process of growth being wholly similar to the formation of true stalagmites over the floors of caverns. A piece of wood taken from the bowl of the Clepsydra was coated with a layer of pure white semi-crystalline silica, resembling the icing used in confectionery.

4. § *Fitful Geyser.*—This geyser is quite near the boiling spring represented in Fig 37, numbered 6. It was in action irregularly all the time we remained in its vicinity. The main orifice is near one side of the top of a small heap of *sinter*, built up by the water somewhat in the shape of a leaning cone. Occasionally the aqueous contents were spurted to the height of three feet above the top, in a coarse jet, but more frequently the ejections were much less forcible than the accompanying sound would seem to warrant. No connecting passage between this and the adjacent boiling bowl was apparent, but the action of the latter was such as to suggest some degree of sympathy in their movements. Some water also escapes from small bowls near the base of the chimney, which are constantly agitated, although they are not necessarily in direct communication with the geyser tube. In pools formed by the falling water, delicate white pebbles of pure *geyserite*, with a concentric structure, have been formed, a polished surface being maintained by the frequent movements to which they are subject. These, as well as portions of the coralline mechanical deposits about the main orifice, are frequently tinged or colored with rich shades of pinkish red, when moist.

5. * *Fountain Geyser.*—While obtaining an interesting specimen of the porcelain silica which forms a jutting ledge in the boiling spring, (No. 6, Fig. 37,) the water in No. 5, which had previously been quiet and not

*These terms are employed in the usual zoological sense, according to Dr. J. D. Dana, (Corals and Coral Islands.) A corallum is a coral-mass or skeleton, the skeleton of each pseudo-individual being called a *corallet.* The *cœnenchyma* is the main connecting mass, which is common to all the polyps of a corallum.

entirely filled, rose suddenly until the bowl was ready to overflow, when a large amount was elevated to a height varying from six to ten feet, in a column of nearly equal diameter. The action began at 4.40 p. m., (August 23,) and the eruption did not cease wholly until 5.40 p. m. Occasionally very sudden impulses would carry smaller but quite large columns twenty-five and thirty feet into the air. Sometimes the whole would gradually die down, and more than once when I thought that the ejection had ended, a vigorous throb would violently throw the water and vapor to its greatest height. The rushing noise produced by the escaping liquid was very loud, and a subsequent eruption, which occurred from 7.30 a. m. to 8.30 a. m. on the following morning, was distinctly audible at our camp near White Dome Geyser, more than a mile distant. At the close of the first eruption the water receded in the bowl, so that we could look down many feet into the large open pit which was thus formed. In this case, as in all other instances of hot springs or geysers, which I was able to examine beneath the surface, the water does not issue perpendicularly beneath the bowl, but in an oblique direction, and, almost invariably, at one side of the bowl. After a time, by a series of alternations of level, an equilibrium is restored and the water comes to rest nearly in its position before the eruption. The agitation takes place mainly in the portion represented at *a* in the cut, *b* being intended to show the outline of an adjacent bowl which receives much of the surplus water, but does not appear to be greatly concerned in the ejection. The ornamentation is peculiar and interesting, varying in fineness of structure according to the distance from the rim of the bowl. The composition of the deposits is not materially different from that of the accumulations about the neighboring bowls. The water in the fountain is very clear, and one obtains a very good view of the interior of the bowl by looking down through it. The common azure tint is present, adding greatly to its beauty. A third eruption of this geyser (apparently) began at 1.20 p. m., August 24, the duration of which was not determined.

6. * *White Dome Geyser.*—The North Branch of White Creek (see chapter XI) is fed toward its lower end by the drainage from two clusters of hot springs and geysers lying at a little distance back from the left bank or edge of the stream. Between these clusters there is a very prominent cone of a once very vigorous geyser, as is evinced by the existence of an old and important channel, now dry, which then carried off the surplus water. The siliceous deposits in this ancient stream-bed are much weathered, and a few small pines are growing directly in its track. The White Dome is a conspicuous object in the landscape, rising nearly or quite 30 feet above the surrounding level. It is composed of a wide mound more than 15 feet in height, surmounted by a narrower chimney near one side, which is open at the top. The geyser is evidently dying out and gradually closing its orifice, although it manifests a certain degree of activity, not sufficient to cause the ejection of very much water. A small amount of vapor is emitted from the chimney without frequent interruption, but there is considerable variation at times in the quantity thus given off.

We slept too soundly to take note of any eruptions which may have occurred during the night, but three were observed on the morning of August 24. The first took place at 8.26 a. m., there being little more than an active sputtering, which continued for two minutes. Almost at the same time, one of the geysers, which had been playing vigorously, in the more southerly cluster, ceased its action. While standing upon the White Dome, at 10.17 a. m., it again sputtered, and threw water 3 feet above the apex of the cone during two minutes. From a distance of half a mile, it was again seen to spout, at 11.20 a. m., with about the same degree of force, the eruption lasting the same length of time as in the preceding instances.

The first two ejections were preceded and followed by a roaring in the tube, (the third was observed beyond the limit of the sound-waves,) each period being of nearly three minutes duration, making the whole time of eruption about eight minutes. Occasional roars were heard for some time afterward at irregular intervals.

A portion of the water falls outside of the chimney and courses down one side, where it has worn a channel in the old deposits of the mound. A few small holes are exposed along this line, through which more or less of vapor is constantly escaping. The material of the mound at this point is a very compact, flinty variety of *geyserite*, arranged irregularly in plates, with a clear *opal* appearing in spots. The exterior is covered with a dark-brown growth of a scummy substance, which turns black upon drying, and a perceptible pink tinge, with a few touches of green, are found beneath and in patches. The recent mechanical deposits about the mouth of the chimney are compactly granular, breaking readily into coarse, uneven joints along no particular lines. The surface-contour is irregular, and the whole when wet has very much the appearance of a mass of white commercial sponge of a mixed variety, *i. e.*, an average mass with frequent spots of a very fine-pored variety. In an ordinary light, small pieces sometimes have a dingy aspect much like the color of coarse granular salt recently removed from a saturated greasy brine, but this changes to an extremely delicate pinkish hue in the full play of the sunlight.

Some excellent specimens of silicified wood were obtained from the bed of the ancient outflow, with all the structure of the original tissue without a visible particle of the substance, which is entirely replaced by the pure white silica. In many cases these are covered by a structureless incrustation of the same material, which has often reached a thickness of more than an inch. The inclosed portion is usually very brittle, the silica showing a tendency toward the granular texture.

7. § *Boiler Geyser.*—Besides the hot springs already described, which lie in a group near the upper end of the vale of White Creek, there are several geysers of some interest. The Boiler and the following bowl are not very extensive, but both appear to be constantly in action. The water in the former rises throbbingly near the center, and falls in a mass almost wholly within the cup, producing its mechanical deposits upon the edges by the action of the successive waves which are thus originated. The resulting formation bears traces of the wavy ridges which would be left upon a horizontal or slightly sloping surface of loose material, as along a lake-beach, but the undulations being here more rapid and restricted in breadth, there is less of uniformity in the surface of the deposit. It is brilliant and glistening, though roughened and much cut into irregular squares, beads, and other forms of relief. Much of the grooving, or, more properly, the separation of the several parts of the relief-work, seems due to the trickling back of the water after it has been thrown up by the waves. By this combined action small gullies are worn out beneath the edges of adjacent raised patches, which give an appearance of overlap beyond what is real. These deposits were slightly pinkish when collected, but the color vanishes when the specimens become dry, although the unexposed portions are often flesh-colored over a surface of fracture. The silica is of a brownish color, usually, except at the surface, much of which is light gray or nearly white.

8. § *Bead Geyser.*—Not far from the Boiler there is a vigorous jet, which issues from a rather long, narrow fissure, the water falling back upon the sides in a fine spray. The mechanical deposit is comparatively even, and it consists of a compact aggregation of minute, shiny, globular grains, which are opaque and of a delicate brown color when dry, but having a rich pink luster as they lie continually moist in their natural position. The vertical edge of the rim is somewhat coarser, with the beady clusters more confusedly arranged. There is a tendency here, as elsewhere for the compacted deposit to split into more or less regular cuboidal blocks, resulting in this case in the production of very limited fissures, and these have been refilled by the infiltration of a pure white silica, which now traverses the mass as an irregular net-work or honey-comb of platy veins, serving to cement the parts more firmly together. Larger fissures, though quite small, are not thus filled, owing to a deficiency in the water-supply.

9. § *Unknown Geyser.*—This name is proposed, provisionally, for a bowl which has been mentioned in a previous chapter under the head of Hot Springs, but which offers such unmistakable evidence of past geyser phenomena that its peculiarities deserve special consideration in this place. No signs of very recent activity were apparent, nor is there any reason to believe that previous observers have witnessed an eruption, and yet the adjacent deposits exhibit very little appearance of extensive weathering. The shallow pools which have received the falling water were wholly dry in 1873, and a large number of the characteristic pebbles of geyserite are present, showing the results of much disturbance, many being lozenge-shaped, others polyhedral. Numerous mammillary pillars project from the surface like so many stalagmites to a height of more than an inch, with horizontal diameters varying from a quarter of an inch to nearly two inches. The tips of these have the glistening leaden hue which characterizes the water-polished siliceous surfaces about active geysers, while the sides possess the peculiar yellowish tints and roughened prickly surface which belong to portions submerged in pools containing hot solutions of silica. The material is a very compact opaliferous geyserite, a cross-section of a pillar presenting a glittering surface, with several concentric bands, caused by the darkening of the color toward the center. The common tints are three, arranged more or less distinctly, with dark gray in the center, brownish-yellow between, and white, with a yellowish-tinge, at the circumference. Little or no agitation of the contents of the bowl was observed at the time of our visit, (August 24.)

10. * *Young Hopeful.*—This name appears in Professor Bradley's report, 1872, designating a small bowl of the group which we are now considering. It spouts rather irregularly, with active and quiescent epochs of one or two minutes duration. The water is thrown in a jet, varying in height from three to nearly ten feet.

The mechanical deposits are not of special interest. Another small geyser near this spot throws the liquid in much the same manner, but with shorter intervals, and to a height of a few inches only. Both of these bowls are probably constant, or perpetual in action, for they seem to have been observed by all the parties which have heretofore visited the locality in which they occur.

11. * *Steady Geyser.*—About a dozen rods eastward from Young Hopeful, there is a basin which receives a portion of its overflow after it has become somewhat cooled by passing through a pool of its own. The contents of this lower basin are almost continually agitated by the ejection of a column of water from beneath a ledge or mound near one side,

causing the jet to rise somewhat obliquely. The extreme altitude of the column at the time of our visit did not exceed twenty feet, and it rarely ascended less than fifteen feet. The falling spray mostly mingles with the contents of the pools, so that the mechanical deposits are less remarkable than in many parts of the Lower Basin. In some of the cooling pools at this point, there occurs a quantity of the yellowish-brown gelatinous material so abundant elsewhere, but it is here so thinly distributed as to give the water the appearance of a yellow liquid at a little distance.

Several other important geysers were observed in action during our stay in the Lower Basin, but we were, in such cases, so far removed from them that it was not possible to obtain any information of sufficient value to merit record here.

In the Half-Way Group, (XIV, chapter XI,) there are one or two apparently constant geysers, in which the water is thrown in fine jets to a height of three or four feet. At first sight, there appears to be no essential difference between such bowls and those spouting springs which have elsewhere been excluded from the class of geysers, but a more careful examination proves that they manifest certain peculiarities of eruption belonging only to veritable geysers. The falling water here returns almost wholly into the bowl, so that no mechanical deposits of importance are formed about their rims.

C.—GEYSERS OF THE UPPER FIRE-HOLE BASIN.

12.† *Old Faithful.*—At the extreme upper end of the Upper Basin, on the left bank of the Fire-Hole River, there are several white mounds or domes which mark the ancient position of as many extinct geysers. One, now active, stands by itself upon a broad table, as it were, with a succession of irregular steps extending downward to the edge of a low cliff at the river-side, some ten rods distant or more. The contents are ejected through an elongated opening in a one-sided chimney, which rises perpendicularly to a height of fifteen feet above the upper step. Its appropriate name was given by Doane and Langford, on account of the approximate regularity of its action. The following table, originally published in the American Naturalist,* gives the particulars of eleven successive eruptions which occurred during a portion of the time which we spent in this locality.†

TABLE.

Number of eruption.	Date.	Eruption began.	Eruption ceased.	Duration.	Intervals of quiet.
		h. m. s.	*h. m. s.*	*m. s.*	*h. m. s.*
1	Aug. 25, 1873	10 38 00 a. m.	10 43 00 a. m.	5 00	
2	....do	11 36 00 a. m.	11 41 30 a. m.	5 30	0 58 00
3	....do	12 39 00 p. m.	12 44 00 p. m.	5 00	0 57 30
4	....do	1 41 15 p. m.	1 45 45 p. m.	4 30	0 57 15
5	....do	2 45 20 p. m.	2 50 00 p. m.	4 40	0 59 35
6	....do	3 53 35 p. m.	3 58 00 p. m.	4 25	1 3 35
7	....do	5 11 10 p. m.	5 15 40 p. m.	4 30	0 47 25
8	....do	6 3 15 p. m.	6 07 45 p. m.	4 30	0 47 25
9	....do	7 12 00 p. m.			1 4 15
10	....do	8 14 00 p. m.			
11	....do	9 17 00 p. m.			
Average duration and quiet interval				4 33⅓	0 56 40

* Vol. viii, March, 1874, p. 160. The first eruption given here was omitted in the Naturalist.

† I take pleasure in acknowledging obligations to Lieut. S. E. Blunt, astronomer, for the record of several of these eruptions, in addition to other favors.

A description of the second eruption will serve as an illustration of the customary phenomena, there being but slight differences in any of the succeeding ejections. At 11.28 a. m. the geyser began to spurt a little, but barely enough to throw a slight amount of water over the sides of the chimney, although a constant rumbling was kept up below. At 11.36 a. m. a heavy mass of water was suddenly thrown out in a magnificent jet to the height of nearly 150 feet, and the accompanying column of vapor ascended to a much greater altitude. This continued quite steadily for two minutes, when the intensity gradually decreased with an occasional vigorous spurt, until 11.41.5 a. m., the rumbling and internal sputtering continuing for some minutes, during which a small amount of vapor quietly escaped from the orifice of the chimney. At least a dozen eruptions of Old Faithful were witnessed without record, for want of accurate observation. In every case the force of the ejection was much the same, but the duration of the premonitory and subsequent sputterings was quite variable. In the third eruption given in the table, the first spurt occurred only three minutes before the ejection began, and the preliminary agitation in the fourth eruption took place but two minutes previously.

The sides of the chimney of this geyser are covered with a very delicate mechanical deposit, which may be compared to an aggregation of immense quantities of minute pearls so arranged as to simulate irregular but crowded masses of grayish-white coral of the finer varieties. In the broad but shallow pools about the base of the chimney, there were no geyserite pebbles, but each pool had a beautiful pinkish bed, tesselated by the falling water in such a manner as to give it the appearance of a pebble-paved floor. There is a distinct cleavage line, marked by the grooves between the pseudo-pebbles. The latter vary in size from that of a grain of wheat to those which have diameters of nearly or quite two inches. The mass of the deposit is composed of remarkably pure, glittering, pearly silica. There is sufficient evidence that the tesselation is caused by ripples induced in the pools by the agitation of the water, and the resulting structure is not widely different from that of the mechanical deposits about the rim of the Boiler Geyser, (*ante*, 7.) Notwithstanding the abundance of the deposits of Old Faithful, it seems certain that it is of comparatively recent origin, for there are large quantities of silicified wood imbedded in the track of its outlet, and even among the outer layers of the chimney itself. As a rule, the cellular texture is not wholly obliterated, although the original form of the wood is often scarcely discernible. Specimens obtained are usually very brittle and much penetrated with intercalated silica.

13.* *Castle Geyser.*—At some distance down the stream, upon the same side as Old Faithful, a prominent mound rises above the general surface to a height of twenty feet, with a huge chimney more than fifteen feet in height, ascending from a point near the center. About the edges of the latter are abundant mechanical deposits, some of which are of the coarse varieties, which everywhere indicate a high fall, or, more commonly, the thud of a heavy column of water. The geyserite is extremely compact, as in No. 12, but, unlike the greater portion about Old Faithful, the exposed surface is here quite generally polished, possessing the peculiar leaden luster noticed in some of the deposits from the Lower Geyser Basin. The same feature is strikingly displayed in parts subjected to the overflow in some steaming pools near the base of the geyser, but with less of the bluish tint, which seems in some way connected with the descent of the water.

When we entered the basin, early on the morning of August 25, the

Castle was roaring vigorously, and a small amount of vapor escaped steadily from the vent at the summit. This gradually dwindled, and no eruption took place until the following day, although spurts of two or three feet only occurred at irregular intervals. Shortly before 4 p. m. on the following day, a large mass of water was ejected in a column which was maintained for ten minutes at a height of nearly thirty feet. Leaving the basin one hour later, the roaring which continued after the eruption was still very audible at a considerable distance. From this it may, perhaps, be justly inferred that an eruption had taken place just before our arrival on the previous day. There was a certain fitfulness of action before and after the main ejection, all of which may properly be considered as part of one eruption lasting more than an hour. We observed the phenomena from a little distance, when we were unable to devote any time to special examination.

There are several small boiling pools near the base of the geyser, and a round steaming caldron on one side. One pool is almost a geyser, throwing the water two feet into the air.

14. † *Giant Geyser.*—Near the edge of the main stream, upon its left bank, below the Castle, there is a large conoid chimney ten feet in height, open down one side, so that one might pass in through the gap. The thickness of the wall is not very great, nor is it remarkably thin. In the past there has evidently been much and vigorous agitation of the pool, which is now in a constant state of ebullition but a little below the surrounding surface-level. Doane, Hayden, Langford and others, have witnessed and described eruptions of great power, but there is no record of important ejections since 1871. In 1873, the action was constant, the water being rarely thrown in successive jets to a height of three feet or less above the summit of the encircling wall, but as a rule the column did not rise sufficiently to throw the liquid over the edges. This is one of the most noticeable geysers in the whole basin, on account of its raised portion, which has been entirely built up by the evaporation of the water ejected from the pool within. The exterior is dark-colored, unlike many of the other chimneys, and the rather coarsely granular geyserite of which the wall is partly composed has a tawny yellow tinge. Smoothly-worn lozenge-shaped and polyhedral pebbles were obtained from shallow pools adjacent to the cone. The cone itself is elevated somewhat above the general surface, resting upon a slight terrace formed of geyser deposits. Several other pools, which seem to have more or less of sympathy in action with the Giant, are situated near it, and some are provided with interesting rims. One large opening of this kind, in a flat-topped mound three feet in height, spurted ten feet in sudden jets.

15.* *Grotto Geyser.*—About thirty rods down the stream from the Giant, and at some distance back from the water, there is an irregular mound with several lateral orifices, through which the water is forced during an eruption. By this means the main current is thrown over a ridge into a pool behind, and a large portion of the ascending column of water is converted into a very fine spray. The markings over a considerable surface are, therefore, exceedingly regular and remarkably fine, resembling a smooth white floor inlaid with glittering pearls. Large slabs of this material, three-fourths of an inch in thickness, can readily be detached without injury, but the geyserite is rather brittle and does not bear transportation well.

We witnessed but one eruption, which began at 2.17 p. m., August 25, continuing uninterruptedly till 3.03 p. m., when it ceased altogether. The water was ejected with much force in two irregularly-alternating columns, proceeding from the two large conical chimneys of which the mound is made up, and from several intermediate openings of small size. The volume of water and vapor was large, and a good-sized stream was formed by the surplus, which ran off down the hill to the river.

The maximum height was nearly twenty-five feet. According to Dr. Peale, the duration of this eruption was less than one-half that of two witnessed by himself in 1872, and the intensity, as measured by the mean height of the eruption, was also less in 1873, judging from his report.

16.* *Riverside Geyser.*—A little below the Grotto, across the river, a geyser which is situated near the edge of the stream began to spout at 2.43 p. m. This is known as the Riverside Geyser. A jet of fine spray was very suddenly thrown more than thirty feet into the air, which continued quite steadily until 2.47.5 p. m., when it ceased acting for one-half minute; then it played weakly for two minutes, ceasing again for half a minute, then played again rather vigorously until 2.53 p. m., (two and one-half minutes). At 2.54 p. m. it roared loudly and became quiet at 2.56 p. m., after which no action occurred. The Riverside has a low, irregular mound, with a small chimney scarcely rising near its center. When quiet, however, there is little about it to attract the attention of the passer along the trail.

17. * *Fan Geyser.*—While watching the pulsations of the Grotto, a column of vapor was evolved from a geyser upon the right bank of the Fire-Hole River, a few rods below the Riverside. This began at 2.43 p. m., almost precisely at the moment when the eruption began in the Riverside. Gradually increasing in intensity, it was throwing a large column of water at 2.49 p. m., which continued, but gradually diminishing, until 2.54 p. m., at which time it almost ceased, sputtering occasionally, however, until 2.56 p. m. This record shows a remarkable similarity or sympathy between the Fan and the Riverside. Dr. Hayden states (Geological Survey of Montana, &c., 1871, p. 124) that the Fan is composed of a close cluster of five orifices which play together. The column is very interesting, spreading out broadly owing to the cross-play of the several streams.

18.* *Grand Geyser.*—Returning to camp, laden with specimens, when nearly opposite the Castle we were recalled by the shouts of several of the party who were standing near that geyser. Passing down the river a few rods, upon the right bank, we saw a heavy mass of water rising in a square pool at the foot of a cliff some ten rods back from the stream. With a rush of wonderful power the column of dark blue liquid ascended nearly two hundred feet, mingled with a cloud of dense white vapor, which rose to a much greater height. This tremendous fountain was kept suspended during five minutes, from 4.01 p. m. to 4.06 p. m., by a series of successive fierce impulses which caused the surrounding platform of geyserite to tremble with the shock. The water then receded in the bowl, passing entirely out of sight and remaining quiet during one-half minute; then playing vigorously for one minute, in the same manner as at first, it again receded and remained quiet for one minute, afterward playing once more even more fiercely than before for two minutes, remaining quiet from 4.11 to 4.12, and then continuing with more or less of vigor until 4.12.5 p. m. At 4.17.5 p. m. vapor issued from the mouth of the bowl, and water was ejected at 4.20.5, continuing until 4.24, when the action ceased, the water, as in every case, receding to a great depth. Spurting took place at 4.28.5, gradually increasing in intensity, with occasional jets, until 4.31, when it again spouted two hundred feet till 4.32.5 p. m. Remaining quiet until 4.48.5, it again spurted several times, less rapidly than before, but very gradually increasing in power and frequency till 5.47 p. m., when the action wholly ceased.

The mechanical deposits about the Grand Geyser are of much beauty, being highly polished and of a glistening ivory tinge. The falling water is very largely broken into fine spray before it reaches the ground, so that the protuberances are often quite delicate, but there is a certain irregularity of arrangement which rather adds to the general effect than otherwise. Perhaps the nearest approach to a satisfactory parallel will be to compare a portion of the common ornamentation to a siliceous base covered with a jumbled arrangement of miniature teeth of various animals without regard to classification. Such comparisons are, however, of little value, at best. There is not a little variation in size of the component parts, according to the action of the water at different points. Sometimes the excrescences are so minute and so densely crowded as to appear globular, giving an irregular surface much the aspect of a coarse oolite or pisolite; other masses, often more or less like small imbedded bowlders, present an appearance upon the upper surface, in many respects similar to the finer varities of *Meandrina*, or "brain-coral." In the wash at a little distance from the geyser, a beautiful specimen of snowy-white silica was obtained, which had been honey-combed by the solvent action of the hot water passing over it. There is more or less of variation in the quality and texture of the deposited material, as is shown by the differences observed in successive layers. Some of the geyserite is pure white, some brown, and green, pink, and even black, are not unfrequently seen in spots or in distinct layers.

It should be remarked, that notwithstanding the expressed contrary opinion of Dr. Hayden, based upon observations of several eruptions, the writer is strongly in favor of the idea that the Grand Geyser is to some extent in sympathy with the three following, for reasons which will be suggested beyond.

19.* *Turban Geyser.*—Just above the Grand Geyser and but a few feet distant there is an oblong pit ten by twenty feet and six feet in depth, with a large passage at one end through which it is fed from below. Shortly before an eruption, as is common in the geyser basins, the water rises so as to fill the pit. At 4.09 p. m., August 25, during one of the spoutings of the Grand Geyser, the water in the Turban was agitated, boiling up in a powerful throb to a height of three feet, with occasional protracted spurts varying from twenty to thirty feet. At 4.12.5 the water receded far down the subterranean passage; at 4.17 p. m. vapor ascended, followed by water at 4.17.5, after which the agitation was variable in degree, being continued without interruption until 5.40. Frequently during the eruption quantities of water poured over the rim of the bowl, a considerable portion flowing directly into the mouth of the Grand Geyser, and apparently producing an important effect upon the action of the latter.

The Turban is named from the occurrence of large globular masses of geyserite within the rim, which are ornamented in such a manner as to suggest the form of the Turkish head-dress to one of an imaginative turn of mind. A fine-grained mechanical deposit taken from near the bottom of the pit after the eruption resembles a piece of sponge with minute "pores," (inhalent apertures,) and quite large "oscula," (exhalent apertures.) In general, the deposits are coarser and quite firm in texture.

20.* *Saw-Mill (?) Geyser.**—Just beyond the Turban, down-stream, a

* The Saw-Mill Geyser laid down on Hayden's Map of the Upper Geyser Basin, published in his report for 1871, is *not* the one referred to here, but Dr. Peale and others have used this name in such connection as to lead me to suppose that this is the one to which the name is applied in their works.

small orifice, not more than 5 or 6 inches in diameter, would be overlooked if not observed during an eruption. The mixed vapor and water ascends in a vigorous jet several feet in height, with a kind of puffing noise, or, more properly, with a sound like the continuous escape of steam under pressure, interrupted by occasional sudden puffs, when the column ascends to a height of 10 or 15 feet. The puffing noise is also present as the eruption dies out by successive irregular spurts. On the 25th of August, this geyser began to play quite suddenly at 4.11 p. m., ceasing action with the Turban and the Grand at 4.17.5 p. m. Vapor again issued at 4.18, and water at 4 19, the eruption continuing constantly until the others also ceased, at 5.40.

21. § *Tardy Geyser.*—A fourth vent near the Saw-Mill (?) gave rise to a small jet during the height of the second eruption of that geyser, and it may be but a waste-pipe for this when full. The Tardy Geyser began to play about 4.26.5 p. m., August 25, and continued in action nearly to 5.40 p. m. The water rose to a maximum height of only 3 feet above the surface.

22, 23, 24. § *Trinity Geysers.*—This name is used for convenience in designating three bowls, which have, perhaps, been otherwise named. So far as can be determined, however, from any writings upon this subject, no record of any eruption has been published. We had left the vicinity of the Grand Geyser late in the afternoon of August 25, and were hastening to our camp at the upper end of the basin, when we were startled by the eruption of another geyser at the edge of a broad terrace just above us. This began at 6.30 p. m., continuing till 6.35.5 p. m. The water proceeded from a mound raised some 3 feet above the terrace, having a diameter of 5 or 6 feet. The water reached a height of 75 feet or thereabout. Another geyser very near spouted at 6.33 p. m., ceasing wholly at 6.35. This had a similar orifice and chimney, not quite as high as the preceding, but the column of water was of nearly the same dimensions. A third geyser, with little or no raised walls, but with a fair-sized pool, but a few feet from the others, spurted at 6.37 for a few minutes, throwing the liquid about 60 feet into the air. From their apparent connection they have received the provisional name of the Trinity Geysers. We were unable to devote sufficient time to their study; hence these few data.

25. † *Giantess.*—This geyser, which is situated on the right bank of the Fire-Hole River, near a portion of our camp, (No. 46, August 25,) was not seen in action by any of our party. In fact, but two or three eruptions have as yet been witnessed, and it is probable that its quiescent intervals are of great duration, although it is one of the most powerful bowls in the world. There is little in its aspect and surroundings to indicate its power, and its subterranean structure is very obscure.

SUMMARY.

The geysers, which have been described from the Upper Fire-Hole Basin, comprise, with the exception of the Giantess, those which were observed in action by the writer of this report. They also constitute the principal members of the great group to which they belong, and several are included which have not before been known to eject a column of water. In the Lower Basin a few of the principal bowls were not seen by the writer; hence, no descriptions of these have been given, but enough has been offered to show all the prominent features of the eruptive springs of the district.

DIFFERENCE BETWEEN HOT SPRINGS AND GEYSERS.

Hot Springs.—We have seen that in some bowls which have been classed as mere thermal springs there is more or less of constant or periodical eruption. A careful examination, however, will almost invariably show a marked difference in the character of the phenomena attendant upon the projection of the elevated liquid.

In the ordinary hot spring the spurting of the liquid, when it occurs, is owing to a resistance offered to the direct escape of the expansive force from below, and this resistance may be found in the tenacity of the liquid contents of the bowl, in the untoward shape of the bowl or its connected passages, or in the sudden restriction of the orifice near the surface of the liquid. In either case the uprising force is condensed, as it were, near one point, and the spurt or eruption is caused by the sudden overcoming of the tension when the force has become sufficiently concentrated to free itself from its confinement. Thus we may meet with a great variety of spouting thermal springs, resulting from two or more of these causes combined, and the force may be produced by heat alone or by the evolution of carbonic acid or other chemical change in addition. (See Fig. 38.)

Geysers.—The phenomena observed in connection with the typical geyser, however, do not admit of such a simple explanation; and there is much doubt whether existing theories are sufficient to account for all the common manifestations of such agitated bowls. Almost without exception, in the true geyser, the action, whether frequent or the reverse, is intermittent, although the successive periods in each case may be quite irregular. Without entering upon a lengthy discussion of this interesting subject, it will be necessary to enumerate several of the peculiar features of geyser-eruptions which serve to distinguish these bowls from the mere eruptive thermal springs. Usually, as the first indications of an approaching eruption, there will be noticed an escape of vapor, soon followed by a sudden rising of a mass of water sufficient to fill the surface-chamber of the geyser. The phenomena which follow are very largely the result of structural features of varying nature, no doubt, but it will invariably be found that the eruption takes place near the center of the bowl, and that the elevation of the column of water is accomplished by continuous or successive throes from one spot, while in the ordinary eruptive springs the column is seldom shot upward from the same point twice in succession. We must, therefore, believe that the propelling power in the geyser acts temporarily and suddenly, while in the common hot spring, quiet, boiling, or eruptive, constant or periodical, the force is evolved with considerable regularity. The idea which the writer desires to convey will be rendered more evident by the comparison of Figs. 38 and 39. Fig. 38 shows the supposed section of a common eruptive spring; and it will readily be seen that jets may even occur in cold springs of this structure, provided a quantity of carbonic-acid or other gas is struggling to free itself from beneath the ledge at *o*. In Fig. 39, which is intended to represent the supposed condition of the subterranean geyser-waters in the first stage of an eruption, the reservoir *a* is supposed to contain water which remains in equilibrium nearly at the level *ss*. By constant accessions of heat from below, the vacant passage above is finally filled with vapor, and by degrees the water in the bent passage *c* becomes heated, and evolves vapor also, as in *o*. After a time, the expansion of the vapor in *b* is able to overcome the combined pressure of the water and vapor in *c* and *o*, when the latter is forced out, followed by a portion of the water in the reservoir *a*. The force thus expended, a vacuum is produced in *b* by the receding of the column of water in *a*, and the foregoing operations

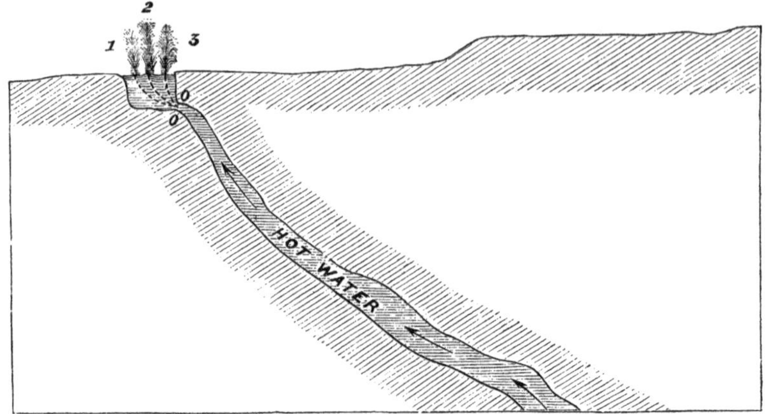

FIG. 38.—Ideal section of a thermal eruptive-spring. The arrows represent the direction of the action of the subterranean force. The channel is constricted at *o oe* the entrance of the surface-bowl. 1, 2, 3 represent the variable positions of successiv, jets.

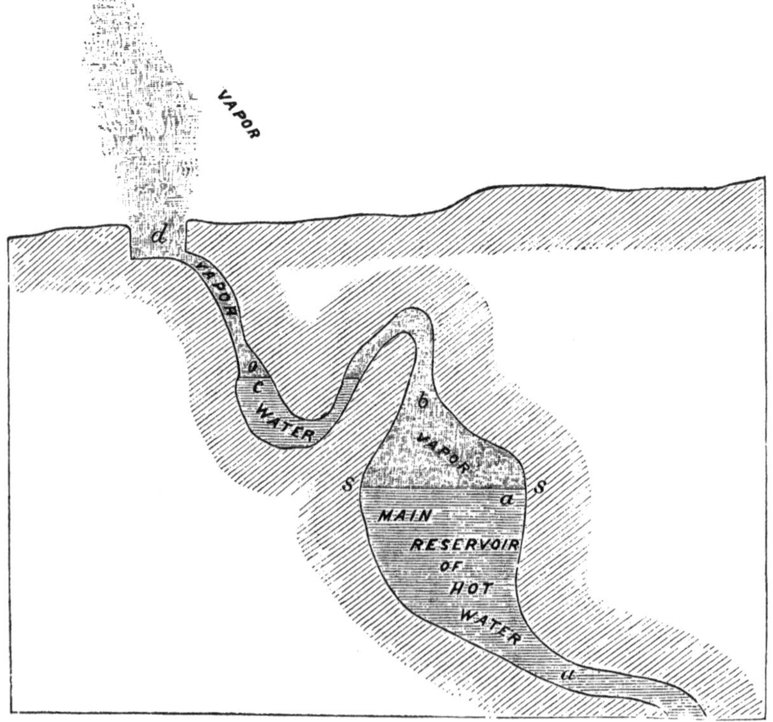

FIG. 39.—Ideal section of an intermittent geyser, to illustrate the phenomena of eruption during the escape of vapor, prior to hot-water ejection.

are indefinitely repeated. This theory seems capable of explaining the facts so far as they are known, and the variations observed in special cases, or even in different eruptions of the same geyser, appear to the writer to require but slight modifications of the section, and none that are of great importance. The passage *c* may be kept filled with water by means of the surplus which falls back into the bowl.

Bunsen's theory of geyser action, which has not yet been proven inadequate to explain the more prominent features of eruptions, does not seem sufficient (to the writer) to account for all the differences between the geyser and the mere hot spring, but it must not be inferred that such excellent authority is disregarded. On the contrary, the author proposes the structural hypothesis simply as a supplement to the superheating theory of Dr. Bunsen, in order to explain surface phenomena common in the Fire-Hole basins, which appear to require an extension of his views. At the same time it must be confessed that there are objections to his theory, based upon these observations, which are difficult to reconcile. It will be impossible to present these here, but an outline of the theories in question is appended. Bunsen has shown that an eruption may be artificially produced by introducing steam near the base of a long, narrow column of water, which causes the water, as it rises under pressure, to become superheated, the surplus heat being used for the production of more steam, which adds to the elevating force. His admirable theory, of which the above experiment is an illustration, is based upon a series of ingenious observations among the hot springs of Iceland. Bischof adopts an opinion almost identical with the structural hypothesis here proposed, and the present author, it will be remarked, combines the two theories, believing both necessary to explain all the facts observed.

ORIGIN AND PRESENT SOURCE OF HEAT-SUPPLY.

It is not to be doubted that the origin of the heat evolved in these springs must be sought in the causes which have led to the pouring out of the immense floods of igneous material which now cover the area over which they are distributed; and yet there are so many elements of uncertainty connected with the distribution of the bowls that a thorough discussion of the subject would scarcely be possible, were it advisable to enter upon it here. The present source of the heat-supply is equally difficult to determine on account of the very meager knowledge which we possess of any of the phenomena, as well as our ignorance of the intimate geological structure of the district. We have now learned just enough to make further investigation most desirable, and it is to be hoped that measures may be taken without delay for the prosecution of researches in a field which promises results of most extraordinary importance if properly cultivated.

Chemical changes, &c.—While it is probable that the seat of the heat-supply is far below the present surface, there is every reason to believe that the character and intensity of the eruptions are very much influenced by the supply of water from above ground, and some data were collected which seem to prove that certain chemical changes under ground produce a very appreciable effect also. Carbonic acid certainly exerts a power in the propulsion of the water in not a few of the springs, and its similar action in some of the geysers is much more than suspected. Some hints of the results of analyses of the various thermal waters, kindly furnished by Dr. Heizmann, lead to suspicions of like results caused by other chemical changes, but little is definitely known concerning them.

MISCELLANEOUS NOTES.

Geyserite pebbles.—As remarked in several places in this chapter, many of the principal geysers in both basins of the Fire-Hole River are surrounded by shallow pools in which are found well-worn pebbles of geyserite, with more or less of a concentric structure. These were at first supposed to be accretions formed by the continual addition of silica from the falling water. Careful observation and the subsequent study of the various mechanical deposits have led me to an opposite conclusion, however. Many of these pebbles are polyhedral, but the concentric layers of these, as in other cases, are arranged in bands, with oval or circular cross-sections, not corresponding with the external configuration. Moreover, an examination of the external layer of polyhedral specimens shows that it has been worn away in parts, proving conclusively that the pebbles have been *reduced* from forms with a more or less curved outline. These pebbles have, therefore, been worn down to their present shape, by attrition in their pools, and they have no doubt been first formed as ordinary mechanical deposits, in the form of protuberances over the general surface, or as divisions of a tesselated patch, like portions of the platform near the base of Old Faithful Geyser. (No. 12, this chapter.)

Silicified wood.—That a very large portion of the petrified wood now found in the volcanic district has become so without the intervention of thermal springs is scarcely to be doubted in the light of the abundant evidence which has been gathered of the more direct action of the waters percolating through the igneous material. Still we are, perhaps, not warranted in adopting the conclusion that the process of silicification was necessarily widely different from that now in progress in the vicinity of many hot springs, for it is probable that very much, if not all of it, was accomplished by the action of heated water. (See chapter IX.) The amount of petrifaction now taking place about the thermal springs is comparatively small, though in some localities a considerable quantity is subjected to the influence of the water. The process is more complete and uniform in the neighborhood of the quieter bowls than usually about the active geysers. In the hot spring the soaking of the wood is much more complete, and, though the silicification may be much retarded, the entrance of the siliceous solution into its substance is thereby greatly facilitated. On the other hand, the outflows from the geysers being more plentiful and vigorous, the fragments of wood are quickly coated with nearly pure silica, but thorough penetration is almost impossible, unless they are so situated as to be almost constantly boiled within the bowl.

Evidences of former floods.—Not only in the geyser basins of the Fire-Hole Valley, but in several other regions of thermal springs, as at Gardiner's River, the locality of the Wayside Group, &c., there are unmistakable signs of inundation at some undetermined time in the past, the extent of which it is very difficult to imagine. In some portions of these districts the trees are marked for two feet above the base of the trunk with a white incrustation, giving them something of the appearance of the whitewashed trees in an orchard. It would certainly be impossible that any such traces should be left by snow remaining upon the ground for any length of time, and there seems no alternative but to regard these markings as a relic of a time not very long gone, when the areas in question were overflowed by siliceous waters to the depth mentioned. If it be true, then, that the overflow from the included bowls has been so enormous during modern times, it becomes a question of very great interest what can have caused such an increase in their intensity. No facts can now be given to aid materially in the solution of this problem, but it may be stated, in closing this lengthy review of the subject of thermo-dynamics, that this is but one of a hundred equally interesting subjects which press upon the attention of the investigator in these parts. When it is considered that all the facts which have thus far been gathered have been recorded during the driest season of the year, and that no observations at any one locality have extended over a period of a single week, it may be well esteemed most fortunate that we have even gained the little knowledge which we now possess of these remarkable phenomena. May the day be not far distant when a complete series of careful, constant, extended, and connected observations may be undertaken, to be continued through all seasons for a number of years.

CHAPTER XIV.

ARCHÆOLOGY, WITH MANNERS AND CUSTOMS OF EASTERN SHOSHONES.

I. Archæology—*a.* Wrought flakes—*b.* Spear-heads and arrow-heads—*c.* Stone circles and other relics of sun-worshipers (?)—*d.* Stone columns, graves, &c.—*e.* Rock-inscriptions. II. Eastern Shoshones or Washakie band—*a.* General and social character—*b.* Traditions and superstitions—*c.* Expression of emotions—*d.* Society, government, &c.—*e.* Musical expression—*f.* Ornament and "medicine" forms.

There are very few portions of our western territory which do not furnish some evidences of the former existence of Indian tribes other than those now occupying the given areas. Relics of various kinds are not absent from the district now under discussion, although such are by no means extremely common in this region. The present and the following chapter are devoted to the very brief discussion of those which have come under the notice of the author, together with some account of the manners, customs, and language of the present inhabitants of the Wind River Valley, commonly known as Washakie's band, or Eastern Shoshones. The material for this review, with one or two exceptions,* consists entirely of personal notes obtained on the march and in camp, in the intervals of more pressing duties, as much time as possible being devoted to the examination of archæological relics wherever they occurred during the trip. It was originally proposed to present this material in a series of several chapters, but this has been rendered impossible for lack of the necessary time for its complete elaboration in connection with outside labors.

I.—ARCHÆOLOGICAL NOTES.

The relative age of the several varieties of the remains to be described under this head may, perhaps, be capable of determination when sufficient data have been gathered, but it will readily be acknowledged that this is now impossible, when it is considered that all the accumulations are superficial and separately distributed, so that two distinct forms are

---

* Dr. J. Van A. Carter, of Fort Bridger, who is well posted concerning the habits and language of the Shoshones and neighboring tribes, has kindly furnished a few notes which have greatly aided in verifying my own, upon the dialect of Washakie's band, besides enabling me to obtain additional hints as to the structure of the language. Wherever comparisons are made with other tribes, due credit is given to the authorities quoted in the text. Mr. J. D. Putnam obtained for me a small list of words from one of our scouts, most of which were verified by comparison with my own notes.

seldom or never found in one locality. We will, therefore, group them according to their character, considering them in their order of occurrence along the trail of Captain Jones's party.

a.—WORKED FLAKES OF QUARTZITE AND OTHER MATERIAL.

The southern portion of the Green River, or Bridger Basin, has the surface strewn with numerous fragments of various rocks, mostly of small size. The greater number of these possess no features of special interest, being evidently the mere accidental products of the natural wear and tear of bowlders *in transitu*, or of rocks subjected to sudden great changes of temperature. Not a few, however, so closely resemble the rough flakes which are produced by striking off small chips upon both sides of a median line that scarcely any one who might view them by themselves in a cabinet would be disposed to question their artificial origin.

Prof. Joseph Leidy has figured and described a number of these wrought flakes in Hayden's Report for 1872*. In speaking of them he says: "These with little doubt may be viewed as rude implements of art. The vast numbers of similar stones to be found on the buttes and plains near Fort Bridger, and their gradation to undoubted accidental fragments with which they are mingled, alone renders it improbable that they should be considered as such."

We can add little or nothing to his careful observations upon the subject, but a little space may, nevertheless, be occupied with a description of these relics and their distribution and mode of occurrence.

The form and size of two average specimens are clearly shown in Figs. 40 and 41, which also afford examples of two of the most common rock varieties observed among the worked fragments in the neighborhood of the Uintah Mountains. Fig. 40 represents a flake of dark, glistening quartzite, with a corroded appearance over a surface of fracture. Fig. 41 is drawn from a specimen composed of a finer-grained variety of quartzite, of a much lighter color, approaching greenish-gray.

Neither of these show remarkable signs of weathering, but there is often much difference in this respect among fragments from the same locality. It is scarcely to be supposed that these rude splinters have ever subserved the purpose of weapons or other implements, although there are many of the flakes of more definite shapes, which may have been so employed. It seems probable, however, that a large proportion of those which can be referred to no particular form, are merely the rejected pieces which have been spoiled during the process of manufacturing more perfect implements, or, in some cases, perhaps, they are pieces from which smaller arrow-heads have been chipped.

Flinty and jaspery flakes are not uncommon, and Professor Leidy reports the occurrence of well-wrought implements in situations which have afforded favorable locations for permanent camping-places of the Indians.

Aside from the freshness of appearance of very many of these stones, there are other reasons for doubting the remote antiquity of the greater portion of them.

It is well known that existing tribes of North American Indians, now mainly removed to the southward of the forty-first parallel, have used

* See his excellent article "on Remains of Primitive Art in the Bridger Basin of Southern Wyoming," Geological Survey of Montana, Idaho, &c., 1872. Washington: 1873, p. 651.

Fig. 40.—Worked flake of dark jaspery quartzite from northern base of Uintah Mts., Green River Basin. Natural size.

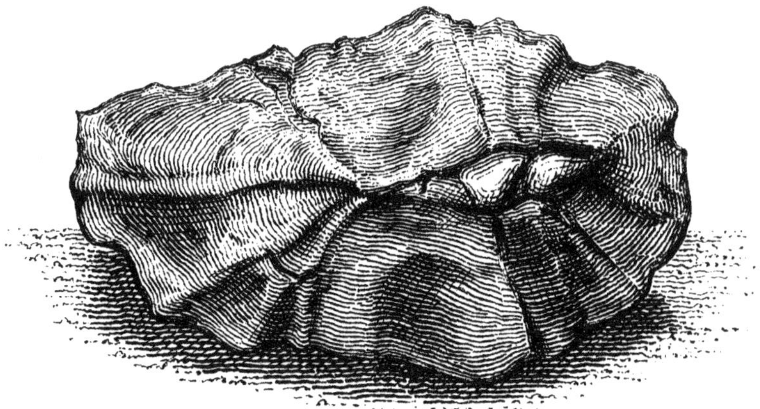

Fig. 41.—Worked flake of light greenish-gray quartzite from northern base of Uintah Mts., Green River Basin. Natural Size.

weapons and other implements of stone, many of which now lie scattered over a wide area, including the territory embraced by our reconnaissance. It is interesting to note that the material of these fairly-fashioned tools, as observed northward along our trail, bears a striking resemblance to the rocks and the rude flakes collected near the northern base of the Uintahs. In fact, not a few of the spear-heads and arrow-heads mentioned beyond could not have been obtained at any point nearer their observed positions than the southern portion of the Green River Basin. Again, certain articles of a very rude character are still in use to some extent among our western Indians, and even in the cases of such tribes as have now entirely discarded the implements of stone and bone, relics of such material are not uncommonly found in graves which cannot be regarded as ancient. The Shoshones, though mostly provided with tools of iron and steel of approved patterns, are still to be seen employing, as a scraper in the dressing of skins, a mere "teshoa," consisting of a small worn bowlder, thinner at one end, split through the middle in such a manner as to furnish a rough cutting-edge at one side. There seems to be a considerable advantage in this over any form of knife or other tool which has yet reached them from without, and it is probable that it will be retained so long as their present method of preparing hides is in vogue.

As a possible offset to the foregoing remarks, it may be mentioned that nothing can be learned of the origin or use of the flakes from the Indians themselves, who appear to know little of them, or, as Dr. Carter observes, they regard them as ancestral possessions bestowed by the Great Spirit directly.

In estimating the value of this element in the determination of the age of these relics, it should be borne in mind that the traditional method of communication is not prevalent among the tribes of the Shoshone Group. But we have barely touched upon the salient points of a subject of great interest, which requires more careful observation and comparison for its further elucidation. We pass somewhat naturally to the next topic.

b.—SPEAR-HEADS AND ARROW-HEADS.

Our route from Fort Bridger to Camp Stambaugh lay along the line of a road which has been much traveled by foot-passengers in the past, and very few of the stone weapons which have doubtless been strewn widely over the Green River Basin by the tribes which have roamed and fought over its area were observed by members of the party. The ever-shifting sands have probably buried large numbers of these implements also, and it is only in peculiarly favorable situations that they are now exposed at the surface. As before mentiond, well-formed spear-heads and arrow-heads may be obtained from many localities in the neighborhood of the Uintah Mountains, where they lie more or less imbedded in the compacted surface-layer, upon the summits of benches, or in the vicinity of hollows, which offer attractive and sheltered situations for camps. North of the Union Pacific Railroad, there are very few chances of obtaining such relics, except upon the tops of rocky buttes or benches not covered by beds of the Bridger-Eocene formation. Fig. 42 represents in outline, with cross-sections taken at base and apex, a portion of a spear-head of gray quartzite, not greatly differing from the material of the flake illustrated in Fig. 41. Very few of the implements made of this material appear to have long retained their original form *in toto*, but the ends are usually more or less fractured, as in figs. 42–44. While running a topographical base-line across the plain near Camp 10, Mr. Le Hardy obtained a fragment of a spear-head of similar substance, three or four times as large as that of Fig. 42. Captain Jones picked up a beautiful arrow-head, very small, of clear opal, from the slope of a low terrace bordering the North Fork of Popo-Agie River, at Camp 17, (Wind River country, southeast of Camp Brown, eight miles.) The fragment shown in Fig. 43 is a portion of an uncertain weapon, which my frequent companion, Pínatsi,* picked up of his own accord from the top of a very high ridge which we had ascended together, north of the trail between Camps 24 and 25, among the foot-hills of the Owl Creek range. He seemed anxious to inform me of its origin, without any hint from myself. Not being able to recall the name of the tribe to which he would refer it, I ran over a list of several well-known Indian nations, including some which had previously roamed over this territory, to all of which he gave a negative answer, but, suddenly brightening, he exclaimed *Apáche! Apáche!* This information cannot, of course, be implicitly relied upon, but it is here given only for what it may be worth. The spear-head represented in Fig. 44 was found partially imbedded in the red sandy talus at the foot of a bluff of the brick-red beds which are generally regarded as Triassic. It is made of gray quartzite, very fine-grained and compact, and shows some signs of weathering. The under surface as it lay had become conspicuously reddened by contact with the soil, and this color is now permanently retained. Between this point and the Yellowstone basin no remains of this character were observed, though it is highly probable that such are not scarce, as there is evidence that this section has been the haunt of many Indians in the past as now. Mr. Creary obtained from the twelfth terrace at the Mammoth Hot Springs of Gardiner's River, a large spear-head of light-drab quartzite, nearly three by four inches. Beyond, in the region occupied by the igneous or eruptive rocks, a new material is provided in the masses of obsidian which occur in places as "volcanic glass." Fig. 45 represents a small specimen of arrow-head with the remains of a shaft, which was

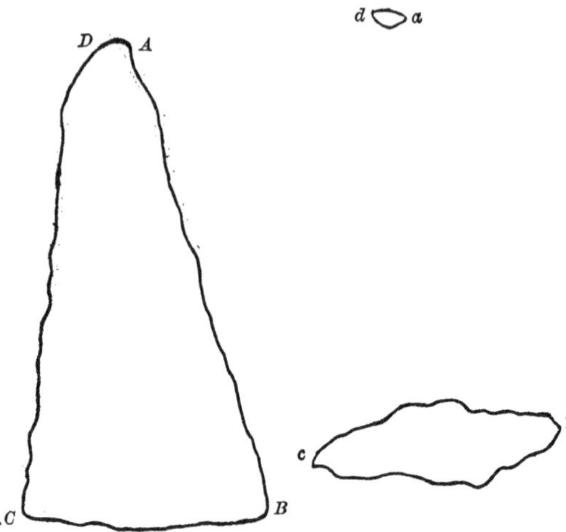

FIG. 42.—Traced outline of a broken spear-head of gray quartzite from a bluff on Little Sandy Creek, one-half mile north of Camp 10, Green River Basin. *a d*, *b c*, sectional outlines at *A D* and *B C*.

FIG. 43.—Outline and end sections of Apáche relic, of greenish gray quartzite, from near Dry Fork, Wind River Valley.

* For pronunciation of Indian words, see vocabulary, Chapter XV, beyond.

picked up by one of the cavalry escort at our camp on Pacific Creek, just below the Two-Ocean Pass. An unbroken arrowhead of pure chal-

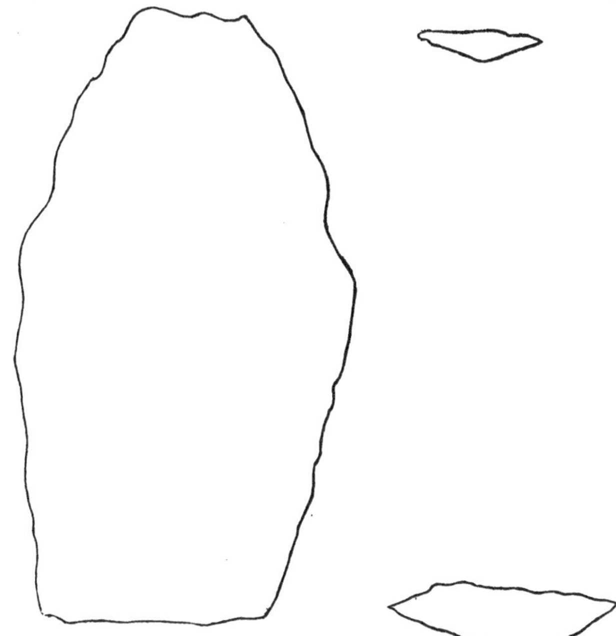

FIG. 44.—Outline of spear-head, with end sections, from the base of a cliff of Triassic beds, beyond Camp 25, at southern base of Owl Creek range.

edony, of the form given in Fig. 46, lay within a few inches of the trail, half way between Camps 53 and 54, not far from Atlantic Creek. The

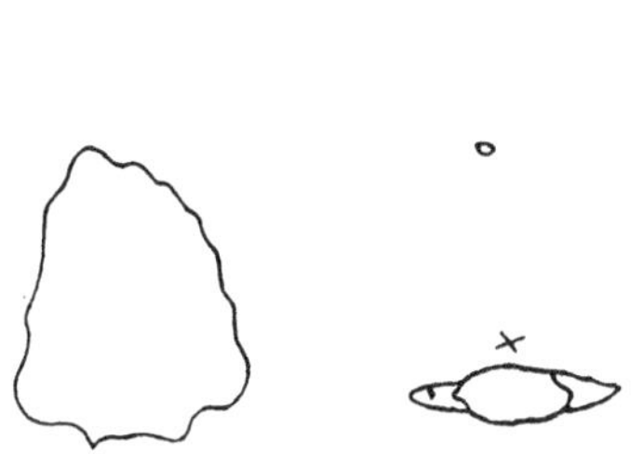

FIG. 45.—Outline and end sections of an obsidian arrow-head. The inner line of the section X is the basal cross-section of the shaft, or neck, of the implement. Locality, Camp 54, on Pacific Creek.

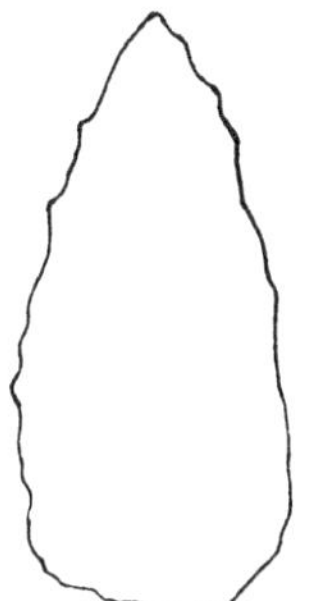

FIG. 46.—Outline, with end sections, of an arrow-head of pure chalcedony obtained on the trail between Camps 53 and 54, near Atlantic Creek, tributary of Upper Yellowstone River.

material of which this is composed is very abundant in regions of Tertiary exposures, and the arrow-heads are usually of extreme beauty, being much more perfect and symmetrical than one would suppose it possible to manufacture from such a substance, while a sharp and jagged edge is secured which cannot fail of accomplishing its intended purpose, when skillfully used. No direct clew to the age of these relics was obtained, nor is it possible to offer any well-founded opinion with respect to the tribes by which they were employed. It may be said, however, that there is little reason for considering them in any degree ancient, for they were all found lying upon the surface of the ground, and mostly showing scarcely any signs of weathering effects. On the other hand, few, if any, are to be regarded as *very* recent, for all were more or less firmly settled in the soil, and it cannot be positively asserted that they had not lain in their observed positions for a century or more. Few would be disposed to regard them, probably, as other than relics of the North American Indians, with the exception, perhaps, of such as were alluded to as occurring in parts of the southern portion of the Green River basin. No weapons of stone were observed in use by the Shoshones, although many of the boys were provided with bows and arrows, with sharpened iron or steel heads for the latter, of the pattern commonly adopted by the western tribes. This consists merely of a thin blade of about the form and dimensions shown in the annexed cut, (Fig. 47,) sharpened along the entire edge, except at the base. Occasional variations in the outline may be observed, and the size is somewhat variable also.

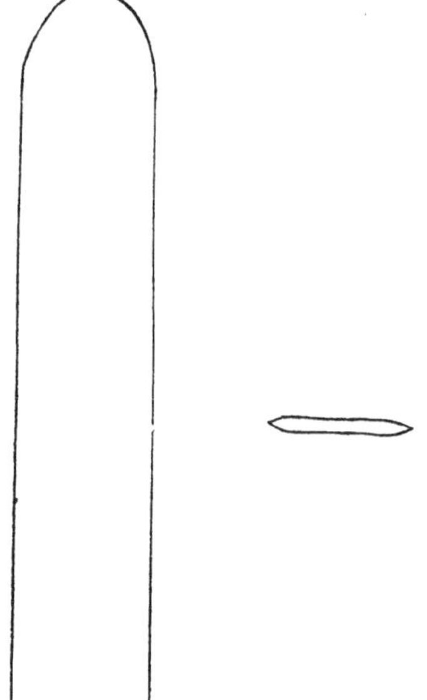

Fig. 47.—Typical shape of knife arrowhead now occasionally employed by young Shoshones, (Eastern.)

c.—STONE CIRCLES, TRIANGLES, ETC.

Since our return from the field, Professor E. D. Cope has presented a paper to the Philadelphia Academy of Science, in which he describes several circles of stones observed by himself in the neighborhood of the Uintah Mountains. In form and size, as well as in their mode of construction, these all appear to differ from those which fall to be described in this place, and indeed, no exactly similar works have been discovered elsewhere, so far as can be learned from the perusal of the writings of leading compilers and authorities.

Strangely enough, the points originally chosen as the termini of a "base-line," marked out by the topographical corps while at Camp Brown, had also been selected at a period long since past, by ruder men, as the locations of simple structures, probably connected with some form of religious ceremonies. The engraving (Fig. 48) represents an oval inclosure formed by the arrangement of flat stones upon the ground in such a manner as to leave an opening toward the east, or in the direction of the rising sun. The circlet is composed of nineteen irregular pieces of limestone, corresponding in character to some of the beds of a neighboring cliff. It is situated upon a rounded bluff in a very commanding position. All the stones were partly imbedded in the soil, and portions of two of them were overgrown with a thick tuft of moss. There was a perceptible depression or hollow near the middle of the inclosure, as if fire had been employed in the rites, but no traces of implements or remains of sacrifices were observed, although a careful search was made. The structure at the northwestern terminus of the base-line is much smaller, and nearly circular, with rather thicker stones, obtained from

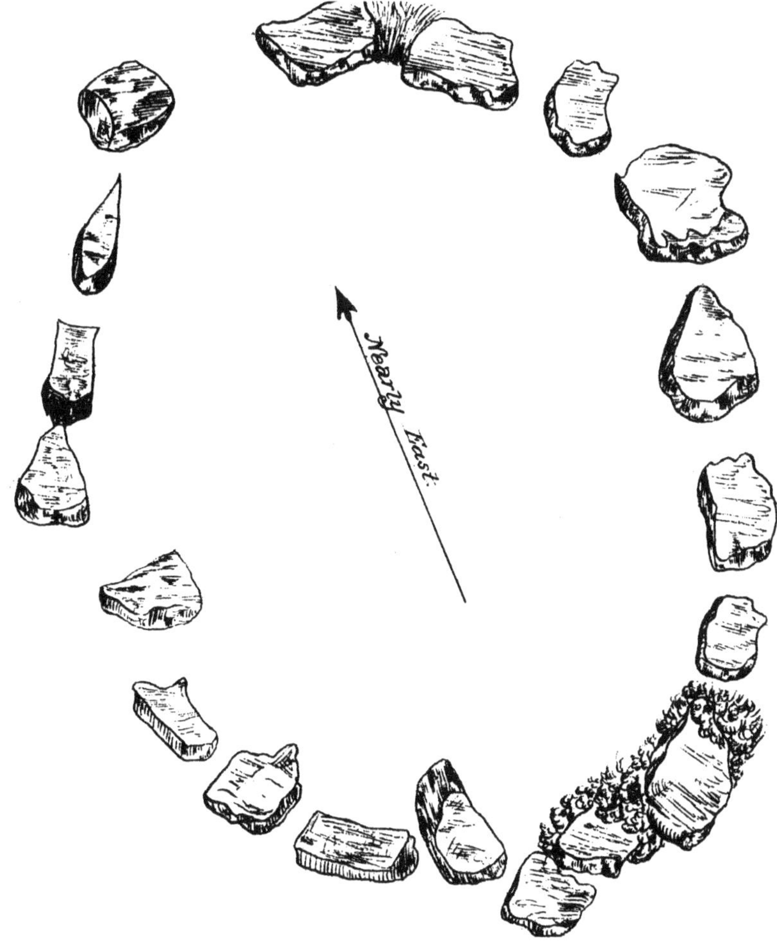

Fig. 48.—Sketch of a rude stone circle on a bluff on right bank of Little Wind River, south of Butte Springs, below Camp Brown.
Dimensions, 3 x 6 feet, inside.

the butte upon the summit of which it is located. The number of stones is nearly as great as in the former instance, but they are more closely crowded. Unfortunately the topographers' monument was built directly upon one side of this circle, two of the stones beyond being also taken to build the pile; hence the writer cannot state positively the number of pieces in the ring. The opening, as before, is toward the east. The butte on which the circle rests is a prominent landmark, though soon shut out from view northward, and it offers a commanding position for such a structure. This hill lies less than a mile to the east of our trail, midway between Camps 19 and 20.

In both cases, rather noticeably, the rings are so placed that access to their level is quite difficult from the west, while the eastward prospect from the flats below is shut off in such a manner as to allow of an earlier view of the rising sun from the more elevated point. It may not be hazardous to regard these inclosures, with others to be mentioned directly, as relics of a race or tribe of sun-worshippers, although we have now no data for assigning them to their proper period or people. They are certainly not very recent, and the Shoshones are unable to account for them, except by referring them, as usual in cases of doubt, to the agency of the Great Spirit, or "*Tam Apa.*"

On the left bank of Wind River, below Camp 58, and a short distance above the entrance of De Noir Creek, there are a number of irregular hillocks or small mound-shaped hills, which overlook a comparatively level area, which offers an attractive spot for temporary camps, but which would scarcely be selected as a site for a more permanent abiding-place. Several of the hills are crowned with low piles of small stones, which furnish but little evidence as to their significance, but the arrangement observed on the summit of one of them, perhaps the most conspicuous, deserves special consideration on account of its apparent relation to the circles before described. The positions of the three clusters of stones in this relic are indicated in Fig. 49, by the letters A, B, C. It will be observed that the base of the triangle is open toward the east, and it has occurred to the writer that these also may have constituted the hastily improvised temple of a tribe of sun-worshippers temporarily encamped in this vicinity. Even were the neighboring flats not wholly unsuitable for a permanent camp, much more favorable and elevated situations for the construction of circles are not wanting at a little distance. The corner heaps are not large, consisting of from two to four rough bowlders of small size, merely thrown together. Whether the single clusters of the same nature upon the surrounding hillocks are identical in origin it is not easy to determine, but it may be remarked that all are easterly from the locality in which the favorable camping-spots occur.

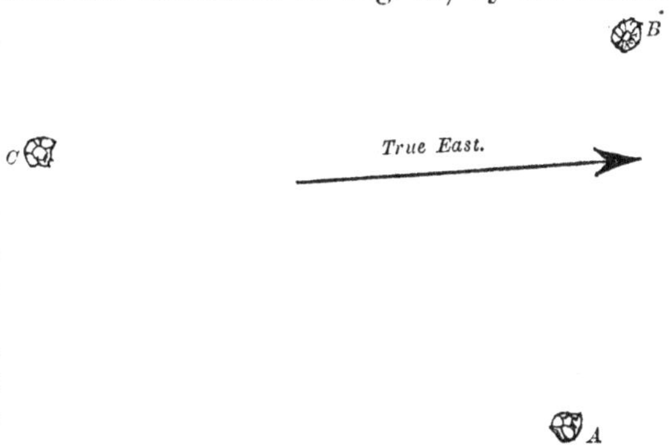

FIG. 49.—Ancient monuments, Wind River Valley, above mouth of De Noir Creek, A, B, C. Heaps or clusters of small bowlders. Distances estimated: A, B, 30 feet; B, C, 50 feet; C, A, 50 feet.

The author is unwilling to press too closely the theory that these circles and triangles have been used in the worship of the sun, although it may be difficult to account for their locations and the position of their openings on any other supposition. Again, although there is every reason to believe that the origin of these relics is not of recent date, it must be confessed that much too little is known of the historical ethnography of the West, and there is danger of giving undue credit to matters of little importance in themselves.

Sir John Lubbock,* in speaking of the *cromlechs*, or circles of upright stones, found in several parts of the world, suggests that the number in each circle may have had some significance, and he credits Dr. Thurnam with the statement that "four circles at Boscawen and adjacent places in Cornwall have each been formed of nineteen stones." It is a coincidence not necessarily anything but accidental to find the same number in the oval inclosure (Fig. 48,) though the ring would have been as complete with less.

d.—MONUMENTS, GRAVES, ETC.

Pillars or columns made of small, flat stones several feet in height, are common along the wagon-roads which traverse the Green River Basin, but these are known in many cases as land-marks established by the early Mormons who marked out the course to be pursued by the converts who were to follow them across the plains on their way to the Salt Lake Valley. Not a few of those monuments have, perhaps, also been built by members of the various topographical parties which have "triangulated" over this area since the date of the first exploration of the region, and a goodly number were added in 1873, by our own corps of surveyors. None of these structures were observed along our route which furnished any indication of a different origin, until we had passed beyond the Owl Creek Mountains, and penetrated the rugged area lying between Owl Creek and Gray Bull River. At a point where the trail led through a peculiar gap in a complicated series of bluffy hills, about three miles before reaching Camp 27, there was a considerable mound of loose fragments of white and red sandstone obtained quite near. There could be no doubt that these stones were placed in their present position by human agency, and it seems proper to regard them as the resting-place of the dead. This opinion is strengthened by the location of the mound, which is in a sheltered nook among the hills, in a spot where no land-mark would be visible even at a distance of several rods only. It should be stated, however, that the trail here made a sudden turn over a hill, and the heap may have been employed as a guide for Indian travelers.

Other monuments were observed in different localities, many of which may readily be dismissed from consideration by regarding them as mere coverts for hunters lying in wait for deer and other game, but there are some which will scarcely admit of so simple an explanation. Such are those which have been erected in such situations that they could never serve as land-marks for travelers or topographers, nor yet as means of concealment from animals. In the absence of any evidence of their real significance, however, these must be passed with a mere allusion to their occasional occurrence, without an attempt to account for them in any way.

It is matter of some surprise that so few Indian graves were noticed during the trip, when we consider the number of burials wh ch must have taken place over the area discussed. The best example of an undoubted sepulchre was seen near the trail, two miles beyond Camp

*"Pre-historic Times," 3d edition, London, 1872, p. 113.

32, on the left bank of North Fork of Stinking Water River. This consisted of a low mound of loose stones lying nearly east and west, with an irregular and broader heap extending a few feet northward from the eastern end. Our Shoshone scout, Nakok, stated that this was the burial-place of a Blackfoot (?) warrior. The stones were small and somewhat broken, having been taken from a collection of washed fragments of limestone spread out over the bed of a flood-stream, which was dry when we passed. Digging down the length of my arm, the stones were found gradually becoming smaller below, and mixed with loose earth, but no human remains nor trinkets were discovered. From the appearance of the adjoining heap, a horse may have been buried near the foot, apparently at a right angle to the warrior's body.

The position of the Indian's body, lying nearly in an east and west direction, may be not wholly accidental. G. Catlin,* speaking of the burial customs among the Mandans, after describing the construction of the scaffold, remarks, "The body is laid * * * on its back, with its feet carefully presented toward the rising sun." The smaller mound in this case, as before stated, had what appeared to be the foot toward the east.

Human skeleton.—While at Camp 28, on Gooseberry Creek, (Shoshone Plateau,) Burt, one of the cavalry escort, brought in the skull of a white man, which he had found on a hill-side near one of the lookout stations. He reported that he found lying with it, at the surface, the prominent bones of the skeleton and laid them together in a secluded spot. We were unable to find these by careful search on the following day; but a story is current among the Indians of the killing of a white man near this locality not many years since, one of three, it is said, who had been driven into the ravines, the others having escaped.

e.—HIEROGLYPHIC ROCK-INSCRIPTIONS.

In the Smithsonian Report, 1872, (page 409 *et seq.*,) Mr. J. G. Bruff gives two views of Indian rock-carvings from the upper portion of the Green River Valley, at some distance northwest of our line of march. These are much more perfect in construction, as well as more true to nature, than any which were observed by us. In fact, none were noticed along our course until we had reached the Little Popo-Agie River, in the Wind River country; and all that were seen by our party occurred within the limits of the Wind River Plateau.

On the left bank of the Little Popo-Agie, just across the road from Fletcher's ranch, above Murphy's, there is a small cavern in light, buff sandstone, which might shelter from three to five men. The mouth of this is well barricaded by a low, curved wall of large, flat stones, placed on edge so as to afford almost complete protection in case of an attack, provided that the besieged were well armed. Inside, on a kind of ledge, a few twigs and leaves were seen, leading to the conclusion that the retreat may have been used as a place of incantation by some Indian medicine-man. On the face of the cliff, above the entrance, and a little to the left, are three hieroglyphic figures, mere daubs of black paint, two being long, thin, characteristic representations of horses, and the third resembling a tapiroid animal without a proboscis, which was probably intended to represent a mule.

Upon a nearly vertical wall of the yellow sandstones just back of Murphy's ranch, at Camp 16, a number of rude figures had been chiseled,

* "North American Indians," Vol. i, p. 89.

apparently at a period not very recent, as they had become much worn. The greater number of these are shown about one-fifth of their size, in

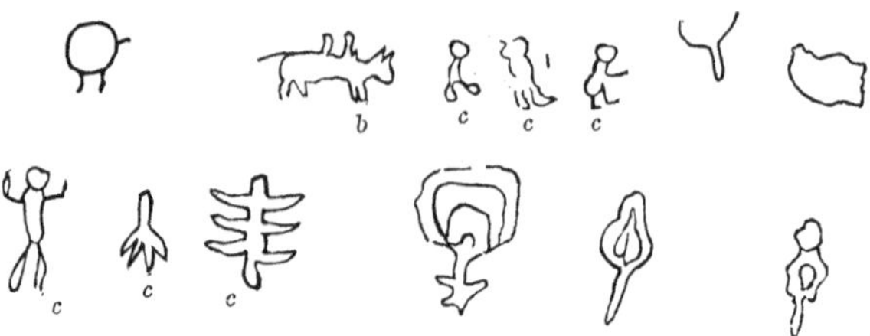

FIG. 50.—Hieroglyphic inscriptions on a cliff of yellowish sandstones back of Murphy's ranch, at Camp 16, on Little Popo-Agie River. (× ⅕ about.)

Fig. 50. No certain clew to the connected meaning of this record was obtained, although Pínatsi attempted to explain it when the sketch was shown to him some days later by Mr. F. W. Bond, who copied the inscriptions from the rocks. The figure on the left, in the upper row, somewhat resembles the design commonly used to represent a shield, with the greater part of the ornamental fringe omitted, perhaps worn away in the inscription. We shall possibly be justified in regarding the whole as an attempt to record the particulars of a fight or battle which once occurred in this neighborhood. Pínatsi's remarks conveyed the idea to Mr. Bond that he understood the figure marked *b* in the cut to signify cavalry, and the six figures marked *c*, to mean infantry, but he did not appear to recognize the hieroglyphs as the copy of any record with which he was familiar. On the side trip to Chimney Rocks, in the nucleus of the Wind River Mountains, (see chapter I,) an interesting hieroglyphic series was discovered carved in a wall of light-buff sandstones overlying the brick-red Triassic beds. The well-traveled woodmen's road from Camp Brown, passes close under this bluff just after crossing Trout Creek. The figure in the cut (Fig. 51) was copied in the afternoon when returning from the mountains. About noon of the following day, an attempt was made to obtain copies of all the others, which are numerous and of several forms, but the light upon them at this hour was so unsatisfactory that only a few of the most prominent figures could be sketched, and these are included in the group in Fig. 52. The story here marked out is more complete, or, perhaps, extends over a greater period than in the Little Popo-Agie record, for the cliffs have very many rude designs cut upon them, a large number of which have now become so indistinct that it is impossible to trace them accurately. Those which are illustrated in the accompanying cuts have been copied as they appear, but it is not certain that they correctly represent the original delineations. The figures are all quite large and the lines are broad and coarse, as if made in haste by some blunt instrument. The rock is very soft and weathers rapidly, being of such a color that the finer markings are only brought out by the direct light of the sun in the afternoon.

FIG. 51.—Hieroglyph roughly cut in light-buff sandstone, on Trout Creek, near crossing of woodmen's road from Camp Brown to Wind River Mountains. (About one-fifth size.)

No information was obtained which can aid in solving the problem of the

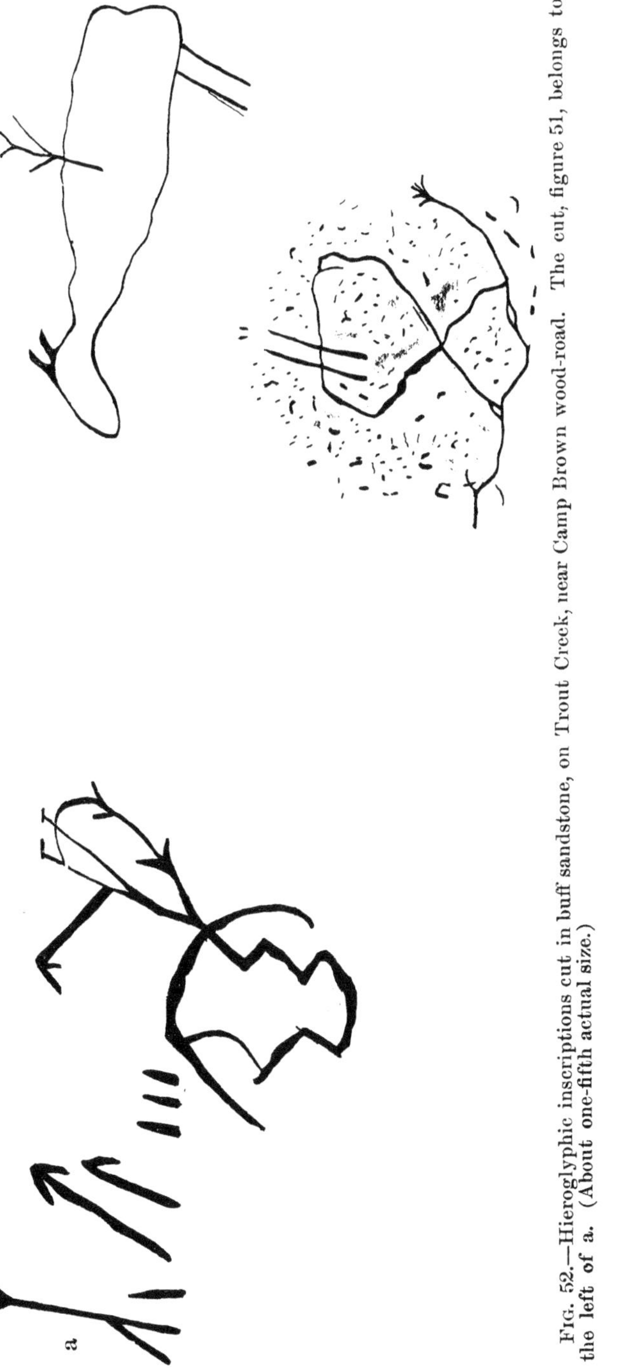

FIG. 52.—Hieroglyphic inscriptions cut in buff sandstone, on Trout Creek, near Camp Brown wood-road. The cut, figure 51, belongs to the left of a. (About one-fifth actual size.)

age, or significance of the picture-writing, as a whole, though the special meaning of certain designs may be inferred from their form, as in the case of the many represented in Fig. 50.

The only remaining instance of rock-sculpturing observed over our route was a set of rough etchings in the upper portion of the valley of Wind River, on the left bank, in the face of a cliff of soft buff-colored sandstones, near the mouth of a creek which enters Wind River a short distance below Camp 59. These are given in Fig. 53, so far as they could be made out, no signs of others being visible. Pínatsi was shown the copy of these in my note-book, and he remarked that they were intended to record the particulars of a fight between the Cheyennes and Shoshones some years since, in which (of course) the latter were victorious. As nearly as could be gathered from his efforts at description, he stated that the upper figure on the right represents a shield, and a

Fig. 53.

FIG. 53.—Hieroglyphs (badly weathered) cut in buff sandstones on left bank of Wind River, at mouth of a creek below Camp 59. (One-fifth actual size, about.)

similar design is rather commonly noticed in many of the engravings of hieroglyphs in the works of authorities on the customs of North American Indians. It would be unwise and futile to attempt any close generalizations upon this scanty material, and it is very unsafe to base any conclusions wholly upon the uncertain testimony of the Indians alone, but there are several points of interest which require at least a passing allusion. It seems a little remarkable that all of these carvings should occur in the Wind River Valley, and, especially, that all should have been recorded upon light-buff sandstones, which are all so soft that the designs are even now greatly obliterated. The general rudeness of workmanship and a certain similarity of construction, as well as the comparative amount of weathering, all point toward a common origin; and the occurrence of the shield in two or three instances would seem to indicate that the work was done at a period prior to the general introduction of fire-arms. There are, however, a few designs which were probably intended to represent guns, from which it may be inferred that their use was also known at the time. We are, therefore, in the absence of other evidence, brought to the conclusion that these relics are of modern date, though pointing backward to an epoch of more primitive Indian culture than the present. The author is strongly of the opinion that they were not made by the Shoshones, for reasons which cannot now be detailed. At the same time the story of Pínatsi, concerning the fight with the Cheyennes, was related in a manner which entitles it to some consideration at least.

II.—MANNERS AND CUSTOMS OF WASHAKIE'S BAND OF EASTERN SHOSHONES.

One of the most important, and now among the most widely-scattered groups of Indians inhabiting the territory of the United States west of the Mississippi, comprises a large number of hostile, semi-hostile, and friendly bands, extending in patches from Oregon to Texas and from the Missouri River to the Pacific Ocean. In the lingual classification of the North American Indians adopted by Schoolcraft, his fifth division, or "Shoshonee group, comprises the Comanches, Shoshones, Snakes, Bonacks, and other tribes of the Rocky Mountains, the higher Red River, and the hill country of Texas."*

Numerous causes, among which may be mentioned the governmental policy of separating and intermingling the various tribes, have rendered this definition obsolete, and it would now be a difficult task to collect the statistics necessary for the enumeration of the numerous bands which properly belong to this group. The names *Snake* and *Shoshone* are interchangeable, and there are given in the report of the Secretary of the Interior for 1873 not less than *thirty-one* distinct bands which are affiliated by their language, comprising in all, (male and female,) only 21,000 individuals. In many cases, where several bands are living upon the same reservation, they have been reported as one, hence the actual number of sects is much greater, no doubt. Even in the district traversed by ourselves, we were frequently called upon in conversation to make distinctions between such companies as Washakie's band, or Eastern Shoshones, and Bannocks, Sheep-Eaters, &c., which were supposed to be roving about. We were, however, thrown in contact principally with the inhabitants of the Eastern Shoshone Agency, at Camp Brown, although some glimpses of Utes, from the Uintah Valley Agency, Utah, were obtained at Fort Bridger and in its vicinity. Fifteen Shoshone scouts were enlisted for the expedition at Camp Brown, who accompanied us during the remainder of the trip, taking with them their families and all their possessions, including a large number of horses. We also passed two days in the neighborhood of Washakie's camp, south of the Stinking Water River, whither he had preceded us with the greater part of his band, for the purpose of hunting buffalo upon the plains. At odd moments upon the march, and when unemployed in camp, the following notes upon the habits, customs, and dialect of these Indians were gathered, and it has been thought that their paucity should not exclude them from publication, when the value of every fact bearing upon these subjects is considered. The opportunities for such observations are fast passing away, and the time will come when even little scraps of this nature will possess a much greater interest than at present.

a.—General character and domestic relations.

The intelligence and susceptibility of cultivation shown by this people is quite generally remarked by those who have had occasion to observe them, and Washakie's band is, perhaps, especially noted for the possession of these traits. This is doubtless owing in large measure to the powerful influence of the chief himself, and partly to their subjugation by the whites several years ago, which has made them realize their comparative weakness; but the Shoshones have held an enviable

*H. R. Schoolcraft, "History of the Indian Tribes of the United States," vol. i, p. 197. (*Bonacks, usually written Bannocks.*)

reputation, with some few exceptions, since the date of the early explorations, notwithstanding the warlike propensities of the allied Comanches, and the degradation of many of the related Pa-Utes. Catlin writes: "Of the Shoshones and Shosokies (Root-Diggers, Yampa-tickaras, [or Pa-Utes? T. B. C.]) all travelers who have spoken of them give them a good character, as a kind and hospitable and harmless people,"* and he cites in proof Rev. Mr. Parker, ("Tour across the Rocky Mountains,") Lewis and Clarke, and Captain Bonneville. "In their domestic relations," as Dr. Carter observes, "there are often cases of tender affection, and I firmly believe them as devoted to each other in all that is practical as are more enlightened nations." The Army officers accompanying our expedition, most of whom were familiar with the habits and customs of other tribes in the West, often expressed great surprise at the numerous exhibitions of paternal and conjugal love which were openly displayed without embarrassment or apparent sense of condescension. While, as is usual among Indians, the squaws belonging to our scouting party were given the charge of domestic affairs, including the packing of luggage and the driving of the animals on the march, young children, especially the boys, were quite commonly carried long distances in their fathers' arms, or in front of them on the saddle, and it was very common to see one or more of the braves strolling about in our camps with their sons tenderly clasped in their arms. Very often, when rough shelters of boughs were made, the material was cut and brought to the spot by the men, and many little acts of kindness of a similar nature were frequently noticed. Cheerfulness and gayety, approaching even to wittiness, are prominent traits of the Shoshone character. An amusing instance occurred on the return-trip shortly before reaching Camp Brown which is worth relating as an illustration of the keen sense of humor often manifested among them. Pínatsi, who was so frequently an attendant of the writer as to earn the appellation of his "man Friday," was riding quietly by my side, when I very soberly asked him, by way of a jest, "Pínatsi, aren't you an arrant humbug?" Without apprehending the question, as he understood English but little, he immediately replied, "Yes, Gum-stóck," (his pronunciation of Comstock.) The derisive shouts of those of our party who were near convinced him of his blunder, when he almost instantly retaliated by putting to me a question in Shoshone, which I answered as unwittingly, bringing down storms of good-natured laughter from his little party upon my own devoted head.

The affections are developed early. One of the little girls of our party carried about with her almost constantly a diminutive "papoose" case, containing a doll with a china head, bestowing much care and attention upon it.

b.—Traditions, legends, and beliefs.

It is always difficult to obtain accurate information regarding the traditions of Indian tribes, and it is somewhat remarkable that this method of preserving history is believed to be almost unemployed among the various divisions of the great Shoshonee Group. This fact, no doubt, has an important bearing upon their capacity for civilization, and their willingness to adopt the manners of the whites with whom they may be associated. Concerning the Comanches, Mr. David G. Burnet remarks that they "have a loose tradition that they came from

* G. Catlin, "North American Indians," 1845, vol. ii, p. 113.

the north."* Jesse Chisholm, a Cherokee, who had lived among them, stated that "his intercourse with the Comanches had impressed him with a high opinion of their intellect. * * * They have an unwavering confidence in the Good Spirit."† Robert S. Neighbors writes: "The Comanches believe they have always lived near the same country they now occupy, and they know of but one migration of their tribes, many years ago, when they traveled from the west and met with what they termed 'Mountain Spaniards' in the mountains of New Mexico. They lived with them many years and intermarried with each other. The first chief they recollect was Ish-shee-shú, (Wolf House,) a great and wise chief. They then lived in Mexico. From thence they visited the prairies for hunting and intermarried with the Wacos, Tah-wac-carros, Torinash, and branches of the Pawnee tribes. * * * When they came from the west there were no people living in Texas. * * * * The first whites they saw were west of the Rio Grande del Norte."‡ He also states that they are "superstitious and worship the Great Spirit, and the sun, moon, and earth." Their "shields are made in imitation of the sun, and before going to war they are stuck upon their lances, facing the rising sun, and no person is permitted to handle or touch them except their owners."

Adam Johnston § says of the Bonaks, (Bannocks,) or Root-Diggers: ‖ "In all my researches among the Indians of this country, I have not found a single relic to mark the past. * * * They seem to have lived in this simple style for ages past, depending on the natural products of the earth for subsistence, and without a single means of recording thought or action—without idols, sacrifices, prayers, or priests."

In the main these statements coincide so nearly with the results of personal observations among the Eastern Shoshones, as to warrant the supposition that these scattered tribes are nearly related, even without the confirmation afforded by similarity of language. Dr. J. Van A. Carter writes me from Fort Bridger as follows: "I have often searched for legends and the like, but without finding any which I regarded as reliably Indian. There was always something to suggest unbelief in the legend or tradition being purely their own—something to stamp it as originally from the fertile brain of some poet or novelist, which had gotten to the Indians by legend-hunters leaving with them what they couldn't honestly find among them. As far as I can see, there is no poetry among them."

Legend of the Gray Bull.—The only legend which we were able to secure, is one which is current in the neighborhood of Camp Brown. It was first obtained from officers at the post, and afterward freely related by intelligent Indians without material alteration, but it could not be certainly ascertained whether it at first came from the imagination of white men or Indians. Some four miles or less above Camps 21 and 22, a stream known as Bull Lake Fork enters Wind River from the right bank. This stream passes down from the mountains through a continuous cañon, without a side channel for several miles. Soon after pass-

* In Schoolcraft's, "History, &c., of Indian Tribes," vol. i, p. 229.

† "Pacific R. R. Reports," vol. iii, part III, p. 35.

‡ H. R. Schoolcraft, *op. cit.*, vol. ii, p. 126.

§ Schoolcraft, *op. cit.*, vol. iv, p. 226.

‖ The term *Root-Diggers*, originally applied to a tribe called Shoshokies, living just west of the Rocky Mountains, in the present Territory of Idaho, has become very indefinite, and it is used indiscriminately to designate the poorer classes of several tribes of Utes and Shoshones, who wander on foot, and are often compelled to subsist upon roots. Their more fortunate brethren call them Yampa-Tickara, (literally, *Root-Eaters*.)

ing through the skirting ridge of Carboniferous limestone, it becomes swollen into a beautiful sheet of water called Bull Lake, or sometimes Gray Bull Lake. Passing along the bottom of the gorge, one hears a low, roaring sound, not unpleasant, caused by the echo from the rushing water, which passes over a series of low cascades near the outlet of the lake. The northern shore of the lake is walled in by a precipitous and rocky bluff, clothed with a thickly scattered growth of scrawling cedar bushes. The legend has it that an old Indian, at midnight, in hot pursuit of a gray bull buffalo, finally drives him down the steep into the water, where the hunter also follows him, and bull, rider, and horse all disappear together. The roarings are supposed to be the dying groans of the vanquished buffalo.

This lake and stream have no connection with the Gray Bull River beyond the Owl Creek Mountains, and it is not impossible that there is some slight confusion in the Indian geography, provided the legend be legitimate.

The Shoshones appear to believe in the Great Spirit, (Tam Apa = *Thou* (?) *Father*,) and to have faith in what may, perhaps, be appropriately styled a rude spiritual philosophy, though the almost entire absence of traditions and legends seems to place them in a peculiarly receptive condition with respect to modifications of belief from time to time. A single illustration of each proposition will suffice to show this more clearly. The dead are usually buried in such a manner as to allow of the return of the spirits to visit their friends, as they say; *i. e.*, by covering their bodies loosely with small stones. It is reported that their "Medicine-Man" once told them that the barking of dogs by night would drive away the spirits of the departed, whereupon these animals were excluded from the camp. This is remarkable indeed, for, as Catlin remarks, dogs "seem to be so near an Indian's heart, as almost to constitute a material link of his existence."* Dogs are again coming into use with them, however, and they now have about half a dozen in the whole band, of which mention is made beyond. These Indians seem very superstitious and are much given to the use of charms and various forms of "Medicine," as it is termed.

c.—*Emotional expression.*

Advantage was taken of the presence of our scouts and their families to observe somewhat closely the character of the men, with their unconscious modes of expression of emotions called out by varying circumstances. It will be understood that the notes under this head are the results of studies of individuals *selected* for their peculiar fitness for the duties imposed upon them, for which reason we can scarcely regard them as representatives of the average of the tribe to which they belong, but rather above the medium standard.

I frequently noticed the children crying and shedding copious tears, with expressions similar to those of white children in like cases. Laughter was very common, both among young and old, its only peculiarities being the very numerous and trifling exciting causes, and its grunting, or guttural, and explosive nature. The voices of the men and women are more nearly alike in pitch than is often found among civilized races.† I never saw anything approaching a kiss, though our Indians were quite affectionate compared with other tribes; nor did I notice the habit of shrugging the shoulders, said to be prevalent with some Indians. Whistling, also, was unobserved. Pouting, with great protrusion of

* G. Catlin, "North American Indians," vol. i, p. 88.
† See "Medicine Song," illustrated, beyond.

the lips, is common with the children when crying or sulky. I have also noticed among the children, particularly with two above fifteen years of age, a look of sullen obstinacy when noticed or patronized by the whites, which is quite different from the usual smiling greeting of the men and women. Can it be that this is an inherited trait? The Shoshones were more or less hostile a few years since, and it may be remarked that this expression was much less common on the faces of the youngest children. "Knitting of the brows," or frowning, was repeatedly observed when an Indian was puzzled, accompanied by a rapid winking of the eyelids, when confused or embarrassed. This incessant winking conveyed to me the idea of embarrassment more than anything else. The expression was not noticed to a great degree, except in the cases of those who were markedly particular in the observance of habits of order and neatness, and other approaches to the refinements of civilization. Such actions would have a tendency to develop a feeling of self-consciousness, which is one great cause of embarrassment. This feeling would probably be more intense in the case of a partially civilized tribe like the Shoshones, for the Indian would have a strong consciousness of being observed, not only by the whites, but also by the members of his own band. Washakie, whose endeavors to introduce the benefits of civilization among his followers entitle him to rank as a real reformer, is a great winker at times. Pínatsi came to my tent while in Camp 31, to reconnoiter. I wrote my name upon a slip of paper, which he took and examined very intently with knitted brow and a confused expression, in which the emotions of doubt, wonder, envy, and perplexity seemed to be but imperfectly conquered by the (to the Indian) stronger emotions of pride and conceit. This peculiar complex expression was often exhibited by the features of this person, more or less modified by the circumstances. When strongly manifested, it gave to his countenance a remarkably perplexed appearance, and, to a certain degree, it betrayed the comparative weakness of his intellect. The same expression, similarly induced, was observed upon the faces of other Indians, and the variations produced by the prevailing traits of their characters were quite striking. In the case of John Le Claire, (French half-breed,) one of the most intelligent of our guides, the prevailing emotion was rather that of disgust or pity, or occasionally even of contempt or conceit. With Luisant, (another French half-breed, very intelligent,) who was affectionate and fond of praise, but very proud at times, this expression was commonly a queer mixture of humility and fear, with a faint lurking sign of suspicion. Tô'*g*ôte, (Mountain Shoshone, or "Sheep-eater" band,) who was rather looked down upon by his companions, on such occasions usually appeared considerably annoyed, but careless, as if habitually accustomed to difficulties, but yet conscious that he was then of much importance on account of his superior knowledge of the country through which he was guiding us. Ná-kŏk, (half-breed,) when thus excited, assumed an air as of conscious superiority, mingled with condescension.

d.—Government, social customs, regulations, etc.

The political economy of this people is comparatively simple, but apparently very effective in a band which numbers barely three hundred warriors. The office of chief is elective, and the popular vote is almost invariably in the favor of the most capable man. Petty chiefs, usually men of some special ability, are not uncommon. Ná-kŏk at one time possessed much influence, which was much lessened by a serious defeat in a fight with the whites on Bear River, several years ago, from which he escaped with the loss of an eye. John Le Claire had a bright-looking boy, of whom he was very fond, who was frequently mentioned by others of our scouting-party as a prospective candidate for the highest office. Washakie's influence is very great indeed, which is not matter of surprise, for his physiognomy indicates an intellect of no mean order. He has steadily favored the civilization of his tribe as far as possible, and lives himself in a neat log house when at Camp Brown. He told Captain Jones that he was dissatisfied with a roving life, and he has since determined to give up the chase as a means of subsistence. It is proper to give to Dr. James Irwin, the esteemed agent at this agency, the credit which is undoubtedly due him for a very large share of the improvement which has taken place of late years in the condition and prospects of these Indians.

Polygamy is not forbidden, but it cannot be very common so long as the proportion of the sexes is so evenly adjusted. Of 1,024 individuals reported by Dr. Irwin in 1873, 489 were given as males, with only 535 females. Bigamy is practiced to some extent, but monogamy is the general rule, perhaps more from necessity than from choice. Adultery, as in other tribes of the Shoshonee group, is punished by cutting off the nose of the guilty female. Young children are carried in cases formed by stretching a skin or cloth over a straight board so as to form a kind of pocket, but no compression of the head is attempted. The case or cradle containing the "papoose" is slung over the mother's back or attached to the front of the saddle so as to hang down by the shoulder of the horse. Persons who are too ill to ride on horseback are carried in litters formed of two poles, with skins stretched across between them. These are used in two ways, either by attaching a horse at each end between the poles, or by placing one horse in front, allowing the other end to drag on the ground. The latter form, called a "wetedda," was used by Nákŏk for several days after leaving Camp Brown, thus providing him with a reclining seat or bed.

The dead are usually buried in shallow graves and covered with a low mound of loose stones.

While in the neighborhood of Washakie's hunting-camp we were informed that there would be a grand "buffalo dance" about the close of the hunting-season, in which both braves and squaws would take part, some going without water for four days. Luisant seemed anxious that we should witness the performance, and after our return to Camp Brown we received special invitations for a specified night, but were several times put off on the plea that Washakie was unwell and could not bear the noise, from which it was concluded that the Indians were unwilling to conduct the exercise in our presence.

When a few of our Indians returned from a visit they had made to the Crow Agency in Montana, while off with the train which went in to Fort Ellis for provisions, they brought a recently captured Sioux scalp given them by the Crows. This was "disgraced" at our camp on the southwest arm of Yellowstone Lake, by elevating it on a pole, and dancing and yelling around it. Ridiculous as was the performance, there was a wild kind of excitement about it which impelled the greater portion of our whole party to join in it with a zest which greatly pleased the Indians.

The general absence of dogs from Washakie's band has already been remarked and explained. The superstition which caused their exclusion seems to be gradually leaving them by association with the whites, as they now have several small curs which bark shrilly and fiercely on the slightest provocation. The allied Utes and Comanches have numerous dogs. In a band of about a dozen Utes (including women and children) near the Uintah Mountains, I saw at least six or eight large, wolfish dogs, while our party of more than forty Shoshones had only a single animal, which if not actually a young coyote, was but a single remove from it. This creature barked, imperfectly, much like those we met in Washakie's camp. The women of the scouting party were several times observed eating with the men. The Utes referred to above were partaking of their noon-day meal when we came upon them, and the men were eating with great gusto, while the women stood idly by or served them when required.

There was a contrast between the appearance of the Shoshones and that of the Utes we saw about Fort Bridger, which was quite favorable to the former. The men among the Utes were of good size and robust, but of low type. Their heads were large and broad across the face, the nose very large and flattened. The women were quite small in comparison. Their habits were in many respects even disgusting. As a rule they were admirable horsemen, but were most awkward and ungainly on foot. The women were roughly treated. One young buck, more attractive than the average, brought a good-looking squaw to the store to trade, evidently for the first time. When he departed, he rode off suddenly at a fast trot, his clumsy wife running behind clinging to his horse's tail. The Shoshone women appear happier and they have certainly much more interesting faces than those of the Ute squaws we met at Fort Bridger.

e.—Songs and Singing.

Singing, if such it may be termed, was of frequent occurrence in the camps of our scouts at night, and occasionally one or more of their number kept up a monotonous series of jerking drawls during the greater part of the day's march. The most of this was found to arise from a faith in its curative properties, or, in other words, such singing was usually considered "great medicine." During Nákŏk's illness a "medicine song" was sung by both braves and squaws almost every night; and we were unable to deny that he steadily improved each day thereafter, all of which was, by the Indians, attributed to the virtues of the music. Through the kindness of Dr. Heizman, this song and a melody sung by the squaws alone have been furnished from his notes, and both are here introduced with his explanations appended. (See Figs. 54

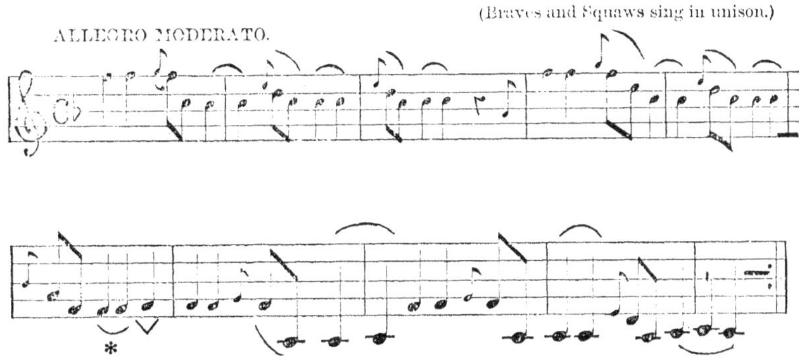

FIG. 54.—Medicine-song of the Shoshones, (arranged by Dr. Chas. L. Heizman assistant surgeon, United States Army.)

and 55.) So far as could be ascertained, no words are used with any of their songs, most of them being sung by the continued repetition of a nasal sound, very near the diphthong *oi* when pronounced through the nose. The men, when singing, or more properly *grunting* alone, often run into a falsetto pitch. The only suspicion of the existence of anything like worded songs or ditties came from observations of the manners of two light-hearted young squaws, (the wives of Nákŏk and Pínatsi,) while on the march. Occasionally as they passed me with some coquettish remark, or comical imitation of English words, which they had heard used by us, I fancied that I detected also the fragment of some merry ditty, but it was impossible to settle the question.

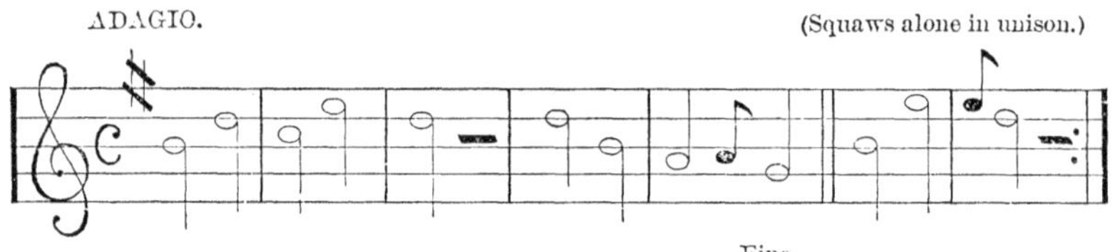

FIG. 55.—Shoshone melody, (arranged by Dr. Chas. L. Heizman, assistant surgeon United States Army.)

f.—Medicine, ornament, etc.

Among the charms and talismans observed in use, several which attracted special attention are given below in the form of simple notes, without attempt at explanation.

An Indian, (Pâka-ké-v'it ?) almost blind from syphilis, carried a "medicine stick" consisting of a slender black-rod, three feet in length, with a small rosette of cut feathers at each end, and a large entire feather hanging loosely from the upper end. Another Indian led a white horse with galled withers, which had its mane and tail stained orange-yellow, and a large feather was tied in the long hair of the tail. Pínatsi one day had a similar feather fastened in the mane of his horse and hanging across its forehead. Singularly enough, all these feathers were black below the middle, with the outer or upper half white, and they were always inverted when in use.

Paint was commonly used for adornment with entire disregard of all principles of refined taste. The material employed was usually an ocherous ore, and much of the earthy hematite from the Green Spring locality on Pelican Creek was collected and used for this purpose. The green, slimy cryptogamic vegetation from the same spot was also daubed in stripes and patches on the horses in some instances. The Indian mentioned above who led the horse with the sore withers, had about ten large rings of brass wire arranged in the fleshy margin of each ear, the largest some eight inches in diameter, at the bottom, the circles gradually diminishing in circumference to the top of the ear, the smallest being not more than two or three inches in diameter. The women generally were fond of display. Nákŏk's squaw seemed supremely happy when gaily dressed in red flannel, riding a noble gray steed, the favorite war-horse of her spouse, with the saddle girt about with a jingling fringe of bits of steel or nails. The decoration reached its climax on the day of their return to Camp Brown, when all rode merrily in to the post, decked in every available fragment of colored garment, with paint and head-dresses of most wonderful arrangement and combination. Nákŏk's favorite head-gear was an old hat from which the top of the crown had been removed, with the upper edge cut in scollops. It is customary for the men to ride with the "breech-clout," *i. e.*, a loose cloth which covers the buttocks when walking, but which allows the bare surface to come in contact with the saddle when riding. Frequently, when given a pair of ordinary pants, the buck cuts out the "seat" on this account, but our scouts, being dressed in the Army uniform, wore their breeches entire during their stay with us.

CHAPTER XV.

PHILOLOGICAL NOTES ON THE EASTERN SHOSHONE DIALECT.

General remarks on pronunciation—Phonic elements of Shoshone dialect, with tables—Comparative vocabulary of two hundred words, with etymology—Brief outline of Shoshone grammar—Compound words—Numerals—Inflection of nouns, verbs, etc.—Illustrative sentences.

There are two not simple obstacles to be overcome in the collection o Indian vocabularies and in the study of the structure of their spoken language. The first difficulty arises from the irregularities of pronunciation, which cannot but exist in dialects communicated only by word of mouth, without any standard of comparison as in the case of written language. Even in our own tongue, with an acknowledged authority of reference, we find great diversities of accent without corresponding differences in orthography. For instance, besides their true pronunciation, the words *yet*, *catch*, *evil*, are often spoken by the illiterate as if spelled yĭt, kĕch or kŏch, evŭl; *god*, even among educated people is pronounced gawd, gahd, and even gŭd, (or nearly so;) *tomahawk* is called variously tŏmăhawk, tŏmĭhawk, tŏmĭhŏk, tŏmĭhawk, etc. Savages are, of course, much less particular than the lower classes of a civilized community, in this respect, and, as they never study their modes of speech, great variations must necessarily occur in the pronunciation of different individuals. It is, therefore, a task of no mean proportions to obtain accurately the sounds of which words are composed. But when it is attempted to represent these words so that others may be able to pronounce them at sight, we are met with a second difficulty which arises from the lack of means to fully express the elementary sounds by the use of ordinary type. It will be necessary, therefore, before proceeding to the vocabulary beyond, to offer some remarks upon the phonic elements of the Shoshone dialect, together with an explanation of the plan which has been adopted for their illustration in the list of words.

A.—PHONIC ELEMENTS, WITH EXPLANATION OF VOCABULARY.

The basis of the system employed in indicating the Shoshone words given in this chapter, is to be found in the excellent "Analytical Alphabet for the Mexican and Central American Languages," which was published as a pamphlet by the American Ethnological Society, New York, 1869. The author, Dr. C. Hermann Berendt, in explaining the principle of this method of phonetic analysis, says, "I call such letters as I am unable to dissolve elements, and I adopt one sign for each." The changes here rendered necessary are almost wholly confined to the substitution of different founts of common type, in the place of certain special characters invented by Dr. Berendt. For convenience of reference, the elements are arranged alphabetically in the following table, with the necessary remarks upon each in a special column.

I.—*Synoptical table of phonic elements.*

Signs of elements.	To be sounded as the equivalent element in—	Remarks.
a	Father, ah	
â	Sack, track	
a̮	Law, talk	
b	Big, bat, ball	*b* and *p* are, in Shoshone, identical, the real sound being apparently between the two.*
c	*Buch*, (German, ch)	Same as the *j* of Dr. Berendt.
d	Did, dot	*d* and *t* are identical; or rather, the actual element is between them, and very difficult to indicate.
e	*Cedro*, (Spanish,) *fée*, (French)	
ê	Met, pet, fret	
f	Fife, fifty	
g	Go, get, gush	In rapid speaking this sound is harsh and guttural.
g	(A grunt like ugh)	Very much like *ch* in the German *buch*, but softer as if spelled *bugh*.
'	(Indefinite grunt)	
h	Hat, behind	A mere rough breathing.
i	Marine, centime	
i	Pin, within	
j	*Je, jardin*, (French)	The combination *dj* is used as the equivalent of *j*, as in *jail*, *jelly*, &c.
k	Kick, docket	
l	Let, lively, long	
m	Mama, mimic	
n	Noun, nine	
n	*Bon*, (French,) *don*, (Spanish)	(Nasal.)
o	Hope, flown, bone	
ô	Hot, not, rot	
ö	*Schön*, (German)	Represents the sound of *modified o* in German, nearly the equivalent of *u* in *urge*.
p	Past, pip, put	Not distinguishable, as a rule, from *b*.*
r	Bear, fear, severe	Final *r*, not *trilled*.
r	Reap, trap, rot	Initial *r*, distinctly *trilled*.
s	Sad, sour, scene	*sh* must not be mistaken for the sound of these letters in *shall*, shot, &c., but the elements are to be separately pronounced as in *dishearten*.
s	Amuse, lose, choose	Equivalent of *z* as ordinarily used in English.
s		Lisped *s*, practically equivalent to *th* in English.
t	Tom, tight, test	Not generally distinguishable from *d*;* *tj* is employed in place of *ch*, as in church.
u	Brute, flute, lute	*u*, as in *Ute*, *unite*, &c., is written *yu*.
û	Uncle, utter, ultra	The sound of *û* combined with *y*, as in *young*, is written *yû*.
u	(oo) foot, hood	
v	Vast, vault, vane	This is not always distinguished from *f*.
(***)		N. B.—A compound sound usually expressed by the use of *w* is otherwise represented here, as explained elsewhere.
x	(sh) shall, shout	
y	Year, young, Nyack	

* The choice of either of these consonants (*b* for *p*, *t* for *d*, and *vice versa*) is usually a mere matter of taste or custom on the part of collectors, but certain words which have become well known among the whites are always pronounced alike, and such have not been altered in the vocabulary. For instance, búngô (horse) is frequently used, while púngô, which is quite as near the Indian pronunciation, would be considered improper in the West. Similarly, pi'apug' (often pronounced pi'up by the whites) would be thought wrongly pronounced bi'abug', which would be no less proper. It has, therefore, been thought best to adopt the commonly-received pronunciation in such cases, rather than to adopt an intermediate sign. This note will also explain some apparent discrepancies in other published lists of words of the Shoshonee group of dialects.

II.—*Table of combinations of elements.*

Symbols.	Pronounced as—	Remarks.
rue diphthongs		Dr. Berendt's method of indicating "true diphthongs" is impracticable in print; hence a different plan is here adopted.*
(ai)	I in *fine*, ei in *zeit* (Germ)	These are the only true diphthongs noticed in the Shoshone dialect, and they evidently occur but seldom.
(au)	Ow in *how*, au in *baum*, (Germ.)	
(ại)	Oi in *oil*, *toil*, &c	
Examples of false diphthongs.		
a^{i}	Áh-ee	"False diphthongs," as Dr. B. calls them, are "combinations of elementary vowels * * * which do not lose their peculiar sounds, and are pronounced one after another; * * * one of the elements is always predominant, the other accessory or half mute." The method of writing these is shown in the left-hand column, and examples of words are given below to illustrate their use. Thus the French word *rien* would be written r^{i}e*n*; the Spanish *reina*, re^{i}na, and the English *lenient*, lê'n^{i}ent.†
e^{u}	Éh-oo	
e^{i}	Éh-ee	
u^{a}	Oó-ah	
^{i}**a**	Ee-áh	
^{e}**o**	Eh-óh	
^{u}**i**†	Oo-e'e (*we*)	
^{u}**a**†	Oo-áh (rapidly wah)	
&c.		

* The accentuation of Indian words being very irregular, the accents are not omitted in the vocabulary except when the pronunciation is sufficiently indicated by the orthography, as in re^{i}na, which must have the accent on the first syllable, and cannot be mistaken for r^{e}ina, with the second syllable accented.

† The false diphthongs, composed of a vowel preceded by a diminished *u*, as ^{u}*e*, ^{u}*i*, &c., are frequently employed without confusion for the sound of *w* followed by the vowel.

B.—VOCABULARY OF TWO HUNDRED AND TWENTY WORDS OF THE DIALECT OF WASHAKIE'S BAND OF EASTERN SHOSHONES, (LOCATED ON THE WIND RIVER RESERVATION, WYOMING.)

The words contained in the annexed list were, with very few exceptions, personally obtained and carefully recorded as they were several times pronounced by the Indians themselves, and by far the greater number have been verified or corrected by comparison and repetition. So far as can be learned from any accessible data, this dialect is more nearly allied to those of the Comanches and the Chemehuévis than to others of the great Shoshonee group. For purposes of ready comparison lists of these words, phonetically spelled, have been prepared from vocabularies already published, and a column is also added to show other affinities which have been traced, and for the purpose of recording incidental notes. The greater part of the information of a comparative nature has been obtained from the Pacific Railroad Reports, Vol. III, Part III, mostly from Chapter V, in which are given vocabularies collected by A. W. Whipple and classified by Wm. W. Turner. Some words were taken from the lists in Schoolcraft's large work on the "History, Condition and Prospects of the Indian Tribes of the United States," but his orthography is in many cases quite unsatisfactory, and indicative of a lack of care in collecting the material on the part of those who recorded the words. To Pínatsi is the author indebted more than to all the other Indians for the unusual zeal which he showed in *teaching* him the words of the language, which is explained by the fact that he was himself an eager pupil in the study of English.

III.—*Comparative vocabulary.*

English.	Washakie band.*	Comanche.*	Chemehuévi.	Notes.
All, any	u'it	ô'ryûk, [oyet]	manoni	u'mîm, (Cahuillo.)
Antelope	m'boa'	[^{u}a'ntsit]		
Ant-lion, (*myrmeleon?*)	êspu'si			
Arrow	pâk	pa'kâu	nu	hul, (Cahuillo;) hul, (netela;) nohu', (Kechi;) t'xuar, nihun, (Kizh.)
Ass	a'x^{u}o			Probably introduced with the donkey; an attempt to pronounce the English word.
Ax, hatchet	hohûnik	ho^{u}ni	taka'benepa	Probably incorrect, as takáb signifies *snow* in Shoshone, &c.
Bad	kîxu^{u}nt			In the sense of dishonorable or of bad character.
Bad	ti'txi	ti'*s*txit	kutxa', katxuxo'a.	
Beads	tso'mo			
Beaver	ha'nitsi	ha'nis	pa^{u}i'nx	
Belly	osûp	pi'spo, usa'p	xapunîm	
Beyond	onu'*n*g^{u}a			
Big, great	pi^{a}pu*g*'	pi'af*s*, [pi'ôp]	akonte'	
Big Horn, (buck)	m'tsambi'			
Big Horn, (female)	tu'kuku'		na*g*'t	
Bison, buffalo	ku'txi, k^{u}i'txi	[ku'txi]	ku'txo	u'txanût, (Cahuillo.)
Bitter	ki'^{u}it	[harxkoni]		
Black	to'ôp't, (tu'o^{u}it)	tu'huft, [to'hop]	xa^{u}a'gare	tu'likx, (Cahuillo.)
Blanket	bo'hu-^{u}a'nûp			Literally, *cloth-cloak*, or *covering.*
Blue	tsa^{iu}u'it, e^{u}u'it	e'fift	x(au)'^{u}a'mök	
Bombycid moth	e^{i}pri'l			
Bow	ho-et	hu''et, [ho^{e}etê]	ats	
Boy	tu'nupûtsi	tu'^{i}nû*s*pûk	(ai)'pats	
Bring, fetch	miya'			
Brown	toganu'mf'			A kind of diminutive of to'gan, *night.*
Brown-black, or dark-brown.	toga'n'-to'ôp't			
Buffalo-robe	kutx'-êmpu'			Literally, *buffalo-skin.*
Bug, beetle	go'nip			
Buprestis, green species.	e^{u}i'ût			
Calloptenus spretus, (insect.)	u'tsik^{u}i			
Camp, town	ka'ni	ka'ne	ka'ni	
Caterpillar, large.	pi'ap'-^{u}ab'			Literally, *large caterpillar.*
Chief	te'k^{u}âni, pi'a'-teg^{u}în.	tekhuêni^{u}op	to'önio	Literally, *talker*, or *great talker.*
Cicada	kö^{u}a'			
Cloak	^{u}a'nup			Used for a loose outer garment, or a blanket when wrapped about the body.
Cloth	(See Skin)			
Cloud	to'mopi	tomork, (plural ?)		
Coat	k^{u}a'xo	[k^{u}axo]		(See note opposite Shirt.)
Colias	o'ôp't-e^{i}pri'l			Literally, *yellow moth*, or *yellow butterfly.*
Colt	do(au)'ts			
Come	pi'tûnt (came)	kim	p(ai)'îk	
Cow	kutx-êm-bu'ngo-êm-pi'a.	^{u}i'stua		Literally, *buffalo-horse mother*, (female.)
Creek, stream	o'gua			
Cricket	mê'xu-^{u}a'nik			^{u}a'nik in Comanche signifies *fox.*
Cricket, (California.)	mê'xu			
Cricket, (spider-like.)	n^{u}enig^{u}î'pa			ane'-go'nip-pi'a(?) *fly-beetle, big*, or *big beetle-fly.*
Crooked	o'nendja, pô'nde^{u}up			
Cry, weep	ya'ga	yaki		
Day	tâ'bi	[ta'arp]	tu'a'ruit	ta'myît, (Cahuillo.)
Do	mehún			
Dog	tsâ^{i}ri	sâ'di [xârdi]	xarîtx	
Eagle	k^{u}ina	[niito]		
Ear	mani'nk	nûk'	n(au)ka'ba	nanô'ka, (Cahuillo;) nona'k, (Kechi;) nanakûm, (Netela;) anana, nadjas, (Kizh.)
Eat	tî'kûp'	tî*s*kadô	teka'ba	
Eater	tï'kura			Also signifies *meal, dinner.*

* Phonetically, ^{u}a's-haki' as pronounced by the Indians. Words within brackets in the Comanche column are taken from Schoolcraft's work.

III.—*Comparative vocabulary*—Continued.

English.	Washakie band.	Comanche.	Chemehuévi.	Notes.
Eight	nai-^{u}atsu′it	nê′me^{u}atsu′t, [na′^{u}e^{u}etxo′te]	nâtx	
Eleven	shu′^{i}ma (sîmitsi) manto′gan.	[xu′mi-meto′i-kut.]		Compounded of shu′^{i}ma, (one,) and mônto′gân (meaning ?)
Eliodes obsoleta, (insect.)	bisu′k^{u}a			kö^{u}a′, (cicada.) Possibly from pi′êtsi-kö^{u}a′, (*little Cicada.*)
Elk, wapiti	parhi′		pari′	
Ephemera	mu′pô			
Eye	nebu′	upu′i	pui′	pusu′nopux, (Kechi;) nopulum, (Netela.)
Far, far off	mânû′ng^{u}a, or mâ′-nûnk.	[me′narki]	mio′ni	There is a surprising similarity between the Shoshone equivalents of *far* and *understand*, (Compare *Beyond.*)
Fast, rapid	nâ′mixa			
Fat	yu	[yu]		
Fat man	yu′putsi			
Father	a′pa	a′puk	mi′o	
Fear	meri′ya-ne′xungên, or meri′ya-xuûnt.			*To feel? fear.*
Feather	titsi′niga	si′e [xia]	pita′o	
Female	pi′a, pi′êtsi			*Mother, or of the mother kind.* One who is *big*, (with young.) See Big, above.
Fight, battle, (noun.)	nâ′vitîng			
Fight, (verb)	nâ′viting mehûn			*To do fight.*
Fifteen	mana′^{i}g^{i}t manto′-gan.	[mo^{u}eke-met-o^{i}küt], m(oi)-beka.		Literally, *five-ten* or its equivalent; exact meaning not ascertained.
Fingers	mana(?)′mo	mo		
Five	ma′n′a^{i}g^{i}t	m(oi)beka [mo-^{u}eke.]		*All the fingers of one hand.* Perhaps from mana (fingers) and u′it (all.)
Fire	ku^{a}na	kun, [ku′ono]	kun	kut, (Cahuillo;) kût, (Kechi;) mug′at, (Netela;) txa^{u}ot,toi-na, (Kizh.)
Fly, (horse)	be′^{i}mi′t			
Fly, (house)	anè′vu			
Fog	pa-gâna′kît			Apparently compounded of pa (water) and a word or words signifying dark or darkness.
Foot	namp′	na′pe [nehâp]	na′mpan	ne′ik, (Cahuillo.)
Foreigner, (white man.)	t(ai)′bo	(ta′rbabo)		
Four	^{u}atsu′it	h(ai)odok^{u}it	^{u}atxu′	^{u}asa′, (Kechi;) ^{u}atsa, (Netela;) ^{u}atsa, (Kizh.)
Fourteen	^{u}a′tsuit-manto′gan	he^{i}aru′k^{u}e-me-to′ikût.		
Friend	hánts	h(ai)itx,[hartx]	te′gibu	
Girl	na^{i}vîtsi	te^{i}st^{u}te-^{u}(ai)′î-spûk, [^{u}(ai)′ epixi.]	n(ai)î′tsît	i′nismal, (Cahuillo;) literally, in Comanche, *little woman.*
Glove	mabu′c′			
Go	mie′r′	[nie′r]	p(ai)′k^{u}e	
God, Great Spirit.	tam′-ápa	[ta-e′pi]′	pua′nt	Literally, *Thou, Father.*
Good	tsant	′txat	at′	at(ai), (Cahuillo.)
Grandmother	gô′gutsi			
Granite	ti′mf′-ana′kit			Literally, *stone-foggy*, (*mixed?*)
Grass	sha′nip	[x(au)′ni′p [xo-nip.]	xu′bût	
Grasshopper	atu′n′			
Great, big	(See Big)			
Green	a^{u}hê′nt	ê′fîft [a^{u}hî′pt].	tup(ai)′	
Gun	pi′a′-et	pi′-(ai)et		Literally, *big-weapon;* usually called merely et in Shoshone.
Hand	mo,ma′su^{u}i′ki	omâ′spân[mo′a]	masi′^{u}anim	nemohemox, (Cahuillo;) mórta, (Kioway;) mana, (*fingers?*) mana′^{i}git, (*fingers all?*) *five;* ma′su^{u}iki, (*fingers open?*) *hand.*
Handsome, pretty	tsant-mabu′ni	[txe-narbu′ni]	n(ai)ts	e′ito, (Cahuillo;) literally, *good seen.*
Hard, (not soft)	kî′tânt			
Hare	ka′mo,ta′b	ta′bon	kam	Rabbit,to′xo-ka′mo,(*white hare.*)
Hat	^{u}a^{i}bha			
Hatchet	(See Ax)			
He	sîk(?)	o′rdtsa [xoku].	einpa′	sî′k, *that.* The Shoshones commonly use *that* in place of *he* when speaking English.
Heavy	pu′ttênt			

III.—*Comparative vocabulary*—Continued.

English.	Washakie band.	Comanche.	Chemehuévi.	Notes.
Here	hîna′			Used also as an imperious exclamation, in the sense of *come here.*
Hieroglyph, picture, drawing, sketch.	mo′ra			
High	pant			
Hill, (see Mountain.)	du^ivana′p′			A low ridge or butte, *not* a considerable elevation.
Horned toad, (*lizard.*)	ama′tsingaha″			
Horse	bu′ngo, tohuetx	tihi′ar		
House, hut, wigwam.	kat	(See Camp)		Used apparently only to distinguish between *camp* and *lodge*; *ka′ni* is used for a single wigwam or a camp.
Hungry	pa′heriân			
I (me)	ni′a, mi	netsa [nur]	nöu′	ne, (Cahuillo;) no, (Kechi;) no, (Netala;) noma, (Kizh;) no, (Kioway.)
Ice, snow	taka′b	ta′′kab [takan]	nuave	
Kettle, pot	^ui′tua	[^uit^ua] pimoro′.	pampu′ni	′tsu, (Kioway.)
Knife	^ui′hi	^ui′, [^ui′it]	^uits	
Lake	pa′-ga^iri		pa-ga′ri	Compound of pa, *water*, and a word unknown.
Lance, spear	tô′*g*ôte(?)			May be a compound word; name of our Sheep-eater guide.
Lariat	t^iyu′nk′			
Laugh, (verb)	yâ′nikên	yâhênet		
Lean	ka′nebîtsi			
Litter, (for the sick.)	^ueté′*s*a			
Little, small	te′tîts^i	te′^a*s*têste [yörtîtx.]	yû′′puîts	
Lost, stray	sôri′go			This *may* mean *loose* rather than *lost.*
Male	no′yogân			
Man	tu′nupa	de′nâspûk		
Many	(See Much)			
Mare	bu′ngo-em-pi′ètsi			Literally, *horse-mother*, or *horse of the mother kind*, or *of the kind that goes big with young.*
Money	pu′e^uêt			
Moon	mer	me′ni, [mûx]	mia′gorokits	men′yil, (Cahuillo;) m(oi)′la, (Kechi;) moi′′u, (Netela;) moa′r, (Kizh.)
Morning, to-morrow.	pêntxiko	pû′etsko	taba′re^uikît	
Mother	pi′a, bi′a	bi′a		
Mountain, (see hill.)	to^iya′b	pi′aps^i-t(oi)yab	te^uitsek(ai)b	
Much	ss^iô′nt	sôrt	ava′t	
Mule	m^iu′na, mu′ra	mu′ra		These are no doubt corruptions of the English and Spanish words for mule.
Muskrat	pa-^uitsi			Literally, (*little water-animal?*)
Name	nâ′nyak			
Near	mi′tîtsi	mi′stîstxi, [me′titx.]	sagâtx	
Negro	to^a-t(ai)′bo	to^o-t(ai)′bo		Literally, *black foreigner.*
Night	to′gan	[tu′kene] tu′-kan.	tu^uû′n	tukma′rpix, (Cahuillo;) literally *shut?*
Nine	shu^ima′-ru′mit	se′^ermano, [sêmomansi.]	u^ui′p	shu^ima, one.
Nineteen	shu^ima-ru′mit-man-to′gan.	[sêmomansi-meto′ikût.]		
No	No. (Spanish, not Shoshone?)	No, (not Comanche? but Spanish.)		In answering questions this form is now generally used, but it is probably introduced from the Spanish.
No, not	ke	ke [ke]	katx	ki^il, (Cahullo.)
Noctuid moth	u′nd^uast			
None, not any, nothing.	ke′-u′it	[keâtx]		Literally, *not all.*
Now	igi′txi			
Old	xo′kôpi	[txokopi], su-kutpur.	nana′per	Inanimate, not used in speaking of animals or persons.
Old, (animate)	xo′kôputsi			Said of persons and animals.
One	shu^ima	sîm′, [sî′mûs]	xu′ix	supli, (Cahuillo;) supul, (Kechi.)
Owl	mu′mpits	[mopi]		
Ox	ku′txi-m-bu′ngo			Literally, *buffalo-horse.*

III.—*Comparative vocabulary*—Continued.

English.	Washakie band.	Comanche.	Chemehuévi.	Notes.
Perhaps	nohô'gâni	[ᵘoha'rkani]		Answers also for "it may be," &c.
Picture	(See Hieroglyph)			
Pipe	toⁱ	tô''i [to'ix]	txu	
Pistol	kivi-et			From kîvirant, (short,) and et, (gun.)
Pretty	(See Handsome)			
Prionus, (beetle)	go'nip-pi'ap'			Literally, *large bug*, (or beetle.)
Rabbit	to'xo-ta'b, (ka'mo)	(See Hare)		Literally, *white hare*, referring to the true rabbit often domesticated.
Rain, (verb)	paema			pa, (water,) *falls*.
Rapid	námixa	(See Fast)		
Red	e'nk-öp't	e'kôfte	enka'garê	
River	(See Creek)			Sometimes distinguished from smaller streams by the prefix pi'apug', (large.)
Run, (verb)	ná'menuk	tu'nes'x, [nokeark.]	nokᵘina	nu'inix, (Cahuillo.)
Saddle	na'de no			
Salmon	arki			
Satchel	mo-ets			*Hand-bag.*
Say, (speak, talk, tell.)	te'kᵘin	te'kᵘaden, [te'kᵘon.]	empa'no	nete'ik, (Cahuillo.)
Sea	pa'ᵘhapa	[pa'hâpᵉe]	otsîp	
See	mabu'ni	okubôn, [narbuni.]	puni'ᵉka	
Seven	ta'tsuc'	ta''tsus, [taetxote.]	mokᵘi'st	
Seventeen	ta'tsuc'-manto'gan.	[taetxote-meto'ikut.]		Literally *seven-ten*. (not exact meaning.)
Short	ki'verânt			
Shirt	kᵘâ'xo	kᵘexi		This seems to apply to any *fitted* garment for the *trunk* of the body, as a *coat*, *vest*, *shirt*, &c. (See also Cloak.)
Shoshone	(See Snake)			
Sit	y(au)nge'ⁱrⁱ	i''kard	kare'	
Six	na''ᵘhᵘt	[na'ᵘa]	nab(ai)'	
Sixteen	na''ᵘhᵘt-manto'gan.	[na'ᵘa-meto'ikut.]		Literally, *six-ten*; (or an equivalent word of uncertain etymology.)
Skin, (cloth)	bo'hu[pu]	[pex]		The pronunciation of this word varies much, particularly in compound words. (See Buffalo-robe, Blanket, &c.)
Sleep, (verb)	ê'pᵘi	ê'rspuidoi	opû'nⁱo	hanetximku'pa, (Cahuillo.)
Slow	ovi'te			
Small	(See Little)			
Snake	Shosho'ni			Name of the tribe; *not* xoxo'ne as frequently pronounced.
Snow	taka'b	(See Ice)		
Soft	yun(ai)'titsⁱ			(?) Possibly made up of yu (fat) and n(ai)'vitsi (girl, or little woman,) with the affix öp't, (meaning a quality.) included. Literally, having the *feeling of a fat girl*.
Soldier	to-kᵘôxû			Literally, *black-coat*; not used in the sense of *warrior*, but to designate a member of the *Army*.
Son	entᵘo'a	etu'ör		atu'a, (Kioway.)
Son-in-law	mu'nôpᵘtsᵉ			In some way formed from tu'nupᵘtse, (*boy*.)
Sour	si'kên-kemû'nt			
Stallion	bu'ngo-no'yogân			Literally, *horse-male*.
Stand	yets	ᵘarn	ᵘinî'na	
Stirrup	na'rati'			Possibly compounded of na'deno (saddle) and a word meaning *to hang*, or the like.
Stone, (rock)	timpf	(tirp)tû'pist	timp	
Straight	to'nânt			
Stream	o'gua	(See Creek, River.)		
Strike, (verb)	m(ai)râ'nîk	[ᵘe'rpur]		
Strong	ne''riânt	ku'tstaᵘi'stonets (kietû.)	kui'tsⁱe	kut, (Kioway.)
Sugar	pi'na			
Sun	ta'bi	ta'bⁱb, [taᵃrp]	ta'bapûts	ta'mit, (Cahuillo;) teme't, (Kechi;) teme't, (Netela;) tamet, (Kizh.)

III.—*Comparative vocabulary*—Continued.

English.	Washakie band.	Comanche.	Chemehuévi.	Notes.
Sunrise	pê'ntxîko-tsis			Literally *morningdawns?* Possibly merely morning personified.
Sunset	ta'bi-yek (?)			
Sweet	pi'na-kemû'nt			Literally, *sugar-like?*
Tail	*mung*^{u}ô'x			
Talk, tell	te'k^{u}in	(See Say; Speak.)		
Ten	shu'^{i}ma''nu''it [xê'-mör.]	se'ermano^{u}um-pnêt, [xu'r-mûm.]	ma'xa	nomatxu'mi, (Cahuillo.) (See observations on numerals elsewhere.) Literally, *one* (once) *fingers-all*, abbreviation of shu'^{i}mana-u''it.
That	sîk	o'rd^{i}t	pê	(See He.)
Thick	pohûndûnt			
Thin	ke-pohûndûnt			Literally, *not thick.*
Thirteen	p(ai)t^{e}-monto'gan	[peh^{u} - meto'^{i}-kut.]		pet^{a}-pa', (Cahuillo;) literally *three-ten*, or equivalent.
Thou—you, (singular.)	im	ûn't' [un]	h(ai)iko	ê, (Cahuillo;) om, (Kechi;) om, (Netela;) oma, (Kizh;) am, (Kioway.)
Three	p(ai)t^{e}	pa'hist (pe'hu)	p(ai)'i	mepa', (Cahuillo;) p(ai), (Kechi:) pahe, (Netela:) pahe, (Kizh; pao, (Kioway.)
Thunder	to'mo-yâ'ga	to'mo-ya'k	to'nâ'nûk	Compounded of to'mopi, (*cloud*,) and yâ'ga, (*to cry*;) literally, *cloud crying*, (*crying-cloud*.)
Tobacco	pa'hêmo	pa'mon, [pahe-mo.]	koa'pe	
To-day	igi'txi-ta'bi	ta'ben, (day)	au'bit	txi'va, [now?] (Cahuillo;) literally, *now-day*, (present day.)
To-morrow, (morning.)	pê'ntxîko	pe'netsko	a'cekuxt	p(ai)'ipa, [coming.] (Cahuillo.)
Tooth	tâ*n*^{u}e	tâ'man [tani]	t(au)''^{u}a	metâ'ma, (Cahuillo:) tun, (Kioway.)
Trail	no'bu			
Tremex, (Hymenopterous insect.)	a''nê'vûts^{i}			Same as *fly*, with animate inflection.
True, (to be)	î'xam			To speak (or tell) truth.
Twelve	h^{u}at^{u}-manto'gan	[^{u}ehe-meto'ik-ut.]		Literally, *two-ten*, (or word of similar meaning.)
Two	h^{u}at^{u}	[^{u}ehe], ^{u}a'hat	^{u}(ai)'i	^{u}e, (Kechi;) ^{u}ehe, (Netela;) ^{u}ehe, (Kizh:) gia, (Kiowa.)
Ugly	titxi-mabu'ni	tistxit (bad)	mama'o	Literally, *bad-seen.*
Understand	nu'ngên, manu'n-gên, xumbû'na.			
Uncle	e^{i}ra			
Very	tibits	[tibits]		
Want—wish, desire—(verb.)	makamu'*nge*'n			
Water	pa'	pa [pa^{a}r]	Pa	pal, (Cahuillo;) Pala. (Kechi;) pal, (Netela;) bar, (Kizh.)
Weep, (cry)	yâ'ga	[ya-ki]		
What, (why?)	hin			
Where	hô'gâni			(See Perhaps.)
Whip	'ni'pa			
White	to'x-ôp't	[to'xop]	tuxa'gare	
White man	tox-op't-t(ai)'bo	[toxop-t(ai)'bu, pabo-t(ai)'bo.]		Literally, *white foreigner.*
Wife	âng^{u}obitsi	k^{u}u^{i}r [k^{u}u'ör].		
Wind	nu^{i}e'^{i}it		nigâ't	
Wolf	i'sha	[ix]	xiina'p	i'so^{u}it, (Cahuillo:) isnut, (Kechi:) isot, (Netela;) ixot, isot, (Kizh.)
Woman	^{u}(ai)'ipe	^{u}(ai)'spûk, [^{u}(ai)'epe.]	maru'k^{u}a	
Yellow	o'-ôp't	[o'hopt]	hö'rbenkare	
Yes	ha'	ha'a, [hâ]	u^{u}(ai)'	hek, (Cahuillo:) oho, (Kechi;) ho^{o}, (Kioway.)
Yesterday	kint	kûto, [kîrt]		
You or ye	ta'me	na'meko	ê'mim	Used also in the singular.

C.—SOME REMARKS ON SHOSHONE GRAMMAR.

The closest study of two or three hundred words of a language could, of course, determine comparatively little of its structure and forms of synthesis, but some broad generalizations may be made concerning the peculiarities of Shoshone grammar, which may prove of some slight value as a contribution to the philology of the North American tribes of Indians. Sufficient data, besides what is given in the accompanying vocabulary, have been collected for a brief review of this subject, from which illustrations will be drawn as we proceed. The matter which follows is arranged under italicized heads, the main topics being but roughly systematized, although an attempt has been made to follow a somewhat logical classification.

a.—Compounding of words, as proper names, etc.

In joining together two or more words for the purpose of expressing their combined meaning by a single term, as in the names of places or persons, or of things fancifully used, the great desideratum in all cases is that the resulting equivalent may possess the quality of euphony, as far as possible without destroying the sense. The greater the original dissimilarity between words, the more radical will be the change required to secure this end, and, to a great extent, the more frequently the compound is used the greater will be the change, and consequently the euphony will be more complete. Thus, in the common names of persons, usually "bestowed by the Indians from some trivial circumstance in domestic life, or hunting, as mere nicknames,"* euphonious combinations are quite the rule, and the same may be said of the fanciful equivalents of such English words as *thunder*, *sunset*, and the like. Examples of both kinds are given in the list below, with their original or extended form.

IV.—*List of euphonic combinations.*†

English.	Complete form, Shoshone.	Euphonic form.
Names of Indians, (though all but the second could be used otherwise :)		
Big Belly	pi′^{a}pu*g*′-osûp	pi′^{o}sûp.
Red Blanket (cloak)	e′nk-ôp′ts^{i}-^{u}a′nûp	e′nkûts^{i}a^{n}a′nûp.
No Arrows	pâ′k-ke′-u′′it	pâ′kake′u′it.
Muddy (bad) Creek	ti′txi-o′gua	tso′gua.
Comanche tribes :		
Root Eaters	ya′mpa-tîkûra	ya′mpatî′kûra.
Buffalo Eaters	ku′txi-tî′kûra	ku′tximtî′kûra.
Honey (sugar) Eaters	pi′na-tî′kûra	pi′naênti′kûra.
Names of streams :		
Stinking Water	pa′-sama′ri (?)	pa′sama′ri.
Wolf's Penis	i′sha-u′a (?)	i′sha^{u}u′a.
Pistol, (short weapon)	ki′v^{e}rânt-et	ki′v^{e}e′t.
Thunder, (cloud cries)	to′mopi-yâ′ga	to′moyâ′ga.
Chief, (big talker)	pi′apu*g*-te′g^{u}în	pi′ate′g^{u}in.

b.—Formation of numerals.

The basis of Shoshone numeration, like that of the North American Indians generally, is to be found in the use of the fingers for counting. There is some difficulty in determining the exact English equivalents of all the terms employed, but enough has been learned to render possible a general explanation of the system, which is given below, in the—

* H. R. Schoolcraft, "American Indians," 1851, p. 87.

† For other examples of euphony in compounded words see in Table III, second and last columns, the equivalents of the words buffalo-robe, caterpillar, (large,) cow, cricket, granite, God, (Great Spirit,) mare, muskrat, negro, ox, rabbit, satchel, soft, soldier.

V.—*Table of Shoshone numerals.*

English.	Shoshone.	Explanations.
One.......	shu^{i}ma............	One? (or first?) finger or forefinger?
Two.......	h^{u}at^{u}.............	
Three......	p(ai)′t^{e}...........	
Four.......	^{u}a′tsuit	From h^{u}at^{u}-shu^{i}ma-u′′it (?) meaning *two-one-all*. Very doubtful.
Five.......	mana′^{i}*g*^{i}t..........	(?) From mana, *fingers*, and u′it, *all*, meaning all of one hand; or perhaps a compound word, meaning *fingers doubled* or closed upon themselves.
Six........	na′^{u}h^{u}t............	
Seven......	ta′tsuc′	
Eight......	na′i-^{u}atsu′it.......	
Nine.......	shu^{i}ma′-ru′mit	(?) From shu^{i}ma-u′′it, *one* (lacking from) *all*.
Ten........	shu′^{i}ma′′nu′^{i}t......	From shu^{i}ma-mana-u′′it, *one*-(once)-*fingers all*, (all the digits open.)
Eleven.....	shu^{i}ma-manto′gan	Shu^{i}ma-mana-togan, *one-fingers night*, (shut,) meaning *fingers shut—then one;* referring to the closing of the fingers before counting the second set of tens.
Twelve to nineteen.	....	The remaining numerals to nineteen, inclusive, are formed by suffixing manto′gan, in the place of ten, to the digits in succession: as, p(ai)′t^{e}-manto′gan, thirteen, &c. Above nineteen the system was not studied, but it is probable that it is very similar to the method in use among the Comanches.

N. B. The Chemehuévis seem to reckon differently. Thus forty is expressed by them ^{u}atxu′-i-maxu′, *four-ten*, fifty mami′-maxu′, *five ten*, equivalent to *fourteen* and *fifteen* in Shoshone and Comanche. The Cahuillos are also reported as counting in the same manner, the multiples of ten.

c.—*Inflection; how and when employed.*

1. *Of the noun and adjective.*—So far as can be learned from the material gathered, no distinction is made in Shoshone between the nominative and objective cases of nouns. For instance, tómopi, cloud, is the same in both the following sentences:

Im sĭk tómopi mabúni? Did you see that cloud?
Sĭk tómopi tŏŏp't. That cloud is black.

No distinction was observed in the terminations of the singular and plural numbers, nor does there appear to be any inflection to denote gender. Certain terminations, however, may be noticed in nouns which do not seem to partake wholly of the nature of compound words, and similar endings will be seen to be characteristic of not a few adjectives as well. Thus the names of the prominent colors are composed of simple prefixes to ŏp't, an expression which may signify the possession of a quality of some kind, perhaps that of color. From this we obtain tŏŏpt, *black;* tóxŏp't, *white;* ŏŏp't, *yellow;* and énkŏp't, red. The names for *brown*, *blue*, and *green*, as given in Table III, are exceptions to this rule, but it is not *certain* that these terms are the exact equivalents of the English words. The suffix is usually dropped in the formation of compound or derivative words, but this is not always done.* Again some words, both nouns and adjectives, end in si, tsi, or tSi preceded by a vowel, and these terminations are not seldom mere affixes to well-known words, as Pína (Pínatsi,) túnupa (túnupûtsi.) The general effect of this addition is to personify the object expressed by the original word, but often it acts the part of a diminutive ending, and it may be that the latter is its principal use. Theoretically there is reason to believe that it partakes of the nature of an animate affix, and it is seldom used in speaking of inanimate objects

* It is interesting to observe that the suffix a′re or ga′re, is similarly employed in several dialects, and it is also used as a termination for the words signifying lake, sea, &c., even in Shoshone.

unless personified, though it is often omitted in connection with persons or the lower animals.

2. *Of the pronoun.*—Little information has been gained concerning pronouns, and it is not easy to arrive at definite conclusions as to their use, owing to the difficulty of correctly interpreting Indian sentences in which they occur. The remarks which follow are, therefore, very crude.

The personal pronouns are:

I, ni'a, or ni^{a}, sometimes pronounced mi. This seems to be equivalent to *me* rather than *I*.

Thou or you, im, (ta'm^{e}, plural, is also used.)

He, sĭk.? The Indians often use *that* for *he* in speaking English. (sĭk= that.)

We, ta'm^{e}-ni^{a}, (sometimes called nam^{e}-mi,) literally, *you–I.*

You, ta'm^{e}.

They, ?.

No inflections, if such occur, are known to the writer. Of pronouns other than personal, no data are available.

3. *Of the verb.*—It is possible to understand the use of the verb without some articulate method of conjugation, though it is not here claimed that such is the case among the Shoshones; but the notes thus far collected afford no clew to anything like a system of verbal inflection in their language. The number and person of the verb are easily determined by the pronoun connected with it, and it is not difficult to distinguish between the infinitive, indicative, and imperative moods by the construction of the sentence, the tone of voice, or the manner of the speaker. The tense, perhaps, is not so readily ascertained, but this can be determined also without trouble in spoken language. In the sentence—

Im sîḳ parh̆i'mabu'ni?

Do (or did) you see that elk?

It is impossible to state whether the verb "mabu'ni" be present, past, or future, but its mode (indicative) is shown by the mark of interrogation. If the speaker wished to change the time or mode merely, it would be accomplished as indicated below by the use of adverbs of time

now you that elk to strike
1. igi'txi im sîk parh̆i' m(ai)râ'nîk? (Present, indicative.)
(Are you striking that elk [wapiti]?)

yesterday
2. kint, im sîk parh̆i' m(ai)râ'nîk? (Past, indicative.)
(Did you strike that elk yesterday?)

3. im sîk parh̆i' pêntxîko m(ai)râ'nîk? (Future, indicative.)
(Will you strike that elk to morrow?)

I not want
4. ni^{a} ke makamu'*n*gen sîk parh̆i' m(ai)râ'nîk. (Present, infinitive.)
(I do not want to strike that elk.)

5. m(ai)râ'nîk sîk parh̆i'! (Present, imperative.)
(Strike that elk!)

The position of the verb in the sentence, then, often is very important but the manner of utterance also plays an important part in the expression of ideas.

d.—Exercises in Shoshone.

The remainder of the notes on the language may best be arranged in the form of sentences which will embody the ideas which it is desired to convey. The substance of all these sentences was obtained from th

Indians or from Dr. Carter, but some few words have been introduced occasionally to illustrate certain points of structure more clearly.

1. Nia ^{u}a′shaki, Shoshone pi′a′te′g^{u}in.
I Wass-ha-kee, S-hó-s-hó-nee Chief.
I am Washakie, the Chief of the Shoshones.

2. Ni′a ke kixuŭnt túnupŭtsi.
I not bad boy. I am not a bad boy.

3. Igi′txi im pa′heriăn? Are you hungry now?

4. Sĭk bu′ngo te′tits^{i} shanip ssiô′nt tĭ′kŭp′. That little horse eats much grass.

5. Im xô′gôpŭts^{i}, ni′a ke yu′pŭts^{i}. You are old; I am not fat.

6. Hin [hŏ′gâni] im ma′kamungen? What do you want?

7. Kint, ni′a ke tam^{e} m^{i}ero, igi′txi ni′a mie′r? I did not go with you yesterday, but now I will go.

8. Kint im sĭk to′-to′mopi mabu′ni. You saw that black cloud yesterday.

9. Pĕ′ntxiko, ss^{i}ônt pa′ema, ni′a te′g^{u}in. I say, it will rain hard to-morrow.

10. Sĭk to^{i}ya′b onu′ng^{u}a, taka′b te′t^{i}ts^{i}. Beyond that mountain there is little snow.

11. Pi^{a}to′k^{u}a′xu, hŏ′gâni im na′nyăk? Big soldier, what is your name?

12. Im kint pi′tŭnt, ni′a igi′txi-ta′bi. You came yesterday, I to-day.

13. Igi′txi-tábi, pĕ′ntxikotsis, sĭk tu′nupŭts^{i} nă′menuk. To-day, at sunrise, that boy ran.

14. Pĕ′ntxiko, ta′m^{e}-ni′a mi′titsi Pa′sama′ri ĕ′p^{u}i? Will we sleep near the Stinking Water to-morrow?

15. Mi′tits^{i} sĭk ka′ni, kint, kutxim-bu′ngo-em-pi′a tibits ss^{i}ŏnt? Were there very many cows near that camp yesterday?

16. Im kĭ′vi-et tibits tsant, ni′a e^{i}ra te′g^{u}in. My uncle says your pistol is very good.

17. Tu′nupa hŏ′gâni me′hŭn? What did the man do?

18. Hŏ′gâni im bo′hu-^{u}a′nŭp? Where is your blanket?

19. Igi′txi-ta′bi tsant, kint pa′ema, pĕ′ntxiko, nohŏ′gĕni, takáb. It is pleasant to-day, yesterday it rained, and perhaps it will snow to-morrow.

20. Im igi′txi no′bu mabúni? Do you see the trail now?

21. Tu′nupŭts^{i} kint yă′ga, n(ai)′vits^{i} igi′txi—tábi yă′nĭkĕn, to′gan, bu′ngo, tsă^{i}ri, u′it′ p^{u}i. The boy laughed yesterday, the girl cries to-day, and at night all horses and dogs sleep.

22. Mabu′ni sĭk ha′nitsi ni pi′a-et miyá. See that beaver bring my gun.

23. Kint ^{u}atsuit-manto′gan bu′ngo-no′yogăn, ^{u}a′shaki′ in-káni shanip tĭbĭts ss^{i}ŏnt tĭ′kŭp′; igi′txi-ta′bi, ke. Yesterday fourteen stallions ate very much grass near Washakie's camp; to-day they do not.

24. Nohŏ′gâni im i′xam nohŏ′gâni ke.
Perhaps (it may be) you to be true.
Perhaps it is as you say, perhaps not.

25. Ni′a bu′ngo to′xŏp′t, hŏ′gĕni im to′-búngo? My horse is white; where is your black horse?

The foregoing sentences, incomplete and unsatisfactory as they certainly are, will serve to show the *general* syntax of the Shoshone dialect, *as these Indians use it in their communication with whites who understand them.* As Dr. Carter remarks, "their communications with each other are, of course, more profoundly Shoshone than when communicating with whites who, as fully as whites can under ordinary circumstances, understand their language." Hence the difficulty of estimating the real value of all the notes obtained from a tribe containing so many who are quite well versed in English. Believing, however, that every item which is authenticated may eventually become of importance in the study of dialects which are much nearer extermination than many believe, this chapter has been prepared, and it is here offered as a slight contribution to one of the most promising of sciences—that of comparative philology.

NOTE EXPLANATORY OF THE COLORED GEOLOGICAL MAP.

The general distribution of the various geological formations in Western Wyoming is sufficiently indicated by the coloring upon the accompanying map, specimens of the tints being separately given with their proper numbers.

It should be remarked that the author lays no claim to strict accuracy in the delineation of outcrops, a task which it is manifestly impossible to accomplish, unaided, in a single season. Believing that such a map, however imperfect in minor details, will serve as an aid in the more complete understanding of the text of this report, and cherishing the hope that it may hereafter prove of some slight value as a guide for future laborers in this field, it is offered as an exponent of the geology of this region with the conviction that it is as nearly correct in its main features as it is possible to make it without more extended research. In fact it is just such a map as the author would use as a basis of operations if he were again to enter the same field.

As far as possible the introduction of conjectural material has been avoided, but in most cases it will be fair to consider that the number of *known* facts is in inverse ratio to the distance from the trail of Captain Jones's party. In some cases the map of Dr. Hayden, accompanying his report to Captain Raynolds, has been followed outside of the limits of this reconnaissance upon the northeast. Prospective maps from competent authorities will doubtless soon render possible quite accurate delineation of the prominent features in the west and south of the dis rict. For this reason the former area has been left uncolored, and the structure of the latter has been but roughly designated.

REPORT ON MINERAL AND THERMAL WATERS.

BY ASSISTANT SURGEON C. L. HEIZMANN, U. S. A.

QUALITATIVE ANALYSES OF RIVER AND SPRING WATERS, SPRING DEPOSITS, ETC.—THERAPEUTICAL CONSIDERATIONS.

SIR: I have the honor to submit the following report of analyses of spring and stream waters, &c., examined *en route* during the summer of 1873 to and from the headwaters of the Yellowstone River through Northwestern Wyoming Territory, together with general observations of the medicinal qualities of the springs within the section known as the National Park.

As a thorough description of the trails and surrounding country will be included in the topographical and geological reports of the expedition under your charge, I confine myself to allusions to the former in localizing waters, and advise references to the latter for particular geological features, instead of incorporating in the report a reiterated account of the route. The date and number of the camp, therefore, will serve to fix the geographical position of streams and springs as well as to guide to the correct appreciation of the natural relations. Moreover, the thermometrical record, which is of the greatest import in the proper estimation of the medicinal value of a water, will be found very incomplete; this on account of the desultory character of observations, necessitated always in a comparatively new and unexplored country. However, the meteorological report of this expedition can be consulted, but it must be remembered that careful readings of instruments for a day or a month in one place are now-a-days deemed insufficient for a strict understanding of climate and its influences. Reference can also be made to the excellent reports and tabulated statements of Dr. A. C. Peale in Hayden's Reports of the United States Geological Survey for 1871 and 1872.

In consequence, and to make easy by a connected account, I have adopted the field system, a recital of observations and notes day after day. A few general quantitative analyses, however, subsequently made, are thought necessary to be incorporated in the body of the report. After our return, I found in Hayden's Report for 1872 analyses of deposits which cover a great deal of the ground of the Yellowstone Basin, and you will find, therefore, that I have only noticed such as have some special relation to a water or have not been analyzed before.

Our journey from Fort Bridger, through South Pass, to Camp Stambaugh, (June 12 to June 24,) over one of the well-worn overland emigrant-routes, crossed the eastern section of the Green River Basin, which is mainly traversed by Green River and five of its branches. All of these streams were greatly swollen and they impeded our progress, particularly the Sandys, whose origin is in the foot-hills of the Wind River Mountains, and which, then violent torrents, in September following had an insignificant flow. The water of these streams at neither period is acid nor alkaline, though bitter to the taste, and causing a burning sensation to the skin. One fluid-ounce of the water of the Little Sandy contained in suspension one-half grain of sand, all of which deposited one hour after standing. The reactions of the clear water showed only the presence of magnesia and sulphuric acid. A bit of the so-called " alkali dust," a white or grayish deposit taken from the banks of this stream, contained lime, magnesia, iron, alumina, sulphuric and carbonic acid, and silica.

Here (June 21) was first noticed a peculiar behavior of the blue litmus-paper used in testing, that of showing after immersion and short exposure to the air an acid reaction; even after wetted with ammonia-water it turned red after a few seconds free exposure.

Ozone papers became of a deep brown color in a few hours, and thus accounted for the phenomenon, which was verified afterward at Camp Stambaugh, and the higher localities of the route, before entering the Yellowstone Valley.

The waters of the Sweetwater, (June 23,) of the streams supplying, and those about Camp Stambaugh, (June 24, July 1,) viz, Beaver, Twin Creek, Little and Big Popo-agie, at this season, and at the points crossed, were pure mountain-streams, exhibiting no reaction though they carried different amounts of sand. In contrast the valley (5,560 feet above sea-level) of the Little Wind River furnished novelties, and I think my regret on leaving it was shared by all of the members of the expedition. The abundance of material for the geologist, botanist, and meteorologist in it makes it a desirable point for their work; and I have no doubt of its possessing advantages for study and discovery for the medical hydrologist, excluding the sources already known there—one large sulphureted lime, (*sulphuric* calcique,) several cold sulphurous springs, and one carbureted and oil spring—but including its mild and invariable climate of summer, (mean average temperature for July, August, and September, 1873, 62°,) and its beautiful surroundings.

The sulphureted-lime spring, two and a half miles from Camp Brown and near the bed of Little Wind River, into which its water flows in a not insignificant stream, is elliptical shaped, (315 feet and 250 feet diameters,) neutral, and contains free carbonic acid, (abundant,) sulphuric acid gas, lime, magnesia, soda, sulphates, chlorides.

Its deposit, hard, stratified, yellowish, contains lime and magnesia carbonates, some chlorine, and a little (not deposited) silica.

The waters, used for bathing only, have the reputation of curing rheumatism and some skin-diseases, and are similar in composition and effects to *Aix-les-Bains*, (Savoy.*) Even a short stay in them for the first time makes one weak, dizzy, and nauseated; afterward, however, after a sensation of depression (rapid beating of the heart) there occur agreeable feelings of cleanliness and strength with mild thirst. The following observations of temperature, taken by Dr. Thomas G. Maghee, United States Army, are interesting:

*Vide Barrault, Eaux Minerales.

Date.	Daily mean, in degrees Fahrenheit.	Temperature of the Hot Springs, in degrees Fahrenheit.		Date.	Daily mean, in degrees Fahrenheit.	Temperature of the Hot Springs, in degrees Fahrenheit.	
		At the shore.	In the center.			At the shore.	In the center.
1874.				1874.			
March 18.....	16.00	106.8	109	April 3.....	35.66	107.2	109.1
March 19.....	13.33	104	106	April 4.....	33.66	104.2	106.2
March 20.....	24.33	107	108.8	April 5.....	29.33	105.4	108
March 21.....	18.00	107.8	109	April 6.....	24.00	108.8	109.9
March 22.....	24.33	106.4	109.4	April 7.....	33.33	108.4	110.1
March 23.....	29.66	107.2	109.8	April 8.....	38.66	106.9	108.5
March 24.....	32.00	106.4	108.9	April 9.....	40.33	108.4	110
March 25.....	35.33	106	107.2	April 10.....	44.33	109.1	110.3
March 26 ...	31.66	107.6	108.1	April 11.....	45.66	107.1	109.2
March 27.....	36.33	109.9	110.1	April 12.....	43.33	101.1	102.4
March 28.....	27.33	103.6	106	April 13.....	38.00	97.2	99.5
March 29.....	27.33	106.2	109.4	April 14.....	34.66	104.6	106.8
March 30.....	25.33	106	107.5	April 15.....	30.00	105	107.5
March 31.....	23.33	107.1	109	April 16.....	32.33	105.1	106.1
April 1.......	30.00	108.6	110.4	April 17.....	28.00	107.6	109.2
April 2.......	36.33	107.2	109.4				

The cold sulphurous springs arise from the base of the foot-hills of the mountains, about six miles from Camp Brown. One, (Tesson's)—temperature 50°—blackish brown deposit, contains lime, magnesia, carbonates, chlorides, sulphates, and abundant sulphureted hydrogen. Doctor Maghee writes that he found its water to be diuretic and mildly laxative.

The carbureted oil-spring about one mile from the camp is remarkable only for its oil and great amount of asphalt making up its shores. With the gases—sulphureted hydrogen and carbureted hydrogen (?)—rising from its sandy bottom (water two feet deep) spring up to the surface plenty of oil-globules, which, floating, are blown ashore, and there become a hard asphalt after some time. The oil, taken as it arises, after evaporation of the water, loses on burning exactly 90 per cent. The water, I think, possesses no interest in a therapeutical point of view, as the bathing or drinking facilities are small, it being constantly filled with the rising globules of oil.

After leaving the Little Wind River Valley and crossing Sage Creek, (Camp 20) Wind River, (21 and 22,) and Dry Creek, (23,) all of no noticeable interest, we passed over the Owl Creek Mountains, which were remarkable for the scarcity of springs and water-courses. One spring, (Camp 25,) the only one on our route over, gave very little water, very hard, and intensely disagreeable to the taste. The water of the Beaver, (28,) a small stream, and Grey Bull, (29,) possessed nothing worthy of note, but a series of little springs were found a few miles south of the latter river, which form a creek (Yellowwater of the Indians) flowing into it. Their sides and bottoms were of deep yellow; their water contained an abundance of iron, some lime, magnesia, sulphuric acid, sulphurets, and carbonic acid combined and disengaged—were neutral, and of 50° temperature. The exterior of their deposit (carbonate of iron) became, after short exposure to the air and light, a white impalpable powder.

Camp 30, July 24, was made on a small stream flowing into the Stinkingwater, and formed by a large number of mountain-springs, with a temperature of 50° (air 70°) neutral and containing lime, magnesia, sulphuric and carbonic acids. The deposit of these, tasteless, was scant, white, and reacted for carbonic acid and hyposulphuric acid.

Camp 32, July 26, was made on the Stinkingwater, near which we found a large spring raised two or three feet above the ground, with an abundant flow of a blackish water of great specific gravity, of strong sulphurous smell, (temperature 56°; of air, 75°,) and depositing black. The water contained soda, sulphates, and sulphides. The deposit was made up of sulphur and hyposulphite of soda. As we approached the river, by Cretaceous bluffs, an odor of sulphuretted hydrogen became distinctly perceptible in the air, observable several miles away. A number of extinct springs occur here, but the existence of numerous active ones near, besides the last mentioned, was indubitable. The Indians stated that many large similar ones could be found at the junction of the forks, about twenty miles east of our trail.

The river, North Fork, which we ascended July 26, August 2, was fed by many pure mountain-streams, flowing abundantly from both the north and south. These often consisted of a succession of falls, sometimes of 100 feet, over the volcanic sides of the cañon; most of them, however, were furious torrents, over steep inclines, broken by great masses of rock.

At the headwaters, where the sources were attainable, the temperature of these was found to be invariably 50°, (air 71° to 80°.) They were pure, or nearly pure, as they exhibited no reaction. The water of one spring, 100 feet beneath the top of the pass over the mountains into the Yellowstone Valley, gushed from a hole in the perpendicular rock and made a perfect fall of 20 feet before reaching its first flowing surface.

The pass into the Yellowstone Basin, August 2. At no time or point of our subsequent trail within the Yellowstone region was spread out for us a more complete or effective view of it than here in the Sierra Shoshonee Mountains. Sufficiently above timber-line to meet with no obstruction, we in wonderment looked upon the great placid lake glimmering in the sun, imbedded in ridges, among bald peaks and timbered hills; a great flowered lawn here, a dense forest there. A large ascending mass of steam marked the Firehole section; others, smaller, the localities of less thermal activity; the course, entrance, and exit of the river, the whole water-shed of the valley as an amphitheater; the scene backed by the Teton range, with its sharp-cut and jagged contour, the three sisters of which stood out grandly in the clear sky.

Nor was our curiosity less gratified when, after a slight descent, we camped (37) (9,000 feet) on a decline whose beautiful clumps of pine and spruce, running streams, and plots variegated by flowers, were suggestive of a cultivated park. Around us buried in the woods we discovered a number of circular springs, 10 to 15 feet in diameter, each on a small terrace. The water of these (temperature 37°–42°) was clear and limpid, revealing a soft grayish bottom pierced here and there by little round holes from which bubbles of gas ascended at intervals of one minute exactly. It showed no reaction of any kind, while the gas collected was suspected to be sulphurous-acid gas, on account of its bleaching litmus paper. Tests for carbonic acid and sulphuretted hydrogen were frequently but fruitlessly applied. These springs were remarkable because of being *sui generis*, none anologous having been found afterward in the other hills or the valleys of this region. What relation they bear to the thermal springs immediately below them (Turbid Lake) could not be discovered either by their deposits or contents in solution. Their outlets gave egress to a small quantity of water, which soon joins the larger streams from the melting snows of the summit.

Turbid Lake is an instance of a class of many thermal *foci*, others existing near Orange Creek, shores of Yellowstone Lake, west side of Yellowstone River, &c., though the surface involved and degree of activity differ in all. A common reservoir for two mountain-streams and innumerable hot springs, it supplies a good stream to the lake. Its clay-colored surface was in constant agitation by the bubbling gases, carbonic acid, and sulphureted hydrogen; its temperature near the shore varied whether taken near the entrance of a hot stream or not, though only a few degrees, the lowest being 60°, highest 70°. Reactions were obtained for iron, alumina, magnesia, sulphates, and sulphides.

The shore of this pond presented, as compared with that of the others to be mentioned, a diminutive representation of the activity of its class. A scaly surface, almost 100 feet wide, was broken by countless springs of all shapes and sizes, temperatures, contents, and deposits, from the emission of a fine puff of steam, or little bubble, to a spring a few feet in diameter, varying from 66° to 192°, sometimes two within six inches of each other differing 20° to 30°, and containing in different proportions lime, magnesia, iron, and alumina, sulphates, chlorides, sulphides, and silica. Indeed, some of the waters tested failed to show the presence of lime or iron, and alumina. Their deposits or surfaces about them, in all cases brilliantly colored, were as various; green, (*Confervoidea*,) yellow, red, or white prominently; and the forms of them were as many as the colors, dry scaly layers, glazed viscous precipitates, and villous or noduled masses. The last, for the most part, consisted of a green base covered with white fungiform protuberances, the manner of the formation of which I could at no time suspect.

A little southeast of the lake, but in the same class, were a number of larger springs than those immediately about it, whose waters flow into it, and two mud-craters in some way connected with it. On the rim of its barren shore, unusually near timber and grass, was a circular hole 20 feet in diameter, borders clean cut, filled to within 1½ feet of its top with a steaming, bubbling, and thudding mass of seemingly plastic and drab-colored mud, (184°.) It had no visible outlet, but its relation to the common reservoir of the surrounding springs may be guessed from the fact of the hollow-sounding surface 25 feet above it, which was broken by small orifices, puffing steam, lined with sulphur crystals. At times, or spasmodically, the mud in the middle of this hole was thrown a foot above the level surface; and strewn on the ground near its border was found a number of chunks of sulphur which is nearly pure, being nearly all soluble in benzole. A specimen of this mud contained iron, alumina, lime, (apparently in small quantity,) magnesia, sulphates, hyposulphites, and sulphur.

The companion of this mud-spring, south of it, differed from it in no respect except by being smaller and puffing like a steam-engine.

Three water springs of large size were found on the banks and in the bottom of one of the mountain streams running into Turbid Lake. One of these was remarkable and curious in its violent ejection of hot water 3 to 5 feet from the midst of a cold, rapid stream. The others (180°–182°) gave large flows to the creek from slightly-elevated banks, but from the enormous mass of deposit (some nearly pure sulphur) about them, I think they will soon become extinct.

The banks of Pelican Creek, which we followed to its mouth to Camp 38, presented for the most part very little of importance until a few miles from its entrance into the lake, where were found remains of extinct springs and a collection of active sources in many respects peculiar.

From a high, large, red bank, flowed into the creek two hot streams beginning in little springs, (average 124°,) depositing the same noduled masses as some waters at Turbid Lake. One, after flowing a few feet, disappeared through a small hole in the bank and re-appeared 70 paces below, when it continued openly its course to the river. Although a few of these springs steamed and gave off the odor of sulphureted hydrogen, none bubbled carbonic acid. Curiously, the red bank contained carbonate of iron. The Indians with us used its material for pigment to ornament themselves and horses. It is of mixed consistency, color, and texture; portions being soft and oily to the touch, others hard and irrefragable; from dark to light red, with purple and brown intermixed; compact or loose; and these differences not owing to the depth from which taken. It is partially soluble in water, (chlorides of lime and magnesia,) partially in acids, (carbonates of iron and lime.) A portion of the hardest intermixed with white, contained: Silica, 70 per cent.; iron, 29.54 per cent.; lime, .13, with traces of magnesia. The hard white noduled deposit from the bed of the flowing spring, a few feet from its source, lost on ignition 9.50 per cent. and contained 75.55 of silica, with iron and alumina, lime and magnesia. A soft green, white, and brown granular specimen, taken from a spring near this, lost on ignition 11 per cent. and contained 83 of silica and other similar contents. The waters contained iron and alumina, magnesia, sulphates, and chlorides.

Here in one of the average (124°) springs animal life was active.

Between the mouth of Pelican Creek and Steamy Point, on the shore of the lake, is a chain of springs (100°–192°) some steaming, most of them with lead-colored deposit and water, all bubbling carbonic acid, and only some sulphureted hydrogen. In one I noticed the gases rising from small holes similar to those of the springs at Camp 37, and from the top of little cones in its bottom. One, (106°,) the largest, and like Turbid Lake a reservoir, bubbled along its shore, while its banks were filled like it with small active, and remains of small extinct springs. One, 20 feet from the last, 3 feet in diameter, temperature 120°, lead-colored deposit, reacted for sulphureted hydrogen, iron, alumina, and soda, sulphides, sulphates, and hyposulphites, and became very acid after standing four hours.

Nearer Steamy Point another like series of springs around a bubbling pond (76°) exists. Steamy Point, covered with large vegetable growth, contained a small number of springs, (184°–192°,) all bubbling violently, and a few holes in the side of a rocky bank, from which issued jets of steam, but little water, depositing a yellowish-brown on the surface. At times, irregularly, the puffing steam was more violent than at others. The ground about these was insecure, as about the mud-springs. The water of one spring, (192°,) lead-colored and slightly acid, (specific gravity great,) contained lime, iron, and alumina, sulphur, sulphates, and hyposulphites. Its smooth, convex bank, 1½ feet deep, was composed of a soft, green, amorphous deposit, which, after having lost most of its water by long keeping, and breaking down into a dry powder, lost on ignition 9.01 per cent. and contained a large quantity of silica, some sulphur, and the same constituents as the water, excepting the hyposulphites.

From Camp 38 we followed the course of the river, east side, downstream, through thick timber and by pure springs, and over beautiful streams (42°) flowing into the river. *En route* were passed many sulphurous springs also. At Camp 39, which was opposite the head of the cañon, were numerous extinct and active springs, the latter materially aiding in the formation of a clear, rapid stream, (70°,) which was very acid and astringent, depositing reddish yellow, and running by a great mound-shaped bank containing both the active and extinct springs.

Its water, taken from below all its sources, contained only iron and alumina, sulphates and chlorides. It is formed by several groups of springs about Camp 39, closely allied, judging by the great prevalence in all of iron and alum. Two springs in one set north of us, (156° and 158°,) each 4 or 5 feet in diameter, muddy bubbling contents, with no outlet visible, emitting a strong odor of sulphureted hydrogen, and ejecting with it sulphurous-acid gas, contained lime, iron, and alumina, magnesia, sulphates, sulphides, chlorides, and hyposulphites. They are surrounded by countless springs and mud-vents of all temperatures; the contents of one of the latter, a very large one, are colored like molasses, and have in agitation a curious intermittent thudding sound. Of the others, the shades are as various as their temperatures, black mud and lead, light and deep green, colorless, &c. Six of those with light green water, (88°–100°,) having an outlet, and very acid, gave only reactions for iron, alumina, magnesia, (abundant,) sulphates, sulphides, (slightly.) Two in the same group had water, blackish, (deposit drab-green,) boiling (170°) and bubbling so violently in deep oblique holes as to be thrown out in great waves, slightly acid, and containing iron and alumina, sulphates, and sulphides. The sulphur was hardly appreciable after the water was taken out, but together with hyposulphites was deposited in great quantity.

Another group, separated from the last by a small ridge filled with the remains of springs and apparent geysers, possessed not so many springs but all of the same kind excepting one, (140°,) which had a colorless water, more acid than any tested, and contained iron, alumina, sulphates, and sulphides, (slightly).

All of these springs tested emitted sulphureted hydrogen, (some steam and sulphurous-acid gas,) the deeper-colored the greater quantity, but none evolved carbonic-acid gas. The deposits of all contained silica in various though small proportions.

Sparsely scattered along the east bank of the river at the bottom of the cañon there are some small springs, pouring their water directly into the river. Sulphureted hydrogen was freely emitted from all, carbonic-acid gas from only a few. Their salts were the same and as differing as those of the springs at Camp 39 and on Turbid Lake. One, however, was remarkable in being something like a geyser in its action, that of ejecting five feet transversely through the air and directly into the river a thin stream from the top of a conical eminence.

August 10—*Camp* 40.—We found a number of springs on the bank of Orange Creek, which where we crossed had a fine appearance, flowing rapidly between rocky and timbered hills, over a bright orange, siliceous bottom, though its valley is redolent with odors of sulphurous gases. All of these differed in temperature; two of the largest, within a few feet of each other, were of 170° and 196°. The first (green-yellow deposit) sending a blackish water into the stream, contained iron and alumina, lime, sulphates, hyposulphites and sulphides, and silica, which last deposited in enormous quantities.

The largest and most numerous steam-jets we saw in the Yellowstone region were found here, in a gap giving egress to a small stream arising from them and flowing from the south into one of the forks of Orange Creek. Its sides and bottom, of deep-red and yellow, included about 50 acres and were filled with hundreds of steam-jets, but contained only a few small holes bubbling hot water. Over the greater portion of its surface the ground was very insecure, often breaking under the tread and exposing soft sulphur crystals, from the midst of which issued a new jet. Hard chips of sulphur, in very great quantities, are strewn about. Scattered in this gorge on firm foundation were rocks of all sizes, some 50 feet high, from beneath most of which violently puffed steam which deposited on the roofs sulphur crystals. There were two very large vents, whose action could be heard a great distance, that of throwing columns of steam from caverns half-way up the declivity, 200 feet into the air.

These, together with a few others not so large, emitted small, clear streams with variegated deposits, which united to form the main one through the gap. Water taken about 20 yards from the greatest jet, as near as one dared to venture, had a temperature of 144°, while the temperature of the steam issuing from the smaller and accessible vents was 196°; of the air 59°. It contained iron and alumina, magnesia, probably, and sulphates.

Six miles from Camp 40 on our trail was found a group of springs in a ravine the upper half of which was filled with extinct springs, where the water flowing through it was potable, the lower half with active sources greatly acidifying it. These were (contents, deposits, &c.) exactly like the last-mentioned. Farther on another group similar to that about Turbid Lake exists. A large central pond, water 100°, with an outlet giving a considerable flow toward a small creek, is surrounded by many small, clear, bubbling springs with nearly the same variety of temperature (86°–150°) and with the same deposits. Near it is a mud-hole (40 by 25 feet) in violent agitation, so much so that the mud in its center is sometimes thrown 2 to 3 feet in the air—great waves of mud being thrown with considerable force against and over its sides—but in other respects having the same characteristics as those at Turbid Lake.

No waters of importance were met with during our journey over the high divide to the East Fork of the Yellowstone River from the camp on which we visited the celebrated Hot Springs at Gardiner's River.

The region about the East Fork of the latter river is one of great beauty. The hills are broken by the stream, which nearly the whole distance to its mouth runs through cañons and over precipices, making fine falls constantly exposing their structure of volcanic rock, basalt, and trachyte, topped by columnar ridges of metamorphic limestone; the falls and rapids alternate in quick succession and give life to the scene. As we approached the mouth of this fork the Great Hot Springs appeared on the west side of the river itself, several miles away, as an enormous dirty-white projection from between two hills, looking like the slag-pile of a giant furnace. Indeed, one's impression is unsatisfactory even after crossing the river at a point facing the springs, and admiration only arises when standing almost at the foot of the great mass of terraces, basins, and cascades.

GREAT HOT SPRINGS, GARDINER'S RIVER.

As these springs have been described and mapped several times as well as a few days' sojourn in their locality permitted—for there is still a great deal of untouched material of all kinds to be observed and examined—I confine myself to a few general remarks.

Each basin is perfect, excluding such as are in a state of forming, composed of crystal-covered walls, from 6 inches to 6 feet high; its sides in columns and consequently its rim scalloped, 1 inch to 5 inches thick; its depth varies 1 inch to 3 feet, its length or breadth from 4 feet to 12 feet. Sometimes its material is snow-white, (when it has just been deprived of water-supply,) at others grayish, (extinct sometimes,) at others brilliant brown or yellow with green-trimmed edges, (when it contains water to its rim, which is either constantly supplied from a main source above, or, if this is cut off, percolates from others in its vicinity, probably through its own bottom, signifying, I think, early extinction.) The deposit on their bottoms is as multiform as the whole system of crystalization. A thin sheet of pure white, looking like rice-paper and breaking to the touch, is very abundant; little white spheres ¼ to ½ inch in diameter, with one small opening, their exterior rough, somewhat like a mulberry, interior smooth—also very fragile—exist in all, and in some cover completely and form the bottom. Many tubs are filled with coralloid crystals springing from the bottom and branching like trees or spreading over the surface in all conceivable shapes. In one basin I observed, attached to a beautiful sandy bottom, an abundant, very thin gelatinous growth 3 inches high, shaped like a mushroom, and of the same bright yellow color as the oscillating silky substance found more frequently. The white deposits are sheets of lime, (mainly,) rapidly precipitated, beneath which become entangled bubbles of rising gas which slowly molded the spheres. Other forms are accounted for by crystalization and deposit of the contents of the water, sometimes modified by intermixture, with minute organic matter, or even by the presence of large growth, as twigs and leaves blown into a basin.

The colors of the granular contents of many bottoms differ wonderfully; white, violet, pink, flesh-color, brown, red, green, yellow, &c. As noticed by observers before, the basin temperatures were curious, often those of two lying together differing 30° to 40°, and the colder, though, in general, not always the farthest removed from its source. Of these the lowest I took was 70°, the highest 144°, with all shades between.

Between basins are smooth covered slopes, which contribute mostly to the general cascade appearance. They are nearly pure white when the water is falling over them. Their structure is as various and as wonderful as that of the basins—generally small radiating crystals giving the mass an asbestos-look, (when the water flows over it from basin to basin;) sometimes a smooth surface becomes rugose by ripples coursing in all directions, (abundant specimens among the extinct springs;) sometimes the exterior is shaped like scales overlapping each other—mailed. Often these slopes terminate abruptly without connecting with a basin below or with a more horizontal surface; their under surface, then, is composed of small, many-colored stalactites, finely fringed, and having the appearance of wings, feathered horns, &c. Sections of level floor have the same structure, forms, colors, &c., but are thicker and have larger stalactites beneath. The temperatures of the sources taken last year do not differ materially from those tabulated by Dr. A. C. Peale, (Hayden's report for 1872,) excepting one, which we succeeded, after considerable trouble, in taking at the center where the water was violently agitated and thrown a foot or more high, (No. 22, 9th terrace of Peale);—it was found to be then 164°. All of the springs on all of the terraces evolved carbonic-acid gas, sulphureted hydrogen, and vapor, all in different proportions. The water of one little spring, on the 12th terrace, (150°,) alum taste and acid, contained silica, lime, magnesia, iron, alumina, carbonates, (slight,) sulphates, sulphides, and chlorides. The water of the springs (13th terrace) flowing from geyser-like tubes on the largest mound contained silica, lime, iron, carbonates, chlorides, and sulphides. There was no spouting, during our stay, from any of these, as witnessed by Peale in 1871, although now and then a rumbling sound from beneath the mound or the more violent gurgling of one or two sources seemed to threaten such an eruption.

A deposit, yellowish-green, scraped from the surface of one of these mound-springs, nearly all soluble in water, contained very little silica, iron and alumina, lime and magnesia, carbonates, hyposulphites, sulphates and sulphides. The white deposit of extinct springs near the "Liberty Cap" reacted for carbonic acid (very abundant) and lime, with a trace of iron and very little silica.

A pure white deposit (powder) of one of the springs on the 11th terrace contained lime and magnesia, carbonates, trace of iron, trace of sulphur, and very little silica.

August 23—*Camp* 44.—Before reaching this point a camp was made on Cascade Creek, which is of no special interest outside of its beautiful fall into the Yellowstone River. Leaving it and the falls of the river, we passed the locality named Mud Volcanoes, where were a number of springs of the same class as and similar to Turbid Lake. Here, flowing into the river, is a small creek, (Alum?) which we followed to near its source in the little divide between the Yellowstone and the Madison, (Firehole.) All along its banks were hundreds of boiling and bubbling springs and remains of extinct ones, all of which may be classed with the last, although there is a greater profusion of clear alum-springs evolving only sulphureted hydrogen, intermixed with the others, than elsewhere. One, near the head of the stream, was for the most part walled (6 feet high) by its deposit on small timber, which, partially silicified, gave it the shape of a yellowish-brown snaggy cone. Although not exactly like a geyser, it nevertheless threw constantly its water (194°) with great violence against its sides and 8 feet into the air. It contained lime, iron, alumina, magnesia, sulphides, sulphates, and chlorides, and evolved no carbonic acid but sulphureted hydrogen. All of the springs surrounding it, very numerous and close together, evolved carbonic-acid gas, but, strangely, some of them only it and sulphureted hydrogen. The creek above, besides being supplied by many small springs (100°–180°) on its banks, contains in its bed many bubbling carbonic-acid gas but no sulphureted hydrogen.

The temperature of the running water here was 84°. However, a tread or the mere piercing with a stick of its sandy bottom anywhere within one-half mile, started a thin, hot, and unbearable stream containing carbonic-acid gas, but no sulphureted hydrogen; of course, as its flow was only momentary, its relative temperature could not be got, but the temperature of the surface-sand where no visible spring existed was the same as that of the water, 84°. Above the point where camp was made and where this phenomenon gradually disappeared, the water of the creek was pure and potable.

Camp 45—*August* 24—in Lower Geyser Basin, and on a little *pure* stream running into the Firehole River. On the hill back of this camp, 100 feet above the open-geyser area, and surrounded by a large growth of timber, was found a number of springs, which for beauty exceeded all in this locality; some large, perfect-shaped funnels, 20 to 50 feet in diameter, at the bottom of which, through the transparent water, could be seen the orifices proportionately as large as the spring, (largest having one of about 1 foot diameter,) venting great bubbles of carbonic-acid gas and vapor. From any point, whether as one approaches them or is directly over them, their bright azure-color strikes one even more pleasantly than the sources (21–32, Peale) on the terraces (9th, 12th) of the Hot Springs at Gardiner's River. This color is not entirely due to sky reflection, but partially to the mixed colors of the deposits. A few deposits were iron-rust, drab, yellow, red, &c., and these were always semi-plastic coatings, (silica just deposited,) which, as they became exposed to the air, hardened. Sometimes the mouths at the bottom were oblique, cavernous-looking holes. A few are surrounded by walls a few feet high, and evidently are, or were, geysers. One spring, (102°,) evolving only carbonic-acid gas, differed from the rest in its sides, not sloping toward its center, but uniformly away from it and under its banks, and was apparently bottomless.

In the most active (geyser) space, the surface surrounding each basin or geyser for 100 yards or more is composed of white, scaly, siliceous deposits, is mound-shaped, gently rising a few feet, and only broken here and there by water trickling down. Frequently at the base there are traces of little basins, something like those at Gardiner's River; at the top they exist whole, but never more than 3 to 4 inches deep, thus in some measure giving to the whole a terraced appearance. The top contains the spring or geyser, averaging in this basin 10 to 30 feet across, irregularly shaped, often like the contour of the human ear, and bordered generally by a corrugated elevation of 2 to 3 inches of various beautiful and brilliant colors. On looking into the limpid water from the rim one can see that he is standing on a thin projecting shelf. The water is constantly boiling and steaming in one or two places, and bubbling great gas globules over the rest of the surface; these were carbonic acid and sulphureted hydrogen. In one case I succeeded in taking the temperature when the geyser was in action, throwing water 30 feet, and found it to be 200°.

In the Lower Basin there are very few springs with rims elevated more than 2 to 3 inches; one, however, was about 12 feet high, dome-shaped, having no water visible, but constantly puffing steam, and only intermittingly ejecting water 5 feet. In all cases in both basins where so great a deposit had formed as to hide from view the water, the internal border of the orifice was composed of from 4 to 10 beautiful rounded surfaces covered with little crystals of white, yellowish, drab, &c.; sometimes surrounding the base of these are small holes, vent probably, giving issue to steam and an occasional spurt of water.

The water of the geyser mentioned above (30 feet) contained silica, iron, alumina, lime, magnesia, (trace of,) sulphates, carbonates, chlorides, and sulphides. A specimen brought home to obtain the quantity of silica for the purpose of comparing with a like specimen from the Upper Basin was unfortunately lost.

The Upper Geyser Basin differed from the Lower in greater activity and larger deposits. As the manner and periods of eruptions of geysers have been described and noted, and as our stay was so brief that few observations only could be taken, I refer you to these descriptions: Doane's, Barlow's, Hayden's, &c., and to Prof. T. B. Comstock's collated tables.*

"Old Faithful," the most notable for its having furnished the best opportunities for transient observations, ejects water containing .14 grammes silica to the litre,† lime, a very small quantity of iron, alumina, and magnesia, carbonates, sulphides, chlorides. The pools at the base of its mound are filled with water, lowering between the eruptions to 70°, while those about the vent (containing pebbles) retain a great deal of heat, varying according to proximity. In some of the latter, just previous to an eruption, the thermometer showed 122°, 130°, 138°.

The water of a spring or geyser, (not determined,) at the opening of

---

* *Vide* Scientific Value of Yellowstone Park, by T. B. Comstock, B. S., Geologist, &c., in American Naturalist, vol. viii, February, 1874.

† The geyser water of Iceland contains 5.40 parts of silica in 10,000 parts of water, the remainder of the total (10.75) constituents being soda principally, (2.74.) In all Yellowstone geysers this base appears to be replaced by lime, there being traces only of soda.

the Upper Basin on the trail along Firehole River, with a drab, nodular deposit, contained iron and alumina, magnesia, carbonates, chlorides and sulphides, but no trace of lime.

By analysis the geyserites of the Upper Basin do not differ essentially from each other in the quantity of silica they contain; the loss on ignition, however, is comparatively small when the specimen is old or taken from the lower layers. *Vide* Doctors Endlich's and Peale's analyses in Hayden's Report for 1872. The results obtained from four analyses since our return are nearly the same as those. I think it, therefore, proper to note only that one of my specimens, a piece which was found broken off for some time from the rim of a little geyser near the "Giantess," and lying loose some distance from it, with a velvety, drab surface and interior of pearly luster, lost on ignition 6 per cent., and contained 93 per cent. of silica. It thus closely resembles in analysis the opaloid, stratiform specimen No. 2 of Doctor Peale, (p. 154 Hayden's Report 1872,) though in description is more like No. 1. However, it has only traces of iron, the remainder consisting of magnesia and lime.

Camp 48, August 28, on west shore of Yellowstone Lake. Two miles of the shelving beach here are filled with thermal springs, which extend a mile back of the lake, with characters generally like those in the Firehole Valley. Many of them are walled high, or are on conical eminences—two perfect ones in the waters of the lake, some distance from shore. The temperatures range from 70° to 180°, and all evolve carbonic acid; a few only, sulphureted hydrogen. One (80°) whitish-water, like slaking lime, clay-colored deposit, and slightly acid, contained silica, (very little,) iron, alumina, lime, magnesia, sulphates, sulphides, and chlorides. Another, near it, (160°,) evolves water, drab deposit, slightly acid, reacted only for iron and alumina, sulphates, and chlorides. Another, (100°,) with reddish-brown, soft, gelatinous, follicular deposit, evolving carbonic acid, contained soda, lime, magnesia, iron, alumina, silica, sulphides, chlorides, and sulphates. This group can be classed with the springs of the Firehole Valley; whether any active geysers are among them has not been determined.

In our course around the southern shore of the lake and up the Yellowstone River there were no springs except pure mountain, among them the source of "Two-Ocean Pass."

On the picturesque slopes of the Snake River sources occurred many springs, but of no especial interest. The springs at Heart Lake were not visited. On the north side of the fork of Wind River, which we followed to Camp Brown, was (September 8) a small, cold, sulphurous spring, like those in the foot-hills of the Wind River Mountains at Camp Brown.

In conclusion, the difficulties of field analyses in so new and interesting a section as the Yellowstone Basin will be remembered. The imperfect means of transportation (pack-animals) for instruments was often a not unforeseen cause of disappointment and annoyance in all the departments of science represented. As an instance, you will recollect the previously-prepared means to measure the gases at the sources, and in failure thereof to imprison them for subsequent laboratory inspection. Both efforts were fruitless: the first on account of breakage of glassware long before our entrance into the valley; the second for the reason that the manner of collecting and sealing in the open air was not well understood by myself, and though repeatedly tried was only partially successful—so little, I ought to say, that it was always found worthless in result, estimating the exact quantity of free gas. The importance of a correct knowledge of this is appreciated not only by medical hydrologists, but more so, probably, by geologists and physicists; for no one who has witnessed the character of geyser-action can fail to suspect an immense influence of subterranean gases (especially carbonic acid) as a motive-power.

Moreover, before starting, through the kindness of Surg. J. B. Brown, U. S. A., medical director of this department, reagents of all kinds—a complete outfit—were supplied for qualitative analyses; for it was very well known that quantitative analyses could not be made on account of our rapid transit and the abundance of material. Indeed, much more than was required was taken with us, and, consequently, much that under the circumstances became a useless burden: several experiences, in other words, are necessary to select what is necessary. In this connection, should any new student in this field (open-air chemistry, under similar circumstances) desire to know what is or is not requisite, I will be glad to furnish him the needed data, since, after discovering the unwelcome facts, I took pains to note wants and superfluities. However, in anticipation of imperfect work, means were suspected and amply taken to bring back waters, deposits, &c. Of the waters (60 specimens in pints) only 20 were brought unbroken to the Union Pacific Railroad, and these, through some oversight or unexpected delay, were all frozen and rendered worthless before reaching Omaha. As an instance, one specimen of geyser-water from the Lower Basin, brought for the purpose of comparison (silica) with that of the Upper Basin, had frozen and was mostly lost, and what remained had deposited all of its silica, as no reaction for it could be obtained.

In consequence of these difficulties experienced, and many others unforeseen, of the great scientific value in innumerable respects of the Yellowstone region, I fear that much that is now passing there will remain unobserved until such times as the permanent residence of observers is secured by appropriations by the Government, and their material preserved likewise by a properly-paid superintendency.

Chemical analysis comes in particularly for mention in assistance to geology* and to medical hydrology, a much-neglected branch of medicine in the United States, except when for the benefit of this or that corporation or landholder.

From my own imperfect analyses, I would classify the thermal points of the Yellowstone Basin as follows, premising that no definite system (prevalence of an acid, gas, or base) has been copied,† and that the numerous springs in the localities mentioned are merely generalized and do not exclude some with them possessing other characters:

For the localities see context.

Neutral and containing— 1. Carbonic acid and Sulphureted hydrogen.	Turbid Lake. East shore of Yellowstone Lake. Eight miles from Orange Creek.
Acid and 2. Sulphureted hydrogen only.	Opposite head of Yellowstone River. Cañon (falls) east side of river. Orange Creek springs, six miles from Orange Creek.

* *Vide* Geology of Northwestern Wyoming, by Theo. B. Comstock, B. S., American Journal of Science and Arts, vol. vi, December, 1873.

†Barrault—Eaux minerales—is probably the best to use because the latest.

Eaux:

1. Chlorines Sodiques, (6 divisions.)
2. Bicarbonates, (3 divisions.)
3. Sulphates, (4 divisions.)
4. Sulphureuses, (2 divisions.)
5. Ferrugineuses, (4 divisions.)

Others, like Dunglison, (Dictionary, art. Waters, Mineral,) or Nysten, (Dictionnaire de Médicine, &c., art. Eaux minerales,) classify, 1. Gaseous or acidulous. 2. Chalybeate. 3. Saline. 4. Sulphureous.

3. Iron, marked. } Pelican Creek springs, six miles from its mouth.

4. Lime and Carbonic acid, marked. } Gardiner's River.

5. Carbonic acid and silica, marked. } Geyser region (Fire Hole Valley,) west side Yellowstone Lake.

From a therapeutic point of view, as there is no recognized system attainable, and elaborate chemical (quantitative) analyses and medical observations are necessary, it is difficult to make comparisons with other well-known sources. Barrault says that "the appreciation of springs is like the science of physiognomy; two sources may have the same constituents in close proportions without being identical from a therapeutical point. In consequence, every analysis must be considered only as relative. Nevertheless, the chemical constituents of a water, the prevalence of one element over another, its temperature, *balneo-th era peutical* means, the climatology of its position, are very valuable indices to the physician in the selection of a water." In this connection Nysten (Dictionnaire art. cit.) remarks of sulphureted waters particularly, that they are the most difficult to imitate, and although their composition is now well known, nevertheless there is something outside of chemical analysis which is not understood, for the manufactured waters do not have exactly the same effect as the natural.

I made several attempts to experiment on the effects of different springs, but as the time allowed was short, nothing was determined.

Gardiner's River prings (external use) seemed to alleviate chronic rheumatism, and, no doubt, would by protracted use cure some forms (syphilitic ?) of dermatoses; both believed by residents and the invalid visitors from Montana.

However, taking the points mentioned by Barrault, I would suggest the probable relation of the following springs to well-known sources:

1. All those which emit carbonic-acid and sulphureted-hydrogen gas, (lose sulphureous principle on keeping,) to Aix-la-Chapelle. Meinberg, (Lippe-Detmold,) in chemical constitution, but not in thermality. Virginia springs, (White Sulphur.)

2. All those which give off sulphureted hydrogen in great quantity, to Bariges, Canterets, Bagnols, (Lozère.)

3. Iron-marked, to all sulphated chalybeate springs, except in temperature, as none but cold springs of this class exist elsewhere.

4. Carbonic acid and silicia-marked, to Rockbridge springs (Virginia) in constituents and effects.

5. Lime and carbonic acid, to Carlsbad, (Bohemia,) in thermality and effects, as the incrustating base of the latter is soda instead of lime. In constituents to Saint Galmier, (Loire.)

By all patients advised or inclined to be hydropathically treated, it is thus seen that the Yellowstone Basin offers all the means, as far as chemical constitution is concerned, with the exception of the unproven existence of manganese, bromine, iodine, and arsenic. The latter element was more than once suspected, but in the hurry tests for all were, unfortunately as the event showed, reserved for a more thorough laboratory analysis. The infinity of springs in all parts, and their great flow, their variety of temperature, any shade of which can easily be got at different points from their source, the facility for all methods of treatment, (inhalation, water-bath, vapor-bath, drinking, douches, &c.,) are remarkable—probably no resort in the world comparing with this region.

A few objections only occur: one, that of the hygienic action of the position. This is defined by Barrault as the influence of altitude, climate, temperature, (relation to water,) &c.

Reference to the meteorological tables will explain the unfitness of this region except for *non-debilitating* diseases, those of the cutaneous and lymphatic systems of the skin, scrofulous (but not tubercular) disorders, rheumatisms, and articular maladies. For asthmatic diseases, bronchial catarrhs, and some forms of dyspepsia; for phthisis, malarial sequelæ, &c., it is evidently inappropriate, and for an additional reason, that of the debilitating result of even a few days' inhalation of the sulphureous air about springs—a constantly-noted fact by many members of your party. At present there is one other objection, remediable, that of the expensive accessibility to invalids of this basin, this to be corrected only by a direct road from the Union Pacific Railroad, and suitable measures for their retention.

Very respectfully, your obedient servant,

C. L. HEIZMANN,
Assistant Surgeon U. S. A.

Capt. W. A. JONES, *U. S. Engineers.*

BOTANICAL REPORT.

By Dr. C. C. Parry.

LIST OF PLANTS COLLECTED.

DEAR SIR: The following comprises a list of the plants collected on the route of the Northwestern Wyoming expedition, under your command, during the season of 1873.

The numbers affixed are those under which the collection has been distributed to the principal *herbaria* of this country and Europe.

A general sketch of the botanical features of the country passed over, with notices of rare plants and descriptions of the new species collected on the expedition, has been published by your permission in the American Naturalist, being included in consecutive numbers of vol. viii, for January, February, March, and April, 1873.

Respectfully, your obedient servant,

C. C. PARRY.

Capt. W. A. JONES,
Engineer Corps, U. S. A.

DAVENPORT, IOWA, *April* 1, 1874.

BOTANICAL LIST.

No. 1. *Clematis Douglasii*, Hook., Camp Stambaugh, June.
No. 2. *Aquilegia flavescens*, Watson, Yellowstone Park, August.
Aquilegia cœrulea, Torr., Owl Creek range, July.
No. 3. *Aquilegia Jonesii*, n. sp., Owl Creek range, July.
No. 4. *Delphinium Menziesii*, DC., Fort Bridger, June.
No. 5. *Delphinium azureum*, Michx., Wind River, July.
No. 6. *Ranunculus occidentalis*, Nutt., Little Sandy, June.
No. 7. *Ranunculus flamula*, L., Stinkingwater, July.
No. 8. *Ranunculus glaberrimus*, Hook., Stinkingwater, July.
No. 9. *Anemone multifida*, DC., Owl Creek, July.
No. 10. *Trollius laxus*, Salisb., Wind River range, July.
No. 11. *Myosurus minimus*, L., Snake River, September.
No. 12. *Thalictrum alpinum*, L., Wind River range, July.
No. 13. *Stanleya tomentosa*, n. sp., Owl Creek, July.
No. 14. *Stanleya viridiflora*, Nutt., Wind River, July.
No. 15. *Draba ventosa*, Gray, n. sp.. Snake Pass, September.
No. 16. *Draba alpina*, var. *densifolia*, Pacific Springs, June.
No. 17. *Smelowskia calycina*, Mey., Stinkingwater divide, August.
No. 18. *Arabis canescens*, Nutt., var., Sweetwater, June.
No. 19. *Sisymbrium junceum*, Bieb., Green River, June.
No. 20. *Vesicaria alpina*, Nutt., Green River, June.
No. 21. *Vesicaria Ludoviciana*, DC., Wind River, July.
No. 22. *Capsella divaricata*, Walp., Little Sandy, June.
No. 23. *Lepidium montanum*, Nutt., South Pass, June.
No. 24. *Thelypodium sagittatum*, Endl., Fort Stambaugh, June.
No. 25. *Physaria didymocarpa*, Hook., Red Cañon, July.

No. 26. *Nasturtium lyratum*, Nutt., Yellowstone, August.
No. 27. *Subularia aquatica*, L., Yellowstone Lake, August.
No. 28. *Arabis Drummondii*, Gray, Stinkingwater Pass, August.
No. 29. *Sisymbrium canescens*, Nutt., Stinkingwater, August.
No. 30. *Arabis canescens*, Nutt., Stinkingwater, August.
No. 31. *Draba alpina*, L., Stinkingwater, August.
No. 32. *Cleome aurea*, Hook., Green River, June.
No. 33. *Viola Nuttallii*, Pursh, Wind River, July.
No. 34. *Viola Nuttallii*, var., Stinkingwater, August.
No. 35. *Arenaria Franklinii*, Dougl., Wind River, July.
No. 36. *Arenaria Hookeri*, Nutt., Wind River, July.
No. 37. *Arenaria congesta*, Nutt., Wind River, July.
No. 38. *Arenaria pungens*, Nutt., Stinkingwater, July.
No. 39. *Arenaria arctica*, Steven, Owl Creek, July.
No. 40. *Arenaria Rossii*, R. Br., Owl Creek range, July.
No. 41. *Cerastium arvense*, L., Owl Creek, July.
No. 42. *Lychnis Drummondii*, Watson, Owl Creek, July.
No. 43. *Lychnis Ajanensis*, Regel., Owl Creek range, July.
No. 44. *Spraguea umbellata*, Torr., Stinkingwater, August.
No. 45. *Lewisia rediviva*, Pursh, Wind River, July.
No. 46. *Calandrina pygmæa*, Gray, Wind River, July.
No. 47. *Calyptridium roseum*, Watson, Green River, June.
No. 48. *Sphæralcea acerifolia*, Nutt., Snake River, September.
No. 49. *Rhamnus alnifolius*, L. Her., Stinkingwater, July.
No. 50. *Lathyrus linearis*, Nutt., Wind River, July.
No. 51. *Thermopsis fabacea*, var., *montana*, Gray, Big Sandy, June.
No. 52. *Lupinus pusillus*, L., Green River, June.
No. 53. *Lupinus minimus*, Doug., var., Stinkingwater, August.
No. 54. *Lupinus sericeus*, Pursh, (?) Wind River, July.
No. 55. *Lupinus argenteus*, Watson, Wind River, July.
No. 56. *Lupinus argenteus*, var., Yellowstone, August.
No. 57. *Lupinus cæspitosus*, Nutt., Stinkingwater, July.
No. 58. *Lupinus cæspitosus*, Nutt., var., Yellowstone Falls, August.
No. 59. *Hedysarum boreale*, Nutt., Owl Creek range, July.
No. 60. *Hedysarum Mackenziei*, Rich., Wind River, July.
No. 61. *Trifolium gymnocarpon*, Nutt., Green River, June.
No. 62. *Trifolium Andinum*, Nutt., Ham's Fork, June.
No. 63. *Trifolium longipes*, Nutt., Sweetwater, June.
No. 64. *Trifolium dasyphyllum*, T. and G., Wind River, July.
No. 65. *Astragalus ventorum*, n. sp., Gray, Wind River, July.
Astragalus megacarpus, Gray, Camp Brown, July.
No. 66. *Astragalus sericoleucus*, Gray, Wind River, July.
No. 67. *Astragalus triphyllus*, Pursh, Owl Creek, July.
No. 68. *Astragalus simplicifolius*, Gray, Green River, June.
No. 69. *Astragalus cæspitosus*, Nutt., Stinkingwater, July.
No. 70. *Astragalus Missouriensis*, Nutt., Wind River, July.
No. 71. *Astragalus glabriusculus*, Gray, Wind River, July.
No. 72. *Astragalus lotiflorus*, Hook., Wind River, July.
No. 73. *Astragalus Geyeri*, Gray, Green River, June.
No. 74. *Astragalus Purshii*, Doug., Green River, June.
No. 75. *Astragalus flavus*, Nutt., Green River, June.
Astragalus Grayi, n. sp., Stinkingwater, July.
No. 76. *Astragalus pubentissimus*, Nutt., Green River, June.
No. 77. *Astragalus Shortianus*, Nutt., Green River, June.
No. 78. *Astragalus hypoglottis*, L., Green River, June.
No. 79. *Astragalus glareosus*, Dougl., Green River, June.

No. 80. *Astragalus junceus*, Nutt., Green River, June.
No. 81. *Astragalus campestris*, Nutt., var., Dry Sandy, June.
No. 82. *Astragalus microcystis*, Gray, Stinkingwater, July.
No. 83. *Astragalus microcystis*, var., Stinkingwater, July.
No. 84. *Astragalus oroboides*, Hornem., Stinkingwater, July.
No. 85. *Astragalus Kentrophyta*, Gray, Stinkingwater, July.
No. 86. *Oxytropis campestris*, L., var., Green River, June.
No. 87. *Oxytropis campestris*, L., var., Yellowstone, August.
No. 88. *Oxytropis campestris*, L., var.(?), Owl Creek, July.
No. 89. *Oxytropis viscida*, Nutt.(?), Wind River, July.
No. 90. *Oxytropis Lamberti*, Pursh, Wind River, July.
No. 91. *Oxytropis Lamberti*, Pursh, var., Yellowstone, August.
No. 92. *Oxytropis lagopus*, Nutt., Pacific Springs, June.
No. 93. *Spiræa betulæfolia*, Pallas, Yellowstone, August.
No. 94. *Spiræa cæspitosa*, Nutt., Owl Creek range, July.
No. 95. *Purshia tridentata*, DC., Pacific Springs, June.
No. 96. *Ivesia Gordoni*, Gray, Stinkingwater Pass, August.
No. 97. *Potentilla Plattensis*, Nutt., Stinkingwater Pass, August.
No. 98. *Parnassia fimbriata*, Banks, Stinkingwater, July.
No. 99. *Heuchera cylindrica*, Dougl., Stinkingwater, July.
No. 100. *Saxifraga Jamesii*, Torr., Owl Creek range, July.
No. 101. *Saxifraga debilis*, Engel., Owl Creek range, July.
No. 102. *Mitella trifida*, Grah., Stinkingwater, July.
No. 103. *Tellima tenella*, Benth. & Hook., Sweetwater, June.
No. 104 *Ribes cereum*, Dougl., Sweetwater, June.
No. 105. *Ribes lacustre*, L., Yellowstone, August.
No. 106. *Ribes setosum*, Dougl., Yellowstone, August.
No. 107. *Ribes leptanthum*, Gray, Wind River, July.
No. 108. *Ribes viscossissimum*, Pursh, Yellowstone, August.
No. 109. *Ribes bracteosum*, Dougl., Wind River, July.
No. 110. *Epilobium alpinum*, L., Stinkingwater, July.
No. 111. *Œnothera Andina*, Nutt., Green River, June.
No. 112. *Œnothera scapoidea*, Nutt., Green River, June.
No. 113. *Œnothera breviflora*, Nutt., Yellowstone, August.
No. 114. *Œnothera cæspitosa*, Nutt., Green River, June.
No. 115. *Zauschneria Californica*, Presl., Stinkingwater, July.
No. 116. *Bupleurium Ranunculoides*, L., Yellowstone, August.
No. 117. *Cymopterus montanus*, Nutt., Green River, June.
No. 118. *Carum Gardineri*, Benth. & Hook., Stinkingwater, July.
No. 119. *Peucedanum leiocarpum*, Hook., Yellowstone, August.
No. 120. *Peucedanum* ———, (?), Stinkingwater, August.
No. 121. *Ligusticum scopulorum*, Gray, Yellowstone, August.
No. 122. *Cymopterus anisatus*, var., Gray, Wind River, July.
No. 123. *Cymopterus Fendleri*, Gray, Green River, June.
No. 124. *Valeriana dioica*, L., Stinkingwater, July.
No. 125. *Kellogia galeoides*, Torr., Stinkingwater, July.
No. 126. *Aster Parryi*, n. sp., Gray, Green River, June.
No. 127. *Aster pulchellas*, D. C. Eaton, Yellowstone, August.
No. 128. *Aster adscendens*, Lindl., Yellowstone, August.
No. 129. *Aster montanus*, Rich., Snake River Pass, September.
No. 130. *Aster conspicuus*, Lindl., Yellowstone, August.
No. 131. *Aster integrifolius*, Nutt., Yellowstone, August.
No. 132. *Machæranthera canescens*, Gray, Yellowstone, August.
No. 133. *Aster elegans*, Nutt., Yellowstone, August.
No. 134. *Aster Engelmanni*, Gray, Yellowstone, August.
No. 135. *Erigeron ursinum*, D. C. Eaton, Yellowstone, August.

No. 136. *Erigeron compositum*, Pursh, Green River, June.
No. 137. *Erigeron radicatus*, Hook. (?), Wind River, July.
No. 138. *Erigeron radicatus*, Hook., var. (?), Wind River, July.
No. 139. *Erigeron canescens*, Hook., Wind River, July.
No. 140. *Erigeron concinum*, T. and Gr., Green River, June.
No. 141. *Solidago Virga-aurea*, L., Yellowstone, August.
No. 142. *Townsendia spathulata*, Nutt., Wind River, July.
No. 143. *Townsendia strigosa*, Nutt., Wind River, July.
No. 144. *Townsendia Parryi*, n. sp., D. C. Eaton, Wind River, July.
No. 145. *Townsendia spathulata*, var. (?), Stinkingwater Pass, August.
Townsendia condensata, n. sp., Washake's Needles, July.
No. 146. *Chænactis Douglasii*, H. and A., Green River, June.
No. 147. *Chrysopsis hispida*, Hook., Yellowstone, August.
No. 148. *Bahia Cucophylla*, DC., Stinkingwater, July.
No. 149. *Aplopappus inuloides*, Nutt., Wind River, July.
No. 150. *Schkuria integrifolia*, n. sp., Gray, Wind River, July.
No. 151. *Grindelia squarrosa*, Dunal., Wind River, July.
No. 152. *Rudbeckia occidentalis*, Nutt., Snake River, September.
No. 153. *Arnica Parryi*, n. sp., Gray, Yellowstone, August.
No. 154. *Arnica angustifolia*, var. (?), Yellowstone, August.
No. 155. *Arnica angustifolia*, var. (?), Fort Stambaugh, June.
No. 156. *Arnica longifolia*, D. C. Eaton, Snake River Pass, September.
No. 157. *Actinella acaulis*, Nutt., Stinkingwater, July.
No. 158. *Actinella grandiflora*, T. and Gr., Wind River, July.
No. 159. *Cosmidium gracile*, T. and Gr., Green River, June.
No. 160. *Tetradymia canescens*, var. *inermis*, Nutt., Green River, June.
No. 161. *Aplopappus suffruticosus*, Gray, Yellowstone, August.
No. 162. *Aplopappus acaulis*, Gray, Green River, June.
No. 163. *Aplopappus Nuttallii*, T. and Gr., Wind River, July.
No. 164. *Aplopappus multicaulis*, Gray, Wind River, July.
No. 165. *Balsamorhiza Hookeri*, Nutt., Pacific Springs, June.
No. 166. *Balsamorhiza sagittata*, Nutt., Wind River, July.
No. 167. *Senecio amplectens*, var. *taraxicoides*, Gray, Yellowstone, Aug.
No. 168. *Senecio Fremontii*, Gray, Stinkingwater, July.
No. 169. *Senecio canus*, Hook., Yellowstone, August.
No. 170. *Senecio Andinus*, Nutt., Yellowstone, August.
No. 171. *Senecio lugens*, Rich., Yellowstone, August.
No. 172. *Antennaria dimorpha*, Nutt., Green River, June.
No. 173. *Antennaria dioica*, Gaertn., Owl Creek, July.
No. 174. *Antennaria luzuloides*, Torr. and Gray, Stinkingwater, July.
No. 175. *Antennaria alpina*, Gærtn., var. (?), Stinkingwater, July.
No. 176. *Antennaria Carpathica*, R. Br., Wind River, July.
No. 177. *Antennaria racemosa*, Hook., Stinkingwater, July.
No. 178. *Tanacetum capitatum*, Nutt., Wind River, July.
No. 179. *Tanacetum Nuttallii*, T. and Gr., Wind River, July.
No. 180. *Artemesia pedatifida*, Nutt., Green River, June.
No. 181. *Artemesia spinescens*, D. C. Eaton, Green River, June.
No. 182. *Artemesia incompta*, Nutt., Owl Creek, July.
No. 183. *Artemesia scopulorum*, Gray, Yellowstone, August.
No. 184. *Artemesia Ludoviciana*, Nutt., var., Yellowstone, August.
No. 185. *Troximon parviflorum*, Nutt., Green River, June.
No. 186. *Macrorrhynchus glaucus*, D. C. Eaton, Green River, June.
No. 187. *Troximon aurantiacum*, Hook. (?), Green River, June.
No. 188. *Hieracium Scouleri*, Hook., Yellowstone, August.
No. 189. *Stephanomeria paniculata*, Nutt., Stinkingwater, July.
No. 190. *Crepis accuminata*, Nutt., Wind River, July.

No. 191. *Crepis occidentalis*, Nutt., Wind River, July.
No. 192. *Porterella carnulosa*, Torr., Yellowstone, August.
No. 193. *Bryanthus Empetriformis*, Gray, Stinkingwater, July.
No. 194. *Ledum glandulosum*, Nutt., Yellowstone, August.
No. 195. *Gaultheria Myrsinites*, Hook., Yellowstone, August.
No. 196. *Monotropa hypopothys*, L., Yellowstone, August.
No. 197. *Lonicera cœrulea*, L., Yellowstone, August.
No. 198. *Pyrola dentata*, Hook., Yellowstone, August.
No. 199. *Dodecatheon Meadia*, L., Wind River, July.
No. 200. *Androsace filiformis*, L., Yellowstone, August.
No. 201. *Androsace Chamajasme*, L., Owl Creek, July.
Douglasia montana, Gray, Washakee's Needles, July.
No. 202. *Phelipæa lutea*, n. sp., Owl Creek, July.
No. 203. *Phelipæa fasciculata*, Nutt., Owl Creek, July.
No. 204. *Pentstemon Menziesii*, Hook., Stinkingwater, August.
No. 205. *Pentstemon Menziesii*, Hook., var., Snake Pass, September.
No. 206. *Pentstemon laricifolius*, H. and A., Owl Creek, July.
No. 207. *Pentstemon deustus*, Dougl., Stinkingwater, July.
No. 208. *Pentstemon gracilis*, Nutt., Pacific Springs, June.
No. 209. *Pentstemon secundiflorus*, Benth., Yellowstone, August.
No. 210. *Pentstemon humilis*, Nutt., Pacific Springs, June.
No. 211. *Pentstemon glaucus*, Graham, Stinkingwater, July.
No. 212. *Mimulus Lewisii*, Pursh, Stinkingwater, July.
No. 213. *Mimulus moschatus*, Dougl., Stinkingwater, July.
No. 214. *Eunanus Fremontii*, Gray, Yellowstone, August.
No. 215. *Pedicularis Parryi*, Gray, var. (?), Yellowstone, August.
No. 216. *Castilleia breviflora*, Nutt., Stinkingwater, July.
No. 217. *Castilleia flava*, Watson, Stinkingwater, July.
No. 218. *Orthocarpus Parryi*, n. sp., Gray, Yellowstone, August.
No. 219. *Castilleia affinis*, H. and A., Nebraska, June.
No. 220. *Echinospermum deflexum*, Lehm., Yellowstone, August.
No. 221. *Echinospermum deflexum*, Lehm., var., Yellowstone, August.
No. 222. *Myosotis alpestris*, L., Stinkingwater, July.
No. 223. *Myosotis alpestris*, L., var., Stinkingwater, July.
No. 224. *Myosotis alpestris*, L., var., Yellowstone, August.
No. 225. *Eritrichium villosum*, var. *aretioides*, DC., Wind River, July.
No. 226. *Mertensia alpina*, Don., Stinkingwater, July.
No. 227. *Mertensia alpina*, Don., var., Stinkingwater, July.
No. 228. *Eritrinchium glomeratum*, DC., var. (?), Green River, June.
No. 229. *Phacelia circinata*, Jacq., Stinkingwater, July.
No. 230. *Phlox bryoides*, Nutt., Pacific Springs, June.
No. 231. *Phlox canescens*, T. and Gr., Green River, June.
No. 232. *Phlox Douglasii*, Hook., Owl Creek, July.
No. 233. *Phlox longifolia*, Nutt., Green River, June.
No. 234. *Gilia liniflora*, Benth., Stinkingwater, July.
No. 235. *Gilia nudicaulis*, Gray, Wind River, July.
No. 236. *Gilia pungens*, Benth., var., Green River, June.
No. 237. *Gilia inconspicua*, Dougl., Green River, June.
No. 238. *Gilia congesta*, Hook., Green River, June.
Gilia iberidifolia, Benth., Green River, September.
No. 239. *Gilia spicata*, Nutt., Green River, June.
No. 240. *Gilia Breweri*, Gray, Dry Sandy, June.
No. 241. *Colomia gracilis*, Dougl., var., Green River, June.
No. 242. *Polemonium confertum*, Gray, Wind River, July.
No. 243. *Polemonium parvifolium*, Nutt., Stinkingwater, July.
No. 244. *Swertia perennis*, L., Yellowstone Falls, August.

No. 245. *Gentiana detonsa*, Fries., Yellowstone, August.
No. 246. *Asclepias brachystephana*, Torr., Green River, June.
No. 247. *Acerates viridiflora*, Ell., Owl Creek, July.
No. 248. *Polygonum imbricatum*, Nutt., Stinkingwater, July.
No. 249. *Rumex paucifolius*, Nutt., Sweetwater, June.
No. 250. *Eriogonum flavum*, Nutt., Owl Creek, July.
No. 251. *Eriogonum brevicaule*, Nutt., Wind River, September.
No. 252. *Eriogonum ovalifolium*, Nutt., Green River, June.
No. 253. *Oxytheca dendroidea*, Nutt., Big Sandy, June.
No. 254. *Paronychia sessilliflora*, Nutt., Wind River, July.
No. 255. *Shepherdia argentea*, Nutt., Wind River, September.
No. 256. *Eleagnus argenteus*, Nutt., Green River, September.
No. 257. *Comandra pallida*, DC., Wind River, July.
No. 258. *Atriplex endolepis*, Watson, ined., Stinkingwater, July.
No. 259. *Grayia polygaloides*, H. and A., Green River, June.
No. 260. *Kochia prostrata*, Schrad., Green River, September.
— —— *Suæda depressa*, Pursh, Green River, September.
No. 261. *Atriplex canescens*, Watson, ined., Green River, June.
No. 262. *Betula occidentalis*, Hook., Green River, June.
No. 263. *Salix* ——(?), Wind River, July.
No. 264. *Juniperus Sabina*, var. *procumbens*, Pursh, Owl Creek, July.
No. 265. *Calochortus Eurycarpus*, Watson, Yellowstone, August.
No. 266. *Fritillaria atropurpurea*, Nutt., Wind River, July.
No. 267. *Fritillaria pudica*, Spreng, Yellowstone, August.
No. 268. *Spiranthes Romanzofiana*, Cham., Yellowstone, August.
No. 269. *Allium brevistylum*, Watson, Yellowstone, August.
No. 270. *Allium Schœnoprasum*, L., Yellowstone, August.
No. 271. *Allium Schœnoprasum*, L., Yellowstone, August.
No. 272. *Allium reticulatum*, (Watson, 1181,) Sweetwater, June.
No. 273. *Allium cernuum*, Roth, Owl Creek, July.
No. 274. *Allium reticulatum*, Fras., Green River, June.
No. 275. *Juncus xiphioides*, E. Mey., Yellowstone, August.
No. 276. *Carex Douglasii*, Boott., Fort Bridger, June.
No. 277. *Carex Raynoldsii*, Dewey, Yellowstone, August.
No. 278. *Carex vitilus*, Fr., Yellowstone, August.
No. 279. *Carex aquatilis*, Wahl., Yellowstone, August.
No. 280. *Carex rigida*, Good., Yellowstone, August.
No. 281. *Carex Hoodii*, Boott., Wind River, July.
No. 282. *Carex festiva*, Dewey, Yellowstone, August.
No. 283. *Carex Douglasii*, Boott., Stinkingwater, July.
No. 284. *Carex tenuirostris*, Olney, ined., Yellowstone, July.
No. 285. *Carex vulgaris*, Fries., Yellowstone, August.
No. 286. *Carex Jamesii*, Torr., Yellowstone, August.
No. 287. *Carex leporina*, L., Stinkingwater, July.
No. 288. *Eriophorum polystachyon*, L., Yellowstone, August.
No. 289. *Kœleria cristata*, Pers., Yellowstone, August.
No. 290. *Poa*, ——, (?), Yellowstone, August.
No. 291. *Tristeum subspicatum*, Beauv., Stinkingwater, July.
No. 292. *Agrostis scabra*, Willd., Yellowstone, August.
No. 293. *Festuca* ——, (?), Yellowstone, August.
No. 294. *Poa tenuifolia*, Nutt. (?), Yellowstone, August.
No. 295. *Melica bulbosa*, Geyer, Yellowstone, August.
No. 296. *Beckmannia cruciformis*, Host., Stinkingwater, July.
No. 297. *Elymus condensatus*, Pursh, Wind River, July.
No. 298. *Poa Andina*, Nutt., Yellowstone, August.
No. 299. *Triticum ægilipoides*, Turck., Yellowstone, August.
No. 300. *Calamagrostis Lapponica*, Trin. (?), Yellowstone, August

FILICES.

No. 301. *Cheilanthes lanuginosa*, Nutt., Owl Creek, July.
No. 302. *Cystopteris fragilis*, Benth, Yellowstone Falls, August.
No. 303. *Woodsia scopulina*, D. C. Eaton, Yellowstone, August.
No. 304. *Woodsia Oregana*, D. C. Eaton, Sweetwater, June.
No. 305. *Botrychium lunaroides*, L., Yellowstone, August.
No. 306. *Botrychium simplex*, Hitchcock, Yellowstone, August.

LYCOPODIACEÆ.

No. 307. *Isoëtes Bolanderi*, n. sp., Engel., Yellowstone, August.

FUNGI.

No. 308. *Trichobasis leguminosarum*, Lk., Wind River, July.
No. 309. *Æcidium Ranuncalacearum*, DC., Wind River, July.
No. 310. *Æcidium Psoraleæ*, n. sp., C. H. Peck, Colorado, June.
No. 311. *Æcidium Parryi*, n. sp., C. H. Peck, Stinkingwater, August.

ENTOMOLOGICAL REPORT.

J. D. PUTNAM.

DEAR SIR: The following list embraces the *Coleoptera* collected during the months of June, July, and August, 1873, on the route from Fort Bridger to the Yellowstone National Park, via Green River, South Pass, Camp Brown, Wind River, and Stinkingwater River; and on the return, in September, via Snake and Wind Rivers. My opportunities for collecting were quite limited, having responsible meteorological duties to perform at all times, and being almost constantly on the march. For these reasons, and also on account of the lack of transportation facilities, the collections are much more imperfect than they should have been. All the regions passed through, and especially the Wind River district, give promise of good yields for future collectors. I am much indebted to the officers on the survey for various kindnesses, and to Mr. Henry Ulke, who very kindly determined the *Coleoptera*, hereafter enumerated, for me. I also annex a list of words used by the Shoshone Indians to designate insects.

Respectfully, your obedient servant,

J. D. PUTNAM.

Capt. W. A. JONES,
United States Corps of Engineers.

LIST OF COLEOPTERA.

☞ *Cicindella tranquebarica*, Herbst,=*vulgaris*, Say, Green River basin, June.

C. duodecimguttata, Dej., Yellowstone basin, August.

Elaphrus Californicus, Mann., Green River basin, June.

Nebria hudsonica, Lec., Yellowstone basin, August.

Calosoma luxatum Say, Wind River basin, June.

Carabus Agassii, Lec., variety of *C. tædatus*, Fort Bridger, May; Wind River and Stinkingwater, July.

Lebia guttula, Lec., Wind River basin, July.

Philotecnus nigricollis, Lec., Green River basin, June.

Pterostichus protractus, Lec., Fort Bridger, May; Yellowstone basin, August.

Pt. Luczotii, Dej., Fort Bridger, May.

Amara lacustris, Lec., Fort Bridger, May.

A. patricia, Dej., Yellowstone basin, August.

Chlænius sericeus, Forster, Green River basin, June.

Harpalus amputatus, Say, Green River basin, June.

H. funistus, Lec., Fort Bridger, May; Yellowstone basin, August.

H. stupidus, Lec., Fort Bridger, May.

H. furtivus, Lec., Fort Bridger, May.

H. obesulus, Lec., Green River basin, June.

Bembidium nebraskense, Lec., Yellowstone basin, August.

B. lucidum, Lec., Green River basin, June.

B. umbratum, Lec., Green River basin, June.

Dytiscus marginicollis, Lec., Yellowstone basin, August.

Silpha lapponica, Herbst, Fort Bridger, May.

S. ramosa, Say, Wind River basin, June.

Aleochara bimaculata, Grav., Green River basin, June.

Creophilus villosus, Grav., Yellowstone basin, August.

Philonthus, (undetermined,) Fort Bridger, May.

Saprinus pratensis, Lec., Green River basin, June.

Phalacrus pennicillatus, Say, Green River basin, June; Wind River, July.

Nitidula ziczac, Say, Wind River basin, July.

Dermestes marmoratus, Say, Green River basin, June.

D. caninus, Germ., Green River basin, June.

Aphodius denticulatus, Hald., Green River basin, June.

Trox alternans, Lec., Fort Bridger, May.

Hoplia laticolis, Lec., Wind River basin, July.

Serica curvata, Lec., Wind River basin, July.

S. frontalis, Lec., Wind River basin, July.

Lachnosterna fusca, Fröhl., Fort Bridger, May.

Polyphylla decemlineata, Say, Owl Creek, July.

Melanophila longipes, Say, Stinkingwater Valley, July; Yellowstone basin, August.

Acmæodera mixta, Lec., Wind River basin, July; abundant in the flowers of the prickly pear, (*Opuntia.*)

Brachys terminans, Fabr., Wind River basin, July.

Dolopius pauper, Lec., Stinkingwater Valley, July.

Corymbites tinctus, Lec., black variety, Yellowstone basin, August.

Podabrus, (undetermined,) Stinkingwater Valley, July.

Collops vittatus, Say, Green River basin, June.

C. cribrosus, Lec., Green River basin, June.

Pristoscellis, near *fuscus* Lec., Wind River basin, July.

Listrus interruptus, Lec., Wind River basin, June.

Dolichosoma foveicollis, Kirby, Wind River basin, July.

Dasytes breviusculus, Motsch., Green River basin, June.

Eleodes obscura, Say, Wind River basin, July.

E. hispilabrus, Say, Green River basin, June; Wind River basin, July.

E. extricata, Say, Green River basin, June; Wind River basin, June. July.

E. nigrina, Lec., Green River basin, June.

E. pimelioides, Mann., Wind River basin, July.

Blapstinus pratensis, Lec., Green River basin, June.

Cœlocnemis dilaticollis, Mann., Yellowstone basin, August.

Corphyra lugubris, Say, Yellowstone basin, August.

C. Lewisii, Horn, Wind River basin, July.

Notoxus serratus, Lec., Wind River basin, July.

N. subtilis, Lec., (?) Green River basin, June.

Anaspis rufa, Say, Wind River basin, July.

Epicauta puncticollis, Mann., Wind River basin, June.

E. maculata, Say, Wind River basin, July.

E. sericans, Lec., Wind River basin, June, July.

Lytta fulgifera, Lec., variety of *Nuttalli*, Say, Wind River basin, July.

Cephaloon lepturides, Newm., variety, Yellowstone basin, August.

[Mr. Ulke says, "Your specimens differ in size and coloration from the Northern-Atlantic types, but I have an intermediate form from Oregon."]

Prionus Californicus, Motsch., Stinkingwater basin, July.

Criocephales productus, Lec., Yellowstone basin, August.
Cr. asperatus, Lec., Yellowstone basin, August.
Monohammus scutellatus, Say, Wind River basin, July.
Oxoplus corallinus, Lec., Yellowstone basin, August.
[Differs from Mr. Ulke's New Mexico type in having the base of the elytra blackish.]
Pachyta liturata, Kirby, Yellowstone basin, August.
Acmæops pratensis, Laich.,=*strigilata*, Fabr., Wind River basin, July.
Ac. subpilosa, Lec., Wind River basin, June.
Galeruca americana, Fabr., Green River basin, June.
Luperus longulus, Lec., Wind River basin, June, July.
Haltica (*Graptodera*,) *inærata*, Lec., Green River basin, June.
Disonycha alternata, Ill., Wind River basin, July.
Saxinus saucia, Lec., Wind River basin, July.
Adoxus vitis, Linn., Wind River basin, July.
Trirhabda alternata, Say, var., Yellowstone basin, August.
Monoxia guttulata, Lec., Green River basin, June.
Hippodamia Lecontei, Muls., Green River basin, June.
H. quinquesignata, Muls., Wind River basin, July.
H. parenthesis, Say, Green River basin, June.
Coccinella picta, Rand., Yellowstone basin, August.
C. trifasciata, Linn., Wind River basin, July; Yellowstone basin, August.
C. transverso-guttata, Fald., Yellowstone basin, August.
C. novemnotata, Herbst., Green River basin, June; Wind River basin, June.
Sphenophorus Ulkei, Horn., Green River basin, June.
Lepyrus colon, Linn., Wind River basin, July.

There were also collected five or six undescribed species of *Curculionidæ*, belonging to the genera *Listroderes*, *Lichenophagus* (?), and *Erirhinus*.

INDIAN NAMES FOR INSECTS.

The following words, used by the Shoshone or Snake Indians to designate insects, were obtained September 14, 1873, at Camp Brown, Wyoming Territory, from Moonharvy, Charlie, and Bob, three Shoshone Indians belonging to Washakie's band:

Large, wingless cricket, (*Anabrus simplex*, Hald.,) Mesch.
Black cricket, (*Gryllus* ———, sp. ?), Mesch; Mes-oo-wan-ich.
Spider-like cricket, (*Stenopelmatus ?*) Nen-i-gúipo.
Pupa of a large grasshopper, (*Œdipoda*,) Át-tung.
Large grasshopper, (*Œdipoda*,) A-dún-ich.
Hateful grasshopper, (*Calaptenus spretus*, Uhler,) Ud-sée-guee.
Tenebrionidæ, (*Cœlœnemus dilaticollis*, Mann,) Bee-sóu-guah.
Cerambycidæ, *Prionus Californicus*, Motsch.,) Gōn-i-pée-ah.
Green buprestid, E-wée-et.
Horse-fly, (*Tabanus*,) Bée-meet.
Common fly, (*Musca*,) (An-é-vou,) An-é-ou.
Tremex, (sp. ?) An-e-góot-tsee.
Cicada, (sp. ?) Kü-ah.
Ant lion (*Myrmelion*,) Es-poú-see.
Day-fly, (*Ephemera*,) Moó-pō.
Various diurnal butterflies and moths, A-e-pril.
Colias philodice, (yellow,) Oabit A-e-pril.
Moths, from Washakie's Needles, (*Arctia*,) Un-dwust.
Large, brown caterpillar, (larva of some *Sphingidæ*,) Beer-waub.

Colors.

White, Tós-it-eh.
Black, Ton-ór-wit.
Brownish-black, Toú-gon-daú-bit.
Brown, Toú-gon-umph.
Red, En-ga-bit.
Yellow, [Oabit,] Orbt.
Green, A went.
Blue, (bright,) Tsoi-wú-it.
Blue, (grayish,) Ah-mú-it.

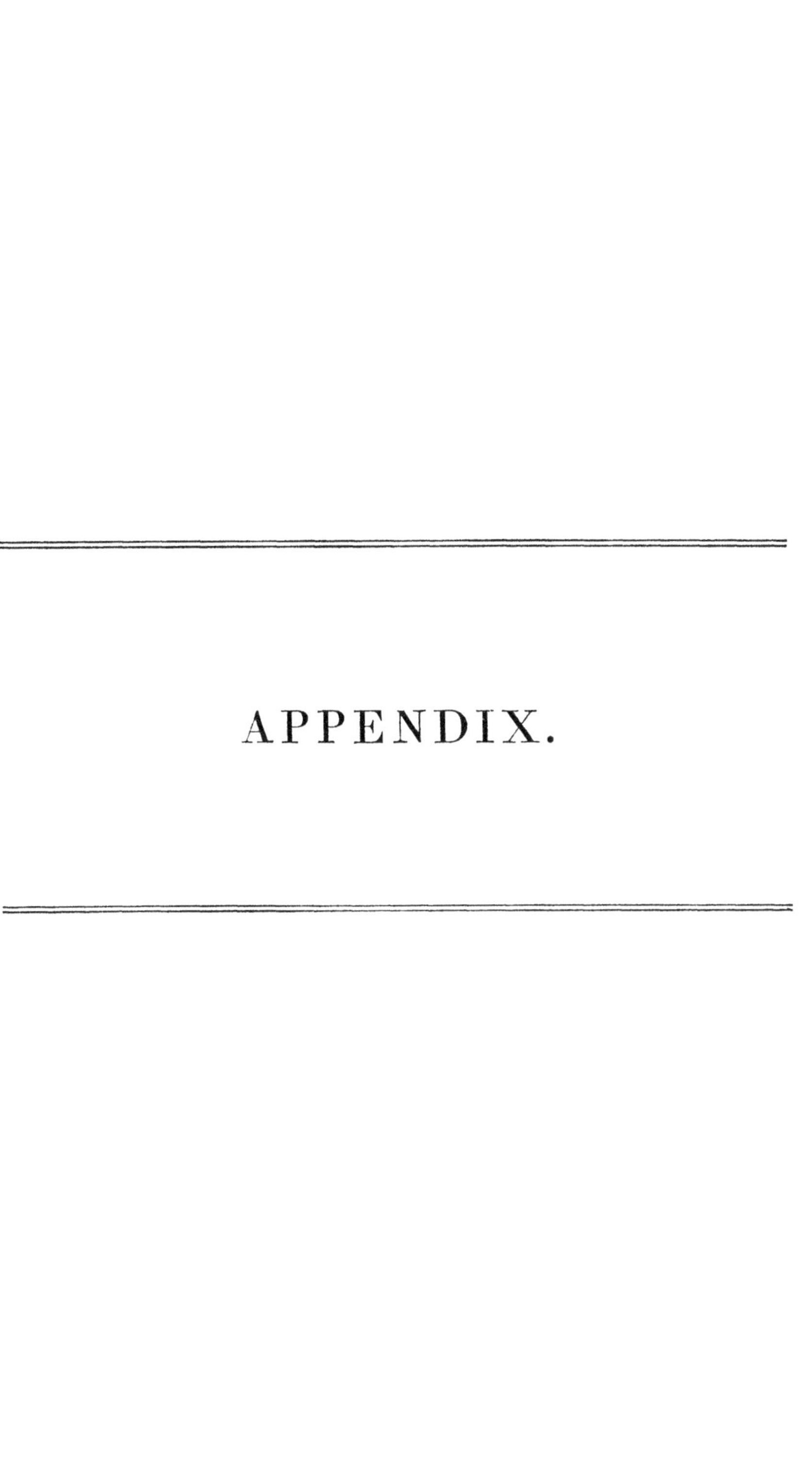

APPENDIX.

APPENDIX.

CORRESPONDENCE RELATIVE TO PRINTING ADDITIONAL CHAPTERS OF THE GEOLOGICAL REPORT.

OFFICE OF THE CHIEF OF ENGINEERS,
Washington, D. C., January 9, 1875.

SIR: Since the printing of the congressional document containing the report of Capt. W. A. Jones upon his reconnaissance in Northwestern Wyoming in 1873, Prof. Theo. B. Comstock, the geologist of the expedition, has prepared eight additional chapters to his geological report.

As these chapters could not be prepared in time to accompany Captain Jones's report, which was transmitted to Congress by the Secretary of War, I would respectfully recommend that one thousand copies of the additional matter be printed by the Public Printer, upon the usual War Department requisition.

Very respectfully, your obedient servant,

A. A. HUMPHREYS,
Brig. Gen., and Chief of Engineers.

Hon. WM. W. BELKNAP,
Secretary of War.

Approved, by order of the Secretary of War.

H. T. CROSBY,
Chief Clerk.

WAR DEPARTMENT, *January* 13, 1875.

WASHINGTON, D. C. *January* 4, 1875.

SIR: I have the honor to transmit herewith a letter of Prof. Theo. B. Comstock, together with the additional manuscript which completes his report to me as geologist of the reconnaissance of Northwestern Wyoming.

Owing to the illness of Professor Comstock, he was unable to complete this manuscript in time for it to be presented with the main report. This latter has gone to press; and as the additional matter is of considerable scientific interest, I would respectfully suggest that it be printed, if possible, in such form that it may be distributed with the main report.

Very respectfully, your obedient servant,

W. A. JONES,
Captain of Engineers.

The CHIEF OF ENGINEERS,
United States Army.

CLEVELAND, OHIO,
December 31, 1874.

SIR: The last installment of my report on the geology, &c., of the district surveyed under your direction in 1873, is herewith transmitted. The construction and arrangement of the several parts is substantially as proposed to you upon our return from the field, more than thirteen months since. The departures from that plan, except in some minor points, have been almost wholly due to the constant state of uncertainty regarding the date of publication. The first eight chapters were sent you in six installments, and as no copy could be retained, under the circumstances, some unnecessary repetitions could scarcely be avoided. The succeeding five chapters (on hot springs and geysers) were completed too late for publication in the first edition of this document, (for the use of Congress,) and the remainder of the report was put in manuscript while the former portion was *in press*. This brief statement will explain to you the necessity for the omission of the intended simple lists of minerals, mammals, and birds, and the lack of the index referred to in the introductory chapter and elsewhere.

The method which has been adopted, of employing head-lines in the text, lessens the need of an index, however, and the subjects are generally so classified as to make reference easy to any part of the work without such a guide.

I have endeavored, in all cases, to give due credit in the body of the work to those who have rendered aid in the collection or elaboration of the material upon which this report is founded, but I cannot let this final opportunity pass without grateful mention of some who have a special claim upon my remembrance. The members of the expedition, without, I believe, one exception, were always ready to assist when called upon, and the officers at Fort Bridger, Camp Stambaugh, and Camp Brown gave me information of value, as well as bestowing kind attentions without stint. Dr. Carter, of Fort Bridger, has laid me under obligations for his very carefully written notes on the Shoshone dialect. Dr. Heisman, of our party, has furnished freely of his notes, besides giving material aid while on the trip. Mr. Charles T. Creary acted as my assistant a portion of the time, and deserves credit for his zeal and endurance of many hardships. I cannot but believe that my life was once saved only by his firmness and presence of mind. Mr. Geo. Hitt, my tent-mate, has my thanks for his consideration and warm-heartedness at all times, which added not a little to the amount that I was able to accomplish during the day.

The Engineer Department at Washington has freely granted more than I have asked, and I would not forget that the publication of this report, in its present form, is due to the charitable opinion of its chief. Lastly, to your own unflagging interest and hearty support, both upon the trip and since our return, is to be attributed the largest portion of the power to make the report even what it is, and as for myself, I can only regret that the result sent herewith is not more worthy of your unselfish generosity and continual encouragement of my efforts.

With esteem, I am sir, your obedient servant,

THEO. B. COMSTOCK,
Geologist N. W. Wyoming Expedition, 1873.

Capt. W. A. JONES,
Corps of Engineers, Commander of Expedition.

MILITARY WAGON-ROAD IN WYOMING AND MONTANA TERRITORIES.*

Letter from the Secretary of War, relative to the bill (*H. R.* 2854) *for the location and construction of a military wagon-road from Green River City, Wyo., to the Yellowstone National Park, and to Fort Ellis, Mont., December* 15, 1874. *Referred to the Committee on Military Affairs and ordered to be printed.*

WAR DEPARTMENT, *December* 10, 1874.

The Secretary of War has the honor to return to the House of Representatives House bill 2854, "For the location and construction of a military wagon-road from Green River City, Wyoming Territory, to the Yellowstone National Park, and to Fort Ellis, Montana Territory," and to transmit, for the information of the Committee on Military Affairs, as requested by the chairman of said committee, under date of June 9, 1874, letter of the Chief of Engineers of the Army, dated June 16, 1874, and copy of report of Capt. W. A. Jones, Corps of Engineers, which fully sets forth the advantages to be derived from the construction of said road.

Under date of November 28, Lieutenant-General Sheridan states: "In forwarding the report of Capt. William A. Jones, Engineer Corps, of his reconnaissance of the route referred to by the within papers from Green River City, Wyoming Territory, or its vicinity, to Fort Ellis, Montana Territory, via the Yellowstone Park, under date of May 10, 1874, I did not express myself as in favor of the projected road. Since that date I have had opportunity to make a personal examination of the road through to Camp Brown, Wyoming Territory, which causes me to reconsider my former action; and I now return these papers with my approval, and recommend that the road, as proposed by the within House bill, introduced by the Hon. W. R. Steele, of Wyoming Territory, be favorably considered by the honorable Secretary of War."

WM. W. BELKNAP,
Secretary of War.

OFFICE OF THE CHIEF OF ENGINEERS,
Washington, D. C., June 16, 1874.

SIR: In compliance with reference to this Office of bill No. 2854, introduced into the House of Representatives on the 6th instant by the Hon. Mr. Steele, for the location and construction of a military wagon-road from Green River City, Wyo., to the Yellowstone National Park and Fort Ellis, Mont., I have the honor to transmit herewith a copy of a letter from Capt. W. A. Jones, of the Corps of Engineers, in which the advantages which are expected to accrue from the construction of said road are fully set forth; and also beg leave to refer to my letter of the 13th instant, forwarding to you a copy of a report by Captain Jones of a reconnaissance of Northwestern Wyoming, made in 1873.

The letter from the Committee on Military Affairs inclosing the bill is returned herewith.

Very respectfully, your obedient servant,

A. A. HUMPHREYS,
Brig. Gen. and Chief of Engineers.

Hon. WM. W. BELKNAP,
Secretary of War.

---

*House of Representatives Ex. Doc. No. 22, 43d Congress, 2d session.

WASHINGTON, D. C., *June* 12, 1874.

SIR: I have the honor to acknowledge the receipt of your letter of this date upon the subject of a proposed military wagon-road in Wyoming.

The road proposed by this bill is over the line discovered by me last year while making the reconnaissance of Northwestern Wyoming. I consider it a perfectly practicable project, which can be attained at a reasonable expense.

The road will leave the Union Pacific Railroad near Green River City, Wyo., at such a point (probably Point of Rocks) as will give the shortest distance from the railroad to the mouth of Wind River Valley. This valley is followed up to its head, where there is a pass over which the grades are perfectly easy and practicable. It is probable that this pass will be practicable for winter travel, as it lies in such position that the prevalent winds are intercepted by neighboring mountain-ranges, and cannot reach it with sufficient force to drive the snow into drifts that will be serious obstructions. It is the testimony of miners, freighters, and others in the Territories, that winter roads can easily be maintained in the mountains, provided the snow does not drift badly. Whether this should prove true or not, the proposed road would remain open as long as the present route via Corinne, and longer than the Missouri River route.

From this pass the road will proceed northerly to Yellowstone Lake, following down its eastern shore, and thence down the Yellowstone River, passing the Great Falls and along the crest of the Grand Cañon, and by the Mammoth Hot Springs on Gardiner's River to Fort Ellis, Bozeman City, and the Crow Indian agency. From here there are good roads to the principal cities and mining towns of Montana. The route traverses the Wind River Valley, (avoiding the present mountain-road between Camp Stambaugh and Camp Brown,) where the soil is quite well adapted to agriculture and grazing, as has been proved by experience, and the climate is exceptionally mild; the Teton Basin, a thoroughly well-watered and well-timbered area of country, where the soil is quite rich, and rain falls with sufficient equability to render irrigation unnecessary probably; the Yellowstone National Park, passing all of its wonderful phenomena except the geyser basins, which can be reached by a short side-road, and a stretch of country in Yellowstone Valley, north of the park, which is now cultivated with success.

Gold, (in veins and diggings,) coal, coal-oil, iron, and gypsum occur in the Wind River country, fine coal in the Teton Basin, and gold, (in veins and diggings,) lead, and silver in the Yellowstone region.

It will thus be seen that this road will open up and develop a country of considerable and varied resources.

It will also furnish the shortest and a most agreeable route to the Yellowstone National Park.

The present approaches to Montana from the East are only two, viz: (1.) The Missouri River route, which involves wagon transportation from Fort Benton, or from Carroll, over a desolate country. This latter affords about the same wagon-road distance to Fort Ellis as the one from Fort Benton, and, should it prove available, will supersede it. (2.) The land-route via the Union and Central Pacific Railroads to Corinne, Utah, and thence to Montana by wagons.

The road proposed by the bill is an improvement upon this, as will be seen from the following tables, and will thus bring the two main routes into a closer competition, giving the mining and agricultural interests of Montana an improved outlet and better competing lines of land and water travel, and affording all of the attendant advantages in the transaction of business, settlement of new country, and the shipment of Army and Indian supplies. It is fraught with lasting benefit to the people of Montana and Northern Idaho, and will hasten the utilization of the Yellowstone National Park as a place of summer resort.

Tables.

			Miles.
I.	By rail:		
	Omaha to Corinne, Union Pacific Railroad		1,055
	Omaha to Point of Rocks, Union Pacific Railroad		805
	Distance saved by rail		250
II.	Omaha to Yellowstone Lake, present route:		
	Omaha to Corinne		1,055
	Corinne to Fort Ellis		403
	Fort Ellis to Yellowstone Lake		118
	Omaha to Yellowstone Lake		1,576
	Proposed route:	Miles.	
	Omaha to Point of Rocks	805	
	Point of Rocks to Yellowstone Lake	289	
	Omaha to Yellowstone Lake		1,094
	Distance saved to Yellowstone Lake		482
	Omaha to Bozeman, Montana, present route:		
	Omaha to Corinne		1,055
	Corinne to { Fort Ellis / Bozeman }		403
	Omaha to { Fort Ellis / Bozeman }		1,458
	Proposed route:	Miles.	
	Omaha to Point of Rocks	805	
	Point of Rocks to { Fort Ellis / Bozeman }	437	
	Omaha to Bozeman		1,242
	Distance saved to { Fort Ellis / Bozeman }		216
III.	* Passenger rates, (railroad:)		
	Omaha to Corinne, Utah		$79 25
	Omaha to Point of Rocks, Wyoming		57 25
	Amount saved per man		22 00
IV.	* Freight rates, (railroad:)		
	Omaha to Corinne, (third-class) per ton		$42 20
	Omaha to Point of Rocks, (third-class) per ton		32 20
	Amount saved per ton		10 00

To sum up: The proposed wagon-road saves 250 miles of railroad; 482 miles of distance to the Yellowstone National Park; and 216 miles to Fort Ellis, Bozeman, and the principal cities of Montana, which is one of the most productive mining regions of the West; is the shortest and most practicable road to the Yellowstone National Park and Montana; is heavily timbered through the belt of country where the heavy

* As the distance (wagon-road) is about the same in the two cases, the saving effected can very fairly be represented by the saving over 250 miles of railroad.

snows fall, indicating a probable winter route, while, at present, there is none; opens up a large tract (2,000,000 acres) of low-lying timber-land—a very important feature; will open to settlement the Wind River Valley, the Teton Basin, and the valley of the Upper Yellowstone; will hasten the attainment of the objects for which the Yellowstone Park was created by law; and will afford better competing lines of travel to the mining and other industries of Montana.

I am, sir, very respectfully, your obedient servant,

W. A. JONES,
Captain of Engineers.

The CHIEF OF ENGINEERS,
United States Army, Washington, D. C.

Forty-third Congress, First Session, H. R. 2854. In the House of Representatives, April 6, 1874. Read twice, referred to the Committee on Military Affairs, and ordered to be printed.

Mr. Steele, on leave, introduced the following bill:

A BILL for the location and construction of a military wagon-road from Green River City, Wyoming Territory, to the Yellowstone National Park, and to Fort Ellis, Montana Territory.

Be it enacted by the Senate and House of Representatives of the United States of America in Congress assembled, That there shall be located and constructed, under the direction of the Secretary of War, a military wagon-road from Green River City, in the Territory of Wyoming, or from such other point in said Territory as may be selected, to the Yellowstone National Park, and to Fort Ellis, in the Territory of Montana. And the Secretary of War is hereby authorized to expend, for the prosecution of said work, any sum of money necessary therefor, not exceeding the sum of sixty thousand dollars; which said sum of money, or so much thereof as may be necessary, is hereby appropriated for that purpose out of any money in the Treasury not otherwise appropriated.

INDEX.

www.ingramcontent.com/pod-product-compliance
Lightning Source LLC
LaVergne TN
LVHW010203110826
845151LV00002B/597
* 9 7 8 1 4 2 5 5 3 6 4 0 4 *